SCOTTISH POETRY, 1730–1830

THIS anthology comprises 218 poems and songs from authors working in the period roughly spanning 1730–1830, a notable era in the literature of Scotland marked by the country's emergence as a leading centre of print culture, while its vibrant oral traditions continued to flower. The period has been particularly associated with Scotland's most famous poet, Robert Burns, as well as one of the most influential novelists of all time, Sir Walter Scott; both of these luminaries are showcased here, but much effort has been made to expand the canon well beyond their shadow. The extraordinary diversity of poets and poetry of the age has been represented by 137 authors, ranging from landed gentry to the working class, from amateurs to professionals, and from those widely published and feted in their lifetimes to those who only achieved recognition posthumously. Long-form poems sit beside shorter ballads, odes, epistles, satires, and sonnets, and themes range from the whimsical and everyday to the overtly political, and much else besides. There is also variety in language, with poems written in English, Scots, and Gaelic; those written fully or partially in Scots have not been glossed, allowing the sounds to speak for themselves, and for those written in Gaelic, modern English translations by leading scholars and poets sit alongside the originals. Full of terrors and wonders, song and satire, love and hate, Scottish poetry of the period 1730–1830 was far livelier than we have cared to remember.

DANIEL COOK is Reader in English Literature and an Associate Dean at the University of Dundee. He is the author of *Thomas Chatterton and Neglected Genius, 1760–1830* (2013), *Reading Swift's Poetry* (2020), and *Walter Scott and Short Fiction* (2021).

T0282103

OXFORD WORLD'S CLASSICS

*For over 100 years Oxford World's Classics have brought
readers closer to the world's great literature. Now with over 700
titles—from the 4,000-year-old myths of Mesopotamia to the
twentieth century's greatest novels—the series makes available
lesser-known as well as celebrated writing.*

*The pocket-sized hardbacks of the early years contained
introductions by Virginia Woolf, T. S. Eliot, Graham Greene,
and other literary figures which enriched the experience of reading.
Today the series is recognized for its fine scholarship and
reliability in texts that span world literature, drama and poetry,
religion, philosophy, and politics. Each edition includes perceptive
commentary and essential background information to meet the
changing needs of readers.*

OXFORD WORLD'S CLASSICS

Scottish Poetry, 1730–1830

Edited by
DANIEL COOK

OXFORD
UNIVERSITY PRESS

OXFORD
UNIVERSITY PRESS

Great Clarendon Street, Oxford, OX2 6DP,
United Kingdom

Oxford University Press is a department of the University of Oxford.
It furthers the University's objective of excellence in research, scholarship,
and education by publishing worldwide. Oxford is a registered trade mark of
Oxford University Press in the UK and in certain other countries

First published as an Oxford World's Classics paperback 2023

Impression: 1

Published in the United States of America by Oxford University Press
198 Madison Avenue, New York, NY 10016, United States of America

British Library Cataloguing in Publication Data

Data available

Library of Congress Control Number: 2022944600

ISBN 978-0-19-880355-3

Printed and bound in the UK by
Clays Ltd, Elcograf S.p.A.

ACKNOWLEDGEMENTS

FOR general guidance on the contents of this anthology I am grateful to a number of Scottish literature scholars, including Murray Pittock, Gerry Carruthers, Valentina Bold, Gerard Lee McKeever, Michael Morris, Rhona Brown, Amy Wilcockson, James Caudle, Murdo Macdonald, Patrick Scott, and Heather Yeung. Numerous Scottish Gaelic scholars have been especially generous with their expertise in textual and contextual matters. Ronald (Ronnie) Black, Michel Byrne, Peter Mackay, and Iain S. MacPherson even supplied new translations of some works, as indicated in the citations, and Donald E. Meek (and the publisher Birlinn Limited) kindly provided permission to include his work. Beyond his own ample body of research, Ronnie also connected me with experts on many of the Gaelic poets, as acknowledged in the relevant biographical headnotes. I'm also thankful to Kate Mathis, William Gillies, Sim Innes, Anja Gunderloch, Rob Dunbar, and Sheila Kidd for answering specific queries. Helen Craik's manuscript piece, 'Here native Genius, gay, unique and strong', and James Shaw's 'Naidheachd na Frainge', appear courtesy of The National Library of Scotland. I'm hopeful that the present book will prove useful to teachers, students, scholars, and anyone keen to discover more about Scottish literature of the eighteenth and nineteenth centuries.

CONTENTS

INTRODUCTION

SCOTTISH poetry of the period 1730–1830 might strike you as at once familiar and unknown. Familiar because it includes among its ranks one of the world's most iconic bards, Robert Burns, as well as one of the most influential novelists of all time, Sir Walter Scott. Unknown because Burns and Scott still overshadow their peers, some of whom have been out of print for decades, even centuries. Struggling to make an impact on the cultural scene of their age, for a variety of personal and social reasons, some of these poets and songwriters published only a single and often small selection of works. A lot of the pieces even appeared posthumously, for the first time, years after the writers' deaths. Other writers found in the following pages remain incredibly famous but in different reading contexts. One of Europe's most respected literary figures, Lord Byron is still feted as a star in the English canon. Raised in part in his maternal home county of Aberdeenshire, Byron was also a roving Scot who remembered with fondness his 'dwelling in my Highland cave, | Or roaming through the dusky wild' ('I would I were a careless child').

As the author of *The Private Memoirs and Confessions of a Justified Sinner* (1824), if nothing else, James Hogg will need little introduction to students of Gothic fiction. The biographer James Boswell also wrote stupendous satirical verses, as did his politician son, Sir Alexander. Joanna Baillie can, with good reason, lay claim to being the leading dramatist of the Romantic period. Her songs here sing again. A picaresque novelist by trade, Tobias Smollett has his roving verse too ('Ode to Leven-Water': 'Pure stream! in whose transparent wave | My youthful limbs I wont to lave'). Other notable novelists join us as poets—Henry Mackenzie, Helen Craik, Mary Brunton, and John Galt among them. Framed within the category of Scottish literature in this anthology, these and other writers ought to be considered in the overlapping contexts of British, Irish, European, North American, and other literatures. They are at once Scots and citizens of the world, inhabiting multiple literary languages at once—Scots, English, and Gaelic, above all, as well as French, German, Italian, and Latin, among others. The pseudo-ancient Ossian poems 'translated' into modern English prose by James Macpherson became a worldwide phenomenon amid a broader Celtomania that thrived in the second half of the eighteenth century and beyond—readers as diverse as Thomas Jefferson and Napoleon Bonaparte were avid fans.

For some, the name of Ossian has become synonymous with controversy—did Macpherson cannibalize genuine relics of oral culture, whether Scottish or Irish, or are the works ingenious fakes?—or Hungarian heavy metal bands and golden ales from Perth. Reading Macpherson's prose poems anew alongside contemporary Gaelic verse, as well as Scots and English imitations, reveals new things about the ebb and flow of literature across the Lowlands, Highlands, and Islands. The present collection contains Gaelic-language texts (in the original form, alongside modern English translations) for the first time in the Oxford World's Classics series. After long neglect by non-Gaelic readers and scholars, six female Gaelic writers take pride of place here—Cairistìona NicFhearghais (Christiana Fergusson), Anna Chaimbeul (Anne Campbell), Bean Torra Dhamh (Mary MacPherson), Mairiread Ghriogarach (Margaret MacGregor), Maighrearad Chamshron (Margaret Cameron), and Anna Ghobha (Ann Gow). They sit alongside the traditional 'big six' male Gaelic poets of the eighteenth and early nineteenth centuries, led by Alastair, mac Mhaighstir Alastair (Alexander MacDonald), followed by Iain mac Fhearchair (John MacCodrum), Rob Donn MacAoidh (Robert Mackay), Dùghall Bochanan (Dugald Buchanan), Donnchadh Bàn Mac an t-Saoir (Duncan Ban Macintyre), and Uilleam Ros (William Ross). Beyond this group, another fifteen male Gaelic poets can be found dispersed across our pages, from Domhnall MacLeòid (Donald MacLeod) down to Iain MacCoinnich (John MacKenzie), more than a century later.

While many Gaelic-language anthologies incorporate anonymous or traditional pieces we focus exclusively on works attributed with some surety to a named person in print, even if the work initially appeared anonymously. One reason for this approach is to encourage further study of the many women and men included, especially when they have been previously overlooked. No book could provide a comprehensive body of a nation's poetry written over the span of an entire century. If we were to apply the rule that Scots, Gaelic, and English should be each represented in roughly equal thirds of the total, Gaelic poetry and song would still be under-represented, though better than in most anthologies. Of the 137 people showcased here, twenty-seven (one-fifth) wrote largely or exclusively in Gaelic. We should also add into the mix Latin and other major Scottish literary languages. For contemporary readers Latin was by no means isolated from Scots, after all. In his *Poems, in English, Scotch, and Latin* (1794), James Grahame even translated

Burns's iconic address 'To a Mouse' into Latin ('Ad Murem'). Scattered throughout verses published in the period we find plenty of casual quotations from the classics, in the original languages typically, whether in the epigraphs or footnotes, or even embedded within or between the lines. Homer, Horace, and Virgil, among other household names, were (and remain) persistent favourites among generations of Scottish poets. Limiting our scope to attributed works across the languages also allows us to rationalize our contents; otherwise, we would be overwhelmed by traditional ballads that were tinkered with, often substantially and with immense ingenuity, throughout our one-hundred-year period. Fortunately, excellent collections of Scottish ballads remain easy to find (see Select Bibliography). Many of the very best ballads and songs can still be heard, in some format or other, in every corner of the world.

Looking at attributed literature also helps us to trace lines of influence across the multiple generations that make up the eighteenth and nineteenth centuries. Burns had scores of admirers among working-class communities and the urban literati alike. One of the country's most under-rated poets, Janet Little the milkmaid, has in our pages been put back into dialogue with the Ayrshire Bard. As the selection offered here makes plain, a lot of people treated (and still treat) Scottish poetry as a living tradition, to which they were contributing (and still contribute) in their own unique ways—sometimes with humility, more often with self-effacing humour. The unduly neglected Christian Milne excelled in this sort of seemingly artless but highly artful metapoetry. Printed in the disarmingly titled collection *Simple Poems, on Simple Subjects* (1805), her epistle 'To a Lady who said it was Sinful to Read Novels', begins 'To love these Books, and harmless Tea, | Has always been my foible', immediately pulling us onside against the bibliophobes. Apparent artlessness has caused us to overlook all sorts of quiet innovators. The hymnist James Montgomery and Margaret Maxwell Inglis penned charmingly solemn verses that more than merit renewed attention from historians of religion and poetry alike—'a purer glow of feeling | Has bid me to rejoice', writes Inglis ('A Morning Sabbath Walk').

Among other achievements, Bean Torra Dhamh (marketed as the Religious Poetess of Badenoch) produced unconventional hymns with strong social commentary, as evidenced in 'Beachd Gràis air an t-Saoghal' ('The Vantage Point of Grace'). Robert Tannahill had a stylistic range that extended far beyond the admittedly unmissable influence of that ingenious fellow labouring poet, Burns. At the other end of the class spectrum, Lady Bury had her own thoughtful songs that will long stay with you ('On Seeing Some Withered Roses Thrown Away':

'Wipe off the yet impassion'd tear, | And turn my heart to peace'). Poets from all walks of life honoured their entire nation (under the labels of 'Scotland', 'Scotia', or 'Caledonia'); others focused on local communities, whether it's Byron's Highlands, Alexander Douglas's Fife, Robert Fergusson's Edinburgh ('Auld Reekie'), Richard Gall's Ayrshire, Alexander Geddes's Linton, John Mayne's Glasgow, David Vedder's Orkney, or Margaretta Wedderburn's Dalkeith. Universal literary and real-world themes sustained their attention, such as the seasons (James Thomson's 'Winter', Michael Bruce's 'Elegy: To Spring', or MacLachlainn's 'An t-Earrach'), nature (Duncan Ban Macintyre's 'Seachran Seilge' or Jean Glover's 'O'er the Muir Amang the Heather'), marriage (Janet Graham's 'Wayward Wife', Joanna Baillie's 'Song, Woo'd and Married and a'', or Robert Lochlore's 'Marriage and the Care o't'), or—the ultimate one—mortality (Robert Blair's *The Grave* or Burns's 'Death and Doctor Hornbook').

On our pages you will find strongly political pieces such as Alexander Robertson of Struan's anti-government poem 'The Careless Good-Fellow' ('Tho' they be call'd the State's Physicians, | They poison all') or Adam Skirving's Jacobite ballad 'Johnnie Cope', which mocks Sir John Cope, the British military commander defeated at Prestonpans. They sit beside comic poems like William Tennant's 'Tammy Little', racy lyrics by Isobel 'Tibbie' Pagan ('Aughlen Spring'), witty verses by Agnes Lyon ('Niel Gow's Farewell to Whisky'), Spenserian visions (William Wilkie's 'A Dream, In the Manner of Spenser'), historical imitations (Henry Mackenzie's 'Duncan, a Ballad'), refurbished tunes (Alison Cockburn's and Jean Elliot's different versions of 'The Flowers of the Forest'), and friendly epistles (Elizabeth Scot's 'To a Friend'), to name but a few. Throughout their careers many of our poets and songwriters addressed serious topics such as religion, war, politics, and emigration; some wrote about drinking and sports. (Some wrote seriously on comic topics, and some wrote comedically about serious ones.) Many celebrated love and friendship. Others lamented the loss of loved ones. Some attacked their enemies with unflinching glee.

Seeking new audiences beyond their domestic or political spheres, some reworked old tunes with astonishing vitality. Elizabeth Grant's popular piece 'Roy's Wife of Aldivalloch' was set to the tune of 'The Ruffian's Rant', Struan's 'The Careless Good-Fellow' to the tune of 'Ne parlez plus de Politique'. One of the earliest entrants in the present collection, Allan Ramsay captured familiar voices with a deceptively straightforward artistry that set the standard for many years to come:

My Soger Laddie is over the Sea,
 And he will bring Gold and Money to me;
And when he comes hame, he'll make me a Lady;
 My Blessing gang with my Soger Laddie.

('The Soger Laddie')

Substantially nostalgic but also forthrightly modern in outlook, Scottish poets and lyricists have always been innovative, whether it's evidenced in a traditional-looking song by Allan Cunningham ('The Thistle's Grown aboon the Rose') or a haunting experimentation with triplets by Walter Sholto Douglas:

His looks were haggard, wild, and bad,
Yet the Owl knew in the man, the lad
Who had destroyed him!—he was glad!

('The Owl')

This book has been stuffed to the brim with odes, ballads, songs, sonnets, satires, metapoems, hymns, fables, pastorals, narrative poems, and much more besides—as well as outrageously ambitious mixtures of various forms, modes and genres.

Placing Scottish Poetry

Each entry comes with a short biographical overview of the author's career pertinent to an understanding of the poems sampled. Not everyone represented here would have considered themselves to be a professional author, let alone an ambassador of Scottish literature. But then, even Scott and Burns had day jobs. People of an elevated social status would not have stomached calling themselves anything but an amateur. Some of those who sought to earn a living by the pen would have judged their burgeoning careers as unsuccessful. Some who were successful at the time, whether critically or commercially, have long fallen out of public view. A younger contemporary of Scott, Thomas Campbell has largely been sidelined, even though he once enjoyed great prestige across continental Europe. Largely forgotten, the Falconar sisters produced two joint collections of highly sophisticated poems when they were barely teenagers. What became of them after 1791 remains a tantalizing mystery. Bringing some newly recovered poets and songwriters into this anthology, I hope to put these and other female writers back into conversation with their male counterparts as much as with themselves. The present anthology is also perhaps the first of its kind to platform a trans male author from the Romantic period—Walter

Sholto Douglas (born Mary Diana Dods), an early exponent of the fantastical turn that would emerge most strongly in late nineteenth-century writing. (If we are mindful of imposing modern categories of gender on people of the past, Douglas/Dods might instead be considered a lesbian furtively married to another woman in an age in which that was not sanctioned by law.)

In the spirit of true inclusivity, I have not prioritized political or religious groups, class, location, age, or other such characteristics. Not everyone here was even born in Scotland. But they all have a substantial connection with the country, whether through family, as a resident, or by inclination. Elizabeth Hamilton was born in Belfast but moved to Perthshire at a young age. Born in London, Lady Bury was raised in a prominent Hiberno-Scottish household. Byron's formative experiences in Aberdeenshire have long been acknowledged, but only in recent years has he appeared more substantially in studies of Scottish writing. Another poet born and raised in England, Susanna Blamire closely engaged with Scottish literary heritage (and the Scots language). Unlike Byron, she appeared—often prominently—in nineteenth-century national anthologies, such as *The Songstresses of Scotland* (1871). With mixed fortunes, some of our poets emigrated to America and Canada. Some even became writers only when living overseas. The poets and songwriters covered here do not constitute a single generation, however defined. Roughly 137 years separates the births of the eldest and youngest of them. We close the anthology with six figures born in the 1790s and at the outset of the 1800s, but neglect writers most associated with the Victorians (Thomas Carlyle and Frances Wright would serve as two high-profile cases). Among those included, Lady Compton and Dorothea Primrose Campbell have been largely ignored by anthologists and scholars alike.

Bringing in poets like Joanna Belfrage Picken and John MacKenzie (a key anthologist in his own right) expands our understanding of the concerns of late Romanticism before it segued into the Victorian period, beyond Wordsworth's circle of disciples. At the other end of the book, we have Alexander Robertson of Struan (born in 1670), who has typically fronted major anthologies of eighteenth-century Scottish literature, including one of the most influential of them all, Joseph Ritson's *Scotish Songs* (1794). As a prominent Jacobite, as both a writer and a military officer, Struan could not publish freely without fear of punishment from the Hanoverian government—his works came out at the end of his life, in the 1740s. Another major early Jacobite writer, William Meston similarly wrote before our period properly begins, but continued to publish, anonymously or pseudonymously on the whole. After Struan, William Hamilton of Bangour was the other major non-Gaelic Jacobite poet to feature regularly in anthologies of the period and well into the next century. A veteran of the 1745 rising, he mingles bloodshed with honour in highly ornate war poetry: 'As over Gladsmuir's blood-stain'd field, | Scotia, imperial goddess, flew' ('Ode on the Battle of Gladsmuir, 1745'). From a different perspective, Cairistìona NicFhearghais (Christiana Fergusson) attests to the fallout of the battles with touching poignancy:

> Och a Thearlaich òig Stiùbhairt,
> Se do chùis rinn mo léireadh,
> Thug thu bhuam gach nì bh' agam
> Ann an cogadh 'nad adhbhar.
>
> ('Mo Rùn Geal Òg')

Ronald Black renders this into English as:

> Och young Charles Edward Stuart,
> Your cause has destroyed me,
> You've taken all I possessed
> For fighting your war.
>
> ('My Heart's Youthful Prize')

Even near contemporaries with shared politics did not necessarily meet in person, let alone collaborate in any sense of the term. While retracing authors' attentive reading of prior literature can greatly enhance our enjoyment as readers, we need to acknowledge that few of the Scots and English speakers could have read the Gaelic poems sampled here. And some pieces that I have gleaned from anthologies, miscellanies, or collections only circulated in small numbers or even among private audiences. We can nevertheless pick up ample strands of intertextuality, in the playful homages to Burns and other leading songwriters, scores of Ossianic imitations, callbacks to Blair and Beattie, or to Ramsay and Ross. We also find clear lines of engagement with old European traditions, from the Quixotic to the Spenserian. In one of the earliest surveys of Scottish writing, from the thirteenth century to the end of the eighteenth, *An Introduction to the History of Scotch Poetry* (1798), Alexander Campbell dubs William Meston the Scottish Butler, in reference to the once highly influential English satirist Samuel Butler, along with other transnational connections. Across the entire present book there are frequent allusions to Shakespeare, Milton, Pope, and Swift, among many other familiar names in an English-language repository shared across the three kingdoms of England, Scotland, and Ireland. While many of our authors wrote in isolation, there are also numerous groups to consider, both real and imagined, formal and informal. Ramsay had many literary followers. In *The Fortunate Shepherdess*, Alexander Ross, for one, honours the recently dead poet in a vibrant manner reminiscent of the master: 'Thou that anes upon a day | Gar'd Allan Ramsay's hungry hart strings play | The merriest sangs that ever yet were sung'. Born the year after Ramsay died, Janet Little still considered the great pastoralist to be the benchmark against whom even Burns had to be judged: 'Old Ramsay's shade, reviv'd again, | In thee we greet' ('An Epistle to Mr Robert Burns').

Andrew Shirrefs was far from alone in curating his own *Poems, Chiefly in the Scottish Dialect* (1790) amid the rise of Burns. (Ironically, considering the seemingly derivative title of his book, Shirrefs's vituperative style feels closer to Ramsay than to the Ayrshire Bard.) Burns encouraged many poets into print, among them John Lapraik, William Dudgeon, David Sillar, and William Reid. Later in the century and into the next, Scott moved in many circles in Edinburgh, including that of his relative Alison Cockburn, who also hosted literary events with the philosopher David Hume and the playwright John Home. Encouraged by James Beattie, Alexander Ross published pastoral poems and some short songs by subscription. If anyone had engaged with the songs during his lifetime, more likely it would have been orally, in the north-east. Influenced by his deep reading of Ramsay and Spenser, he replicates in print that vital orality even while contemplating his future, and the future of all Scots poets:

> Sae I begins, my pen into my hand,
> Just ready hearkning, as she should command.
> But then about her, there was sic a dinn,
> Some seeking this, some that, some out some in.
> That its nae wonder, tho' I aft gae wrang,
> An' for my ain, set down my neiper's sang,
> For hundreds mair were learning at her school,
> And some wrote fair, an' some like me wrote foul.

> ('Invocation', *The Fortunate Shepherdess*)

As the biographical headnotes indicate, many of our poets idolized their forerunners from afar. Burns was a teenager when Robert Fergusson died, but he felt that young man's formal influence keenly throughout his entire career. John Tait's 'The Bards of Scotland' offers a veritable who's who of Scottish poetry, with Ramsay, Thomson,

Macpherson, Hamilton, and others addressed as though part of a living tradition available to all.

This period in literary history generated many leading songwriters whose lyrics were designed to be sung in the taverns, churches, or clubs, and even at events. Even popular songs needed a lot of help to reach print, however. 'Auld Robin Gray' had appeared in David Herd's indispensable *Ancient and Modern Scottish Songs* in 1776, and remained a fixture of Scottish anthologies throughout the ensuing decades. Not until Walter Scott produced an authoritative edition for the Bannatyne Club in 1825, having quoted it in his 1823 novel *The Pirate*, did Lady Anne Barnard receive the credit due to her. A conventional love ballad in some ways, the unfurling of plot over repeated units of sound creates an utterly captivating effect:

> My heart it said na, and I look'd for Jamie back;
> But hard blew the winds, and his ship was a wrack;
> His ship was a wrack! Why didna Jenny dee?
> Or, wherefore am I spared to cry out, Woe is me!

Another popular songwriter, Anne Hunter, had a canny knack for inhabiting all sorts of voices—among them, Mary Stuart, Queen of Scots ('I Sigh, and lament me in vain') and a mermaid ('Come with me, and we will go | Follow, follow, follow me'). A mainstay of nineteenth-century anthologies though she composed anonymously, Carolina Oliphant, Lady Nairne had set many of her most memorable songs to traditional tunes:

> Sweet's the laverock's note and lang,
>   Lilting wildly up the glen;
> But aye to me he sings ae sang,—
>   Will ye no come back again?
>
>   ('Will ye no come back again?')

For all of its world-famous songs and songlike poetry, Scottish literature from this period also looks and sounds bookish. As Little sings, 'A milk maid poem-books to print; | Mair fit she wad her dairy tent' ('Given to a Lady Who Asked Me to Write a Poem').

Critics haunt everyone, Little continues: 'So much I dread their cruel spite, | My hand still trembles when I write'. Not everyone writes for professional reasons ('Critics, be dumb', writes Isabella Kelly). Poetry can be a private distraction, though it does not always come easily:

> Heigho! I'm wond'rous dull; in truth I'm wond'rous sad—
> Little amusement, and the weather bad;

What shall I do? I'll write—Come, ready friend—
I mean my pen—Good folks, I pray attend:
Still at a loss, I do not wish to teaze;—
My muse, assist me—teach me how to please—
My thoughts are free—then, fancy, take thy range—

(Isabella Kelly, 'The Choice; or, Dull Hour Past')

For Anne Ross, the obligations imposed on poetry-making could seem
unwelcome, even among friends and family: 'for it suits not well, | In
verse, the language of my heart to tell' ('One Being Desired by a Friend,
in the Year 1785, to Make a Poem on a Family Residing Near the Banks
of Clyde'). As the poem unfolds on the page before her—before
us—self-doubt ebbs into wistful memory-making, 'when remembrance
calls past scenes to view, | Tho' happy here, I cannot help to mourn'.
Education meant a lot to poets like Margaret MacGregor:

Cha robh neach air bhith 'g iarraidh orm triall gu machair nan Gall,
Ach thuig mi gum b' fheàrrd mi ràith an t-samhraidh thoirt ann;
'S mòr an stàth tha san ionnsach', bheir e tionnsgal don dràic,
'S neach sam bith ga bheil tùr cha leig à chuimhne e gu bràth.

('Òran 's i an sgoil am Peart')

No one demanded I journey to the Lowlanders' country,
But I realised it would benefit me to spend a summer season there;
Schooling is of great use, it gives ambition to the drudge,
And anyone of intelligence will retain it for life.

('A song composed when she was attending a school in Perth'
[translated by Michel Byrne])

A working woman, Christian Milne ingeniously demonstrates a talent
for punchy quatrains even as she anticipates a muted reception from
middle-class readers:

I'm gratify'd to think that you
    Should wish to see my Songs,
As few would read my Book, who knew
    To whom this Book belongs.

('To a Gentleman Desirous of
Seeing My Manuscript')

A lot of printed poetry retained the rhythms of oral verse. We see this
in Alexander Geddes's use of calmly insistent refrain within the lines of
'Linton, a Tweedale Pastoral': 'Calm is the air, and cloudless is the sky'.
But the text also includes explanatory footnotes from the author, and
even in-text quotations. Print mattered to poets.

Scotland was home to widely circulated periodicals that teemed with aspiring writers based throughout the country and beyond, from *The Scots Magazine* (1739–1817) to *Blackwood's Edinburgh Magazine* (1817–1980). Publishers and booksellers like Thomas and Walter Ruddiman, Andrew Millar, William Blackwood, and John Murray, many of whom owned the periodicals, also worked tirelessly to circulate literature by their countrymen and countrywomen in book form. Often they did so from their bases in Edinburgh and other major northern cities. Often they did so in collaboration with the largest print houses London had to offer. (Browsing the texts' citations you will detect the strong presence of just some of these leading periodicals and publishers across the years.) Some of the poets knew each other as students or academics at one of the universities in Edinburgh, St Andrews, Glasgow, or Aberdeen. Some groups operated down south, in London typically, and overlapped with established circles of prominent English and Irish figures. David Mallet and James Thomson enjoyed great success down south, for a time shaping literary mores across the three kingdoms and over in America. A patron and a poet in his own right, Sir Gilbert Elliot furthered the careers of Home and Hume, among other fellow Scots. Some poets who benefited from early guidance often paid it forward to their younger peers. A student of divinity at Edinburgh, Thomas Blacklock found active mentors in David Hume and Joseph Spence. In turn, he supported Burns and Scott, both of whom credited him with helping with significant career decisions.

Beyond the university towns, many poets hailed from, or were raised in, regions right across the nation. The shires have their champions, though some of them have since been renamed or rezoned (Aberdeenshire, Banffshire, Dumfriesshire, Dunbartonshire, Haddingtonshire, Kincardineshire, Kirkcudbrightshire, Lanarkshire, Perthshire, Renfrewshire, Roxburghshire, Selkirkshire, among them). Bannoch, Dundee, Inverness, Kelso, Kilmarnock, Paisley, and other towns and cities provided thriving intellectual milieux. Angus, Argyll, and Fife have had their fair share of literary stars too, though many of them have yet to be publicly commemorated in any noticeable way. Then there are the Highlands and islands—Orkney, Shetland, Skye, and more. Booksellers and music collectors placed around the country often encouraged, and even commissioned at large expense, respected writers to compile under their own brand multi-author anthologies of their fellow Scots or of people associated with specific locales. Chief among these projects were Ramsay's *Tea-Table Miscellany* (1723–37), Scott's *Minstrelsy of the Scottish Border* (1802–3),

Hogg's *The Jacobite Relics of Scotland* (1819–21), and Cunningham's *The Songs of Scotland, Ancient and Modern* (1825). James Johnson's *The Scots Musical Museum* (1787–1803) was driven by the formidable songwriter Robert Burns. Burns, along with Laing and Nicol and others, also takes pride of place in John Struthers's widely imitated collection *The Harp of Caledonia* (1821).

One of the country's leading anthologists, Robert Anderson gained key connections in Edinburgh, as his colossal edition of *The Works of the British Poets* (1792–1807) attests. Other important collections that shaped the terrain of Scottish literature within the period range from David Herd's *Ancient and Modern Scottish Songs, Heroic Ballads, Etc.* (1776) to Robert Chambers's *The Scottish Songs* (1829), both of which were plundered by editors for many years to come, myself included. The antiquary John Pinkerton rejigged a series of volumes of ancient (and some pseudo-ancient) ballads, as in *Select Scottish Ballads* (1783). Following Anderson's monolithic *Works of the British Poets*, other collections by Scottish editors conflated Scottish and English writing under a British label, as in Thomas Campbell's *Specimens of the British Poets* (1819). There were key Gaelic anthologies, too, such as John Gillies's *Collection of Ancient and Modern Gaelic Poems and Songs* (1786) and Alexander and Donald Stewart's *Cochruinneacha Taoghta de Shaothair nam Bard Gaëleach* (1804). Other books brought Scots together around genres or themes, as in the Thomas Blacklock-helmed *Collection of Original Poems. By Scotch Gentlemen* (1760–2). Lesser known miscellanies, such as *The Caledoniad* (1775), offered some intriguing pieces with the faintest of attributions. Just who is the mysterious poet known as Miss B—ce of Fife? (In his *Introduction to the History of Scotch Poetry*, Alexander Campbell makes a plausible guess: Eliza Bruce. We will probably never know for sure.) Readers who sought Scottish poems and songs could find them everywhere, in bookshops and coffee houses, in pamphlets and periodicals, right across the world.

Reading Scottish Poetry

Only an audacious poet like Robert Fergusson could declare the death of an entire nation's music in perfectly pitched lines:

> On Scotia's plains, in days of yore,
> When lads and lasses *tartan* wore,
> Saft Music rang on ilka shore,
>   In hamely weid;

> But harmony is now no more,
> And *music* dead.
>
> ('Elegy, on the Death of
> Scots Music')

Little wonder Burns often adopted that flexible stanza structure, too—it allows for, and encourages, rhythmic dexterity even while it uses fewer rhymes (a-a-a-b-a-b, in the above). Fergusson used that seemingly restrictive pattern to create different effects in such poems as 'The King's Birth-Day in Edinburgh', where the lines flow at unsettling speed:

> The hills in terror wou'd cry out,
> And echo to thy dinsome rout;
> The herds wou'd gather in their nowt,
>   That glowr'd wi' wonder,
> Haflins afraid to bide thereout
>   To hear thy thunder.

Burns's 'Address to the Deil' has its own rapidly delivered terrors:

> An' how ye gat him i' your thrall,
> An' brak him out o' house and hal',
> While scabs an' blotches did him gall,
>   Wi' bitter claw,
> An' lows'd his ill-tongu'd, wicked Scawl,
>   Was warst ava?

Often known as the Habbie Stanza, the form could also accommodate Burns's cheeky comedy:

> Fair fa' your honest, sonsie face,
> Great Chieftain o' the Puddin-race!
> Aboon them a' ye tak your place,
>   Painch, tripe, or thairm:
> Weel are ye wordy o' a *grace*
>   As lang 's my arm.
>
> ('Address to a Haggis')

The Habbie Stanza was the perfect vehicle for conversational sincerity in Janet Little's overview of modern Scottish poetry centred on her idol:

> The task I'll drop; wi' heart sincere
> To heav'n present a humble prayer,
> That a' the blessings mortals share
>   May be, by turns,
> Dispens'd with an indulgent care
>   To Robert Burns.
>
> ('An Epistle to Mr Robert Burns')

Homage, horror, comedy, satire, or prayer: this robust stanzaic form proved ideal for the Scottish imagination over many decades. Fergusson, like Burns and Little after him and Ramsay before him, could with consummate ease also switch to different forms entirely. In one of his longest poems, 'Auld Reekie', Fergusson builds up a vivid picture of life in Edinburgh over brisk couplets:

> Auld Reekie! wale o' ilka town
> That Scotland kens beneath the moon;
> Where couthy chiels at e'enin' meet,
> Their bizzin' craigs and mous to weet;
> And blythely gar auld care gae by
> Wi' blinkit and wi' bleerin' eye.

Many of the poems and songs included in the present book have been nabbed from single and multi-author collections, anthologies and miscellanies, periodicals and magazines, and standalone broadsheets. The longest were published in book-length form. Found early on, Robert Blair's *The Grave* (1743), in blank verse, is a prime example of a literary work that demands to be read as a complete text, as the meditative quality of the writing rewards our attention and resists the extraction of easy homilies. To establish the solemn atmosphere of the setting, some sentences run to well over a dozen lines, often with multiple clauses within each ('Oft, in the lone Church-yard at Night I've seen | By Glimpse of Moon-shine . . .'). Blair punctures other sentences with dramatic sounds, jolting our mood: 'Again! the Screech-Owl shrieks: Ungracious Sound! | I'll hear no more, it makes one's Blood run chill'. While *The Grave* appears in its entirety, other important long poems have been inserted piecemeal. One of the four parts of James Thomson's *The Seasons* (1730) can be found in full—'Winter'. We also have significant sampling from John Armstrong's medical georgic *The Art of Preserving Health* (1744), Macpherson's *Fingal* (1761), William Falconer's *The Shipwreck* (1762), Ross's *The Fortunate Shepherdess* (1768), Beattie's *The Minstrel* (1771–4), Mayne's *Glasgow: A Poem* (1803), Scott's *The Lady of the Lake* (1810), and 'Kilmeny' from Hogg's *The Queen's Wake* (1813). Against Blair's slow-building lines, Falconer uses the long form to encapsulate the relentlessness of sea voyaging:

> Her gnawing worms corrode the human breast,
> And multiply the pangs of the distress'd:
> Or forming o'er the deep th' imbattl'd line,
> Where hostile Ships in dire commotion join;

> While dying victims agonize in pain,
> And fierce Destruction lords it o'er the main.

> ('Proem', *The Shipwreck*)

Unlike Falconer, James Beattie and James Macpherson, his near contemporaries, influenced their peers in profound if markedly different
ways, a quick examination of which might prove instructive for an
introduction to poetry of the mid-eighteenth century. Beattie's *The
Minstrel* revisited an earlier fascination with old British bards, while
Macpherson's faux-ancient revivalism attracted imitators for many
more decades to come, some of whom appear later in this anthology.
Attentive to wider communities, Ossianic poetry still centres on indi-
vidual experience ('Immortal youth, beyond the power of years!', as
Michael Bruce has it in 'Ossian's Hymn to the Sun'). It champions
heroes, but never loses sight of those left behind. In form, it changes
a lot. Favouring rhyming quatrains over Macpherson's prose in
'Another Extract from Ossian', Christian Gray nevertheless retained
the sentimentalist imagery and tone well into the 1820s: 'Like flowers
which nightly mildews blight, | And scorching suns consume'. Beattie's
minstrelsy prolonged a nostalgic view of poetry that at once revisited
Spenser and looked ahead to Scott, and even Byron.

> Along this narrow valley you might see
> The wild deer sporting on the meadow ground,
> And, here and there, a solitary tree,
> Or mossy stone, or rock with woodbine crown'd.
> Oft did the cliffs reverberate the sound
> Of parted fragments tumbling from on high;
> And from the summit of that craggy mound
> The perching eagle oft was heard to cry,
> Or on resounding wings to shoot athwart the sky.

> ('Canto 2', *The Minstrel*)

For all the formal differences, eighteenth-century poets circled back
to common interests, both natural and supernatural. Nature is a force
to be reckoned with in Alastair, mac Mhaighstir Alastair's 'Iorram
Cuain' ('Ocean Oar-Song'):

> An fhairge molach bronnach torrach
>   Giobach corrach ràpalach.

> Is cruaidh ri stiùradh beul-mhuir dhùldaidh
>   Teachd le brùchdail chàrsanaich.

Ronald Black has translated this into English for us:

The sea is rough, it swells and bulges,
  It's shaggy, steep and clamorous.

It's hard to steer through gloomy front-waves
  That hiss ahead with flatulence.

For James Thomson, nature emphatically shapes the poetic mind—'How mighty, how majestic are thy works!', even Winter:

See *WINTER* comes, to rule the varied Year,
Sullen, and sad, with all his rising train,
Vapours, and *Clouds*, and *Storms*. Be these my theme,
These, that exalt the soul to solemn thought,
And heavenly musing. Welcome, kindred glooms!

(*The Seasons*)

William MacMurchy's 'Moladh Chinntìre' ('In Praise of Kintyre') presents a wonderful, enviable harmony between poets and their fellow singers, the birds:

'S ealcarach binnghobach ordail
  Sheinneas an smeòrach san fheasgar,
'N uiseag os a cionn gu h-uallach,
  'N lon 's a' chuach a' cur beas leatha.

(The song-thrush sings in the afternoon,
  Art-skilful, beak-tuneful, regular,
The lark is above her in its gaiety,
  Blackbird and cuckoo serve her as bass.

[translated by Ronald Black])

Often immortalized in poetry around the world, birds can also die on the page. James Montgomery's 'On Finding the Feathers of a Linnet Scattered on the Ground' opens with the 'murder' committed by some 'hovering kite', into whose 'rapacious maw' the eponymous linnet finds 'thy timeless grave'. Set up as a more conventional celebration of birdsong—'let the softest notes rehearse'—Rebekah Carmichael's 'On the St. Bernard's Canary Birds' kills off her 'pretty birds' with the frost: 'They fell, for ever lost'. Mary McMorine's speaker finds lingering comfort in the presence of a linnet that once belonged to her deceased nephew: 'Think not to fly, ah! we must never part' ('On the Death of Her Nephew, Addressed to his Linnet'). A grim and utterly enchanting take on the animal fable genre, Douglas's/Dods's 'The Owl' employs varied rhythms and choppy inter-jections to build a world of chaos from the owl's perspective:

He was digging a grave—the Bird
Shriek'd aloud—the Murderer heard

> Once again that boding scream,
> And saw again those wild eyes gleam—
> And 'Curse on the Fiend!' he cried, and flung
> His mattock up—it caught and hung—
> The Felon stood a while aghast—
> Then fled through the forest, fast, fast, fast!

For all its violence, nature needs protection from us. Thomas Campbell lamented the 'sooty exhalations' that threatened the natural beauty of his native Clyde ('Lines on Revisiting a Scottish River'). Like animals, flowers can have strong political meaning in literature, as we see so raucously expressed in Cunningham's 'It's Hame, and it's Hame':

> The green leaf o' loyaltie 's beginning for to fa',
> The bonnie white rose it is withering an' a';
> But I'll water 't wi' the blude of usurping tyrannie,
> An' green it will grow in my ain countree.

The bonnie white rose brings to mind Bonnie Prince Charlie and the 'withering' of the Jacobite cause in the face of the immense machinery of the Hanoverian government. Other flowers symbolize the universal fragility of the human body. 'E'en thy bright charms must lose their boasted bloom', writes Maria Falconar in 'The Dying Rose'. Beauty and death go hand in hand in Blair's *The Grave*, as expressed with quick precision in the evocative image of the wilting flowers: 'Thy Charms expung'd, | Thy Roses faded, and thy Lillies soil'd'.

Equally adept with narrative poems and philosophical verse, Anne Bannerman could chill the bones or expand the minds of her readers at will. Framed in a flexible ballad format, 'The Dark Ladie' flits between soldierly mirth and fear. A knight's quest can only end with death; here it comes with shameless suddenness:

> And to the alarmed guests she turn'd,
> No breath was heard, no voice, no sound,
> And in a tone, so deadly deep,
> She pledg'd them all around,
> That in their hearts, and thro' their limbs,
> No pulses could be found.

Bannerman's contemplative poetry feels no less unsettling: 'For Nature is nought to the eye of despair | But the images of hope that have vanish'd in air' ('Exile'). James Hogg often celebrated the beauties of the Scottish landscape, 'thou land of the mountain and rock, | Of the ocean, the mist, and the wind' ('Caledonia'). But he too gave voice to the Gothic imagination:

> I hear a small voice from the hill,
> The vapour is deadly, pale, and still—
> A murmuring sough is on the wood,
> And the witching star is red as blood.
>
> ('A Witch's Chant')

Alongside her peers Hogg, Scott, and Bannerman, we find the Canadian immigrant Ann Cuthbert Knight, author of the largely forgotten but brilliantly disturbing narrative poem 'Geraldine':

> All darkly lours the wintry sky,
> And thick the stormy showers descend,
> And, waving to the wild wind's sigh,
> With sullen sound the branches bend.
>
> Chill blows the blast—fast falls the shower,
> But in the hall the fire burns gay,
> And oft, to steal the wintry hour,
> The aged minstrel pours the lay.

'Ah! would some native bard arise', entreats David Vedder in his ode 'To Orkney', 'To sing with all a poet's fire'. The countryside of the mainland and the islands is not simply a source of poetic inspiration, however high in value, and whether dark or light or something else entirely; it is a place where poetry happens. 'To many a mingled sound at once', Scott writes in *The Lady of the Lake*, 'The awakened mountain gave response'. Full of terrors and wonders, song and satire, love and hate, Scottish poetry of the period 1730–1830 was far livelier than we have cared to remember.

NOTE ON THE TEXTS

THIS anthology comprises 218 poems and songs by 137 different people. For established authors I have consulted authoritative critical editions of works where available. As some of the pieces given here have only been published once before, for consistency I have mainly used first editions for my base texts. Where possible, I have also examined substantially revised editions from within the period. In some cases, I have followed a particularly popular, widely circulated or influential version of a poem or song. The base text is indicated below the title of the author's first item. Unless stated otherwise, the subsequent works given in that author's section, if they have multiple pieces, come from the same anthology, single-author collection, book, or periodical. I have kept original spelling where period variations exist, though I have silently corrected any obvious errors and removed inconsistencies within the same texts. The original grammar has been retained, though repeated quotation marks at the start of new lines (a common feature in eighteenth-century print) have been omitted, and punctuation (most often commas, colons, semi-colons, and dashes) adjusted for consistency. Other changes have been made across the collection in the interest of formal regularity. In most cases, as signalled where relevant, the footnotes belong to the original authors, and have only been lightly edited to remove ambiguity caused by the new print context.

Unlike many modern anthologists, I have not glossed Scots words as I want to mimic the clean pages of early editions, and let the sounds speak for themselves. In addition to numerous print dictionaries, the online *Dictionaries of the Scots Language* (DSL) will aid the non-Scots speaker. English versions of all the Gaelic texts have been translated by leading modern scholars and poets. If you would like to learn more about the language, Edward Dwelly's *Illustrated Gaelic-English Dictionary* (1911) remains the standard source. Two densely packed dual-language anthologies covering our period, Ronald Black's *An Lasair* (2001) and Donald E. Meek's *Caran an t-Saoghail* (2003), have proven invaluable for my research—and I would strongly urge readers with a concern for the fullness of Scottish literature to seek them out. Another useful book is a smaller and more recent collection covering five hundred years of Gaelic love and transgressive verse, Peter Mackay and Iain S. MacPherson's *An Leabhar Liath* (2016). An older book, Derick

Thomson's *Gaelic Poetry in the Eighteenth Century: A Bilingual Anthology* (1993), remains indispensable. Narrower in its focus, John Lorne Campbell's *Highland Songs of the Forty-Five* (1933) is similarly vital for any reader interested in Jacobite culture. These collections identify the poets, however tentatively, and expertly place them within different regional and national milieux.

In order to strike a better balance between male-presenting and female-presenting writers than is common in anthologies even today, I have excluded a number of highly accomplished if over-represented male poets. In some cases, those men cover ground amply taken up by poets and songwriters included here—usually Burns or his imitators. In others, their inclusion would lead to over-clustering in specific decades. Many eligible people missing here—especially men—can be found in the most comprehensive modern anthology of Scottish writing, David McCordick's *Scottish Literature* (1996), which runs to 2,497 pages (excluding a subsequent volume of twentieth-century literature), though it does not make room for Gaelic texts in translation or in the original. Roderick Watson's *The Poetry of Scotland* (1995), which does cover Gaelic (and Scots and English), takes in poetry produced between 1380 and 1980 across its 714 pages. By design, it is therefore highly selective. To aid a more appropriate gender balance, especially when dealing with a period renowned for producing circles of mutually supportive female and male authors, I have relied heavily on meticulous anthologies devoted to Scottish women's writing. The chief such collections are Moira Burgess's *The Other Voice* (1987), Catherine Kerrigan's *An Anthology of Scottish Women Poets* (1991), and Nancy Kushigan and Stephen Behrendt's *Scottish Women Poets of the Romantic Period* (2001), as well as Roger Lonsdale's groundbreaking edition, *Eighteenth-Century Women Poets* (1989).

A partial and far from exhaustive list of alternative inductees might contain Lord Gardenstone, Andrew Erskine, Robert Alves, John Dunlop, Andrew Scott, John Hamilton, William Cameron, John Pinkerton, Alexander Wilson, Alexander Balfour, James Scadlock, Joseph Train, George Beattie, Thomas Pringle, William Glen, and William Motherwell, all of whom were successful, in different ways, on their own terms. Pringle has even been dubbed the father of South African poetry. Wilson became a respected ornithologist in America. Despite the necessary restriction on space in the pursuit of breadth, I am pleased to showcase some important long poems in their entirety. Other anthologies have accommodated a small band of long poems, and I would encourage you to track them down: Thomas Crawford, David

Hewitt, and Alexander Law's *Longer Scottish Poems*, volume II: *1650–1830* (1987) and Robert Irvine's *The Edinburgh Anthology of Scottish Literature* (2009). Lesser known longer poems of the period miss out, but they more than merit new attention (and republication)—to name but two: John Ogilvie's Hebridean epic *Rona, a Poem, in Seven Books* (1777) and George Skene's *Donald Bane: An Heroic Poem, in Three Books* (1796). (Ogilvie is instead represented by one of his shorter odes.) Running to 2,560 lines over four books, James Grainger's georgic poem *The Sugar Cane* (1764) would be a useful historical document for its copious footnotes alone. The Select Bibliography that follows comprises key books and articles suitable for a study of the literature made available here. Together these materials provide a new introduction to the field of Scottish poetry written in the eighteenth and nineteenth centuries.

SELECT BIBLIOGRAPHY

Dictionaries and Other Resources

Aitken, W. R., *Scottish Literature in English and Scots: A Guide to Information Sources* (Detroit: Gale, 1982).

Campbell, Alexander, *An Introduction to the History of Scotch Poetry* (Edinburgh: Printed for Andrew Foulis, 1798).

Dictionaries of the Scots Language (DSL) <http://www.dsl.ac.uk>.

Dwelly, Edward, *The Illustrated Gaelic-English Dictionary* (Edinburgh: Birlinn, 1993; first published in 1911).

Ewan, Elizabeth, Rose Pipes, Jane Rendall, and Siân Reynolds (eds), *The New Biographical Dictionary of Scottish Women* (Edinburgh: Edinburgh University Press, 2018).

Ferguson, Mary, and Ann Matheson, *Scottish Gaelic Union Catalogue: A List of Books Printed in Scottish Gaelic from 1567 to 1973* (Edinburgh: National Library of Scotland, 1984).

Glen, Duncan, *The Poetry of the Scots: An Introduction and Bibliographical Guide to Gaelic, Scots, Latin and English* (Edinburgh: Edinburgh University Press, 1991).

Irving, David, *The Lives of the Scottish Poets, with Dissertations on the Literary History of Scotland and the Early Scottish Drama*, 2nd edn (London: Longman, Hurst, Rees & Orme, 1810; first published in 1804).

Oxford Dictionary of National Biography (ODNB) <http://www.oxforddnb.com>.

Robertson, Joseph, *Lives of Scottish Poets, with Portraits and Vignettes*, 6 vols (London: Printed for Thomas Boys, 1822).

Robinson, Mairi, *The Concise Scots Dictionary* (Aberdeen: Aberdeen University Press, 1985).

Smith, Dennis, assisted by Paul Barnaby and Ulrike Morét, *Scotland: World Bibliographical Series* (Oxford, Santa Barbara, and Denver: Clio Press, 1998).

18th- and 19th-Century Anthologies

Anderson, Robert (ed.), *The Works of the British Poets, with Prefaces Biographical and Critical*, 14 vols (London: Printed for John and Arthur Arch; Edinburgh: Bell & Bradfute and J. Mundell & Co., 1792–1807).

The Caledoniad. A Collection of Poems, Written Chiefly by Scottish Authors, 3 vols (London: W. Hay, 1775).

Campbell, Thomas (ed.), *Specimens of the British Poets*, 7 vols (London: John Murray, 1819).

Chambers, Robert (ed.), *The Scottish Songs*, 2 vols (Edinburgh: William Tait, 1829).

Cromek, R. H. (ed.), *Select Scotish Songs, Ancient and Modern*, 2 vols (London: Printed for T. Cadell and W. Davies, 1810).

Cunningham, Allan (ed.), *Songs: Chiefly in the Rural Language of Scotland* (London: Printed for the Author, 1813).

Cunningham, Allan (ed.), *The Songs of Scotland, Ancient and Modern*, 4 vols (London: Printed for John Taylor, 1825).

Donaldson, Alexander (ed.), *A Collection of Original Poems. By Scotch Gentlemen*, 2 vols (Edinburgh: Printed for A. Donaldson, and sold by R. and J. Dodsley, and J. Richardson, 1760–2).

Gillies, John (ed.), *A Collection of Ancient and Modern Gaelic Poems and Songs* (Perth: Printed for John Gillies, 1786).

Herd, David (ed.), *Ancient and Modern Scottish Songs, Heroic Ballads, Etc.*, 2 vols (Edinburgh: Printed for James Dickson and Charles Elliot, 1776).

Hogg, James (ed.), *The Jacobite Relics of Scotland*, 2 vols (Edinburgh: Printed for William Blackwood; London: T. Cadell and W. Davies, 1819–21).

Jamieson, Robert (ed.), *Popular Ballads and Songs, from Tradition, Manuscripts, and Scarce Editions*, 2 vols (Edinburgh: Archibald Constable and Co., Cadell and Davies; London: John Murray, 1806).

Johnson, James (ed.), *The Scots Musical Museum*, 6 vols (Edinburgh: James Johnson & Co., 1787–1803).

Mac-an-Tuairneir, Paruig (ed.), *Comhchruinneacha do dh' Orain Taghta, Ghaidhealach* (Edinburgh: Stewart, 1813).

MacDomhnuill, Raonuill (ed.), *Comh-Chruinneachidh Orannaigh Gaidhealach* (Edinburgh: Walter Ruddiman, 1776).

MacKenzie, John (ed.), *Sar-Obair nam Bard Gaelach; or, The Beauties of Gaelic Poetry, and Lives of the Highland Bards*, 4th edn (Edinburgh: Maclachlan & Stewart, 1877).

Mackintosh, Duncan (ed.), *Co-Chruinneach dh' Orain Thaghte Ghaeleach* (Edinburgh: John Elder, 1831).

Maclean Sinclair, Alexander (ed.), *Clàrsach na Coille: A Collection of Gaelic Poetry* (Glasgow: Archibald Sinclair, 1881).

Maclean Sinclair, A. (ed.), *The Gaelic Bards from 1715 to 1765* (Charlottetown: Haszard & Moore, 1892).

Mac-na-Ceàrdadh, Gilleasbuig (ed.), *An t-Oranaiche* (Glasgow: Archibald Sinclair, 1879).

Malcolm, Robert (ed.), *Jacobite Minstrelsy* (Glasgow: R. Griffin & Co., 1829).

Park, Thomas (ed.), *The Works of the British Poets, Collated with the Best Editions*, 48 vols (London: J. Sharpe, 1808–9).

Pinkerton, John (ed.), *Select Scottish Ballads*, 2 vols (London: J. Nichols, 1783).

Ramsay, Allan (ed.), *The Tea-Table Miscellany*, 3 vols (Edinburgh: Thomas Ruddiman, 1723–37).

Ritson, Joseph (ed.), *Scotish Songs*, 2 vols (London: Printed for J. Johnson and J. Egerton, 1794).

Rogers, Charles (ed.), *The Modern Scottish Minstrel; or, The Songs of Scotland of the Past Half Century*, 6 vols (Edinburgh: Adam & Charles Black, 1857).

A Select Collection of Scots Poems Chiefly in the Broad Buchan Dialect (Edinburgh: T. Ruddiman, 1785).

Smith, R. A. (ed.), *The Scotish Minstrel. A Selection from the Vocal Melodies of Scotland, Ancient and Modern*, 6 vols (Edinburgh: Robt. Purdie, 1821–4).

Stewart, Alexander, and Donald Stewart (ed.), *Cochruinneacha Taoghta de Shaothair nam Bard Gaëleach. A Choice Collection of the Works of the Highland Bards, Collected in the Highlands and Isles*, 2 vols (Edinburgh: Charles Stewart, 1804).

Struthers, John (ed.), *The Harp of Caledonia: A Collection of Songs, Ancient and Modern, Chiefly Scottish*, 2 vols (Glasgow: E. Khull, 1821).

Tytler, Sarah, and J. L. Watson (ed.), *The Songstresses of Scotland*, 2 vols (London: Strahan & Co., 1871).

Wilson, James Grant (ed.), *The Poets and Poetry of Scotland, from the Earliest to the Present Time*, 4 vols (London, Glasgow, and Edinburgh: Blackie & Son, 1877).

Modern Anthologies

Black, Ronald (ed.), *An Lasair: Anthology of 18th Century Scottish Gaelic Verse* (Edinburgh: Origin, 2019; first published in 2001).

Burgess, Moira (ed.), *The Other Voice: Scottish Women's Writing since 1808* (Edinburgh: Polygon, 1987).

Campbell, John Lorne (ed.), *Highland Songs of the Forty-Five* (Edinburgh: John Grant, 1933).

Crawford, Robert, and Mick Imlah (eds), *The Penguin Book of Scottish Verse* (London: Penguin, 2006; first published in 2000).

Crawford, Thomas (ed.), *Love, Labour and Liberty: The Eighteenth-Century Scottish Lyric* (Cheadle: Carcanet Press, 1976).

Crawford, Thomas, David Hewitt, and Alexander Law (eds), *Longer Scottish Poems*, Volume II: *1650–1830* (Edinburgh: Scottish Academic Press, 1987).

Irvine, Robert (ed.), *The Edinburgh Anthology of Scottish Literature*, 2 vols (Glasgow: Kennedy & Boyd, 2010; first published in 2009).

Kerrigan, Catherine (ed.), *An Anthology of Scottish Women Poets* (Edinburgh: Edinburgh University Press, 1991).

Kushigan, Nancy, and Stephen Behrendt (eds), *Scottish Women Poets of the Romantic Period* (Alexandria, VA: Alexander Stress Press, 2001).

Lindsay, Maurice (ed.), *Scotland: An Anthology* (London: Robert Hale, 1989; first published in 1974).

Lonsdale, Roger (ed.), *Eighteenth-Century Women Poets* (Oxford: Oxford University Press, 1990; first published in 1989).

Lonsdale, Roger (ed.), *The New Oxford Books of Eighteenth-Century Verse* (Oxford: Oxford University Press, 2009; first published in 1984).

Lyle, Emily B. (ed.), *Andrew Crawfurd's Collection of Ballads and Songs* (Edinburgh: Scottish Text Society, 1975–6).

Lyle, Emily B. (ed.), *Scottish Ballads* (Edinburgh: Canongate, 1997; first published in 1993).

McCordick, David (ed.), *Scottish Literature: An Anthology*, 2 vols (New York: Peter Lang, 1996).

MacDiarmid, Hugh (ed.), *The Golden Treasury of Scottish Poetry* (London: Macmillan, 1940).

Mackay, Peter, and Iain S. MacPherson (eds), *An Leabhar Liath: The Light Blue Book: 500 Years of Gaelic Love and Transgressive Verse* (Edinburgh: Luath Press, 2016).

MacLachlan, Christopher (ed.), *Before Burns: Eighteenth-Century Scottish Poetry* (Edinburgh: Canongate, 2002).

MacQueen, John, and Tom Scott (eds), *The Oxford Book of Scottish Verse* (Oxford: Oxford University Press, 1991; first published in 1966).

Meek, Donald E. (ed.), *Caran an t-Saoghail: The Wiles of the World: Anthology of 19ᵗʰ Century Scottish Gaelic Verse* (Edinburgh: Birlinn, 2003).

Moore, Dafydd (ed.), *Ossian and Ossianism in Britain and Ireland, 1750–c.1820*, 4 vols (London: Routledge, 2004).

Thomson, Derick S. (ed.), *Gaelic Poetry in the Eighteenth Century: A Bilingual Anthology* (Aberdeen: Association for Scottish Literary Studies, 1993).

Watson, Roderick (ed.), *The Poetry of Scotland: Gaelic, Scots and English 1380–1980* (Edinburgh: Edinburgh University Press, 1995).

Watson, William J. (ed.), *Bardachd Ghaidhlig*, 3rd edn (Stirling: A. Learmonth, 1959).

Period Surveys and Studies

Christian, George S., *Beside the Bard: Scottish Lowland Poetry in the Age of Burns* (Lewisburg: Bucknell University Press, 2020).

Craig, David, *Scottish Literature and the Scottish People, 1680–1830* (London: Chatto & Windus, 1961).

Crawford, Robert, *Devolving English Literature* (Edinburgh: Edinburgh University Press, 2001; first published in 1992).

Crawford, Thomas, *Society and the Lyric: A Study of the Song Culture of Eighteenth-Century Scotland* (Edinburgh: Scottish Academic Press, 1979).

Daiches, David, *The Paradox of Scottish Culture: The Eighteenth-Century Experience* (London: Oxford University Press, 1964).

Davis, Leith, Ian Duncan, and Janet Sorensen (eds), *Scotland and the Borders of Romanticism* (Cambridge: Cambridge University Press, 2004).

Donaldson, William, *The Jacobite Song: Political Myth and National Identity* (Aberdeen: Aberdeen University Press, 1988).

Gifford, Douglas (ed.), *The History of Scottish Literature*, Volume 3: *Nineteenth Century* (Aberdeen: Aberdeen University Press, 1989; first published in 1988).

Gifford, Douglas, and Dorothy McMillan (eds), *A History of Scottish Women's Writing* (Edinburgh: Edinburgh University Press, 1997).

Hook, Andrew (ed.), *The History of Scottish Literature*, Volume 2: *1660–1800* (Aberdeen: Aberdeen University Press, 1989; first published in 1987).

McLean, Ralph, Ronnie Young, and Kenneth Simpson (eds), *The Scottish Enlightenment and Literary Culture* (Lewisburg: Bucknell University Press, 2016).

Manning, Susan (ed.), *The Edinburgh History of Scottish Literature*, Volume 2: *Enlightenment, Britain and Empire (1707–1918)* (Edinburgh: Edinburgh University Press, 2007).

Pittock, Murray (ed.), *The Edinburgh Companion to Scottish Romanticism* (Edinburgh: Edinburgh University Press, 2011).

Pittock, Murray, *Poetry and Jacobite Politics in Eighteenth-Century Britain and Ireland* (Cambridge: Cambridge University Press, 2006; first published in 1994).

Pittock, Murray, *Scottish and Irish Romanticism* (Oxford: Oxford University Press, 2011; first published in 2008).

Sher, Richard B., *The Enlightenment and the Book: Scottish Authors and Their Publishers in Eighteenth-Century Britain, Ireland & America* (Chicago: University of Chicago Press, 2006).

Simpson, Kenneth, *The Protean Scot: The Crisis of Identity in Eighteenth Century Scottish Literature* (Aberdeen: Aberdeen University Press, 1988).

Thomson, Derick, *An Introduction to Gaelic Poetry* (Edinburgh: Edinburgh University Press, 1989; first published in 1974).

Walker, Marshall, *Scottish Literature since 1707* (London and New York: Longman, 1996).

CHRONOLOGY

Year	Historical Events	The Poets
1723–37		Allan Ramsay, *The Tea-Table Miscellany*
1730		James Thomson, *The Seasons*
1732	The First Secession from the established Church of Scotland	
1736	The Porteous Riots shake Edinburgh	
1739	*The Scots Magazine* enters circulation Formation of the Black Watch regiment	
1740		David Mallet, *Alfred: A Masque*
1741	Robert Foulis sets up a publishing business in Glasgow	
1743		Robert Blair, *The Grave* Death of Chevalier Ramsay
1744		John Armstrong, *The Art of Preserving Health*
1745	Second Jacobite rising (the '45), led by Charles Edward Stuart The Battle of Prestonpans Jacobites capture Carlisle	Death of William Meston
1746	The Battle of Culloden The Act of Proscription The Heritable Jurisdictions (Scotland) Act	Deaths of Lady Grizel Baillie and Robert Blair
1747	A theatre is established at Playhouse Close in Edinburgh	
1748	David Hume, *An Enquiry Concerning Human Understanding*	Tobias Smollett, *Roderick Random* James Thomson, *The Castle of Indolence* Death of James Thomson
1749	A stage coach service between Edinburgh and Glasgow now runs	Alexander Robertson of Struan, *Poems, on Various Subjects and Occasions* Death of Alexander Robertson of Struan

Year	Historical Events	The Poets
1751	John Smith opens a bookshop in Glasgow (John Smith & Son remains the oldest bookselling company in the English-speaking world)	Alastair, mac Mhaighstir Alastair, *Ais-Eiridh na Sean Chánoin Albannaich*
1754	Building of the Royal Exchange (later known as Edinburgh City Chambers)	Death of William Hamilton of Bangour
1756–63	The Seven Years' War	
1756		Thomas Blacklock, *Poems* Death of Jerome Stone
1757	Death of Thomas Ruddiman, printer to the University of Edinburgh	William Wilkie, *The Epigoniad*
1758		Death of Allan Ramsay
1759	William Robertson, *The History of Scotland 1542–1603* Adam Smith, *The Theory of Moral Sentiments*	John Ogilvie, *The Day of Judgment* Death of Domhnall MacLeòid (Donald MacLeod)
1760	George III becomes King of Great Britain and of Ireland	James Macpherson, *Fragments of Ancient Poetry Collected in the Highlands of Scotland* William Hamilton of Bangour, *Poems on Several Occasions*
1761	Thomas Gillespie founds the Relief Church	James Macpherson, *Fingal*
1762	Land reform leads to the Highland Clearances Lord Bute becomes the first Scottish Prime Minister of Britain Hugh Blair becomes the Regius Chair of Rhetoric and Belles Lettres at Edinburgh (arguably the world's first professorship of English Literature)	James Boswell, *The Cub, at New-market* William Falconer, *The Shipwreck*
1763	Scotland's first purpose-built concert hall, St Cecilia's Hall, is built	
1764		James Grainger, *The Sugar Cane*
1765		James Macpherson, *The Works of Ossian* Deaths of David Mallet and Jean Adam
1766		William Julius Mickle, *Pollio: An Elegiac Ode*

Year	Historical Events	The Poets
1767	Adam Ferguson, *An Essay on the History of Civil Society*	Dùghall Bochanan (Dugald Buchanan), *Spiritual Songs* Death of Michael Bruce
1768–81	First edition of *Encyclopædia Britannica* produced in Edinburgh	
1768	Walter Ruddiman establishes *Weekly Magazine*	Alexander Ross, *The Fortunate Shepherdess*
	Death of Andrew Millar (publisher)	Death of Dùghall Bochanan (Dugald Buchanan)
1769	The *Millar v Taylor* case upholds perpetual common law copyright Opening of the first Theatre Royal in Edinburgh	
1770		William Falconer is lost at sea and presumed dead Death of Alastair, mac Mhaighstir Alastair
1771–4		James Beattie, *The Minstrel*
1771		Henry Mackenzie, *The Man of Feeling* Tobias Smollett, *The Expedition of Humphry Clinker* Death of Tobias Smollett
1772		Michael Bruce, *Poems on Several Occasions* Deaths of James Graeme and William Wilkie
1773	*Hinton v Donaldson* disputes the existence of a common-law copyright	Robert Fergusson, *Poems* James Graeme, *Poems on Several Occasions*
1774	*Donaldson v Becket* rules against perpetual copyright	Death of Robert Fergusson
1775–83	American Revolutionary War	
1776	Adam Smith, *The Wealth of Nations*	Raonuill MacDomhnuill, *Comh-Chruinneachidh Orannaigh Gaidhealach* David Herd, *Ancient and Modern Scottish Songs*
	Death of Robert Foulis (printer)	James Beattie, *Poems on Several Occasions* Death of Ailean Stiùbhart (Allan Stewart)
1777		Tobias Smollett, *Plays and Poems*

Year	Historical Events	The Poets
1778	The Papists Act 1778	Deaths of Rob Donn (Robert Mackay) and Uilleam MacMhurchaidh (William MacMurchy)
	The Highland Society of London is created	
1779		Deaths of John Armstrong and Iain mac Fhearchair (John MacCodrum)
1780	Formation of the Society of Antiquaries of Scotland	Death of Iain MacRath (John MacRae)
1781	Death of Walter Ruddiman (printer and newspaper proprietor)	Alexander Geddes, *Linton, a Tweedale Pastoral*
1783	Creation of the Glasgow Chamber of Commerce, the first in Britain The Royal Society of Edinburgh is founded Thomas Bell patents roller printing	John Pinkerton, *Select Scottish Ballads*
1784		Death of Alexander Ross
1786		John Gillies, *A Collection of Ancient and Modern Gaelic Poems and Songs* Robert Burns, *Poems, Chiefly in the Scottish Dialect* Death of Dùghall Bochanan (Dugald Buchanan)
1787–1803		James Johnson, *The Scots Musical Museum*
1788–99	The French Revolution and Terror	
1788		Gavin Turnbull, *Poetical Essays* Maria and Harriet Falconar, *Poems* Deaths of William Julius Mickle and James Mylne
1789		Death of Elizabeth Scot
1790		Joanna Baillie, *Poems* Death of Andrew Macdonald
1791–1804	The Haitian Revolution	
1791	The Roman Catholic Relief Act 1791	Death of Thomas Blacklock
1792–1807		Robert Anderson, *The Works of the British Poets*
1792	The Year of the Sheep (*bliadhna nan caorach*)	

Year	Historical Events	The Poets
	The Friends of the People Society meets for the first time	
1793	Thomas Muir of Huntershill is sentenced to transportation Death of John Murray (publisher and bookseller)	George Thomson, *A Select Collection of Original Scottish Airs*
1794	Death of Alexander Donaldson (bookseller)	Isabella Kelly, *Collection of Poems and Fables on Several Occasions* James Grahame, *Poems, in English, Scotch, and Latin* Deaths of Susanna Blamire and Alison Cockburn
1795		Death of James Boswell
1796	The Royal Technical College (now the University of Strathclyde) is founded	Deaths of Robert Burns and James Macpherson
1798	The Irish Rebellion of 1798	Alexander Campbell, *An Introduction to the History of Scotch Poetry* Joanna Baillie, *De Monfort* Anne Ross, *A Collection of Poems*
1799		Thomas Campbell, *The Pleasures of Hope*
1801	The kingdoms of Great Britain and Ireland merge to form the United Kingdom Greenock Burns Club is established	James Hogg, *Scottish Pastorals, Poems, Songs* Deaths of Jean Glover and Richard Gall
1802–3		Walter Scott, *Minstrelsy of the Scottish Border*
1802	*Edinburgh Review* re-established	Anne Bannerman, *Tales of Superstition and Chivalry* Anne Hunter, *Poems* Death of Alexander Geddes
1803–15	The Napoleonic Wars	
1803	The Irish Rebellion of 1803	James Ballantyne and Walter Scott establish a publishing office in Edinburgh Alexander Boswell, *Songs, Chiefly in the Scottish Dialect* Isobel Pagan, *A Collection of Songs and Poems on Several Occasions* John Mayne, *Glasgow: A Poem* Death of James Beattie
1804		David Irving, *The Lives of the Scottish Poets*

Year	Historical Events	The Poets
		Alexander and Donald Stewart, *Cochruinneacha Taoghta de Shaothair nam Bard Gaëleach*
		James Grahame, *The Sabbath*
1805	*The Glasgow Herald* newspaper begins circulation	Walter Scott, *The Lay of the Last Minstrel*
		James Nicol, *Poems, Chiefly in the Scottish Dialect*
		Robert Tannahill, *The Soldier's Return*
		Deaths of Janet Graham and Jean Elliot
1806		Robert Jamieson, *Popular Ballads and Songs*
		Alexander Douglas, *Poems, Chiefly in the Scottish Dialect*
		James Montgomery, *The Wanderer of Switzerland and Other Poems*
1807	The Hunterian Museum and Art Gallery opens in Glasgow	James Hogg, *The Mountain Bard*
		Death of John Skinner
1808–9		John Jamieson, *Etymological Dictionary of the Scottish Language*
1808		Elizabeth Hamilton, *The Cottagers of Glenburnie*
		Anne Grant, *The Highlanders, and Other Poems*
		Walter Scott, *Marmion*
		Deaths of John Home and James Muirhead
1809		Lord Byron, *English Bards and Scotch Reviewers*
1810		R. H. Cromek, *Select Scotish Songs, Ancient and Modern*
		Walter Scott, *The Lady of the Lake*
		Deaths of Robert Tannahill and Anna Gordon (Mrs Brown of Falkland)
1811		Anne Grant, *Essays on the Superstitions of the Highlanders*
		Deaths of John Leyden and James Grahame
1812–15	The War of 1812	
1812	Henry Bell builds Europe's first passenger steamboat	Lord Byron, *Childe Harold's Pilgrimage*
		John Wilson, *The Isle of Palms, and Other Poems*

Year	*Historical Events*	*The Poets*
		William Tennant, *Anster Fair*
		Death of Donnchadh Bàn Mac an
		t-Saoir (Duncan Ban Macintyre)
1813		Walter Scott declines the position of Poet
		Laureate
		Paruig Mac-an-Tuairneir,
		Comhchruinneacha do dh' Orain Taghta,
		Ghaidhealach
		James Hogg, *The Queen's Wake*
		Deaths of John Ogilvie and Janet Little
1814		Walter Scott, *Waverley*
		Mary Brunton, *Discipline*
		Deaths of Alastair MacFhionghain
		(Alexander MacKinnon) and Patricia
		Rolland Darling
1815	Death of William Creech	Christian Johnstone, *Clan-Albin*
	(publisher)	Death of Bean Torra Dhamh (Mary
		MacPherson) Lord Byron, *Hebrew*
		Melodies
1816		John Wilson, *The City of the Plague, and*
		Other Poems
		Ann Cuthbert Knight, *A Year in*
		Canada, and Other Poems
		Dorothea Primrose Campbell, *Poems*
		Deaths of Elizabeth Hamilton, Gavin
		Turnbull, Ebenezer Picken, and
		Christian Milne
1817	*Blackwood's Edinburgh*	Death of John Tait
	Magazine is launched	
	The Scotsman enters circulation	
1818		Susan Ferrier, *Marriage*
		Deaths of Hector Macneill and Mary
		Brunton
1819–21	James Hogg, *The Jacobite*	
	Relics of Scotland	
1819		Thomas Campbell, *Specimens of the*
		British Poets
		John Gibson Lockhart, *Peter's Letters to*
		His Kinsfolk
		Death of James Nicol
1820	George IV becomes King of	Walter Scott receives a baronetcy from
	the United Kingdom	George IV
	The Celtic Society (later The	James Hogg, *Winter Evening Tales*
	Royal Celtic Society) is	
	founded	

Year	Historical Events	The Poets
	The Radical War (also known as the Scottish Insurrection), in which artisans sought economic and political reform	
	Formation of the United Secession Church	
1821–9	The Greek War of Independence	
1821	William Fairbairn builds the first iron-hulled steamship	John Galt, *The Annals of the Parish*
	Founding of the School of Arts of Edinburgh (Heriot-Watt University)	John Struthers, *The Harp of Caledonia*
		Deaths of Anne Hunter, Isobel Pagan, and Alexander Douglas
1822	King George IV visits Scotland	Allan Cunningham, *Sir Marmaduke Maxwell*
	The first Highland and Agricultural Show takes place	Death of Eòghann MacLachlainn (Ewen MacLachlan)
1823	Founding of the Bannatyne Club	William Grant Stewart, *Popular Superstitions*
		The Poems of James Grahame, John Logan, and William Falconer
1824		James Hogg, *The Private Memoirs and Confessions of a Justified Sinner*
		Death of Lord Byron
1825–6	Financial and publishing industries collapse, affecting Constable, the Ballantynes, and other Scottish printers and booksellers	
1825		Allan Cunningham, *The Songs of Scotland, Ancient and Modern*
		Lady Anne Barnard, *Auld Robin Gray*
		Deaths of Lady Anne Barnard, Helen Craik, William Gillespie, and William Knox
1826	The Scottish Academy (later known as the Royal Scottish Academy) is founded	
	The Irvine Burns Club formed	
1827	Death of Archibald Constable (publisher and bookseller)	Death of Margaret Chalmers
1828	Burke and Hare arrested for the West Port Murders	Deaths of Elizabeth Grant and Ailean Dùghallach (Allan MacDougall)

SCOTTISH POETRY, 1730–1830

ALEXANDER ROBERTSON OF STRUAN

(1670–1749)

—

THE Jacobite army officer Alexander Robertson of Struan was the thirteenth holder of the barony of Struan or Strowan and chief of Clan Robertson—and a prolific poet. Amid heightened anxieties about sedition, few of his poems appeared in the public domain during his lifetime, however. A decent selection of his works was finally published in 1749, mostly taken from his manuscripts, not long after his death at the age of seventy-nine. And he has been a staple of Jacobite anthologies ever since. A highly educated man, Struan wrote poetry with consummate ease in several languages, including Gaelic, English, French, Italian, and Latin. *Poems, on Various Subjects and Occasions* (1749; revised in 1752) traverses an astonishing array of genres, modes, and tones, from the elegiac to the angry, and includes imitations of Horace, Virgil, Catullus, and others. Struan could write with great skill in either the long or short form, but the latter best captures the rapidity of his intellect.

—

'Liberty Preserved: or, Love Destroyed. A Song'

Poems, on Various Subjects and Occasions (Edinburgh: Ch. Alexander, 1752).

> At length the Bondage I have broke
>   Which gave me so much Pain;
> I've slipt my Heart out of the Yoke,
>   Never to drudge again;
> And, conscious of my long Disgrace,
> Have thrown my Chain at CUPID's Face.
>
> If ever he attempt again
>   My Freedom to enslave,
> I'll court the Godhead of Champain
>   Which makes the Coward brave,
> And, when that Deity has heal'd my Soul,
> I'll drown the little Bastard in my Bowl.

'An Ode in the Time of a Storm'

Now Jove in his Ire is dealing with his Thunder,
And the Weight of his Palm breaks the Clouds all asunder,
High Lightning he scatters, and Pails full of Rain
Showers down to destroy the Delights of the Swain.

Our Days are so clouded, some Times, that the Light
Of Noontide is chang'd to the Shades of the Night,
And at Night, with the Lightning, so fatally gay,
You'd swear that the Shades were converted to Day.

But, ye Gods, who reside in our Altars so high,
Where Wine is still offer'd as oft as you're dry,
For your Pleasure and Profit defend from all Harm
The innocent Grape in Despite of the Storm.

'The Careless Good-Fellow'

(Tune: "Ne parlez plus de Politique")

Plague on the Race of Politicians,
    Both great and small.
Tho' they be call'd the State's Physicians,
    They poison all:
Let them be fraudfully espousing
    Or George or James;
We'll here, in Peace of Mind carousing,
    Dismiss their Claims.

Why should we mind King Stanislaus,
    Or him of France,
Their Harmony shall never draw us
    To join their Dance.
Ev'n let the Saxon, with the Russian,
    The Vistula pass,
We'll to themselves leave the Discussion,
    And drink our Glass.

If Don Phillippo should recover
    What was his own,
While little Carlos makes a Pother
    To mount a Throne,

Let them repine who feel their Losses,
    The Toper sings;
While rosy Wine's a Cure for Crosses,
    A Fig for Kings.

Let the poor Herd of German Princes
    Their Bacon save,
And leave his Head that no more Sense has
    Than God him gave.
If Berwick (much averse to Plunder)
    Harass the Rhine,
We'll beg him spare his Fire and Thunder,
    To save the Vine.

Let the Sardinian Hero caper,
    And cast his Coat,
Nor seek in Armour keen to vapour;
    He like it not,
Let him bestir his Limbs to conquer
    The Milanese;
Give us of Burgundy a Bumper,
    We're much at Ease.

Should the Grand Turk with Janizaries
    His Limit cross,
And drive August o'er all his Ferries,
    'Twere no great Loss:
And should he broach his vile Opinions,
    What must we do?
We have much worse in our Dominions;
    Come here's to you.

Let old Papa, with Crown like Steeple,
    His Sons advise,
And curb his much believing People,
    With Truth or Lies:
Let him ride on, and keep the Saddle,
    'Tis none of mine;
With nought that's Romish will we meddle,
    Except his Wine.

Myn-Heer-Van-Frog no Salamander
    Appears to be,
And hates the Toils of Alexander,

As much as we
Who'd live in Flames, and push the Quarrel
    With France and Spain;
'Tis safer far to pierce yon Barrel
    Of stout Champain.

And now let Discord far be from us
    In any Shape,
Nor Christian Blood be drawn among us,
    But from the Grape.
Come fill the Bowl, for in such Measure
    As Wine does rise,
We'll, rich in so divine a Treasure,
    The World despise.

ALLAN RAMSAY
(1684–1758)

━━

A LANARKSHIRE native, Allan Ramsay was the most influential Scottish poet of his generation. As many as 143 original and subsequent editions of his works were published in his lifetime alone. Moving to Edinburgh for an apprenticeship to a wigmaker, Ramsay took on various jobs before finally settling on bookselling. In 1712 he became a founding member of the Easy Club, through which he made important connections with Jacobite men of letters. As a bookseller, Ramsay was able to issue his own work on his terms, particularly vernacular literature with *Scots Songs* (1718). He quickly followed up with a handsome quarto volume of *Poems* (1721), as well as *Fables and Tales* and *A Tale of Three Bonnets* (both 1722), and *Fair Assembly* (1723). With the widespread success of his three-volume *Tea-Table Miscellany* (1723–7), his reputation as a leading Scottish poet and collector was fully assured. (A fourth volume appeared in 1737, by which time the original set had reached ten editions.) By the 1730s Ramsay had become a household favourite in Scotland. His influence on later poets, particularly the folk revivalists of the second half of the eighteenth century, continued to grow.

━━

'The Last Speech of a Wretched Miser'

Poems: Volume II (Edinburgh: Thomas Ruddiman, 1728).

> O Dool! and am I forc'd to die,
> And nae mair my dear Siller see,
> That glanc'd sae sweetly in my Eye!
>   It breaks my Heart;
> My Gowd! my Bands! alackanie!
>   That we shou'd part.
>
> For you I labour'd Night and Day,
> For you I did my Friends betray,

For you on stinking Caff I lay,
  And Blankets thin;
And for your Sake fed mony a Flea
  Upon my Skin.

Like *Tantalus* I lang have stood
Chin deep into a Siller Flood;
Yet ne'er was able for my Blood,
  But Pain and Strife,
To ware ae Drap on Claiths or Food,
  To cherish Life.

Or like the wissen'd beardless Wights,
Wha herd the Wives of Eastern Knights,
Yet ne'er enjoy the saft Delights
  Of Lasses bony;
Thus did I watch lang Days and Nights
  My lovely Money.

Altho' my Annual rents cou'd feed
Thrice forty Fowk that stood in Need,
I grudg'd my sell my daily Bread:
  And if frae hame,
My Pouch produc'd an Ingan Head,
  To please my Wame.

To keep you cosie in a Hoord,
This Hunger I with Ease endur'd;
And never dought a Doit afford
  To ane of Skill,
Wha for a Dollar might have cur'd
  Me of this Ill.

I never wore my Claiths with brushing,
Nor wrung away my Sarks with washing;
Nor ever sat in Taverns dashing
  Away my Coin,
To find out Wit or Mirth by clashing
  O'er dearthfu' Wine.

Abiet my Pow was bald and bare,
I wore nae frizl'd Limmer's Hair,
Which takes of Flower to keep it fair
  Frae reesting Free,

As meikle as wad dine and mair,
       The like of me.

Nor kept I Servants, Tales to tell,
But toom'd my Coodies a' my sell;
To hane in Candle I had a Spell
       Baith cheap and bright,
A Fish-head, when it 'gins to smell,
       Gives curious Light.

What Reason can I shaw, quo' ye,
To save and starve, to cheat and lie,
To live a Beggar, and to die
       Sae rich in Coin?
That's mair than can be gi'en by me,
       Tho' *Belzie* join.

Some said my Looks were groff and sowr,
Fretfu', drumbly, dull, and dowr:
I own it was na in my Power,
       My Fears to ding;
Wherefore I never cou'd endure
       To laugh or sing.

I ever hated bookish reading,
And musical or dancing breeding,
And what's in either Face or Cleading,
       Of painted things;
I thought nae Pictures worth the heeding,
       Except the King's.

Now of a' them the Eard e'er bure,
I never Rhimers cou'd endure,
They're sic a sneering Pack, and poor,
       I hate to ken 'em;
For 'gainst us thrifty Sauls they're sure
       To spit their Venom.

But waster Wives, the warst of a',
Without a Youk they gar ane claw,
When wickedly they bid us draw
       Our Siller Spungs,
For this and that, to make them braw,
       And lay their Tongues.

Some loo the Courts, some loo the Kirks,
Some loo to keep their Skins frae Lirks,
Some loo to woo beneath the Birks
    Their Lemans bony;
For me, I took them a' for Stirks
    That loo'd na Money.

They ca'd me Slave to Usury,
Squeez, cleave the Hair, and peel the Flea,
Clek, flae the Flint, and Penury,
    And sauless Wretch;
But that ne'er skaith'd or troubled me,
    Gin I grew rich.

On Profit a' my Thoughts were bent,
And mony Thousands have I lent,
But sickerly I took good tent,
    That double Pawns,
With a Cudeigh, and ten *per Cint*
    Lay in my Hands.

When Borrow'rs brak, the Pawns were Rug,
Rings, Beads of Pearl, or Siller Jug,
I sald them aff, ne'er fash'd my Lug
    With Girns or Curses,
The mair they whing'd, it gart me hug
    My swelling Purses.

Sometimes I'd sigh, and ape a Saint,
And with a lang Rat-rhime of Cant,
Wad make a Mane for them in want;
    But for ought mair,
I never was the Fool to grant
    Them ony Skair.

I thought ane freely might pronounce
That Chiel a very silly Dunce,
That cou'd not Honesty renounce,
    With Ease and Joys,
At ony time, to win an Ounce
    Of yellow Boys.

When young I some Remorse did feel,
And liv'd in Terror of the Deel,

His Furnace, Whips, and racking Wheel;
      But by Degrees,
My Conscience grown as hard as Steel,
      Gave me some Ease.

But Fears of Want, and carking Care
To save my Stock,—and Thirst for mair,
By Night and Day opprest me sair,
      And turn'd my Head;
While Friends appear'd like Harpies Gare,
      That wish'd me dead.

For fear of Thieves I aft lay waking
The live lang Night till Day was breaking,
Syne throu' my Sleep, with Heart sair aking,
      I've aften started,
Thinking I heard my Windows cracking,
      When *Elspa* f——.

O Gear! I held ye lang thegither;
For you I starv'd my good auld Mither,
And to *Virginia* sald my Brither,
      And crush'd my Wife;
But now I'm gawn I kenna whither,
      To leave my Life.

My Life! my God! my Spirit earns,
Not on my Kindred, Wife or Bairns,
Sic are but very laigh Concerns,
      Compar'd with thee!
When now this mortal Rotle warns
      Me I maun die.

It to my Heart gaes like a Gun,
To see my Kin and graceless Son,
Like Rooks already are begun
      To thumb my Gear,
And Cash that has not seen the Sun
      This fifty Year.

Oh! oh! that spendthrift Son of mine,
Wha can on roasted Moorfowl dine,
And like Dub-water skink the Wine,
      And dance and sing;

He'll soon gar my dear Darlings dwine
　　Down to nathing.

To that same Place, where e'er I gang,
O could I bear my Wealth alang!
Nae Heir shou'd e'er a Farthing fang,
　　That thus carouses,
Tho' they shou'd a' on Woodies hang,
　　For breaking Houses.

Perdition! *Sathan!* is that you?
I sink—am dizzy!—Candle blue.
Wi' that he never mair play'd pew,
　　But with a Rair,
Away his wretched Spirit flew,
　　It maksna where.

'Lass with a Lump of Land'

Gi'e me a Lass with a Lump of Land,
　　And we for Life shall gang thegither;
Tho' daft or wise I'll ne'er demand,
　　Or black or fair it maksna whether.
I'm aff with Wit, and Beauty will fade,
　　And Blood alane is no worth a Shilling;
But she that's rich, her Market's made,
　　For ilka Charm about her is killing.

Gi'e me a Lass with a Lump of Land,
　　And in my Bosom I'll hug my Treasure;
Gin I had anes her Gear in my Hand,
　　Shou'd Love turn dowf, it will find Pleasure.
Laugh on wha likes, but there's my Hand,
　　I hate with Poortith, tho' bonny, to meddle;
Unless they bring Cash, or a Lump of Land,
　　They'se never get me to dance to their Fiddle.

There's meikle good Love in Bands and Bags,
　　And Siller and Gowd's a sweet Complection;
But Beauty, and Wit, and Vertue in Rags,
　　Have tint the Art of gaining Affection.
Love tips his Arrows with Woods and Parks,

And Castles, and Riggs, and Moors, and Meadows;
And nathing can catch our modern Sparks,
But well tocher'd Lasses, or jointer'd Widows.

'The Soger Laddie'

My Soger Laddie is over the Sea,
    And he will bring Gold and Money to me;
And when he comes hame, he'll make me a Lady;
    My Blessing gang with my Soger Laddie.

My doughty Laddie is handsome and brave,
    And can as a Soger and Lover behave:
True to his Country, to Love he is steady;
    There's few to compare with my Soger Laddie.

Shield him, ye Angels, frae Death in Alarms,
    Return him with Lawrels to my langing Arms,
Syne frae all my Care ye'll pleasantly free me,
    When back to my Wishes my Soger ye gi'e me.

O soon may his Honours bloom fair on his Brow,
    As quickly they must, if he get his Due;
For in noble Actions his Courage is ready,
    Which makes me delight in my Soger Laddie.

'The Spring and the Skye'

Fed by a living *Spring*, a Rill
Flow'd easily adown a Hill;
A thousand Flowers upon its Bank
Flourish'd fu' fair, and grew right rank:
Near to its Course a *Skye* did ly,
Whilk was in Simmer aften dry,
And ne'er recover'd Life again,
But after soaking Showers of Rain;
Then wad he swell, look big and sprush,
And o'er his Margine proudly gush.
Ae Day, after great Waughts of Weet,
He with the Chrystal Current met,
And ran him down with unco' Din,

Said he, How poorly does thou rin?
See with what State I dash the Brae,
Whilst thou canst hardly make thy Way.
      The *Spring*, with a superior Air,
Said, Sir, your Brag gives me nae Care;
For soon's ye want your foreign Aid,
Your paughty Cracks will soon be laid.
Frae my ain Head I have Supply;
But you must borrow, else rin dry.

'Bonny Christy'

How sweetly smells the Simmer green?
    Sweet taste the Peach and Cherry;
Painting and Order please our Een,
    And Claret makes us merry:
But finest Colours, Fruits and Flowers,
    And Wine, tho' I be thirsty,
Lose a' their Charms and weaker Powers,
    Compar'd with those of *Christy*.

When wand'ring o'er the flowry Park,
    No nat'ral Beauty wanting;
How lightsome is't to hear the Lark,
    And Birds in Concert chanting?
But if my *Christy* tunes her Voice,
    I'm rapt in Admiration;
My Thoughts with Extasies rejoice,
    And drap the hale Creation.

When e'er she smiles a kindly Glance,
    I take the happy Omen,
And aften mint to make Advance,
    Hoping she'll prove a Woman.
But dubious of my ain Desert,
    My Sentiments I smother,
With secret Sighs I vex my Heart,
    For fear she love another.

Thus sang blate *Edie* by a Burn,
    His *Christy* did o'er-hear him;

She doughtna let her Lover mourn,
  But e'er he wist drew near him.
She spake her Favour with a Look,
  Which left nae Room to doubt her:
He wisely this white Minute took,
  And flang his Arms about her.

My *Christy!*—witness bonny Stream,
  Sic Joys frae Tears arising;
I wish this may na be a Dream:
  O Love the maist surprising
Time was too precious now for Tauk,
  This Point of a' his Wishes;
He wadna with set Speeches bauk,
  But wair'd it a' on Kisses.

WILLIAM MESTON
(1688–1745)

———

BORN in Midmar, Aberdeenshire, William Meston was a teacher and poet of unflinching satirical skill. He fought in the Jacobite rising of 1715, before taking up a professorship at Marischal College, Aberdeen. Later, he co-founded a series of private schools at Elgin, Turriff, Montrose, and Perth, before tutoring the children of a prominent Jacobite family, the Oliphants of Gask. Anti-Whig and religious satire chiefly occupied Meston's pen, most strikingly in *The Tale of a Man and his Mare* (1721), *The Knight of the Kirk* (1723), *Old Mother Grim's Tales* (1737), and *Mob contra Mob* (?1714; 1738). But he also wrote sensitive elegies, panegyrics, and odes, among other things. His works were first collected posthumously, by all accounts, in *The Poetical Works of the Ingenious and Learned William Meston* (1767). However, many of the major poems had appeared separately in print, anonymously, since at least 1714.

———

Old Mother Grim's Tales *(1737)*, *'Tale VIII: A Lochaber Tale'*

The Poetical Works of the Ingenious and Learned William Meston, A.M., 6th edn (Edinburgh: Walt. Ruddiman, 1767).

> *Sunt quos curriculo pulverem olympicum*
> *Collegisse juvat; metaque fervidis*
> *Evitata rotis, palmaque nobilis*
> *Terrarum dominos evehit ad Deos.*

> Who can believe, how small affairs
> Will sometimes set friends by the ears!
> And then, how small an incident,
> Will loss of limb and life prevent?
> Which, if you only please to hear,
> Will by the following tale appear.

Upon a time, no matter where,
Some Glunimies met at a fair,
As deft and tight as ever wore
A durk, a targe, and a claymore,
Short hose, and belted plaid, or trews,
In Uist, Lochabar, Sky, or Lewis,
Or cover'd hard head with a bonnet,
(Had you but known them, you would own it);
But sitting too long by the barrel,
MacBane and Donald Dow did quarrel,
And in a culleshangee landed.
The dispute, you must understand it,
Was, which of them had the best blood,
When both, 'tis granted, had as good
As ever yet stuff'd a black-pudding;
So out came broad swords on a sudden,
Keen to decide the controversy,
And would have shed blood without mercy,
Had not a crafty Highland Demon,
MacGilliwrae, play'd the Palemon;
Who lighted on a pleasant fancy
To end the strife, and no man can say,
But that the plot shew'd his invention,
His pious purpose and intention.
Hold, hold! quoth he, I'll make your vermin
This paultry quarrel soon determine;
Come each of you reach me a louse,
For she that's found to be most crouse,
Without dispute, has had the best food,
As so her master has the best blood.
Both listened to this fine orison,
Which, if you'll mark it, was a wise one;
Their swords they sheath'd by this advice,
And fell to work to hunt for lice;
And very easily found twenty,
For of these cattle they had plenty,
Which from their bosom they did pull out,
Of which Palemon two did cull out,
In shape and size that were most egal,
To make the louse-race fair and legal;
MacBane's was marked on the back,

From head to tail, with strip of black,
By which she was from Donald's known;
So every master knew his own.

   Habbie, for he was at the sport,
On bagpipe play'd the horseman's sport,
While wise Palemon try'd a trick,
To spur them up with fiery stick
Such running yet was never seen,
On Leith sands, or Strathbogie green,
At Coupar, Perth, and other places,
Which men frequent to see horse races;
In fine MacBane's louse wan the race,
Who still of Donald takes the place.

   Now, should the wisdom of the nation,
Take this into consideration,
And ratify it by the law,
That no man sword nor durk should draw,
But leave it to their proper vermin,
Their paultry quarrels to determine,
As well the greater as the small ones,
Of Christian blood it might save gallons,
And give diversion by such races,
In country fairs and market places;
And better shew their zeal and skill,
Than hunting out more blood to spill.
If any rogue deserv'd a banging,
Or, for atrocious crimes, a hanging,
And justly is sentenc'd to die;
But who shall hang him? You, or I?
If, in this point, we are divided,
A louse race fairly might decide it,
Without expence of time or trouble,
About a thing not worth a bubble.

   Yea, who can tell, as things improve,
But this, at last, might princes move,
Such races for their crowns to run,
If once the practice was begun;
For so to get a crown's no worse,
Than by the neighing of a horse,

Or by the flying of the crows;
And yet my gentle reader knows,
Darius could no title bring,
But that, to make him Persia's king;
And Romulus, the story's famous,
By this means got the *pas* of Remus.

Our foreign mails might bring advice
Of races run by foreign lice;
The German, Dutch, the Saxon, Russian,
The French, the Spanish, and the Prussian,
The Cossack, Calmuck, and the Tartars,
Who run with neither hose nor garters;
The Persian, and the Janizaries,
Which gains the race, and which miscarries,
In Italy who gain'd the races,
Who on the Rhine, and other places;
At Philipsburg tell how they ran,
Who had the rear, and who the van;
How Eugene, by his art and cunning,
Could trace the German lice to running,
And such accomplish'd racers make them;
The French could never overtake them;
How Russian vermin could advance,
Against the mighty powers of France,
And slowly into Dantzick crept,
When French lice either dreamt or slept;
Who gain'd the race at Sheriff-muir,
Where both sides ran right well, 'tis sure.
How Highland lice could play a prankie,
And win the race at Killycrankie:
Then we might see recruiters trudging,
And their recruits in bosom lodging.

Well might this project free all nations
From great expences and taxations;
One million'th part might raise lice forces,
Of what is spent on men and horses.

ALASTAIR, MAC MHAIGHSTIR ALASTAIR / ALEXANDER MACDONALD

(C.1693–C.1770)

———

THE Scottish Gaelic poet Alexander MacDonald (Alastair, mac Mhaighstir Alastair; or Alexander, the son of Master Alexander) was probably born in Ardnamurchan. MacDonald is said to have attended the University of Glasgow, like his minister father, who may have intended his son for a career in the Church. By 1729 he was employed as teacher and catechist, and held posts in a variety of locations in Ardnamurchan, until 1745. MacDonald took part in three major battles during the Jacobite rising of 1745, as well as the march to Derby. He held a captain's commission, made the acquaintance of Bonnie Prince Charlie soon after his landing, and even acted as the prince's chief Gaelic tutor. Approximately 6,000 lines of verse ascribed to MacDonald have survived. That is likely to represent only a fraction of his total output, which ranges over a vast array of topics. Much of the surviving poetry includes many songs and poems connected with the '45 and with the political events of 1745–8 more broadly, though he may have also participated in the earlier rising of 1715.

———

'Iorram Cuain'

Comh-Chruinneachidh Orannaigh Gaidhealach, ed. Raonuill MacDomh-nuill (Edinburgh: Walter Ruddiman, 1776).

> Gur neo-aoigheil turas faoillich
> Ged bhiodh na daoine tàbhachdach.
>
> > *Tha m' fhearann saoibhir, hó a hó,*
> > *Ho-rì hi-ró nam b' àill leat mi,*
> > *Tha m' fhearann saoibhir, hó a hó.*
>
> An fhairge molach bronnach torrach
> Giobach corrach ràpalach.

Is cruaidh ri stiùradh beul-mhuir dhùldaidh
    Teachd le brùchdail chàrsanaich.

Cladh a' chùlain cha b'e 'n sùgradh
    'S e ri bùirean bàcanach.

An cùlanach fhéin chan e as fhasa
    Agus lasan àrdain air,

Teachd gu dlùth an déidh a-chéile
    Agus geumraich dàr' orra.

An fhairge phaiteach, 's a beul farsaing,
    Agus acras àraidh oirr'.

'S mairg a choimeas muir ri mòintich,
    Ged bhiodh mór shneachd stràct' oirre.

Neòil a' gealladh oidhche shalaich
    Gun aon chala sàbhailte.

Dubh rath-dorcha, gun dad gealaich,
    Oirthir aineol àrdchreagach.

Gaoth a' séideadh, muir ag éirigh,
    'S fear ag éigheach àrdghuthach:

"Siud e tighinn, 's chan ann righinn—
    Cròcmhuir frithearr' bàsanach;

Cum ceann-caol a fiodha dìreach
    Ri muir dìleann dàsanach!"

Ach dh'aithnich sinn gun sheòl sinn fada
    A-mach san tabh, 's bu ghàbhaidh sin.

Leag sinn a croinn is a h-aodach—
    'S bu ghnìomh dhaoine càileachdach.

'S chuir sinn a-mach cliathan rìghne—
    'S bu ghrinn an t-àlach iad.

'S shuidh orr' ochdar shonna troma
    'S sgoilteadh tonnan stàplainneach.

Heig air chnagaibh, hùg air mhaidean,
    'S cogal bhac air àbranaibh.

Iad a' mosgladh suas a-chéile
   'S masgadh treun air sàl aca.

Sgeanan locrach ràmh á Lochlainn
   Bualadh bhoc air bàirlinnean.

Iad a' traoghadh suas na dìle
   Le neart fìor-gharg ghàirdeanan.

Cathadh-mara 's marcach-sìne
   'S stoirm nan sìon d'an sàrachadh.

Lasraichean srad teine-sionnachain
   Dearg on iomradh chàileachdach.

Iad ag obair ás an léintean—
   'Hùg' is 'héig' d'a ràdhainn ac'.

Iorram àrd bhinn shuas aig Eumann
   Ann an cléith ràmh bràghada.

Aonghas mac Dhonnchaidh d'a réir sin—
   A rìgh, bu treun a thàirneadh e.

Donnchadh Mac Uaraig a' luadh leo
   'S b' fhada buan a spàlagan.

Bha fuaim aon mhaide air cléith ac',
   Bualadh spéicean tàbhachdach.

Ràimh d'am pianadh 's fir d'an spìonadh
   'N glacadh iarnaidh àrdthonnach.

Gallain chiatach leobhar-liaghach
   'S fuirbidh dian d'an sàrachadh.

Lunnan mìne 's dùirn d'an sìneadh,
   Seile sìos air dheàrnaichean.

Muir ag osnaich shuas m'a toiseach,
   Chuip-gheal, choip-gheal ghàirbheucach.

Suas le sgùradh, saidh ri bùirean
   Le sìor dhùrachd sàr iomraidh.

Slabhraidh chùirneineach ri dùrdail
   Shìos—rinn stiùir a fàgail ann.

Gaoth 'na deannadh 's i ri feannadh
　　Nan tonn ceannfhionn ràsanach.

Na fir lùthmhor 'n déidh an rùsgadh
　　A' cur smùid dhe'n àlaichean.

Chaoidh cha mheataicheadh am misneach,
　　Na fir sgibidh thàbhachdach.

Rìgh an eagail, Neptiun ceigeach,
　　Ri sìor sgreadadh, "Bàthar sibh."

Gum b' fhàth uamhainn muir ri nuallraich
　　'S cathadh cuain a' stràcadh orr'.

Ghuidh an sgioba geur na dùilean
　　'S fhuair an ùrnaigh gràsan daibh.

Smachdaich Éolus na speuran
　　'S a bhuilg-shéididh àrdghaothach,

'S gun d'rinn Neptiun fairge lomadh
　　Mar bhiodh gloine-sgàthain ann.

Sgaoil na neòil bha tonnghorm cìordhubh
　　'S shoillsich grian mar b' àbhaist di,

'S mhothaich an sgioba do dh'fhearann
　　'S ghlac iad cala sàbhailte;

Ghabh iad pronn, is deoch is leaba,
　　'S rinn iad cadal sàmhach oirr'.

'Ocean Oar-Song' (translated by Ronald Black)

A wolftime* voyage is uninviting
　　Despite the men being competent.

My land is wealthy, hó a hó,
Ho-rì hi-ró if you'd have me,
My land is wealthy, hó a hó.

The sea is rough, it swells and bulges,
　　It's shaggy, steep and clamorous.

It's hard to steer through gloomy front-waves
    That hiss ahead with flatulence.

The back-wave trough is no fun either
    As it roars along derisively.

The back-wave itself isn't easier
    With its fiery gleam of haughtiness,

Coming close one after another
    And roaring like the deer in rutting.

The hunchbacked sea, its mouth wide open,
    Has a voracious appetite.

Sad is he who likened ocean
    To mountains, even snow-covered.

Clouds promising a dirty night
    With no safe port available.

A black interlunation, no moon whatsoever,
    An unknown, high-cliffed litoral.

A wind is blowing, the sea is rising,
    And a man shouts as loud as possible:

"There it comes, and it's far from sluggish—
    The foaming sea, lethal, impetuous;

Hold the prow of her timber steady
    Into the waves, their flood and insanity!"

Then we realised we'd sailed too far out
    From the land, and that was dangerous.

We lowered her masts and all her sailcloth—
    It was a task for men of ability.

And we extended our supple oar-banks—
    What an elegant set they were.

And there sat at them eight heavy heroes
    And splashing waves were pulverised.

Thole-pins creaking, oar-blades crashing,
    Wood-waste on the gunwale-sheaths.

They invigorate each other
  And make the seas commingle.

Plane-like blades of oars from Norway
  Inflicting blows on billow-tops.

They propel the water upwards
  By sheer strength of arms and stamina.

The sea-spray, spindrift and tempest
  Of the elements oppressing them.

Flames of sparks and phosphorescence
  Spring red from rowing so intuitive.

They labour on in their shirt-sleeves
  With "heave" and "hawl" for utterance.

Loud and sweet is Eumann's singing
  As he plies his oar up for'ard.

Angus Robertson responding—
  My God, his pull was phenomenal.

Duncan Kennedy waulked with them
  And his strokes went on eternally.

There was only one sound at a time from their oar-bank,
  They made their strokes with effectiveness.

Men pulling so hard that oars were tortured
  In high-waved iron mastery.

Beautiful slim-feathered saplings
  With fierce warriors tormenting them.

Smooth handles and the fists to stretch them,
  And palms on which to salivate.

Up round her bow the sea was sighing,
  Foam-white, froth-white and loud-bellowing.

Rising scoured, the stern-post roaring
  With sound rowing's steady earnestness.

Beneath, a spangled trail was fizzing—
  It was the helm that had put it there.

The wind was sweeping by and flaying
  The white loquacious billow-heads.

Once stripped, the energetic strongmen
  Pulled their oar-banks mightily.

Never would their courage fail them,
  These men who were tidy and effective.

The king of horror, rugged Neptune,
  Shrieked steadily, "I'm drowning you."

The howling sea was the cause of terror
  With ocean spindrift raking them.

The crew sent up a mighty prayer
  Which got them grace from the elements.

Aeolus calmed down the heavens
  And his high-winded bellow-bags,

And Neptune smoothed down the ocean
  As if it were a looking-glass.

The wave-blue jet-black clouds dissolved
  And the sun shone as it was accustomed to,

And the crew caught a sight of land then
  And got to a safe anchorage;

Food, drink and bed they now enjoyed,
  And went to sleep in quietness.

'Prasgan nan Garbh-Chrìoch?'

Donald Mackinnon, 'Unpublished Poems by Alexander Macdonald
(Mac Mhaighstir Alastair) III. Poems hitherto unpublished', *The Celtic
Review*, 5 (1908–9).

O! gu'n tigeadh a-nall dhuinn
  Ar cabhlach garbh daoineach
Le Fhrangaichibh caothaich,
  Le gleadhar na gaoitheadh—
Gum falbhadh ar mulad,
  'S bhiodh curaids 'nar n-aodann,

'S bhiodh armailt Dhiùc Uilleam
    'Nan cuileagaibh taobh-dearg.

A Mhiùsagan binne
    Nam fil-fhaclan bòidheach,
Is tric a rinn sibh mo thadhal
    A chur lathailt air òran;
Bhon a leig sibh ur rùn rium,
    Sin is dùrachd ur n-eòlais,
Na tréigibh a-nis mi
    'S mi tric ann am chlòsaid.

Ach có rinn an ealain sa
    Thug sgeith air mo chluasaibh?
Chan fhaod gun do shruth i
    Bho shruthan glan fuarain:
Bhon bhreun-lón a bhrùchd i
    Le sgiùrdan de thuaileas—
Cha robh 'na ciad ùghdar
    Aon driùchd de dh'uaisle.

Am baisteach bochd mìomhail
    As mì-shìobhalta giùlan,
Ge fàth gàir' anns an tìr ud
    I dhìobhairt a sprùillich,
'S iad na pileachan mìoruin
    Seo dhìleadh le Iùdas
Thug sgéith air an strìopaich
    A h-inntinn a rùsgadh.

'S ged a rùisg thu mar chranna-mhadadh
    Sgaiteach do dheud ruinn
A dhèanamh dìchill gar gearradh
    'S nach b' urr' thu d'ar reubadh,
Chan eil ann am' eòlas
    Té sheòrsa fon ghréin sa
Dhèanadh tiunnail an òrain sa
    Ach am pòr tha thu fhéin dhiubh.

Breun-mhonstar de dh'ealain
    Gun mhiosar gun òrdan,
Eanghlas shearbh shalach
    De bharrasglaich còmhraidh:

Is beag a bhuineadh don chaillich,
  Nighean Chailein ri Seònaid,
Dol a chàineadh a' Phrionnsa—
  Cha do dh'ionnsaich i eòlas.

An cluiche sa a phasadh
  A' chearraich, gun earbainn,
Sann a bhéist thu na cairtean
  Le d' bhras-iomairt chealgaich;
Na bhuannaich thu chliù leis
  Cuir ad' phùidse gu staillichdeil,
'S mur eil ortsa seun dùbailt'
  Gun cuidhtichear t' earraghlòir.

Aig a thainead 's tha 'm pòr ud
  An-dràst' ann ad' dhùthaich,
Gu bheil mios ort an Latharn'
  Gur tu rogha nan ùghdar;
Ma tha iad le soileas
  Sìor-mholadh do bhùrdain,
An dùthaich eile cha b' fhiach e
  Thogail cian thar an ùrlair.

A bhana-mhinistear ascaoin
  A fhuair blas air an t-searbhaig,
'S i mhiosgainn an teacsta
  'N do shocraich do shearmoid;
'S e 'n deamhan a las thu
Chuir gart ort fìor fheargach
  Le t' aoir dol a chagnadh
Threun-ghaisgeach nan Garbh-Chrìoch.

A bhan-rògaire Dheòrsach
  Le h-òrdan bhios sgiùrsta,
Sann a thoill thu bhith ròiste
  Air ròis-bhior am fùirneis;
Tha togradh do sgòrnain
  Gu d' gheòcaich bhith rùchdan
Dol a dhèanamh an òrain
  Le h-òrdainean Iùdais.

Is nàr do bhan-eaglaisich
  Beadachd is tiunnsgal

Le spiorad na beag-nàir'
  Labhairt sgeigeil air prionnsa;
Do chreideamh cha teagaisg dhuit
  Cead thoirt do d' sgiùrsadh
Droch cainnt chur an eagar
  Le t' fheagal a mhùchar.

Dh'ainneoin dìchill do chinnidh
  Anns an iomairt sa 'n-dràsta,
A' torradh suas an cuid chillean
  Le gionaich' na sàstachd,
Gun crùnar Righ Seumas
  Le éirigh nan Spàinneach
'S nam Frangach dearg-chreuchdach
  'S còmhnadh gleusta nan Gàidheal.

'S ged a bhitheadh tu cho caise
  'S clobha dathte 'nad earball,
Bidh an gnothach sa paisgte
  Le ascall nan Earraghaidh'l;
Bidh móran de t' aitim
  Air an spadadh le fearaghnìomh
'S cuid eile dhiubh 'n glasaibh
  'S cuibhreach rag air an sealbhan.

Chaidh na mucan gu rochdail
  'S an socan air rùsgadh,
Ri rùrach nan soithche,
  'S nam pocannan plùchte;
Ach se Cumberland plocach
  Le 'ochd mìle dùbailte
Rinn an *conquest* cho socair
  'S nach stopt' air am bùrach.

'S mur bhith Diùc Uilleam
  An Cille Chuimein 'na chùrraig
A bhith cho dìolt' air fuileachd,
  Bhiodh cullaich gan sgiùrsadh;
Gun rachamaid gu h-ullamh
  Air chullainn m'ur tùrlach,
'S bhiodh dearg-chroisean fuileach
  Le'r buillean 'nur crùnaibh.

Cha tèarm thigeadh ceart oirnn
   "Prasgan nan Garbh-Chrìoch"
Ach cruithneachd nan gaisgeach
   Chuir ceartas á fearaghnìomh,
Fìor eitean nan curaidh
   'N àm curaids a dhearbhadh—
Luchd bualaidh nam buillean
   Ann an cumasg nan dearg-chneadh.

Tha thusa gle bhòstail
   Ás do sheòrsa gu cruadal:
Daoine staideile, còire,
   Ach fior Dheòrsach gu buannachd;
Ach is cinnteach mar as beò sinn
   Tha sinn deònach san uair seo
Sinn a tharraing an òrdugh
   Chun nan srònan as cruaidhe.

Ged a thuirt thu le blaisbheum
   Ruinn "prasgan nan Garbh-Chrìoch",
Chum sinn cogadh ri Sasainn
   Ré tachdain, 's ri h-Albainn;
Cuim' ruinn nach do chas sibh
   Aig Glascho le'r n-armaibh?
Chuir sinn eagal ur cac oirbh
   'S thàrr sibh ás mar an earba.

Ach nuair choinnich Diùc Uilleam
   Le'r trì uiread de shluagh sinn,
Le ceud anacothrom cumaisg
   Gun do dh'iomain e ruaig oirnn;
Ach is fada mun cumadh iad
   Buillean aon uair ruinn,
Ach uiread is uiread
   Dhol a bhuilleachais chruaidh ruinn.

Taisbean dhòmhsa milisia
   An-ceartuair san Eòrpa
Nach rachamaid 'nan dosan
   Ann an cosgar na còrach;
'S ged a thogadh tu fhathast
   Fir Latharna 's Chòmhaill,

B' fhasa cat chur an triubhas
  Na 'n cur an uidheam 'nar còmhdhail.

Na biodh bòst oirbh mu na thog sibh
  De spréidh anns an dùthaich:
Mura bhitheadh an armailte
  Mhòr bh' air ur cùlaibh,
Cha dèanainn fad' iarraidh
  Air cóig ciad bhcireadh cùis dhiobh,
Luchd a dhìoghlaim nan ceirslean
  'S ìm brachain 'nam pùidse.

Luchd a thogail nam binid
  'S gan dinneadh 'nam pòca
G'am bruich air na h-éibhlibh
  Mar ghréidhteachan feòla,
Na Hottentots bhreuna
  Bu déisinneach còmhroinn
An cuinneag an déircich
  'S an creutair ga sgròbadh.

Bha ìomhaigh na gealtachd
  Air a cailceadh 'nur gnùisibh,
Fìor chlamhain na h-ealtainn
  Gu cearcan a phlùchadh;
Nan dèant' ur n-ath-bhaisteadh
  B' ainm ceart dhuibh na giùdain,
Bu lìonmhor mu'r brataich
  Fìor ghealtairean fùidseach.

Pàigheadh dùbailte ás teachd oirbh
  Bheirear dhachaigh 'nar fairgneadh
Ás na Mìn-Chrìochan feachd-bhog
  Air son peacadh nan Earraghaidheal;
Le riadh thig na creachan
  Le gaisgich nan Garbh-Chrìoch,
'S bidh claidheamh is lasair
  Mu'r n-aitreabh bhios gailbheach.

Cha leóghainn ach caoirich
  Thug a' chaoireachd sa bhuainne:
Na liùgachan plamach
  'S crois sgamhain 'nan spruaicibh;

Bu bhuige na slaman
    Toirt lannan á truaill iad,
Fìor fheòdar ri tharraing
    Nach gearradh am buachar.

Chreach na ceallairean òtraich
    Snàtha 's clòimh gacha tùrlaich,
Càis, ìm agus uibhean
    Dèanamh gruithim 'nam pùidse;
Cha d'fhàg iad balg abhrais
    No ball ann gun spùilleadh—
Buaidh-làraich cha choltach
    Bhith 'm fochair nam brùidean.

Is còmhdach mollachd bhan bochda
    Deòir is osnaich gach bantraich:
An déis an rùsgaidh 's an dochainn
    Gum bu lochdach ur n-ainneart;
Thig plàigh agus gort oirbh
    'S claidheamh prosnaicht' o'r naimhdibh—
Lannar ás sibh mar choirce,
    Eadar stoc agus mheanglan.

Gur geur tha ur cogais
    A' cogadh ri'r reusan,
Gur h-e Seumas gun teagamh
    Rìgh Bhreatainn is Éireann;
Thug an saoghal a dh'ainneoin
    Corp is anam nam béistean—
Gun do ghràdhaich iad Mammon,
    'S mar sin daingeann san eucoir.

'The Rabble of the Rough-Bounds?'
(translated by Ronald Black)

Oh let our big, soldier-filled
    Fleet come over to save us
With its battle-crazed Frenchmen,
    By the rattle of the wind—
Our depression would leave us,
    We'd show pluck in our faces,

And Duke William's army
    Would be all red-bodied flies.

You sweet-throated Muses
    Of the beautiful poet-words,
You have often come to visit me
    To lick a song into shape;
Since you've revealed your intentions
    And the blessings of knowing you,
Please don't now forsake me
    When I'm often in my closet.

But who made this ditty
    That was retched in my ears?
It cannot have flowed
    From the clean spring of a fountain:
It belched out of a quagmire
    With squirts of foul slander—
Its creator possessed
    Not one drop of gentility.

The poor impudent baptist
    Of uncivilised behaviour,
Though they laugh in that country
    At the rubbish she vomits,
It's these pills of ill-will
    Digested by Judas*
That put wings on the slut
    To lay bare her mind.

And though you've shown us your fangs
    Like a hound-bitch that bites
To do your best to cut us
    Though unable to tear us,
I do not know any female
    Of any race on this planet
Who'd make the likes of this song
    Save the tribe *you* belong to.

A foul beast of a ditty
    Without measure or order,
A mixture, bitter and dirty,
    Of ranting, raving opinions:

It ill becomes the old woman,
    Colin's daughter by Janet,
To try to slander the Prince—
    She never made his acquaintance.

To get this game past
    The gambler, I'm sure,
You've corrupted the cards
    With your bold cheating play;
Whatever fame it has won you
    Put very fast in your pouch,
For unless you're twice charmed
    Your bold talk will be paid for.

Though that race is thin-spread
    Just now in your country,
You're respected in Lorn
    As the best of all authors;
But if they are with flattery
    Ever-praising your jingle,
Nowhere else do they stoop to
    Raise it far off the floor.

You coarse female minister
    With an appetite for acid,
Spite is the text
    That your sermon has fixed on;
It's Auld Nick who inspired you
    To threaten so fiercely
And insult with your satire
    The Rough Bounds' brave heroes.

You Hanoverian harlot
    Who's ordained to be whipped,
You deserve to be roasted
    In a fire on a spit;
Your throat's inclination
    Is to belch at your gluttons
In composing the song
    On the orders of Judas.

It's disgrace for a churchwoman
    To show impudence and industry

In a spirit of shamelessness
    To speak with cheek of a prince;
Your faith does not teach you
    To countenance your whipping
By expressing bad language
    Which your fear will then smother.

Despite your clan's diligence
    In this ongoing enterprise,
Heaping up hoards of wealth
    With the greed leisure gives them,
King James will be crowned
    By the aid of the Spaniards
And the red-wounding Frenchmen
    With skilled help from the Gael.

And despite your ferocity
    With red-hot tongs in your tail,
This affair will be ended with
    The loss of the Argylls;
Many of your kindred will
    Be slaughtered by manly deeds
While the rest are imprisoned
    With stiff chains round their throats.

The pigs started grunting*
    When their snouts were unmuzzled,
Ransacking the dishes
    With the bags pressed flat;
But it's fat-cheeked Cumberland
    With his double eight thousand
Who made the conquest so easy
    That their grubbing wasn't stopped.

And were it not for Duke William
    In his neuk in Fort Augustus
Being so sated with bloodshed,
    Boars would have been scourged;
We'd have set about willingly
    Kicking your fat arses,
And with bloody red crosses
    Our blows would have crowned you.

"The rabble of the Rough Bounds"
    Is not a term that would suit us
But the wheat of the heroes
    Who brought justice by man-deeds,
The very essence of warriors
    When time came to show courage—
The strikers of blows
    In the fight of the red wounds.

You boast a great deal
    Of the toughness of your tribe:
They are plump, decent people,
    But true Whigs for a profit;
But as sure as we are living
    We are willing at this time
To march in good order
    Towards the hardest of noses.

Though you called us with blasphemy
    "The rabble of the Rough Bounds",
We made war with England
    For a while, and with Scotland;
Why did you not engage us
    At Glasgow with your weapons?
We had you scared shitless
    And you ran off like the roe.

But when Duke William engaged us
    With your triple-sized army
And a hundred advantages,
    He sent us down to defeat;
But far ahead is the day
    When even once they could hold us
If the fighting, though fierce,
    Were equal in numbers.

Show to me a militia
    At this instant in Europe
That we could not engage with
    In waging battle for justice;
You'd find it easier, if you raised
    The Lorn and Cowal men again,

To put a cat into breeches
    Than to train them to fight us.

Let you not boast of the cattle
    That you drove in the country:
Were it not for the massive
    Army behind you,
I'd soon have had five hundred
    Men to dispose of you,
You putters of wool-yarns
    And rancid butter in pouches.

These purloiners of rennets
    Who stuff them in pockets
To cook them on embers
    Like gobbets of meat,
Foul Hottentots sharing
    The revolting repast
In the mendicant's bucket
    While the creature is fleeced.

The image of cowardice
    Was chalked in your faces,
The true buzzards of birds
    For smothering hens;
If you were rebaptised
    You'd be well named the worthless,
For many under your banner
    Were both craven and gutless.

Double pay from attacking you
    Will be brought home to our hearths
From the soft-armied Smooth Bounds
    For the sins of the Argylls;
The heroes of the Rough Bounds
    Will take plunder with interest,
And sword and flame full of wrath
    Will surround your abodes.

It's not lions but lambs
    Who stole all our sheep-stuff:
The slippery sneaks with
    A mean cross in their skulls;

They are softer than curds
    When unsheathing their swords,
Pure pewter for drawing
    That couldn't cut cow-dung.

These dunghill-cellarers stole
    The thread and wool from each closet,
Cheese, eggs and butter
    Making curd-pie in their pouches;
Not a spinning-bag or scrap
    Did they leave without plundering—
Being in those brutes' presence
    Is not like victory in battle.

The proof of poor women's curses
    Is the tears and sighs of each widow:
After stripping and beating them
    Your abuse of them was criminal;
Plague and famine will get you
    And your foes' sword of vengeance—
You'll be cut down like oats,
    Both your trunk and your branches.

How fiercely your conscience
    Is at war with your reason,
For James is indeed
    King of Britain and Ireland;
The world deems irrelevant
    These beasts' bodies and souls—
It's been judged they love Mammon,
    So they're guilty as charged.

'An Cnocan'

Alastair Donullach (Mac Mhaighstir Alastair), *Eiseirigh na Seann Chanain Albannaich; no, An Nuadh Oranaiche Gaidhealach*, 7th edn (Edinburgh: Maclachlan & Stewart, 1874).

Bu mhath gach crosachd gus a-nochd
    Thachair riumsa, 'n-oir no 'n-iar;
Lùths mo choise sgaradh rium
    Chrùn suim mo mhì-fhortain riamh.

Ach galar, gun dealta gun ghréin
   Gun fheur, gun riasg thig á h-ùir
Air a' chnocan dhòite liath
   Thug bho m' chois-sa trian a lùiths.

Fallas nan seangan 's nan daol
   Gad fheannadh gu daor bho d' rùsg;
Guma h-e do phiseach is d' fheum
   Bhith 'd chon-tom breun aig gach cù.

'S ma gheibh Lucifer a chead
   Teachd bharr a shlabhraidh bho nead,
Gheibh e còir is òrdugh rag
   Bhith mùn 's a' cac air do bhiod.

Mo mhallachd sa 's mallachd na gaoith'
   Shéideas sìontan daor nan speur
Gus am fail thu cho lom
   Ri aotraman lom am bi séid.

Conasg, fòghnan, agus dris
   'S gach dreamsgal gun mheas gun sùgh
Laomadh air a' chnocan liath—
   Cha ghabh neòinean friamh ad' ùir.

Mo mhallachd-sa 's mallachd nam baobh
   'S mallachd nan aoir, bhon as ì as mò,
Dh'fhaileadh do mhullaich 's do thaobh
   Gun duilleach mu d' chraoibh, no cnò.

Gun mheas gun toradh gun bhlàth
   Asad a dh'fhàs de'm bi spéis;
Crann-shneachd a spìonadh do chluas,
   'Nad lòbhran 's ad' fhuath don spréidh.

Peileirean beathracha cruaidh
   'S teine-dealain luath nan speur
Gad losgadh suas ad' luaith ruaidh
   'S tuath-ghaoth gad fhuadach bho chéil'.

Còinneach odhar 's cnotal ruadh
   'S iteodha mu'm fuathach spréidh
Chinntinn mu d' losaidean cruaidh
   'S nathraichean 'nan cuaich ad' sgéith.

'The Hillock' (translated by Ronald Black)

Until tonight all obstacles I've met,
    East or west, were bearable;
Losing the power of my foot has crowned
    All the misfortunes I ever had.

But a plague, without dew or sun
    Or grass, or sedge that comes from the soil,
Be upon the burnt grey hillock
    That robbed my foot of a third of its strength.

May the sweat of the ants and beetles
    Strip you dearly of your turf;
May your fate and your function be
    To be a foul dog's hillock for every cur.

And if Lucifer gets permission
    To come off his chain and out of his lair,
He will have title and strict command
    To pee and shit upon your summit.

My curse on you and the curse of the wind
    That blows the costly storms of the skies
Until you're peeled as naked and bare
    As a round bladder blown up with air.

May gorse, and thistle, and briar
    And every fruitless sapless scrub
Go to seed upon the grey hillock—
    No daisy will take root in your soil.

May my curse and the curse of the witches
    And the curse of the satires, since it's supreme,
Flay your summit and your hillside,
    Leaving your tree without foliage or nut.

With no fruit or crop or blossom
    To grow out of you with any respect;
May a fall of snow pluck out your ears
    And make you a leper loathsome to cows.

May the hard bullets of thunderbolts
    And the quick lightning of the skies

Burn you up into red glowing ashes
    While a north wind tears you apart.

May dun-coloured moss and yellow crotal
    And hemlock repellent to cattle
Grow around your rock-hard haunches
    With coiled-up serpents in your flanks.

DOMHNALL MACLEÒID /
DONALD MACLEOD
(1698–1759)

THE Reverend Donald MacLeod (Domhnall MacLeòid) was heredi-
tary tacksman (tenant) of Greshornish in Skye. A graduate of King's
College, Aberdeen, he served as missionary in Benbecula, then as parish
minister successively of South Uist, North Uist, and Duirinish in Skye.
He is believed to have composed many Gaelic poems, but only two,
'Beannachadh Baird' ('A Poet's Blessing') and 'An Dealachadh' ('The
Parting'), appear to have survived. Both show the poet performing a formal social function appropriate to his status. In 'An Dealachadh'
MacLeod bids an elegant if rather old-fashioned farewell to a party of
gentlemen who have come from Skye to North Uist for the hunting.
North Uist was part of the estate of Sir James MacDonald of Sleat, but
the individuals named seem to be Donald MacLeod of Bernera (an old
Jacobite warrior of the '45) and Roderick MacLeod of Talisker (Professor
of Philosophy at King's College). Also in the party are a 'cleric', presumably Presbyterian, and a 'parson', presumably Episcopalian. (Thanks to
Ann Loughran and Andrew P. MacLeod for assistance with this entry.)

'An Dealachadh'

The Gaelic Bards from 1715 to 1765, ed. A. Maclean Sinclair (Charlottetown:
Haszard & Moore, 1892).

> Ge subhach comann nan càirdean,
>   'S tùrsach an sgànradh o chéile—
> Air son ana-mèinneachd pàirtidh
>   Ceangal gràidh agus dheagh bheusan.
>
> B' éibhneach sinn ri'r teachd d'ar talmhainn,
>   B' éibhneach bhur tàmh 'nar bunadh,
> B' éibhneach sinn a-raoir nam fanadh,
>   'S cìs cha ghabhamaid de thuilleadh.

An-diugh ar sòlas dh'fhògair bròn,
  Ar dochair gur h-éiginn triall;
Chì sinn air fhad 's gum fan seòid
  Dealachadh fa-dheòidh gur rian.

Dealachadh ri còmhlan gun fhiamh
  Anns gach gnìomh gu fearail borb,
Gu bàidheach 's nach sòradh sìth—
  'S an nàmh as faobharach colg.

Mo chion Domhnall, ionmhainn Ruairidh,
  Ceann agus aidmheil ua Leòid,
Dà urla gun smùr 'nan sealladh,
  Cuim dheagh-ghlan o'n tamall pleòid.

'S ionmhainn bhur cléireach, ge ruadh,
  'S bhur pearsan, ge fuar a bhrìgh,
'S ionmhainn bhur n-òigridh 's bhur liath—
  Ar gean leibh 'nur triall gu Sgì.

Comann 'tha ìosal is àrd,
  Comann 'tha garbh agus mìn,
Comann 'tha gòrach is glic,
  Comann 'tha miosail neo-chrìon.

Comann 'tha bàidheil ri bochd,
  Comann 'tha gun lochd 'nan gné,
Comann 'tha ceanail mu Ròid,
  Comann còir an comann réidh.

Comann ri'n leigeamaid ar rùn
  Gun imcheist air cùl ar cinn,
An comann glan a dh'imich bhuainn—
  Air ur geàrd gach uair bidh sinn.

Thog ar meanmna ri bhur teachd,
  O chaidh sibh tuitidh ar sprochd;
Ait leinn sibh 'bhith treun 'nur neart
  Le ceart ge trom sinn a-nochd.

Ach 's e ar guidh' ri Rìgh nan Slògh
  O mheachainn nan tonn bhur dìon
Gu 'n uair an dèan éibhneas làn
  Ar comainn chàirdeil subhach sinn.

'The Parting' (translated by Ronald Black)

The friendship of kinsfolk is happy,
    But it's sad when they have to disperse—
They replace sectarian passions
    With ties of love and good conduct.

We welcomed your trip to our land,
    We welcomed your stay in our house;
We'd have welcomed your staying last night
    And taken no payment for more.

Today our joy has banished our grief,
    Our pain that you have to go;
We see when heroes have stayed so long
    That parting at last is the way.

Parting from folk without fear
    Who're manly and bold in each deed,
Who're loving and wouldn't grudge peace—
    Though the foe has a sharp-bladed sword.

My darling is Donald, beloved is Rory,
    Head and confession of Leod's descendants,
Two faces of unblemished appearance,
    Shapes good and pure that cause brief anxiety.

Dear is your cleric, though red-haired,
    And your parson, though cold is his message,
Dear are your young and your grey-haired,
    We wish you well on your voyage to Skye.

A party that's low and that's high,
    A party that's rough and that's smooth,
A party that's foolish and wise,
    A party that's worthy and generous.

A party that's kind to the poor,
    A party of faultless character,
A party that's civil round Roodsmas—
    The peaceful party's the kind one.

A party we'd share our thoughts with
    Without qualms in the backs of our minds,

The excellent party that's left us—
   We'll back you on every occasion.

Our spirits rose at your coming,
   Now you've gone we'll be depressed;
We're happy for you to be brave and strong
   Although for sure we're sad tonight.

But we pray that the King of Hosts
   Protect you from the power of the waves
Until the time that the full contentment
   Of our friendly kinsfolk will bring us joy.

ROBERT BLAIR

(1699–1746)

———

Born and educated in Edinburgh, and later minister in Haddington presbytery at Athelstaneford, Robert Blair is now remembered for his long blank verse poem *The Grave* (1743). At Athelstaneford, the reclusive Blair worked slowly on the meditative masterpiece, which he had begun while living in Edinburgh many years prior. An evangelical revival in the 1740s encouraged the author to seek publication, with the aid of the English hymnist and fellow minister Dr Isaac Watts, who failed to gain the interest of the London booksellers. Finally, in 1743, with the help of another divine, Dr Philip Doddridge, Blair saw *The Grave* published in a handsome quarto edition. Frequently printed thereafter, later with iconic images by the poet and printer William Blake, the work enjoyed instant and longstanding success. Luxuriantly gloomy, the poem includes stunningly imaginative if highly morbid descriptions of death and dying.

———

The Grave *(1743)*

The Grave. A Poem, 2nd edn (London: M. Fenner, 1743).

> Whilst some affect the Sun, and some the Shade,
> Some flee the City, some the Hermitage;
> Their Aims as various, as the Roads they take
> In Journeying thro' Life; the Task be mine
> To paint the gloomy Horrors of the *Tomb*;
> Th' appointed Place of Rendezvous, where all
> These Travellers meet. Thy Succours I implore,
> Eternal King! whose potent Arm sustains
> The Keys of Hell and Death. THE GRAVE, dread Thing!
> Men shiver, when thou'rt named: Nature appal'd
> Shakes off her wonted Firmness. Ah! how dark
> Thy long-extended Realms, and rueful Wastes!
> Where nought but Silence reigns, and Night, dark Night,

Dark as was *Chaos*, 'ere the Infant Sun
Was roll'd together, or had try'd his Beams
Athwart the Gloom profound! The sickly Taper
By glimmering thro' thy low-brow'd misty Vaults,
(Furr'd round with mouldy Damps, and ropy Slime),
Lets fall a supernumerary Horror,
And only serves to make thy Night more irksome.
Well do I know thee by thy trusty *Yew*,
Chearless, unsocial Plant! that loves to dwell
'Midst Sculls and Coffins, Epitaphs and Worms:
Where light-heel'd Ghosts, and visionary Shades,
Beneath the wan cold Moon (as Fame reports)
Embody'd, thick, perform their mystick Rounds.
No other Merriment, Dull Tree! is thine.
      See yonder Hallow'd Fane! the pious Work
Of Names once fam'd, now dubious or forgot,
And buried 'midst the Wreck of Things which were:
There lie interr'd the more illustrious Dead.
The Wind is up: Hark! how it howls! Methinks
Till now, I never heard a Sound so dreary:
Doors creak, and Windows clap, and Night's foul Bird
Rook'd in the Spire screams loud: The gloomy Isles
Black-plaster'd, and hung round with Shreds of 'Scutcheons
And tatter'd Coats of Arms, send back the Sound
Laden with heavier Airs, from the low Vaults
The Mansions of the Dead. Rous'd from their Slumbers
In grim Array the grizly Spectres rise,
Grin horrible, and obstinately sullen
Pass and repass, hush'd as the Foot of Night.
Again! the Screech-Owl shrieks: Ungracious Sound!
I'll hear no more, it makes one's Blood run chill.
Quite round the Pile, a Row of Reverend Elms,
Coeval near with that, all ragged shew,
Long lash'd by the rude Winds: Some rift half down
Their branchless Trunks: Others so thin at Top,
That scarce Two Crows could lodge in the same Tree.
Strange Things, the Neighbours say, have happen'd here:
Wild Shrieks have issued from the hollow Tombs,
Dead men have come again, and walk'd about,
And the Great Bell has toll'd, unrung, untouch'd.
(Such Tales their Chear, at Wake or Gossiping,

When it draws near to Witching Time of Night.)
        Oft, in the lone Church-yard at Night I've seen
By Glimpse of Moon-shine, chequering thro' the Trees,
The School-boy with his Satchel in his Hand,
Whistling aloud to bear his Courage up,
And lightly tripping o'er the long flat Stones
(With Nettles skirted, and with Moss o'ergrown),
That tell in homely Phrase who lie below;
Sudden! he starts, and hears, or thinks he hears
The Sound of something purring at his Heels:
Full fast he flies, and dares not look behind him,
Till out of Breath he overtakes his Fellows;
Who gather round, and wonder at the Tale
Of horrid *Apparition*, tall and ghastly,
That walks at Dead of Night, or takes his Stand
O'er some new-open'd *Grave*; and, strange to tell!
Evanishes at Crowing of the Cock.
        The new-made *Widow* too, I've sometimes spy'd,
Sad Sight! slow moving o'er the prostrate Dead:
Listless, she crawls along in doleful Black,
Whilst Bursts of Sorrow gush from either Eye,
Fast-falling down her now untasted Cheek.
Prone on the lowly Grave of the Dear Man
She drops; whilst busy-meddling Memory,
In barbarous Succession, musters up
The past Endearments of their softer Hours,
Tenacious of its Theme. Still, still she thinks
She sees him, and indulging the fond Thought,
Clings yet more closely to the senseless Turf,
Nor heeds the Passenger who looks that Way.
        Invidious *Grave!* how do'st thou rend in sunder
Whom Love has knit, and Sympathy made one;
A Tie more stubborn far than Nature's Band!
Friendship! Mysterious Cement of the Soul!
Sweetener of Life! and Solder of Society!
I owe thee much. Thou hast deserv'd from me,
Far, far beyond what I can ever pay.
Oft have I prov'd the Labours of thy Love,
And the warm Efforts of the gentle Heart
Anxious to please. Oh! when my Friend and I
In some thick Wood have wander'd heedless on,

Hid from the vulgar Eye; and sat us down
Upon the sloping Cowslip-cover'd Bank,
Where the pure limpid Stream has slid along
In grateful Errors thro' the Under-wood
Sweet-murmuring: Methought! the shrill-tongu'd Thrush
Mended his Song of Love; the sooty Black-bird
Mellow'd his Pipe, and soften'd every Note:
The Eglantine smell'd sweeter, and the Rose
Assum'd a Dye more deep; whilst ev'ry Flower
Vy'd with its Fellow-Plant in Luxury
Of Dress. Oh! then the longest Summer's Day
Seem'd too too much in Haste: Still the full Heart
Had not imparted half: T'was Happiness
Too exquisite to last. Of Joys departed
Not to return, how painful the Remembrance!
        Dull *Grave!* thou spoil'st the Dance of Youthful Blood,
Strik'st out the Dimple from the Cheek of Mirth,
And ev'ry smirking Feature from the Face;
Branding our *Laughter* with the Name of *Madness.*
Where are the *Jesters* now? the Men of Health
Complexionally pleasant? Where the *Droll?*
Whose ev'ry Look and Gesture was a Joke
To clapping Theatres and shouting Crouds,
And made even thick-lip'd musing Melancholy
To gather up her Face into a Smile
Before she was aware? Ah! Sullen now,
And Dumb, as the green Turf that covers them!
        Where are the mighty Thunderbolts of War?
The *Roman Cæsars,* and the *Grecian Chiefs,*
The Boast of Story? Where the hot-brain'd Youth?
Who the *Tiara* at his Pleasure tore
From Kings of all the then discover'd Globe;
And cry'd forsooth, because his Arm was hamper'd,
And had not Room enough to do its Work?
Alas! how slim, dishonourably slim!
And cramm'd into a Space we blush to name.
Proud *Royalty!* how alter'd in thy Looks?
How blank thy Features, and how wan thy Hue?
Son of the Morning! whither art thou gone?
Where hast thou hid thy many-spangled Head,
And the majestick Menace of thine Eyes

Felt from afar? Pliant and powerless now,
Like new-born Infant wound up in his Swathes,
Or Victim tumbled flat upon its Back,
That throbs beneath the Sacrificer's Knife:
Mute, must thou bear the Strife of little Tongues,
And coward Insults of the base-born Croud;
That grudge a Privilege, thou never hadst,
But only hop'd for in the peaceful *Grave*,
Of being unmolested and alone.
Arabia's Gums and odoriferous Drugs,
And Honours by the *Heralds* duly paid
In Mode and Form, ev'n to a very Scruple;
Oh cruel *Irony!* These come too late;
And only mock, whom they were meant to honour.
Surely! There's not a Dungeon-Slave, that's bury'd
In the High-way, unshrouded and uncoffin'd,
But lies as soft, and sleeps as sound as He.
Sorry Pre-eminence of high Descent
Above the vulgar-born, to rot in State!
          But see! the well-plum'd *Herse* comes nodding on
Stately and slow; and properly attended
By the whole Sable Tribe, that painful watch
The sick Man's Door, and live upon the Dead,
By letting out their Persons by the Hour
To mimick Sorrow, when the Heart's not sad.
How rich the Trappings, now they're all unfurl'd,
And glittering in the Sun! Triumphant Entrys
Of Conquerors, and Coronation Pomps,
In Glory scarce exceed. Great Gluts of People
Retard th' unweildy Show; whilst from the Casements
And Houses Tops, Ranks behind Ranks close-wedg'd
Hang bellying o'er. But! tell us, Why this Waste?
Why this ado in Earthing up a Carcase
That's fall'n into Disgrace, and in the Nostril
Smells horrible? Ye *Undertakers!* tell us,
'Midst all the gorgeous Figures you exhibit,
Why is the Principal conceal'd, for which
You make this mighty Stir? 'Tis wisely done:
What would offend the Eye in a good Picture
The Painter casts discreetly into Shades.
          Proud *Lineage!* now how little thou appear'st!

Below the Envy of the Private Man!
Honour! that meddlesome officious Ill,
Pursues thee ev'n to Death; nor there stops short.
Strange Persecution! when the *Grave* itself
Is no Protection from rude Sufferance.
    Absurd! to think to over-reach the *Grave*,
And from the Wreck of Names to rescue ours!
The best concerted Schemes Men lay for Fame
Die fast away: Only themselves die faster.
The far-famed *Sculptor*, and the lawrell'd *Bard*,
Those bold Insurancers of Deathless Fame,
Supply their little feeble Aids in vain.
The tapering *Pyramid!* th' *Egyptian*'s Pride,
And Wonder of the World! whose spiky Top
Has wounded the thick Cloud, and long out-liv'd
The angry Shaking of the Winter's Storm;
Yet spent at last by the Injuries of Heaven,
Shatter'd with Age, and furrow'd o'er with Years,
The Mystick Cone with Hieroglyphicks crusted
Gives Way. Oh! lamentable Sight! at once
The Labour of whole Ages lumbers down;
A hideous and mishapen Length of Ruins.
Sepulchral Columns wrestle but in vain
With all-subduing Time: Her cank'ring Hand
With calm deliberate Malice wasteth them:
Worn on the Edge of Days, the Brass consumes,
The Busto moulders, and the deep-cut Marble,
Unsteady to the Steel, gives up its Charge.
Ambition! half convicted of her Folly,
Hangs down the Head, and reddens at the Tale.
    Here! all the mighty *Troublers of the Earth,*
Who swam to Sov'reign Rule thro' Seas of Blood;
Th' oppressive, sturdy, Man-destroying Villains!
Who ravag'd Kingdoms, and laid Empires waste,
And in a cruel Wantonness of Power
Thinn'd States of half their People, and gave up
To Want the rest: Now like a Storm that's spent,
Lye hush'd, and meanly sneak behind thy Covert.
Vain Thought! to hide them from the general Scorn,
That haunts and doggs them like an injur'd Ghost
Implacable. Here too the *petty Tyrant*

Whose scant Domains *Geographer* ne'er noticed,
And, well for neighbouring Grounds, of Arm as short;
Who fix'd his Iron Talons on the Poor,
And grip'd them like some Lordly Beast of Prey;
Deaf to the forceful Cries of gnawing Hunger,
And piteous plaintive Voice of Misery:
(As if a *Slave* was not a Shred of Nature,
Of the same common Nature with his *Lord*):
Now! tame and humble, like a Child that's whipp'd,
Shakes Hands with Dust, and calls the Worm his Kinsman;
Nor pleads his Rank and Birthright. Under Ground
Precedency's a Jest; Vassal and Lord
Grossly familiar, Side by Side consume.

　　　When Self-Esteem, or others' Adulation,
Would cunningly persuade us we are Something
Above the common Level of our Kind;
The *Grave* gainsays the smooth-complexion'd Flatt'ry,
And with blunt Truth acquaints us what we are.

　　　Beauty! thou pretty Play-thing! dear Deceit!
That steals so softly o'er the Stripling's Heart,
And gives it a new Pulse, unknown before!
The *Grave* discredits thee: Thy Charms expung'd,
Thy Roses faded, and thy Lillies soil'd,
What hast thou more to boast of? Will thy Lovers
Flock round thee now, to gaze and do thee Homage?
Methinks! I see thee with thy Head low laid,
Whilst surfeited upon thy Damask Cheek
The high-fed *Worm* in lazy Volumes roll'd
Riots unscar'd. For this, was all thy Caution?
For this, thy painful Labours at thy Glass?
T' improve those Charms, and keep them in Repair,
For which the Spoiler thanks thee not. Foul-feeder!
Coarse Fare and Carrion please thee full as well,
And leave as keen a Relish on the Sense.
Look! how the Fair One weeps! the conscious Tears
Stand thick as Dew-drops on the Bells of Flow'rs:
Honest Effusion! the swoln Heart in vain
Works hard to put a Gloss on its Distress.

　　　Strength too! thou surly, and less gentle Boast
Of those that laugh loud at the Village-ring!
A Fit of common Sickness pulls thee down

With greater Ease, than e'er thou didst the Stripling
That rashly dar'd thee to th' unequal Fight.
What Groan was that I heard? Deep Groan indeed!
With Anguish heavy-laden! Let me trace it:
From yonder Bed it comes, where the Strong Man,
By stronger Arm belabour'd, gasps for Breath
Like a hard-hunted Beast. How his great Heart
Beats thick! his roomy Chest by far too scant
To give the Lungs full Play! What now avail
The strong-built sinewy Limbs, and well-spread Shoulders?
See! how he tugs for Life, and lays about him,
Mad with his Pain! Eager he catches hold
Of what comes next to Hand, and grasps it hard,
Just like a Creature drowning! Hideous Sight!
Oh! how his Eyes stand out, and stare full ghastly!
Whilst the Distemper's rank and deadly Venom
Shoots like a burning Arrow cross his Bowels,
And drinks his Marrow up. Heard you that Groan?
It was his last. See how the great *Goliath*,
Just like a Child that brawl'd itself to Rest,
Lies still. What mean'st thou then, O mighty Boaster!
To vaunt of Nerves of thine? What means the Bull,
Unconscious of his Strength, to play the Coward,
And flee before a feeble Thing like Man;
That knowing well the Slackness of his Arm,
Trusts only in the well-invented Knife?

       With *Study* pale, and Midnight Vigils spent,
The Star-surveying *Sage*, close to his Eye
Applies the Sight-invigorating Tube;
And travelling through the boundless Length of Space
Marks well the Courses of the far-seen Orbs,
That roll with regular Confusion there,
In Extasy of Thought. But Ah! proud Man!
Great Heights are hazardous to the weak Head:
Soon, very soon, thy firmest Footing fails;
And down thou dropp'st into that darksome Place,
Where *nor Device, nor Knowledge* ever came.

       Here! the *Tongue-Warrior* lies, disabled now,
Disarm'd, dishonour'd, like a Wretch that's gagg'd,
And cannot tell his Ail to Passers by.
Great Man of Language! whence this mighty Change?

This dumb Despair, and drooping of the Head?
Tho' strong Persuasion hung upon thy Lip,
And sly Insinuation's softer Arts
In Ambush lay about thy flowing Tongue;
Alas! how Chop-fall'n now? Thick Mists and Silence
Rest, like a weary Cloud, upon thy Breast
Unceasing. Ah! Where is the lifted Arm,
The Strength of Action, and the Force of Words,
The well-turn'd Period, and the well-tun'd Voice,
With all the lesser Ornaments of Phrase?
Ah! fled for ever, as they ne'er had been!
Raz'd from the Book of Fame: Or, more provoking,
Perchance some Hackney hunger-bitten Scribler
Insults thy Memory, and blots thy Tomb
With long flat Narrative, or duller Rhimes
With heavy-halting Pace that drawl along;
Enough to rouse a Dead Man into Rage,
And warm with red Resentment the wan Cheek.

    Here! the great Masters of the *healing Art*,
These mighty Mock-Defrauders of the *Tomb!*
Spite of their *Juleps* and *Catholicons*
Resign to Fate. Proud *Æsculapius'* Son!
Where are thy boasted Implements of Art,
And all thy well-cramm'd Magazines of Health?
Nor Hill, nor Vale, as far as Ship could go,
Nor Margin of the Gravel-bottom'd Brook,
Escap'd thy rifling Hand: From stubborn Shrubs
Thou wrung'st their shy retiring Virtues out,
And vex'd them in the Fire: Nor Fly, nor Insect,
Nor writhy Snake, escap'd thy deep Research.
But why this *Apparatus*? Why this Cost?
Tell us, thou doughty Keeper from the *Grave!*
Where are thy *Recipes* and *Cordials* now,
With the long List of Vouchers for thy Cures?
Alas! thou speakest not. The bold Impostor
Looks not more silly, when the Cheat's found out.

    Here! the lank-sided *Miser*, worst of Felons!
Who meanly stole, discreditable Shift!
From Back and Belly too, their proper Cheer;
Eas'd of a Tax, it irk'd the Wretch to pay
To his own Carcase, now lies cheaply lodg'd,

By clam'rous Appetites no longer teaz'd,
Nor tedious Bills of Charges and Repairs.
But Ah! Where are his Rents, his Comings-in?
Ay! now you've made the Rich Man Poor indeed:
Robb'd of his Gods, what has he left behind!
Oh! Cursed Lust of Gold! when for thy Sake
The Fool throws up his Int'rest in both Worlds,
First starv'd in this, then damn'd in that to come.
     How shocking must thy Summons be, O *Death!*
To him that is at Ease in his Possessions;
Who, counting on long Years of Pleasure here,
Is quite unfurnish'd for that World to come!
In that dread Moment, how the frantick Soul
Raves round the Walls of her Clay Tenement,
Runs to each Avenue, and shrieks for Help,
But shrieks in vain! How wishfully she looks
On all she's leaving, now no longer her's!
A little longer, yet a little longer,
Oh! might she stay, to wash away her Stains,
And fit her for her Passage! Mournful Sight!
Her very Eyes weep Blood; and every Groan
She heaves is big with Horror: But the Foe,
Like a staunch Murth'rer steady to his Purpose,
Pursues her close through ev'ry Lane of Life,
Nor misses once the Track, but presses on;
Till forc'd at last to the tremendous Verge,
At once she sinks to everlasting Ruin.
     Sure! 'tis a serious Thing *to Die!* My Soul!
What a strange Moment must it be, when near
Thy Journey's End, thou hast the Gulf in View?
That awful Gulf, no Mortal e'er repass'd
To tell what's doing on the other Side!
Nature runs back, and shudders at the Sight,
And every Life-string bleeds at Thoughts of parting!
For part they must: *Body* and *Soul* must part;
Fond Couple! link'd more close than wedded Pair.
This wings its Way to its Almighty Source,
The Witness of its Actions, now its Judge:
That drops into the dark and noisome *Grave*,
Like a disabled Pitcher of no Use.
     If *Death* was nothing, and nought *after Death*;

If when Men dy'd, at once they ceas'd to Be,
Returning to the barren Womb of Nothing
Whence first they sprung; then might the Debauchee
Untrembling mouth the Heav'ns: Then might the Drunkard
Reel over his full Bowl, and when 'tis drain'd,
Fill up another to the Brim, and laugh
At the poor Bug-bear *Death*: Then might the Wretch
That's weary of the World, and tir'd of Life,
At once give each Inquietude the Slip
By stealing out of Being, when he pleas'd,
And by what Way; whether by Hemp, or Steel:
Death's thousand Doors stand open. Who could force
The ill-pleas'd Guest to sit out his full Time,
Or blame him if he goes? Sure! he does well
That helps himself as timely as he can,
When able. But if there is an *Hereafter*,
And that there is, Conscience, uninfluenc'd,
And suffer'd to speak out, tells ev'ry Man;
Then must it be an awful Thing *to die*:
More horrid yet, to die by one's own Hand.
Self-Murther! name it not: Our Island's Shame!
That makes her the Reproach of neighbouring States.
Shall Nature, swerving from her earliest Dictate
Self-Preservation, fall by her own Act?
Forbid it, Heav'n! Let not upon Disgust
The shameless Hand be foully crimson'd o'er
With Blood of its own Lord. Dreadful Attempt!
Just reeking from self-slaughter, in a Rage
To rush into the Presence of our Judge!
As if we challeng'd him to do his worst,
And matter'd not his Wrath. Unheard of Tortures
Must be reserv'd for such: These herd together;
The Common Damn'd shun their Society,
And look upon themselves as Fiends less foul.
Our Time is fix'd; and all our Days are number'd;
How long, how short, we know not: This we know,
Duty requires we calmly wait the Summons,
Nor dare to stir till Heav'n shall give Permission:
Like Centrys that must keep their destin'd Stand,
And wait th' appointed Hour, till they're reliev'd.
Those only are the Brave, that keep their Ground,

And keep it to the last. To run away
Is but a Coward's Trick: To run away
From this World's Ills, that at the very worst
Will soon blow o'er, thinking to mend ourselves
By boldly vent'ring on a World unknown,
And plunging headlong in the dark; 'tis Mad:
No Frenzy half so desperate as this.

      Tell us! ye Dead! Will none of you in Pity
To those you left behind disclose the Secret?
Oh! that some courteous Ghost would blab it out!
What 'tis You are, and We must shortly be.
I've heard, that Souls departed have sometimes
Forewarn'd Men of their Death: 'Twas kindly done
To knock, and give th' Alarum. But what means
This stinted Charity? 'tis but lame Kindness
That does its Work by halves. Why might you not
Tell us what 'tis *to Die*? Do the strict Laws
Of your Society forbid your speaking
Upon a Point so nice? I'll ask no more;
Sullen, like Lamps in Sepulchres, your Shine
Enlightens but yourselves: Well,—'tis no Matter;
A very little Time will clear up all,
And make us learn'd as you are, and as close.

      Death's Shafts fly thick! Here falls the Village Swain,
And there his pamper'd Lord! The Cup goes round;
And who so artful as to put it by?
'Tis long since *Death* had the Majority;
Yet strange! *the Living lay it not to Heart*.
See! yonder Maker of the Dead Man's Bed,
The *Sexton!* hoary-headed Chronicle,
Of hard unmeaning Face, down which ne'er stole
A gentle Tear; with Mattock in his Hand
Digs through whole Rows of Kindred and Acquaintance,
By far his Juniors! Scarce a Scull's cast up,
But well he knew its Owner, and can tell
Some Passage of his Life. Thus Hand in Hand
The Sot has walk'd with *Death* twice Twenty Years;
And yet ne'er Yonker on the Green laughs louder,
Or clubs a Smuttier Tale: When Drunkards meet,
None sings a merrier Catch, or lends a Hand
More willing to his Cup. Poor Wretch! he minds not,

That soon some trusty Brother of the Trade
Shall do for him what he has done for Thousands.
       On this Side, and on that, Men see their Friends
Drop off, like Leaves in Autumn; yet launch out
Into fantastic Schemes, which the long Livers,
In the World's hale and undegenerate Days,
Could scarce have Leisure for! Fools that we are!
Never to think of *Death*, and of *Ourselves*
At the same Time! As if to learn *to Die*
Were no Concern of ours. Oh! more than Sottish!
For Creatures of a Day, in gamesome Mood
To frolick on Eternity's dread Brink,
Unapprehensive; when for aught we know
The very first swoln Surge shall sweep us in.
Think we, or think we not, *Time* hurries on
With a resistless unremitting Stream,
Yet treads more soft than e'er did Midnight Thief,
That slides his Hand under the Miser's Pillow,
And carries off his Prize. What is *this World*?
What? but a spacious *Burial-Field* unwall'd,
Strew'd with Death's Spoils, the Spoils of Animals
Savage and Tame, and full of Dead Men's Bones?
The very Turf on which we tread, once liv'd;
And we that live must lend our Carcases
To cover our own Offspring: In their Turns
They too must cover theirs. 'Tis *here* all meet!
The shiv'ring *Icelander*, and Sun-burnt *Moor*;
Men of all Climes, that never met before;
And of all Creeds, the *Jew*, the *Turk*, and *Christian*.
Here the proud *Prince*, and *Favourite* yet prouder,
His Sov'reign's Keeper, and the People's Scourge,
Are huddled out of Sight. *Here* lie abash'd
The great *Negotiators* of the Earth,
And celebrated *Masters of the Ballance*,
Deep read in Stratagems, and Wiles of Courts:
Now vain their *Treaty-Skill!* Death scorns to treat.
Here the o'erloaded *Slave* flings down his Burthen
From his gall'd Shoulders; and when the cruel Tyrant,
With all his Guards and Tools of Pow'r about him,
Is meditating new unheard-of Hardships,
Mocks his short Arm, and quick as Thought escapes

Where Tyrants vex not, and the Weary rest.
Here the warm *Lover* leaving the cool Shade,
The Tell-tale Echo, and the babbling Stream,
Time out of Mind the favo'rite Seats of Love,
Fast by his gentle Mistress lays him down
Unblasted by foul Tongue. *Here* Friends and Foes
Lie close; unmindful of their former Feuds.
The Lawn-rob'd *Prelate*, and plain *Presbyter*,
E'er while that stood aloof, as shy to meet,
Familiar mingle *here*, like Sister-Streams
That some rude interposing Rock had split.
Here is the large-limb'd *Peasant*: *Here* the *Child*
Of a Span long, that never saw the Sun,
Nor press'd the Nipple, strangled in Life's Porch.
Here is the *Mother* with her Sons and Daughters;
The barren *Wife*; and long-demurring *Maid*,
Whose lonely unappropriated Sweets
Smil'd like yon Knot of Cowslips on the Cliff,
Not to be come at by the willing Hand.
Here are the *Prude* severe, and gay *Coquet*,
The sober *Widow*, and the young green *Virgin*,
Cropp'd like a Rose, before 'tis fully blown,
Or half its Worth disclos'd. Strange Medley *here!*
Here garrulous *Old Age* winds up his Tale;
And jovial *Youth* of lightsome vacant Heart,
Whose ev'ry Day was made of Melody,
Hears not the Voice of Mirth: The shrill-tongu'd Shrew,
Meek as the Turtle-Dove, forgets her Chiding.
Here are the Wise, the Generous, and the Brave;
The Just, the Good, the Worthless, the Profane;
The downright Clown, and perfectly Well-bred;
The Fool, the Churl, the Scoundrel, and the Mean;
The supple Statesman, and the Patriot stern;
The Wrecks of Nations, and the Spoils of Time,
With all the Lumber of Six Thousand Years.

     Poor *Man!* how Happy once in thy *first State!*
When yet but warm from thy great Maker's Hand,
He stamp'd thee with his Image, and well-pleas'd
Smil'd on his last fair Work. Then all was Well.
Sound was the *Body*, and the *Soul* serene;
Like Two sweet Instruments ne'er out of Tune,

That play their several Parts. Nor Head, nor Heart,
Offer'd to ache: Nor was there Cause they should;
For all was pure within: No fell Remorse,
Nor anxious Castings up of what might be,
Alarm'd his peaceful Bosom: Summer Seas
Shew not more smooth, when kiss'd by Southern Winds
Just ready to expire. Scarce importun'd,
The generous Soil with a luxuriant Hand
Offer'd the various Produce of the Year,
And every Thing most perfect in its Kind.
Blessed! thrice blessed Days! But Ah, how short!
Bless'd as the pleasing Dreams of Holy Men;
But fugitive like those, and quickly gone.
Oh! slipp'ry State of Things! What sudden Turns?
What strange Vicissitudes, in the first Leaf
Of Man's sad History? To-day most Happy,
And 'ere To-morrow's Sun has set, most Abject!
How scant the Space between these vast Extremes!
Thus far'd it with *our Sire*: Not long he enjoy'd
His Paradise! Scarce had the happy Tenant
Of the fair Spot due Time to prove its Sweets,
Or summ them up; when strait he must be gone
Ne'er to return again. And must he go?
Can nought compound for the first dire Offence
Of erring Man? Like one that is condemn'd
Fain would he trifle Time with idle Talk,
And parley with his Fate. But 'tis in vain.
Not all the lavish Odours of the Place
Offer'd in Incense can procure his Pardon,
Or mitigate his Doom. A mighty Angel
With flaming Sword forbids his longer Stay,
And drives the Loiterer forth; nor must he take
One last and farewel Round. At once he lost
His Glory, and his God. If Mortal now,
And sorely maim'd, No Wonder! *Man has Sinn'd*.
Sick of his Bliss, and bent on new Adventures,
Evil he wou'd needs try: Nor try'd in vain.
(Dreadful Experiment! Destructive Measure!
Where the worst Thing could happen, is Success.)
Alas! too well he sped: The *Good* he scorn'd
Stalk'd off reluctant, like an ill-used Ghost,

Not to return; or if it did, its Visits
Like those of *Angels* short, and far between:
Whilst the black *Dæmon* with his Hell-'scap'd Train,
Admitted once into its better Room,
Grew loud and mutinous, nor would be gone;
Lording it o'er the *Man*, who now too late
Saw the rash Error, which he could not mend:
An Error fatal not to him alone,
But to his future Sons, his Fortune's Heirs.
Inglorious Bondage! Human Nature groans
Beneath a Vassalage so vile and cruel,
And its vast Body bleeds through ev'ry Vein.
          What Havock hast thou made? Foul Monster, *Sin!*
Greatest and first of Ills! The fruitful Parent
Of Woes of all Dimensions! But for *thee*
Sorrow had never been. All noxious Thing!
Of vilest Nature! Other Sorts of Evils
Are kindly circumscrib'd, and have their Bounds.
The fierce *Volcano*, from his burning Entrails
That belches molten Stone and Globes of Fire,
Involv'd in pitchy Clouds of Smoke and Stench,
Marrs the adjacent Fields for some Leagues round,
And there it stops. The big-swoln *Inundation*,
Of Mischief more diffusive, raving loud,
Buries whole Tracts of Country, threat'ning more;
But that too has its Shore it cannot pass.
More dreadful far than these! *Sin* has laid waste
Not here and there a Country, but *a World*:
Dispatching at a wide extended Blow
Entire Mankind; and for their Sakes defacing
A whole Creation's Beauty with rude Hands;
Blasting the foodful Grain, the loaded Branches,
And marking all along its Way with Ruin.
Accursed Thing! Oh, where shall Fancy find
A proper Name to call thee by, expressive
Of all thy Horrors? Pregnant Womb of Ills!
Of Temper so transcendantly malign,
That Toads and Serpents of most deadly Kind
Compar'd to thee are harmless. Sicknesses
Of ev'ry Size and Symptom, racking Pains,
And bluest Plagues, are thine! See! how the Fiend

Profusely scatters the Contagion round!
Whilst deep-mouth'd Slaughter bellowing at her Heels
Wades deep in Blood new-spilt; yet for To-morrow
Shapes out new Work of great uncommon Daring,
And inly pines till the dread Blow is struck.
      But hold! I've gone too far; too much discover'd
My Father's Nakedness, and Nature's Shame.
Here let me pause! and drop an honest Tear,
One Burst of filial Duty, and Condolence,
O'er all those ample Deserts *Death* hath spread,
This *Chaos* of Mankind. O Great *Man-Eater!*
Whose ev'ry Day is *Carnival*, not sated yet!
Unheard of *Epicure!* without a Fellow!
The veryest *Gluttons* do not always cram;
Some Intervals of Abstinence are sought
To edge the Appetite: *Thou* seekest none.
Methinks! the countless Swarms thou hast devour'd,
And Thousands at each Hour thou gobblest up;
This, less than *this*, might gorge thee to the full!
But Ah! rapacious still, thou gap'st for more:
Like One, whole Days defrauded of his Meals,
On whom lank Hunger lays her skinny Hand,
And whets to keenest Eagerness his Cravings.
(As if Diseases, Massacres, and Poison,
Famine, and War, were not thy Caterers!)
      But know! that Thou must *render up thy Dead*,
And with high Int'rest too! They are not thine;
But only in thy Keeping for a Season,
Till the Great promis'd Day of Restitution;
When loud diffusive Sound from brazen Trump
Of Strong-lung'd Cherub shall alarm thy Captives,
And rouse the long, long Sleepers into Life,
Day-Light, and Liberty.———
Then must thy Gates fly open, and reveal
The Mines, that lay long forming under Ground,
In their dark Cells immur'd; but now full ripe,
And pure as Silver from the Crucible,
That twice has stood the Torture of the Fire
And Inquisition of the Forge. We know,
The illustrious Deliverer of Mankind,
The Son of God, thee foil'd. Him in thy Pow'r

Thou couldst not hold: Self-vigorous he rose,
And, shaking off thy Fetters, soon retook
Those Spoils, his voluntary Yielding lent.
(Sure Pledge of our Releasement from thy Thrall!)
Twice Twenty Days he sojourn'd here on Earth,
And shew'd himself alive to *chosen Witnesses*
By Proofs so strong, that the most slow-assenting
Had not a Scruple left. This having done,
He mounted up to Heav'n. Methinks! I see him
Climb the Aërial Heights, and glide along
Athwart the severing Clouds: But the faint Eye
Flung backwards in the Chace, soon drops its Hold;
Disabled quite, and jaded with pursuing.
Heaven's Portals wide expand to let him in;
Nor are his Friends shut out: As some great Prince
Not for himself alone procures Admission,
But for his Train: It was his Royal Will,
That where He is, there should his Followers be.
Death only lies between! A gloomy Path!
Made yet more gloomy by our Coward Fears!
But not untrod, nor tedious: The Fatigue
Will soon go off. Besides, there's no By-road
To Bliss. Then why, like ill-condition'd Children,
Start we at transient Hardships, in the Way
That leads to purer Air, and softer Skies,
And a ne'er Setting Sun? Fools that we are!
We wish to be, where Sweets unwith'ring bloom;
But strait our Wish revoke, and will not go.
So have I seen upon a Summer's Even,
Fast by the Riv'let's Brink, a Youngster play:
How wishfully he looks! To stem the Tide
This Moment resolute, next unresolv'd:
At last! he dips his Foot; but as he dips,
His Fears redouble, and he runs away
From th' inoffensive Stream, unmindful now
Of all the Flow'rs, that paint the further Bank,
And smil'd so sweet of late. Thrice welcome *Death!*
That after many a painful bleeding Step
Conducts us to our Home, and lands us safe
On the long-wish'd for Shore. Prodigious Change!
Our Bane turn'd to a Blessing! *Death* disarm'd

Loses his Fellness quite: All Thanks to him
Who scourg'd the Venom out. Sure! *the last End*
Of the Good Man is *Peace*. How calm his *Exit!*
Night-Dews fall not more gently to the Ground,
Nor weary worn out Winds expire so soft.
Behold him! in the Evening-Tide of Life,
A Life well-spent, whose early Care it was
His riper Years should not upbraid his Green:
By unperceiv'd Degrees he wears away;
Yet like the Sun seems larger at his Setting!
High in his Faith and Hopes, look! how he reaches
After the Prize in View! and, like a Bird
That's hamper'd, struggles hard to get away!
Whilst the glad Gates of Sight are wide expanded
To let new Glories in, the first fair Fruits
Of the fast-coming Harvest. *Then!* Oh *Then!*
Each Earth-born Joy grows vile, or disappears,
Shrunk to a Thing of Nought. Oh! how he longs
To have his Passport sign'd, and be dismiss'd!
'Tis done; and now he's Happy: The glad *Soul*
Has not a Wish uncrown'd. Ev'n the lag *Flesh*
Rests too *in Hope* of meeting once again
Its better Half, never to sunder more.
Nor shall it hope in vain: The Time draws on
When not a single Spot of Burial-Earth,
Whether on Land, or in the spacious Sea,
But must give back its long-committed Dust
Inviolate: And faithfully shall these
Make up the full Account; not the least Atom
Embezzl'd, or mislaid, of the whole Tale.
Each *Soul* shall have a *Body* ready furnish'd;
And each shall have his own. Hence ye Prophane!
Ask not, how this can be? Sure the same Pow'r
That rear'd the Piece at first, and took it down,
Can re-assemble the loose scatter'd Parts,
And put them as they were. Almighty God
Has done much more; nor is his Arm impair'd
Thro' Length of Days: And what he can, he will:
His Faithfulness stands bound to see it done.
When the dread Trumpet sounds, the slumb'ring Dust,
Not unattentive to the Call, shall wake:

And ev'ry Joint possess its proper Place,
With a new Elegance of Form, unknown
To its first State. Nor shall the conscious *Soul*
Mistake its Partner; but amidst the Croud
Singling its other Half, into its Arms
Shall rush, with all th' Impatience of a Man
That's new-come Home, who having long been absent
With Haste runs over ev'ry different Room,
In Pain to see the whole. Thrice happy Meeting!
Nor *Time*, nor *Death*, shall ever part them more.

    'Tis but a Night, a long and moonless Night,
We make the *Grave* our Bed, and then are gone.

    Thus at the Shut of Ev'n, the weary Bird
Leaves the wide Air, and in some lonely Brake
Cow'rs down, and dozes till the Dawn of Day,
Then claps his well-fledg'd Wings, and bears away.

ALEXANDER ROSS
(1699–1784)

———

ALEXANDER ROSS hailed from the parish of Kincardine O'Neil, Aberdeenshire. In his early thirties, after various teaching roles, Ross was appointed parish schoolmaster at Lochlee in Forfarshire, a remote village at the head of Glenesk in the Grampian Mountains. Ross wrote large quantities of poetry, much of it unpublished, though his songs circulated orally throughout northeast Scotland. In 1766 he met the poet James Beattie, the son of his late friend. Sharing poems, Beattie encouraged Ross to publish *The Fortunate Shepherdess* and some short songs. They appeared by subscription in 1768, followed by a revised edition in 1778 under the new title *Helenore*. The long narrative poem follows the skirmishes between shepherds and Highland raiders against the backdrop of stunning Grampian scenery. Often compared with Ramsay, Ross here displays plenty of other major literary influences, Spenser among them.

———

The Fortunate Shepherdess *(1768)*, *'Invocation'*

The Fortunate Shepherdess, a Pastoral Tale. In Three Cantos, in the Scotish Dialect (Aberdeen: Francis Douglas, 1768).

> Say, SCOTA, Thou that anes upon a day
> Gar'd Allan Ramsay's hungry hart strings play
> The merriest sangs that ever yet were sung,
> Pity anes mair, for I'm outthrow as clung.
> 'Twas that grim gossip, chandler chafted want,
> With threed-bair claithing, and an ambry scant,
> Made him cry o' thee, to blaw throw his pen,
> Wi' leed, that well might help him to come ben,
> An' crack amo' the best of ilka sex,
> An' shape his houghs to gentle bows and becks.
> He wan thy heart, well wordy o't poor man,
> Take yet another gangrell by the hand;

As gryt's my mister, an' my duds as bair,
And I as sib as he was ilka hair:
Mak me but half as canny, there's no fear,
Tho' I be auld, but I'll yet gather gear.
　　　　O gin thou hadst not heard him first o'erwell,
When he got maughts to write The Shepherd's Tale,
I meith ha had some chance of landing fair,
But O that sang, the mither of my care!
What wad I geen, that thou hadst put thy thumb,
Upo' the well tauld tale, till I had come;
Then led my hand alongst it line for line,
O to my dieing day, how I wad shine;
An' as far yont it, as syn Habbi plaid,
Or Ga'in on Virgil matchless skill display'd:
An' mair I wadna wiss. But Ramsay bears
The gree himsel, an' the green laureals wears:
Well mat he brook them, for piece ye had spair'd,
The task to me, Pate meith na been a laird:
'Tis may be better, I's take what ye gee
Ye're nae toom handed gin your heart be free:
But I's be willing as ye bid me write,
Blind horse they say ride hardy to the fight;
And by good hap, may come awa, but scorn
They are na kempers a' that shear the corn.
Then Scota heard, and said your rough spun ware
Sounds but right douft an' fowsome to my ear;
Do ye pretend to write like my ain bairn,
Or onie ane that wins beyont the Kairn;
Ye're far mistaen gin ye think sick a thought,
The Gentle Shepherd's nae sae easy wrought;
There's scenes an' acts, there's drift an' there's design,
An' a' maun like a new ground whittle shine;
Sick wimpl'd wark, would crack a pow like thine.
Kind mistris, says I, gin this be your fear,
Charge nae mair shot, than what the piece'll bear.
Something but scenes or acts, than kittle game,
Yet what may please, bid me sit down an' frame,
Gae, then; she says, nor deave me with your dinn,
PUFF—I inspire you, sae you may begin.
If ye oe'r forthersome, turn tapsie turvy
Blame you ain haste, an' say not that I spur ye.

But sound and feelfu' as I bid you write,
An' ready hae you pen when I indite:
Speak my ain leed, 'tis gueed auld Scots I mean,
Your Southren gnaps, I count not worth a preen.
We've words a fouth, that we can ca' our ain,
Tho' frae them now my childer fair refrain.
An' are to my gueed auld proverb confeerin,
Neither gueed fish nor flesh, nor yet fa't herrin.
Gin this ye do an lyn your rime wi' sense
But ye'll make friends of freemet fouk, fa' kens?
Wi' thir injunctions ye may set you down:
Mistress, says I, I'm at your bidding boun.

　　　Sae I begins, my pen into my hand,
Just ready hearkning, as she should command.
But then about her, there was sic a dinn,
Some seeking this, some that, some out some in.
That its nae wonder, tho' I aft gae wrang,
An' for my ain, set down my neiper's sang,
For hundreds mair were learning at her school,
And some wrote fair, an' some like me wrote foul.

JAMES THOMSON

(1700–1748)

AN EDNAM native, James Thomson remains best known for his book-length poems *The Seasons* (1730) and *The Castle of Indolence* (1748), and for the lyrics of 'Rule, Britannia!' (*Alfred: A Masque* [1740], with David Mallet), though he wrote a wide range of shorter poems and songs. Owing in large part to his friend David Malloch (now known as Mallet), Thomson made the acquaintance of Aaron Hill, John Dyer, Alexander Pope, and other leading English poets. During his first year in London, in 1725, he produced early versions of his popular *Hymn on Solitude* (after Milton) and *Winter*, a blank-verse poem about nature with strong devotional overtones. *Summer* (1727) followed *Winter* (1726) in a matter of months. In January 1728 the poet issued proposals to publish *The Seasons* by subscription, though he published *Spring* on his own accord a few months later. (He had little success with it.) A steady stream of poems, largely philosophical in nature, followed; and he worked on his first play, *Sophonisba*, which opened at Drury Lane on 28 February 1730. That summer, a glittering list of subscribers had signed up for a revised version of *The Seasons*, which, with *Autumn* now written, appeared to great acclaim.

The Seasons *(1730)*, 'Winter'

The Seasons, A Hymn, A Poem to the Memory of Sir Isaac Newton, and Britannia, a Poem (London: J. Millan and A. Millar, 1730).

> See *WINTER* comes, to rule the varied Year,
> Sullen, and sad, with all his rising train,
> *Vapours*, and *Clouds*, and *Storms*. Be these my theme,
> These, that exalt the soul to solemn thought,
> And heavenly musing. Welcome, kindred glooms!
> Congenial horrors, hail! with frequent foot,
> Pleas'd have I, in my chearful morn of life,
> When nurs'd by careless *Solitude* I liv'd,

And sung of Nature with unceasing joy,
Pleas'd, have I wander'd thro' your rough domain;
Trod the pure virgin-snows, myself as pure;
Heard the winds roar, and the big torrent burst;
Or seen the deep, fermenting tempest brew'd
In the red evening-sky. Thus pass'd the time,
Till thro' the lucid chambers of the south
Look'd out the joyous *Spring*, look'd out, and smil'd.

To thee, the patron of her first essay,
The muse, O *Wilmington!* renews her song.
Since has she rounded the revolving *Year*:
Skim'd the gay *Spring*; on eagle-pinions borne,
Attempted thro' the *Summer*-blaze to rise;
Then swept o'er *Autumn* with the shadowy gale,
And now among the *Wintry* clouds again,
Roll'd in the doubling storm, she tries to soar;
To swell her note with all the rushing winds;
To suit her sounding cadence to the floods;
As is her theme, her numbers wildly great:
Thrice happy! could she fill thy judging ear
With bold description, and with manly thought.
For thee the Graces smooth; thy softer thoughts
The Muses tune; nor art thou skill'd alone
In awful schemes, the management of states,
And how to make a mighty people thrive:
But equal goodness; sound integrity;
A firm, unshaken, uncorrupted soul,
Amid a sliding age; and burning strong,
Not vainly blazing, for thy country's weal,
A steady spirit, regularly free;
These, each exalting each, the statesman light
Into the patriot; and, the publick hope
And eye to thee converting, bid the muse
Record what envy dares not flattery call.

When *Scorpio* gives to *Capricorn* the sway,
And fierce *Aquarius* fouls th' inverted year;
Retiring to the verge of heaven, the sun
Scarce spreads o'er other the dejected day.
Faint are his gleams, and ineffectual shoot
His struggling rays, in horizontal lines,
Thro' the thick air; as at dull distance seen,

Weak, wan, and broad, he skirts the southern sky;
And, soon descending, to the long dark night,
Wide-shading all, the prostrate world resigns.
Nor is the night unwish'd; while vital heat,
Light, life, and joy the dubious day forsake.
Mean-time, in sable cincture, shadows vast,
Deep-ting'd, and damp, and congregated clouds,
And all the vapoury turbulence of heaven
Involve the face of things. Thus *Winter* falls,
A heavy gloom oppressive o'er the world,
Thro' nature shedding influence malign,
And rouses all the seeds of dark disease.
The soul of man dies in him, loathing life,
And black with horrid views. The cattle droop
The conscious head; and o'er the furrow'd land,
Red from the plow, the dun discolour'd flocks,
Untended spreading, crop the wholesome root.
Along the woods, along the moorish fens,
Sighs the sad genius of the coming storm;
And up among the loose, disjointed cliffs,
And fractur'd mountains wild, the brawling brook,
And cave, presageful, send a hollow moan,
Resounding long in listening fancy's ear.
          Then comes the father of the tempest forth,
Striding the gloomy blast. First rains obscure
Drive thro' the mingling skies, with vapour vile;
Dash on the mountain's brow, and shake the woods,
That grumbling wave below. Th' unsightly plain
Lies a brown deluge; as the low-bent clouds
Pour flood on flood, yet unexhausted still
Combine, and deepening into night shut up
The day's fair face. The wanderers of heaven,
Each to his home, retire; save those that love
To take their pastime in the troubled air,
Or skimming flutter round the dimply pool.
The cattle from th' untasted fields return,
And ask, with meaning lowe, their wonted stalls,
Or ruminate in the contiguous shade.
Thither the houshold, feathery people crowd,
The crested cock, with all his female train,
Pensive, and wet. Mean-while the cottage-swain

Hangs o'er th' enlivening blaze, and taleful there
Recounts his simple frolick: much he talks,
And much he laughs, nor recks the storm that blows
Without, and rattles on his humble roof.
       Wide o'er the brim, with many a torrent swell'd,
And the mix'd ruins of its banks o'erspread,
At last the rous'd-up river pours along,
Resistless, roaring; dreadful down it comes
From the chapt mountain, and the mossy wild,
Tumbling thro' rocks abrupt, and sounding far;
Then o'er the sanded valley floating spreads,
Calm, sluggish, silent; till again constrain'd,
Betwixt two meeting hills it bursts a way,
Where rocks, and woods o'erhang the turbid stream;
There gathering triple force, rapid, and deep,
It boils, and wheels, and foams, and thunders thro'.
       Nature! great parent! whose continual hand
Rolls round the seasons of the changeful year,
How mighty, how majestic are thy works!
With what a pleasing dread they swell the soul!
That sees astonish'd! and astonish'd sings!
Ye too, ye winds! that now begin to blow,
With boisterous sweep, I raise my voice to you.
Where are your stores, ye subtil beings! say,
Where your aerial magazines reserv'd,
Against the day of tempest perilous?
In what far-distant region of the sky,
Hush'd in dead silence, sleep you when 'tis calm?
Late in the lowring sky, red, fiery streaks
Begin to flush about; the reeling clouds
Stagger with dizzy poise, as doubting yet
Which master to obey: while rising slow,
Blank, in the leaden-colour'd east, the moon
Wears a wan circle round her sully'd orb.
The stars obtuse emit a shivering ray;
Snatch'd in short eddies plays the fluttering straw;
Loud shrieks the soaring hern; and, skreaming wild,
The circling sea-fowl rise; while from the shore,
Eat into caverns by the restless wave,
And forest-rustling mountain, comes a voice,
That solemn-sounding bids the world prepare.

Then issues forth the storm, with mad controul,
And the thin fabrick of the pillar'd air
O'erturns at once. Prone, on the passive main,
Descends th' ethereal force, and with strong gust
Turns from the bottom the discolour'd deep.
Thro' the loud night, that bids the waves arise,
Lash'd into foam, the fierce, conflicting brine
Seems, as it sparkles, all around to burn.
Mean-time whole oceans, heaving to the clouds,
And in broad billows rolling gather'd seas,
Surge over surge, burst in a general roar,
And anchor'd navies from their stations drive,
Wild as the winds athwart the howling waste
Of mighty waters. Now the hilly wave
Straining they scale, and now impetuous shoot
Into the secret chambers of the deep,
The full-blown *Baltick* thundering o'er their head.
Emerging thence again, before the breath
Of all-exerted heaven they wing their course,
And dart on distant coasts; if some sharp rock,
Or sand insidious break not their career,
And in loose fragments fling them floating round.
Nor raging here alone unrein'd at sea,
To land the tempest bears; and o'er the cliff,
Where screams the sea-mew, foaming unconfin'd,
Fierce swallows up the long-resounding shore.

      The mountain growls; and all its sturdy sons
Stoop to the bottom of the rocks they shade.
Lone on its midnight side, and all aghast,
The dark, way-faring stranger breathless toils,
And, often falling, climbs against the blast.
Low waves the rooted forest, vex'd, and sheds
What of its tarnish'd honours yet remain;
Dash'd down, and scatter'd, by the tearing wind's
Assiduous fury, its gigantic limbs.
Thus struggling thro' the dissipated grove,
The whirling tempest raves along the plain;
And on the cottage thatch'd, or lordly roof,
Keen-fastening, shakes them to the solid base.
Sleep frighted flies; and round the rocking dome,
For entrance eager, howls the savage blast.

Then too, they say, thro' all the burthen'd air,
Long groans are heard, shrill sounds, and distant sighs,
That, utter'd by the demon of the night,
Warn the devoted wretch of woe, and death.
Huge *Uproar* lords it wide. The clouds commix'd
With stars swift-gliding sweep along the sky.
All nature reels. Till nature's *King*, who oft
Amid tempestuous darkness dwells alone,
And on the wings of the careering wind
Walks dreadfully serene, commands a calm;
Then straight air, sea, and earth are hush'd at once.

As yet, 'tis midnight waste. The weary clouds,
Slow-meeting, mingle into solid gloom.
Now, while the drowsy world lies lost in sleep,
Let me associate with the serious *Night*,
And *Contemplation* her sedate compeer;
Let me shake off th'intrusive cares of day,
And lay the meddling senses all aside.

And now, ye lying Vanities of life!
Ye ever-tempting, ever-cheating train!
Where are ye now? and what is your amount?
Vexation, disappointment, and remorse.
Sad, sickening thought! and yet deluded Man,
A scene of crude disjointed visions past,
And broken slumbers, rises still resolv'd,
With new-flush'd hopes, to run the giddy round.

Father of light, and life! thou Good supreme!
O teach me what is good! teach me thyself!
Save me from folly, vanity, and vice,
From every low pursuit! and feed my soul
With knowledge, conscious peace, and virtue pure;
Sacred, substantial, never-fading bliss!

The keener tempests rise: and fuming dun
From all the livid east, or piercing north,
Thick clouds ascend; in whose capacious womb
A vapoury deluge lies, to snow congeal'd.
Heavy they roll their fleecy world along;
And the sky saddens with the gather'd storm.
Thro' the hush'd air the whitening shower descends,
At first thin-wavering; till at last the flakes
Fall broad, and wide, and fast, dimming the day,

With a continual flow. Sudden the fields
Put on their winter-robe, of purest white.
'Tis brightness all; save where the new snow melts,
Along the mazy stream. The leafless woods
Bow their hoar Heads. And, ere the languid sun
Faint from the west emits his evening ray,
Earth's universal face, deep-hid, and chill,
Is one wild, dazzling waste. The labourer-ox
Stands cover'd o'er with snow, and then demands
The fruit of all his toil. The fowls of heaven,
Tam'd by the cruel season, crowd around
The winnowing store, and claim the little boon
That Providence allows. The Red-breast sole,
Wisely regardful of th' embroiling sky,
In joyless fields, and thorny thickets, leaves
His shivering fellows, and to trusted man
His annual visit pays. New to the dome
Against the window beats, then brisk alights
On the warm hearth, and hopping o'er the floor
Eyes all the smiling *Family* askance,   ·
And pecks, and starts, and wonders where he is;
Till, more familiar grown, the table-crumbs
Attract his slender feet. The foodless wilds
Pour forth their brown inhabitants. The hare,
Tho' timorous of heart, and hard beset
By death in various forms, dark snares, and dogs,
And more unpitying men, the garden seeks,
Urg'd on by fearless want. The bleating kind
Eye the bleak heaven, and next the glistening earth,
With looks of dumb despair; then sad, dispers'd,
Dig for the whither'd herb thro' heaps of snow.
        Now, shepherds, to your helpless charge be kind,
Baffle the raging year, and fill their pens
With food at will; lodge them below the storm,
And watch them strict: for from the bellowing east,
In this dire season, oft the whirlwind's wing
Sweeps up the burthen of whole wintry plains
In one wide waft, and o'er the hapless flocks,
Hid in the hollow of two neighbouring hills,
The billowy tempest whelms; till upwards urg'd,
The valley to a shining mountain swells,

Tript with a wreath, high-curling in the sky.
      As thus the snows arise; and foul, and fierce,
All winter drives along the darken'd air;
In his own loose-revolving fields, the swain
Disaster'd stands; sees other hills ascend
Of unknown joyless brow; and other scenes,
Of horrid prospect, shag the trackless plain:
Nor finds the river, nor the forest, hid
Beneath the white abrupt; but wanders on
From hill to dale, still more and more astray:
Impatient flouncing thro' the drifted heaps,
Stung with the thoughts of home; the thoughts of home
Rush on his nerves, and call their vigour forth
In many a vain effort. How sinks his soul!
What black despair, what horror fills his heart!
When for the dusky spot, that fancy feign'd
His tufted cottage rising thro' the snow,
He meets the roughness of the middle waste,
Far from the tract, and blest abode of man:
While round him night resistless closes fast,
And every tempest, howling o'er his head,
Renders the savage wilderness more wild.
Then throng the busy shapes into his mind,
Of cover'd pits, unfathomably deep,
A dire descent! beyond the power of frost,
Of faithless boggs; of precipices huge,
Smooth'd up with snow; and, what is land unknown,
What water, of the still unfrozen eye,
In the loose marsh, or solitary lake,
Where the fresh fountain from the bottom boils.
These check his fearful steps; and down he sinks
Beneath the shelter of the shapeless drift,
Thinking o'er all the bitterness of death,
Mix'd with the tender anguish nature shoots
Thro' the wrung bosom of the dying man,
His wife, his children, and his friends unseen.
In vain for him th' officious wife prepares
The fire fair-blazing, and the vestment warm;
In vain his little children, peeping out
Into the mingling rack, demand their sire,
With tears of artless innocence. Alas!

Nor wife, nor children more shall he behold,
Nor friends, nor sacred home. On every nerve,
The deadly winter seizes; shuts up sense;
And, o'er his stronger vitals creeping cold,
Lays him along the snows, a stiffen'd corse,
Unstretch'd, and bleaching in the northern blast.
     Ah little think the gay licentious proud,
Whom pleasure, power, and affluence surround;
They, who their thoughtless hours in giddy mirth,
And wanton, often cruel, riot waste;
Ah little think they, while they dance along,
How many feel this very moment, death
And all the sad variety of pain.
How many sink in the devouring flood,
Or more devouring flame. How many bleed,
By shameful variance betwixt man and man.
How many pine in want, and dungeon glooms;
Shut from the common air, and common use
Of their own limbs. How many drink the cup
Of baleful grief, or eat the bitter bread
Of misery. Sore pierc'd by wintry winds,
How many shrink into the sordid hut
Of chearless poverty. How many shake
With all the fiercer tortures of the mind,
Unbounded passion, madness, guilt, remorse;
Whence tumbled headlong from the height of life,
They furnish matter for the tragic muse.
Even in the vale, where Wisdom loves to dwell,
With Friendship, Peace, and Contemplation join'd,
How many, rackt with honest passions, droop
In deep retir'd distress. How many stand
Around the death-bed of their dearest friends,
Like wailing pensive ghosts awaiting theirs,
And point the parting pang. Thought but fond man
Of these, and all the thousand nameless ills,
That one incessant struggle render life,
One scene of toil, of anguish, and of fate,
Vice in his high career would stand appall'd,
And heedless rambling impulse learn to think;
The conscious heart of Charity would warm,
And his wide wish Benevolence dilate;

The social tear would rise, the social sigh;
And into clear perfection, gradual bliss,
Refining still, the social passions work.
             And here can I forget the generous few,
Who, touch'd with human woe, redressive sought
Into the horrors of the gloomy jail?
Unpitied, and unheard, where Misery moans;
Where Sickness pines; where Thirst and Hunger burn,
And poor Misfortune feels the lash of Vice.
While in the land of liberty, the land
Whose every street, and public meeting glows
With open freedom, little tyrants rag'd:
Snatch'd the lean morsel from the starving mouth;
Tore from cold, wintry limbs the tatter'd robe;
Even robb'd them of the last of comforts, sleep;
The free-born *Briton* to the dungeon chain'd,
Or, as the lust of cruelty prevail'd,
At pleasure mark'd him with inglorious stripes;
And crush'd out lives, by various nameless ways,
That for their country would have toil'd, or bled.
Hail patriot-band! who, scorning secret scorn,
When Justice, and when Mercy led the way,
Dragg'd the detected monsters into light,
Wrench'd from their hand Oppression's iron rod,
And bade the cruel feel the pains they gave.
Yet stop not here, let all the land rejoice,
And make the blessing unconfin'd, as great.
Much still untouch'd remains; in this rank age,
Much is the patriot's weeding hand requir'd.
The toils of law, (what dark insidious men
Have cumbrous added to perplex the truth,
And lengthen simple justice into trade),
Oh glorious were the day! that saw these broke,
And every man within the reach of right.
             Yet more outragious is the season still,
A deeper horror, in *Siberian* wilds;
Where *Winter* keeps his unrejoicing court,
And in his airy hall the loud misrule
Of driving tempest is for ever heard.
There thro' the ragged woods absorpt in snow,
Sole tenant of these shades, the shaggy bear,

With dangling ice all horrid, stalks forlorn;
Slow-pac'd and sourer as the storms increase,
He makes his bed beneath the drifted snow;
And, scorning the complainings of distress,
Hardens his heart against assailing want.
While tempted vigorous o'er the marble waste,
On sleds reclin'd, the furry *Russian* sits;
And, by his rain-deer drawn, behind him throws
A shining kingdom in a winter's day.
        Or from the cloudy *Alps*, and *Appenine*,
Capt with grey mists, and everlasting snows;
Where nature in stupendous ruin lies,
And from the leaning rock, on either side,
Gush out those streams that classic song renowns:
Cruel as death, and hungry as the grave!
Burning for blood! bony, and ghaunt, and grim!
Assembling wolves in torrent troops descend;
And, pouring o'er the country, bear along,
Keen as the north-wind sweeps the glossy snow.
All is their prize. They fasten on the steed,
Press him to earth, and pierce his mighty heart.
Nor can the bull his awful front defend.
Or shake the murdering savages away.
Rapacious, at the mother's throat they fly,
And tear the screaming infant from her breast.
The godlike face of man avails him nought. ·
Even beauty, force divine! at whose bright glance
The generous lyon stands in soften'd gaze,
Here bleeds, a hapless, undistinguish'd prey.
But if, appriz'd of the severe attack,
The country be shut up, lur'd by the scent,
On church-yards drear (inhuman to relate!)
The disappointed prowlers fall, and dig
The shrowded body from the tomb; o'er which,
Mix'd with foul shades, and frighted ghosts, they howl.
        Now, all amid the rigours of the year,
In the wild depth of *Winter*, while without
The ceaseless winds blow ice, be my retreat,
Between the groaning forest and the shore,
Beat by a boundless multitude of waves,
A rural, shelter'd, solitary, scene;

Where ruddy fire and beaming tapers join,
To chase the cheerless gloom. There let me sit,
And hold high converse with the mighty dead;
Sages of antient time, as gods rever'd,
As gods beneficent, who blest mankind
With arts, and arms, and humaniz'd a world.
Rous'd at th' inspiring thought, I throw aside
The long-liv'd volume; and, deep-musing, hail
The sacred shades, that slowly-rising pass
Before my wondering eyes.—First *Socrates*,
Whose simple question to the folded heart
Stole unperceiv'd, and from the maze of thought
Evolv'd the secret truth—a god-like man!
Solon the next, who built his common-weal
On equity's wide base. *Lycurgus* then,
Severely good; and him of rugged *Rome*,
Numa, who soften'd her rapacious sons.
Cimon sweet-soul'd, and *Aristides* just;
With that attemper'd Hero,* mild, and firm,
Who wept the brother while the tyrant bled.
Unconquer'd *Cato*, virtuous in extreme.
Scipio, the human warrior, gently brave;
Who soon the race of spotless glory ran,
And, warm in youth, to the poetic shade,
With friendship, and philosophy, retir'd.
And, equal to the best, the *Theban* twain,*
Who, single rais'd their country into fame.
Thousands behind, the boast of *Greece* and *Rome*,
Whom Virtue owns, the tribute of a verse
Demand; but who can count the stars of heaven?
Who sing their influence on this lower world?
But see who yonder comes! in sober state,
Fair, mild, and strong, as is a vernal sun:
'Tis *Phoebus* self, or else the *Mantuan* swain!
Great *Homer* too appears, of daring wing,
Parent of song! and equal by his side,
The *British* muse; join'd hand in hand they walk,
Darkling, full up the middle steep to fame.
Nor absent are those tuneful shades, I ween,
Taught by the Graces, whose inchanting touch
Shakes every passion from the various string;

Nor those, who solemnize the moral scene.
        First of your kind! society divine!
Still visit thus my nights, for you reserv'd,
And mount my soaring soul to deeds like yours.
Silence, thou lonely power! the door be thine;
See on the hallow'd hour that none intrude,
Save *Lycidas* the friend, with sense refin'd,
Learning digested well, exalted faith,
Unstudy'd wit, and humour ever gay.
Or from the muses' hill will *Pope* descend,
To raise the sacred hour, to make it smile,
And with the social spirit warm the heart:
For tho' not sweeter his own *Homer* sings,
Yet is his life the more endearing song.
        Thus in some deep retirement would I pass
The winter-glooms, with friends of various turn,
Or blithe, or solemn, as the theme inspir'd:
With them would search, if this unbounded frame
Of nature rose from unproductive night,
Or sprung eternal from th' *eternal Cause,*
Its springs, its laws, its progress and its end.
Hence larger prospects of the beauteous whole
Would gradual open on our opening minds;
And each diffusive harmony unite,
In full perfection, to th' astonish'd eye.
Thence would we plunge into the moral world;
Which, tho' more seemingly perplex'd, moves on
In higher order; fitted, and impell'd,
By Wisdom's finest hand, and issuing all
In universal good. Historic truth
Should next conduct thro' the deeps of time:
Point us how empire grew, revolv'd, and fell,
In scatter'd states; what makes the nations smile,
Improves their soil, and gives them double suns;
And why they pine beneath the brightest skies,
In nature's richest lap. As thus we talk'd,
Our hearts would burn within us, would inhale
That portion of divinity, that ray
Of purest heaven, which lights the glorious flame
Of patriots, and of heroes. But if doom'd,
In powerless humble fortune, to repress

These ardent risings of the kindling soul;
Then, even superior to ambition, we
Would learn the private virtues; how to glide
Thro' shades and plains, along the smoothest stream
Of rural life: or snatch'd away by hope,
Thro' the dim spaces of futurity,
With earnest eye anticipate those scenes
Of happiness, and wonder; where the mind,
In endless growth and infinite ascent,
Rises from state to state, and world to world.
And when with these the serious soul is foil'd,
We, shifting for relief, would play the shapes
Of frolic fancy; and incessant form
Unnumber'd pictures, fleeting o'er the brain,
Yet rapid still renew'd, and pour'd immense
Into the mind, unbounded without space:
The great, the new, the beautiful; or mix'd,
Burlesque, and odd, the risible and gay;
Whence vivid Wit, and Humour, droll of face,
Call laughter forth, deep-shaking every nerve.

      Mean-time the village rouzes up the sire;
While well attested, and as well believ'd,
Heard solemn, goes the goblin-story round;
Till superstitious horror creeps o'er all.

      Or, frequent in the sounding hall, they wake
The rural gambol. Rustic mirth goes round:
The simple joke that takes the shepherd's heart,
Easily pleas'd; the long loud laugh, sincere;
The kiss, snatch'd hasty from the sidelong maid,
On purpose guardless, or pretending sleep;
The leap, the slap, the haul; and, shook to notes
Of native music, the respondent dance.
Thus jocund fleets with them the winter-night.

      The city swarms intense. The publick haunt,
Full of each theme, and warm with mixt discourse,
Hums indistinct. The sons of riot flow
Down the loose stream of false inchanted joy,
To swift destruction. On the rankled soul
The gaming fury falls; and in one gulph
Of total ruin, honour, virtue, peace,
Friends, families, and fortune headlong sink.

Rises the dance along the lighted dome,
Mix'd, and evolv'd, a thousand sprightly ways.
The glittering court effuses every pomp;
The circle deepens; rain'd from radiant eyes,
A soft effulgence o'er the palace waves:
While, thick as insects in the summer-shine,
The fop, light-fluttering, spreads his mealy wings.
    Dread o'er the scene the ghost of *Hamlet* stalks;
Othello rages; poor *Monimia* mourns;
And *Belvidera* pours her soul in love.
Assenting terror shakes; the silent tear
Steals o'er the cheek: or else the *comic Muse*
Holds to the world the picture of itself,
And raises sly the fair impartial laugh.
    Clear frost succeeds; and thro' the blue serene,
For sight too fine, th' ethereal nitre flies:
Killing infectious damps, and the spent air
Storing afresh with elemental life.
Close crowds the shining atmosphere; and binds
Our strengthen'd bodies in its cold embrace,
Constringent; feeds, and animates our blood;
Refines our spirits, thro' the new-strung nerves,
In swifter sallies darting to the brain;
Where sits the soul, intense, collected, cool,
Bright as the skies, and as the season keen.
All nature feels the renovating force
Of *Winter*, only to the thoughtless eye
In desolation seen. The vacant glebe
Draws in abundant vegetable soul,
And gathers vigour for the coming year.
A strong glow sits on the lively cheek
Of ruddy fire: and luculent along
The purer rivers flow; their sullen deeps,
Amazing, open to the shepherd's gaze,
And murmur hoarser at the fixing frost.
    What art thou, Frost? and whence are thy keen stores
Deriv'd, thou secret all-invading Power,
Whom even th' illusive fluid cannot fly?
Is not thy potent energy, unseen,
Myriads of little salts, or hook'd, or shap'd
Like double wedges, and diffus'd immense

Thro' water, earth and ether? Hence at eve,
Steam'd eager from the red horizon round,
With the still rage of *Winter* deep suffus'd,
An icy gale, oft shifting, o'er the pool
Breathes a blue film, and in its mid career
Arrests the bickering stream. The loosen'd ice,
Let down the flood, and half-dissolv'd by day,
Rustles no more; but to the sedgy bank
Fast grows, or gathers round the pointed stone,
A crystal pavement, by the breath of heaven
Cemented firm; till seiz'd from shore to shore,
The whole detruded river growls below.
Loud rings the frozen earth, and hard reflects
A double noise; while, at his evening-watch,
The village-dog deters the nightly thief;
The heifer lows; the distant water-fall
Swells in the breeze; and, with the hasty tread
Of traveller, the many sounding plain
Shakes from afar. The full ethereal round,
Infinite worlds disclosing to the view,
Shines out intensely keen; and, all one cope
Of starry glitter, glows from pole to pole.
From pole to pole the rigid influence falls,
Thro' the still night, incessant, heavy, strong,
And seizes nature fast. It freezes on;
Till morn, late rising o'er the drooping world,
Lifts her pale eye unjoyous. Then appears
The various labour of the silent night:
Prone from the dripping eave, and dumb cascade,
Whose idle torrents only seem to roar,
The pendant isicle; the frost-work fair,
Where transient hues, and fancy'd figures rise;
The liquid kingdom all to solid turn'd;
Wide-spouted o'er the brow, the frozen brook,
A livid tract, cold-gleaming on the morn;
The forest bent beneath the plumy wave;
And by the frost refin'd the whiter snow,
Incrusted hard, and sounding to the tread
Of early shepherd, as he pensive seeks
His pining flock, or from the mountain-top,
Pleas'd with the slippery surface, swift descends.

On blithesome frolicks bent, the youthful swains,
While every work of man is laid at rest,
Fond o'er the river rush, and shuddering view
The doubtful deeps below. Or where the lake
And long canal the cerule plain extend,
The city pours her thousands, swarming all,
From every quarter: and, with him who slides;
Or skating sweeps, swift as the winds, along,
In circling poise; or else disorder'd falls,
His feet, illuded, sprawling to the sky,
While the laugh rages round; from end to end,
Encreasing still, resounds the crowded scene.

      Pure, quick, and sportful, is the wholesome day;
But soon elaps'd. The horizontal sun,
Broad o'er the south, hangs at his utmost noon;
And, ineffectual, strikes the gelid cliff.
The mountain still his azure gloss maintains,
Nor feels the feeble touch. Perhaps the vale
Relents a while to the reflected ray;
Or from the forest falls the cluster'd snow,
Myriads of gem, that, by the breeze diffus'd,
Gay-twinkle thro' the gleam. Heard thick around,
Thunders the sport of those, who, with the gun,
And dog impatient bounding at the shot,
Worse than the season, desolate the fields;
And, adding to the ruins of the year,
Distress the footed, or the feather'd game.

      But what is this? these infant tempests what?
The mockery of *Winter:* should our eye
Astonish'd shoot into the frozen zone;
Where more than half the joyless year is night;
And, failing gradual, life at last goes out.
There undissolving, from the first of time,
Snows swell on snows amazing to the sky;
And icy mountains there, on mountains pil'd,
Seem to the shivering sailor from afar,
Shapeless, and white, an atmosphere of clouds.
Projected huge, and horrid, o'er the main,
Alps frown on Alps; or rushing hideous down,
As if old Chaos was again return'd,
Shake the firm pole, and make an ocean boil.

Whence heap'd abrupt along the howling shore,
And into various shapes (as fancy leans)
Work'd by the wave, the crystal pillars heave,
Swells the blue portico, the gothic dome
Shoots fretted up; and birds, and beasts, and men,
Rise into mimic life, and sink by turns.
The restless deep itself cannot resist
The binding fury; but, in all its rage
Of tempest taken by the boundless frost,
Is many a fathom to the bottom chain'd,
And bid to roar no more: a bleak expanse,
Shag'd o'er with wavy rocks, chearless, and void
Of every life, that from the dreary months
Flies conscious southward. Miserable they!
Who, here entangled in the gathering ice,
Take their last look of the descending sun;
While, full of death, and fierce with tenfold frost,
The long long night, incumbent o'er their head,
Falls horrible. Such was the *Briton*'s fate,
As with first prow, (What have not *Britons* dar'd!),
He for the passage sought, attempted since
So much in vain, and seeming to be shut
By jealous nature with eternal bars.
In these fell regions, in *Arzina* caught,
And to the stony deep his idle ship
Immediate seal'd, he with his hapless crew,
Each full exerted at his several task,
Froze into statues; to the cordage glued
The sailor, and the pilot to the helm.

        Hard by these shores, the last of mankind live;
And, scarce enliven'd by the distant sun,
(That rears and ripens man, as well as plants),
Here Human Nature just begins to dawn.
Deep from the piercing season sunk in caves,
Here by dull fires, and with unjoyous chear,
They wear the tedious gloom. Immers'd in furs,
Ly the gross race. Nor sprightly jest, nor song,
Nor tenderness they know; nor ought of life,
Beyond the kindred bears that stalk without.
Till long-expected morning looks at length
Faint on their fields (where *Winter* reigns alone)

And calls the quiver'd savage to the chace.
     Muttering, the winds at eve, with hoarser voice
Blow blustering from the south. The frost subdu'd,
Gradual, resolves into a trickling thaw.
Spotted the mountains shine; loose sleet descends,
And floods the country round. The rivers swell,
Impatient for the day. Broke from the hills,
O'er rocks and woods, in broad brown cataracts,
A thousand snow-fed torrents shoot at once;
And, where they rush, the wide-resounding plain
Is left one slimy waste. Those sullen seas,
That wash th' ungenial pole, will rest no more
Beneath the shackles of the mighty north;
But, rousing all their waves, resistless heave—
And hark! the lengthening roar continuous runs
Athwart the rifted main: at once it bursts,
And piles a thousand mountains to the clouds.
Ill fares the bark, the wretch's last resort,
That, lost amid the floating fragments, moors
Beneath the shelter of an icy isle,
While night o'erwhelms the sea, and horror looks
More horrible. Can human force endure
Th' assembled mischiefs that besiege them round:
Heart-gnawing hunger, fainting weariness,
The roar of winds and waves, the crush of ice,
Now ceasing, now renew'd with louder rage,
And in dire echoes bellowing round the main.
More to embroil the deep, Leviathan,
And his unwieldy train, in horrid sport,
Tempest the loosen'd brine; while thro' the gloom;
Far, from the bleak inhospitable shore,
Loading the winds, is heard the hungry howl
Of famish'd monsters, there awaiting wrecks.
Yet *Providence,* that ever-waking eye,
Looks down with pity on the fruitless toil
Of mortals lost to hope, and lights them safe,
Thro' all this dreary labyrinth of fate.
'Tis done!—dread *Winter* has subdu'd the year,
And reigns tremendous o'er the desart plains.
How dead the vegetable kingdom lies!
How dumb the tuneful! Horror wide extends

His solitary empire. Here, fond man!
Behold thy pictur'd life; pass some few years,
Thy flowering *Spring*, thy *Summer*'s ardent strength,
Thy sober *Autumn* fading into age,
And pale concluding *Winter* comes at last,
And shuts the scene. Ah! whither now are fled,
Those dreams of greatness? those unsolid hopes
Of happiness? those longings after fame?
Those restless cares? those busy bustling days?
Those gay-spent, festive nights? those veering thoughts,
Lost between good and ill, that shar'd thy life?
All now are vanish'd! *Virtue* sole survives,
Immortal, mankind's never-failing friend,
His guide to happiness on high.—And see!
'Tis come, the glorious morn! the second birth
Of heaven, and earth! Awakening nature hears
The new-creating word, and starts to life,
In every heighten'd form, from pain and death
For ever free. The great eternal scheme,
Involving all, and in a perfect whole
Uniting, as the prospect wider spreads,
To reason's eye refin'd clears up apace.
Ye vainly wise! ye blind presuming! now,
Confounded in the dust, adore that *Power*,
And *Wisdom* oft arraign'd: see now the cause,
Why unassuming Worth in secret liv'd,
And dy'd, neglected: why the good man's share
In life was gall, and bitterness of soul:
Why the lone widow, and her orphans pin'd,
In starving solitude; while Luxury,
In palaces, lay prompting his low thought,
To form unreal wants: why heaven-born Truth,
And Moderation fair, wore the red marks
Of Superstition's scourge: why licens'd Pain,
That cruel spoiler, that embosom'd foe,
Imbitter'd all our bliss. Ye good distrest!
Ye noble few! who here unbending stand
Beneath life's pressure, yet a little while,
And what you reckon evil is no more;
The storms of *Wintry time* will quickly pass,
And one unbounded SPRING encircle all.

IAIN RUADH STIÙBHART /
JOHN ROY STEWART

(1700–?1749)

━━━

THE Scottish Gaelic poet John Roy Stewart (Iain Ruadh Stiùbhart) was born at Knock in Strathspey, near the modern village of Aviemore. He became a professional soldier, first serving King George in the Royal Scots Greys, then King Louis in the Écossais Royales. As soon as the '45 broke out he returned to Scotland to offer his services to Charles Edward Stuart (Bonnie Prince Charlie), who asked him to form an Edinburgh Regiment, which in fact consisted mainly of men from Perthshire and Strathspey. As one of the Jacobites' best military strategists, he plays a prominent part in all histories of the '45. He had apparently hoped to be given the leadership of the army at Culloden, but in this as in much else he was disappointed. Many of the stories about him, and many of his poems (including the one that follows here), date from the time after Culloden when he was on the run in Strathspey. He died in obscurity in France, probably in 1749.

━━━

'Ùrnaigh Iain Ruaidh'

Sar-Obair nam Bard Gaelach; or, The Beauties of Gaelic Poetry, and Lives of the Highland Bards, ed. John MacKenzie, 4th edn (Edinburgh: Maclachlan & Stewart, 1877).

Aig taobh sruthain 'na shuidhe 's e sgìth
    Tha an Crìostaidh bochd, Iain Ruadh—
'Na cheatharnach, fhathast gun sìth,
    'S a chas air tuisleadh san tìm gu truagh.

Ma thig Duibhnich no Cataich am' dhàil
    Mun slànaich mo luigheannan truagh,
Ged thig iad cho trice 's as àill
    Cha chuir iad orm làmh le luaths.

Nì mi an ubhaidh rinn Peadar do Phàl
    Is a luighean air fàslomadh bruaich—

Seachd paidir an ainm sagairt is pàp'
    Ga chur ris 'na phlàst mun cuairt.

Ubhaidh eile, ás leth Muire nan Gràs
    As urrainn creideach dhèanamh slàn ri uair:
"Tha mise am' chreideamh gun teagamh gun dàil
    Gun toir sinn air ar naimhdean buaidh."

Sgeul eile 's gur h-oil leam gur fìor
    Tha an-dràst' anns gach tìr mun cuairt:
Gach fear gleusta bha feumail don rìgh
    Bhith ga ruith feadh gach frìth air ruaig.

Bodaich dhona gun onair gun bhrìgh
    Ach gionach gu nì air son duais
Gabhail fàth oirnn 's gach àit' anns am bì—
    Cuir a' chuibhle seo, Chrìost, mun cuairt.

Ma thionnd'as i deiseil an-dràst'
    'S gum faigh Frangaich am Flànras buaidh,
Tha m' earbs' ás an targanachd bhà
    Gun tig armailt nì stàth dhuinn thar chuain.

Gun toir Fortan dha dìdean le gràs
    Mar Mhaois nuair a thràigh a' Mhuir Ruadh
'S gum bi Deòrsa le dhreòlanaibh bàitht'
    Mar bha 'n t-amadan Phàraoh 's a shluagh.

Nuair bha Israël sgìth 's an staid ghràis
    Rinneadh Saul an là sin 'na rìgh—
Thug e sgiùrsadh le miosgainn is plàigh
    Orra fhéin, air an àl 's air an nì.

Is amhail bha Breatainn fo bhròn
    On a thréig iad a' chòir is an rìgh;
Ghabh Flaitheas rinn corraich ro-mhòr—
    Crom an Donais! Chaidh 'n seòrsa an dìosg.

A Rìgh shocraich Muire nan Gràs,
    Crom riumsa le bàidh do chluas
'S mi 'g ùmhladh le m' ghlùn air an làr—
    Gabh achanaich àraidh bhuam.

Chan eil sinn a' sireadh ach còir,
    Thug Cuigs' agus Deòrsa bhuainn;

Réir do cheartais thoir neart dhuinn is treòir
Is cum sinn o fhòirneart sluaigh.

'John Roy's Prayer' (translated by Ronald Black)

Sitting tired at the side of a stream
    Is this wretched Christian, John Roy—
A fighting man, still without peace,
    Because his foot has just badly slipped.

If I'm found by Campbells or Sutherland men
    Before my wretched ligaments heal,
Should they even come as much as they like,
    They will not catch me any time soon.

I'll make the charm made by Peter for Paul
    With his ankle on a hillside ledge—
Seven prayers in name of priest and pope
    Applied like a poultice to protect it.

Another charm, ascribed to Mary of Graces
    Who can make a believer instantly whole:
"I believe without any doubt or delay
    That we will triumph over our foes."

Another bit of news which I fear must be true
    Is currently in all the districts around:
That each able man who has served the king
    Is now being chased all over the hills.

Evil serfs without honour or worth
    But greedy for some kind of prize
Are attacking us wherever we go—
    Please turn this wheel, O Christ, around.

If it turns sunwise right away
    To let the French in Flanders win,
My faith is in the ancient prophecy
    That the force we need will come over the sea.

May Fortune protect him with grace
    Like Moses when the Red Sea went dry
So that George and his thugs will be drowned
    Like that fool Pharaoh and his host.

The day she tired of the state of grace
    Is when Israël made Saul her king—
He scourged with malice and with plague
    Her people, their children and their stock.

Thus has Britain been depressed
    Since forsaking justice and their king;
Heaven vented upon us its rage—
    The Devil! Their likes have turned barren.

O King who made Mary of Graces,
    Bend kindly to me Thine ear
As I submit with my knee to the ground—
    Accept from me a special prayer.

The only thing we seek is our rights,
    Which George and his Whigs have removed;
By Thy justice grant guidance and strength
    And keep us safe from mob misrule.

UILLEAM MACMHURCHAIDH / WILLIAM MACMURCHY

(c.1700–1778)

———

WILLIAM MACMURCHY was from Largie in Kintyre. In addition to being a poet in his own right, he was at various times a schoolmaster, tailor, piper, harper, and collector of verse, song, and proverbs. MacMurchy probably served on the government side in the '45, with the statutory piper's pay of 1s per day. He served as a soldier again some time later, probably in Montgomerie's regiment (the 77th) in America. He subsequently worked as a 'musicianer' in Campbeltown, providing pipe and harp accompaniment for dance-classes and balls. There is some evidence that he was known as *Uilleam Grinn* (Handsome William) and was a personal friend of Alastair, mac Mhaighstir Alastair. His poetic output was broad but not unconventional, including religious verse, love, humour, satire, and praise of Campbells, MacDonalds, and MacNeills. In 'Moladh Chinntìre' he views the beauties of Kintyre from a westerly standpoint (at Largie, or perhaps in America), shows off his knowledge of musical terminology, echoes the ship motifs of an old song in praise of an earl of Argyll, the 'Duanag Ullamh' ('Pre-Prepared Little Poem'), and ends with a shameless hint that he expects payment for his work. (Thanks to Keith Sanger and Barnaby Brown for information.)

———

'Moladh Chinntìre'

Translator's transcription

Soraidh soir uam gu Cinntìre
  Le caoine, dìsl' agus fàilte,
Gun ard no ìosal a dhearmad
  Eadar an Tairbeart 's Àbhart.

Banaltra Galldachd 's Gaidhealtachd,
  Ged a thréig i nis a h-àbhaist,

Bha drùdhadh gach tìr d'a h-ionnsaigh
  'S cha dùraig aon neach a fàgail.

'S cubhraidh 's is fallain a fàile,
  'G éirigh thar blàthaibh 's thar geugaibh,
Measarr' a samhradh 's a geamhradh
  Gun ainiochd stoirme no gréine.

'S aoibhinn a cnoca 's a cruacha,
  'S àirigheach 's is buailteach a glinne,
Bóthach laoghach meannach uanach
  Gruthach bainneach uachdrach imeach.

Gheibhte prostan àlainn uasal
  A' ruagadh a' bhuic uallaich cheannaird,
Le coin ghradcharach ro-lùthmhor
  Ga chur gu dubhshlan air a charaibh.

Bidh 'n coileach san tom gu sàmhach
  'S gadhar nan àmhailt ga chealgadh,
'S gus an glacar anns an lìon e
  Cha smuain e inntleachd an t-sealgair.

Á glinn as binne durdan, srutha
  Seinn tro shrathaibh fasgach feurach
Luibheach craobhach meangach duilleach
  Caorach cnuthach subhach smeurach.

'S ealcarach binnghobach ordail
  Sheinneas an smeòrach san fheasgar,
'N uiseag os a cionn gu h-uallach,
  'N lon 's a' chuach a' cur beas leatha.

Chan eil fear ciùil sa choille chubhraidh
  Nach seinn le dùrachd a chòras
Gu fileant', ealant', dìonach, siubhlach,
  A' roinn na h-ùine gu h-eòlach.

An caomh chomhsheinn pongail ordail
  Freagairt a móramh 's a minim,
Gu h-eagnaidh geibnigh teibnigh ceòlmhor—
  Òran as glòrmhoire sa chruinne.

Gu feart-tarnach ceart-tarnach ceutach
  Gun bhuige no géire no dìochuimhn',
A' stad 's ag aideachadh gu h-eòlach,
  A' mealtainn sòlais 's sìothchaint.

A' freagairt a-chéile mun inbhir
  'M bi 'm breac 's am bradan gu suilbhir,
Gu h-iteach, lannach, ballach, bruinngheal,
  A' mire 's a' leumnaich ri'n urball.

'S fochlasach biolaireach a fuarain
  An achlais gach cluain 's gach tulaich,
A' brùchdadh mar chriostal an uachdar
  'Nan ìocshlaint fhionnair bhuadhaich mhilis.

A magha seisneil deisneil rìoghail
  An lìonmhor fear sìolchuir san earrach;
San fhoghar, greadhnach meadhrach uallach
  Dualach sguabach cruachach torrach.

A creaga truideach crotach calmnach,
Murbhuach'leach sgarbhnach a calaidh,
Gèadhach lachach de gach seòrsa,
Dobhranach rònanach ealach.

Nuallan a tonna mar orgain
  Teachd leis a' mhonmhar as binne,
Druim air dhruim a' ruith a-chéile
  'S gàir éibhinn am beul gach aoinfhir.

A cuain-long gu longach lànmhor
  Luchdmhor làidir dealbhach dìonach;
'S lìonmhor corda, crois 's crannag
  Ris na crannaibh fallain fìorard.

Gu bàrcannach ardchrannach croiseach,
  Gu bàtannach coiteach ràmhach,
Cuplach tairrneach staghmhor beartach
  Ulagach acaireach càblach.

'S lìonmhor diùlnach lùthmhor treòrach
  An àm an seòlaidh gam beartadh,
Gan tulgadh sna crannagaibh guanach
  Le'n coimhdheis fuaradh no fasgadh.

Se a glòir 's a sgèimh thar gach aoin-ni
  A h-uaisle flathail rìoghail stàtail;
'S an cùirtibh maiseach meadhrach muirneach
  Bha 'n sinnseara cliùiteach gan àiteach—

Clann Domhnaill na féile 's an t-suaircis
  'G am buaine ceannas nan Innse;
'S cian bunadh na treibh' as uaisle
  San tìr mhaisich bhuadhaich rìoghail.

An fhin' a bu teinne ri dórainn
  'S nach iomaireadh foirneart air fainne,
Thoirbheartach air luchd an céilidh—
  Onair 's féile gun ghainne!

'In Praise of Kintyre' (translated by Ronald Black)

Hail to the east from me to Kintyre,
  With goodwill, loyalty and greeting
And no neglecting of high or low
  Between the Tarbert and Dunaverty.

Nursing mother of Lowlands and Highlands,
  Although she has now forsaken her custom,
The pressure of every land is towards her
  And no one ever wishes to leave her.

Her air is full of balm and good health,
  Rising over blossoms and branches,
Mild is her summer and her winter
  With no great force of storm or of sun.

Her hillocks and mountains are pleasant,
  Her glens are full of shielings and folds,
Of cows and calves, of kids and lambs,
  Of curds and milk, of cream and butter.

A handsome noble band could be found
  Chasing the haughty high-headed buck,
With swift-moving dogs of great agility
  Matching the twists and turns he makes.

The woodcock stays silent in tufted ground
  While the hound with its tricks detects it,

And until it's entangled in the net
    It cannot predict the hunter's intelligence.

Streams from musically murmuring glens
    Sing through straths sequestered and grassy,
Full of herbs, trees, branches and foliage,
    Of berries, nuts, fruit and blackcurrants.

The song-thrush sings in the afternoon,
    Art-skilful, beak-tuneful, regular,
The lark is above her in its gaiety,
    Blackbird and cuckoo serve her as bass.

All the musicians in the scented wood
    Sing their chorus with heartfelt emotion,
Fluent, expert, dry-throttled and smooth,
    Keeping time as well they know how,

In sweet pitch-perfect regular harmony
    Responding to her whole and her half note,
Skilfully, trippingly, smartly, tunefully—
    A song as glorious as any in the world,

Of powerful tone, of true pitch, beautiful,
    With no softness, sharpness, forgetfulness,
Deliberately pausing, enunciating clearly,
    Enjoying happiness and tranquillity,

Echoing each other around the estuary
    Where the trout and salmon happily swim,
Finned, scaled, speckled and belly-white,
    Sporting, leaping and chasing their tails.

Rich in brook-lime and cress are her springs
    Under the arm of each meadow and hillock,
Bursting like crystal up to the surface
    As cool, sweet, curative medicine.

Her sense-pleasing, south-facing, royal plains
    Are full of men at the sowing in springtime;
In harvest they're cheerful, merry, delightful,
    Many-sheaved, fecund, heaped-up and fruitful.

Her rocks teem with starlings, curlews and doves,
    Her coves with scarts and great northern divers,

She's full of geese and duck of each kind,
   Not to mention otters, seals and swans.

The sound of her waves is like harpsichords,
   Coming in with the sweetest murmur,
Crest upon crest pursuing each other
   With a joyful cry in the mouth of each one.

Her harbours are large, with plenty of ships
   Filled with cargo, strong, picturesque, watertight,
With countless ropes, cross-trees, crows' nests
   Up on the sturdy high-towering masts.

Full of barques, high-masted, cross-tree'd,
   Full of cobles, dinghies and oars,
Full of couples, nails, stays and tackle,
   Full of pulleys, anchors and cables.

Numerous strong and vigorous heroes
   Get them ready in time of sailing,
They're swayed around in the giddy cross-trees
   And don't care whether to windward or leeward.

Her glory and beauty beyond other things
   Is her princely, royal, stately nobility;
It's in splendid, magnificent, joyful courts
   Their illustrious ancestors were reared—

Clan Donald of generosity and civility,
   The longest-lasting lords of the Isles,
Far distant's the root of the noblest tribe
   In the lovely, prosperous, loyal land.

To the clan that was toughest in face of peril,
   Who would never practise violence on weakness,
And who always give gifts to their visitors,
   Be honour and entertainment unstinting!

IAIN MAC FHEARCHAIR /
JOHN MACCODRUM

(C.1700–1779)

━━━

THE poet John MacCodrum (Iain mac Fhearchair) was born in North Uist. His outstanding knowledge of the Ossianic ballads brought him to the notice of his chief, Sir James MacDonald of Sleat, who made him his official poet. Such an appointment encouraged MacCodrum to see himself as spokesman for the Clan Donald. Sir James was succeeded in 1766 by his brother Sir Alexander, who earned the dislike and disapproval of Johnson and Boswell when they visited him in 1773. Johnson and Boswell commented on the fever of emigration which had gripped the West Highlands. The prevailing cause of the emigration from the area, the subject of the following poem, was a steep rise in rents which took place in 1769. Sir Alexander's tacksmen (tenants) formed themselves into a kind of company, which bought 100,000 acres of land in South Carolina, to which they emigrated *en masse*, taking many of their sub-tenants with them. Over two hundred people left the island between 1771 and 1775. In addition to songs of praise for chiefs and lairds, MacCodrum specialized in satirical songs about local events and people.

━━━

'Òran do na Fògarraich'

Cochruinneacha Taoghta de Shaothair nam Bard Gaëleach. A Choice Collection of the Works of the Highland Bards, Collected in the Highlands and Isles, ed. Alexander and Donald Stewart, 2 vols (Edinburgh: Charles Stewart, 1804).

> Togaibh misneach is sòlas,
> Bithibh inntinneach ceòlmhor
> Agus cuiribh ur dòchas
>   Ann an còmhnadh an Àirdrigh,
> On as fheudar dhuibh seòladh
> ('S nach ann do ur deòin e)

Do rìoghachd nach eòl duibh
    Mar a thòisich ur càirdean.
O nach fuiling iad beò sibh
Ann an crìochaibh ur n-eòlais,
S fheàrr dhuibh falbh do ur deòin
    Na bhith fodha mar thràillean;
Siad na h-uachdarain ghòrach
A chuir fuaradh fo'r srònaibh—
A bhris muineal Rìgh Deòrsa
    Nuair a dh'fhògradh na Gàidhil!

Ma thig cogadh is creachan
(Mar as minig a thachair)
Sann a bhios sibh 'nur starsaich
    Fo chasaibh ur nàmhaid;
Tha sibh soirbh ri bhur casgairt
'S gun neach ann gu'm bacadh,
Tha bhur guaillean gun tacsa
    'S na gaisgich gur fàgail.
Rìgh, gur sgiolta ri'm faicinn
'Nan seasamh air faithche
Le'n aodaichean gasta
    De bhreacanan càrnaid
Na tha falbh uaibh an ceartuair
De dh'òganaich dhreachmhor—
Gun truailleadh, gun ghaiseadh,
    Gun taise gun tàire.

Thug siud sgrìob air MacDhòmhnaill,
Thug e spùilleadh air Mòrar,
Thug e lomadh air Cnòideart,
    Thug e leòn air Clann Raghnaill:
Falbh nam fear òga,
Falbh nam fear mòra,
Falbh nam fear cròdha
    'N àm na tòrachd a phàigheadh.
Bidh cinn-chinnidh 'nan ònar,
'S an slinnean gun chòmhdach,
Gun treise gun chòmhnadh
    Nuair thig fòirneart an làthair,
Ur naimhdean gu spòrsail

Gur stampadh fo'm bhrògan—
Luchd fòirneart gu treòrach
   Gun neach beò gus an àicheadh.

S truagh an gnothach ri smaoineach',
Tha 'm fearann ga dhaoradh—
Ghrad dh'fhalbh ar cuid dhaoine
   'S thàinig caoirich 'nan àite;
S lag an sluagh iad, 's is faoin iad
Dol an carraid no 'n caonnaig,
Làn bracsaidh is caoile
   'S iad fo dhraoidh ghille-màrtainn.
Cha dèan smiùradh ur saoradh
'N làthair batail air raonaidh,
No fead cìobair an aonaich
   Gnè chaochladh dhe'r n-ànradh,
'S ged a chruinnicheadh sibh caogad
Mholt is reitheachan maola
S beag a thogadh a h-aon diubh
   Claidheamh faobharach stàilinn.

Ciod am fàth dhomh bhith 'g innse
Gun d'fhàs sibh cho mìodhar
'S gun spothadh sibh frìghde
   Far an dìreadh i fàrdan?
Dh'fhalbh na ceannardan mìleant'
Dh'an robh sannt air an fhìrinn,
Dh'an robh geall air an dìlsean
   Agus cuing air an nàmhaid,
Air an tuath bha iad cuimhneach
(Cha b'ann gus an sgrìobadh),
Bhiodh bantraichean 's dìlleachdain
   Dìolta gu saidhbhir;
Gach truaghan gun dìth air
Mun cuairt air na suinn sin
Nach sealladh gu h-ìseal—
   Bha 'n inntinn ro stàtail.

Dia a stiùireadh ur gnothaich
Air gach taobh agus romhaibh,
A-null air chuan domhain
   As coimhiche gàire—

Thugadh Eölus earail
Don ghaoith a bhith tairis
Gun giùlain i thairis
 Ur mnathan 's ur pàistean;
Biodh an fhairge le mothar
Toirt an spìd ás an reothairt,
Biodh Neiptean ga clothadh
 Gun tomhas ro àrd oirr'
Gus an ruig sibh am fearann
Gun eagal a ghabhail,
Dol air tìr mar as math leibh
 Ann an calaichean sàbhailt.

Triallaibh nis, fhearaibh,
Gu dùthaich gun ghainne,
Cuiribh cùl ris an fhearann
 Chaidh thairis am màl oirbh
Gu dùthaich a' bhainne,
Gu dùthaich na meala,
Gu dùthaich an ceannaich sibh
 Fearann gu'r n-àilgheas,
Gu dùthaich gun aineis,
Gun chrìonadh gun stanard,
Far an cnuasaich sibh barrachd
 'S a mhaireas ri'r làithean—
Se 'n saighdeir glic fearail
Nuair chitheadh e barrachd
A theicheadh le 'anam
 'S nach fanadh air làraich.

Seallaibh mun cuairt duibh
Is faicibh na h-uaislean
Gun iochd annt' ri truaghain,
 Gun suairceas ri dàimhich;
Sann a tha iad am barail
Nach buin sibh don talamh,
'S ged dh'fhàg iad sibh falamh
 Chan fhaic iad mar chall e:
Chaill iad an sealladh
Air gach reachd agus gealladh
Bha eadar na fearaibh

Thug am fearann s' on nàmhaid—
Ach innseadh iad dhòmhsa
Nuair théid sibh air fògradh
Mur caill iad an còir air
    Gun dòigh air a theàrnadh.

'A Song to the Exiles' (translated by Ronald Black)

Pluck up courage and joy,
Be hopeful and cheerful
And put your reliance
    In the help of the High King,
Because you must sail
(Though it's not what you want)
To a land you don't know
    In the wake of your kinsfolk.
Since they won't let you live
In the country you know,
You had better leave willingly
    And not be trampled like slaves;
How stupid are landlords
Who set your bows to the wind—
Who broke the neck of King George
    When the Gael were expelled!

If war and plundering come
(As has frequently happened)
You'll be a threshold
    Under enemy feet;
You are easy to slaughter
When there's no one to stop them,
You've no support at your shoulders
    As the heroes are leaving you.
O King, how trim to be seen
Standing on greensward
With their splendid attire
    Of red tartan plaids
Are those handsome young men
Who are leaving you soon—
Uncorrupted, unblemished,
    Without fear or reproach.

What has ravaged MacDonald,
Brought destruction to Morar,
Laid Knoydart waste
    And wounded Clanranald
Is the going of the young men,
The going of the big men,
The going of the brave men
    Who'd pay their rent in the battlefield.
Chiefs will be isolated,
Their shoulderblades naked,
Without strength or support
    When violence appears,
Your enemies gleefully
Trampling all over you—
Oppressors will thrive
    With none alive to oppose them.

It's sad to reflect how
The land's being enslaved—
Our people suddenly went
    And sheep came in their place;
They're weak troops, ineffective
In attack or in battle,
Full of braxy and famine
    And under foxes' enchantments.
No smearing will save you*
In time of battle on battlefield,
No shepherd's whistle on mountain
    Will relieve your distress,
And if you mustered fifty
Hornless rams and wedders
Not one of them would lift
    A bladed sword of steel.

What's the point of my telling
That you've grown so short-sighted
That you'd geld a louse if it gained
    A farthing in value?
Gone are the warrior chiefs
Who yearned for the truth,
Who respected their followers
    And held back their enemies,

They remembered their tenants
(But not so as to fleece them),
Widows and orphans were
    Richly maintained;
Each pauper looked after
Surrounding those heroes
Who would never look low—
    Their minds were too stately.

God guide your affairs
On each side and before you,
Across the deep ocean
    Of most terrible roar—
May Æolus command
The wind to be gentle
And carry across
    Your wives and your children;
Let the sea with her murmur
Take the sting from the spring-tide,
Let Neptune restrain it
    From rising too high
Until you reach land
Without taking fright,
Going ashore in good order
    In sequestered harbours.

Go now, my lads,
To a realm without want,
Abandon the land
    Whose rent's gone beyond you
For the realm of the milk,
For the realm of the honey,
For a realm where you'll buy
    All the land you desire,
For a realm without poverty,
Without blight or rationing,
Where you'll glean more
    Than can last all your days—
It's the wise manly soldier
When he saw more arriving
Who'd escape with his life
    And not stay on the field.

Look all around you
And behold the nobility
With no pity for paupers
    Or kindness to kinsfolk;
They are convinced that
You don't belong to the land,
And though they've left you with nothing
    They don't see it as loss:
They have lost sight
Of each law and commitment
Binding the men
    Who took this land from the foe—
But let them just tell me
When you go into exile
If they won't cease to own it
    With no way to save it.

WILLIAM HAMILTON OF BANGOUR

(1704–1754)

———

THE Jacobite army officer and poet William Hamilton of Bangour was born in Linlithgowshire. As a student at the University of Edinburgh he produced his earliest known verse, a translation of the Mezentius episode in the *Aeneid*, which was Jacobite code for unjust kingship. In Edinburgh he made the acquaintance of leading literary figures, most notably Allan Ramsay, Thomas Ruddiman, and David Hume. He participated in the 1745 Jacobite rising, before fleeing to France after Culloden. A poorly edited and seemingly unauthoritative collection of Hamilton's verse appeared towards the end of his life, *Poems on Several Occasions* (1748), while the poet was abroad. He died before issuing a corrected version, though a 1760 edition with the same name claimed to fulfil the task. Hamilton's works appeared prominently alongside Struan's in Ramsay's *Tea-Table Miscellany* (1723–37), as well as in later, more explicitly Jacobite anthologies. Corrected or otherwise, *Poems* reveals an author adept with different modes and tones. Odes jostle with parodies, epigrams with epitaphs, songs with Shakespearean soliloquies, and more.

———

'Ode on the Battle of Gladsmuir, 1745'

The Works of the British Poets, Collated with the Best Editions, ed. Thomas Park, 48 vols (London: J. Sharpe, 1808–9).

> As over Gladsmuir's blood-stain'd field,
>   Scotia, imperial goddess, flew;
> Her lifted spear and radiant shield
>   Conspicuous blazing to the view:
>   Her visage, lately clouded with despair,
>   Now reassum'd its first majestic air.
>
> Such seen as oft in battle warm
>   She glow'd through many a martial age;
> Or mild to breathe the civil charm,

In pious plans and counsel sage:
  For, o'er the mingling glories of her face,
  A manly greatness heighten'd female grace.

Loud as the trumpet rolls its sound,
  Her voice the power celestial rais'd;
Whilst her victorious sons around
  In silent joy and wonder gazed:
    The sacred Muses heard the immortal lay,
    And thus to earth the notes of fame convey:

" 'Tis done! my sons! 'tis nobly done!
  Victorious over tyrant power;
How quick the race of fame was run!
  The work of ages in one hour:
    Slow creeps the oppressive weight of slavish reigns;
    One glorious moment rose, and burst your chains.

But late, forlorn, dejected, pale,
  A prey to each insulting foe;
I sought the grove and gloomy vale,
  To vent in solitude my woe;
    Now to my hand the balance fair restor'd;
    Once more I wield on high the imperial sword:

What arm has this deliverance wrought?
  'Tis he! the gallant youth appears;
O warm in fields, and cool in thought!
  Beyond the slow advance of years!
    Haste, let me, rescued now from future harms,
    Strain close the filial virtue in my arms.

Early I nurs'd this royal youth,
  Ah! ill detain'd on foreign shores;
I fill'd his mind with love of truth,
  With fortitude and wisdom's stores:
    For when a noble action is decreed,
    Heav'n forms the hero for the destin'd deed.

Nor could the soft seducing charms
  Of mild Hesperia's blooming soil
E'er quench his noble thirst of arms,
  Of generous deeds and honest toil;
    Fir'd with the warmth a country's love imparts,
    He fled their weakness, but admir'd their arts.

With him I plow'd the stormy main;
　My breath inspir'd the auspicious gale;
Reserv'd for Gladsmuir's glorious plain,
　　Through dangers wing'd his daring sail:
　　　Where, form'd with inborn worth, he durst oppose
　　　His single valour to an host of foes.

He came! he spoke! and all around,
　As swift as Heav'ns quick-darted flame,
Shepherds turn'd warriors at the sound,
　　And every bosom beat for fame:
　　　They caught heroic ardour from his eyes,
　　　And at his side the willing heroes rise.

Rouse, England! rouse, Fame's noblest son,
　In all thy ancient splendour shine;
If I the glorious work begun,
　　O let the crowning palm be thine:
　　　I bring a prince, for such is Heav'n's decree,
　　　Who overcomes but to forgive and free.

So shall fierce wars and tumults cease,
　While plenty crowns the smiling plain;
And Industry, fair child of peace,
　　Shall in each crowded city reign;
　　　So shall these happy realms for ever prove
　　　The sweets of union, liberty, and love."

'Epigram. On a Lion Enraged at Seeing a Lad in the Highland Dress'

Poems on Several Occasions (Edinburgh: W. Gordon, 1760).

　　　　Calm and serene th' imperial lion lay
　　　　Mildly indulging in the solar ray,
　　　　On vulgar mortals with indiff'rence gaz'd,
　　　　All unconcern'd, nor angry, nor amaz'd;
　　　　But when the Caledonian lad appear'd,
　　　　Sudden alarm'd, his manly mane he rear'd,
　　　　Prepar'd in fierce encounter to engage
　　　　The only object worthy of his rage.

DAVID MALLET

(1705–1765)

———

HAILING from Perthshire, David Mallet (formerly known as Malloch) was a well-connected playwright and poet in the period. Mallet met James Thomson as a student at the University of Edinburgh. He was also befriended by the leading poet of his generation, Allan Ramsay. After university, Mallet moved south in 1723 to tutor the Duke of Montrose's sons. At the same time, Mallet had some early literary success with 'William and Margaret', a free adaption of a traditional ballad. The piece caught the attention of Aaron Hill, who brought the young Scot into his circle of English poets. Many more poems and plays followed. For the rest of his career, Mallet enjoyed due prominence in the literary scene of London, especially when writing for the British government, alongside his friend Thomson.

———

'A Fragment'

The Works of David Mallet Esq; In Three Volumes. A New Edition corrected (London: A. Millar and P. Vaillant, 1759).

> Fair morn ascends: soft zephyr's wing
> O'er hill and vale renews the spring:
> Where, sown profusely, herb and flower,
> Of balmy smell, of healing power,
> Their souls in fragrant dews exhale,
> And breathe fresh life in every gale.
> Here, spreads a green expanse of plains,
> Where, sweetly-pensive, *Silence* reigns;
> And there, at utmost stretch of eye,
> A mountain fades into the sky;
> While winding round, diffus'd and deep,
> A river rowls with sounding sweep.
> Of human art no traces near,
> I seem alone with *Nature* here!

Here are thy walks, O sacred HEALTH!
The monarch's bliss, the beggar's wealth!
The seasoning of all good below!
The sovereign friend in joy or woe!
O *Thou*, most courted, most despis'd,
And but in absence duly priz'd!
Power of the soft and rosy face!
The vivid pulse, the vermil grace,
The spirits when they gayest shine,
Youth, beauty, pleasure, all are thine!
O *sun* of life! whose heavenly ray
Lights up, and chears, our various day,
The turbulence of hopes and fears,
The storm of fate, the cloud of years,
Till *Nature*, with thy *parting* light,
Reposes late in *Death*'s calm night:
Fled from the trophy'd roofs of state,
Abodes of splendid pain, and hate;
Fled from the couch, where, in sweet sleep,
Hot *Riot* would his anguish steep,
But tosses thro the midnight-shade,
Of death, of life, alike afraid;
For ever fled to shady cell,
Where *Temperance*, where the *Muses* dwell;
Thou art seen, at early dawn,
Slow-pacing o'er the breezy lawn:
Or on the brow of mountain high,
In silence feasting ear and eye,
With song and prospect, which abound
From birds, and woods, and waters round.

But when the sun, with noontide ray,
Flames forth intolerable day;
While *Heat* sits fervent on the plain,
With *Thirst* and *Languor* in his train;
All nature sickening in the blaze:
Thou, in the wild and woody maze,
That clouds the vale with umbrage deep,
Impendent from the neighbouring steep,
Wilt find betimes a calm retreat,
Where breathing *Coolness* has her seat.

There, plung'd amid the shadows brown,

Imagination lays him down;
Attentive, in his airy mood,
To every murmur of the wood:
The bee in yonder flowery nook;
The chidings of the headlong brook;
The green leaf shivering in the gale;
The warbling hill, the lowing vale;
The distant woodman's echoing stroke;
The thunder of the falling oak.
From thought to thought in vision led,
He holds high converse with the Dead;
Sages, or Poets. See they rise!
And shadowy skim before his eyes.
Hark! ORPHEUS strikes the lyre again,
The soften'd savages to men:
Lo! SOCRATES, the *Sent* of heaven,
To whom it's *moral will* was given.
Fathers and friends of human kind,
They form'd the nations or refin'd,
With all that mends the head and heart,
Enlightening truth, adorning art.
            While thus I mus'd beneath the shade,
At once the sounding breeze was laid:
And *Nature*, by the *unknown law*,
Shook deep with reverential awe.
Dumb silence grew upon the hour;
A browner night involv'd the bower:
When issuing from the inmost wood,
Appear'd fair *Freedom*'s GENIUS good.
O *Freedom!* sovereign boon of heaven;
Great Charter, with our being given;
For which the patriot, and the sage,
Have plan'd, have bled thro every age!
High privilege of human race,
Beyond a mortal monarch's grace:
Who could not give, nor can reclaim,
What but from God immediate came!

JOHN ARMSTRONG

(1708/9–1779)

THE physician and poet John Armstrong was born in Castleton, Roxburghshire. Armstrong took his medical degree at the University of Edinburgh, and practised in London by 1735, though unlicensed by the College of Physicians. In this decade and the next he published both serious medical papers and satires on quacks. Anonymously published, *Oeconomy of Love* is an explicit sex manual in blank verse that ran to numerous editions. Armstrong kept it out of his two-volume *Miscellanies* (1771), even though it had been greatly toned down by the seventeenth edition in 1768. An Italian translation appeared in 1744, the year in which Armstrong's far more respectable blank-verse georgic *The Art of Preserving Health* was published. Further literary publications followed: *The Muncher's and Guzler's Diary* (1749), a mock-almanac, and then two verse epistles in heroic verse: *Of Benevolence* (1751) and *Taste* (1753). In 1754 Armstrong wrote a tragedy, *The Forced Marriage*, which was never staged, much to his chagrin. His *Sketches, or, Essays on Various Subjects*, consisting of short pieces, some no more than jottings, on language, literature, and aesthetics, was published in 1758 under the pen-name Launcelot Temple. After the College of Physicians effectively ended his medical career, as he practised without a license, he enjoyed leisurely tours of Scotland and Wales, then the Continent. As Temple, he wrote a satirical *Short Ramble through some Parts of France and Italy* (1771). Divided into four books, on air, diet, exercise, and the passions, *The Art of Preserving Health* is an important example of the century's interest in the medical humanities.

The Art of Preserving Health *(1744)*, 'Air'

The Art of Preserving Health: A Poem (London: A. Millar, 1744).

> Daughter of Paeon, queen of every joy,
> HYGEIA;* whose indulgent smile sustains
> The various race luxuriant nature pours,

And on th' immortal essences bestows
Immortal youth; auspicious, O descend!
Thou, chearful guardian of the rolling year,
Whether thou wanton'st on the western gale,
Or shak'st the rigid pinions of the north,
Diffusest life and vigour thro' the tracts
Of air, thro' earth, and ocean's deep domain.
When thro' the blue serenity of heav'n
Thy power approaches, all the wasteful host
Of pain and sickness, squalid and deform'd,
Confounded sink into the loathsome gloom,
Where in deep Erebus involv'd the fiends
Grow more profane. Whatever shapes of death,
Shook from the hideous chambers of the globe,
Swarm thro' the shuddering air: whatever plagues
Or meagre famine breeds, or with slow wings
Rise from the putrid watry element,
The damp waste forest, motionless and rank,
That smothers earth, and all the breathless winds,
Or the vile carnage of th' inhuman field;
Whatever baneful breathes the rotten south;
Whatever ills th' extremes or sudden change
Of cold and hot, or moist and dry produce;
They fly thy pure effulgence: they, and all
The secret poisons of avenging heaven,
And all the pale tribes halting in the train
Of vice and heedless pleasure: or if aught
The comet's glare amid the burning sky,
Mournful eclipse, or planets ill–combin'd,
Portend disastrous to the vital world;
Thy salutary power averts their rage,
Averts the general bane: and but for thee
Nature would sicken, nature soon would die.

Without thy chearful active energy
No rapture swells the breast, no poet sings,
No more the maids of Helicon delight.
Come then with me, O Goddess heavenly gay!
Begin the song; and let it sweetly flow,
And let it wisely teach thy wholesome laws:
"How best the fickle fabric to support

Of mortal man; in healthful body how
A healthful mind the longest to maintain."
'Tis hard, in such a strife of rules, to chuse
The best, and those of most extensive use;
Harder in clear and animated song
Dry philosophic precepts to convey.
Yet with thy aid the secret wilds I trace
Of nature, and with daring steps proceed
Thro' paths the muses never trod before.

Nor should I wander doubtful of my way,
Had I the lights of that sagacious mind
Which taught to check the pestilential fire,
And quell the dreaded Python of the Nile.
O Thou belov'd by all the graceful arts,
Thou long the fav'rite of the healing powers,
Indulge, O MEAD! a well-design'd essay,
Howe'er imperfect: and permit that I
My little knowledge with my country share,
Till you the rich Asclepian stores unlock,
And with new graces dignify the theme.

Ye who amid this feverish world would wear
A body free of pain, of cares a mind;
Fly the rank city, shun its turbid air;
Breathe not the chaos of eternal smoke
And volatile corruption, from the dead,
The dying, sickning, and the living world
Exhal'd, to sully heaven's transparent dome
With dim mortality. It is not air
That from a thousand lungs reeks back to thine,
Sated with exhalations rank and fell,
The spoil of dunghills, and the putrid thaw
Of nature; when from shape and texture she
Relapses into fighting elements:
It is not air, but floats a nauseous mass
Of all obscene, corrupt, offensive things.
Much moisture hurts; but here a sordid bath,
With oily rancour fraught, relaxes more
The solid frame than simple moisture can.
Besides, immur'd in many a sullen bay

That never felt the freshness of the breeze,
This slumbring deep remains, and ranker grows
With sickly rest: and (tho' the lungs abhor
To drink the dun fuliginous abyss)
Did not the acid vigour of the mine,
Roll'd from so many thundring chimneys, tame
The putrid salts that overswarm the sky;
This caustick venom would perhaps corrode
Those tender cells that draw the vital air,
In vain with all their unctuous rills bedew'd;
Or by the drunken venous tubes, that yawn
In countless pores o'er all the pervious skin,
Imbib'd, would poison the balsamic blood,
And rouse the heart to every fever's rage.
While yet you breathe, away! the rural wilds
Invite; the mountains call you, and the vales,
The woods, the streams, and each ambrosial breeze
That fans the ever undulating sky;
A kindly sky! whose fost'ring power regales
Man, beast, and all the vegetable reign.
Find then some woodland scene where nature smiles
Benign, where all her honest children thrive.
To us there wants not many a happy seat;
Look round the smiling land, such numbers rise
We hardly fix, bewilder'd in our choice.
See where enthron'd in adamantine state,
Proud of her bards, imperial Windsor sits;
There chuse thy seat, in some aspiring grove
Fast by the slowly-winding Thames; or where
Broader she laves fair Richmond's green retreats,
(Richmond that sees an hundred villas rise
Rural or gay.) O! from the summer's rage,
O! wrap me in the friendly gloom that hides
Umbrageous Ham! But if the busy town
Attract thee still to toil for power or gold,
Sweetly thou mayst thy vacant hours possess
In Hampstead, courted by the western wind;
Or Greenwich, waving o'er the winding flood;
Or lose the world amid the sylvan wilds
Of Dulwich, yet by barbarous arts unspoil'd.
Green rise the Kentish hills in chearful air;

But on the marshy plains that Essex spreads
Build not, nor rest too long thy wandering feet.
For on a rustic throne of dewy turf,
With baneful fogs her aching temples bound,
Quartana there presides; a meagre fiend
Begot by Eurus, when his brutal force
Compress'd the slothful Naiad of the fens.
From such a mixture sprung this fitful pest,
With feverish blasts subdues the sick'ning land:
Cold tremors come, and mighty love of rest,
Convulsive yawnings, lassitude, and pains
That sting the burden'd brows, fatigue the loins,
And rack the joints, and every torpid limb;
Then parching heat succeeds, till copious sweats
O'erflow; a short relief from former ills.
Beneath repeated shocks the wretches pine;
The vigour sinks, the habit melts away;
The chearful, pure and animated bloom
Dies from the face, with squalid atrophy
Devour'd, in sallow melancholy clad.
And oft the sorceress, in her fated wrath,
Resigns them to the furies of her train;
The bloated Hydrops, and the yellow fiend
Ting'd with her own accumulated gall.

In quest of sites, avoid the mournful plain
Where osiers thrive, and trees that love the lake;
Where many lazy muddy rivers flow:
Nor for the wealth that all the Indies roll
Fix near the marshy margin of the main.
For from the humid soil, and watry reign,
Eternal vapours rise; the spungy air
For ever weeps; or, turgid with the weight
Of waters, pours a sounding deluge down.
Skies such as these let every mortal shun
Who dreads the dropsy, palsy, or the gout,
Tertian, corrosive scurvy, or moist catarrh;
Or any other injury that grows
From raw-spun fibres, idle and unstrung,
Skin ill-perspiring, and the purple flood
In languid eddies loitering into phlegm.

Yet not alone from humid skies we pine;
For air may be too dry. The subtle heaven
That winnows into dust the blasted downs,
Bare and extended wide without a stream,
Too fast imbibes th' attenuated lymph
Which, by the surface, from the blood exhales.
The lungs grow rigid, and with toil essay
Their flexible vibrations; or inflam'd,
Their tender ever-moving structure thaws.
Spoil'd of its limpid vehicle, the blood
A mass of lees remains, a drossy tide
That slow as Lethe wanders thro' the veins,
Unactive in the services of life,
Unfit to lead its pitchy current thro'
The secret mazy channels of the brain.
The melancholic fiend, (that worst despair
Of physic), hence the rust-complexion'd man
Pursues, whose blood is dry, whose fibres gain
Too stretch'd a tone: And hence in climes adust
So sudden tumults seize the trembling nerves,
And burning fevers glow with double rage.

Fly, if you can, these violent extremes
Of air; the wholesome is nor moist nor dry.
But as the power of chusing is deny'd
To half mankind, a further task ensues;
How best to mitigate these fell extreams,
How breathe unhurt the withering element,
Or hazy atmosphere: Tho' custom moulds
To every clime the soft Promethean clay;
And he who first the fogs of Essex breath'd
(So kind is native air) may in the fens
Of Essex from inveterate ills revive
At pure Montpelier or Bermuda caught.
But if the raw and oozy heaven offend,
Correct the soil, and dry the sources up
Of watry exhalation; wide and deep
Conduct your trenches thro' the spouting bog;
Solicitous, with all your winding arts,
Betray th' unwilling lake into the stream;
And weed the forest, and invoke the winds

To break the toils where strangled vapours lie;
Or thro' the thickets send the crackling flames.
Mean time, at home with chearful fires dispel
The humid air: And let your table smoke
With solid roast or bak'd; or what the herds
Of tamer breed supply; or what the wilds
Yield to the toilsome pleasures of the chase.
Generous your wine, the boast of rip'ning years,
But frugal be your cups; the languid frame,
Vapid and sunk from yesterday's debauch,
Shrinks from the cold embrace of watry heavens.
But neither these, nor all Apollo's arts,
Disarm the dangers of the dropping sky,
Unless with exercise and manly toil
You brace your nerves, and spur the lagging blood.
The fat'ning clime let all the sons of ease
Avoid; if indolence would wish to live.
Go, yawn and loiter out the long slow year
In fairer skies. If droughty regions parch
The skin and lungs, and bake the thick'ning blood;
Deep in the waving forest chuse your seat,
Where fuming trees refresh the thirsty air;
And wake the fountains from their secret beds,
And into lakes dilate the running stream.
Here spread your gardens wide; and let the cool,
The moist relaxing vegetable store
Prevail in each repast: Your food supplied
By bleeding life, be gently wasted down,
By soft decoction, and a mellowing heat,
To liquid balm; or, if the solid mass
You chuse, tormented in the boiling wave;
That thro' the thirsty channels of the blood
A smooth diluted chyle may ever flow.
The fragrant dairy from its cool recess
Its nectar acid or benign will pour
To drown your thirst; or let the mantling bowl
Of keen Sherbet the sickle taste relieve.
For with the viscous blood the simple stream
Will hardly mingle; and fermented cups
Oft dissipate more moisture than they give.
Yet when pale seasons rise, or winter rolls

His horrors o'er the world, thou may'st indulge
In feasts more genial, and impatient broach
The mellow cask. Then too the scourging air
Provokes to keener toils than sultry droughts
Allow. But rarely we such skies blaspheme.
Steep'd in continual rains, or with raw fogs
Bedew'd, our seasons droop; incumbent still
A ponderous heaven o'erwhelms the sinking soul.
Lab'ring with storms in heapy mountains rise
Th' imbattled clouds, as if the Stygian shades
Had left the dungeon of eternal night,
Till black with thunder all the south descends.
Scarce in a showerless day the heavens indulge
Our melting clime; except the baleful east
Withers the tender spring, and sourly checks
The fancy of the year. Our fathers talk
Of summers, balmy airs, and skies serene.
Good heaven! for what unexpiated crimes
This dismal change! The brooding elements
Do they, your powerful ministers of wrath,
Prepare some fierce exterminating plague?
Or is it fix'd in the Decrees above
That lofty Albion melt into the main?
Indulgent nature! O dissolve this gloom!
Bind in eternal adamant the winds
That drown or wither: Give the genial west
To breathe, and in its turn the sprightly north:
And may once more the circling seasons rule
The year; not mix in every monstrous day.

Mean time, the moist malignity to shun
Of burthen'd skies; mark where the dry champain
Swells into chearful hills; where Marjoram
And Thyme, the love of bees, perfume the air;
And where the Cynorrhodon with the rose
For fragrance vies; for in the thirsty soil
Most fragrant breathe the aromatic tribes.
There bid thy roofs high on the basking steep
Ascend, there light thy hospitable fires.
And let them see the winter morn arise,
The summer evening blushing in the west;

While with umbrageous oaks the ridge behind
O'erhung, defends you from the blust'ring north,
And bleak affliction of the peevish east.
O! when the growling winds contend, and all
The sounding forest fluctuates in the storm,
To sink in warm repose, and hear the din
Howl o'er the steady battlements, delights
Above the luxury of vulgar sleep.
The murmuring rivulet, and the hoarser strain
Of waters rushing o'er the slippery rocks,
Will nightly lull you to ambrosial rest.
To please the fancy is no trifling good,
Where health is studied; for whatever moves
The mind with calm delight, promotes the just
And natural movements of th' harmonious frame.
Besides, the sportive brook for ever shakes
The trembling air; that floats from hill to hill,
From vale to mountain, with incessant change
Of purest element, refreshing still
Your airy seat, and uninfected Gods.
Chiefly for this I praise the man who builds
High on the breezy ridge, whose lofty sides
Th' etherial deep with endless billows laves.
His purer mansion nor contagious years
Shall reach, nor deadly putrid airs annoy.

But may no fogs, from lake, or fenny plain,
Involve my hill. And wheresoe'er you build;
Whether on sun-burnt Epsom, or the plains
Wash'd by the silent Lee; in Chelsea low,
Or high Blackheath with wintry winds assail'd;
Dry be your house: but airy more than warm.
Else every breath of ruder wind will strike
Your tender body thro' with rapid pains;
Fierce coughs will teize you, hoarseness bind your voice,
Or moist Gravedo load your aching brows.
These to defy, and all the fates that dwell
In cloister'd air tainted with steaming life,
Let lofty ceilings grace your ample rooms;
And still at azure noontide may your dome
At every window drink the liquid sky.

Need we the sunny situation here,
And theatres open to the south, commend?
Here, where the morning's misty breath infests
More than the torrid noon? How sickly grow,
How pale, the plants in those ill-fated vales
That, circled round with the gigantic heap
Of mountains, never felt, nor never hope
To feel, the genial vigour of the sun!
While on the neighbouring hill the rose inflames
The verdant spring; in virgin beauty blows
The tender lily, languishingly sweet;
O'er every hedge the wanton woodbine roves,
And autumn ripens in the summer's ray.
Nor less the warmer living tribes demand
The fost'ring sun: whose energy divine
Dwells not in mortal fire; whose generous heat
Glows thro' the mass of grosser elements,
And kindles into life the pond'rous spheres.
Chear'd by thy kind invigorating warmth,
We court thy beams, great majesty of day!
If not the soul, the regent of this world,
First-born of heaven, and only less than God!

JEAN ADAM

(1710–1765)

HAILING from Cartsdyke, near Greenock in Renfrewshire, Jean Adam (sometimes anglicized as Jean or Jane Adams) was largely self-educated, until the minister of West Kirk, Greenock, whose service she entered after her father's death, encouraged her to read more formally. Later keeping a day school, Adam was remembered fondly by a former pupil, Mrs Fullarton, who claimed the poet often sang her own songs for the children. Although little heralded upon publication in Glasgow, Adam's *Miscellany Poems* (1734), in two volumes, comprises a hefty body of work, mainly on religious and moral subjects. But it is a short song ascribed to her, 'There's Nae Luck about the House', for which she is most fondly remembered.

'There's Nae Luck about the House'

The Songstresses of Scotland, ed. Sarah Tytler and J. L. Watson, 2 vols (London: Strahan & Co., 1871).

> And are ye sure the news is true?
> And are ye sure he's weel?
> Is this a time to think o' wark?
> Ye jauds, fling by your wheel.
> Is this a time to think o' wark,
> When Colin's at the door?
> Rax me my cloak, I'll to the quay,
> And see him come ashore.
> For there's nae luck about the house,
> There's nae luck at a';
> There's little pleasure in the house
> When our gudeman's awa'.
>
> And gie to me my bigonet,
> My bishop-satin gown;

For I maun tell the bailie's wife
    That Colin's come to town.
My turkey slippers maun gae on,
    My hose o' pearl blue;
It's a' to pleasure my ain gudeman,
    For he's baith leal and true.

Rise up and mak a clean fireside,
    Put on the muckle pot;
Gie little Kate her Sunday gown,
    And Jock his button coat;
And mak their shoon as black as slaes,
    Their hose as white as snaw;
It's a' to please my ain gudeman,
    For he's been long awa'.

There's twa fat hens upo' the bauk,
    They've fed this month and mair,
Mak haste and thraw their necks about,
    That Colin weel may fare;
And spread the table neat and clean,
    Gar ilka thing look braw;
For wha can tell how Colin fared
    When he was far awa'?

Sae true his heart, sae smooth his speech,
    His breath like caller air;
His very foot has music in't
    As he comes up the stair.
And will I see his face again?
    And will I hear him speak?
I'm downricht dizzy wi' the thocht,
    In troth I'm like to greet.

Since Colin's weel, I'm weel content,
    I hae nae mair to crave;
Could I but live to mak him blest,
    I'm blest aboon the lave:
And will I see his face again?
    And will I hear him speak?
I'm downricht dizzy wi' the thocht,
    In troth I'm like to greet.
        For there's nae luck, &c.

ALISON COCKBURN

(?1713–1794)

THE writer and literary hostess Alison Cockburn (*née* Rutherford) was born in Fairnilee, Selkirkshire. Cockburn wrote poetry and songs throughout her life, but only a few pieces were published for a wider audience beyond her circle of friends. After her husband's death, Cockburn relocated to Edinburgh, where she discussed literature with leading Scottish authors, including David Hume, John Home, and Walter Scott, a cousin on her mother's side. The poem for which she is now remembered, 'The Flowers of the Forest', was belatedly published in *The Lark*, in 1765, and initially not even under her name. Many commentators believed it to be an old ballad, but Burns and others recognized (and praised) its modern craftsmanship. Another version of 'The Flowers of the Forest', by Jean Elliot, is markedly different in form and content. Both versions were published side by side, with attributions, in Robert Chambers's *The Scottish Songs* (1829), among many other old and modern collections.

'The Flowers of the Forest'

The Scottish Songs, ed. Robert Chambers, 2 vols (Edinburgh: William Tait, 1829).

> I've seen the smiling
> Of Fortune beguiling,
> I've felt all its favours, and found its decay;
> Sweet is its blessing,
> Kind its caressing;
> But now 'tis fled—fled far away.
>
> I've seen the forest
> Adorned the foremost
> With flowers of the fairest, most pleasant and gay;
> Sae bonnie was their blooming!

Their scent the air perfuming!
But now they are wither'd and weeded away.

I've seen the morning
With gold the hills adorning,
And loud tempest storming before the mid-day.
I've seen Tweed's silver streams,
Shining in the sunny beams,
Grow drumly and dark as he row'd on his way.

Oh, fickle Fortune,
Why this cruel sporting?
Oh, why still perplex us, poor sons of a day?
Nae mair your smiles can cheer me,
Nae mair your frowns can fear me;
For the Flowers of the Forest are a' wede away.

ROB DONN MACAOIDH / ROBERT MACKAY
(1714–1778)

══

THE poet Robert Mackay (known as Rob Donn) was born at Allt na Caillich, in Strathmore, which lies between the north coast of Sutherland and the inland Ben Hope. The earliest work ascribed to him is a mocking quatrain about a tailor said to have been composed when he was just three years old. Aged seven, according to the memoir in an 1829 edition of his works, Rob Donn was taken into the family of John Mackay (Iain Mac Eachainn), where he helped to herd calves and revelled in the musical habits of those around him. Throughout his life he worked as herdsman, drover, and gamekeeper; for some time he was directly employed by Lord Reay near Durness, and made the acquaintance of the Reverend Murdo Macdonald, who encouraged his talents further. Rob Donn wrote some love poems and many elegies but, above all, he was a born satirist.

══

'Is trom leam an àirigh'

Robert Mackay, *Songs and Poems, in the Gaelic Language* (Inverness: Kenneth Douglas, 1829).

Is trom leam an àirigh 's a' ghàir seo a th' innt'
Gun a' phàirtinn a dh'fhàg mi bhith 'n-dràst' air mo chinn—
Anna chaol-mhalach chìoch-chorrach shlìob-cheannach chruinn
Is Iseabail a' bheòil mhilis, mhànranaich bhinn.
Heich! Mar a bhà air mo chinn,
A dh'fhàg mi cho cràidhteach 's nach stàth dhomh bhith 'g inns'.

Shiubhail mis' a' bhuaile 's a suas feadh nan craobh,
'S gach àit' anns am b' àbhaist bhith pàgadh mo ghaoil;
Nuair chunnaic mi 'm fear bàn ud 's e mànran r' a mhnaoi
B' fheàrr leam nach tiginn idir làimh riu', no 'n gaoith—
'S e mar a bhà, air mo chinn,
A dh'fhàg mi cho cràidhteach 's nach stàth dhomh bhith 'g inns'.

On chualas gun gluaiseadh tu uam leis an t-saor
Tha mo shuain air a buaireadh le bruadraichean gaoil,
Den chàirdeas a bhà siud chan fhàir mi bhith saor—
Gun bhàrnaigeadh làimh riut tha 'n gràdh dhomh na mhaor,
Air gach tràth 's mi ann an strì
A' feuchainn r' a àicheadh 's e fàs rium mar chraoibh.

Ach Anna Bhuidhe nighean Dòmhnaill, nam b' eòl duit mo nì
'S e do ghràdh gun bhith pàight' leag a-bhàn uam mo chlì;
Tha e dhomh à d' fhianais cho gnìomhach 's nuair chì,
A' diogalladh 's a' smùsach gur ciùrrtach mo chrìdh—
Nis ma thà mi ga do dhìth
Gum b' fheàrirrde mi pàg uait mus fàgainn an tìr.

Ach labhair i gu fàiteagach àilgheasach rium:
'Chan fhàir thu bhith làimh rium do chàradh mo chinn—
Tha sianar gam iarraidh o bhliadhna de thìm
'S cha b' àraidh le càch thu thoirt bàrr os an cinn.
Ha ha hà! An d' fhàs thu gu tinn?
'N e 'n gaol-s' a bheir bàs ort? Gum pàigh thu d' a chinn!'

Ach cionnas bheir mi fuath dhuit ged dh'fhuaraich thu rium?
Nuair as feargaich' mo sheanchas mu d' ainm air do chùl,
Thig d' ìomhaigh le h-annsachd na samhladh nam ùidh:
Saoilidh mi 'n sin gun dèan an gaol sin an tùrn
'S thèid air a ràdh gu h-às ùr—
Is fàsaidh e 'n tràth sin cho àrda ri tùr.

'I'm depressed by the sheiling' (translated by Peter Mackay and Iain S. MacPherson)

I'm depressed by the sheiling and the laughing inside,
The party I've left still troubles my mind:
Anna with the sleek hair, pert breasts, round behind,
Isobel, sweet-talking, whispering, refined.
Aich! The state of my mind—
I'm not cured by talking, I'm aching inside.

I wandered the paddock and up through the trees
To all of the places we'd go on a spree,
Overheard a blonde bloke and his wife's pleasantries;

No wish to be seen, I passed them down-breeze.
That was the state of my mind—
I'm not cured by talking, I was aching inside.

Since I heard the joiner would steal you from me
My sleep's been broken by love-baffled dreams.
Yon affair now means I'll never be free:
Without your summons, love's a bailiff to me.
All day long I'm besieged:
I try to deny it, but it grows like a tree.

You don't know what I'm worth, Donald's daughter, blonde Anne,
The way you snub my love leaves me at your command:
With you absent or present, my heart's flames are fanned,
They tickle and suckle and smart like firebrands.
Without you I'm unmanned,
Yet still dream of a kiss before I leave this land.

But full of disdain, condescending, you said:
"You've no chance of caressing my head,
Six men are fighting to be in your stead
And they're all sure *you* won't get close to my bed.
Ha ha! Are you sick in the head?
You think this love'll kill you? Then you'll end up dead."

You're cold to me, but still I don't hate you,
And though behind your back I slag and slate you
In my mind there's an affectionate you
And I still think my love could elate you.
It's still true:
My love grows tall as a tower for you.

DÙGHALL BOCHANAN /
DUGALD BUCHANAN

(1716–1768)

DUGALD BUCHANAN (Dùghall Bochanan) was a native of Strathyre, Perthshire. After the '45 he was appointed by the Society in Scotland for the Propagating of Christian Knowledge as its schoolmaster and catechist in Rannoch. He used his poetic gift to bring the Gospel to the people in a way that they could understand, and his *Spiritual Songs* (1767) became a bestseller that ran to forty separate printings. It consists of just eight hymns, in theological order, from God to man. The third in the sequence, 'Am Bruadar', deals with the vanity of earthly wishes. Falling victim to an epidemic of fever, he died in 1768 while helping to see the Gaelic translation of the New Testament through the press.

'Am Bruadar'

Translator's transcription

Air bhith dhòmhsa ann am' shuain
    A' bruadar dìomhain, mar tha càch,
Bhith glacadh sonais o gach nì
    'S e gam dhìbreadh anns gach àit',

Ar leam gun tàinig neach am' chòir
    'S gun tuirt e rium gur gòrach mì
Bhith smuainteach' greim a ghléidheadh den ghaoith
    No gun lìon an saoghal mo chrìdh.

"S dìomhain duit bhith 'g iarraidh sàimh
    'N aon nì no 'n àit' air bith fon ghréin;
Cha chlos do d' chorp an taobh seo 'n uaigh
    No t' anam 'n taobh seo shuaimhnis Dé.

An tràth dh'ith Àdhamh 'm meas an tùs,
    Am peacadh dhrùidh e air gach nì,

Lìon e a h-uile nì le saothair
    'S dh'fhàg e 'n saoghal 'na bhristeadh crìdh.

Air sonas anma chaill e chòir
    Mar ris gach sòlas bha sa ghàr':
O sin ta shliochd 'nan deòraibh truagh,
    Mar uain am mearachd air am màthair—

Ri mèilich chruaidh, ta 'd ruith gach nì,
    An dùil gum faigh an inntinn clos;
Ach dhaibh ta 'n saoghal gun iochd no truas
    Mar mhuime choimhich fhuair gun tlus.

Mar sin tha iad gun fhois no tàmh,
    Gan sàrach' glacadh faileas bréig'
'S a' deoghal toil-inntinn o gach nì
    Is iad mar chìochan seasg 'nam beul.

Bidh teanndachd éigin ort am-feast'
    'S do dhòchas faicinn fuasgladh t' fheum
An còmhnaidh dhuit mar fhad na làimh'—
    Ach gu bràth chan fhaigh dheth greim.

Cha teagaisg deuchainn 's dearbhadh thu
    O dhùil is earbsa chur sa bhréig
A rinn do mhealladh mìle uair—
    S cho fada uait an-diugh 's an-dé.

An nì bu mhó don tug thu miann,
    Nach d'fhàg a mhealtainn riamh e searbh?
Tha tuilleadh sonais ann an dùil
    Na th' ann an crùn le bhith 'na shealbh.

Ceart mar an ròs ata sa ghàr',
    Seargaidh a bhlàth nuair théid a bhuain:
Mun gann a ghlacas tu e 'd làimh
    Tréigidh àile e 's a shnuadh.

Nì bheil neach o thrioblaid saor
    Am measg a' chinne-daonn' air fad:
S cho lìonmhor osna aig an rìgh
    Is aig an neach as ìsle staid.

Tha smùdan fhéin ás ceann gach fòid
    Is dòrainn ceangailt' ris gach math,

Tha 'n ròs a' fàs air drisibh geur
   'S an taic a–chéil' tha mhil 's an gath.

Ged chì thu neach an saidhbhreas mòr,
   Na meas a shòlas bhith thar chàch:
An tobar as glaine chì do shùil,
   Tha ghrùid 'na ìochdar gabhail tàmh.

'S ma chuireas t' anail e 'na ghluais,
   Le tarrainn chabhaig suas ad' bheul,
Dùisgidh an ruadhan dearg a–nìos
   'S le gaineamh lìonaidh e do dheud.

'S ged chì thu neach an inbhe àird
   Tha e mar nead am bàrr na craoibh':
Gach stoirm a' bagradh thilgeadh nuas
   'S e air a luasgadh leis gach gaoith.

An neach as fheàrr tha 'n saoghal a' riar',
   Tha fiaradh éigin ann a staid
Nach dèan a sheòltachd is a shrì
   Am-feast' a dhìreachadh air fad.

Mar bhata fiar an aghaidh chéil'
   Ata o shuidheach' fhéin do chur:
A réir mar dhìreas tu a bhàrr
   S cho cinnteach nì thu cam a bhun.

Na h-Iùdhaich thionail beag no mòr
   Den Mhana dhòirteadh orra nuas;
Nuair chuir gach neach a chuid sa chlàr
   Cha robh air bàrr no dadam uaith'.

Mar sin ata gach sonas saoghalt'
   Ata thu faotainn ann ad' làimh:
Fa chomhair saidhbhris 's inbhe cùirt
   Tha caitheamh, cùram agus cràdh.

Ged chàrn thu òr ad' shlige suas,
   Fa chomhair fàsaidh 'n luaidh' d'a réir,
Is ged a chuir thu innte rìoghachd,
   A' mheidh cha dìrich i 'na déidh.

Tha cuibhreann iomchaidh aig gach neach,
   'S ged tha thu meas gur tuille b' fheàrr,

Cha toir an t-anabharr th' ann a-siud
   Am-feast' an cudthrom ás a' chràdh.

O iomluas t' inntinn tha do phian
   A' diùltadh 'n-diugh na dh'iarr thu 'n-dé:
Cha chomasach don t-saoghal do riar'
   Le t' anamianna 'n aghaidh chéil'.

Nam faigheadh toil na feòl' a rùn
   D'a mianna brùideil dh'iarradh sàth:
Flaitheas a b' àird' chan iarradh ì
   Na annta siud bhith sìorraidh 'snàmh.

Ach ged a b' ionmhainn leis an fheòil
   Air talamh còmhnachadh gach ré,
Bhiodh dùrachd t' àrdain agus t' uaill'
   Cho àrd a-suas ri cathair Dhé.

Ach nam b' àill leat sonas buan,
   Do shlighe tabhair suas do Dhia,
Le dùrachd, creideamh agus gràdh—
   Is sàsaichidh e t' uile mhiann.

Tha 'n cuideachd siud gach nì san t-saoghal
   Tha 'n comas dhaoine shealbhach' fìor:
Biadh is aodach agus slàint',
   Is saorsa, càirdeas agus sìth."

An-sin do mhosgail ás mo shuain
   Is dh'fhàg mo bhruadar mi air fad,
Is leig mi dhiom bhith ruith gach sgàil
   Is dh'fhàs mi toilichte le m' staid.

'The Dream' (translated by Ronald Black)

Once when I had been asleep
   Dreaming idly, as do others,
Of seizing happiness from everything
   While it forsakes me everywhere,

I thought a being came where I was
   And said to me that I'm a fool
To think that I can grasp the wind
   Or that the world can fill my heart.

"It's vain for you to be seeking joy
    In any thing or place on the earth;
Your body won't rest this side of the grave
    Nor your soul this side of the peace of God.

When Adam ate the fruit at the start,
    The sin penetrated everything,
It filled all that there is with toil
    And left the world a broken heart.

He lost the right to contentment of soul
    Along with the garden's happiness:
From that his race are wretched exiles,
    Like lambs who cannot find their mother—

Bleating hard, they chase everything,
    Thinking they will get peace of mind;
But the world is as merciless to them
    As a cold, unloving, alien nurse.

So they go without peace or rest,
    Anxiously clutching any false shadow
And sucking pleasure from worldly things
    Resembling milkless breasts in their mouths.

Some distress or other will always beset you
    While your hope sees the answer to your need
Always an arm's length away from you—
    But you will never be able to seize it.

Trial and hardship won't warn you away
    From putting faith and trust in the lie
That has deceived you a thousand times—
    It's as far from you now as yesterday.

The thing you had always wanted most,
    Didn't enjoying it leave it bitter?
There's more happiness in looking ahead
    Than in real possession of a crown.

Just like the rose that's in the garden,
    Its blossom withers when it's plucked:
You've scarcely grasped it in your hand
    When it loses its scent and hue.

No one person is free from oppression
    Throughout the whole of the human race:
Just as frequently sighs the king
    As does he of the lowest state.

Each lump of peat emits its smoke
    And grief to every good is tied,
The rose it grows upon sharp thorns
    With sting and honey side by side.

If you see a person of great wealth,
    Don't imagine he's happier than others:
The purest well that your eye can see,
    Sediment lies down there in its depths.

And if your breath should stir it up,
    By drawing it quickly into your mouth,
The red scurf will waken up from below
    And come and fill up your teeth with sand.

And if you see a person of high degree
    He'll be like a nest in the top of the tree:
Each tempest threatening to throw him down
    While he's tossed around by every wind.

The one most satisfied by the world,
    There's some kink or other in his condition
Which all his cunning and endeavour
    Will never altogether straighten.

Like a stick deviating this way and that
    From its own direction is your state:
According as you straighten its tip
    Just as surely you bend its base.

The Jews they gathered more or less
    Of the Manna that was poured upon them;
When everyone put his bit on the board
    There was no excess nor any missing.*

Like that is every worldly joy
    That you can pick up in your hand:
For all the wealth and rank at court
    There's loss, there's worry and there's pain.

Even if you've heaped up gold in your scale,
    Opposite it lead grows proportionately,
And even if you've put a whole kingdom in,
    The balance won't tilt up consequentially.

Everyone has some suitable portion,
    And even if you think that more would be better,
No such excess can ever take
    Any of the weight out of the pain.

Your anguish is caused by your fickle mind
    Refusing today what yesterday you sought:
To satisfy you the world is unable
    When your cravings contradict each other.

If fleshly desire were to get its way
    It would try to fulfil its brutish lusts:
No higher kingdom would it seek
    Than forever swimming around in those.

But though the flesh would be delighted
    To live at all times upon the earth,
Your pride's and vanity's desire
    Would be up as high as the throne of God.

But if you'd like to have joy eternal,
    Your path surrender now to God,
With sincerity, faith and love—
    And He will fulfil your every wish.

That's what brings all things in the world
    That men can genuinely possess:
Food and clothing and health,
    And freedom, friendship and peace."

Then I woke up from my sleep
    And my dream left me completely,
And I ceased to chase each spectre
    And grew content with my condition.

AILEAN STIÙBHART / ALLAN STEWART
(1716–1776)

A POET in English, Gaelic, and Latin, Allan Stewart (Ailean Stiùbhart) was born at the manse of Blair Atholl, son of the Reverend Duncan Stewart of Invernahyle, Episcopalian minister of Blair Atholl. After attending Edinburgh University he became tacksman (tenant) of Innerhadden in Rannoch, then in 1745–6 he served Prince Charles as a captain in John Roy Stewart's Edinburgh Regiment. 'Cìs nan Cnàmh' reflects the chaos in Rannoch following Culloden, in the course of which some soldiers of the Black Watch on a 'punitive expedition' led by Lt John Campbell of Glenlyon (the Younger), burned down the poet's house and plundered his land. There is only one source for the song, Turner's collection of 1813, and it appears to lack its beginning, probably because the editor omitted a description of exactly what had happened. Stewart's other known surviving song was composed much later. It praises the poet-catechist Dugald Buchanan and (by implication) the Forfeited Estates Commissioners for bringing education, peace, and the Gospel to Rannoch in place of the redcoats' reign of terror. What these two songs have in common, therefore, is Stewart's craving for the rule of law when provided by sensible parliaments, as opposed to that of August 1746, which prohibited the wearing of Highland dress, the only clothes the people had.

'Cìs nan Cnàmh'

Comhchruinneacha do dh' Orain Taghta, Ghaidhealach, ed. Paruig Mac-an-Tuairneir (Edinburgh: Stewart, 1813).

Ach nan tigeadh Tearlach Stiùbhart
  Leis gu sunndach bhiomaid falbh,
Dh'éireadh ar cridhe 's ar tiunnsgal
  Mar sa bhurn am bradan bàn;
Chan eil gearastan san dùthaich
  Nach biodh ciurrte dheth, gun dàil,

'S bhiomaid pàighte anns a' phlunndrainn
    'S anns an rùsgadh rinn na Caim.

Tha chòir air leaghadh anns na crìochan
    'S tha i ìosal uile 'n-dràst',
Sinn gar leònadh aig na biastan,
    Leis 'm bu mhiann ar slugadh slàn—
Ach nuair rùisgear riu na h-iarainn
    Tha fos n-ìosal feadh nan càrn,
Bidh ar cornaibh air an lìonadh
    'S bidh iadsan sianail thun a' bhàis.

Ach 's léir an leus air Clanna Ghaidheal
    A' pharlamaid seo tha gan cràdh,
Gun airm, gun éideadh, gun earlaid,
    Gun a' chearbag théid mu'm màs;
Ged rinn dìoghaltas ar tearbadh,
    'S earbsach mi gu bheil e 'n dàn—
Gum bi sinn an uachdar le'r feara-ghnìomh
    'S dearganaich fo chìs nan cnàmh.

Mosglaibh uile gach treunlaoch,
    'S bithibh gleusda mar a b' àbhaist,
Mar thràillean na deanaibh géilleadh
    Fhad 's bhios fuil 'nur féithean blàth;
Chuala mi a bhith leughadh
    Bharr air Reumair iomadh fàidh
Gu bheil curaidhnean aig Seumas
    Nì treubhantas an déidh bhith marbh.

Mosglaibh uile, gach duine,
    Anns a' chumasg bithibh garg,
Deòrsa 's Uilleam rinn ar guineadh,
    Siud na cuileinean gun dealbh;
Choidhch' cha toir a' chràin no 'n cullach
    Am-feast buinig ás ur n-arm—
'S fuadaichibh a' mhuc le gusgal
    Mar ri h-uirceinean thar fairg'.

'N Rìgh ga dhìdean is a dhìslean,
    Air an fhìor-fhuil gun robh sealbh,
Air crùn Alba o linn Raibeirt,

A réir nan eachdraidhean as fhearr;
Bidh cinn-fheadhna 's iad gu greadhnach
    Feadh do theaghlaich sa *Whitehall*—
Mar bhalla praise mun cuairt duit
    Cabhlach cruadalach air sàl.

Nuair a théid an crùn mun òigear
    'S lìonmhor mòr-fhear bhios mu d' shàil,
Seanalairean le 'n campa 'n ordugh
    'S iad gun sgur ag òl do shlàint';
Gloineachean gan lìonadh, 's bòlaibh,
    Le fìon òr-chostach na Spainnt
'S iad gan aiseag sìos air bordaibh
    Measg an t-slòigh, o làimh gu làimh.

'The Tax of Bones' (translated by Ronald Black)

But if Charles Stuart should come
    With him we'd gladly be going,
Our hearts and minds would leap as high
    As the white salmon in the burn;
With that, each garrison in the land
    Would be swiftly out of action,
And we'd be paid back for the plunder
    And the rape the Campbells committed.

The rule of law has disappeared here
    And is low in every place now,
We're being gored by those animals,
    Who'd love to swallow us completely—
But every rock hides hidden blades,
    And when they've been revealed to them
We will fill our drinking-cups
    And they will scream their way to death.

But this parliament that's torturing them
    Is a visible blister on the sons of the Gael,
Who have neither arms, nor clothes, nor hope,
    Nor even a scrap to cover their arse;
Although sweet revenge has eluded us,
    I still have faith that it is in store—

That we will prevail with our manly deeds
    While redcoats succumb to the tax of bones.

Awaken all you gallant heroes
    And be nimble like you used to be,
Don't surrender as if you were slaves
    As long as warm blood runs through your veins;
I heard that somebody had read
    Many a prophet as well as Rhymer*
Saying that James has mighty warriors
    Who will do great deeds even after death.

Awaken ye all, every one of ye,
    In the struggle be ferocious,
For George and William* who've wounded us
    Are unprepossessing puppies;
Never again will the sow or the boar
    Be triumphant over your army—
Just drive away the pig with its squealing
    Along with its piglets over the sea.

May the King be defended and his kin,
    May fortune favour the true royal blood
Of the Scottish crown from King Robert's time
    According to the best genealogies;
The Highland chiefs will exultingly mix
    Along with your family in Whitehall—
Like a wall of brass that's raised around you
    Is a hardy navy upon the sea.

When that young man receives the crown
    Many great men will be at your heel,
Generals with their camps in order
    Will forever be drinking your health;
Glasses will be filled, and bowls,
    With Spanish wine that's paid for in gold
And they will pass them down the tables
    Amongst the army, from hand to hand.

ADAM SKIRVING

(1719–1803)

———

BAPTIZED at Athelstaneford in Haddingtonshire, and educated at
Prestonkirk, Adam Skirving became a substantial farmer at Garleton
near Haddington. He is credited with two of the most popular songs
from the Jacobite rising of 1745: 'Tranent Muir' and 'Johnnie Cope'.
The latter song, included here, mocks the plight of General Sir John
Cope, the government commander at the battle of Prestonpans. The
song appeared in Johnson's *Scots Musical Museum* (1790) and, as two
separate versions, in Joseph Ritson's *Scotish Songs* (1794). It is not
obvious which—if any—of these may have been Skirving's creation
since Scotland's popular song culture encouraged collective composition long before a piece saw print (and often beyond that point). The
version printed here comes from James Hogg's canon-defining collection *The Jacobite Relics of Scotland* (1819, 1821).

———

'Johnnie Cope'

*The Jacobite Relics of Scotland; Being the Songs, Airs, and Legends, of the
Adherents to the House of Stuart*, ed. James Hogg, second series (Edinburgh:
William Blackwood; London: T. Cadell and W. Davies, 1821).

Cope sent a challenge frae Dunbar,
"Charlie, meet me an ye daur;
And I'll learn ye the art of war,
    If you'll meet me i' the morning."
    Hey, Johnnie Cope, are ye wauking yet?
    Or are your drums a-beating yet?
    If ye were wauking I would wait,
        To gang to the coals i' the morning.

When Charlie look'd the letter upon,
He drew his sword the scabbard from:
"Come, follow me, my merry merry men,

And we'll meet Johnnie Cope i' the morning."
    Hey, Johnnie Cope, &c.

"Now, Johnnie, be as gude's your word:
Come, let us try baith fire and sword,
And dinna rin like a frighted bird,
    That's chas'd frae its nest i' the morning."
    Hey, Johnnie Cope, &c.

When Johnnie Cope he heard o' this,
He thought it wadna be amiss,
To have a horse in readiness
    To flee awa i' the morning.
    Hey, Johnnie Cope, &c.

"Fy, now, Johnnie, get up and rin;
The Highland bagpipes make a din.
It's best to sleep in a hale skin,
    For 'twill be a bludie morning."
    Hey, Johnnie Cope, &c.

When Johnnie Cope to Dunbar came,
They speer'd at him, "Where's a' your men?"
"The deil confound me gin I ken,
    For I left them a' this morning."
    Hey, Johnnie Cope, &c.

"Now, Johnnie, troth ye wasna blate,
To come wi' news o' your ain defeat,
And leave your men in sic a strait,
    So early in the morning."
    Hey, Johnnie Cope, &c.

"I'faith," quo' Johnnie, "I got a fleg
Wi' their claymores and philabegs.
If I face them again, deil break my legs!
    So I wish you a gude-morning."
    Hey, Johnnie Cope, are ye wauking yet?
    Or are your drums a-beating yet?
    If ye were wauking I would wait,
        To gang to the coals i' the morning.

CAIRISTÌONA NICFHEARGHAIS / CHRISTIANA FERGUSSON

(FL. 1746)

━━

CHRISTIANA FERGUSSON (Cairistìona NicFhearghais) may have been born about 1720, but the date of her death is unknown. A blacksmith's daughter from the Ross-shire parish of Contin, she had married William Chisholm, who was said by John MacKenzie to have been tacksman (tenant) of Innis nan Ceann in Strathglass, but who is perhaps more likely to have been a landless cottar. 'Mo Rùn Geal Òg' is a song by a widow who had lost her husband at Culloden. There is some evidence that Chisholm was goaded by his wife into following his kinsmen to Culloden, where he fought well and was killed. Other than Culloden and Hanover, the only place-names mentioned in the song are Trotternish and Sleat in Skye, but this can be resolved by assuming that the poet fled to the safety of relatives in that island and made the song there.

━━

'Mo Rùn Geal Òg'

Cochruinneacha Taoghta de Shaothair nam Bard Gaëleach. A Choice Collection of the Works of the Highland Bards, Collected in the Highlands and Isles, ed. Alexander and Donald Stewart, 2 vols (Edinburgh: Charles Stewart, 1804).

> Och a Thearlaich òig Stiùbhairt,
>   Se do chùis rinn mo léireadh,
> Thug thu bhuam gach nì bh' agam
>   Ann an cogadh 'nad adhbhar;
> Cha chrodh is cha chairdean
>   Rinn mo chràdh, ach mo chéile
> On là dh'fhàg e mi 'm aonar
>   Gun sìon san t-saoghal ach léine,
>   Mo rùn geal òg.

Có nis thogas an claidheamh
   No nì a' chathair a lìonadh
'S gann gur e a th' air m' aire
   O nach maireann mo chiadghràdh;
Ach ciamar gheibhinn o m' nàdar
   A bhith 'g àicheadh nas miann leam
'S mo thogradh cho làidir
   Bhith cur an àite mo rìgh mhath
     Mo rùn geal òg?

Bu tu 'm fear slinneanach, leathann,
   Bu chaoile meadhain 's bu dealbhaich:
Cha bu tàillear gun eòlas
   Dhèanadh còta math geàrr dhut
No dhèanadh dhut triubhas
   Gun bhith cumhang, no gann dhut—
Mar ghealbhradain do chosan
   Le d' gheàrr-osan mu d' chalpa,
     Mo rùn geal òg.

Bu tu 'm fear mór bu mhath cumachd
   O d' mhullach gu d' bhrògan,
Bha do shlios mar an eala
   'S blas na meal' air do phògan;
T' fhalt dualach donn lurach
   Mu do mhuineal an òrdagh
'S e gu cama-lubach cuimir
   'S gach aon toirt urram d'a bhòidhchead,
     Mo rùn geal òg.

Bu tu iasgair na h-abhann,
   'S tric a thathaich thu fhéin i,
Agus sealgair a' mhunaidh,
   Bhiodh do ghunn' air dheagh ghleusadh;
Bu bhinn leam tabhann do chuilean
   Bheireadh fuil air mac éilde,
Ás do làimh bu mhór m' earbsa—
   Gur tric a mharbh thu le chéil' iad,
     Mo rùn geal òg.

Bu tu pòiteir na dibhe
   'N àm suidhe 's taigh òsta—
Ge b'e dh'òladh, 's tu phàigheadh

Ged thuiteadh càch mu na bòrdaibh;
Bhith air mhisg chan e b' fhiù leat,
   'S cha do dh'ionnsaich thu òg i,
'S cha do dh'iarr thu riamh mùthadh
   Air cùl do mhnà pòsta,
      Mo rùn geal òg.

Bha mi greis ann am barail
   Gum bu mhaireann mo chéile
'S gun tigeadh tu dhachaigh
   Le aighear 's le faoilteachd;
Ach tha 'n t-àm air dol thairis
   'S chan fhaic mi fear t' eugais,
'S gus an cuir iad mi 's talamh
   Cha dealaich do ghaol rium,
      Mo rùn geal òg.

Och is och, gur mi Bochdag
   'S mi làn osnaich an comhnaidh,
Chaill mi dùil ri thu thighinn,
   Thuit mo chridhe gu dòrtadh—
Cha tog fidheall no clàrsach,
   Pìob no tàileasg no ceòl mi;
Nis o chuir iad thu 'n tasgaidh,
   Cha dùisg caidreabh dhaoin' òg' mi,
      Mo rùn geal òg.

Gura mis' th' air mo sgaradh,
   'S ged a chanam, cha bhreug e:
Chaidh mo shùgradh gu sileadh
   O nach pillear bhon eug thu;
Fear do chéille 's do thuigse
   Cha robh furast' r'a fheutainn—
'S cha do sheas an Cùil Lodair
   Fear do choltais bu tréine,
      Mo rùn geal òg.

'S iomadh baintighearna phrìseil
   Le'n sìoda 's le'n sròltaibh
Do'n robh mise 'm chùis fharmaid
   Chionns gun tairgeadh tu pòg dhomh;
Ged a bhithinn cho sealbhmhor
   'S gum bu leam airgead Hanòbhair,

Bheirinn cnac anns na h-àithntean
    Nan cumadh càch bhuam do phògan,
        Mo rùn geal òg.

'S iomadh bean a bha brònach
    Eadar Tròndairnis is Sléibhte,
'S iomadh té bha 'na bantraich
    Nach d'fhuair samhla do m' chéile;
Bha mise làn sòlais
    Fhads bu bheò sinn le chéile,
Ach a-nis o'n a dh'fhalbh thu
    Cha chùis fharmaid mi fhéin daibh,
        Mo rùn geal òg.

'My Heart's Youthful Prize' (translated by Ronald Black)

Och young Charles Edward Stuart,
    Your cause has destroyed me,
You've taken all I possessed
    For fighting your war;
It's not for cattle nor kinsfolk
    I'm distraught, but my husband
Since he left me bereft
    With no world save a shirt,
        My heart's youthful prize.

Who will now lift the sword
    Or cause the throne to be filled
Is scarce my concern
    Since my first love's been killed;
But how could I find in my nature
    To deny what I want
When my desire is so strong
    To put in place of my sovereign
        My heart's youthful prize?

You were a broad man, big-shouldered,
    Of slimmest waist, and most shapely:
It took an experienced tailor

To make you a short coat that fitted
Or to make you some trews
    That wouldn't be tight, or inadequate—
Like bright salmon your legs
    With short hose round your calves,
        My heart's youthful prize.

You were a big well-made man
    From your crown to your shoes,
Your side like the swan's
    With honey's taste on your kisses;
Your wavy hair brown and lovely
    All arranged round your neck
In neat curly tresses
    Admired by all for its beauty,
        My heart's youthful prize.

You were the fisher of the river,
    You frequented it often,
While as hunter of the moor
    Well primed was your gun;
I loved the bark of your whelps
    Who would blood a hind's son,
I fully trusted your hand—
    You often shot them together,
        My heart's youthful prize.

You were the man for the drink
    In time of sitting in tavern—
Whoever drank, you would pay
    When others fell round the tables;
You cared not for drunkenness,
    You learned it not in your youth,
And you never philandered
    Behind your wife's back,
        My heart's youthful prize.

I believed for a while
    That my husband was living
And that you would come home
    With a joke and a greeting;
But the time has gone past
    And I don't see your likeness—

But until I am buried
   I will love you for ever,
      My heart's youthful prize.

Och, my name's 'Little Wretch'
   And I'm constantly sighing,
I've lost hope of your coming,
   My heart's fallen to weeping—
No harp or fiddle will lift me,
   No pipe, chess or music;
Now that they've buried you,
   Young folk's banter can't rouse me,
      My heart's youthful prize.

I've been torn apart,
   And though I say it, it's true:
My flirting's turned into tears
   Since death won't release you;
A man of your sense and wisdom
   Wasn't easy to find—
And there stood not at Culloden
   A braver man in your mould,
      My heart's youthful prize.

Many well-to-do women
   With their silk and their satins
Would behold me with envy
   When you gave me a kiss;
Were I lucky enough
   To have Hanover's money,
I'd still have breached the commandments
   Had others kept you from kissing me,
      My heart's youthful prize.

Many women were mournful
   From Trotternish to Sleat,
Many wives became widows
   Whose men were nothing to mine;
I was full of contentment
   While we lived together,
But now since you're gone
   I've no cause to be envied,
      My heart's youthful prize.

TOBIAS SMOLLETT

(1721–1771)

—

HAILING from Dunbartonshire, Tobias Smollett wrote prose and verse across multiple genres. Today he is best known as the author of the picaresque novels *The Adventures of Roderick Random* (1748), *The Adventures of Peregrine Pickle* (1751), and *The Expedition of Humphry Clinker* (1771). But 'The Tears of Scotland' in particular was a popular poem. Outwardly a lament for Scotland after the decisive battle of Culloden, the piece was ambiguous enough to find its way into Jacobite and Hanoverian anthologies alike. 'Ode to Leven-Water', meanwhile, captures Smollett's talent for description. The following poems come from a handsome posthumous collection of Smollett's works titled *Plays and Poems* (1777).

—

'The Tears of Scotland. Written in the Year 1746'

Plays and Poems (London: T. Evans and R. Baldwin, 1777).

I

Mourn, hapless Caledonia, mourn
Thy banish'd peace, thy laurels torn!
Thy sons, for valour long renown'd,
Lie slaughter'd on their native ground;
Thy hospitable roofs no more,
Invite the stranger to the door;
In smoaky ruins sunk they lie,
The monuments of cruelty.

II

The wretched owner sees afar
His all become they prey of war;
Bethinks him of his babes and wife,
Then smites his breast, and curses life.

Thy swains are famish'd on the rocks,
Where once they fed their wanton flocks:
Thy ravish'd virgins shriek in vain;
Thy infants perish on the plain.

III

What boots it then, in every clime,
Thro' the wide spreading waste of time,
Thy martial glory, crown'd with praise,
Still shone with undiminish'd blaze?
Thy tow'ring spirit now is broke,
Thy neck is bended to the yoke.
What foreign arms could never quell,
By civil rage, and rancour fell.

IV

The rural pipe, and merry lay
No more shall chear the happy day:
No social scenes of gay delight
Beguile the dreary winter night:
No strains, but those of sorrow flow,
And nought be heard but sounds of woe,
While the pale phantoms of the slain
Glide nightly o'er the silent plain.

V

O baneful cause, oh, fatal morn,
Accurs'd to ages yet unborn!
The sons, against their fathers stood,
The parent shed his children's blood.
Yet, when the rage of battle ceas'd,
The victor's soul was not appeased:
The naked and forlorn must feel
Devouring flames, and murd'ring steel!

VI

The pious mother doom'd to death,
Forsaken wanders o'er the heath,
The bleak wind whistles round her head,

Her helpless orphans cry for bread;
Bereft of shelter, food, and friend,
She views the shades of night descend,
And stretch'd beneath the inclement skies,
Weeps o'er her tender babes and dies.

VII

While the warm blood bedews my veins,
And unimpair'd remembrance reigns,
Resentment of my country's fate,
Within my filial breast shall beat;
And, spite of her insulting foe,
My sympathizing verse shall flow:
"Mourn, hapless Caledonia, mourn
Thy banish'd peace, thy laurels torn."

'Ode to Leven-Water'

On Leven's banks, while free to rove,
And tune the rural pipe to love;
I envied not the happiest swain
That ever trod the Arcadian plain.
        Pure stream! in whose transparent wave
My youthful limbs I wont to lave;
No torrents stain thy limpid source;
No rocks impede thy dimpling course,
That sweetly warbles o'er its bed,
With white, round, polished pebbles spread;
While, lightly pois'd, the scaly brood
In myriads cleave thy chrystal flood;
The springing trout in speckled pride,
The salmon, monarch of the tide;
The ruthless pike, intent on war;
The silver eel, and motled par.
Devolving from thy parent lake,
A charming maze thy waters make,
By bowers of birch, and groves of pine,
And edges flower'd with eglantine.
        Still on thy banks so gayly green,
May num'rous herds and flocks be seen,

And lasses chanting o'er the pail,
And shepherds piping in the dale,
And ancient faith that knows no guile,
And industry imbrown'd with toil,
And hearts resolv'd, and hands prepar'd,
The blessings they enjoy to guard.

WILLIAM WILKIE

(1721–1772)

——

KNOWN as the Scottish Homer, William Wilkie was born in Linlithgowshire and educated at Edinburgh. In 1757 he produced perhaps his most accomplished work, the *Epigoniad*, which deals with the Epigoni, the sons of seven heroes who fought against Thebes. His other publications include *Moral Fables in Verse* (1768). In 1756 he became a Church minister at Ratho in Midlothian, and, not long after, was appointed Professor of Natural Philosophy at the University of St Andrews (in 1759). 'A Dream. In the Manner of Spenser' appeared in the 1759 revised edition of the *Epigoniad*. A persistent influence on Scottish poets since the sixteenth century, Spenser exerted a powerful pull over Wilkie's aesthetics, form and content included. Wilkie in turn influenced important poets that followed in his stead, his former student Robert Fergusson among them.

——

'A Dream. In the Manner of Spenser'

The Epigoniad. A Poem. In Nine Books, 2nd edn (London: A. Millar; Edinburgh: A. Kincaid and J. Bell, 1759).

I

One ev'ning as by pleasant Forth I stray'd,
　　In pensive mood, and meditated still
On poets learned toil, with scorn repaid
　　By Envy's bitter spite, and want of skill;
　　A cave I found, which open'd in a hill.
The floor was sand, with various shells yblended,
　　Through which, in slow meanders, crept a rill;
The roof, by Nature's cunning slight suspended:
Thither my steps I turn'd, and there my journey ended.

II

Upon the ground my listless limbs I laid,
　　Lull'd by the murmur of the passing stream:

Then sleep, soft stealing, did my eyes invade;
   And waking thought, soon ended in a dream.
   Transported to a region I did seem,
Which with Thessalian Tempe might compare;
   Of verdant shade compos'd, and wat'ry gleam:
Not even Valdarno, thought so passing fair,
Might match this pleasant land, in all perfections rare.

III

One, like a hoary palmer, near a brook,
   Under an arbor, seated did appear;
A shepherd swain, attending, held a book,
   And seem'd to read therein that he mote hear.
   From curiosity I stepped near;
But ere I reach'd the place where they did sit,
   The whisp'ring breezes wafted to my ear
The sound of rhymes which I myself had writ:
Rhymes much, alas, too mean, for such a judge unfit.

IV

For him he seem'd who sung Achilles' rage,
   In lofty numbers that shall never die,
And wise Ulysses' tedious pilgrimage,
   So long the sport of sharp adversity:
   The praises of his merit, Fame on high,
With her shrill trump, for ever loud doth sound;
   With him no bard, for excellence, can vie,
Of all that late or ancient e'er were found;
So much he doth surpass ev'n bards the most renown'd.

V

The shepherd swain invited me to come
   Up to the arbor where they seated were;
For Homer call'd me: much I fear'd the doom
   Which such a judge seem'd ready to declare.
   As I approach'd, with meikle dread and care,
He thus address'd me: Sir, the cause explain
   Why all your story here is told so bare?
Few circumstances mix'd of various grain;
Such, surely, much enrich and raise a poet's strain.

VI

Certes, quoth I, the critics are the cause
    Of this, and many other mischiefs more;
Who tie the Muses to such rigid laws,
    That all their songs are frivolous and poor.
    They cannot now, as oft they did before,
Ere pow'rful prejudice had clipt their wings,
    Nature's domain with boundless flight explore,
And traffick freely in her precious things:
Each bard now fears the rod, and trembles while he sings.

VII

Though Shakespear, still disdaining narrow rules,
    His bosom fill'd with Nature's sacred fire,
Broke all the cobweb limits fix'd by fools,
    And left the world to blame him and admire.
    Yet his reward few mortals would desire;
For, of his learned toil, the only meed
    That ever I could find he did acquire,
Is that our dull, degenerate, age of lead,
Says that he wrote by chance, and that he scarce could read.

VIII

I ween, quoth he, that poets are to blame
    When they submit to critics tyranny:
For learned wights there is no greater shame,
    Than blindly with their dictates to comply.
    Who ever taught the eagle how to fly,
Whose wit did e'er his airy tract define,
    When with free wing he claims his native sky,
Say, will he steer his course by rule and line?
Certes, he'd scorn the bounds that would his flight confine.

IX

Not that the Muses' art is void of rules:
    Many there are, I wot, and stricter far,
Than those which pedants dictate from the schools,
    Who wage with wit and taste eternal war:
    For foggy ignorance their flight doth mar;
Nor can their low conception ever reach

To what dame Nature, crown'd with many a star,
Explains to such as know her learned speech;
But few can comprehend the lessons she doth teach.

X

As many as the stars that gild the sky,
    As many as the flow'rs that paint the ground,
In number like the insect tribes that fly,
    The various forms of beauty still are found;
    That with strict limits no man may them bound,
And say that this, and this alone, is right:
    Experience soon such rashness would confound,
And make its folly obvious as the light;
For such presumption sure becomes not mortal wight.

XI

Therefore each bard should freely entertain
    The hints which pleasing fancy gives at will;
Nor curb her sallies with too strict a rein,
    Nature subjecting to her hand-maid Skill:
    And you yourself in this have done but ill;
With many more, who have not comprehended
    That Genius, crampt, will rarely mount the hill,
Whose forked summit with the clouds is blended:
Therefore, when next you write, let this defect be mended.

XII

But, like a friend, who candidly reproves
    For faults and errors which he doth espy,
Each vice he freely marks; yet always loves
    To mingle favor with severity.
    Certes, quoth he, I cannot well deny,
That you in many things may hope to please:
    You force a barbarous northern tongue to ply,
And bend it to your purposes with ease;
Tho' rough as Albion's rocks, and hoarser than her seas.

XIII

Nor are your tales, I wot, so loosely yok'd,
    As those which Colin Clout did tell before;

Nor with description crouded so, and choak'd,
  Which, thinly spread, will always please the more.
  Colin, I wot, was rich in Nature's store;
More rich than you, had more than he could use:
  But mad Orlando taught him had his lore;
Whose flights, at random, oft misled his muse:
To follow such a guide, few prudent men would chuse.

XIV

Me you have follow'd: Nature was my guide;
  To this the merit of your verse is owing:
And know for certain, let it check your pride,
  That all you boast of is of my bestowing.
  The flow'rs I see, thro' all your garden blowing,
Are mine; most part, at least: I might demand,
  Might claim them, as a crop of my own sowing,
And leave but few, thin scatter'd o'er the land:
A claim so just, I wot, you could not well withstand.

XV

Certes, quoth I, that justice were full hard,
  Which me alone would sentence to restore;
When many a learned sage, and many a bard,
  Are equally your debtors, or much more.
  Let Tityrus himself produce his store,
Take what is thine, but little will remain:
  Little, I wot, and that indebted sore
To Ascra's bard, and Arethusa's swain;
And others too beside, who lent him many a strain.

XVI

Nor could the modern bards afford to pay,
  Whose songs exult the champions of the Cross:
Take from each hoard thy sterling gold away,
  And little will remain but worthless dross.
  Not bards alone could ill support the loss;
But sages too, whose theft suspicion shunn'd:
  E'en that sly Greek, who steals and hides so close,
Were half a bankrupt, if he should refund.
While these are all forborn, shall I alone be dunn'd.

XVII

He smil'd; and from his wreath, which well could spare
    Such boon, the wreath with which his locks were clad,
Pluck'd a few leaves to hide my temples bare;
    The present I receiv'd with heart full glad.
    Henceforth, quoth I, I never will be sad;
For now I shall obtain my share of fame:
    Nor will licentious wit, or envy bad,
With bitter taunts, my verses dare to blame:
This garland shall protect them, and exalt my name.

XVIII

But dreams are short; for as I thought to lay
    My limbs, at ease, upon the flow'ry ground,
And drink, with greedy ear, what he might say,
    As murm'ring waters sweet, or music's sound,
    My sleep departed; and I, waking, found
Myself again by Fortha's pleasant stream.
    Homewards I stepp'd, in meditation drown'd,
Reflecting on the meaning of my dream;
Which let each wight interpret as him best doth seem.

THOMAS BLACKLOCK

(1721–1791)

———

THE Reverend Thomas Blacklock, of Annan in Dumfriesshire, loved literature from a young age. At the University of Edinburgh he studied philosophy and then divinity, while also pursuing interests in French, Greek, Latin, and Italian. Blacklock's first book, *Poems on Several Occasions*, was published in Glasgow in 1746, and contains juvenile pieces as well as more recent fare on the Jacobite rising of 1745. David Hume and Joseph Spence were early and active admirers. In turn, Blacklock supported his younger contemporaries, including Burns and Scott, who both credit him with influencing important career decisions. In addition to fellow poets, Blacklock provided a powerful voice in the advocacy of improved education for visually impaired children—the cause mattered to him: he lost his eyesight in early infancy. Throughout his life, Blacklock produced poems, reviews, articles, sermons, translations, and other prose works, much of which remains in manuscript.

———

'A Pastoral Song'

Poems, 3rd edn (London: R. and J. Dodsley, 1756).

> Sandy, the gay, the blooming swain,
>   Had lang frae love been free;
> Lang made ilk heart that fill'd the plain
>   Dance quick with harmless glee.
>
> As blythsome lambs that scour the green,
>   His mind was unconstrain'd;
> Nae face could ever fix his een,
>   Nae sang his ear detain'd.
>
> Ah! luckless youth! a short-liv'd joy
>   Thy cruel fates decree:
> Fell tods shall on thy lambkins prey,
>   And love mair fell on thee.

'Twas e'er the sun exhal'd the dew,
    Ae morn of chearful May,
Forth Girzy walk'd, the flow'rs to view,
    A flow'r mair sweet than they!

Like sun-beams sheen her waving locks;
    Her een like stars were bright;
The rose lent blushes to her cheek;
    The lily purest white.

Jimp was her waist, like some tall pine
    That keeps the woods in awe;
Her limbs like iv'ry columns turn'd,
    Her breasts like hills of snaw.

Her robe around her loosely thrown,
    Gave to the shepherd's een
What fearless innocence would show;
    The rest was all unseen.

He fix'd his look, he sigh'd, he quak'd,
    His colour went and came;
Dark grew his een, his ears resound,
    His breast was all on flame.

Nae mair yon glen repeats his sang,
    He jokes, and smiles nae mair;
Unplaited now his cravat hung,
    Undrest his chesnut hair.

To him how lang the shortest night!
    How dark the brightest day!
Till, with the slow consuming fire,
    His life was worn away.

Far, far frae shepherds and their flocks,
    Opprest with care, he lean'd;
And, in a mirky, beachen shade;
    To hills and dales thus plean'd:

At length, my wayward heart, return,
    Too far, alas! astray;
Say, whence you caught that bitter smart,
    Which works me such decay.

Ay me! 'twas Love, 'twas Girzy's charms,
    That first began my woes;
Could he sae saft, or she sae fair,
    Prove such relentless foes?

Fierce winter nips the sweetest flower;
    Keen lightning rives the tree;
Bleak mildew taints the fairest crop,
    And love has blasted me.

Sagacious hounds the foxes chace;
    The tender lambkins they;
Lambs follow close their mother ewes,
    And ewes the blooms of May.

Sith a' that live, with a' their might,
    Some dear delight pursue;
Cease, ruthless maid! to scorn the heart
    That only pants for you.

Alas! for griefs to her unken'd,
    What pity can I gain?
And should she ken, yet love refuse,
    Could that redress my pain?

Come, death, my wan, my frozen bride,
    Ah! close those wearied eyes:
But death the happy still pursues,
    Still from the wretched flies.

Could wealth avail; what wealth is mine
    Her high-born mind to bend?
Her's are those wide delightful plains,
    And her's the flocks I tend.

What tho', whene'er I tun'd my pipe,
    Glad fairies heard the sound,
And, clad in freshest April green,
    Aft tript the circle round:

Break, landward clown, thy dinsome reed,
    And brag thy skill nae mair:
Can aught that gies na Girzy joy,
    Be worth thy lightest care?

Adieu! ye harmless sportive flocks!
  Who now your lives shall guard?
Adieu! my faithful dog, who oft
  The pleasing vigil shar'd:

Adieu, ye plains, and light, anes sweet,
  Now painful to my view:
Adieu to life; and thou, mair dear,
  Who caus'd my death; adieu!

JOHN SKINNER

(1721–1807)

THE songwriter and ecclesiastical historian Reverend John Skinner was born in Aberdeenshire. From 1739 he worked as assistant teacher in Monymusk, where some of his early poetry was written, and soon after that a family tutor in Shetland. Ordained in 1742, he was appointed to Longside, near Peterhead, where he acted as the minister for the rest of his life. In 1746 the episcopal chapel at Longside was destroyed by government soldiers, even though Skinner opposed Jacobitism. Horrified, Skinner wrote a series of scathing satires on the event. During the 1750s and 1760s Skinner enjoyed increasing influence due to his steady stream of prose, much of which addressed ecclesiastical controversy. A nimble verse-maker in Latin, English, and Scots, Skinner championed the literary use of northeast Scots. He even supplied materials for *The Scots Musical Museum*. Burns was especially fond of Skinner's song 'Tullochgorum'.

'Tullochgorum'

Amusements of Leisure Hours: or Poetical Pieces, Chiefly in the Scottish Dialect (Edinburgh: John Moir, 1809).

I

> Come gi'e's a sang, Montgomery cry'd,
> And lay your disputes all aside,
> What signifies't for folks to chide
>   For what was done before them:
> Let Whig and Tory all agree,
>   Whig and Tory, Whig and Tory,
>   Let Whig and Tory all agree,
>   To drop their Whig-mig-morum;
> Let Whig and Tory all agree
> To spend the night wi' mirth and glee,

And cheerful sing alang wi' me
      The Reel o' Tullochgorum.

II

O' Tullochgorum's my delight,
It gars us a' in ane unite,
And ony sumph that keeps a spite,
      In conscience I abhor him:
For blythe and cheerie we'll be a',
   Blythe and cheerie, blythe and cheerie,
   Blythe and cheerie we'll be a',
      And make a happy quorum,
For blythe and cheerie we'll be a'
As lang as we hae breath to draw,
And dance till we be like to fa',
      The Reel o' Tullochgorum.

III

What needs there be sae great a fraise
Wi' dringing dull Italian lays,
I wadna gie our ain Strathspeys
      For half a hunder score o' them;
They're dowf and dowie at the best,
   Dowf and dowie, dowf and dowie,
   Dowf and dowie at the best,
      Wi' a' their variorum;
They're dowf and dowie at the best,
Their *allegros* and a' the rest,
They canna' please a Scottish taste
      Compar'd wi' Tullochgorum.

IV

Let warldly worms their minds oppress
Wi' fears of want and double cess,
And sullen sots themsells distress
      Wi' keeping up decorum:
Shall we sae sour and sulky sit,
   Sour and sulky, sour and sulky,
   Sour and sulky shall we sit,
      Like auld philosophorum!

Shall we sae sour and sulky sit,
Wi' neither sense, nor mirth, nor wit,
Nor ever try to shake a fit
      To th' Reel o' Tullochgorum?

V

May choicest blessings ay attend
Each honest, open hearted friend,
And calm and quiet be his end,
      And a' that's good watch o'er him;
May peace and plenty be his lot,
  Peace and plenty, peace and plenty,
  Peace and plenty be his lot,
      And dainties a great store o' them;
May peace and plenty be his lot,
Unstain'd by any vicious spot,
And may he never want a groat,
      That's fond o' Tullochgorum!

VI

But for the sullen frumpish fool,
That loves to be oppression's tool,
May envy gnaw his rotten soul,
      And discontent devour him;
May dool and sorrow be his chance,
  Dool and sorrow, dool and sorrow,
  Dool and sorrow be his chance,
      And nane say, wae's me for him!
May dool and sorrow be his chance,
Wi' a' the ills that come frae *France*,
Wha e'er he be that winna dance
      The Reel o' Tullochgorum.

LACHLANN MAC A' PHEARSAIN /
LACHLAN MACPHERSON

(C.1723–C.1767)

———

LACHLAN MACPHERSON of Strathmashie (the Younger), was a distinguished member of the Highland 'tacksman' class. That is to say, his family did not own their land, but had held it for generations from their chief, MacPherson of Cluny, on the basis that they and their sub-tenants would provide military aid when required. Strathmashie was an intelligent, well-read man who gained fame in the 1760s for assisting James Macpherson with his Ossianic pseudo-translations. He also sang to his own fiddle accompaniment, portraying himself toiling or carousing side by side with his people, and indulged in endearing bouts of self-mockery. Strathmashie and his father had been out for Prince Charles in the '45, serving as officers in Cluny's regiment, and it is entirely natural that he should resent Hardwicke's Disclothing Act of 1746. The first few verses of 'A' Bhriogais Lachdann' concentrate on the difficulties presented by breeches in the area of the crotch, and the last two evoke memories of the march from Derby in December 1745, during which the MacPhersons distinguished themselves at Clifton.

———

'A' Bhriogais Lachdann'

Translator's transcription

'S coma leam a' bhriogais lachdann—
B' annsa 'm féile beag 's am breacan;
'S beag a ghabh mi riamh de thlachd
  Den fhasan a bh' aig clann nan Gall.

Cha chléirichean 's chan easbaigean
Chum a bharr an t-Seisein mi,
Ach a' bhriogais leibideach
  Nach deanadh anns na preasan clann!

Ged tha bhriogais mìothlachdar,
Gur feumail anns na crìochan i—

Gach fear a bhios ri dìolanas
         Gun toir i strìochdadh air gun taing.

Ach cuiribh air na mnathan i!
Sann orr' as fhearr a laigheas i—
Gur sgiobalt' air feadh taighe i
         'S b'e 'n ceòl am faighinn innt' a' danns.

Gur mise b' anns an éisteachd
'S na mnathan 'g ràdh ri chéile
Gum b' fhearr leo orra fhéin i
         Na bhith ceusadh an fhir chaim!

Cha mhath gu dìreadh bruthaich i
'S chan fhiach leinn thun an t-siubhail i,
'S chan eil mi idir buidheach
         Air an fhear a ludhaig i bhith ann.

Cha mhath an t-éideadh idir i
Nuair théid sinn anns an uisge leatha—
Nuair lùbas i mu'r n-iosgaidean
         Gun toir i niosgaid air gach ball.

A' bhriogais dhubh gun sianadh
A chuir ás an t-aodach briagha
Bhiodh fosgailt air ar bialaibh
         'S nach iarradh a chumail teann.

Chuir i mach do Shasann sinn
Le surd a bhitheadh sgairteil oirnn,
'S leig i rithist dhachaigh sinn
         Gun fhiù a' chaiptein air ar ceann.

Ged thug iad dhuinn san fhasan i,
Chan eil i idir taitneach leinn;
'S truagh, a Rìgh, nach robh e tachdt'—
         Am fear a thug an t-Achd a-nall.

'The Hodden Breeks' (translated by Ronald Black)

I much dislike the hodden breeks—
Better filabeg and plaid;
I never took much pleasure in
         That fashion of the Lowland folk.

It's not ministers nor bishops
Who've kept the Session off my back,
But those irritating breeches
    That make no babies in the bushes!

Though the breeks are tasteless, coarse,
They're quite useful hereabouts—
They force each man in search of skirt
    To give it up without a fight.

But why not put them on the girls?
They will fit them perfectly—
They'll be quicker round the house
    And fun to wear when dancing.

It so happened that I overheard
The women saying to each other
They'd rather put them on themselves
    Than have men's willies crucified.

They're no good for climbing hills
And little use for travelling,
And I'm not well inclined at all
    To the man who introduced them.

They're not suitable for wearing
When we enter water in them—
When they wrap around our thighs
    They bring out sores on every limb.

The damned unhallowed breeks
That replaced the gorgeous clothes
Which gave us empty space in front
    And never needed to be tightened.

Those clothes brought us into England
With sky-high morale and energy,
Then they brought us home again
    Without even a captain at our head.

Although they gave us breeks to wear,
We don't think much of them at all;
Alas, O Lord, that no one choked him—
    That man who introduced the Act.*

JANET GRAHAM

(1723–1805)

A NATIVE of Annandale, Dumfriesshire, Janet Graham lived in Dumfries for a time and latterly in Edinburgh; like many genteel maiden ladies of the period she stayed with different families. Her only work to have survived in print is the humorous song 'Wayward Wife', which appeared, in slightly abbreviated form, in David Herd's seminal *Ancient and Modern Scottish Songs* (1776), as well as in later anthologies, such as Allan Cunningham's *The Songs of Scotland* (1825). A curious example of the wedlock advice genre, 'Wayward Wife' showcases Graham's unashamedly contrarian sense of humour.

'Wayward Wife'

Ancient and Modern Scottish Songs, Heroic Ballads, Etc., ed. David Herd, 2 vols (Edinburgh: James Dickson and Charles Elliot, 1776).

> Alas! my son, you little know,
> The sorrows that from wedlock flow.
> Farewell to every day of ease,
> When you've gotten a wife to please:
>> *Sae bide you yet, and bide you yet,*
>> *You little ken what's to betide you yet,*
>> *The half of that will gain you yet,*
>> *If a wayward wife obtain you yet.*
>
> [Your hopes are high, your wisdom small,
> Woe has not had you in its thrall;]
> The black cow on your foot ne'er trod,
> Which gars you sing alang the road,
>> *Sae bide you yet*, &c.
>
> Sometimes the rock, sometimes the reel,
> Or some piece of the spinning wheel,
> She will drive at ye wi' good will,

And then she'll send you to the deil.
  Sae bide you yet, &c.

When I like you was young and free,
I valu'd not the proudest she;
Like you I vainly boasted then,
That men alone were born to reign;
  But bide you yet, &c.

Great Hercules and Samson too,
Were stronger men than I or you;
Yet they were baffled by their dears,
And felt the distaff and the sheers;
  Sae bide you yet, &c.

Stout gates of brass, and well-built walls,
Are proof 'gainst swords and cannon-balls,
But nought is found by sea or land,
That can a wayward wife withstand:
  Sae bide you yet, &c.

DONNCHADH BÀN MAC AN T-SAOIR / DUNCAN BAN MACINTYRE

(1724–1812)

———

HAILING from the southern shore of Loch Tulla in Argyll, Duncan Ban Macintyre (Donnchadh Bàn Mac an t-Saoir) displayed an early adeptness in verse-making across different genres. Macintyre had made the acquaintance of James Stewart, the Killin minister who translated the *New Testament* into Gaelic (in 1767), and his son, John, who was to see the poet's first edition of his poems through the press in 1768. Donald MacNicol, the minister of Lismore, meanwhile, had already written down many of Macintyre's poems as the author was illiterate. These friends also introduced Macintyre to the works of another leading Gaelic poet, Alastair, mac Mhaighstir Alastair, we might presume, since there are clear signs of their influence on the younger poet. During the period 1746–66, Macintyre served as forester (gamekeeper) in three of the Earl of Breadalbane's deer-forests—*Coire a' Cheathaich* (the 'Misty Corrie' above Glen Lochay), Beinn Dobhrain, and Glen Etive—probably in that order. Macintyre has always been the best loved of the Gaelic poets, owing, no doubt, to the optimistic note with which many of his poems end.

———

'Seachran Seilge'

Translator's transcription

Chunnaic mi 'n damh donn 's na h-éildean
Dìreadh a' bhealaich le chéile;
Chunnaic mi 'n damh donn 's na h-éildean.

'S mi teàrnadh á Coir' a' Cheathaich,
'S mór mo mhìghean 's mi gun aighear,
Siubhal frìthe ré an latha:
Thilg mi 'n spraigh nach d'rinn feum dhomh.

Ged tha bacadh air na h-armaibh,
Ghléidh mi 'n Spàinteach chun na sealga,
Ged a rinn i orm de chearbaich'
Nach do mharbh i mac na h-éilde.

Nuair a dh'éirich mi sa mhadainn,
Chuir mi innte fùdar Ghlascho,
Peileir teann, is trì puist Shas'nach,
Cuifean asgairt air a dhéidh sin.

Bha 'n spor ùr an déis a breacadh,
Chuir mi ùille ris an acainn;
Eagal drùchd bha mùdan craicinn
Cumail fasgaidh air mo chéile.

Laigh an eilid air an fhuaran,
Chaidh mi farasta mun cuairt dhith,
Leig mi 'n deannal ud m'a tuairme—
Leam as cruaidh gun d'rinn i éirigh.

Ràinig mise taobh na bruaiche
'S chost mi rithe mo chuid luaidhe,
'S nuair a shaoil mi i bhith buailte,
Sin an uair a b' àird' a leum i.

'S muladach bhith siubhal frìthe
Ri là gaoithe 's uisge 's dìle,
'S òrdugh teann ag iarraidh sìdhne
Cur nan gìomanach 'nan éiginn.

'S mithich teàrnadh do na gleannaibh
On tha gruamaich' air na beannaibh
'S ceathach dùinte mu na meallaibh
A' cur dalladh air ar léirsinn.

Bidh sinn beò an dòchas ra-mhath
Gum bi chùis nas fheàrr an t-ath-lath',
Gum bi gaoth, is grian, is talamh
Mar as math leinn air na sléibhtibh.

Bidh an luaidhe ghlas 'na deannaibh,
Siubhal réidh aig conaibh seanga
'S an damh donn a' sileadh fala
'S àbhachd aig na fearaibh gleusta.

'The Abortive Hunt' (translated by Ronald Black)

I've seen the brown stag and the hinds
Climbing up the pass together;
I've seen the brown stag and the hinds.

As I come down from Misty Corrie,
I feel distressed, and much disheartened—
I scoured the hillsides all day long,
   Released the charge, and it misfired.

Though weapons are against the law,
I kept my Spanish gun for hunting,
Yet still she messed up on her duty
   And failed to kill the hind's son.

When I got out of bed this morning,
I filled her up with Glasgow powder,
Tight-fitting ball, three English slugs,
   All packed in with a wad of tow.

The fresh flint had just been roughened,
The mechanism lubricated,
And from the dew I kept my spouse
   Protected by a leather cover.

The hind lay down beside the spring,
So I went carefully around her
And fired the charge in her direction—
   I am annoyed that up she jumped.

I moved to down beside the brae
And gave her all the lead I had,
Then when I thought that she'd been hit,
   That was when she jumped the highest.

It's wretched, wandering the hills
On days of wind and rain and deluge,
With strict demands for venison
   Driving foresters demented.

It's time to go down to the glens
As the hills are turning gloomy,
With mist enveloping the summits
   And zero visibility.

But we will live in earnest hope
Of a better day tomorrow,
With the wind, and sun, and earth
    As we like them on the mountains.

Grey lead will hasten to its target
And lean hounds will run unhindered
While the brown stag sheds his blood
    And skilful men enjoy their sport.

'Do a Mhusg, air dha gabhail ann an Geàrd Bhaile Dhùn Éideann'

'S iomadh car a dh'fhaodas tighinn air na fearaibh,
'S theag' gun gabh iad gaol air an té nach fhaigh iad;
Thug mi fichead bliadhna don chiad té ghabh mi,
'S chuir i rithist cùl rium is bha mi falamh.

Is thàinig mi Dhùn Éideann a dh'iarraidh leannain,
Is thuirt an Caiptean Caimbeul 's e 'n Geàrd a' Bhaile
Gum b' aithne dha bantrach an àite falaich,
'S gun dèanadh e àird' air a cur am' charaibh.

Rinn e mar a b' àbhaist cho math 's a ghealladh—
Thug e dhomh air làimh i, 's am pàigheadh mar rith',
'S ge b'è bhios a' feòrach a h-ainm no sloinneadh,
Their iad rithe Seònaid, 's b'e Deòrs' a seanair.

Tha i soitheamh suairce, gun ghruaim gun smalan,
'S i cho àrd an uaisle ri mnaoi san fhearann;
'S culaidh am' chumail suas i, on tha i mar rium,
'S mór an t-adhbhar smuairein don fhear nach fhaigh i.

Leig mi dhiom Nic Còiseim, ged tha i maireann,
Is leig mi na daimh chròcach an taobh bha 'n aire,
Is thaobh mi ris an ògmhnaoi, 's ann leam nach aithreach,
Chan eil mi gun stòras on phòs mi 'n ainnir.

Bheir mi fhéin mo bhriathar gu bheil i ra-mhath
'S nach d'aithnich mi riamh oirre cron am falach,
Ach gu foinneamh fìnealta dìreach fallain,
'S i gun ghaoid gun ghiamh, gun char fiar, gun chamadh.

Bidh i air mo ghiùlan, 's gur math an airidh,
Nì mi fhéin a sgùradh gu math, 's a glanadh;
Chuirinn rithe 'n t-ùilleadh ga cumail ceanalt',
'S cuiridh mi ri m' shùil i, 's cha diùlt i aingeal.

Nuair bhios cion an stòrais air daoinibh ganna,
Cha leigeadh nighean Deòrsa mo phòca falamh—
Cumaidh i rium òl anns na taighibh leanna,
'S pàighidh i gach stòpan a nì mi cheannach.

Nì i mar bu mhiann leam a h-uile car dhomh,
Chan innis i breug dhomh no sgeul am mearachd,
Cumaidh i mo theaghlach cho math 's bu mhath leam,
Ge nach dèan mi saothair no obair shalach.

Sgìthich mi ri gnìomh, ge nach d'rinn mi earras,
Thug mi bòid nach b' fhiach leam bhith ann am sgalaig;
Sguiridh mi dham' phianadh, on thug mi 'n aire
Gur h-e 'n duine dìomhain as fhaide mhaireas.

'S i mo bheanag ghaolach nach dèan mo mhealladh,
'S fóghnaidh i dhomh daonnan a dhèanamh arain;
Cha bhi fàilinn aodaich orm no anairt,
'S chaidh cùram an t-saoghail a-nis ás m' aire.

'To his Musket, on Joining the Edinburgh City Guard' (translated by Ronald Black)

There can be many twists and turns in the lives of men—
They may fall in love with a woman they can't have;
I spent twenty years with the first one that I had,
But then she turned her back on me and left me bereft.

So I came to Auld Reekie to look for a sweetheart,
And Captain Campbell of the City Guard said
That he knew of a widow in some secret location,
And would take some steps to put her in my possession.

As usual, he did just as good as he'd promised—
He put her in my hands, and paid me her dowry,
And if anyone asks for her name or her forebears,
They call her Janet. And George was her grandad.

She's modest and gentle, without gloominess or grief,
And as high in dignity as any woman in the land;

She's my way to earn a living, just because she's with me—
The man who can't have her has great cause for regret.

I parted from Nic Còiseim, although she still survives,
And I let the antlered stags go wherever they wanted;
I preferred the younger woman, and no, I don't regret it,
For I'm not without an income since I married the girl.

I'll swear upon my oath that she's good in all respects,
That I've never detected in her any hidden fault—
In fact, she's shapely, graceful, straight and full of health
And has no defect or blemish, no bent bit or distortion.

I carry her around, for she thoroughly deserves it,
And I clean her myself, I give her a good scouring;
I make sure she's well oiled to keep her in good shape,
And when I put her to my eye, she never fails to spark.

When men who are broke are short of the needful,
George's daughter doesn't allow my pocket to be empty—
She keeps me in drink when I go into the alehouse
And pays for every flagon that I may care to buy.

She always attends to every notion that I get,
She never tells me a lie or gets a story wrong,
She supports my family as well as I could wish,
Though I never soil my hands with toil or manual labour.

I got tired of working, though I didn't make much money,
I swore that being a labourer was beneath my station;
I'm going to stop worrying, because I have noticed
That the man who is idle is the one who lasts the longest.

My beloved little woman will never let me down,
She'll always be what I need to earn my daily bread;
Never more will I suffer from lack of clothes or linen,
And the cares of the world have now gone out of my mind.

'Muinntir Hopetoun'

Translator's transcription

Fhuair mi sgeul air muinntir Hopetoun,
Cha sgeul beag e,

Is dona b' fhiach iad riamh an togail—
Sluagh nach freagradh,
Gealtairean nan eudann boga,
Sìol na bleide
A dh'iarras pàigheadh 's nach dèan obair
Leis an eagal.

Dh'iarradh orra dol do Shasann
An cinnseal cogaidh,
Gum faigheadh iad saor an t-aiseag,
Air ghaol socair:
Leag iad air caoineadh 's air basraich,
Is trom an osnaich—
Tha iad ré 'n saoghail fo mhasladh,
Dh'fhaodt' an crochadh.

Ma gheibh na Gaidhil an tairgse
Fhuair na daoin' ud,
Cha sòradh iad druim na fairge
Le seòl gaoithe,
Siùbh'lidh iad Sasann is Albainn,
Sunndach, eutrom,
Gun fhiamh, gun eagal, gun chearbaich',
Gun leisg saoithreach.

Sliochd nam fineachan as ainmeil'
Tha air an t-saoghal,
Is mór an cruadal a bha 'n earbsa
Riutha daonnan,
Is onair d'ar dùthaich gun d'fhalbh sibh
Thigh'nn an taobh sa—
'S ann an-dràst' tha cùis ri dhearbhadh
'S cliù ri fhaotainn.

'The Hopetoun Fencibles' (translated by Ronald Black)

I've heard news of Hopetoun's men,
   It's no small matter,
They were never worth recruiting—
   Bunch of misfits,

Cowards with namby-pamby faces,
    Cheeky beggars
Who ask for pay then do no work
    Because they're frightened.

They were asked to go to England
    On war footing,
They'd be ferried there for nought,
    Being fond of leisure:
They started weeping and hand-clapping,*
    Their sighs are deep—
They're disgraced for all their lives
    And could be strung up.

Should the Gael receive the offer
    Those men received,
They'd not refuse to sail the high seas
    At wind's mercy,
They'll march through England and through Scotland,
    Cheerful, lively,
Courageous, fearless, in good order,
    Not sparing effort.

The most celebrated clansmen
    Upon the planet,
Great hardihood has been vouchsafed
    To them at all times,
Our land is honoured that you left
    To come down here—
Now's the time for trying a case
    And winning glory.

JEROME STONE

(1727–1756)

JEREMIAH (JEROME) STONE was baptized in the parish of Scoonie in Fifeshire. After a basic education, Stone travelled the country as a chapman. Later, Stone gained the mentorship of the Reverend Thomas Tullidelph, who arranged for Stone to access free lectures at the University of St Andrews. During his studies Stone wrote poetry with some regularity, as the manuscript folio held in the University of Edinburgh Library attests. He also published some poems and prose in the *Scots Magazine*. In January 1756 he wrote an open letter for *Scots Magazine* in which he praised ancient Irish poetry—as an example he translated the Gaelic poem 'Fraoch's Death', which he titled 'Albin and the Daughter of Mey'. (This item appeared four years before James Macpherson published his volume of *Fragments of Ancient Poetry Collected in the Highlands of Scotland and Translated from the Galic or Erse Language*.) This version is taken from *A Collection of Original Poems* (1762).

'Albin and the Daughter of Mey. An old tale, translated from the Irish'

A Collection of Original Poems. By Scotch Gentlemen, 2 vols (Edinburgh: A. Donaldson and J. Reid; London: R. and J. Dodsley, and J. Richardson, 1762).

> Whence come these dismal sounds that fill our ears!
>   Why do the groves such lamentations send!
> Why sit the virgins on the hill of tears,
>   While heavy sighs their tender bosoms rend!
> They weep for ALBIN with the flowing hair,
>   Who perish'd by the cruelty of *Mey*;
> A blameless hero, blooming, young, and fair;
>   Because he scorn'd her passion to obey.
> See on yon western hill the heap of stones,
> Which mourning friends have raised o'er his bones!

O woman! bloody, bloody was thy deed;
    The blackness of thy crime exceeds belief;
The story makes each heart but thine to bleed,
    And fills both men and maids with keenest grief!
Behold thy daughter, beauteous as the sky
    When early morn transcends yon eastern hills,
She lov'd the youth who by thy guile did die,
    And now our ears with lamentations fills:
'Tis she, who sad, and grov'ling on the ground,
Weeps o'er his grave, and makes the woods resound.

A thousand graces did the maid adorn:
    Her looks were charming, and her heart was kind;
Her eyes were like the windows of the morn,
    And Wisdom's habitation was her mind.
A hundred heroes try'd her love to gain;
    She pity'd them, yet did their suits deny:
Young ALBIN only courted not in vain,
    ALBIN alone was lovely in her eye:
Love fill'd their bosoms with a mutual flame;
Their birth was equal, and their age the same.

Her mother *Mey*, a woman void of truth,
    In practice of deceit and guile grown old,
Conceiv'd a guilty passion for the youth,
    And in his ear the shameful story told:
But o'er his mind she never could prevail;
    For in his life no wickedness was found;
With shame and rage he heard the horrid tale,
    And shook with indignation at the sound:
He fled to shun her, while with burning wrath
The monster, in revenge, decreed his death.

Amidst Lochmey, at distance from the shore,
    On a green island, grew a stately tree,
With precious fruit each season cover'd o'er,
    Delightful to the taste, and fair to see:
This fruit, more sweet than virgin honey found,
    Serv'd both alike for physic and for food;
It cur'd diseases, heal'd the bleeding wound,
    And hunger's rage for three long days withstood.

But precious things are purchas'd still with pain,
And thousands try'd to pluck it, but in vain.

For at the root of this delightful tree,
    A venomous and awful dragon lay,
With watchful eyes, all horrible to see,
    Who drove th' affrighted passengers away.
Worse than the viper's sting its teeth did wound,
    The wretch who felt it soon behov'd to die;
Nor could physician ever yet be found
    Who might a certain antidote apply:
Ev'n they whose skill had sav'd a mighty host,
Against its bite no remedy could boast.

Revengeful *Mey*, her fury to appease,
    And him destroy who durst her passion slight,
Feign'd to be stricken with a dire disease,
    And call'd the hapless ALBIN to her sight:
"Arise, young hero! Skill'd in feats of war,
    On yonder lake your dauntless courage prove;
To pull me of the fruit, now bravely dare,
    And save the mother of the maid you love.
I die without its influence divine;
Nor will I taste it from a hand but thine."

With downcast look the lovely youth reply'd,
    "Though yet my feats of valour have been few,
My might in this adventure shall be try'd;
    I go to pull the healing fruit for you."
With stately steps approaching to the deep,
    The hardy hero swims the liquid tide;
With joy he finds the dragon fast asleep,
    Then pulls the fruit, and comes in safety back;
Then with a chearful countenance, and gay,
He gives the present to the hands of *Mey*.

"Well have you done, to bring me of this fruit;
    But greater signs of prowess must you give:
Go pull the tree entirely by the root,
    And bring it hither, or I cease to live."
Though hard the task, like lightning fast he flew,
    And nimbly glided o'er the yielding tide;
Then to the tree with manly steps he drew,

And pull'd, and tugg'd it hard, from side to side:
Its bursting roots his strength could not withstand;
He tears it up, and bears it in his hand.

But long, alas! ere he could reach the shore,
    Or fix his footsteps on the solid land,
The monster follow'd with a hideous roar,
    And like a fury grasp'd him by the hand.
Then, gracious God! what dreadful struggling rose!
    He grasps the dragon by th' invenom'd jaws,
In vain: for round the bloody current flows,
    While its fierce teeth his tender body gnaws.
He groans through anguish of the grievous wound,
And cries for help; but, ah! no help was found!

At length, the maid, now wond'ring at his stay,
    And rack'd with dread of some impending ill,
Swift to the lake, to meet him, bends her way;
    And there beheld what might a virgin kill!
She saw her lover struggling on the flood,
    The dreadful monster gnawing at his side;
She saw young ALBIN fainting, while his blood
    With purple tincture dy'd the liquid tide!
Though pale with fear, she plunges in the wave,
And to the hero's hand a dagger gave!

Alas! too late; yet gath'ring all his force,
    He drags, at last, his hissing foe to land.
Yet there the battle still grew worse and worse,
    And long the conflict lasted on the strand.
At length he happily descry'd a part,
    Just where the scaly neck and breast did meet;
Through this he drove a well-directed dart,
    And laid the monster breathless at his feet.
The lovers shouted when they saw him dead,
While from his trunk they cut the bleeding head.

But soon the venom of his mortal bite
    Within the hero's bosom spreads like flame;
His face grew pale, his strength forsook him quite,
    And o'er his trembling limbs a numbness came.
Then fainting on the slimy shore he fell,
    And utter'd, with a heavy, dying groan,

These tender words, "My lovely maid, farewell!
    Remember ALBIN; for his life is gone!"
These sounds, like thunder, all her sense oppress'd,
And swooning down she fell upon his breast.

At last, the maid awak'ning as from sleep,
    Felt all her soul o'erwhelm'd in deep despair,
Her eyes star'd wild, she rav'd, she could not weep,
    She beat her bosom, and she tore her hair!
She look'd now on the ground, now on the skies,
    Now gaz'd around, like one imploring aid:
But none was near in pity to her cries,
    No comfort came to soothe the hapless maid!
Then grasping in her palm, that shone like snow,
The youth's dead hand, she thus express'd her wo.

Burst, burst, my heart! the lovely youth is dead,
    Who, like the dawn, was wont to bring me joy;
Now birds of prey will hover round his head,
    And wild beasts seek his carcase to destroy;
While I who lov'd him, and was lov'd again,
    With sighs and lamentable strains must tell,
How by no hero's valour he was slain,
    But struggling with a beast inglorious fell!
This makes my tears with double anguish flow,
This adds affliction to my bitter wo!

Yet fame and dauntless valour he could boast;
    With matchless strength his manly limbs were bound;
That force would have dismay'd a mighty host,
    He show'd, before the dragon could him wound.
His curling locks, that wanton'd in the breeze,
    Were blacker than the raven's ebon wing;
His teeth were whiter than the fragrant trees,
    When blossoms clothe them in the days of spring;
A brighter red his glowing cheeks did stain,
Than blood of tender heifer newly slain.

A purer azure sparkled in his eye,
    Than that of icy shoal in mountain found;
Whene'er he spoke, his voice was melody,
    And sweeter far than instrumental sound.
O he was lovely! fair as purest snow,

Whose wreaths the tops of highest mountains crown;
His lips were radiant as the heav'nly bow;
   His skin was softer than the softest down;
More sweet his breath than fragrant bloom, or rose,
Or gale that cross a flow'ry garden blows.

But when in battle with our foes he join'd,
   And fought the hottest dangers of the fight,
The stoutest chiefs stood wond'ring far behind,
   And none durst try to rival him in might!
His ample shield then seem'd a gate of brass,
   His awful sword did like the lightning shine!
No force of steel could through his armour pass,
   His spear was like a mast, or mountain-pine!
Ev'n kings and heroes trembled at his name,
And conquest smil'd where-e'er the warrior came!

Great was the strength of his unconquer'd hand,
   Great was his swiftness in the rapid race;
None could the valour of his arm withstand,
   None could outstrip him in the days of chace.
Yet he was tender, merciful, and kind;
   His vanquish'd foes his clemency confess'd;
No cruel purpose labour'd in his mind,
   No thought of envy harbour'd in his breast.
He was all glorious, bounteous, and benign,
And in his soul superiour to a king!

But now he's gone! and nought remains but wo
   For wretched me; with him my joys are fled,
Around his tomb my tears shall ever flow,
   The rock my dwelling, and the clay my bed!
Ye maids, and matrons, from your hills descend,
   To join my moan, and answer tear for tear;
With me the hero to his grave attend,
   And sing the songs of mourning round his bier.
Through his own grove his praise we will proclaim,
And bid the place for ever bear his name.

JEAN ELLIOT

(1727–1805)

———

THE poet Jean (or Jane) Elliot was born at Minto House, near Hawick, Roxburghshire. During the Jacobite rising of 1745 she, when only eighteen, entertained a party of Jacobites at Minto while her father took refuge among the neighbouring crags. Her claim to fame rests upon one poem written, according to legend, as the result of a wager with her brother and fellow poet Gilbert. Discussing the battle of Flodden during a coach journey, Gilbert challenged his sister to write a ballad on the subject, which she did before the journey's end. Whether that story is true or not, Elliot would have been familiar with the traditional air of *The Flowers of the Forest*, as well as two surviving lines of 'The Battle of Flodden', which she incorporated into her work ('I've heard them lilting at the yowe-milking' and 'The flowers of the forest are a' wede away'). The originality of Elliot's version becomes evident when compared with another song of the same name, by Alison Cockburn, as the works differ markedly in tone and form.

———

'The Flowers of the Forest'

The Scottish Songs, ed. Robert Chambers, 2 vols (Edinburgh: William Tait, 1829).

(Tune: "The Flowers of the Forest")

I've heard the lilting at our yowe-milking,
  Lasses a-lilting before the dawn of day;
But now they are moaning on ilka green loaning—
  The Flowers of the Forest are a' wede away.

At buchts, in the morning, nae blythe lads are scorning,
  The lasses are lonely, and dowie, and wae;
Nae daffin', nae gabbin', but sighing and sabbing,
  Ilk ane lifts her leglen and hies her away.

In hairst, at the shearing, nae youths now are jeering,
    The bandsters are lyart, and runkled, and grey;
At fair, or at preaching, nae wooing, nae fleeching—
    The Flowers of the Forest are a' wede away.

At e'en, at the gloaming, nae swankies are roaming,
    'Bout stacks wi' the lasses at bogle to play;
But ilk ane sits drearie, lamenting her dearie—
    The Flowers of the Forest are a' wede away.

Dule and wae for the order, sent our lads to the Border!
    The English, for ance, by guile wan the day;
The Flowers of the Forest, that foucht aye the foremost,
    The prime o' our land, are cauld in the clay.

We hear nae mair lilting at our yowe-milking,
    Women and bairns are heartless and wae;
Sighing and moaning on ilka green loaning—
    The Flowers of the Forest are a' wede away.

ELIZABETH SCOT

(1729–1789)

━━

Elizabeth Scot (*née* Rutherford) was born at Hermiston Hall, her family's country mansion, near Edinburgh. Scot studied Latin and Greek at home, and showed a precocious interest in literature, writing poetry from the age of eleven. Allan Ramsay encouraged her efforts in verse, and she corresponded with Thomas Blacklock and Robert Burns. An inveterate experimenter, Scot wrote in quatrains and heroic couplets, and produced elegies and topical tales. For plot, she adopted ancient legends or reworked modern works. Family members published a posthumous collection of her work, *Alonzo and Cora, with Other Original Poems, Principally Elegiac*, in 1801.

━━

'To a Friend'

Alonzo and Cora, with Other Original Poems, Principally Elegiac (London: Bunney and Gold, 1801).

> How various are the parts, by heaven assign'd
> To fill the motley drama of mankind!
> To some 'tis given, apart from noise and state,
> And all the pains and pleasures of the great,
> To taste what joys to rural life belong;
> The Muse solicit to inspire the song;
> With simple swains to pass the careless day,
> And gently trifle life's short dream away.
> *You* nobler toils and harder tasks demand:
> To plan the glory of your native land;
> From listening senates to extort applause,
> And guard the monarch's rights and country's laws,
> Your rank, your name, your talents, heaven design'd
> To bless your friends, your sovereign, and mankind,
> Yet from these higher cares some moments spare;
> Let friendless merit claim your fostering care:

'Tis yours to give to genius honours due;
Genius, that finds its noblest theme in you.

'The Lover's Complaint'

Me, from the source of every comfort torn,
Condemn'd in pensive solitude to mourn,
Me, a devoted prey to pain and grief,
E'en the false flatterer hope denies relief.
Oh! look propitious on these lines, that flow
From love sincere and undissembled woe.
No certain aim my wishes now pursue;
To weep and mourn is all I now can do.
In sorrow sunk, dismay'd by hopeless love,
Thro' fancy's endless labyrinth I rove;
Review those happy scenes of past delight,
Where oft you sooth'd mine ear and charm'd my sight.
        When winter's rage the smiling year deforms,
And blackens all the skies with gathering storms,
Spring's opening dawn the dismal prospect cheers,
When she, in smiles array'd, serene appears.
But will no spring for me its joys renew,
And chase the gloom of sorrow from my view?
For me has fate no happy time in store?
Will joy and ORAN* greet mine eyes no more?
Each well-known spot recals you to my mind,
Where oft you walk'd, or where you oft reclin'd.
But, absent you, I gaze on empty air,
Yet think I hear your voice, and see you there.
Lovers these unavailing arts essay,
When fancy gives what fortune takes away.
        As some fond mother, who distracted eyes
Her dying babe, yet scarce believes it dies;
Views each faint sign of life with dire delight
And obstinately hopes in nature's spite:
Thus, when thy cruel coldness I survey'd,
When first I found my easy faith betray'd,
Alarm'd, and still reluctant to believe,
I tried each art that could my fears deceive:
Hop'd what I wish'd, and form'd thee to my mind,

Of truth tenacious, and for ever kind.
But soon the sad conviction grew too strong;
For falsehood, tho' it please, supports not long.
Yet, say? what wonder, thou shouldst win the heart,
Endow'd by nature, and adorn'd by art.
I thought thee best, as comeliest of thy kind,
A faultless form with every virtue join'd.
Oh! had the work been perfect, as it seem'd;
Prais'd for its beauty, for its worth esteem'd;
On thee each eye with fond delight had hung,
Each ear had caught the music of thy tongue.
Why, led astray by vanity and youth,
Could'st thou with treacherous aims dissemble truth?
Why try each pleasing charm, each winning art,
To pierce with grief a fond believing heart,
Whose warmest vows were all to heaven address'd,
To crown thy wishes, and pronounce thee bless'd?
Thy fond endearments more than all I priz'd,
And, if but ORAN lov'd, the world despis'd.

  Too long, alas! by dire misfortune cross'd,
On a wide sea of adverse chances toss'd,
In thee I hop'd one faithful plank to find,
And brave secure the rage of wave and wind:
On this I trusted all that yet remain'd,
Safe from the shipwreck I so late sustain'd.
Ah! foolish hope, and, Ah! believing maid,
By thine own truth and honest heart betray'd:
For soon dark clouds of ever-during night
Swept all the pleasing vision from my sight.
Thus, when the merchant, in pursuit of gain,
Attempts the dangers of the faithless main,
Lo! sudden storms his air-built hopes betray,
And all his wealth becomes at once their prey.
To one rich casket still he fondly cleaves,
And, grasping that, the rest to ruin leaves:
This dearest to his soul, and valued most,
Consoles him for the mighty treasures lost.
But if some swelling wave ev'n this denies,
And sweeps his darling casket from his eyes,
Despondent now, he strives with fate no more,
But fainting gives the hopeless struggle o'er:

All lost for ever he resigns his breath,
And seeks a last and safe retreat in death.
          If souls above with fond affection glow,
If spirits mingle in affairs below,
To me, kind heaven, one happy lot assign;
To guard my best-lov'd ORAN still be mine.
For ever near him let my soul preside,
Repel each danger, and each action guide;
Direct what path to shun, and what pursue;
From errour and from passion clear his view.
No distance then thy presence shall deny,
Nor shall this hated form offend thine eye;
But, veil'd in some soft mist of melting air,
Be still invisible, tho' ever near.

EACHANN MACLEÒID /
HECTOR MACLEOD

(*FL*. 1750)

—

LITTLE is known about Hector MacLeod (Eachann MacLeòid). He is said to have been from South Uist, but his surname was (and is) unusual there, and there is no trace of that island in his surviving work. According to the Gaelic historian John MacKenzie, MacLeod served the Jacobites as a spy at Fort William during the '45, bringing to the role a mixture of real intelligence and feigned naivety—especially when interrogated by the governor of the fort. The same dichotomy characterizes his poems, of which only four survive: 'Moladh do Choileach Smeòraich' ('The Praise of a Cock-Thrush'), 'Moladh do Eas Mòrair' ('The Praise of the Falls of Morar'), 'Moladh Choille Chros' ('The Praise of Cross Wood'), and 'An Taisbean' ('The Vision'). 'An Taisbean' reads like a Jacobite scrapbook: it includes natural description, a nod to the Irish *aisling* ('vision') verse of the period, heraldry and animal symbolism, a vignette of Prince Charles, an imitation of Lachlann MacMhuirich's medieval 'Brosnachadh' ('incitement') to the battle of Harlaw, an evocation of Mac Mhaighstir Alastair's 'Smeòrach Chlann Raghnaill' ('The Mavis of Clanranald'), a passage of prose (typical of the satirical tradition), and a glimpse of the Arcadian bliss that will follow a new and successful rising.

—

'An Taisbean'

Sar-Obair nam Bard Gaelach; or, The Beauties of Gaelic Poetry, and Lives of the Highland Bards, ed. John MacKenzie, 4th edn (Edinburgh: Maclachlan & Stewart, 1877).

> Moch madainn Chéitein ri ceò
>   'N àm don ghréin togail bho neòil,
> Chunnaic mi sealladh sa bheinn—
>   Is éibhinn ri éisteachd mo sgeòil.

Bha dearrsadh le teas a' cur smùid
Á bruachannan molach fraoich
'S bha deàlradh nan gathannan blàth
Cur sgèimh air cuirnean nam braon.

Bha dealt a' driùchdadh gu grinn
'N àm sgapadh do dhubhlachd a' cheò—
Na paidirean air an fheur
Mar leugan fo sgèimh an òir.

Bha abhainn a' ruith troimh ghleann
De dh'fhìor fhìon-uisge nan ard,
Bu lìonmhor geala-bhradan luath—
Sgèimh airgid dh'a shnuadh air an t-snàmh.

Bha maghannan mìlteach feòir
Bu mheilbheagach dhìtheanach blàth
Air gach taobh dhen uisge chruaidh
Bu luath mu thuath a' ruith balbh.

Bha neòinein is sòbhrach gu dlùth,
Creamh agus biolair a' fàs
Air àileanaibh aimhréidh 's air lóin
Far 'm bu lìonmhoire ròs geal is dearg.

Bu cheòlmhor ceileireach eòin
Air ghriananan eireachdail ard',
A' freagradh a-chéile gu grinn—
Chan fhaighte an cùirt rìgh na b' fheàrr.

Chunnaic mi, 'n uaigneas leis fhéin,
Ag éisteachd ri torghan nan eun,
Ar leam, den chruthaigheachd bheò,
An aon duin' òg a b' àillidh sgèimh.

O nach robh de dh'fhearaibh chàich
Ach esan is mi fhéin sa ghleann,
Smuaintich mi gun gabhainn sgeul
Có e fhéin, nam faighinn deth cainnt.

Thàinig e gu tostach mall,
Gu foidhidneach foistinneach ciùin.
Labhair e fosgarra réidh:
"A ghabhail sgeula thàinig thù?

"Mas math leat naidheachd a thoirt uam
　　Gu maithean Alba gu léir,
Amhairc gu geur fada bhuat
　　'S chì thu na sluaigh 'nan làn fheirg."

Chunnaic mi 'n fhairge mar choill
　　Le crannaibh loingis làn àrd
Le brataichean annasach ùr—
　　Ar leam gum b'ann ás an Spàinn.

Chunnaic mi cabhlach ro mhór
　　Gu gàireach gabhail gu tìr,
Bu luchdmhor, làn athaiseach iad,
　　Suaicheantas Frangach 'nan croinn.

Thàinig na sluaigh sin gu tìr
　　'S cha b' uaigneach an gluasad o thràigh—
Bha làmhach nan canan 's am fuaim
　　A' gluasad air chrith nam beann ard'.

Chuala mi coileach 's e gairm
　　'S e bualadh a sgiathan gu cruaidh,
'S thuirt an duine math sin rium:
　　"Cluinn Coileach na h-Àirde Tuath!"

Chunnaic mi tighinn air thùs
　　Stiùbhartaich, cinneadh an rìgh,
'Nam bòcanan gioraig san leirg
　　A dhearg an airm le fuil san t-srì.

Thàinig Clann Dòmhnaill 'nan déidh
　　Mar chonaibh confach gun bhiadh,
'Nam beithrichean guineach geur
　　An guaillean a-chéile gu gnìomh.

B' àlainn dealbhach am bréid sròil
　　Air a cheangal ri crann caol,
An robh caisteal, bradan is long,
　　Làmh dhearg, iolair is craobh.

Bha fraoch os cionn sin gu h-ard
　　Ceangailt' am barr a' chroinn chaoil:
Bha sin ann, is leóghann dearg—
　　'S cha b' àite tearmainn a chraos!

Thairrneadh na slòigh air sliabh Fiobha
    An coinneamh ri cath a chur;
Fhuair iad brosnachadh fìor mhear
    Thug éirigh le buirbe 'nam fuil:

"A chlannaibh Mìlidh, mosgailibh.
    Is somalta cian ur cadal.
Teannaibh ri dìoladh Chùil Lodair.
    Dh'at na fiachan sa fada.

"Tòisichibh gu h-ardanach,
gu bras-rìoghail móralach,
gu mear-leumnach dearg-chneadhach,
gu luath-làmhach treun-bhuilleach,
gu h-aigneach innsginneach,
gu h-anathach nàmhadach,
gu mion-chuimhneach dìoghaltach,
gu gruamach fiata an-tròcaireach,
gun tearmann gun mhathanas,
gun ath-thruas gun bhuigeachas,
gun innidh gun eagal,
gun umhail gun fhaicill,
gun fhiamh gun anamhisnich,
gun chùram gun ghealtachd,
gun taise gun fhaiteachas,
gun saidealtachd gun uabhann,
gun eisimeil gun umhlachd,
gun athadh do nàmhaid
ach a' gabhail romhaibh thoirt iubhair,
a' cosnadh na cath-làraich."

Chunnaic mi air leth o chàch
    Trì leóghainn a b' fharsainge craois;
Thug iad trì sgairtean cho ard
    'S gun sgàin creagan aig meud an glaodh.

Bha leóghann diubh sin air Creig Ghuirm
    Dha'm b' ainm Iain Mùideartach òg
On Chaisteal Thioram 's o Bhorgh
    De shliochd nan Collaidh bu bhorb colg.

Thog seann leóghann luath a cheann
    'S a chas rìoghail an Dùn Tuilm

Dha'm bu sheann eireachdas riamh
  Buaidh nan sliabh an càs a' chrùin.

Thàinig an treas leóghann dhiùbh
  On choill 's o Gharaidh nam bàrc.
Is dh'ordaich iad pàirt dhe'n cuid sluaigh
  Dhol a thiodhlacadh nam marbh.

Sann an-sin a thagh iad oifigich an-diadhaidh an-tròcaireach an-aobhach an-athach an-iochdmhor. Agus thagh iad cuideachd de bhorb-bhrothach bhodach dha'm b' airm chosanta spaidean agus sluasaidean gu tìodhlacadh nam marbh agus gu glanadh na h-àraich: Aonghas Amharra á Éigneig, Calum Crosta á Grùlainn, Eóghann Iargalta á Crasabhaig, Dùghall Ballach á Gallabaidh, Niall Eangharra á Raimisgearraidh, agus Dòmhnall Durrgha á Gearas.

Chunnaic mi 'n gleann soilleir uam
  An robh eireachdas thar gach glinn,
B' airde cheileirich' cheòlmhoire fuaim
  Glaodhaich nan cuach os a chinn.

Théid fargradh feadh Bhreatainn gu léir.
  Éiridh gu feachd fir gu leòir.
Chì sibh na Gàidhil a' triall
  Le rìoghalachd mar bu chòir.

'The Vision' (translated by Ronald Black)

One early May morning in mist
  When the sun was above her clouds,
I saw a vision in the mountains—
  My news is joyful to hear.

Her shining with heat had brought mist
  Out of shaggy heathery braes
While the gleam of radiant sunbeams
  Adorned the droplets of dew.

Dew was bespangling its beauty
  As the gloom of the mist dispersed—
The prayer beads on the grass
  Were like jewels with the beauty of gold.

A river that ran through a glen
   Was of true wine-water from summits,
With swift silver salmon aplenty—
   Their hue was bright beauty swimming.

Innumerable patches of grass
   With poppies and daisies for blooms
Lined each side of the vehement stream
   That flowed swiftly and silently north.

Daisies and primroses grew
   With garlic and cress in profusion
On disordered meadows and lawns
   Where white and red roses abounded.

Melodious and musical were birds
   On beautiful sun-bowers above,
Answering each other with elegance—
   No king's court offered anything better.

I saw, far away from the crowd,
   Listening to the sound of the birds,
I thought, out of all humankind,
   The young man of handsomest form.

Since no other people's men
   Were in the glen but myself and he,
I thought I would try to enquire
   Who he was, if he'd speak with me.

He came in a quiet, stately way,
   With patience, repose and calm.
He spoke openly, in a measured tone:
   "Is it to get news that you have come?

"If you're willing to carry my message
   To all of the leaders of Scotland,
Look far far away in the distance
   And you'll see armies in battle rage."

I then saw the sea as a forest
   Full and tall with the masts of a fleet,
And banners new, unfamiliar—
   I thought they might be from Spain.

I saw a huge navy of ships
   Noisily coming to land,
Capacious, most stately they were,
   The emblem of France at their masts.

Those armies then disembarked
   And loud was their march from the strand—
The cannonfire and their noise
   Caused the high mountains to shake.

I heard a cock as he crowed
   Striking his wings hard together,
And that good man remarked to me:
   "Hear ye the Cock o' the North!"

I saw advancing in front
   The Stewarts, the tribe of the king,
Like goblins haunting the highway
   Who bloodied their arms in the fight.

Next to come were Clan Donald
   Like mad dogs deprived of their food,
As thunderbolts wounding and sharp
   Shoulder to shoulder for strife.

A gorgeous, intricate silk flag
   Was attached to a slender mast,
Showing castle, salmon and ship,
   And red hand, eagle and tree.

Above that, a bunch of heather
   Had been tied to the slender mast's top.
There it was, and the red lion standard—
   It's maw was no place of escape!

The hosts were deployed on the moor of Fife*
   With the aim of giving battle;
They received a fiery incitement
   That made their blood rise with passion:

"O kindreds of Mìle, awaken.
   Large and long is your slumber.
Begin to avenge Culloden.
   These debts have accumulated.

"Begin with pride,
brashly-royal and magnificent,
lively-leaping, red-wounding,
swift-handed, brave-striking,
spirited and vigorous,
courageous and aggressive,
minutely remembering and vengeful,
surly, fierce and unmerciful,
without sanctuary or forgiveness,
without compassion or tenderness,
without softness or timidity,
without caution or carefulness,
without hesitation or fear,
without cowardice or care,
without weakness or reluctance,
without sheepishness or terror,
without dependency or meekness,
not afraid of the enemy
but getting in within bowshot range,
winning the battlefield."

I saw apart from the rest
    Three lions with jaws open wide;
They gave three roars so loud
    That rocks split with the sound of their cries.

One of the lions on Creag Ghorm
    Was young John of Moidart by name
From Castle Tirrim and Borve
    Of the Collas' race of fierce rage.

An old swift lion reared his head
    With his royal foot in Duntulm
Whose old virtue had always been
    Victory in battle in the cause of the crown.

The third of these lions came
    From the wood and from Garry of the boats.
And they ordered some of their troops
    To go and bury the dead.

That was when they chose officers who were ungodly, unmerciful,
unamiable, unfearing and unfeeling. And they chose a company of mad

mangy serfs whose defensive weapons were spades and shovels to bury
the dead and to cleanse the battlefield: Ill-Tempered Angus from
Éigneag, Cross-Grained Calum from Grulin, Obstinate Ewen from
Crasavaig, Spotted Dugald from Gallabaidh, Short-Tempered Neil
from Raimisgearraidh, and Dour Donald from Gearas.

> I saw the bright glen far away,
>   The most beautiful of all glens,
> Where the cries of the cuckoos above
>   Were loudest, sweetest, most musical.
>
> Word will go round the whole of Britain.
>   Enough men will join to fight.
> You will see the Gael on the march
>   With royalty as is their right.

IAIN MACRATH (IAIN MAC MHURCHAIDH) / JOHN MACRAE
(c.1730–1780)

━━

'DÈAN CADALAN SÀMHACH' is reputed to be the first Gaelic song ever made in America. Its probable author, John MacRae, was the son of a man who was hanged by Cumberland's forces at Inverness shortly after the Battle of Culloden. MacRae was born and grew up in Kintail, where he served Seaforth as gamekeeper, stalker, and forester until emigrating to North Carolina in or around 1774. Astonishingly, he chose to serve King George in the American War of Independence, taking part as a lieu-tenant at the Battle of Moore's Creek Bridge. It is possible, of course, that he did this purely for the money, given that he says in our poem that 'We're in distress from deserting King George'. He went from prison to prison, and appears to have been exchanged in 1778. He rejoined the army, only to be captured and exchanged again. Now a captain, he fell ill and died at Camden in South Carolina shortly before the Battle of King's Mountain. Most of his surviving thirty songs discuss hunting, drinking, distilling, love, and friendship in Kintail. His songs of farewell, emigra-tion, and America strike a very different note; their worried tone is set by 'Dèan Cadalan Sàmhach', which became the Highland settlers' anthem.

━━

'Dèan Cadalan Sàmhach'

Translator's transcription

Dèan cadalan sàmhach, a chuilein mo rùin,
Dèan fuireach mar thà thu 's tu 'n-dràst' an àit' ùr;
Bidh òigearan againn làn beartais is cliù,
'S ma bhios tu 'nad airidh, 's leat feareigin dhiùbh.

Gur ann an Ameireagaidh tha sinn an-dràst',
Fo dhubhar na coille nach teirig gu bràth;
Nuair dh'fhalbhas an dubhlachd 's a thionndainneas blàths,
Bidh cnothan, bidh ubhlan, bidh siùcar a' fàs.

'S ro bheag orm fhìn na daoine seo th' ann,
Le còtaichean drògaid, ad mhór air an ceann,
Le briogaisean goirid 's iad sgoilte gu'm bonn,
Chan fhaicear an t-osan, 's i bhochdainn a th' ann.

Gu bheil sinne 'nar n-Innseanaich cinnteach gu leòr,
Fo dhubhar nan craobh, cha bhi h-aon againn beò;
Madraidh-allaidh is béistean ag éigheach 's gach fròig—
Gu bheil sinne 'nar n-éiginn bhon thréig sinn Rìgh Deòrs'.

Thoir soraidh le fàilte Chinntàile nam bò,
Far an d'fhuair mi greis m' àrach 's mi 'm phàisteachan òg;
'S am biodh na buachaillean a' cuallach nam bò
'S na h-ighneagan guanach 's an gruaidh mar an ròs.

An toiseach an fhoghair bu chridheil nar sunnd,
Am fiadh anns an fhireach 's am bradan air grunnd;
Bhiodh luingeas an sgadain a' tighinn fo sheòl—
Bu bhòidheach an sealladh 's fir dhonna air am bord.

'Have a Quiet Sleep' (translated by Ronald Black)

Have a quiet sleep, little pup whom I love,
Stay as you are, as you're now in a new place,
We'll have young men full of riches and fame,
And if you deserve it, one of them will be yours.

For it's in America we are at this time,
In the shade of the forest that never ends;
When midwinter goes and the warmth returns
Nuts will grow, apples, and sugar as well.

I don't think much of these men here at all,
With drugget coats, big hats on their heads,
Short breeches split right down to the bottom,
And no sign of hose, because of their poverty.

We are Indians, there's no doubt about it,
In the shade of the trees none of us will survive
With wolves and beasts howling in every cranny—
We're in distress from deserting King George.

Bring farewell and greeting to Kintail of the cows
Where I was raised for a while as a very young child,

Where you'd find herdboys watching the cows
And fun-loving girls with cheeks like the rose.

At the beginning of autumn we used to be happy
With deer in the forest, salmon on river-bed,
And the herring-fleet coming in under full sail—
What a beautiful sight, with fine men on board.

WILLIAM FALCONER

(1732–?1770)

━━

LITTLE is known about William Falconer's childhood in Edinburgh except that he had some rudimentary schooling before he went to sea as an apprentice. His long narrative poem *The Shipwreck* (1762), by the author's own claim, remains the best record of his seafaring years. He was almost certainly at sea in merchant ships, and (if we follow the poem) served in the Royal Navy. Even though *The Shipwreck* received favourable reviews, Falconer returned to the sea—or at least, he tried to. He entered a period of appointments as purser of laid-up vessels. With leave to pursue some further literary pursuits, he produced *The Universal Dictionary of the Marine* (1769), an undertaking rooted in the copious notes of technical explanation he had attached to *The Shipwreck*. Both books secured Falconer's literary fame—Byron and Coleridge were notable fans. The fate of Falconer's corporeal form remains unclear, however. We presume that he died on the frigate *Aurora*, which went missing in 1770.

━━

The Shipwreck *(1762), Proem*

The Shipwreck. A Poem. In Three Cantos (London: A. Millar, 1762).

> While jarring int'rests wake the world to arms,
> And fright the peaceful plains, with fierce alarms;
> While Neptune hears Britannia's Thunders roll
> In vengeance, o'er the deep, from pole to pole:
> Declining martial strains and hostile rage,
> An unknown Author treads th' Aonian stage;
> Far other lays of sad Distress to sing
> Than ever trembled on the lyric string:
> To paint a scene, the MUSES never knew;
> A scene, where never Phocian laurel grew:
> Where adverse elements dire conflict wage,
> And swelling surges brave the Tempest's rage;

Where Dangers, in one sad succession, rise,
And Hope immers'd in present Anguish lies.
          Ye ever-tuneful Nine! Whose sacred lyrics
Bid vernal groves resound with heavenly choirs;
Whose golden viols, fraught with endless Fame,
Arts, Arms, and Heroes to all space proclaim;
Or to soft sounds, in softer notes, express
The variegated pang of deep distress:
Amidst the mournful tales of plaintive woe,
That, from your harps, in melting numbers flow;
To nautic strains th' untutor'd song inspire!
And deign a ray of your Promethean fire!
The fate, in lively sorrow, to deplore,
Of wand'rers shipwreck'd on a leeward shore.
          Alas! unheeded by th' Aonian Train,
Their heavenly presence I implore in vain.
Ah! will they leave Pieria's flow'ry vales,
To visit frowning skies and ruthless gales?
Where dreadful surges roll beneath the storm,
And horrid tempests all the deep deform:
With them perpetual harmony remains,
While endless Discord fills these dire domains.
          Unknown to PHOEBUS or the sacred Nine,
Too bold, the Youth approaches Delphos' shrine;
Doom'd, far oh far! from Phocis' happy shore,
The vast and trackless deep to wander o'er:
Alternate change of climates has he known,
And felt the fierce extremes of either zone;
Where arctic storms congeal eternal snow,
Or aequinoctial Suns intensely glow.
Thro' Poland, Denmark, Norway he has stray'd,
And Sweden, France, and Russia each survey'd;
His wand'ring steps have press'd Iberian strands,
And Greece, and Italy's delightful lands,
Nor left untrod the Tagus' golden sands:
He oft has track'd the burning Lybian soil;
And view'd the fruitful margin of the Nile;
The fertile plains of either Asia seen;
And of America, the wide domain,
From where th' Atlantic lashes Labrador,
To where Peruvian surges loudly roar:

From where fam'd Sidon, on Phoenicia's plain,
Stoops her proud neck beneath the Turkish chain;
To where the Isthmus, lav'd by adverse tides,
Atlantic and Pacific seas divides.
But while he measur'd o'er th' unbounded race,
In Fortune's vast illimitable chace,
Adversity, companion of his way!
Pursu'd his weary steps, with iron sway:
Bid new distresses ev'ry instant grow,
Marking each change of place, with change of woe.
In regions where th' ALMIGHTY's scourging Hand
With raging pestilence, afflicts the land;
Where winged deaths, in dreadful myriads, fly,
And fierce contagion taints the morbid sky:
Or where pale famine blasts the hopeful year,
Diffusing want of misery severe;
Her gnawing worms corrode the human breast,
And multiply the pangs of the distress'd:
Or forming o'er the deep th' imbattl'd line,
Where hostile Ships in dire commotion join;
While dying victims agonize in pain,
And fierce Destruction lords it o'er the main.
Such adverse fate, in early youth indur'd,
The orient dawn of mental day obscur'd;
Each vivid passion of the soul, supprest,
And quench'd the kindling ardor of the breast:
Then censure not severe th' unvaunted song!
Tho' jarring sounds the lab'ring verse prolong:
Tho' terms uncouth shou'd strike th' offended ear,
For sake of truth, the uncouth measures bear!
No laurel wreaths he asks, nor does he claim
To stand recorded in the rolls of Fame:
The MUSES' aid he supplicates no more;
But trusts alone to MEM'RY's ample store.
  Upborn from earth, the light IDEA springs,
Cleaving smooth air, on intellectual wings:
The sacred groves of Phocis hovers o'er,
Castalian vales and fam'd Boetotia's shore;
Corinthian and Athenian plains descries,
And o'er the dreadful scene of Shipwreck flies,
Then, back recoiling from the dismal sight,

For tall Colonne she directs her flight;
Where marble columns, by rude Time defac'd,
In order, on the lofty cape are plac'd;
That, now o'er-grown with moss, did once sustain,
In antient times, TRITONIA's sacred fane;
And, hence the name, the neighb'ring fields retain:
Where, high in clouds, its topmost cliffs is rear'd,
Array'd in robes divine, a Nymph appear'd:
Pensive her look, around her heavenly head
A radiant orb of lucid glory play'd:
Her spacious wings were dipt in Iris' bow,
Where various hues in rich profusion glow:
In her right hand, an ample roll she held,
Where all Antiquity stood forth reveal'd,
With ev'ry wise and noble art of Man,
Since first the circling hours their course began;
Her left, a silver wand erected bore,
Whose magic touch dispels Oblivion's pow'r:
At sight of her, the sable Goddess shrinks,
And all her deadly efficacy sinks.
Borne on seraphic wings along the skies,
Swift o'er th' immensity of space she flies;
Unknown effects, to her decisive law
Referr'd, all hence their just conclusions draw:
To things long past, a second date she gives,
And hoary Time, from her, fresh youth receives:
Coeval with, and sister of bright FAME,
She shares her pow'r, and MEM'RY is her name.
On the yet-roaring flood her eyes were cast,
Reflecting on the fatal Shipwreck past.
Soon as IDEA had the Goddess seen,
She, conscious of her form, and heavenly mien,
The well-known vision, instant recollects,
And thus submissive, her address directs.

　　　　O! elder daughter of primeval Time!
By whom transmitted down, in ev'ry clime,
Annals of ages long elaps'd, are known,
And blazon'd glories spread from zone to zone;
Who, from thy airy height, so late hast been
Spectatress of this melancholy scene;
Say! whence this ruin'd wreck? and wither bound?

And, whence these lifeless victims strew'd around?
What dire distress was felt? what tempest blew?
And of what Nation were the hapless Crew?
      She ceas'd, and saw her modest suit prevail;
And MEM'RY thus began the piteous tale.

JOHN OGILVIE
(1732–1813)

THE Church of Scotland minister and poet John Ogilvie was born and educated in Aberdeen. Ordained to the parish of Lumphanan in 1759, he moved to the neighbouring parish of Midmar a year later. There he remained as minister for fifty-three years. He enjoyed an early literary friendship with fellow Aberdonian James Beattie, while Lord Hailes evidently advised on and corrected some of his works. Ogilvie's earliest published poems, including *The Day of Judgment* (1753), were written before the age of seventeen. *Providence* (1764) is a blank verse theodicy in which he justifies God's cosmic plan. Later he turned to an epic style with *Rona* (1777), a Hebridean tragedy; *The Fane of the Druids* (1787–9), a partly mythical early history of Scotland; and *Britannia, a National Epic Poem* (1801). The following piece is a descriptive ode in nine Pindaric stanzas that owes much to Thomas Gray's influential mid-century masterpiece *The Bard*.

'Ode to Time, occasioned by seeing the Ruins of an Old Castle'

The Day of Judgment. A Poem. In Two Books, 3rd edn (London: G. Keith, 1759).

I.I

STROPHE.
O Thou who mid' the world-involving gloom,
Sit'st on yon solitary spire!
Or slowly shak'st the sounding dome,
Or hear'st the wildly-warbling lyre;
Say when thy musing soul
Bids distant times unroll,
And marks the flight of each revolving year,
That saw the race of Glory run,
That mark'd Ambition's setting sun,

That shook old Empire's tow'ring pride,
That swept them down the floating tide,
Say when these long-unfolding scenes appear,
Streams down thy hoary cheek the pity-darting tear?

I.2

Cast o'er yon trackless waste thy wand'ring eye:
Yon Hill whose gold-illumin'd brow
Just trembling thro' the bending sky,
O'erlooks the boundless wild below;
Once bore the branching wood
That o'er yon murm'ring flood
Hung wildly-waving to the rustling gale;
The naked heath with moss o'ergrown,
That hears the 'lone owl's nightly moan,
Once bloom'd with Summer's copious store,
Once rais'd the lawn-bespangling flow'r,
Or heard some Lover's plaintive lay,
When by pale Cynthia's silver ray,
All wild he wander'd o'er the lonely dale,
And taught the list'ning moon the melancholy tale.

I.3

Ye wilds where heav'n-rapt Fancy roves,
Ye sky-crown'd hills, and solemn groves!
Ye low-brow'd vaults, ye gloomy cells!
Ye caves where night-bred Silence dwells!
Ghosts that in yon lonely hall,
Lightly glance along the wall;
Or beneath yon ivy'd tow'r,
At the silent mid-night hour,
Stand array'd in spotless white,
And stain the dusky robe of Night;
Or with now solemn pauses, roam
O'er the long, sounding, hollow dome!
Say mid yon desert' solitary round,
When Darkness wraps the boundless spheres,
Does ne'er some dismal dying sound
On Night's dull serious ear rebound,
That mourns the ceaseless lapse of life-consuming years?

2.1

O call th' inspiring glorious hour to view,
When Caledonia's martial train,
From yon steep rock's high-arching brow
Pour'd on the heart-struck flying Dane!
When War's blood-tinctur'd spear
Hung o'er the trembling rear;
When light-heel'd Terror wing'd their headlong flight:
Yon Tow'rs then rung with wild alarms!
Yon Desert gleam'd with shining arms!
While on the bleak hill's brightning spire,
Bold Vict'ry flam'd, with eyes of fire;
Her limbs celestial robes infold,
Her wings were ting'd with spangling gold,
She spoke:—her words infus'd resistless might,
And warm'd the bounding heart, and rouz'd the soul of fight.

2.2

But ah, what hand the smiling prospect brings!
What voice recalls th' expiring day!
See darting swift on eagle-wings,
The glancing Moment bursts away!
So from some mountain's head,
In mantling gold array'd,
While bright-ey'd Fancy stands in sweet surprize:
The vale where musing Quiet treads,
The flow'r-clad lawns, and bloomy meads,
Or streams where Zephyr' loves to stray
Beneath the pale Eve's twinkling ray;
Or waving woods detain the sight:—
—When from the gloomy cave of Night
Some cloud sweeps shadowy o'er the dusky skies,
And wraps the flying scene that fades, and swims, and dies.

2.3

Lo! rising from yon dreary tomb,
What spectres stalk across the gloom!
With haggard eyes, and visage pale,
And voice that moans with feeble wail!
O'er yon long resounding plain

Slowly moves the solemn train;
Wailing-wild with shrieks of woe
O'er the bones that rest below!
While the dull Night's startled ear
Shrinks, aghast with thrilling fear!
Or stand with thin robes wasting soon,
And eyes that blast the sick'ning moon!
Yet these, ere Time had roll'd their years away,
Ere death's fell arm had mark'd its aim;
Rul'd yon proud tow'rs with ample sway,
Beheld the trembling swains obey;
And wrought the glorious deed that swell'd the trump of Fame.

3 . 1

But why o'er these indulge the bursting sigh?
Feels not each shrub the Tempest's pow'r?
Rocks not the dome when whirl-winds fly?
Nor shakes the hill when thunders roar?
Lo! mould'ring, wild, unknown,
What Fanes, what Tow'rs o'erthrown,
What tumbling chaos marks the waste of Time!
I see Palmyra's temples fall!
Old Ruin shakes the hanging wall!
Yon waste where roaming lions howl,
Yon aisle where moans the grey-ey'd Owl,
Shows the proud Persian's great abode:
Where scepter'd once, an earthly God!
His pow'r-clad arm controul'd each happier clime,
Where sports the warbling Muse, and Fancy soars sublime.

3.2

Hark!—what dire sound rolls murm'ring on the gale?
Ah! what soul-thrilling scene appears!
I see the column'd arches fail!
And structures hoar, the boast of years!
What mould'ring piles decay'd
Gleam thro' the moon-streak'd shade,
Where Rome's proud Genius rear'd her awful brow!
Sad monument!—Ambition near,
Rolls on the dust and pours a tear;

Pale Honour drops the flutt'ring plume,
And Conquest weeps o'er Caesar's tomb,
Slow Patience sits with eye deprest,
And Courage beats his sobbing breast;
Ev'n War's red check the gushing streams o'erflow,
And Fancy's list'ning ear attends the plaint of Woe.

3·3

Lo on yon Pyramid's sublime,
Whence lies Old Egypt's desert clime,
Bleak, naked, wild! where Ruin low'rs,
Mid' Fanes, and Wrecks, and tumbling tow'rs:
On the steep height waste and bare,
Stands the Pow'r with hoary hair!
O'er His scythe He bends;—His hand
Slowly shakes the flowing sand,
While the Hours, an airy ring
Lightly flit with downy wing;
And sap the works of man;—and shade
With silver'd locks his furrow'd head;
Thence rolls the mighty Pow'r His broad survey,
And seals the Nations awful doom;
He sees proud Grandeur's meteor-ray,
He yields to Joy the festive day;
Then sweeps the length'ning shade, and marks them for the tomb.

WILLIAM JULIUS MICKLE
(1734–1788)

———

THE poet and translator William Julius Mickle (formerly Meikle) was born in Langholm, Dumfriesshire, and educated there and in Edinburgh. After leaving school he worked as a clerk in the family brewery, where he became chief partner, and then owner after his father's death in 1757. In 1763 he secretly travelled to London to pursue a literary career, though he sought patronage with little success. After the under-rated *Pollio* (1766), Mickle's first poetical work to garner genuine interest was the neo-Spenserian poem *The Concubine* (1767). This was followed by a yet more ambitious work, *The Lusiad, or, The Discovery of India* (1776), after Luís de Camões's sixteenth-century epic poem *Os Lusíadas*. A flurry of publications helped Mickle support his family and pay off lingering debts. Aside from *The Prophecy of Queen Emma* (1782), a satire on the American War of Independence, though, he produced few new poems in his final years. *The Poetical Works of William Mickle* appeared in 1799, more than a decade after the author's death.

———

'Pollio: An Elegiac Ode'

Pollio: An Elegiac Ode. Written in the Wood near Roslin Castle, 1762 (Oxford: Clarendon Press, 1766).

I

The peaceful Evening breathes her balmy store,
  The playful School-boys wanton o'er the Green;
Where spreading Poplars shade the Cottage Door,
  The Villagers in rustic joy convene.

II

Amid the secret Windings of the Wood,
  With solemn Meditation let me stray;
This is the Hour, when, to the Wise and Good,
  The heavenly Maid repays the Toils of Day.

III

The River murmurs, and the breathing Gale
   Whispers the gently waving Boughs among,
The Star of Evening glimmers o'er the Dale,
   And leads the silent Host of Heaven along.

IV

How bright, emerging o'er yon broom-clad Height,
   The silver Empress of the Night appears!
Yon limpid Pool reflects a stream of Light,
   And faintly in its breast the Woodland bears.

V

The Waters tumbling o'er their rocky Bed,
   Solemn and constant, from yon Dell resound;
The lonely Hearths blaze o'er the distant Glade;
   The Bat, low-wheeling, skims the dusky Ground.

VI

August and hoary, o'er the sloping Dale,
   The Gothic Abbey rears its sculptur'd Towers;
Dull through the Roofs resounds the whistling Gale;
   Dark Solitude among the Pillars lowers.

VII

Where yon old Trees bend o'er a Place of Graves,
   And solemn shade a Chapel's sad remains,
Where yon scath'd Poplar through the Window waves,
   And, twining round, the hoary Arch sustains;

VIII

There, oft, at Dawn, as One forgot behind,
   Who longs to follow, yet unknowing where,
Some hoary Shepherd, o'er his Staff reclin'd,
   Pores on the Graves, and sighs a broken Prayer.

IX

High o'er the Pines, that with their dark'ning shade
   Surround yon craggy Bank, the Castle rears

Its crumbling Turrets: still its towery Head
A warlike mien, a sullen grandeur wears.

X

So, midst the snow of Age, a boastful air
Still on the war-worn Veteran's Brow attends;
Still his big Bones his youthful Prime declare,
Though, trembling o'er the feeble Crutch, he bends.

XI

Wild round the Gates the dusky Wall-flowers creep,
Where oft the Knights the beauteous Dames have led;
Gone is the Bower, the Grot a ruin'd heap,
Where Bays and Ivy o'er the fragments spread.

XII

'Twas here our Sires exulting from the Fight,
Great in their bloody arms, march'd o'er the Lea,
Eying their rescued Fields with proud delight;
Now lost to them! and, ah how chang'd to me!

XIII

This Bank, the River, and the fanning Breeze,
The dear Idea of my POLLIO bring;
So shone the Moon through these soft nodding Trees,
Where here we wander'd in the Eves of Spring.

XIV

When April's smiles the flowery Lawn adorn,
And modest Cowslips deck the Streamlet's side,
When fragrant Orchards to the roseate Morn
Unfold their Bloom, in Heaven's own Colours dy'd:

XV

So fair a Blossom gentle POLLIO wore,
These were the Emblems of his healthful Mind;
To Him the letter'd Page display'd its Lore,
To Him bright Fancy all her Wealth resign'd:

XVI

Him, with her purest Flames, the Muse endow'd,
　　Flames never to th' illiberal Thought allied;
The sacred Sisters led where Virtue glow'd
　　In all her Charms; he saw, he felt, and died.

XVII

Oh Partner of my Infant Griefs and Joys!
　　Big with the Scenes now past my Heart o'erflows,
Bids each Endearment, fair as once, to rise,
　　And dwells luxurious on her melting Woes.

XVIII

Oft with the rising Sun when Life was new,
　　Along the Woodland have I roam'd with Thee;
Oft by the Moon have brush'd the Evening Dew,
　　When all was fearless Innocence and Glee.

XIX

The sainted Well where yon bleak Hill declines,
　　Has oft been conscious of those happy Hours;
But now the Hill, the River crown'd with Pines,
　　And sainted Well have lost their cheering Powers,

XX

For Thou art gone—My Guide, my Friend, oh where,
　　Where hast thou fled, and left me here behind!
My tenderest Wish, my Heart to Thee was bare,
　　Oh, now cut off each passage to thy Mind!

XXI

How dreary is the Gulph, how dark, how void,
　　The trackless Shores that never were repast!
Dread Separation! on the Depth untry'd
　　Hope faulters, and the Soul recoils aghast.

XXII

Wide round the spacious Heavens I cast my eyes;
　　And shall these Stars glow with immortal fire,

Still shine the *lifeless* glories of the Skies,
   And could thy bright, thy LIVING Soul expire?

XXIII

Far be the thought—the Pleasures most sublime,
   The Glow of Friendship, and the virtuous Tear,
The tow'ring Wish that scorns the bounds of Time,
   Chill'd in this Vale of Death, but languish here.

XXIV

So plant the Vine on Norway's wintery Land,
   The languid Stranger feebly buds, and dies:
Yet there's a Clime where Virtue shall expand
   With godlike strength, beneath her native Skies.

XXV

The lonely Shepherd on the Mountain's side,
   With patience waits the rosy opening Day;
The Mariner at Midnight's darksome tide,
   With chearful hope expects the Morning Ray.

XXVI

Thus I, on Life's storm-beaten Ocean tost,
   In mental vision view the happy Shore,
Where POLLIO beckons to the peaceful Coast,
   Where Fate and Death divide the Friends no more.

XXVII

Oh that some kind, some pitying kindred Shade,
   Who now, perhaps, frequents this solemn Grove,
Would tell the awful Secrets of the Dead,
   And from my Eyes the mortal Film remove!

XXVIII

Vain is the Wish—yet surely not in vain
   Man's Bosom glows with that celestial Fire,
Which scorns Earth's Luxuries, which smiles at Pain,
   And wings his Spirit with sublime Desire.

XXIX

To fan this Spark of Heaven, this Ray divine,
    Still, oh my Soul! still be thy dear Employ;
Still thus to wander through the Shades be thine,
    And swell thy Breast with visionary Joy.

XXX

So to the dark-brow'd Wood, or sacred Mount,
    In ancient days, the holy Seers retir'd,
And, led in vision, drank at SILOE'S Fount,
    While rising Ecstasies their Bosoms fir'd;

XXXI

Restor'd Creation bright before them rose,
    The burning Desarts smil'd at EDEN'S Plains,
One friendly Shade the Wolf and Lambkin chose,
    The flowery Mountains sung—"MESSIAH REIGNS!"

XXXII

Though fainter Raptures my cold Breast inspire,
    Yet, let me oft frequent this solemn Scene,
Oft to the Abbey's shatter'd Walls retire,
    What time the Moonshine dimly gleams between.

XXXIII

There, where the Cross in hoary ruin nods,
    And weeping Yews o'ershade the letter'd Stones,
While midnight Silence wraps these drear Abodes,
    And soothes me wand'ring o'er my kindred Bones,

XXXIV

Let kindled Fancy view the glorious Morn,
    When from the bursting Graves the Just shall rise,
All Nature smiling, and, by Angels borne,
    MESSIAH'S Cross fair blazing o'er the Skies.

JAMES BEATTIE

(1735–1803)

━━

LONG recognized as a leading poet and philosopher, James Beattie's life began humbly in Laurencekirk, Kincardineshire. At fourteen the gifted student won a bursary to Marischal College in Aberdeen, where he studied Greek under Thomas Blackwell and moral philosophy under Alexander Gerard. After graduating, he became village school-master and parish clerk at Fordoun. In this period he submitted poetry to the *Scots Magazine* and the *Edinburgh Magazine*, and was soon appointed a professor of moral philosophy and logic at Aberdeen. His early poetry was collected in *Original Poems and Translations* (1760). Shortly after that he began work on one of his most cele-brated works, *The Minstrel*, which eventually appeared in print in two books, in 1771 and 1774. In effect, the Spenserian poem is Beattie's autobiography of his poetic growth. The poetic growth of Edwin inspired a host of poets, Wordsworth and Coleridge among them, for many generations to come. Beattie wrote little new poetry after 1770, due to illness and other commitments. Instead, he revised older pieces. *Poems on Several Occasions* (1776), from which the following three poems come, captures Beattie's skill in some of the dominant forms of Romantic-period poetry: the ode and the elegy, as well as the verse autobiography.

━━

'Ode to Hope'

Poems on Several Occasions (Edinburgh: W. Creech, 1776).

I. 1

O Thou, who glad'st the pensive soul,
More than Aurora's smile the swain forlorn,
Left all night long to mourn
Where desolation frowns, and tempests howl;
And shrieks of Woe, as intermits the storm,

Far o'er the monstrous wilderness resound,
And cross the gloom darts many a shapeless form,
And many a fire-eyed visage glares around.
O come, and be once more my guest.
Come, for thou oft thy suppliant's vow hast heard,
And oft with smiles indulgent chear'd
And soothed him into rest.

I. 2

Smit by thy rapture-beaming eye
Deep flashing through the midnight of their mind,
The sable bands combined,
Where Fear's black banner bloats the troubled sky,
Appall'd retire. Suspicion hides her head,
Nor dares th' obliquely gleaming eyeball raise;
Despair, with gorgon-figured veil o'erspread,
Speeds to dark Phlegethon's detested maze.
Lo, startled at the heavenly ray,
With speed unwonted Indolence upsprings,
And, heaving, lifts her leaden wings,
And sullen glides away:

I. 3

Ten thousand forms, by pining Fancy view'd,
Dissolve.—Above the sparkling flood
When Phoebus rears his awful brow,
From lengthening lawn and valley low
The troops of fen-born mists retire.
Along the plain
The joyous swain
Eyes the gay villages again,
And gold-illumined spire;
While on the billowy ether borne
Floats the loose lay's jovial measure;
And light along the fairy Pleasure,
Her green robes glittering to the morn,
Wantons on silken wing. And goblins all
To the damp dungeon shrink, or hoary hall,
Or westward, with impetuous flight,
Shoot to the desert realms of their congenial Night.

II. I

When first on Childhood's eager gaze
Life's varied landscape, stretch'd immense around,
Starts out of night profound,
Thy voice incites to tempt th' untrodden maze.
Fond he surveys thy mild maternal face,
His bashful eye still kindling as he views,
And, while thy lenient arm supports his pace,
With beating heart the upland path pursues:
The path that leads, where, hung sublime,
And seen afar, youth's gallant trophies, bright
In Fancy's rainbow ray, invite
His wingy nerves to climb.

II. 2

Pursue thy pleasurable way,
Safe in the guidance of thy heavenly guard,
While melting airs are heard,
And soft-eyed cherub forms around thee play:
Simplicity, in careless flowers array'd,
Prattling amusive in his accent meek;
And Modesty, half turning as afraid,
The smile just dimpling on his glowing cheek;
Content and Leisure, hand in hand
With Innocence and Peace, advance, and sing;
And Mirth, in many a mazy ring,
Frisks o'er the flowery land.

II. 3

Frail man, how various is thy lot below!
To-day though gales propitious blow,
And Peace soft gliding down the sky
Lead Love along and Harmony,
To-morrow the gay scene deforms;
Then all around
The thunder's sound
Rolls rattling on through heaven's profound,
And down rush all the storms.
Ye days, that balmy influence shed,
When sweet Childhood, ever sprightly,

In paths of pleasure sported lightly,
Whither, ah whither are ye fled!
Ye cherub train, that brought him on his way,
O leave him not midst tumult and dismay;
For now youth's eminence he gains;
But what a weary length of lingering toil remains!

III. 1

They shrink, they vanish into air.
Now Slander taints with pestilence the gale;
And mingling cries assail,
The wail of Woe, and groan of grim Despair.
Lo, wizard Envy from his serpent eye
Darts quick destruction in each baleful glance;
Pride smiling stern, and yellow Jealousy,
Frowning Disdain, and haggard Hate advance;
Behold, amidst the dire array,
Pale wither'd Care his giant-stature rears,
And lo, his iron hand prepares
To grasp its feeble prey.

III. 2

Who now will guard bewilder'd youth
Safe from the fierce assault of hostile rage?
Such war can Virtue wage,
Virtue, that bears the sacred shield of Truth?
Alas! full oft on Guilt's victorious car
The spoils of Virtue are in triumph borne;
While the fair captive, mark'd with many a scar,
In lone obscurity, oppress'd, forlorn,
Resigns to tears her angel form.
Ill-fated youth, then whither wilt thou fly?
No friend, no shelter now is nigh,
And onward rolls the storm.

III. 3

But whence the sudden beam that shoots along?
Why shrink aghast the hostile throng?
Lo, from amidst Affliction's night,
Hope bursts all radiant on the sight:

Her words the troubled bosom soothe.
"Why thus dismay'd?
Though foes invade,
Hope ne'er is wanting to their aid
Who tread the path of truth.
'Tis I, who smooth the rugged way,
I, who close the eyes of Sorrow,
And with glad visions of to-morrow
Repair the weary soul's decay.
When Death's cold touch thrills to the freezing heart,
Dreams of heaven's opening glories I impart,
Till the freed spirit springs on high
In rapture too severe for weak Mortality."

'Elegy'

Still shall unthinking man substantial deem
The forms that fleet through life's deceitful dream?
On clouds, where Fancy's beam amusive plays,
Shall heedless Hope the towering fabric raise?
Till at Death's touch the fairy visions fly,
And real scenes rush dismal on the eye;
And from Elysium's balmy slumber torn
The startled soul awakes, to think, and mourn.

  O ye, whose hours in jocund train advance,
Whose spirits to the song of gladness dance,
Who flowery vales in endless view survey
Glittering in beams of visionary day;
O, yet while Fate delays th' impending woe,
Be roused to thought, anticipate the blow;
Lest, like the lightning's glance, the sudden ill
Flash to confound, and penetrate to kill;
Lest, thus encompass'd with funereal gloom,
Like me, ye bend o'er some untimely tomb,
Pour your wild ravings in Night's frighted ear,
And half pronounce Heaven's sacred doom severe.

  Wise, Beauteous, Good! O every grace combined,
That charms the eye, or captivates the mind!
Fair as the floweret opening on the morn,
Whose leaves bright drops of liquid pearl adorn!

Sweet, as the downy-pinion'd gale, that rove
To gather fragrance in Arabian groves!
Mild, as the strains, that, at the close of day
Warbling remote, along the vales decay!—
Yet, why with these compared? What tints so fine,
What sweetness, mildness, can be match'd with thine?
Why roam abroad? Since still, to Fancy's eyes,
I see, I see thy lovely form arise.
Still let me gaze, and every care beguile,
Gaze on that cheek, where all the Graces smile;
That soul-expressing eye, benignly bright,
Where meekness beams ineffable delight;
That brow, where Wisdom sits enthroned serene,
Each feature forms, and dignifies the mien:
Still let me listen, while her words impart
The sweet effusions of the blameless heart,
Till all my soul, each tumult charm'd away,
Yields, gently led, to Virtue's easy sway.

     By thee inspired, O Virtue, Age is young,
And musick warbles from the faltering tongue:
Thy ray creative cheers the clouded brow,
And decks the faded cheek with rosy glow,
Brightens the joyless aspect, and supplies
Pure heavenly lustre to the languid eyes:
But when Youth's living bloom reflects thy beams,
Resistless on the view the glory streams,
Love, Wonder, Joy, alternately alarm,
And Beauty dazzles with angelic charm.

     Ah whither fled!—ye dear illusions stay—
Lo, pale and silent lies the lovely clay.—
How are the roses on that cheek decay'd,
Which late the purple light of youth display'd!
Health on her form each sprightly grace bestow'd;
With life and thought each speaking feature glow'd.—
Fair was the flower, and soft the vernal sky;
Elate with hope, we deem'd no tempest nigh;
When lo, a whirlwind's instantaneous gust
Left all its beauties withering in the dust.

     All cold the hand, that soothed Woe's weary head!
And quench'd the eye, the pitying tear that shed!
And mute the voice, whose pleasing accents stole,

Infusing balm, into the rankled soul!
O Death, why arm with cruelty thy power,
And spare the idle weed, yet lop the flower!
Why fly thy shafts in lawless error driven!
Is Virtue then no more the care of Heaven!—
But peace, bold thought! be still my bursting heart!
We, not Eliza, felt the fatal dart.
Scaped the dark dungeon does the slave complain,
Nor bless the hand that broke the galling chain?
Say, pines not Virtue for the lingering morn,
On this dark wild condemn'd to roam forlorn?
Where Reason's meteor-rays, with sickly glow,
O'er the dun gloom a dreadful glimmering throw?
Disclosing dubious to th' affrighted eye
O'erwhelming mountains tottering from on high,
Black billowy seas in storm perpetual toss'd,
And weary ways in wildering labyrinths lost.
O happy stroke that bursts the bonds of clay,
Darts through the rending gloom the blaze of day,
And wings the soul with boundless flight to soar,
Where dangers threat, and fears alarm no more.
          Transporting thought! here let me wipe away
The tear of grief, and wake a bolder lay.
But ah! the swimming eye o'erflows anew,
Nor check the sacred drops to pity due;
Lo, where in speechless, hopeless anguish, bend
O'er her loved dust, the Parent, Brother, Friend!
How vain the hope of man!—But cease thy strain,
Nor Sorrow's dread solemnly profane;
Mix'd with yon drooping Mourners, on her bier
In silence shed the sympathetick tear.

The Minstrel *(1771–4)*, *Canto 2*

I

Of chance or change O let not man complain,
Else shall he never never cease to wail:
For, from the imperial dome, to where the swain
Rears the lone cottage in the silent dale,
All feel th' assault of fortune's fickle gale;

Art, empire, earth itself, to change are doom'd;
Earthquakes have raised to heaven the humble vale,
And gulphs the mountain's mighty mass entomb'd,
And where th' Atlantick rolls wide continents have bloom'd.

II

But sure to foreign climes we need not range,
Nor search the antient records of our race,
To learn the dire effects of time and change,
Which in ourselves, alas, we daily trace.
Yet at the darken'd eye, the wither'd face,
Or hoary hair, I never will repine:
But spare, O Time, whate'er of mental grace,
Of candour, love, or sympathy divine,
Whate'er of fancy's ray, or friendship's flame is mine.

III

So I, obsequious to Truth's dread command,
Shall here without reluctance change my lay,
And smite the Gothic lyre with harsher hand;
Now when I leave that flowery path for aye
Of childhood, where I sported many a-day,
Warbling and sauntering carelessly along;
Where every face was innocent and gay,
Each vale romantick, tuneful every tongue,
Sweet, wild, and artless all, as Edwin's infant song.

IV

"Perish the lore that deadens young desire"
Is the soft tenor of my song no more.
Edwin, though loved of heaven, must not aspire
To bliss, which mortals never knew before.
On trembling wings let youthful fancy roar,
Nor always haunt the sunny realms of joy;
But now and then the shades of life explore;
Though many a sound and sight of woe annoy,
And many a qualm of care his rising hopes destroy.

V

Vigour from toil, from trouble patience grows.
The weakly blossom, warm in summer bower,

Some tints of transient beauty may disclose;
But ah it withers in the chilling hour.
Mark yonder oaks! Superiour to the power
Of all the warring winds of heaven they rise,
And from the stormy promontory tower,
And toss their giant arms amid the skies,
While each assailing blast increase of strength supplies.

VI

And now the downy cheek and deepen'd voice
Gave dignity to Edwin's blooming prime;
And walks of wider circuit were his choice;
And vales more wild, and mountains more sublime.
One evening, as he framed the careless rhyme,
It was his chance to wander far abroad,
And o'er a lonely eminence to climb,
Which heretofore his foot had never trode;
A vale appear'd below, a deep retired abode.

VII

Thither he hied, enamour'd of the scene:
For rocks on rocks piled, as by magic spell,
Here scorch'd with lightning, there with ivy green,
Fenced from the north and east this savage dell;
Southward a mountain rose with easy swell,
Whose long long groves eternal murmur made;
And toward the western sun a streamlet fell,
Where, through the cliffs, the eye, remote, survey'd
Blue hills, and glittering waves, and skies in gold array'd.

VIII

Along this narrow valley you might see
The wild deer sporting on the meadow ground,
And, here and there, a solitary tree,
Or mossy stone, or rock with woodbine crown'd.
Oft did the cliffs reverberate the sound
Of parted fragments tumbling from on high;
And from the summit of that craggy mound
The perching eagle oft was heard to cry,
Or on resounding wings to shoot athwart the sky.

IX

One cultivated spot there was, that spread
Its flowery bosom to the noonday beam,
Where many a rose-bud rears its blushing head,
And herbs for food with future plenty teem.
Sooth'd by the lulling sound of grove and stream
Romantick visions swarm on Edwin's soul:
He minded not the sun's last trembling gleam,
Nor heard from far the twilight curfew toll;—
When slowly an his ear these moving accents stole.

X

"Hail, awful scenes, that calm the troubled breast,
And woo the weary to profound repose;
Can passion's wildest uproar lay to rest,
And whisper comfort to the man of woes!
Here Innocence may wander, safe from foes,
And Contemplation soar on seraph wings.
O Solitude, the man who thee foregoes,
When lucre lures him, or ambition stings,
Shall never know the source whence real grandeur springs."

XI

"Vain man, is grandeur given to gay attire?
Then let the butterfly thy pride upbraid:—
To friends, attendants, armies, brought with hire?
It is thy weakness that requires their aid:—
To palaces, with gold and gems inlay'd?
They fear the thief, and tremble in the storm:—
To hosts, through carnage who to conquest wade?
Behold the victor vanquish'd by the worm!
Behold, what deeds of woe the locust can perform!"

XII

"True dignity is his, whose tranquil mind
Virtue has raised above the things below,
Who, every hope and fear to heaven resign'd,
Shrinks not, though Fortune aim her deadliest blow."
—This strain from midst the rocks was heard to flow
In solemn sounds. Now beam'd the evening star;

And from embattled clouds emerging slow
Cynthia came riding on her silver car;
And hoary mountain-cliffs shone faintly from afar.

XIII

Soon did the solemn voice its theme renew;
(While Edwin wrapt in wonder listening stood)
"Ye tools and toys of tyranny, adieu,
Scorn'd by the wise, and hated by the good!
Ye only can engage the servile brood
Of Levity and Lust, who, all their days,
Ashamed of truth and liberty, have woo'd,
And hug'd the chain, that glittering on their gaze
Seems to outshine the pomp of heaven's empyreal blaze."

XIV

"Like them, abandon'd to Ambition's sway,
I sought for glory in the paths of guile;
And fawn'd and smiled, to plunder and betray,
Myself betray'd and plunder'd all the while;
So gnaw'd the viper the corroding file.
But now with pangs of keen remorse I rue
Those years of trouble and debasement vile.—
Yet why should I this cruel theme pursue!
Fly, fly, detested thoughts, for ever from my view."

XV

"The gusts of appetite, the clouds of care,
And storms of disappointment, all o'erpast,
Henceforth no earthly hope with heaven shall share
This heart, where peace serenely shines at last.
And if for me no treasure be amass'd,
And if no future age shall hear my name,
I lurk the more secure from fortune's blast,
And with more leisure feed this pious flame,
Whose rapture far transcends the fairest hopes of fame."

XVI

"The end and the reward of toil is rest.
Be all my prayer for virtue and for peace.

Of wealth and fame, of pomp and power possess'd,
Who ever felt his weight of woe decrease!
Ah! what avails the lore of Rome and Greece,
The lay heaven-prompted, and harmonious string,
The dust of Ophir, or the Tyrian fleece,
All that art, fortune, enterprise, can bring,
If envy, scorn, remorse, or pride the bosom wring!"

XVII

"Let Vanity adorn the marble tomb
With trophies, rhymes, and scutcheons of renown,
In the deep dungeon of some Gothic dome,
Where night and desolation ever frown.
Mine be the breezy hill that skirts the down;
Where a green grassy turf is all I crave,
With here and there a violet bestrown,
Fast by a brook, or fountain's murmuring wave;
And many an evening sun shine sweetly on my grave."

XVIII

"And thither let the village swain repair;
And, light of heart, the village maiden gay,
To deck with flowers her half-dishevel'd hair,
And celebrate the merry morn of May.
There let the shepherd's pipe the live-long day
Fill all the grove with love's bewitching wo;
And when mild Evening comes with mantle grey,
Let not the blooming band make haste to go,
No ghost nor spell my long and last abode shall know."

XIX

"For though I fly to scape from Fortune's rage,
And bear the scars of envy, spite, and scorn,
Yet with mankind no horrid war I wage,
Yet with no impious spleen my breast is torn:
For virtue lost, and ruin'd man, I mourn.
O Man, creation's pride, heaven's darling child,
Whom nature's best divinest gifts adorn,
Why from thy home are truth and joy exiled,
And all thy favourite haunts with blood and tears defiled!"

XX

"Along yon glittering sky what glory streams!
What majesty attends night's lovely queen!
Fair laugh our vallies in the vernal beams;
And mountains rise, and oceans roll between,
And all conspire to beautify the scene.
But, in the mental world, what chaos drear!
What forms of mournful, loathsome, furious mien!
O when shall that Eternal Morn appear,
These dreadful forms to chase, this chaos dark to clear!"

XXI

"O Thou, at whose creative smile, yon heaven,
In all the pomp of beauty, life, and light,
Rose from th' abyss; when dark Confusion, driven
Down down the bottomless profound of night,
Fled, where he ever flies thy piercing sight!
O glance on these sad shades one pitying ray,
To blast the fury of oppressive might,
Melt the hard heart to love and mercy's sway,
And chear the wandering soul, and light him on the way."

XXII

Silence ensued: and Edwin raised his eyes
In tears, for grief lay heavy at his heart.
"And is it thus in courtly life (he cries)
That man to man acts a betrayer's part!
And dares he thus the gifts of heaven pervert,
Each social instinct, and sublime desire!—
Hail Poverty! if honour, wealth, and art,
If what the great pursue, and learn'd admire,
Thus dissipate and quench the soul's ethereal fire!"

XXIII

He said, and turn'd away; nor did the Sage
O'erhear, in silent orisons employ'd.
The Youth, his rising sorrow to assuage,
Home as he hied, the evening scene enjoy'd:
For now no cloud obscures the starry void;

The yellow moonlight sleeps on all the hills;
Nor is the mind with starting sounds annoy'd,
A soothing murmur the lone region fills,
Of groves, and dying gales, and melancholy rills.

XXIV

But he from day to day more anxious grew.
The voice still seem'd to vibrate on his ear.
Nor durst he hope the Hermit's tale untrue;
For man he seem'd to love, and heaven to fear;
And none speaks false, where there is none to hear.
"Yet, can man's gentle heart become so fell!
No more in vain conjecture let me wear
My hours away, but seek the Hermit's cell;
Tis he my doubt can clear, perhaps my care dispel."

XXV

At early dawn the Youth his journey took,
And many a mountain pass'd, and valley wide,
Then reach'd the wild; where, in a flowery nook,
And seated on a mossy stone, he spied
An antient man: his harp lay him beside.
A stag sprang from the pasture at his call,
And, kneeling, lick'd the wither'd hand, that tied
A wreathe of woodbine round his antlers tall,
And hung his lofty neck with many a floweret small.

XXVI

And now the hoary Sage arose, and saw
The wanderer approaching: innocence
Smiled on his glowing check, but modest awe
Depress'd his eye, that fear'd to give offence.
"Who art thou, courteous stranger? and from whence?
Why roam thy steps to this abandon'd dale?"
"A shepherd-boy (the Youth replied), far hence
My habitation; hear my artless tale;
Nor levity nor falsehood shall thine ear assail."

XXVII

"Late as I roam'd, intent on Nature's charms,
I reach'd at eve this wilderness profound;

And, leaning where yon oak expands her arms,
Heard these rude cliffs thine awful voice rebound,
(For in thy speech I recognise the sound.)
You mourn'd for ruin'd man, and virtue lost,
And seem'd to feel of keen remorse the wound,
Pondering on former days, by guilt engross'd,
Or in the giddy storm of dissipation toss'd."

XXVIII

"But say, in courtly life can craft be learn'd,
Where knowledge opens, and exalts the soul?
Where Fortune lavishes her gifts unearn'd,
Can selfishness the liberal heart control?
Is glory there achiev'd by arts, as foul,
As those which felons, fiends, and furies plan?
Spiders ensnare, snakes poison, tygers prowl;
Love is the godlike attribute of man.
O teach a simple Youth this mystery to scan."

XXIX

"Or else the lamentable strain disclaim,
And give me back the calm, contented mind;
Which, late, exulting, view'd, in Nature's frame,
Goodness untainted, wisdom unconfined,
Grace, grandeur, and utility combined.
Restore those tranquil days, that saw me still
Well pleased with all but most with humankind;
When Fancy roam'd through Nature's works at will,
Uncheck'd by cold distrust, and uninform'd of ill."

XXX

"Wouldst thou (the Sage replied) in peace return
To the gay dreams of fond romantick youth,
Leave me to hide, in this remote sojourn,
From every gentle ear the dreadful truth:
For if my desultory strain with ruth
And indignation make thine eyes o'erflow,
Alas! what comfort could thy anguish sooth,
Shouldst thou th' extent of human folly know.
Be ignorance thy choice, where knowledge leads to wo."

XXXI

"But let untender thoughts afar be driven;
Nor venture to arraign the dread decree:
For know, to man, as candidate for heaven,
The voice of The Eternal said, Be free:
And this divine prerogative to thee
Does virtue, happiness, and heaven convey;
For virtue is the child of liberty,
And happiness of virtue; nor can they
Be free to keep the path who are not free to stray."

XXXII

"Yet leave me not. I would allay that grief,
Which else might thy young virtue overpower;
And in thy converse I shall and relief,
When the dark shades of melancholy lower;
For solitude has many a dreary hour,
Even when exempt from grief, remorse, and pain:
Come often then; for, haply, in my bower,
Amusement, knowledge, wisdom thou may'st gain:
If I one soul improve I have not lived in vain."

XXXIII

And now, at length, to Edwin's ardent gaze
The Muse of history unrolls her page.
But few, alas! the scenes her art displays,
To charm his fancy, or his heart engage.
Here Chiefs their thirst of power in blood asswage,
And straight their flames with tenfold fierceness born:
Here smiling Virtue prompts the patriot's rage,
But lo, erelong, is left alone to mourn,
And languish in the dust, and clasp th' abandon'd urn.

XXXIV

"Ah, what avails (he said) to trace the springs
That whirl of empire the stupendous wheel!
Ah, what have I to do with conquering kings,
Hands drench'd in blood, and breasts begirt with steel!
To those, whom Nature taught to think and feel,
Heroes, alas, are things of small concern.

Could History man's secret heart reveal,
And what imports a heaven-born mind to learn,
Her transcripts to explore what bosom would not yearn!"

XXXV

"This praise, O Cheronean Sage, is thine.
(Why should this praise to thee alone belong!)
All else from Nature's moral path decline,
Lured by the toys that captivate the throng;
To herd in cabinets and camps, among
Spoil, carnage, and the cruel pomp of pride;
Or chaunt of heraldry the drowsy song,
How tyrant blood, o'er many a region wide,
Rolls to a thousand thrones its execrable tide."

XXXVI

"O who of man the story will unfold,
Ere victory and empire wrought annoy,
In that elysian age (misnamed of gold)
The age of love, and innocence, and joy,
When all were great and free! man's sole employ
To deck the bosom of his parent earth;
Or toward his bower the murmuring stream decoy,
To aid the floweret's long-expected birth,
And lull the bed of peace, and crown the board of mirth."

XXXVII

"Sweet were your shades, O ye primeval grove,
Whose boughs to man his food and shelter lent,
Pure in his pleasures, happy in his loves,
His eye still smiling and his heart content.
Then, hand in hand, Health, Sport, and Labour went.
Nature supply'd the wish she taught to crave.
None prowl'd for prey, none watch'd to circumvent.
To all an equal lot Heaven's bounty gave:
No vassal fear'd his lord, no tyrant fear'd his slave."

XXXVIII

"But ah! th' Historick Muse has never dared
To pierce those hallow'd bowers: 'tis Fancy's beam

Pour'd on the vision of th' enraptured Bard,
That paints the charms of that delicious theme.
Then hail sweet Fancy's ray! and hail the dream
That weans the weary soul from guilt and woe!
Careless what others of my choice may deem,
I long where Love and Fancy lead to go,
And meditate on heaven; enough of earth I know."

XXXIX

"I cannot blame thy choice (the Sage replied)
For soft and smooth are Fancy's flowery ways.
And yet even there, if left without a guide,
The young adventurer unsafely plays.
Eyes dazzled long by Fiction's gaudy rays
In modest Truth no light nor beauty find.
And who, my child, would trust the meteor-blaze,
That soon must fail, and leave the wanderer blind,
More dark and helpless far, than if it ne'er had shined?"

XL

"Fancy enervates, while it sooths, the heart,
And, while it dazzles, wounds the mental sight:
To joy each heightening charm it can impart,
But wraps the hour of wo in tenfold night.
And often, where no real ills affright,
Its visionary fiends, an endless train,
Assail with equal or superior might,
And through the throbbing heart, and dizzy brain,
And shivering nerves, shoot stings of more than mortal pain."

XLI

"And yet, alas, the real ills of life
Claim the full vigour of a mind prepared,
Prepared for patient, long, laborious strife.
Its guide Experience, and Truth its guard.
We fare on earth as other men have fared:
Were they successful? Let not us despair.
Was disappointment oft their sole reward?
Yet shall their tale instruct, if it declare,
How they have born the load ourselves are doom'd to bear."

XLII

"What charms th' Historick Muse adorn, from spoils,
And blood, and tyrants, when she wings her flight,
To hail the patriot Prince, whose pious toils
Sacred to science, liberty, and right,
And peace, through every age divinely bright
Shall shine the boast and wonder of mankind!
Sees yonder sun, from his meridian height,
A lovelier scene, than Virtue thus inshrined
In power, and man with man for mutual aid combined?"

XLIII

"Hail sacred Polity, by Freedom rear'd!
Hail sacred Freedom, when by Law restrain'd!
Without you what were man? A groveling herd
In darkness, wretchedness, and want enchain'd.
Sublimed by you, the Greek and Roman reign'd
In arts unrival'd: O, to latest days,
In Albion may your influence unprofaned
To godlike worth the generous bosom raise,
And prompt the Sage's lore, and fire the poet's lays."

XLIV

—"But now let other themes our care engage.
For lo, with modest yet majestick grace,
To curb Imagination's lawless rage,
And from within the cherish'd heart to brace,
Philosophy appears. The gloomy race
By Indolence and moping Fancy bred,
Fear, Discontent, Solicitude give place,
And Hope and Courage brighten in their stead,
While on the kindling soul her vital beams are shed."

XLV

"Then waken from long lethargy to life
The seeds of happiness, and powers of thought;
Then jarring appetites forego their strife,
A strife by ignorance to madness wrought.
Pleasure by savage man is dearly bought
With fell revenge, lust that defies controul,

With gluttony and death. The mind untaught
Is a dark waste, where fiends and tempests howl;
As Phebus to the world, is Science to the soul."

XLVI

"And Reason now through Number, Time, and Space,
Darts the keen lustre of her serious eye,
And learns, from facts compared, the laws to trace,
Whose long progression leads to Deity.
Can mortal strength presume to boast so high!
Can mortal sight, so oft bedim'd with tears,
Such glory bear!—for lo, the shadows fly
From nature's face; Confusion disappears,
And order charms the eyes, and harmony the ears."

XLVII

"In the deep windings of the grave, no more
The hag obscene, and griesly phantom dwell;
Nor in the fall of mountain-stream, or roar
Of winds, is heard the angry spirit's yell;
No wizard mutters the tremendous spell,
Nor sinks convulsive in prophetick swoon;
Nor bids the noise of drums and trumpets swell,
To ease of fancied pangs the labouring moon,
Or chace the shade that blots the blazing orb of noon."

XLVIII

"Many a long-lingering year, in lonely isle,
Stun'd with th' eternal turbulence of waves,
Lo, with dim eyes, that never learn'd to smile,
And trembling hands, the famish'd native craves
Of heaven his wretched fare: shivering in caves,
Or scorch'd on rocks, he pines from day to day
But Science gives the word; and lo, he braves
The surge and tempest, lighted by her ray,
And to a happier land wafts merrily away."

XLIX

"And even where Nature loads the teeming plain
With the full pomp of vegetable store,

Her bounty, unimproved, is deadly bane:
Dark woods and rankling wilds, from shore to shore,
Stretch their enormous gloom; which to explore
Even Fancy trembles, in her sprightliest mood;
For there, each eyeball gleams with lust of gore,
Nestles each murderous and each monstrous brood,
Plague lurks in every shade, and steams from every flood."

L

"Twas from Philosophy man learn'd to tame
The soil, by plenty to intemperance fed.
Lo, from the echoing ax, and thundering flame,
Poison and plague and yelling rage are fled.
The waters, bursting from their slimy bed,
Bring health and melody to every vale:
And, from the breezy man, and mountain's head,
Ceres and Flora, to the sunny dale,
To fan their glowing charms, invite the fluttering gale."

LI

"What dire necessities on every hand
Our art, our strength, our fortitude require!
Of foes intestine what a numerous band
Against this little throb of life conspire!
Yet Science can elude their fatal ire
A while, and turn aside Death's level'd dart,
Sooth the sharp pang, allay the fever's fire,
And brace the nerves once more, and cheer the heart,
And yet a few soft nights and balmy days impart."

LII

"Nor less to regulate man's moral frame
Science exerts her all-composing sway.
Flutters thy breast with fear, or pants for fame,
Or pines to Indolence and Spleen a prey,
Or Avarice, a fiend more fierce than they?
Flee to the shade of Academus' grove;
Where cares molest not, discord melts away
In harmony, and the pure passions prove
How sweet the words of truth breath'd from the lips of Love."

LIII

"What cannot Art and Industry perform,
When Science plans the progress of their toil!
They smile at penury, disease, and storm;
And oceans from their mighty mound recoil.
When tyrants scourge, or demagogues embroil
A land, or when the rabble's headlong rage
Order transforms to anarchy and spoil,
Deep-versed in man the philosophick Sage
Prepares with lenient hand their phrenzy to asswage."

LIV

"Tis he alone, whose comprehensive mind,
From situation, temper, soil, and clime
Explored, a nation's various powers can bind
And various orders, in one Form sublime
Of polity, that, midst the wrecks of time,
Secure shall lift its head on high, nor fear
Th' assault of foreign or domestick crime,
While publick faith, and publick love sincere,
And Industry and Law maintain their sway severe."

LV

Enraptured by the Hermit's strain, the Youth
Proceeds the path of Science to explore.
And now, expanding to the beams of Truth,
New energies, and charms unknown before,
His mind discloses: Fancy now no more
Wantons on fickle pinion through the skies;
But, fix'd in aim, and conscious of her power,
Sublime from cause to cause exults to rise,
Creation's blended stores arranging as she flies.

LVI

Nor love of novelty alone inspires,
Their laws and nice dependencies to scan;
For, mindful of the aids that life requires,
And of the services man owes to man,
He meditates new arts on Nature's plan;
The cold desponding breast of Sloth to warm,

The flame of Industry and Genius fan,
And Emulation's noble rage alarm,
And the long hours of Toil and Solitude to charm.

LVII

But She, who set on fire his infant heart,
And all his dreams, and all his wanderings shared
And bless'd, the Muse, and her celestial art,
Still claim th' Enthusiast's fond and first regard.
From Nature's beauties variously compared
And variously combined, he learns to frame
Those forms of bright perfection, which the Bard,
While boundless hopes and boundless views inflame,
Enamour'd consecrates to never-dying fame.

LVIII

Of late, with cumbersome, though pompous show,
Edwin would oft his flowery rhyme deface,
Through ardour to adorn; but Nature now
To his experienced eye a modest grace
Presents, where Ornament the second place
Holds, to intrinsick worth and just design
Subservient still. Simplicity apace
Tempers his rage: he owns her charm divine,
And clears th' ambiguous phrase, and lops th' unwieldy line.

LIX

Fain would I sing (much yet unsung remains)
What sweet delirium o'er his bosom stole,
When the great Shepherd of the Mantuan plains
His deep majestick melody 'gan roll:
Fain would I sing, what transport storm'd his soul,
How the red current throb'd his veins along,
When, like Pelides, bold beyond controul,
Gracefully terrible, sublimely strong,
Homer raised high to heaven the loud, th' impetuous song.

LX

And how his lyre, though rude her first essays,
Now skill'd to sooth, to triumph, to complain,

Warbling at will through each harmonious maze,
Was taught to modulate the artful strain,
I fain would sing:—but ah! I strive in vain.—
Sighs from a breaking heart my voice confound.—
With trembling step, to join yon weeping train,
I haste, where gleams funereal glare around,
And, mix'd with shrieks of woe, the knells of death resound.

LXI

Adieu, ye lays, that fancy's flowers adorn,
The soft amusement of the vacant mind!
He sleeps in dust, and all the Muses mourn,
He, whom each Virtue fired, each grace refined,
Friend, teacher, pattern, darling of mankind!—
He sleeps in dust.—Ah, how should I pursue
My theme!—To heart-consuming grief resign'd
Here on his recent grave I fix my view,
And pour my bitter tears.—Ye flowery lays, adieu!

LXII

Art thou, my G,******* for ever fled!
And am I left to unavailing woe!
When fortune's storms assail this weary head,
Where cares long since have shed untimely snow,
Ah, now for comfort whither shall I go!
No more thy soothing voice my anguish chears:
Thy placid eyes with smiles no longer glow,
My hopes to cherish, and allay my fears.—
'Tis meet that I should mourn:—flow forth afresh my tears.

JAMES MACPHERSON

(1736–1796)

———

HAILING from Badenoch, Macpherson grew up in a stronghold of Jacobitism. The nearby Ruthven barracks had kept the Jacobite soldiers in check until the army set fire to it in February 1746, when Macpherson was not yet ten years old. As a student in Aberdeen he read divinity, but he also developed an interest in satirical and humorous poetry. In this period he wrote imitations of Robert Blair and Horace, among others. Encouraged by leading intellectuals of the age, Adam Ferguson and Hugh Blair among them, Macpherson produced *Fragments of Ancient Poetry Collected in the Highlands of Scotland* (1760). Avid readers quickly established funds so that Macpherson could explore the literary culture of the area more thoroughly. Further collections of ancient Gaelic poetry 'translated' into English prose followed—to great acclaim, and then, great controversy. Taken from *The Works of Ossian* (1765), the following pieces showcase the emotional range of the Ossianic poems, from the elegiac to the angry, while also allowing us to trace common tropes, themes, and images. The footnotes, taken almost wholesale from the original publication, ought to be read as both commentary and para-poetry.

———

Fingal, An Ancient Epic Poem *(1761), book 1*

The Works of Ossian, the Son of Fingal. In Two Volumes. Translated from the Galic Language by James Macpherson, 3rd edn (London: T. Becket and P. A. Dehondt, 1765).

Cuchullin* sat by Tura's wall; by the tree of the rustling leaf.—His spear leaned against the mossy rock. His shield lay by him on the grass. As he thought of mighty Carbar,* a hero whom he slew in war; the scout* of the ocean came, Moran the son of Fithil.*

    Rise, said the youth, Cuchullin, rise; I see the ships of Swaran. Cuchullin, many are the foe: many the heroes of the dark-rolling sea.

Moran! replied the blue-eyed chief, thou ever tremblest, son of Fithil: Thy fears have much increased the foe. Perhaps it is the king* of the lonely hills coming to aid me on green Ullin's plains.

I saw their chief, says Moran, tall as a rock of ice. His spear is like that blasted fir. His shield like the rising moon. He sat on a rock on the shore: his dark host rolled, like clouds, around him.—Many, chief of men! I said, many are our hands of war.—Well art thou named, the Mighty Man, but many mighty men are seen from Tura's windy walls.—He answered, like a wave on a rock, who in this land appears like me? Heroes stand not in my presence: they fall to earth beneath my hand. None can meet Swaran in the fight but Fingal, king of stormy hills. Once we wrestled on the heath of Malmor,* and our heels overturned the wood. Rocks fell from their place; and rivulets, changing their course, fled murmuring from our strife. Three days we renewed our strife, and heroes stood at a distance and trembled. On the fourth, Fingal says, that the king of the ocean fell; but Swaran says, he stood. Let dark Cuchullin yield to him that is strong as the storms of Malmor.

No: replied the blue-eyed chief, I will never yield to man. Dark Cuchullin will be great or dead. Go, Fithil's son, and take my spear: strike the sounding shield of Cabait.* It hangs at Tura's rustling gate; the sound of peace is not its voice. My heroes shall hear on the hill.

He went and struck the bossy shield. The hills and their rocks replied. The sound spread along the wood: deer start by the lake of roes. Curach* leapt from the sounding rock; and Connal of the bloody spear. Crugal's* breast of snow beats high. The son of Favi leaves the dark-brown hind. It is the shield of war, said Ronnar, the spear of Cuchullin, said Lugar.—Son of the sea, put on thy arms! Calmar lift thy sounding steel! Puno! horrid hero, rise: Cairbar from thy red tree of Cromla. Bend thy white knee, O Eth; and descend from the streams of Lena.—Ca-olt stretch thy white side as thou movest along the whistling heath of Mora: thy side that is white as the foam of the troubled sea, when the dark winds pour it on the murmuring rocks of Cuthon.*

Now I behold the chiefs in the pride of their former deeds; their souls are kindled at the battles of old, and the actions of other times. Their eyes are like flames of fire, and roll in search of the foes of the land.—Their mighty hands are on their swords; and lightning pours from their sides of steel.—They came like streams from the mountains; each rushed roaring from his hill. Bright are the chiefs of battle in the armour of their fathers.—Gloomy and dark their heroes followed, like the gathering of the rainy clouds behind the red meteors of heaven.—The sounds of crashing arms ascend. The grey dogs howl

between. Unequally bursts the song of battle; and rocking Cromla*
echoes round. On Lena's dusky heath they stood, like mist* that shades
the hills of autumn: when broken and dark it settles high, and lifts its
head to heaven.

Hail, said Cuchullin, sons of the narrow vales, hail ye hunters of the
deer. Another sport is drawing near: it is like the dark rolling of that
wave on the coast. Shall we fight, ye sons of war! or yield green Innisfail*
to Lochlin? —O Connal* speak, thou first of men! thou breaker of
the shields! thou hast often fought with Lochlin; wilt thou lift up thy
father's spear?

Cuchullin! calm the chief replied, the spear of Connal is keen. It
delights to shine in battle, and to mix with the blood of thousands. But
tho' my hand is bent on war, my heart is for the peace of Erin.* Behold,
thou first in Cormac's war, the sable fleet of Swaran. His masts are as
numerous on our coast as reeds in the lake of Lego. His ships are like
forests cloathed with mist, when the trees yield by turns to the squally
wind. Many are his chiefs in battle. Connal is for peace.—Fingal would
shun his arm the first of mortal men: Fingal that scatters the mighty, as
stormy winds the heath; when the streams roar thro' echoing Cona: and
night settles with all her clouds on the hill.

Fly, thou chief of peace, said Calmar* the son of Matha; fly, Connal,
to thy silent hills, where the spear of battle never shone; pursue the
dark-brown deer of Cromla: and stop with thine arrows the bounding
roes of Lena. But, blue-eyed son of Semo, Cuchullin, ruler of the war,
scatter thou the sons of Lochlin,* and roar thro' the ranks of their
pride. Let no vessel of the kingdom of Snow bound on the dark-rolling
waves of Inis-tore.* O ye dark winds of Erin rise! roar ye whirlwinds of
the heath! Amidst the tempest let me die, torn in a cloud by angry
ghosts of men; amidst the tempest let Calmar die, if ever chace was
sport to him so much as the battle of shields.

Calmar! slow replied the chief, I never fled, O Matha's son. I was
swift with my friends in battle, but small is the fame of Connal. The
battle was won in my presence, and the valiant overcame. But, son of
Semo, hear my voice, regard the ancient throne of Cormac. Give wealth
and half the land for peace, till Fingal come with battle. Or, if war be
thy choice, I lift the sword and spear. My joy shall be in the midst of
thousands, and my soul brighten in the gloom of the fight.

To me, Cuchullin replies, pleasant is the noise of arms: pleasant as
the thunder of heaven before the shower of Spring. But gather all the
shining tribes that I may view the sons of war. Let them move along
the heath, bright as the sun-shine before a storm; when the west

wind collects the clouds, and the oaks of Morven echo along the shore.

But where are my friends in battle? The companions of my arm in danger? Where art thou, white-bosom'd Cathbat? Where is that cloud in war, Duchomar?* and hast thou left me, O Fergus!* in the day of the storm? Fergus, first in our joy at the feast! son of Rossa! arm of death! comest thou like a roe* from Malmor. Like a hart from the echoing hills?—Hail thou son of Rossa! what shades the soul of war?

Four stones,* replied the chief, rise on the grave of Cathbat.—These hands have laid in earth Duchomar, that cloud in war. Cathbat, thou son of Torman, thou wert a sun-beam on the hill.—And thou, O valiant Duchomar, like the mist of marshy Lano; when it sails over the plains of autumn and brings death to the people. Morna, thou fairest of maids! calm is thy sleep in the cave of the rock. Thou hast fallen in darkness like a star, that shoots athwart the desart, when the traveller is alone, and mourns the transient beam.

Say, said Semo's blue-eyed son, say how fell the chiefs of Erin? Fell they by the sons of Lochlin, striving in the battle of heroes? Or what confines the chiefs of Cromla to the dark and narrow house?*

Cathbat, replied the hero, fell by the sword of Duchomar at the oak of the noisy streams. Duchomar came to Tura's cave, and spoke to the lovely Morna.

Morna,* fairest among women, lovely daughter of Cormac-cairbar.* Why in the circle of stones; in the cave of the rock alone? The stream murmurs hoarsely. The old tree's groan is in the wind. The lake is troubled before thee, and dark are the clouds of the sky. But thou art like snow on the heath; and thy hair like the mist of Cromla; when it curls on the rocks, and it shines to the beam of the west.—Thy breasts are like two smooth rocks seen from Branno of the streams. Thy arms like two white pillars in the halls of the mighty Fingal.

From whence, the white-armed maid replied, from whence, Duchomar the most gloomy of men? Dark are thy brows and terrible. Red are thy rolling eyes. Does Swaran appear on the sea? What of the foe, Duchomar?

From the hill I return, O Morna, from the hill of the dark-brown hinds. Three have I slain with my bended yew. Three with my long bounding dogs of the chace.—Lovely daughter of Cormac, I love thee as my soul.—I have slain one stately deer for thee.—High was his branchy head; and fleet his feet of wind.

Duchomar! calm the maid replied, I love thee not, thou gloomy man.—Hard is thy heart of rock, and dark thy terrible brow. But Cathbat, thou son of Torman,* thou art the love of Morna. Thou art like a sun-beam on the hill in the day of the gloomy storm. Sawest thou the son of Torman, lovely on the hill of his hinds? Here the daughter of Cormac waits the coming of Cathbat.

And long shall Morna wait, Duchomar said, his blood is on my sword.—Long shall Morna wait for him. He fell at Branno's stream. High on Cromla I will raise his tomb, daughter of Cormac-cairbar; but fix thy love on Duchomar, his arm is strong as a storm.—

And is the son of Torman fallen? said the maid of the tearful eye. Is he fallen on his echoing heath; the youth with the breast of snow? he that was first in the chace of the hill; the foe of the strangers of the ocean.—Duchomar thou art dark* indeed, and cruel is thy arm to Morna. But give me that sword, my foe; I love the blood of Caithbat.

He gave the sword to her tears; but she pierced his manly breast. He fell, like the bank of a mountain-stream; stretched out his arm and said;

Daughter of Cormac-cairbar, thou hast slain Duchomar. The sword is cold in my breast: Morna, I feel it cold. Give me to Moina* the maid; Duchomar was the dream of her night. She will raise my tomb; and the hunter shall see it and praise me. But draw the sword from my breast; Morna, the steel is cold.

She came, in all her tears, she came, and drew it from his breast. He pierced her white side with steel; and spread her fair locks on the ground. Her bursting blood sounds from her side: and her white arm is stained with red. Rolling in death she lay, and Tura's cave answered to her groans.—

Peace, said Cuchullin, to the souls of the heroes; their deeds were great in danger. Let them ride around* me on clouds; and shew their features of war: that my soul may be strong in danger; my arm like the thunder of heaven.—But be thou on a moon-beam, O Morna, near the window of my rest; when my thoughts are of peace; and the din of arms is over.—Gather the strength of the tribes, and move to the wars of Erin.—Attend the car of my battles; rejoice in the noise of my course.—Place three spears by my side; follow the bounding of my steeds; that my soul may be strong in my friends, when the battle darkens round the beams of my steel.

As rushes a stream* of foam from the dark shady steep of Cromla; when the thunder is rolling above, and dark-brown night on half the hill. So fierce, so vast, so terrible rushed on the sons of Erin. The chief like a whale of ocean, whom all his billows follow, poured valour forth as a stream, rolling his might along the shore.

The sons of Lochlin heard the noise as the sound of a winter-stream. Swaran struck his bossy shield, and called the son of Arno. What

murmur rolls along the hill like the gathered flies of evening? The sons
of Innis-fail descend, or rustling winds* roar in the distant wood. Such
is the noise of Gormal before the white tops of my waves arise. O son of
Arno, ascend the hill and view the dark face of the heath.

He went, and trembling, swift returned. His eyes rolled wildly round.
His heart beat high against his side. His words were faultering, broken,
slow.

Rise, son of ocean, rise chief of the dark-brown shields. I see the
dark, the mountain-stream of the battle: the deep-moving strength of
the sons of Erin.—The car, the car of battle comes, like the flame of
death; the rapid car of Cuchullin, the noble son of Semo. It bends
behind like a wave near a rock; like the golden mist of the heath. Its
sides are embossed with stones, and sparkle like the sea round the boat
of night. Of polished yew is its beam, and its seat of the smoothest
bone. The sides are replenished with spears; and the bottom is the foot-
stool of heroes. Before the right side of the car is seen the snorting
horse. The high-maned, broad-breasted, proud, high-leaping, strong
steed of the hill. Loud and resounding is his hoof; the spreading of his
mane above is like that stream of smoke on the heath. Bright are the
sides of the steed, and his name is Sulin-Sifadda.

Before the left side of the car is seen the snorting horse. The dark-
maned, high-headed, strong-hoofed, fleet, bounding son of the hill:
his name is Dusronnal among the stormy sons of the sword.—A thousand thongs bind the car on high. Hard polished bits shine in a wreath
of foam. Thin thongs bright-studded with gems, bend on the stately
necks of the steeds.—The steeds that like wreaths of mist fly over the
streamy vales. The wildness of deer is in their course, the strength of
the eagle descending on her prey. Their noise is like the blast of winter
on the sides of the snow-headed Gormal.

Within the car is seen the chief; the strong stormy son of the sword;
the hero's name is Cuchullin, son of Semo king of shells. His red cheek
is like my polished yew. The look of his blue-rolling eye is wide beneath
the dark arch of his brow. His hair flies from his head like a flame, as
bending forward he wields the spear. Fly, king of ocean, fly; he comes,
like a storm, along the streamy vale.

When did I fly, replied the king, from the battle of many spears?
When did I fly, son of Arno, chief of the little soul? I met the storm of
Gormal when the foam of my waves was high; I met the storm of the
clouds and shall I fly from a hero? Were it Fingal himself my soul
should not darken before him.—Rise to the battle, my thousands; pour
round me like the echoing main. Gather round the bright steel of your

king; strong as the rocks of my land; that meet the storm with joy, and stretch their dark woods to the wind.

As autumn's* dark storms pour from two echoing hills, towards each other approached the heroes.—As two dark streams from high rocks meet, and mix and roar on the plain; loud, rough and dark in battle meet Lochlin and Innis-fail. Chief mixed his strokes with chief, and man with man; steel, clanging, sounded on steel, helmets are cleft on high. Blood bursts and smoaks around.—Strings twang on the polished yews. Darts rush along the sky. Spears fall like the circles of light that gild the stormy face of the night.

As the troubled noise of the ocean when roll the waves on high; as the last peal of the thunder of heaven, such is the noise of battle. Though Cormac's hundred bards were there to give the war to song; feeble were the voices of a hundred bards to send the deaths to future times. For many were the falls of the heroes; and wide poured the blood of the valiant.

Mourn, ye sons of the song, the death of the noble Sithallin.*—Let the sighs of Fiöna rise on the dark heaths of her lovely Ardan.—They fell, like two hinds of the desert, by the hands of the mighty Swaran; when, in the midst of thousands he roared; like the shrill spirit of a storm, that sits dim, on the clouds of Gormal, and enjoys the death of the mariner.

Nor slept thy hand by thy side, chief of the isle of mist;* many were the deaths of thine arm, Cuchullin, thou son of Semo. His sword was like the beam of heaven when it pierces the sons of the vale; when the people are blasted and fall, and all the hills are burning around.— Dusronnal* snorted over the bodies of heroes; and Sifadda* bathed his hoof in blood. The battle lay behind them as groves overturned on the desart of Cromla; when the blast has passed the heath laden with the spirits of night.

Weep on the rocks of roaring winds, O maid of Inistore,* bend thy fair head over the waves, thou fairer than the spirit of the hills; when it moves in a sun-beam at noon over the silence of Morven. He is fallen! thy youth is low; pale beneath the sword of Cuchullin. No more shall valour raise the youth to match the blood of kings.—Trenar, lovely Trenar died, thou maid of Inistore. His gray dogs are howling at home, and see his passing ghost. His bow is in the hall unstrung. No sound is in the heath of his hinds.

As roll a thousand waves to the rocks, so Swaran's host came on; as meets a rock a thousand waves, so Innis-fail met Swaran. Death raises all his voices around, and mixes with the sound of shields.—Each hero is a pillar of darkness, and the sword a beam of fire in his hand. The field echoes from wing to wing, as a hundred hammers that rise by turns on the red son of the furnace.

Who are these on Lena's heath that are so gloomy and dark? Who are these like two clouds,* and their swords like lightning above them? The little hills are troubled around, and the rocks tremble with all their moss.—Who is it but Ocean's son and the car-borne chief of Erin? Many are the anxious eyes of their friends, as they see them dim on the heath. Now night conceals the chiefs in her clouds, and ends the terrible fight.

It was on Cromla's shaggy side that Dorglas placed the deer;* the early fortune of the chace, before the heroes left the hill.—A hundred youths collect the heath; ten heroes blow the fire; three hundred chuse the polish'd stones. The feast is smoking wide.

Cuchullin, chief of Erin's war, resumed his mighty soul. He stood upon his beamy spear, and spoke to the son of songs; to Carril of other times, the gray-haired son of Kinfena.* Is this feast spread for me alone and the king of Lochlin on Ullin's shore, far from the deer of his hills, and sounding halls of his feasts? Rise, Carril of other times, and carry my words to Swaran; tell him from the roaring of waters, that Cuchullin gives his feast. Here let him listen to the sound of my groves amidst the clouds of night.—For cold and bleak the blustering winds rush over the foam of his seas. Here let him praise the trembling harp, and hear the songs of heroes.

Old Carril went, with softest voice, and called the king of dark-brown shields. Rise from the skins of thy chace, rise, Swaran king of groves.— Cuchullin gives the joy of shells; partake the feast of Erin's blue-eyed chief.

He answered like the sullen sound of Cromla before a storm. Though all thy daughters, Innis-fail! should extend their arms of snow; raise high the heavings of their breasts, and softly roll their eyes of love; yet, fixed as Lochlin's thousand rocks, here Swaran shall remain; till morn, with the young beams of my east, shall light me to the death of Cuchullin. Pleasant to my ear is Lochlin's wind. It rushes over my seas. It speaks aloft in all my shrowds, and brings my green forests to my mind; the green forests of Gormal that often echoed to my winds, when my spear was red in the chace of the boar. Let dark Cuchullin yield to me the ancient throne of Cormac, or Erin's torrents shall shew from their hills the red foam of the blood of his pride.

Sad is the sounds of Swaran's voice, said Carril of other times:—

Sad to himself alone, said the blue-eyed son of Semo. But, Carril, raise thy voice on high, and tell the deeds of other times. Send thou the night away in song; and give the joy of grief. For many heroes and maids of love have moved on Innis-fail. And lovely are the songs of woe that are heard on Albion's rocks; when the noise of the chace is over, and the streams of Cona answer to the voice of Ossian.*

In other days,* Carril replies, came the sons of Ocean to Erin. A thousand vessels bounded over the waves to Ullin's lovely plains. The sons of Innis-fail arose to meet the race of dark-brown shields. Cairbar, first of men, was there, and Grudar, stately youth. Long had they strove for the spotted bull, that lowed on Golbun's* echoing heath. Each claimed him as their own; and death was often at the point of their steel.

Side by side the heroes fought, and the strangers of Ocean fled. Whose name was fairer on the hill than the name of Cairbar and Grudar!—But ah! why ever lowed the bull on Golbun's echoing heath? They saw him leaping like the snow. The wrath of the chiefs returned.

On Lubar's* grassy banks they fought, and Grudar like a sun-beam, fell. Fierce Cairbar came to the vale of the echoing Tura, where Brassolis,* fairest of his sisters, all alone, raised the song of grief. She sung of the actions of Grudar, the youth of her secret soul.—She mourned him in the field of blood; but still she hoped for his return.

Her white bosom is seen from her robe, as the moon from the clouds of night. Her voice was softer than the harp to raise the song of grief. Her soul was fixed on Grudar; the secret look of her eye was his.—When shalt thou come in thine arms, thou mighty in the war?—

Take, Brassolis, Cairbar came and said, take, Brassolis, this shield of blood. Fix it on high within my hall, the armour of my foe. Her soft heart beat against her side. Distracted, pale, she flew. She found her youth in all his blood; she died on Cromla's heath. Here rests their dust, Cuchullin; and these two lonely yews, sprung from their tombs, wish to meet on high. Fair was Brassolis on the plain, and Grudar on the hill. The bard shall preserve their names, and repeat them to future times.

Pleasant is thy voice, O Carril, said the blue-eyed chief of Erin; and lovely are the words of other times. They are like the calm shower* of spring, when the sun looks on the field, and the light cloud flies over the hills. O strike the harp in praise of my love, the lonely sun-beam of Dunscaich. Strike the harp in the praise of Bragela, of her that I left in the Isle of Mist, the spouse of Semo's son. Dost thou raise thy fair face from the rock to find the sails of Cuchullin?—The sea is rolling far distant, and its white foam shall deceive thee for my sails. Retire, for it is night, my love, and the dark winds sigh in thy hair. Retire to the halls of my feasts, and think of the times that are past: for I will not return till the storm of war is ceased. O Connal, speak of wars and arms, and send her from my mind, for lovely with her raven-hair is the white-bosomed daughter of Sorglan.

Connal, slow to speak, replied, Guard against the race of Ocean. Send thy troop of night abroad, and watch the strength of Swaran.—Cuchullin! I am for peace till the race of the desert come; till Fingal come, the first of men, and beam, like the sun, on our fields.

The hero struck the shield of his alarms—the warriors of the night moved on. The rest lay in the heath of the deer, and slept amidst the dusky wind.—The ghosts* of the lately dead were near, and swam on gloomy clouds. And far distant, in the dark silence of Lena, the feeble voices of death were heard.

'Berrathon: A Poem'

Bend thy blue course, O stream, round the narrow plain of Lutha.* Let the green woods hang over it from their mountains: and the sun look on it at noon. The thistle is there on its rock, and shakes its beard to the wind. The flower hangs its heavy head, waving, at times, to the gale. Why dost thou awake me, O gale, it seems to say, I am covered with the drops of heaven? The time of my fading is near, and the blast that shall scatter my leaves. Tomorrow shall the traveller come, he that saw me in my beauty shall come; his eyes will search the field, but they will not find me?—So shall they search in vain, for the voice of Cona, after it has failed in the field. The hunter shall come forth in the morning, and the voice of my harp shall not be heard. "Where is the son of car-borne Fingal?" The tear will be on his cheek.

Then come thou, O Malvina,* with all thy music, come; lay Ossian in the plain of Lutha: let his tomb rise in the lovely field.—Malvina! where art thou, with thy songs: with the soft sound of thy steps?—Son* of Alpin art thou near? where is the daughter of Toscar?

I passed, O son of Fingal, by Tar-lutha's mossy walls. The smoke of the hall was ceased: silence was among the trees of the hill. The voice of the chace was over. I saw the daughters of the bow. I asked about Malvina, but they answered not. They turned their faces away: thin darkness covered their beauty. They were like stars, on a rainy hill, by night, each looking faintly through her mist.

Pleasant* be thy rest, O lovely beam! soon hast thou set on our hills! The steps of thy departure were stately, like the moon on the blue, trembling wave. But thou hast left us in darkness, first of the maids of

Lutha! We sit, at the rock, and there is no voice; no light but the meteor of fire! Soon hast thou set, Malvina, daughter of generous Toscar!

But thou risest like the beam of the east, among the spirits of thy friends, where they sit in their stormy halls, the chambers of the thunder.—A cloud hovers over Cona: its blue curling sides are high. The winds are beneath it, with their wings; within it is the dwelling* of Fingal. There the hero sits in darkness; his airy spear is in his hand. His shield half covered with clouds, is like the darkened moon; when one half still remains in the wave, and the other looks sickly on the field.

His friends sit around the king, on mist; and hear the songs of Ullin: he strikes the half-viewless harp; and raises the feeble voice. The lesser heroes, with a thousand meteors, light the airy hall. Malvina rises, in the midst; a blush is on her cheek. She beholds the unknown faces of her fathers, and turns aside her humid eyes.

Art thou come so soon, said Fingal, daughter of generous Toscar? Sadness dwells in the halls of Lutha. My aged son* is sad. I hear the breeze of Cona, that was wont to lift thy heavy locks. It comes to the hall, but thou art not there; its voice is mournful among the arms of thy fathers. Go with thy rustling wing, O breeze! and sigh on Malvina's tomb. It rises yonder beneath the rock, at the blue stream of Lutha. The maids* are departed to their place; and thou alone, O breeze, mournest there.

But who comes from the dusky west, supported on a cloud? A smile is on his gray, watry face; his locks of mist fly on the wind: he bends forward on his airy spear: it is thy father, Malvina! Why shinest thou, so soon, on our clouds, he says, O lovely light of Lutha!—But thou wert sad, my daughter, for thy friends were passed away. The sons of little men* were in the hall; and none remained of the heroes, but Ossian king of spears.

And dost thou remember Ossian, car-borne Toscar* son of Conloch? The battles of our youth were many; our swords went together to the field. They saw us coming like two falling rocks; and the sons of the stranger fled. There come the warriors of Cona, they said; their steps are in the paths of the vanquished.

Draw near, son of Alpin, to the song of the aged. The actions of other times are in my soul: my memory beams on the days that are past. On the days of the mighty Toscar, when our path was in the deep. Draw near, son of Alpin, to the last sound* of the voice of Cona.

The king of Morven commanded, and I raised my sails to the wind. Toscar chief of Lutha stood at my side, as I rose on the dark-blue wave. Our course was to sea-surrounded Berrathon,* the isle of many storms.

There dwelt, with his locks of age, the stately strength of Larthmor. Larthmor who spread the feast of shells to Comhal's mighty son, when he went to Starno's halls, in the days of Agandecca. But when the chief was old, the pride of his son arose, the pride of fair-haired Uthal, the love of a thousand maids. He bound the aged Larthmor, and dwelt in his sounding halls.

Long pined the king in his cave, beside his rolling sea. Morning did not come to his dwelling; nor the burning oak by night. But the wind of ocean was there, and the parting beam of the moon. The red star looked on the king, when it trembled on the western wave. Snitho came to Selma's hall: Snitho companion of Larthmor's youth. He told of the king of Berrathon: the wrath of Fingal rose. Thrice he assumed the spear, resolved to stretch his hand to Uthal. But the memory* of his actions rose before the king, and he sent his son and Toscar. Our joy was great on the rolling sea; and we often half-unsheathed our swords.* For never before had we fought alone, in the battles of the spear. Night came down on the ocean; the winds departed on their wings. Cold and pale is the moon. The red stars lift their heads. Our course is slow along the coast of Berrathon; the white waves tumble on the rocks.

What voice is that, said Toscar, which comes between the sounds of the waves? It is soft but mournful, like the voice of departed bards. But I behold the maid,* she sits on the rock alone. Her head bends on her arm of snow: her dark hair is in the wind. Hear, son of Fingal, her song, it is smooth as the gliding waters of Lavath.—We came to the silent bay, and heard the maid of night.

How long will ye roll around me, blue-tumbling waters of ocean? My dwelling was not always in caves, nor beneath the whistling tree. The feast was spread in Torthóma's hall; my father delighted in my voice. The youths beheld me in the steps of my loveliness, and they blessed the dark-haired Nina-thoma. It was then thou didst come, O Uthal! like the sun of heaven. The souls of the virgins are thine, son of generous Larthmor! But why dost thou leave me alone in the midst of roaring waters. Was my soul dark with thy death? Did my white hand lift the sword? Why then hast thou left me alone, king of high Finthormo!*

The tear started from my eye, when I heard the voice of the maid. I stood before her in my arms, and spoke the words of peace.—Lovely dweller of the cave, what sigh is in that breast? Shall Ossian lift his sword in thy presence, the destruction of thy foes?—Daughter of Torthóma, rise, I have heard the words of thy grief. The race of Morven are around thee, who never injured the weak. Come to our dark-bosomed ship, thou brighter than that setting moon. Our course is to the rocky Berrathon, to the echoing walls of Finthormo.—She came in her beauty, she came with all her lovely steps. Silent joy brightened in her face, as when the shadows fly from the field of spring; the blue-stream is rolling in brightness, and the green bush bends over its course.

The morning rose with its beams. We came to Rothma's bay. A boar rushed from the wood; my spear pierced his side. I rejoiced over the blood,* and foresaw my growing fame.—But now the sound of Uthal's train came from the high Finthormo; they spread over the heath to the chace of the boar. Himself comes slowly on, in the pride of his strength. He lifts two pointed spears. On his side is the hero's sword. Three youths carry his polished bows: the bounding of five dogs is before him. His warriors move on, at a distance, admiring the steps of the king. Stately was the son of Larthmor! but his soul was dark. Dark as the troubled face of the moon, when it foretels the storms.

We rose on the heath before the king; he stopt in the midst of his course. His warriors gathered around, and a gray-haired bard advanced. Whence are the sons of the strangers? begun the bard. The children of the unhappy come to Berrathon; to the sword of car-borne Uthal. He spreads no feast in his hall: the blood of strangers is on his streams. If from Selma's walls ye come, from the mossy walls of Fingal, chuse three youths to go to your king to tell of the fall of his people. Perhaps the hero may come and pour his blood on Uthal's sword; so shall the fame of Finthormo arise, like the growing tree of the vale.

Never will it rise, O bard, I said in the pride of my wrath. He would shrink in the presence of Fingal, whose eyes are the flames of death. The son of Comhal comes, and the kings vanish in his presence; they are rolled together, like mist, by the breath of his rage. Shall three tell to Fingal, that his people fell? Yes!—they may tell it, bard! but his people shall fall with fame.

I stood in the darkness of my strength; Toscar drew his sword at my side. The foe came on like a stream: the mingled sound of death arose. Man took man, shield met shield; steel mixed its beams with steel.—Darts hiss through air; spears ring on mails; and swords on broken bucklers bound. As the noise of an aged grove beneath the roaring wind, when a thousand ghosts break the trees by night, such was the din of arms.—But Uthal fell beneath my sword; and the sons of Berrathon fled.—It was then I saw him in his beauty, and the tear hung in my eye. Thou art fallen,* young tree, I said, with all thy beauty round thee. Thou art fallen on thy plains, and the field is bare. The winds come from the desart, and there is no sound in thy leaves! Lovely art thou in death, son of car-borne Larthmor.

Nina-thoma sat on the shore, and heard the sound of battle. She turned her red eyes on Lethmal the gray-haired bard of Selma, for he had remained on the coast, with the daughter of Torthóma. Son of the times of old! she said, I hear the noise of death. Thy friends have met with Uthal and the chief is low! O that I had remained on the rock, inclosed with the tumbling waves! Then would my soul be sad, but his death would not reach my ear. Art thou fallen on thy heath, O son of high Finthormo! thou didst leave me on a rock, but my soul was full of thee. Son of high Finthormo! art thou fallen on thy heath?

She rose pale in her tears, and saw the bloody shield of Uthal; she saw it in Ossian's hand; her steps were distracted on the heath. She flew; she found him; she fell. Her soul came forth in a sigh. Her hair is spread on his face. My bursting tears descend. A tomb arose on the unhappy; and my song was heard.

Rest, hapless children of youth! and the noise of that mossy stream. The virgins will see your tomb, at the chace, and turn away their weeping eyes. Your fame will be in the song; the voice of the harp will be heard in your praise. The daughters of Selma shall hear it; and your renown shall be in other lands.—Rest, children of youth, at the noise of the mossy stream.

Two days we remained on the coast. The heroes of Berrathon convened. We brought Larthmor to his halls; the feast of shells was spread.—The joy of the aged was great; he looked to the arms of his fathers; the arms which he left in his hall, when the pride of Uthal arose.—We were renowned before Larthmor, and he blessed the chiefs of Morven; but he knew not that his son was low, the stately strength of Uthal. They had told that he had retired to the woods, with the tears of grief; they had told it, but he was silent in the tomb of Rothma's heath.

On the fourth day we raised our sails to the roar of the northern wind. Larthmor came to the coast, and his bards raised the song. The joy of the king was great, he looked to Rothma's gloomy heath; he saw the tomb of his son; and the memory of Uthal rose.—Who of my heroes, he said, lies there: he seems to have been of the kings of spears? Was he renowned in my halls, before the pride of Uthal rose?

Ye are silent, ye sons of Berrathon, is the king of heroes low?—My heart melts for thee, O Uthal; though thy hand was against thy father.—O that I had remained in the cave! that my son had dwelt in Finthormo!—I might have heard the tread of his feet, when he went to the chace of the boar.—I might have heard his voice on the blast of my cave. Then would my soul be glad: but now darkness dwells in my halls.

Such were my deeds, son of Alpin, when the arm of my youth was strong; such were* the actions of Toscar, the car-borne son of Conloch. But Toscar is on his flying cloud; and I am alone at Lutha: my voice is like the last sound of the wind, when it forsakes the woods. But Ossian shall not be long alone, he sees the mist that shall receive his ghost. He beholds the mist that shall form his robe, when he appears on his hills. The sons of little men shall behold me, and admire the stature of the chiefs of old. They shall creep to their caves, and look to the sky with fear; for my steps shall be in the clouds, and darkness shall roll on my side.

Lead, son of Alpin, lead the aged to his woods. The winds begin to rise. The dark wave of the lake resounds. Bends there not a tree from Mora with its branches bare? It bends, son of Alpin, in the rustling blast. My harp hangs on a blasted branch. The sound of its strings is mournful.—Does the wind touch thee, O harp, or is it some passing ghost!—It is the hand of Malvina! but bring me the harp, son of Alpin; another song shall rise. My soul shall depart in the sound; my fathers shall hear it in their airy hall.—Their dim faces shall hang, with joy, from their clouds; and their hands receive their son.

The aged oak* bends over the stream. It sighs with all its moss. The withered fern whistles near, and mixes, as it waves, with Ossian's hair.—Strike the harp and raise the song: be near, with all your wings, ye winds. Bear the mournful sound away to Fingal's airy hall. Bear it to Fingal's hall, that he may hear the voice of his son; the voice of him that praised the mighty.—The blast of north opens thy gates, O king, and I behold thee sitting on mist, dimly gleaming in all thine arms. Thy form now is not the terror of the valiant: but like a watery cloud; when we see the stars behind it with their weeping eyes. Thy shield is like the aged moon: thy sword a vapour half-kindled with fire. Dim and feeble is the chief, who travelled in brightness before.—

But thy steps* are on the winds of the desert, and the storms darken in thy hand. Thou takest the sun in thy wrath, and hidest him in thy clouds. The sons of little men are afraid; and a thousand showers descend.—

But when thou comest forth in thy mildness; the gale of the morning is near thy course. The sun laughs in his blue fields; and the gray stream winds in its valley.—The bushes shake their green heads in the wind. The roes bound towards the desert.

But there is a murmur in the heath! the stormy winds abate! I hear the voice of Fingal. Long has it been absent from mine ear!—Come, Ossian, come away, he says: Fingal has received his fame. We passed away, like flames that had shone for a season, our departure was in renown. Though the plains of our battles are dark and silent; our fame is in the four gray stones. The voice of Ossian has been heard; and the harp was strung in Selma.—Come Ossian, come away, he says, and fly with thy fathers on clouds.

And come I will, thou king of men! the life of Ossian fails. I begin to vanish on Cona; and my steps are not seen in Selma. Beside the stone of Mora I shall fall asleep. The winds whistling in my grey hair shall not waken me.—Depart on thy wings, O wind: thou canst not disturb the rest of the bard. The night is long, but his eyes are heavy; depart, thou rustling blast.

But why art thou sad, son of Fingal? Why grows the cloud of thy soul? The chiefs of other times are departed; they have gone without their fame. The sons of future years shall pass away; and another race arise. The people are like the waves of ocean: like the leaves* of woody Morven, they pass away in the rustling blast, and other leaves lift their green heads.—

Did thy beauty last, O Ryno?* Stood the strength of car-borne Oscar? Fingal himself passed away; and the halls of his fathers forgot his steps.—And shalt thou remain, aged bard! when the mighty have failed?—But my fame shall remain, and grow like the oak of Morven; which lifts its broad head to the storm, and rejoices in the course of the wind.

'The Songs of Selma'

Star of the descending night! fair is thy light in the west! thou liftest thy unshorn head from thy cloud: thy steps are stately on thy hill. What dost thou behold in the plain? The stormy winds are laid. The murmur of the torrent comes from afar. Roaring waves climb the distant rock. The flies of evening are on their feeble wings, and the hum of their course is on the field. What dost thou behold, fair light? But thou dost smile and depart. The waves come with joy around thee, and bathe thy lovely hair. Farewel, thou silent beam!—Let the light of Ossian's soul arise.

And it does arise in its strength! I behold my departed friends. Their gathering is on Lora, as in the days that are past.—Fingal comes like a watry column of mist; his heroes are around. And see the bards of the song, gray-haired Ullin; stately Ryno; Alpin,* with the tuneful voice, and the soft complaint of Minona!—How are ye changed, my friends, since the days of Selma's feast! when we contended, like the gales of the spring, that, flying over the hill, by turns bend the feebly-whistling grass.

Minona* came forth in her beauty; with down-cast look and tearful eye; her hair flew slowly on the blast that rushed unfrequent from the hill.—The souls of the heroes were sad when she raised the tuneful voice; for often had they seen the grave of Salgar,* and the dark dwelling of white-bosomed Colma.* Colma left alone on the hill, with all her voice of music! Salgar promised to come: but the night descended round.—Hear the voice of Colma, when she sat alone on the hill!

COLMA.

It is night;—I am alone, forlorn on the hill of storms. The wind is heard in the mountain. The torrent shrieks down the rock. No hut receives me from the rain; forlorn on the hill of winds.

Rise, moon! from behind thy clouds; stars of the night appear! Lead me, some light, to the place where my love rests from the toil of the chace! his bow near him, unstrung; his dogs panting around him. But here I must sit alone, by the rock of the mossy stream. The stream and the wind roar; nor can I hear the voice of my love.

Why delays my Salgar, why the son of the hill, his promise? Here is the rock, and the tree; and here the roaring stream. Thou didst promise with night to be here. Ah! whither is my Salgar gone? With thee I would fly, my father; with thee, my brother of pride. Our race have long been foes; but we are not foes, O Salgar!

Cease a little while, O wind! stream, be thou silent a while! let my voice be heard over the heath; let my wanderer hear me. Salgar! it is I who call. Here is the tree, and the rock. Salgar, my love! I am here. Why delayest thou thy coming?

Lo! the moon appeareth. The flood is bright in the vale. The rocks are grey on the face of the hill. But I see him not on the brow; his dogs before him tell not that he is coming. Here I must sit alone.

But who are these that lie beyond me on the heath? Are they my love and my brother?—Speak to me, O my friends! they answer not. My soul is tormented with fears.—Ah! they are dead. Their swords are red from the fight. O my brother! my brother! why hast thou slain my Salgar? why, O Salgar! hast thou slain my brother? Dear were ye both to me! what shall I say in your praise? Thou wert fair on the hill among thousands; he was terrible in fight. Speak to me; hear my voice, sons of my love! But alas! they are silent; silent for ever! Cold are their breasts of clay!

Oh! from the rock of the hill; from the top of the windy mountain, speak ye ghosts of the dead! speak, I will not be afraid.—Whither are ye gone to rest? In what cave of the hill shall I find you? No feeble voice is on the wind: no answer half-drowned in the storms of the hill.

I sit in my grief. I wait for morning in my tears. Rear the tomb, ye friends of the dead; but close it not till Colma come. My life flies away like a dream: why should I stay behind? Here shall I rest with my friends, by the stream of the sounding rock. When night comes on the hill; when the wind is on the heath; my ghost shall stand in the wind, and mourn the death of my friends. The hunter shall hear from his booth. He shall fear but love my voice. For sweet shall my voice be for my friends; for pleasant were they both to me.

Such was thy song, Minona softly-blushing maid of Torman. Our tears descended for Colma, and our souls were sad.—Ullin came with the harp, and gave the song of Alpin.—The voice of Alpin was pleasant: the soul of Ryno was a beam of fire. But they had rested in the narrow house: and their voice was not heard in Selma.—Ullin had returned one day from the chace, before the heroes fell. He heard their strife on the hill; their song was soft but sad. They mourned the fall of Morar, first of mortal men. His soul was like the soul of Fingal; his sword like the sword of Oscar.—But he fell, and his father mourned: his sister's eyes were full of tears.—Minona's eyes were full of tears, the sister of car-borne Morar. She retired from the song of Ullin, like the moon in the west, when she foresees the shower, and hides her fair head in a cloud.—I touched the harp, with Ullin; the song of mourning rose.

RYNO.

The wind and the rain are over: calm is the noon of day. The clouds are divided in heaven.

Over the green hills flies the inconstant sun. Red through the stony vale comes down the stream of the hill. Sweet are thy murmurs, O stream! but more sweet is the voice I hear. It is the voice of Alpin, the son of the song, mourning for the dead. Bent is his head of age, and red his tearful eye. Alpin, thou son of the song, why alone on the silent hill? why complainest thou, as a blast in the wood; as a wave on the lonely shore?

ALPIN.

My tears, O Ryno! are for the dead; my voice, for the inhabitants of the grave. Tall thou art on the hill; fair among the sons of the plain. But thou shalt fall like Morar;* and the mourner shall sit on thy tomb.

The hills shall know thee no more; thy bow shall lie in the hall, unstrung.

Thou wert swift, O Morar! as a roe on the hill; terrible as a meteor of fire. Thy wrath was as the storm. Thy sword in battle, as lightning in the field. Thy voice was like a stream after rain; like thunder on distant hills. Many fell by thy arm; they were consumed in the flames of thy wrath.

But when thou didst return from war, how peaceful was thy brow! Thy face was like the sun after rain; like the moon in the silence of night; calm as the breast of the lake when the loud wind is laid.

Narrow is thy dwelling now; dark the place of thine abode. With three steps I compass thy grave, O thou who wast so great before! Four stones, with their heads of moss, are the only memorial of thee. A tree with scarce a leaf, long grass which whistles in the wind, mark to the hunter's eye the grave of the mighty Morar. Morar! thou art low indeed. Thou hast no mother to mourn thee; no maid with her tears of love. Dead is she that brought thee forth. Fallen is the daughter of Morglan.

Who on his staff is this? who is this, whose head is white with age, whose eyes are red with tears, who quakes at every step.—It is thy father,* O Morar! the father of no son but thee. He heard of thy fame in battle; he heard of foes dispersed. He heard of Morar's fame; why did he not hear of his wound? Weep, thou father of Morar! weep; but thy son heareth thee not. Deep is the sleep of the dead; low their pillow of dust. No more shall he hear thy voice; no more shall he awake at thy call. When shall it be morn in the grave, to bid the slumberer awake?

Farewel, thou bravest of men! thou conqueror in the field! but the field shall see thee no more; nor the dark wood be lightened with the splendor of thy steel. Thou hast left no son. But the song shall preserve thy name. Future times shall hear of thee; they shall hear of the fallen Morar.

The grief of all arose, but most the bursting sigh of Armin.* He remembers the death of his son, who fell in the days of his youth. Carmor* was near the hero, the chief of the echoing Galmal. Why bursts the sigh of Armin, he said? Is there a cause to mourn? The song comes, with its music, to melt and please the soul. It is like soft mist, that, rising from a lake, pours on the silent vale; the green flowers are filled with dew, but the sun returns in his strength, and the mist is gone. Why art thou sad, O Armin, chief of sea-surrounded Gorma?

Sad! I am indeed: nor small my cause of woe!—Carmor, thou hast lost no son; thou hast lost no daughter of beauty. Colgar the valiant lives; and Annira fairest maid. The boughs of thy family flourish,

O Carmor! but Armin is the last of his race. Dark is thy bed, O Daura! and deep thy sleep in the tomb.—When shalt thou awake with thy songs? with all thy voice of music?

Rise, winds of autumn, rise; blow upon the dark heath! streams of the mountains, roar! howl, ye tempests, in the top of the oak! walk through broken clouds, O moon! show by intervals thy pale face! bring to my mind that sad night, when all my children fell; when Arindal the mighty fell; when Daura the lovely failed.

Daura, my daughter! thou wert fair; fair as the moon on the hills of Fura;* white as the driven snow; sweet as the breathing gale. Arindal, thy bow was strong, thy spear was swift in the field: thy look was like mist on the wave; thy shield, a red cloud in a storm. Armar, renowned in war, came, and sought Daura's love; he was not long denied; fair was the hope of their friends.

Erath, son of Odgal, repined; for his brother was slain by Armar. He came disguised like a son of the sea: fair was his skiff on the wave; white his locks of age; calm his serious brow. Fairest of women, he said, lovely daughter of Armin! a rock not distant in the sea, bears a tree on its side; red shines the fruit afar. There Armar waits for Daura. I came to carry his love along the rolling sea.

She went; and she called on Armar. Nought answered, but the son of the rock.* Armar, my love! my love! why tormentest thou me with fear? hear, son of Ardnart, hear: it is Daura who calleth thee! Erath the traitor fled laughing to the land. She lifted up her voice, and cried for her brother and her father. Arindal! Armin! none to relieve your Daura.

Her voice came over the sea. Arindal my son descended from the hill; rough in the spoils of the chace. His arrows rattled by his side; his bow was in his hand: five dark gray dogs attended his steps. He saw fierce Erath on the shore: he seized and bound him to an oak.

Thick bend the thongs* of the hide around his limbs; he loads the wind with his groans.

Arindal ascends the deep in his boat, to bring Daura to land. Armar came in his wrath, and let fly the gray-feathered shaft. It sung; it sunk in thy heart, O Arindal my son! for Erath the traitor thou diedst. The oar is stopped at once; he panted on the rock and expired. What is thy grief, O Daura, when round thy feet is poured thy brother's blood.

The boat is broken in twain by the waves. Armar plunges into the sea, to rescue his Daura or die. Sudden a blast from the hill comes over the waves. He sunk, and he rose no more.

Alone, on the sea-beat rock, my daughter was heard to complain. Frequent and loud were her cries; nor could her father relieve her. All night I stood on the shore. I saw her by the faint beam of the moon. All night I heard her cries. Loud was the wind; and the rain beat hard on the side of the mountain. Before morning appeared, her voice was weak. It died away, like the evening-breeze among the grass of the rocks. Spent with grief she expired. And left thee Armin alone: gone is my strength in the war, and fallen my pride among women.

When the storms of the mountain come; when the north lifts the waves on high; I sit by the sounding shore, and look on the fatal rock. Often by the setting moon I see the ghosts of my children. Half-viewless, they walk in mournful conference together. Will none of you speak in pity? They do not regard their father. I am sad, O Carmor, nor small my cause of woe!

Such were the words of the bards in the days of the song; when the king heard the music of harps, and the tales of other times. The chiefs gathered from all their hills, and heard the lovely sound. They praised the voice* of Cona! the first among a thousand bards. But age is now on my tongue; and my soul has failed. I hear, sometimes, the ghosts of bards, and learn their pleasant song. But memory fails on my mind; I hear the call of years. They say, as they pass along, why does Ossian sing? Soon shall he lie in the narrow house, and no bard shall raise his fame.

Roll on, ye dark-brown years, for ye bring no joy on your course. Let the tomb open to Ossian, for his strength has failed. The sons of the song are gone to rest: my voice remains, like a blast, that roars, lonely, on a sea-surrounded rock, after the winds are laid. The dark moss whistles there, and the distant mariner sees the waving trees.

ALEXANDER GEDDES
(1737–1802)

——

A CATHOLIC priest and biblical scholar, Alexander Geddes was born
in the parish of Rathven, Banffshire. As a teenager he entered the minor
seminary of Scalan in the Braes of Glenlivet; at twenty-one, he entered
the Scots College at Paris, and attended lectures at the Collège de
Navarre. He also studied Hebrew at the Sorbonne, where he also
excelled in Greek and Latin. Returning to Scotland in 1764, Geddes
spent several months ministering in Dundee before being appointed
chaplain to Traquair House in Peeblesshire. Within four years he was
removed from his post, having fallen in love with one of the ladies of
the house and for apparently criticizing church authorities. After
some years of financial hardship, he had some success with *Select
Satires of Horace Translated into English Verse* (1779). He also produced religious and anti-slavery pamphlets, as well as reams of satirical poetry for the radical press. 'Linton, a Tweedale Pastoral' is
a patronage poem in the manner of Virgil's *Pollio eclogue*, though
aligned with the habits of Scottish Spenserianism. An uneven mixture
of sincerity and sarcasm, the poem ends with a vision of Catholics
and Protestants living in harmony.

——

'Linton, a Tweedale Pastoral'

Linton, a Tweedale Pastoral (Edinburgh: C. Elliot, 1781).

Ye NYMPHS and NAIADS of the silver TWEED,
To louder notes attune the vocal reed!*

No more the limpid brook, and purling rill,
The flow'ry meadow, and the green-topt hill,
The mossy fountain, and the shadowy grove,
And all the other scenes of rural love,
Invite my song—A nobler theme inspires
A shepherd's breast with more than shepherd's fires!

Oh! did the muse, that erst, on Mincio's plains,
Taught heav'nly numbers to the Mantuan swains,
But deign, propitious, on my verse to smile,
And breathe the beauties of a courtly stile,
Not *Tityrus* self should sing a loftier lay,
Nor *Pollio* bear the past'ral palm away.

For now approaches that expected age
So clearly mark'd in THOMAS' mystic page—
THOMAS *the True*,* who never told a lie.
Read!—and revere the well-known prophecy!

"When from the RAVEN* and the ROOK* shall spring
An EAGLET-BIRD, (the forest's future king),
Then, men of *Tweedale*, banish ev'ry fear;
For gladsome days and glorious times are near."

He said—and streight the sister-Fates begin
Those gladsome days and glorious times to spin.
Already swells the glomerating clue,
And the last threads are of a finer hue!
But let them of a finer still be drawn,
To usher in young LINTON'S natal dawn.
With richer colours mark th' auspicious morn
On which the HOPE *of swains* is to be borne.

'Tis done—The Heav'ns assume a brighter dye;
Calm is the air, and cloudless is the sky:
With such a splendour Phoebe never shone,
And stars display a lustre not their own!

At length the Sun starts from his nuptial bed,*
With beams of new-born radiance round his head:
Joyous he springs to run th' ethereal course,
And, like a giant, glories in his force.*
The *Hours* and *Seasons* wait upon his nod,
And own the empire of the ruling God!

Lo! *Winter* quits a part of his domain,
And gives the year to *Spring*'s more gentle reign:
All nature feels the Spring's more gentle sway,
And sickly *Februa* blooms like healthful *May!*
If such a Winter, such a Spring, we see;
What must our *Summers* and our *Autumns* be?

Yet still remain some dregs of former times,*
(The just atonement of our Fathers crimes):
Still horrid *Mars*, besprent with human gore,
Drives the swoln tide of blood from shore to shore;
And grins with joy, to see his thunder hurl'd,
In spite of *Jove*, o'er all th' astonish'd world!
Still Lux'ry, seated on her silken throne,
Calls half the great-ones of the earth her own!
Still, some few Ministers betray their trust!
Still, some few Judges are not always just!
Still, some few Consciences are to be sold!
Still, some few Patriots may be brib'd with gold!
Still, some few Fair Ones scruple not to spread
A pair of antlers on their Husbands head!
More than *one* Lawyer—Doctor—and Divine,
Still meanly cringe at Mammon's dirty shrine!
More than *one* purse-proud Fool, and titled Knave,
To needy Worth with insolence behave!
Not only B * * cheats and circumvenes!
Not only T * * speaks not as he means!
Ev'n in the Muses and the Swains retreat,
O shame! remain some falsehood and deceit!
Nor shall the promis'd BLISS complete appear,
'Till the fair YOUTH have reach'd his twentieth year.

Then war, and discord, and domestic strife,
And all the other woes of human life,
Dearth, famine, plague, mortality, shall cease;
And all be health—and harmony—and peace.

No more *Religion*, with fanatic hand,
Shall fan the fire of Faction in the land;
But, mild and gentle, like her heav'nly SIRE,
No other flames but those of LOVE inspire.
Papist and *Protestant* shall strive to raise,
In diff'rent notes, ONE great CREATOR'S praise.
Polemic volumes on their shelves shall rot;
And *Hays* and *Abernethies* be forgot.

No more the weeping mother shall bemoan
Her sons, unburied, on some coast unknown:

Nor widow'd matron curse the fatal day
That tore her dearest—best-belov'd away.

No more the injur'd maiden shall complain
Of broken vows, and promises in vain;
But ev'ry swain shall, like the turtle, prove
Faithful and constant to his constant love.
No more th' oppressed villager shall roam
To seek, in foreign climes, a kindlier home;
But, fixt for ever to his native spot,
To sons of sons transmit his happy lot.

Old mother EARTH shall (now no longer curst)
Become as fecund as she was at first;
And yield, as erst in *Eden's* virgin soil,
Her fruits to man's amusement—not his toil.
Each barren heath, each thistle-bearing plain,
Shall wave with harvests of the bearded grain.
On bitter crabs shall golden apples glow,
And grapes hang clust'ring with the misletoe;
Sweet-smelling balsams every shrub adorn,
And Sharon-roses grow on ev'ry thorn;
Clear crystal springs from ev'ry mountain gush,
And Philomela chant in ev'ry bush.

No pois'nous herb shall taint our pregnant ewes,*
Nor early lambkins feel the noxious dews:
With sportive kids shall sportive foxes play,
(As artless and as innocent as they):
The timid goslin shall no longer dread
The rav'nous vulture and rapacious glede:
Nor shall the trembling linnet cease his lay,
Altho' the hawk be on the neighb'ring spray.

No snarling cur shall guard the fleecy store,
Nor fright the weary pilgrim from the door:
But spread shall be the hospitable board
To all alike—the peasant and the lord.
Plenty, and peace, and genuine joy, shall reign
From *Tweed* to *Teviot*—over all the plain.
SATURN shall smile—and wonder, to behold,
In *iron* days, a little age of *gold*;
And TWEEDALE then shall be what *Latium* was of old.

ANNA CHAIMBEUL / ANNE CAMPBELL
(D. 1768?)

ANNA CHAIMBEUL (Anna, Anne or Annie Campbell) was a Gaelic singer-songwriter best known for a lament composed for a sole female voice, 'Ailein Duinn' ('Dark-haired Alan' or 'Brown-haired Alan'). A sea captain from Lewis, Ailean Moireasdan (Alan Morrison) set sail from Stornoway in the spring of 1768 where he intended to meet his fiancée, Chaimbeul, for their betrothal party in Scalpay, Harris. Sailing into a storm, the vessel and its crew sank off the coast of the Shiant Islands. Heart-broken, Chaimbeul died a few months after producing this lament.

'Ailein Duinn'

Translator's transcription

Ailein Duinn, ò hi shiùbhlainn leat,
   Hao ri rì iu ò hì o hù gò rionn ò
   Ailein Duinn, ò hì shiùbhlainn leat.

'S mòr an diù tha tighinn fa-near dhomh
Fuachd na sìneadh 's meud na gaillinn
A dh'fhuadaich na fir on charraig
'S a chuir iad a bhòid' gan ainneoin –

Cha b' e siud mo rogha cala
Caolas Shiadair anns na Hearadh
Far am faicte fèidh air bearraidh,
Coileach dubh air bhàrr gach meangain.

Ailein Duinn, a mhiann nan leannan,
Chuala mi gun deach thu fairis
Air a' bhàta chrìon dhubh dharaich;
Mas fìor sin, cha bhi mi fallain –
O, a-chaoidh cha dèan mi banais.

Gura mise tha gu deurach:
Chan e bàs nan uan sa Chèitein
No tainead mo bhuaile sprèidheadh
Ach an fhlichead tha ad lèinidh
'S tu air bàrr nan stuagh ag èirigh
'S mucan-mara ga do reubadh.

'S truagh, a Rìgh, nach mì bha là' riut –
Ge b' e sgeir no bogh' an tàmh thu,
Ge b' e tiùrr am fàg an làn thu –
Cùl do chinn am bac mo làimheadh.

Ailein Duinn, gun tug mi spèis dhut
Nuair a bha thu 'n sgoil na Beurla
Far an robh sinn òg le chèile.

Ailein Duinn, gun d' fhuair thu 'n urram,
Fhuair thu 'n urram air na fearaibh:
An ruith 's an leum 's an streup 's an carachd,
'S ann an cur na cloiche fairis.

Ailein Duinn, gun tug mi gràdh dhut
Nach tug mi dh'athair no mhàthair,
'S nach tug mi phiuthar no bhràthair,
'S nach tug mi chinneadh no chàirdean.

Nar dhìoladh Dia siud air d' anam—
Na fhuair mi dhe d' shùgradh falaich,
'S na fhuair mi dhe d' chuid gun cheannach:
Pìosan daora caol' an anairt,
'S nèapaigear dhen t-sìoda bhallach
'S ribinn gus mo ghruag a cheangal.

'S dh'òlainn deoch, ge b' oil le m' chàirdean,
Chan ann de dh'uisge, no de shàile,
'S chan ann de dh'fhìon dearg na Spàinneadh –
A dh'fhuil do chuim, do chlèibh 's do bhràghad,
A dh'fhuil do chuim, 's tu 'n dèis do bhàthadh.

M' iarratas air Rìgh na Cathrach
Gun mo chur an ùir no 'n gaineamh
No an talamh toll no 'n àite falaich
Ach sa bhall a bheil thus', Ailein,
Ged a b' ann san liadhaig fheamainn
No am broinn na muice-mara.

'Brown-haired Alan' (translated by Peter Mackay and Iain S. MacPherson)

Brown-haired Alan, I'd go with you,
Hao ri rì iu ò hì o hù gò rionn ò
Brown-haired Alan, I'd go with you.

Huge worries are wracking me.
The storm's cold, the strong gale,
Has cleared men from the rocks
And carried them away helpless.

I'd not have chosen your harbour
In Harris, in the straits of Shader,
Where deer are seen on ridges
And black cockerels sit on the branches.

Brown-haired Alan, desire of lovers,
I heard that you were drowned.
The mean black oak boat went over,
If it's true I'll never come round.
Oh, I'll never be married.

My heart is broken
Not from the death of lambs in May
Or my cattlefold, empty and bare,
But the soaking of your plaid
As you're carried over the waves,
Whales tearing you apart.

God, I wish I was with you
Whichever rock or reef holds you,
Whatever wreck the tides leave you:
Your head crooked in my arm.

Brown-haired Alan, I admired you
When you were in the English school
When we were together in our youth.

Alan, you won each honour,
Honour over all the others:
You ran, jumped, played, wrestled,
And threw the stone better.

I loved you more than any other
More than a father or mother
More than a sister or brother
More than kith and kin.

Let God not damn your soul
For our secret flirtation,
What you gave me without condition:
Scarfs of flecked silk and satin,
And strips of dearest, fine linen
To tie my hair in ribbons.

Despite my people I'd drink
Not water or brine,
Or red Spanish wine –
But the blood of your breast,
Of your sea-drowned chest.

I ask, King of us all,
Don't bury me in sand or soil,
Or in an earthy hole,
But wherever Alan, you are;
Whether in the tangled sea-oak
Or the belly of the whale.

JAMES MYLNE
(1738/9–1788)

———

BORN into a farming family in Haddingtonshire, James Mylne harboured poetic ambitions from a young age. Many of his surviving juvenile odes, epistles, and fables address class issues in a forthright, calmly passionate tone. But Mylne's unseemly overtures to his idol Burns, a fellow farmer poet, has overshadowed his own accomplishments. Burns considered it impudent opportunism, and many observers apparently took that view. A posthumous edition of Mylne's works appeared fairly soon after his death, titled *Poems, Consisting of Miscellaneous Pieces and Two Tragedies* (1790), from which 'A Scots Song' is taken.

———

'A Scots Song'

Poems, Consisting of Miscellaneous Pieces, and Two Tragedies (Edinburgh: William Creech; London. T. Cadell, 1790).

I

How pleasant ance were Lothian's plains!
    Joy sung in ev'ry cottage there!
Trig were our maidens, blyth our swains,
    At ev'ry wedding, feast, and fair!
Nae wedding now, nae fair, nae feast,
    Can fill our maids or swains wi' glee.
Care sighs in ev'ry thoughtfu' breast,
    And sadness lours in ilka eye.

II

These views of Forth nae mair can please;
    Now summer fields nae mair seem gay:
Joy flies, with competence and ease,
    Frae Lothian's groaning swains away!
Ance winter's sharpest frost and snaw,

In plenty warm, we didna fear;
But now the blasts of poortith blaw,
   Mair sharp than winter's a' the year.

III

Now nappy ale and punch nae mair,
   At Christmas, shall our swains solace;
Where vig'rous age forgot his care,
   Amidst his childrens pratling race.
Nae sturdy youth at bullets plies;
   Unhanded wastes the curling-stane;
Useless in stour the golf-club lies,
   And pipers waste their wind in vain.

IV

Nae mair shall love-pair'd couples glow,
   With raptures down the rural dance;
And marks of artless passion flow
   From heart to heart, with ev'ry glance!
In joyful clubs nae mair we stroll,
   The garden of its sweets to strip;
Where happy Love aft slyly stole
   Far dearer sweets frae Beauty's lip.

V

Nae mair the swain by flow'ry pease,
   Or whitening hedge, the virgin leads.
How sweet the fragrance of the breeze!
   Her breath that sweetness far exceeds!
When lasses wade, or wash their claes,
   With kilted coats upon the knee,
Nae pawky swains keek o'er the braes
   Or cares the whitest legs to see!

VI

And when they to the milking gang,
   Nae jokesome shepherd brings the cow:
Alane they hum some dreary sang;
   What swains dow kiss or towzle now?
Dark Winter hears nae sang mair gay,
   Than *Margaret's Ghost*, or *Forest Flowers*,

Which in their prime were wed away
　　By cruel fate—Ah! fae are ours!

VII

Sing nae blyth sangs, yea beauteous quire!
　　Each fair-wrought lad as stiff's a rung,
Wad fa' asleep beside the fire,
　　Though *John, come kiss me now* ye sung!
But ken ye whence our sorrow's spring?
　　Our greedy laids bear a' the blame.
What ance made mony a tenant sing,
　　Now hardly steghs ae landlord's wame!

VIII

While sumptuously ye eat and drink,
　　Does it ne'er sting your conscious breast,
Ah, cruel luxury! to think
　　He starves whose toil procur'd the feast.
Here heartless coofs may toil and pine,
　　Some rigid tyrant's willing slaves;
But freedom shall be ever mine?
　　There's freedom yet beyond the waves!

JAMES BOSWELL

(1740–1795)

━━━

THE lawyer, diarist, and author James Boswell (9th Laird of Auchinleck) was born into a prominent family in Edinburgh. As a young man, and a student at the University of Edinburgh, Boswell delighted in his home city's cultural scene. As a teenager, he began his lifelong habit of recording detailed journals, as well as publishing poetry and theatre reviews. Intent on becoming a Catholic priest or monk, in 1760, he fled to London, where he met Samuel Johnson, the subject of his most famous biography. In the next few years he took a grand tour of Europe, which informed his highly successful travel writing. In 1769 he became a co-proprietor of *London Magazine*, for which he later wrote a series of monthly essays under the byline of The Hypochondriack. By August 1783 he had amassed a total of seventy pieces. Dr Johnson hoped to see his friend's articles revised for book form, but he died soon after. As a poet, Boswell displayed a keen cosmopolitan wit, as in the following chatty satire on modern authors, *The Cub, at New-market*.

━━━

The Cub, at New-market: A Tale *(1762)*

The Cub, at New-market: A Tale (London: R. and J. Dodsley, 1762).

> POETS, for most part, have been poor;
> Experience tells us;—Proof too sure.
> "Ay, may be so," Lord RICH exclaims,
> Who Fortune's Will incessant blames,
> "It may be so; but yet, confound 'em,
> They still have Jollity around 'em."
>
> PRAY, my good Lord!—'tis no Offence
> To ask by rules of common sense,—
> Is not this distribution right?—
> At least I view it in that light;
> For 'tis but just that ev'ry Creature
> Should have *some* favour from Dame Nature.

RICH shrugs his shoulders;—"Why, perhaps,
'Tis as you say"—then sudden slaps
His fist upon his buff-clad thigh,
And surly grunts, "Don't know, not I.
But come, don't you your Promise fail,
Do, give us now that same new Tale
Of Mirth;—'twill serve my spleen t' appease,
And set my troubled mind at ease."

I will, my Lord! but hope you'll make
Allowance for a Youngster's sake.
"O never fear."—Don't look so grim,
You seem dispos'd my back to trim;
That Cudgel looks so wondrous strong,
'Twould sweep a dozen Tars along.

"POH! Poh! this idle trifling! nay,
Come, Sir, you dine with me to-day."

BRAVO! my Lord! Oh, now I'm fee'd,
Wise as a Lawyer I'll proceed.

LORD E*******N, who has, you know,
A little dash of whim, or so;
Who thro' a thousand scenes will range
To pick up any thing that's strange,
By chance a curious CUB had got,
On SCOTIA's Mountains newly caught;
And, after driving him about
Thro' London, many a diff'rent rout,
The comic Episodes of which
Would tire your Lordship's Patience each;
New-market Meeting being near,
He thought 'twas best to have him there;
And, that your Time I mayn't consume,
View him in the New Coffee-Room!

THERE soon his noble Patron gay
Flies to his sportive Friends away:
While the Poor Being hums a song,
Astonish'd to behold a Throng
Of DUKES and LORDS!—Bless me! he thought;
Enchantment surely here has wrought!

SOMETIMES stock-still he stood amaz'd,
And with a stupid wonder gaz'd;
Admir'd at ev'ry thing he saw,
Ev'n Spurs would his attention draw;
Much more MILITIA COL'NELS GREAT!
The Bulwarks of BRITANNIA's State!
Whose strut majestic made him shrink,
As on a Promontory's brink:
In short, size, colour, voice, and shape,
Made our *Prodigious Hero* gape!
Such charms in Novelty we find,
Such it's effect on ev'ry mind.

SOMETIMES, he, with an awkward stride,
Would lift his legs, from side to side;
While Stars reflecting Phoebus' light
With beamy radiance struck his sight:
Then, as his visive orbs grew dim,
Began to think some look'd at him;
And Bashfulness, he knew not why,
Brought tears into his sheepish eye.

WHAT could the luckless fellow do?
For not a single soul he knew.
At last a corner pure and snug
He chanc'd to spy, which made him hug
Himself with joy.—There down he sat,
Of Solitude fond as a Bat:
And like a man at point of death,
Scarcely squeez'd forth above his breath,
"Here, get me *Paper*, *Pen* and *Ink*,
For, *Waiter*, I will write, I think."

AND now, my Story, pause awhile;
Till I, in *Hudibrastic* stile,
Attempt to give you as I can,
The Portraiture of this Wild Man.

HE was not of the iron Race,
Which sometimes CALIDONIA grace,
Tho' he to Combat could advance—
Plumpness shone in his Countenance;
And Belly prominent declar'd,

That he for Beef and Pudding car'd.
He had a large and pond'rous head,
That seem'd to be compos'd of lead;
From which hung down such stiff, lank hair,
As might the crows in Autumn scare.

TWO hours thus studious past or more;
Afraid to venture on the floor,
He rather thought on something new,
Nor dreamt he any notice drew.

SEDLEY, a truly worthy Knight,
In whom strong sense quick parts unite,
Whose humour of peculiar cast
Surprizes you from first to last;
Who, tho' few really are more wise,
To look a little foolish tries;
And likes *Exotics* to discover,
As a fine Lady a new Lover;
To the consounded Put comes near,
Tips him at once a friendly leer,
And thus accosts him: "How now, Squire?
Why, you've already wrote a Quire;
Yet still continue to go on:
What! will your labours ne'er be done?
'Tis said that you and EGLINTOUN
Our History are handing down:
No doubt, 'twill be a Work compleat;
All former Authors will be beat:
Out with *Proposals*—for my share,
I'll instantly subscribe, I swear."

JUST in the moment as he spoke,
The sprightly PEER, with switch of oak,
Popt in his nose—"Faith, good enough,
Sir CHARLES my friend! You *Jockey* bluff!
We'll give you leave—no favour light—
Here to throw in a willing mite.
You, to *Parnassus* who resort,
And the *Pierian* Ladies court,
Come, touch us up a sketch in rhime,
And shew your genius—now's the time.

To the best JUSTICE in the Nation—
The Squire I mean—make Dedication;
And I, who have a knack that way,
Will whistle Notes to what you say:
Nay, more, in attitude burlesque,
Will draw the CALIBAN grotesque;
Who in the Frontispiece shall stand,
And, ludicrous, your mirth command."

THIS last Design was scarcely broach'd,
When, lo! the MONSTER fell approach'd!
The Justice in one arm he lugs,
And the thin Spectre onward tugs.

OUR CLOWN (like country mouse of old,
'Bout which in HORACE we are told)
Quak'd timid, as, with horrid grin,
He saw HIM shake his triple chin;
Th' affrighted *Animal* would skulk,
And hide him from th' ENORMOUS BULK.

YOU'll easily believe, *My Lord!*
That this could no small fun afford;
And set—nay call me not queer Dog—
Their *Gelasticity* agog.

AT first the circle held but few;
Till, as the loud laugh stronger grew,
DUKES, LORDS, and COMMONS fondly join'd,
Eager the mighty joke to find:
Not one of 'em a sentence spoke,
With peals of laughter like to choak;
Each as he came th' infection seiz'd,
And by his friend behind was teaz'd
With "What's the matter?"—All at once,
The friend behind turns equal Dunce.

IN short, the Hounds, when in full cry,
Ne'er struck with so much force the sky,
As this blithe Chorus did assault
The Coffee-Room's resounding Vault.

MEANTIME, Sir CHARLES, who *seem'd* to pry
Into the Jest, with aspect sly;

His visage veiling with a gloom,
Slip'd to the middle of the room,
Pull'd half a dozen by the sleeve,
And whisper'd each; "You may believe,
I'm forc'd to tell you what is true,
Why, damn it, Sir! they laugh at *You*."

AND now, my Lord!—And now, in end,
To what does all this Story tend?

IF you're so good as to allow,
I'd willingly the Moral show.
"Ha! ha! my Boy! with all my heart;—
You're now to play a serious part.
Wisdom to learn from such as you,
Is surely something very new."

YOUR Lordship here then may observe,
That Nonsense frequently will serve
To set a table on a roar,
And drive dull Sadness out of door.
From whence, that Folly is at least
Harmless, I think should be confest;
And that in life it may be well,
Sometimes to hunt the *Bagatelle*.

LIKEWISE we see that Fate ne'er fails
To weigh things in impartial scales:
For, tho' some People are more blest,
With Understanding than the rest,
She some external Oddity
Bestows, which they themselves can't see,
Or some particular defect,
Which, while they indolent neglect,
To Mortals of inferior sort,
In harmless Satire serves for sport.

THUS is the Ballance render'd even;
Here view the equity of Heaven.

BEAN TORRA DHAMH /
MARY MACPHERSON
(C.1740–1815)

———

BORN in Badenoch, the Gaelic poet Mary MacPherson (Bean Torra Dhamh), also known as Mary Clark, received a good education from her schoolmaster father. She married young—and was early widowed. One by one her children grew up and went away, leaving her with little but her faith, which was evidently very strong. Her poems present the classic religious experience of passing through hardship to find great joy. The present poem is not a typical hymn, however, in that it contains a strong element of social commentary.

———

'Beachd Gràis air an t-Saoghal'

Translator's transcription

S mìle marbhphaisg ort, a shaoghail,
S carach, baoghalach do chleachdadh—
’S gar nach eil mi sean no aosmhor
S lìonmhor caochladh tha mi faicinn:
S tric am bàs le shaighdibh dùbhlanach
A’ tionndadh mùirn gu airtneal
’S a’ toirt aoibhnis mhóir gu bròn
Nuair bhios ar sùil ri sòlas fhaicinn.

’S tha gach là a’ teagasg iùil dhuinn
Chum ar cùp a ghiùlan faic’lleach—
Mas e ’s gum faigh sinn làine chuimseach
S cuibhreann iomchaidh e gu’r n-astar;
’M fad ’s a bhios sinn anns an fhàsach
Gheibh sinn aran ’s pàirt ri sheachnadh,
’S cuim’ am biodh ar gearan uaibhreach
Bho nach lìon e suas ar beairteas?

Gar na ghlac mi móran stòrais
Cha do chrìon mo chòir gu airceas:
   An t-aran lathail fhuair mi 'n còmhnaidh
'S math gu leòir gun stòr chur seachad;
   An tì rinn tadhal mór san fhàsach,
Cha do thàrr e maoin a thasgaidh—
   S fheàrr am beagan buain le gràs
Na oighreachd 's achanna chàich thoirt dhachaigh.

S gàbhaidh 'bhuaidh a th' air cloinn dhaoin'
A h-uile h-aon air saod a' bheairtis,
   'M fad 's am fagas 'falbh ga fhaotainn
'S cogadh 's caonnag ga thoirt dhachaigh;
   S lìonmhor neach tha 'cost a shaothrach
Nach do bhlais a mhaoin le 'taitneas—
   S mairg a ghlacas creach nam feumnach
Chum e fhéin a dhèanamh beairteach.

An tì a thaisgeas sìol na truaill'eachd,
Cha bhi 'stòras buan gu mairsinn:
   Ged a dhùin e glaiste suas e,
Gheibh e sgiathan luath chum astair;
   Mar an iolair 'shiùbhlas bhuainn
Chum nan nèamh le fuaim 's le clapraich,
   S amhlaidh beairteas thig le foill—
Ge mór a shraighlich, s faoin a mhairsinn.

S tric tha 'm beairteas 'na chùis-dhìtidh
Dha na mìltean tha ga ghlacadh,
   Càrnadh suas le cruas droch innleachd
Cuid an dìlleachdain gun taice:
   Bidh a' bhantrach dhaibh fo chìs,
S tric a dhìobair i 'n t-each-toiseach—
   S cruaidh an cridh' a bh' aig an linn
A dh'òrdaich lagh cho millteach crosta.

Chuir iad cas air reachd na fìrinn
'S ghluais iad dìcheallach san droch-bheart,
   'Claoidh nam bochd 's gan lot le mìorun—
Bantraich 's dìlleachdain gun choiseachd;
   B' uabhasach an cleachdadh tìre
Croich is binn air àird gach cnocain,

Cùirt nan spleagh gun lagh gun fhìrinn
As tric a dhìt an tì bha neochiont'.

Nuair bhios gràs ann an luchd-riaghlaidh,
Bidh na h-ìochdarain làn aitis,
   'S bidh gach prionnsa 's diùc is iarla
'Seasamh na còir fo sgiath a' cheartais;
   Cha bhi duine bochd gun phòrsan
'S cha bhi deòiridh truagh gun taice
   'S bidh gach cealgair air am fògradh
'S chan fhaigh luchd an fhòirneirt fasgadh.

An-sin bidh sonas anns gach rìoghachd
'S cùirt gach rìgh mar fhìonan taitneach,
   Torach, làn le gràdh 's le fìrinn
'S bheir gach sluagh deagh ìobairt seachad:
   Tionnda'idh 'n t-Àrabach 's an t-Inns'nach
Fo thrompaid bhinn an t-soisgeil
   'S cumaidh 'm Pàp na h-àithntean dìreach
'S cha bhi ìomhaigh ann no croisean;

Ach bidh 'n soisgeal air a leughadh
Anns a' bheus an robh e 'n toiseach
   'S bidh 'n luchd-teagaisg làn de dh'éifeachd
'Toirt an léirsinn do na bochdaibh;
   S binn am fuaim 's gach cluas bhith 'g éisteachd
Ait-sgeul aoibhinn cléir nan abstol
   Anns 'n do shuidh iad cruinn gu léir
Le Spiorad Dhé, 'toirt géill dh'a fhocal.

'S thusa, dhuine, cluinn is leugh seo,
'S cuimhnich fhéin bhith ceum air thoiseach,
   'S thu cho pailt de stòr 's de dh'fheudail,
'S banc' gu d' ghéill, 's cóig ceud air ocar:
   A mheud 's ged thionail thu ri chéile,
Do mhac gun chéill is d' oighre costail—
   B' fheàrr dhuit beannachd bho luchd-déirce
Na na dh'fhàg thu 'd dhéidh gu droch-bhuil.

'S bhon a shiùbhlas sinn gu léir
Don chill bhon d'éirich sinn an toiseach,
   Anns an uaigh 's nach luaidh sinn feudail
'S nach bi feum againn air costas,

S faoin gach fasan is deagh éideadh,
S tan' an léin' an téid an corp sa
    'S nì na daola cuilm den chreubhaig
'M fad 's a mhaireas reud gun chost dhith.

An-sin gach duine chuir san eucoir,
Buainidh e le deuraibh goirte,
    'S bidh an duais gu truagh mar thoill iad—
S àrd a chluinnear caoidh an ochan;
    Bidh an lochd 'na chrois 's gach eudann
'S an cogais reubach fhéin gan lotadh,
    Sgiùrsar iad gu sloc na péine
'S corraich Dhé mar leus gan losgadh;

Ach na fìreanaich gu aoibhneas,
Crùn is oighreachd gheibh gach neach dhiubh,
    'S còmhnaidh ait an teach na soillse—
Sona soim' bhios cloinn na maise
    A chliùthachadh ùr-Mhac na Maighdinne
A choisinn saibhreas dhaibh le 'ghaisgeachd
    'S a thug buaidh bhon uaigh le 'threun-làimh,
'S geat an éig le 'ghàirdean spealg e.

'S chaidh e suas le buaidh-ghàir aoibhnis
A dh'ullachadh dha chloinn an dachaigh,
    'S thug e àithntean d'a luchd-muinntir
'Uain 's a chaoraich a stiùradh faic'lleach;
    'S nuair a thig e rìs 'na mhòrachd
A thoirt am pòrsan do gach neach dhiubh,
    An seirbheiseach rinn ceilg 's fòirneart,
Sgiùrsar e le còrdaibh gorta.

'The Vantage Point of Grace' (translated by Ronald Black)

A thousand curses on you, world,
Subtle, risky is your way—
    And though I'm not yet old or aged
It's many changes I can see:
    Often death with his fierce arrows
Turns gladness into misery

And makes great happiness into gloom
When we're hoping to see contentment.

Each day teaches us advice
To carry our cup carefully—
    If we get a reasonable fill
It's a fit portion for our journey;
    As long as we are in the desert
We'll get bread with some to spare,
    And why complain haughtily
When it won't augment our riches?

Although I've not obtained much wealth
My lot has not shrivelled into poverty:
    Daily bread I've always enjoyed
And adequate income without having to save;
    He who's seen much of the desert
Has stored away but little wealth—
    Better to reap a little with grace
Than to bring home others' goods and fields.

It has a dangerous effect on man
For all to be going in search of riches,
    Seeking near and far to find them
With war and strife to bring them home;
    Many people waste their labour
Whose wealth has given them no pleasure—
    Cursed be he who robs the needy
In order to enrich himself.

Whoever stores corrupted seed,
His wealth will never last forever:
    Even if he's closed it, locked it up,
It will find swift wings to travel;
    Like the eagle flying away from us
To the skies with sound and flapping,
    Thus is wealth that comes unfairly—
For all its rattle, it can't continue.

Wealth is often cause for condemnation
To the thousands who embrace it,
    Raking in with cruel duplicity
The share of the unsupported orphan:

They extract tax from the widow
Who has often lost her heriot horse—
   Hard was the heart of the generation
That ordained a law so severe and perverse.

   They have trampled the laws of truth
And moved diligently to do evil,
   Oppressing the poor and viciously harming them—
Even disabled widows and orphans;
   Dreadful was the local custom
Of gallows and judgement on each hilltop,
   The court of lies without law or truth
Which often condemned the innocent.

   When there is grace in those who rule,
Those below will be fully content,
   With every prince and duke and earl
Defending rights under justice's wing;
   None of the poor will lack a share
And no wretched beggar will lack support
   And every criminal will be banished
And oppressors will have no place to hide.

   There will be joy then in every kingdom
With each king's court like a pleasant vine,
   Fruitful, full of love and truth
And each people will give good sacrifice:
   The Arab and Indian will convert
Under the gospel's melodious trumpet
   And the Pope will properly keep the commandments
And no images or crosses will there be;

   But the gospel will be read
In the good way in which it was at first
   And preachers will have effective power
In bringing their vision to the poor;
   It's a lovely sound in each ear to be hearing
The sweet good news of apostolic clergy
   In which they sat round all together
With God's Spirit, yielding to His word.

   And you, my friend, listen and read this,
And remember to keep a step in front,

You being so full of wealth and treasure,
Commanding a bank, with five hundred at interest:
    For all that you have gathered together,
Your son's an oaf and your heir's expensive—
    You'd benefit more from the beggars' blessing
Than from all your legacy, which won't end well.

    And because we all must travel on
To the clay from which we were made at first,
    Into the grave where we'll speak not of wealth
And in which we will have no need to spend,
    Vain are all fashions and pricy dresses,
Thin is the shirt that this body goes into,
    And the beetles will have a feast on the flesh
As long as any of it's left unused.

    Then all of those who sowed unjustly
Will reap a harvest of bitter tears,
    Their prize will be as sad as they've earned—
Loud will be heard the wail of their groans;
    Their crime will be a cross in each face
As their own guilty conscience torments them,
    They'll be scourged into the pit of pain
While God's wrath burns them like a fireball;

    But the righteous will go to happiness,
They'll all have a crown, an inheritance,
    And a pleasant abode in a well-lit house—
Beauty's children happy and eager
    To glorify the Virgin's newborn Son
Who won riches for them with His courage,
    Robbed the grave of its power with His brave hand
And smashed death's gate by the strength of his arm.

    He went up with a shout of joy and triumph
To prepare His children's eternal home,
    Giving commandments to His disciples
To guide His lambs and sheep with care;
    And when He returns in magnificence
To give every one of them their share,
    The servant who practised deceit and violence
Will get a scourging with painful cords.

ISOBEL PAGAN

(1740/1–1821)

———

A NATIVE of New Cumnock in Ayrshire, Isobel, popularly known as Wicked Tibbie, was famed in her own lifetime for possessing keen satirical skills. Abandoned early by her parents, she received little formal education, though she was a keen reader, especially of the Bible. As an adult, Pagan lived in an old brick store in Muirkirk, where she sold whisky and regaled onlookers with dramatic monologues and bawdy songs. In 1805 her *Collection of Songs and Poems on Several Occasions* was published in Glasgow. But, with much of her audience being illiterate, many of her songs circulated through performance. Having heard 'Ca' the Yowes to the Knowes', Burns wrote his own version for *The Scots Musical Museum*, with an additional verse of his own. But he did not acknowledge Pagan as the original source. 'Aughlen Spring' has appeared in previous anthologies, but it remains less well known. Set to the bouncy tune 'Bush aboon Traquair', it aptly showcases Pagan's humour and lyrical dexterity.

———

'Aughlen Spring'

A Collection of Songs and Poems on Several Occasions (Glasgow: Niven, Napier & Khull, 1803).

(Tune: "Bush aboon Traquair")

Give ear to me of each degree,
  Pity my lamentation,
The youth I lov'd is gone from me,
  Which causes great vexation.
He is design'd to share his fate,
  Out o'er the trackless ocean,
He's cross'd the sea, and gone from me,
  When love was in the blossom.

Near Aughlen Spring where birds do sing,
  While he was here beside me,

I had no fear while he was near,
    Whatever might betide me.
I'll visit aft the hawthorn tree,
    Where calmly first he told me,
Fine tales of love so comely,
    Whiles round he did enfold me.

His handsome shape and manly wit,
    His love refin'd and tender,
Superior far, I vow and swear,
    To the wealth of Alexander.
And I myself, for want of wealth,
    Was frown'd on by his mother,
But for his sake I'll single live,
    And ne'er wed any other.

O! may the powers preserve him still,
    And keep him safe from danger,
His eyes from viewing youthful toys,
    His heart from every stranger.
But if that Fate do favour him,
    That he advance in treasure,
And soon return, I'll cease to mourn,
    Renewing former pleasure.

JAMES MUIRHEAD
(1742–1808)

———

BORN at East Logan Farm in the parish of Buittle in Kirkcudbrightshire, and schooled in Dumfries, James Muirhead read theology
at the University of Edinburgh. In 1770 he was ordained minister of
the parish of Urr in Kirkcudbrightshire. Muirhead's one published
song, 'Bess the Gawkie' (that is, 'fool'), appeared in Herd's *Ancient
and Modern Scottish Songs* (1776). Burns praised it as one of
Scotland's great pastorals. However, some years later, the two men
entered into an unsavoury spat in the press after Muirhead objected to
being implicated in Burns's satire on freeholders, *Ballads on Mr Heron's
Election, 1795*. Muirhead retaliated with a brochure in which he ques-
tioned Burns's principles, before Burns retaliated in turn.

———

'Bess the Gawkie'

The Scottish Songs; Collected and Illustrated, ed. Robert Chambers,
2 vols (Edinburgh: William Tait, 1829).

> Blythe young Bess to Jean did say,
> Will ye gang to yon sunny brae,
> Where flocks do feed, and herds do stray,
>   And sport a while wi' Jamie?
> Ah, na, lass, I'll no gang there,
> Nor about Jamie tak a care,
> Nor about Jamie tak a care,
>   For he's ta'en up wi' Maggie.
>
> For hark and I will tell you, lass,
> Did I not see young Jamie pass,
> Wi' mickle blytheness in his face,
>   Out ower the muir to Maggie.
> I wat he gae her mony a kiss,
> And Maggie took them ne'er amiss,

'Tween ilka smack pleas'd her wi' this,
    That Bess was but a gawkie—

For when a civil kiss I seek,
She turns her head, and thraws her cheek,
And for an hour she'll hardly speak;
    Wha'd no ca' her a gawkie?
But sure my Maggie has mair sense,
She'll gie a score without offence;
Now gie me ane into the mense,
    And ye shall be my dawtie.

O Jamie, ye hae monie ta'en,
But I will never stand for ane
Or twa when we do meet again;
    So ne'er think me a gawkie.
Ah, na, lass, that canna be;
Sic thoughts as thae are far frae me,
Or ony thy sweet face that see,
    E'er to think thee a gawkie.

But, whisht, nae mair o' this we'll speak,
For yonder Jamie does us meet;
Instead o' Meg he kiss'd sae sweet,
    I trow he likes the gawkie.
O, dear Bess, I hardly knew,
When I cam' by, your gown sae new;
I think you've got it wet wi' dew.
    Quoth she, That's like a gawkie!

It's wet wi' dew, and 'twill get rain,
And I'll get gowns when it is gane;
Sae ye may gang the gate ye came,
    And tell it to your dawtie.
The guilt appeared in Jamie's cheek:
He cried, O cruel maid, but sweet,
If I should gang anither gate,
    I ne'er could meet my dawtie.

The lasses fast frae him they flew,
And left poor Jamie sair to rue
That ever Maggie's face he knew,

Or yet ca'd Bess a gawkie.
As they gaed ower the muir, they sang,
The hills and dales wi' echoes rang,
The hills and dales wi' echoes rang,
     Gang o'er the muir to Maggie.

CHRISTIAN CARSTAIRS

(*FL.* 1763–1786)

———

HAILING from Kinross, Christian Carstairs is said to have been a governess. What little is known of her derives from her anonymously published collection *Original Poems* (1786). Many of the surviving copies of that book have been signed with her name at the end. Dedicated to Ann Henderson and with a small list of subscribers, mostly made up of young governesses, the volume appears to have circulated privately. The earliest poem dates from 1763, and that decade, the 1760s, appears to have been Carstairs's most productive. Handsomely presented, *Original Poems* contains a pleasing mixture of epistles, epitaphs, and ballads, among other things.

———

'On Seeing Lady H—after the Death of a Favourite Daughter'

Original Poems. By a Lady, Dedicated to Miss Ann Henderson. A Tribute to Gratitude and Friendships (Edinburgh: Andrew Shortrede, 1786).

> Not death so common, or an infant lost,
> The turn of mind by tender feelings tost;
> Deep by regret each happy scene reflect,
> For her my life all other joys neglect.
> Blows there a rose so sweet? each flower recalls,
> A day how gay, then droops its head and falls.
> Bleak winter comes! the lifeless trees no shade,
> A dreary night; how cold, how chang'd a bed!
> How then to sleep, to peace, my mind compose!
> At once depriv'd for ever of repose.
> What have I done? to blast my early hope,
> Torn thus my life, the cause of my hard lot?
> Oh! awful thought, to question thy decree!
> Prostrate to earth, my spirit flies to thee;

The mystic dove in clouds ascends above,
Come, little children, come, and share my love.
Around her couch in innocence descend,
Thy guardian wings to comfort and defend.
Resign'd her mind, in slumbers quiet impart
Thy heavenly scenes to raise again her heart.
But how these scenes, these joys, conceiv'd below?
For aught in earth would I these scenes forego,
Already blest, yet wants one blessing more,
When we shall meet, and you these scenes explore.

ANNE HUNTER

(1742/3–1821)

———

ANNE HUNTER (*née* Home) was probably born in Waterford, as her father served as an army surgeon in that part of Ireland. The family moved to Hull in England next, and then settled in Scotland sometime after 1758, and then turned back to England (London), where the poet met and married the Scottish surgeon John Hunter. Before then, the poet had gained notice for her lyrical pieces, though they appeared anonymously. Her 'Adieu ye streams that softly glide', to the air of 'The Flowers of the Forest', appeared in *The Black Bird* (1764) and in two Edinburgh periodicals, *The Lark* and *The Charmer* (both 1765). Hunter wrote steadily throughout the 1770s and 1780s, by which time she had initiated a series of literary gatherings. She counted the writers Elizabeth Carter, Mary Delany, Elizabeth Montagu, Hester Thrale, and Joanna Baillie among her closest friends. In the early 1790s she became acquainted with Joseph Haydn, who set some of her most beloved songs to music, including 'My mother bids me bind my hair'. Hunter collected sixty works in her *Poems* in 1802, less than a third of her larger oeuvre.

———

'Song [My mother bids me bind my hair]'

Poems (London: T. Payne, 1802).

My mother bids me bind my hair
　　With bands of rosy hue,
Tie up my sleeves with ribbons rare,
　　And lace my bodice blue.

For why, she cries, sit still and weep,
　　While others dance and play?
Alas! I scarce can go or creep,
　　While Lubin is away.

'Tis sad to think the days are gone,
　　When those we love were near;

I sit upon this mossy stone,
    And sigh when none can hear.

And while I spin my flaxen thread,
    And sing my simple lay,
The village seems asleep, or dead,
    Now Lubin is away.

'The Lamentation of Mary Stuart, Queen of Scots, adapted to a very Ancient Scottish Air, Supposed to have been her own Composition'

I Sigh, and lament me in vain,
    These walls can but echo my moan;
Alas! it increases my pain,
    To think of the days that are gone.

Through the grates of my prison I see
    The birds as they wanton in air;
My heart, how it pants to be free,
    My looks they are wild with despair.

Ye roofs, where cold damps and dismay
    With silence and solitude dwell;
How comfortless passes the day,
    How sad tolls the evening bell!

The owls from the battlements cry,
    Hollow winds seem to murmur around,
"O Mary, prepare thee to die!"
    My blood it runs cold at the sound.

Unchang'd by the rigors of fate,
    I burn with contempt for my foes,
Though fortune has clouded my state,
    This hope shall enlighten its close.

False woman! in ages to come
    Thy malice detested shall be;
And when we are cold in the tomb,
    The heart still shall sorrow for me.

'A Mermaid's Song'

Now the dancing sunbeams play
  On the green and glassy sea;
Come, and I will lead the way,
  Where the pearly treasures be.
Come with me, and we will go
  Follow, follow, follow me.

Come, behold what treasures lie
  Deep below the rolling waves,
Riches hid from human eye
  Dimly shine in ocean's caves;
Stormy winds are far away,
Ebbing tides brook no delay;
  Follow, follow, follow me.

HENRY MACKENZIE
(1745–1831)

===

Born and educated in Edinburgh, Henry Mackenzie is remembered for his sentimental novella *The Man of Feeling* (1771). But the Addison of the North, as some dubbed him, was also a keen periodical writer. Between 1785 and 1787 he edited *The Lounger*, to which he contributed several influential short stories and essays. In an effusive memoir of the author, Walter Scott, somewhat diplomatically, praised Mackenzie's skills as a prose writer. But he also highlighted Mackenzie's early efforts in imitating old Scots ballads, one of which follows here.

===

'Duncan, a Ballad'

The Works of Henry Mackenzie, Esq., 8 vols (Edinburgh: James Ballantyne and Co., 1808).

"Saw ye the thane o' meikle pride,
    Red anger in his e'e?"—
"I saw him not, nor care," he cry'd,
    "Red anger frights na' me.

"For I have stuid whar honour bade,
    Though death trade on his heel:
Mean is the crest that stoops to fear,
    Nae sic may Duncan feel."

Hark! hark! or was it but the wind
    That through the ha' did sing?
Hark! hark again! a warlike shout!
    The black woods round do ring.

" 'Tis na for nought," bauld Duncan cry'd,
    "Sic shoutings, on the wind";
Syne up he started frae his seat,
    A thrang o' spears behind.

"Haste, haste, my valiant hearts," he said,
  "Anes mair to follow me;
We'll meet thae shouters by the burn,
  I guess wha they may be."

But wha is he that speeds sae fast,
  Frae the slaw marching thrang?
Sae frae the mirk cloud shoots a beam
  The sky's blue face alang.

Some messenger it is, mayhap;
  Then not of peace I trow:—
"My master, Duncan, bade me rin,
  And say these words to you.

Restore again that bluming rose
  Your rude hand pluckt awa;
Restore again my Mary fair,
  Or you shall rue the fa."

Three strides the gallant Duncan tuik,
  And shuik his forward spear;
"Gae tell thy master, saft-chin'd youth,
  We are na wont to fear:

He comes na on a wassel rout
  Of revel, sport, and play;
Our swords gart fame proclaim us men,
  Lang ere this ruefu' day.

The rose I pluckt of right was mine;
  Our hearts together grew
Like twa sweet roses on ae stalk,
  Frae hate to love she flew."

Swift as a winged shaft he sped:—
  "Bald Duncan said in jeer,
'Gae tell thy master, saft-chin'd youth,
  We are na wont to fear:

He comes na on a wassel rout
  Of revel, sport, and play;
Our swords gart fame proclaim us men,
  Lang ere this ruefu' day.

The rose I pluckt of right was mine;
   Our hearts together grew
Like twa sweet roses on ae stalk,
   Frae hate to love she flew'."

He stampt his foot upo' the ground,
   And thus in wrath did say,
"God strike my saul, if frae this field
   We baith in life shall gae!"

He waved his hand, the pipes they play'd,
   The targets clatter'd round;
And now between the meeting faes
   Was little space of ground.—

But wha is she that rins sae fast?
   Her feet nae stap they find;
Sae swiftly rides the milky cloud
   Upon the summer's wind.

Her face a mantle screen'd before,
   She shaw'd of lily hue;
Sae frae the grey mist breaks the sun,
   To drink the morning dew.

"Alake! my friends, what sight is this?
   O stap your rage," she cry'd;
"Whar love with honey'd lip should be,
   Mak not a breach sae wide.

Can then my uncle draw his sword,
   My husband's breast to bleed?
Or can my sweet lord do to him,
   Sic foul and ruthless deed?

Bethink thee, uncle, of the time,
   My gray-hair'd father died;
Frae whar your shrill horn struik the wood,
   He sent for you wi' speed.

'My brother! Guard my bairn,' he said,
   'She has nae father soon;
Regard her, Donald, as your ain,
   I'll ask nae ither boon.'

Can these brave men, who but of late
    Together chaced the deer,
Against their comrades bend their bows
    In bluidy hunting here?"

She spake, while trickling ran the tears
    Her blushing cheek alang;
And silence, like a heavy cloud,
    O'er a' the warriors hang.

Then stapt the red-haired Malcolm forth,
    Threescore his years and three,
Yet a' the strength of strongest youth,
    In sic an eld had he.

Nae pity was there in his breast,
    For war alane he loved;
His grey een sparkled at the sight
    Of plunder, death, and bluid.

"What, shall our hearts of steel," he said,
    "bend to a woman's sang?
Or can her words our honour quit,
    For sic dishonest wrang?

For this did a' thae warriors come,
    To hear an idle tale?
And o'er our death-accustom'd arms,
    Shall silly tears prevail?"

They gied a shout, their bows they tuik,
    They clash'd their steely swords,
Like the loud waves of Barra's shore,
    There was nae room for words.

A cry the weeping Mary gied,—
    "O uncle, hear my prayers!
Heed na' t hat man o' bluidy luik"—
    She had nae time for mair.

For in the midst anon there came
    A blind unweeting dart,
That glanc'd frae aff her Duncan's targe,
    And strack her to the heart.

A while she stagger'd, syne she fell,
    And Duncan see'd her fa';
Astound' he stuid, for in his limbs
    There was nae power at a':

The spear he meant at fraes to fling,
    Stuid fix'd within his hand,
His lips, half open, cou'd na' speak,
    His life was at a stand.

Sae the black stump of some auld aike,
    With arms in triumph dight,
Seems to the traveller like a man;

    * * * * * * * *

      Caetera desunt.

ELIZABETH GRANT
(1745/6–1828)

———

HAILING from Banffshire, Elizabeth Grant was a much-admired song-writer. Today her reputation largely rests on 'Roy's Wife of Aldivalloch', set to the tune 'The Ruffian's Rant'. Aldivalloch is a Banffshire farm and, according to sleuths for the *Inverness Courier*, a Roy of Aldivalloch did indeed marry a much younger bride in 1727. Robert Burns praised 'Roy's Wife' for its irregularity, a feature sometimes referred to as a Scotch snap. As testimony to his admiration, Burns wrote his own variants for *The Scots Musical Museum*.

———

'Roy's Wife of Aldivalloch'

The Songs of Scotland, Ancient and Modern; with An Introduction and Notes, Historical and Critical, and Characters of the Lyric Poets, ed. Allan Cunningham, 4 vols (London: John Taylor, 1825).

> Roy's wife of Aldivalloch!
> Roy's wife of Aldivalloch!
> Wat ye how she cheated me,
> As I came o'er the braes of Balloch?
> She vow'd, she swore she wad be mine,
> Said that she lo'ed me best of ony;
> But, oh! the fickle, faithless quean,
> She's ta'en the carle and left her Johnie.
>
> Roy's wife of Aldivalloch!
> Roy's wife of Aldivalloch!
> Wat ye how she cheated me,
> As I came o'er the braes of Balloch?
> She was a kind and cantie queen,
> Weel could she dance the highland walloch;
> How happy I, had she been mine,
> Or I been Roy of Aldivalloch!

Roy's wife of Aldivalloch!
Roy's wife of Aldivalloch!
Wat ye how she cheated me,
As I came o'er the braes of Balloch?
Her hair sae fair, her een sae clear,
Her wee bit mou sae sweet and bonnie!
To me she ever will be dear,
Though she's for ever left her Johnie.

MICHAEL BRUCE

(1746–1767)

———

A PRECOCIOUS child, Michael Bruce could read from the Bible before he started at the village school in Portmoak, where he formed signifi-cant friendships with David Pearson and William Arnot. The Laird of Portmoak inspired a love of English literature and Latin in Bruce, who later studied Greek and other subjects at the University of Edinburgh. While teaching at the Forest Mill school in Clackmannanshire, Bruce composed some of his most skilled works, including 'Lochleven'. Weakened by the damp weather he encountered there, he returned to Kinnesswood, where he later died of consumption. Amid rapidly declining health, he wrote his final poem, a self-elegy, 'Elegy: To Spring'. Bruce published no poems in his lifetime. A former schoolfriend, John Logan, produced a notably stunted posthumous collection of Bruce's works, *Poems on Several Occasions* (1770), which did little to attract an audience. To add insult to injury, Bruce's 'Ode to the Cuckoo' subsequently appeared in print twice under different names, including Logan's in his own 1781 *Poems*. In that volume Bruce's erstwhile editor also appropriated many of Bruce's hymns.

———

'Elegy: To Spring'

Poems on Several Occasions (Edinburgh: W. Anderson, 1770).

I

'Tis past: the iron North has spent his rage;
    Stern Winter now resigns the length'ning day;
The stormy howlings of the winds assuage,
    And warm o'er ether western breezes play.

II

Of genial heat and chearful light the source,
    From southern climes, beneath another sky,

The sun, returning, wheels his golden course;
   Before his beams all noxious vapours fly.

III

Far to the north grim Winter draws his train
   To his own clime, to ZEMBLA's frozen shore;
Where, thron'd on ice, he holds eternal reign;
   Where whirlwinds madden, and where tempests roar.

IV

Loos'd from the bands of frost, the verdant ground
   Again puts on her robe of chearful green,
Again puts forth her flow'rs; and all around,
   Smiling, the chearful face of Spring is seen.

V

Behold! the trees new-deck their wither'd boughs;
   Their ample leaves the hospitable plane,
The taper elm, and lofty ash disclose;
   The blooming hawthorn variegates the scene.

VI

The lily of the vale, of flow'rs the Queen,
   Puts on the robe she neither sew'd nor spun:
The birds on ground, or on the branches green,
   Hop to and fro, and glitter in the sun.

VII

Soon as o'er the eastern hills the morning peers,
   From her low nest the tufted lark upsprings;
And, cheerful singing, up the air she steers;
   Still high she mounts, still loud and sweet she sings.

VIII

On the green furze, cloth'd o'er with golden blooms
   That fill the air with fragrance all around,
The linnet flies, and tricks his glossy plumes,
   While o'er the wild his broken notes resound.

IX

While the sun journeys down the western sky,
    Along the greensward, mark'd with ROMAN mound,
Beneath the blithesome shepherd's watchful eye,
    The chearful lambkins dance and frisk around.

X

Now is the time for those who wisdom love,
    Who love to walk in Virtue's flow'ry road,
Along the lovely paths of Spring to rove,
    And follow Nature up to Nature's GOD.

XI

Thus ZOROASTER studied Nature's laws;
    Thus SOCRATES, the wisest of mankind;
Thus heav'n-taught PLATO thrac'd th' Almighty cause,
    And left the wond'ring multitude behind.

XII

Thus ASHLEY gather'd Academic bays;
    Thus gentle THOMSON, as the Seasons roll,
Taught them to sing the great CREATOR's praise,
    And bear their poet's name from pole to pole.

XIII

Thus have I walk'd along the dewy lawn;
    My frequent foot the blooming wild hath worn;
Before the lark I've sung the beauteous dawn,
    And gather'd health from all the gales of morn.

XIV

And, even when Winter chill'd the aged year,
    I wander'd lonely o'er the hoary plain;
Tho' frosty Boreas warn'd me to forbear,
    Boreas, with all his tempests, warn'd in vain.

XV

Then sleep my nights, and quiet bless'd my days;
    I fear'd no loss, my MIND was all my store;

No anxious wishes e'er disturb'd my ease;
    Heav'n gave content and health—I ask'd no more.

XVI

Now Spring returns: but not to me returns
    The vernal joy my better years have known;
Dim in my breast life's dying taper burns,
    And all the joys of life with health are flown.

XVII

Starting and shiv'ring in th' inconstant wind,
    Meagre and pale, the ghost of what I was,
Beneath some blasted tree I lie reclin'd,
    And count the silent moments as thy pass:

XVIII

The winged moments, whose unstaying speed
    No art can stop, or in their course arrest;
Whose flight shall shortly count me with the dead,
    And lay me down in peace with them that rest.

XIX

Oft morning-dreams presage approaching fate;
    And morning-dreams, as poets tell, are true.
Led by pale ghosts, I enter Death's dark gate,
    And bid the realms of light and life adieu.

XX

I hear the helpless wail, the shriek of wo;
    I see the muddy wave, the dreary shore,
The sluggish streams that slowly creep below,
    Which mortals visit, and return no more.

XXI

Farewell, ye blooming fields! ye chearful plains!
    Enough for me the church-yard's lonely mound,
Where Melancholy with still Silence reigns,
    And the rank grass waves o'er the chearless ground.

XXII

There let me wander at the shut of eve,
   When sleep sits dewy on the labourer's eyes,
The world and all its busy follies leave,
   And talk with wisdom where my DAPHNIS lies.

XXIII

There let me sleep forgotten in the clay,
   When death shall shut these weary aching eyes,
Rest in the hopes of an eternal day,
   Till the long night's gone, and the last morn arise.

'Weaving Spiritualized'

*Lochleven, and Other Poems, with a Life of the Author from Original
Sources*, ed. William Mackelvie (Edinburgh: M. Paterson, 1837).

A web I hear thou hast begun,
And know'st not when it may be done—
So death uncertain see ye fear—
For ever distant, ever near.

See'st thou the shuttle quickly pass—
Think mortal life is as the grass,—
An empty cloud—a morning dream—
A bubble rising on the stream.

The knife still ready to cut off
Excrescent knots that mar the stuff,
To stern affliction's rod compare—
'Tis for thy good, so learn to bear.

Too full a quill oft checks the speed
Of shuttle flying by the reed—
So riches oft keep back the soul,
That else would hasten to its goal.

Thine eye the web runs keenly o'er
For things amiss, unseen before,—
Thus scan thy life—mend what's amiss—
Next day correct the faults of this.

For when the web is at an end,
'Tis then too late a fault to mend—
Let thought of this awaken dread,—
Repentance dwells not with the dead.

'Ossian's Hymn to the Sun'

The Cabinet of Poetry, Containing the Best Entire Pieces to be Found in the Works of the British Poets, 6 vols (London: Richard Phillips, 1808).

O thou whose beams the sea-girt earth array,
King of the sky, and father of the day!
O sun! what fountain, hid from human eyes,
Supplies thy circle round the radiant skies,
For ever burning and for ever bright,
With heav'n's pure fire, and everlasting light?
What awful beauty in thy face appears!
Immortal youth, beyond the power of years!
        When gloomy darkness to thy reign resigns,
And from the gates of morn thy glory shines,
The conscious stars are put to sudden flight,
And all the planets hide their heads in night;
The queen of heaven forsakes th' ethereal plain,
To sink inglorious in the western main.
The clouds refulgent deck thy golden throne,
High in the heavens, immortal and alone!
Who can abide the brightness of thy face!
Or who attend thee in thy rapid race?
The mountain-oaks, like their own leaves, decay;
Themselves the mountains wear with age away;
The boundless main that rolls from land to land,
Lessens at times, and leaves a waste of sand;
The silver moon, refulgent lamp of night,
Is lost in heaven, and emptied of her light:
But thou for ever shalt endure the same,
Thy light eternal, and unspent thy flame.
        When tempests with their train impend on high,
Darken the day, and load the labouring sky;
When heaven's wide convex glows with lightnings dire,
All ether flaming and all earth on fire;

When loud and long the deep-mouthed thunder rolls,
And peals on peals redoubled rend the poles;
If from the opening clouds thy form appears,
Her wonted charm the face of nature wears;
Thy beauteous orb restores departed day,
Looks from the sky, and laughs the storm away.

HECTOR MACNEILL

(1746–1818)

———

A NATIVE of Midlothian, Hector Macneill spent his early youth near
Loch Lomond, where his father tenanted a farm, and schooled in
Stirling. As a young teenager Macneill spent some time in St Kitts, in
the West Indies, where his relatives traded. After living and working
across the Caribbean and Bermuda, in Guadeloupe, Antigua, and
St George's Town, for more than a decade, he returned to Scotland
after the death of his mother and sister, before setting off to sea again,
sporadically, in the pursuit of funds. Macneill finally gained literary
notice when his ballad against drinking, 'Scotland's Skaith, or, The
History of Will and Jean', appeared to wide acclaim in 1795. Fourteen
editions followed in barely twelve months. By this point, Macneill had
become a regular contributor to the *Scots Magazine*. First published in
1801, *The Poetical Works of Hector Macneill* was reprinted twice in his
lifetime, and again in 1856. *The Pastoral or Lyric Muse of Scotland*,
afterwards called *The Scottish Muse*, follows here.

———

'The Scottish Muse'

The Poetical Works of Hector Macneill, Esq., 2 vols (London: T. N.
Longman and O. Rees, et al., 1801).

> Now, good Cesario, but that piece of song,
> That old and antique song we heard last night:
> Methought it did relieve my passion much:
> More than light airs, and recollected terms
> Of these more brisk and giddy paced times.—
>
> SHAKSPEARE.

> O welcome simply soothing treasure!
> In midst o' pain my lanely pleasure!
> Tutor'd by thee, and whispering leisure,
>   I quit the thrang,

And, wrapt in bless'd retirement, measure
      Thy varied sang!

Kind, leil companion! without thee,
Ah welladay! what should I be!
Whan jeer'd by fools wha canna see
      My inward pain,
Aneath thy sheltering wing I flee
      And mak my mane.

There seated, smiling by my side,
For hours thegither wilt thou bide,
Chanting auld tales o' martial pride
      And luve's sweet smart!
Till glowing warm thy numbers glide
      Streight to the heart.

'Tis then wi' powerfu' plastic hand
Thou wav'st thy magic-working wand;
And stirring up ideas grand
      That fire the brain,
Aff whirl'st me swith to fairy land
      'Mang fancy's train.—

Scar'd by disease whan balmy rest
Flees trembling frae her downy nest;
Starting frae horror's dreams opprest,
      I see thee come
Wi' radiance mild that cheers the breast
      And lights the gloom!

Heart'ning thou com'st, wi' modest grace,
Hope, luve, and pity, in thy face,
And gliding up wi' silent pace
      My plaints to hear,
Whisper'st in turn thae soothing lays
      Saft in my ear.

Ill-fated wand'rer! doom'd to mane!
Wan sufferer! bleach'd wi' care and pain!
How chang'd alas! since vogie vain,
      Wi' spirits light,
Ye hail'd me first in untaught strain
      On STREVLIN's height!

—Ah me! how stark! how blithe! how bauld
Ye brattl'd then through wind and cauld!
Reckless, by stream, by firth and fauld
   Ye held your way;
By passion rul'd; by luve enthrall'd,
   Ye pour'd the lay.

'Twas then, entranc'd in am'rous sang,
I mark'd you midst the rural thrang;
Ardent and keen, the hail day lang
   Wi' NATURE tane,
Slip frae the crowd and mix amang
   Her simple train.

'Twas then I saw (alas! owre clear!)
Your future thriftless, lost career!
And while I blam'd, wi' boding fear,
   The tunefu' art,
Your moral pride and truth sincere
   Aye wan my heart.

"He ne'er can lout," I musing said,
To ply the fleeching, fawning trade;
Nor bend the knee, nor bow the head
   To *walth or power!*
But backward turn wi' scornfu' speed
   Frae flatt'ry's door.

He'll never learn his bark to steer
'Mid *passion's* sudden, wild career;
Nor try at times to tack or veer
   To *int'rest's* gale,
But hoist the sheet, unaw'd by fear,
   Tho' storms prevail.

Owre proud to ask;—owre bauld to yield!
Whar will he find a shelt'ring beild?
Whan poortith's blast drifts cross the field
   Wi' wintry cauld,
Whar will he wone—poor feckless chield!
   Whan frail and auld?

Year after year in youtheid's prime,
Wander he will, frae clime to clime,

Sanguine wi' hope on wing sublime
    Mount heigh in air!
But than—waes me! there comes a time
    O' dool and care!

There comes a time!—or soon, or late,
O' serious thought and sad debate;
Whan blighted hope and adverse fate
    Owrespread their gloom,
And mirk despair, in waefu' state,
    Forsees the doom!

—And maun he fa'! (I sighing cried)
Wi' guardian honour by his side!
Shall fortune frown on guiltless pride
    And straits owrtake him!
—Weel! blame wha like—whate'er betide
    I'se ne'er forsake him!

Ardent I spake! and frae the day
Ye hail'd me smiling; youthfu' gay
On *Aichil's* whin-flower'd fragrant brae,
    I strave to cheer ye!
Frae morn's first dawn to e'en's last ray
    I ay was near ye.

Frae west to east—frae isle to isle,
To India's shore and sultry soil;
'Mid tumult, battle, care, and toil,
    I following flew;
Ay smooth'd the past, and wak'd the smile
    To prospects new.

Whan warfare ceas'd its wild uproar
To Elephanta's far-fam'd shore
I led ye ardent to explore
    Wi' panting heart,
Her idol monuments o' yore
    And sculptur'd art.

Sweet flew the hours! (the toil your boast)
On smiling Salsett's cave-wrought coast!—
Though hope was tint—tho' a' was cross'd
    Nae dread alarms

Ye felt—fond fool! in wonder lost
     And nature's charms!

Frae east to west, frae main to main,
To Carib's shore return'd again;
In sickness, trial, hardship, pain,
     Ye ken yoursell,
Drapt frae the muse's melting strain
     Peace balmy fell.

Fell sweet! for as she warbling flew,
Hope lent her heav'ns refreshing dew;
Fair virtue close, and closer drew
     To join the lay;
While conscience bright, and brighter grew,
     And cheer'd the way!—

Whether to east or westward borne,
(Or flush'd wi' joy, or wae-forlorn)
Ye hail'd the fragrant breath o' morn
     Frae orange flower,
Or cassia-bud, or logwood thorn,
     Or Guava bower:

Or frae the mist-cap'd mountain blue
Inhal'd the spicy gales that flew
Rich frae Pimento's groves that grew
     In deep'ning green
Crown'd wi' their flowers o' milk-white hue
     In dazzling sheen!

Whether at midnoon panting laid,
Ye woo'd coy zephyr's transient aid
Under the Banyan's pillar'd shade,
     On plain or hill,
Or Plantain green, that rustling play'd
     Across the rill:

Or 'neath the tam'rind's shelt'ring gloom,
Drank coolness wafted in perfume,
Fresh frae the shaddack's golden bloom,
     As flutt'ring gay
Humm'd saft the bird o' peerless plume,
     Frae spray to spray!

—Whether at eve, wi' raptur'd breast
The shelving palm-girt beach ye prest,
And e'ed, entranc'd, the purpling west
    Bepictur'd o'er,
As ocean murm'ring, gently kiss'd
    The whitening shore:

Whether at twilight's parting day
Ye held your solenm musing way,
Whar through the gloom in myriad ray
    The fire-flies gleam;
And 'thwart the grove in harmless play
    The light'nings stream!

Or, by the moon's bright radiance led,
Roam'd late the Guinea-verdur'd glade
Where tower'd the giant Ceiba's shade;
    And, loflier still,
The Cabbage rears its regal head
    Owre palm-crown'd hill.

Still following close, still whisp'ring near
The muse aye caught your list'ning ear;
'Mid tempest's rage and thunder's rair
    Aye cheering sang:—
Touch'd by her hand (unchill'd by fear)
    The Harp strings rang.

Return'd at last frae varied clime,
Whar youth and hope lang tint their time,
Ance mair to Strevlin's height sublime
    We wing'd our way;
Ance mair attun'd the rural rhime
    On Aichil brae.

'Twas then my native strains ye lear'd,
For passion spake while fancy cheer'd;
A while wi' flaunting airs ye flar'd
    And thought to shine;
But Nature—judging nature sneer'd
    And ca'd it—*fine!*

Stung wi' the taunt, ye back recoil'd,
Pensive ye mus'd; I mark'd and smil'd;

Daund'ring depress'd 'mang knows flower'd wild,
          My aten reed
Ye faund ae bonny morning mild
          'Tween Ayr and Tweed.

'Tween past'ral Tweed and wand'ring Ayr,
Whar unbusk'd nature blooms sae fair!
And mony a wild note saft and clear
          Sings sweet by turns,
Tun'd by my winsome Allan's ear
          And fav'rite Burns.

Trembling wi' joy ye touch'd the reed,—
Doubtfu' ye sigh'd and hang your head;
Fearfu' ye sang till some agreed
          The notes war true;
Whan grown mair bauld, ye gae a screed
          That pleas'd nae few.

By Forth's green links bedeck'd wi' flowers,
By Clyde's clear stream and beechen bowers;
Heartsome and healthfu' flew the hours
          In simple sang,
While Lossit's braes and Eden's towers
          The notes prolang!

—Thae times are gane!—ah! welladay!
For health has flown wi' spirits gay;
Youth too has fled! and cauld decay
          Comes creeping on:
October's sun cheers na like May
          That brightly shone!

Yet autumn's gloom, though threat'ning bleak
Has joys, gin folk calm joys wad seek;
Friendship and worth then social cleek
          And twine thegither.
And gree and crack by ingle cheek
          Just like twin-brither.

'Tis then (youth's vain vagaries past,
That please a while, but fash at last)

Serious, our ee we backward cast
    On bygane frays,
And, marvelling, mourn the thriftless waste
    O' former days!

Then too, wi' prudence on our side,
And reas'ning virtue for our guide,
Calmly we view the restless tide
    O' warldly care,
And cull, wi' academic pride,
    The flow'rs o' lare.

And while, wi' sure and steady pace,
Coy science's secret paths we trace,
And catch fair nature's beauteous face
    In varied view,
Ardent, though auld, we join the chace,
    And pleas'd pursue.—

'Tis sae through life's short circling year,
The seasons change, and, changing, cheer;
Journeying we jog, unaw'd by fear:
    Hope plays her part!
Forward we look, though in the rear
    Death shakes the dart.

Catch then the dream! nor count it vain,
Hope's dream's the sweetest balm o' pain:
Heav'n's unseen joys may yet remain,
    And yet draw near ye:
Meanwhile, ye see, I hear your mane,
    And flee to cheer ye.

Ane too's at hand, to wham ye fled
Frae Britain's cauld, frae misery's bed;
Owre seas tempestuous shivering sped,
    To Friendship's flame;
Whar kindling warm, in sunbeams clad,
    She hails her Graham.

Wi' him (let health but favouring smile)
Ance mair ye'll greet fair Albion's isle!
In some calm nook life's cares beguile

        Atween us twa:
Feed the faint lamp wi' virtue's oil—
        Then—slip awa!

The flatterer ceas'd, and smil'd adieu,
Just wav'd her hand, and mild withdrew!
Cheer'd wi' the picture (fause or true)
        I check'd despair,
And frae that moment made a vow
        To—mourn nae mair.

SUSANNA BLAMIRE

(1747–1794)

===

BORN and raised in Cumberland and Carlisle, Susanna Blamire spent considerable time in Stirlingshire, and even wrote in Scots. Among the best known of the Scots songs are 'What ails this heart o' mine?', 'The Siller Croun', and 'The Nabob', which was set to the air 'The Traveller's Return'. Blamire published little in her lifetime, other than anonymously in magazines and collections such as *Calliope* (1788) and *The Scots Musical Museum* (1790). Her authorship of popular pieces only gained wider acknowledgement with the posthumous publication of her *Poetical Works* (1842). A high-profile admirer, the poet Hugh MacDiarmid praised Blamire for her unsentimental, mirthful Scottish songs.

===

'What ails this heart o' mine?'

The Poetical Works of Susanna Blamire: 'The Muse of Cumberland', ed. Henry Lonsdale (Edinburgh: John Menzies, 1842).

> What ails this heart o' mine?
>   What ails this watery ee?
> What gars me a' turn cauld as death
>   When I take leave o' thee?
> When thou art far awa
>   Thou'lt dearer grow to me;
> But change o' place and change o' folk
>   May gar thy fancy jee.
>
> When I gae out at een,
>   Or walk at morning air,
> Ilk rustling bush will seem to say
>   I us'd to meet thee there.
> Then I'll sit down and cry,
>   And live aneath the tree,

And when a leaf fa's i' my lap
   I'll ca't a word frae thee.

I'll hie me to the bower
   That thou wi' roses tied,
And where wi' mony a blushing bud
   I strove mysell to hide.
I'll doat on ilka spot
   Where I hae been wi' thee;
And ca' to mind some kindly word
   By ilka burn and tree!

Wi' sic thoughts i' my mind,
   Time through the world may gae,
And find my heart in twenty years
   The same as 'tis to-day.
'Tis thoughts that bind the soul,
   And keep friends i' the ee;
And gin I think I see thee aye,
   What can part thee and me!

'The Siller Croun'

And ye shall walk in silk attire,
   And siller hae to spare,
Gin ye'll consent to be his bride,
   Nor think o' Donald mair.
O wha wad buy a silken goun
   Wi' a poor broken heart!
Or what's to me a siller croun,
   Gin frae my love I part!

The mind wha's every wish is pure
   Far dearer is to me;
And ere I'm forc'd to break my faith
   I'll lay me doun an' dee!
For I hae pledg'd my virgin troth
   Brave Donald's fate to share;
And he has gi'en to me his heart,
   Wi' a' its virtues rare.

His gentle manners wan my heart,
   He gratefu' took the gift;

Could I but think to seek it back
 It wad be waur than theft!
For langest life can ne'er repay
 The love he bears to me;
And ere I'm forc'd to break my troth
 I'll lay me doun an' dee.

ANNA GORDON (MRS BROWN)
(1747–1810)

———

ALSO known as Mrs Brown of Falkland, the Aberdeen native Anna Gordon was one of the most important Scottish ballad collectors of the eighteenth century. Francis James Child later adopted twenty-seven of her works as 'A' texts in his definitive *English and Scottish Popular Ballads* (1882–98). Gordon learned the bulk of her repertoire in childhood from her mother, Lilias Forbes, and her aunt, Anne Forbes (Mrs Farquharson of Allanaquoich). Some fifty of Gordon's songs were written down between about 1783 and 1801, and eventually found their way through various intermediaries to Walter Scott and Robert Jamieson, who published a selection of them in *Minstrelsy of the Scottish Border* (1802–3) and *Popular Ballads and Songs* (1806) respectively.

———

'Alison Gross'

Popular Ballads and Songs, from Tradition, Manuscripts, and Scarce Editions, ed. Robert Jamieson, 2 vols (Edinburgh: Archibald Constable and Co., Cadell and Davies; London: John Murray, 1806).

> O Alison Gross, that lives in yon tower,
>   The ugliest witch in the northern countrie,
> Has trysted me ae day up to her bower,
>   And mony a fair speech she made to me.
>
> She straiked my head, and she kembed my hair,
>   And she set me down saftly on her knee,
> Says,—"Gin ye will be my lemman sae true,
>   Sae mony braw things as I would you gi'e."
>
> She shaw'd me a mantle o' red scarlet,
>   Wi' gouden flowers and fringes fine,

Says,—"Gin ye will be my lemman sae true,
    This goodly gift it sall be thine."

"Awa, awa, ye ugly witch,
    Haud far awa, and lat me be;
I never will be your lemman sae true,
    And I wish I were out of your company."

She neist brocht a sark o' the saftest silk,
    Weel wrought wi' pearls about the band;
Says,—"Gin ye will be my lemman sae true,
    This goodly gift ye sall command."

She shaw'd me a cup o' the good red goud,
    Weel set wi' jewels sae fair to see;
Says,—"Gin ye will be my lemman sae true,
    This goodly gift I will you gie."

"Awa, awa, ye ugly witch!
    Haud far awa, and lat me be;
For I wadna ance kiss your ugly mouth
    For a' the gifts that ye cou'd gie."

She's turned her richt and round about
    And thrice she blew on a grass-green horn;
And she sware by the moon and the stars aboon,
    That she'd gar me rue the day I was born.

Then out she has ta'en a silver wand,
    And she's turned her three times round and round;
She's muttered sic words, that my strength it fail'd,
    And I fell down senseless on the ground.

She's turn'd me into an ugly worm,
    And gar'd me toddle about the tree;
And ay, on ilka Saturday's night,
    My sister Maisry came to me,

Wi' silver bason, and silver kemb,
    To kemb my headie upon her knee;
But or I had kiss'd her ugly mouth,
    I'd rather hae toddled about the tree.

But as it fell out on last Hallowe'en,
    When the Seely Court was ridin' by,

The queen lighted down on a gowan bank,
    Nae far frae the tree whare I wont to lye.

She took me up in her milk-white hand,
    And she straiked me three times o'er her knee;
She changed me again to my ain proper shape,
    And I nae mair maun toddle about the tree.

ELIZABETH KEIR

(1747–1834)

THE novelist Elizabeth Keir was born in Edinburgh, and raised there and in Corstorphine. She lived for a time in England with her Scottish husband, a physician at St Thomas Hospital in London, but returned to Corstorphine after his sudden death in 1783. Through her friends Ann and Margaret Keith, Keir developed notable connections with leading literary figures in Edinburgh, including Alison Cockburn and Walter Scott. She published two unattributed novels, *Interesting Memoirs* (1785) and *The History of Miss Greville* (1787). The novels offer fairly conventional fare: stuffed with sentimental and didactic passages, they didn't sell well. As a poet, Keir was far more innovative. Apart from the anonymous epistle to Lady Perth reproduced here, little to no poetry has appeared in print. Two large volumes comprised of almost nine-hundred manuscript pages are now held at the National Library of Scotland. Many of the poems in the first volume are addressed to female friends, including the Keiths, as well as family members. In the second volume William Keir, Elizabeth's future husband, gradually emerges as the primary addressee of the works. After her husband's death, she turned to her children, nieces, and nephews for inspiration. With the death of her youngest son in 1810, Keir appears to have all but abandoned her craft.

'To the Right Honourable, Lady Perth, on the Much Lamented Death of Her Only Son, aged Seven Years and Ten Months'

To the Right Honourable, Lady Perth, on the Much Lamented Death of Her Only Son, aged Seven Years and Ten Months (London, 1799).

> Permit a Stranger, distant and unknown,
> Acquainted with thy deep distress alone,
> In these sincere though lifeless lines, to show,

Her power to feel, not mitigate thy woe.
Forgive th' attempt some comfort to suggest,
To thy grief-harrowed, deeply wounded breast;
Truths, from the mind, distracting passions blot,
Truths, when most needed often most forgot,
Truths, by experience long endear'd to me,
Oh! may they fruitful prove of heavenly peace to thee!

Possest of all the graces that adorn,
And promise fair, in life's sweet opening morn,
Thou mourn'st a blossom cropt in beauty's bloom,
Torn from thy arms and hurried to the tomb;
Heir of illustrious titles, ample wealth,—
But say,—could these ensure peace, virtue, health?

Could they exemption from one pang procure,
Of all the number mortals here endure?—
Let not these objects swell th' account of grief,
Which bring not virtue aid, nor pain relief;
Ah! better taught, and wiser, rather deem,
These glittering shadows are not what they seem.

Thus Reason argues, but her pleas how vain;
While bleeds the heart with agonizing pain.
An only Son!—there fell the direful blow,
That laid all joy, all hope, all comfort low.

Till time a portion of that grief shall steal,
And mitigate these pangs it ne'er can heal,
Let blest Religion bring her heavenly aid,
On her be all thy hopes and wishes staid.

That voice which oft has charm'd a mother's ear,
Could'st thou as erst that voice delighted hear,
Methinks—Ah! do not my presumption blame,
Would in such language thy attention claim.

"O thou! beheld with pity from above,
By the blest object of thy fondest love,
Could I withdraw the veil which sense supplies,
Unfold those glories hid from mortal eyes,
How would'st thou blush to sigh and weep for me;
Could Angels weep, such tears were shed for thee!"

"For thee, ordain'd to struggle still below,
Expos'd to sickness, sin, remorse, and woe,
Whilst I, freed from a mortal's weak embrace,
Behold the brightness of my Father's face,
His matchless love enjoy, his works of wonder trace!
Instead of human science, dark at best,
With error mingled, anxious care imprest,
From the pure fount of light, of truth, and love,
I drink of sacred WISDOM FROM ABOVE;
All useful truths intuitively gain,
Without distraction, lassitude, or pain;
Through various scenes of glorious beauty range;
High transports taste, without the fear of change;
In the wide scale of being still ascend,
With kindred orbs that to perfection tend,
And bliss enjoy, without degree, or end."

"As sinful, God condemns not virtuous woe;
Who gave thee tears, permits these tears to flow:
Tears, sinking nature's first though short relief;
Tears, the last refuge of desponding grief;
Yet, tears, a thousand trifles oft supply,
When heaviest ills that poor relief deny."

"Enough to nature's keen distress is given,
Now rouse to duty, and submit to heaven.
Friends, kindred, Daughter, thy attention claim,
And nearer still, a Husband's tender name."

"Be these the objects of thy love and care,
Who share thy sorrows should thy comforts share.
Dispel all doubts, all murmurs from thy breast;
Be God's unblemish'd rectitude confest;
All-wise to know, all powerful to protect,
Convinc'd that mercy all his ways direct,
With heavenly hope solace thy restless mind,
And thus submissive, patient, and resign'd,
To a firm stay convert the chastening rod,
And recognize thy FATHER in thy GOD."

JOHN TAIT

(1748–1817)

━━

JOHN TAIT was a Writer to the Signet and afterwards judge of the Edinburgh Police Court. Evidently a popular and reliable poet too, his works regularly appeared in Walter Ruddiman's *Weekly Magazine*, the *London Magazine*, the *Scots Magazine*, and *Westminster Magazine*. 'The Bards of Scotland' appeared in both the *Weekly Magazine* and *Scots Magazine* in November 1770. Featuring many prominent literary figures of the century, such as Ramsay, Thomson, Hamilton, and Macpherson, the poem is a veritable who's who of Scottish poetry.

━━

'The Bards of Scotland. An Elegy'

Weekly Magazine or Edinburgh Amusement (29 November 1770): 276–7.

—those who tuneful wak'd th' enchanting lyre.
                                    THOMSON

Blest be the fields renown'd in ancient days,
    Where thousand bards have own'd the muses smile,
Who once with glory sung their simple lays,
    Tho' now they add to dark oblivion's spoil.

Blest be the isle where OSSIAN rais'd the song!
    As nature taught him in fair fancy's grove;
Whose Muse could thunder with the warlike throng,
    Or melt the soul with softest tales of love.

Blest be the plains where DOUGLAS sought the Muse,
    And courted fame in MARO's sacred guise;
Who painted *May* of every bliss profuse,
    When o'er the hills the morning beams arise!

Blest shades! where RAMSAY with his shepherd's reed,
    Bid Peggy's love from echo's hills resound,

Where gentle HAMILTON travers'd the mead,
    And charm'd each scene with just harmonic sound!

Blest be the plains where THOMSON first essay'd
    To court the Muse, in native splendour dress'd,
Where first he su'd for fancy's powerful aid,
    And pour'd the song with ardour from his breast!

Blest be the groves where MALLET's polish'd lay,
    First burst delightful on th' astonished ear;
Where first he sung the *Birks of Invermay*,
    Or first attended *Margaret*'s mournful bier!

Hail, native SCOTIA! ever glorious coast!
    These Bards are thine, and thine their growing fame,
For 'mid thy rocks, in airy visions lost,
    Sweet inspiration oft has nurs'd their flame.

Sooth'd by the gales that fragrant blew around,
    Their thoughts were gentle as the vernal day,
While from their breasts the numbers burst profound,
    Mature and powerful as the summer ray.

Ye mighty names! to you I'll rear a shrine,
    Sacred to science and her peaceful train,
There for your brows, my humble wreaths I'll twine,
    There for your glory, raise my feeble strain.

Should fancy warm me with her genial rays,
    Then should my raptur'd numbers soar sublime,
Then should I give your names a worthy praise,
    To mock the power of all-subduing time.

Still of thy beauties, SCOTIA, should I sing,
    Thy rural haunts, thy sweetly flowing streams,
Thy fertile fields, where plenty spreads her wings,
    And health and fragrance dance in sunny beams.

Nor should my verse forget thy sons of fame,
    Who now with rapture warble on the dale,
Whose feeling breasts confess the Muse's flame,
    And pour profuse the sweetly varying tale.

I'd praise thy BLACKLOCK, hid in endless night,
    Yet greatly eminent in virtuous song;

Thy ARMSTRONG sage, thy BEATTIE flaming bright,
  Thy HOME, thy WILKIE—all thy tuneful throng.

Come then, ye Muses, lead me by the hand,
  While I attempt your THOMSON's worth to tell,
Attune my lyre, give me the magic wand,
  Which can dark Error's gath'ring clouds dispel.

Tutor my numbers, fire my youthful mind,
  Exalt my soul on Fancy's airy wing,
Then shall my accents flow in strains refin'd,
  And not unworthy of the theme I sing.

Ye sons of SCOTIA, venerate your Bards,
  And give them glory, give them high renown;
To ev'ry name devote the just rewards,
  For ev'ry brow prepare the sacred crown.

Thus shall the blissful genius of the isle,
  Applauding view the glories of her shore;
Thus bounteous SCIENCE on the land shall smile,
  And give with lib'ral hand, profuse, her boundless store.

JAMES GRAEME

(1749–1772)

———

JAMES GRAEME, of Carnwath in Lanarkshire, studied at the grammar
schools of Carnwath, Libberton, and Lanark. Intended for a career in
the Church, he studied at the University of Edinburgh. There he met
his lifelong friend, and future biographer, Robert Anderson, who
fanned his interests in the classics, philosophy, and literature. In 1771,
Graeme became a tutor to the sons of Major Martin White of Milton,
near Lanark, but his health quickly ailed. He died of consumption
within a matter of months. An influential anthologist in his own right,
Anderson included a selection of Graeme's poems, together with some
of his own, in *Poems on Several Occasions* (1773), where we find 'The
Mortified Genius'.

———

'The Mortified Genius'

Poems on Several Occasions (Edinburgh: W. Somerville, 1773).

> What now avails, to gain a woman's heart,
> The sage's widow, or the poet's art!
> Pox on the times! the genius of old
> Would whip you off a girl in spite of gold;
> In spite of liv'ries, equipage, and lace,
> And all the Gothic grandeur of a race.
> But now the mill'ner's 'prentice, with a sneer,
> Blessing herself, cries, Heav'ns! what have we here?
> A man of rhyme, worth—fifty lines a-year.
>   Our wit still pleases; but 'tis dev'lish hard,
> What saves the elegy should damn the bard;
> *That* gains access to dressing, drawing-rooms,
> A wish'd-for, welcome guest where'er it comes;
> But *me*, the luckless author, scorn'd and poor,
> Each surly porter drives from e'ry door.
>   Conscious of secret worth, I hurry home,

And now the master damn, and now the dome;
Firmly resolv'd, whatever shall betide,
No more to ask what has been deny'd;
Resolved, indeed! but ev'ry pow'r above
Laughs at our weak resolves, and chiefly Love.
"Brush the brown hat, and darn the breeches knee;
The wealthy, pride may suit, but suits not thee:
Papa, I own, looked mighty sour and grim;
But if the daughter smile, a fig for him!
Mark'd you the secret motions of her eye?
How kind yon glance had been, had none been by!
Yon proud reserve, yon shyness, I could swear,
Is prudence all, and pure pretence with her:
'Tis right—old fellows, that can thousands give,
May claim, at least, some rev'rence while they live;
A few, few years lays FUSCUS in his grave,
And MIRA's yours perhaps, and all he gave!"

      Intent on future harm, thus said the god,
Who bends the stubborn purpose with a nod;
Constrains the stiffest gladly to obey,
Makes the gay gloomy, and the gloomy gay.
Resist who will, I knew too well his pow'r,
In vain resisted, to resist it more!
My hands instinctive, at the forceful call,
At once seize gloves, and hat, and staff, and all;
Then forth I walk, and ever, as I go,
Con o'er my manners, and practise a bow;
Spread, careful spread, the cravat on my breast,
As prim and formal as a parish priest.

      The knocker clacks.—"Who's there?"—"'Is Miss within?"
"Confound the booby, what a monstrous din!
She has no time, she says, to speak with you;
For Mr FLORIMEL came here just now."
My heart beat thick, and ev'ry word he said
Distain'd my hollow cheeks with foreign red;
O, brutish times! and is that thing of silk,
That sapless sipper of an ass's milk;
That tea-nursed grinner, whose consumptive cough,
Should he but mint a laugh, would cut him off;
Preferr'd to me! in whose athletic grasp
Ten thousand buzzing beaux were but a wasp.

Sure wit and learning greater honour claim;
No wit, no learning, ever smil'd on him:
I'll lay my Lexicon, for all his airs,
That fellow cannot read the arms he bears;
Nor, kneeling, MIRA! on his trembling knee,
Explain one half of all he says to thee.
"No matter, he has gold; whose precious hue
Is beauty, virtue, wit and learning too:
O, blind to worth! what lovelier than a chaise,
Two bowing footmen, and a pair of bays?
What virtue like an handsome country-seat,
A good *per annum*, and a course of plate?
And then for wit—a clever library;
He cannot read a book; but he can buy:
A fig for learning! Learning does he lack,
Whose factor both can write and sign—a tack?
Besides, you know, for ten or less *per ann.*
Ev'n you, or any scholar, is his man." '
          Bear me, ye gods! O, bear me where you please!
To unknown regions, over unknown seas;
Place me where dews refreshing never drop,
On NIGER's banks, a swarthy ÆTHIOP;
Or melt me to the fashionable size,
Below the scorching heat of Indian skies:
No; there, ev'n there, the lust of gold prevails,
Each river groans with ships, each breeze with sails;
The land abounds, nay ocean's farthest creeks,
With dirt that's sought for, or with dirt that seeks.
Fix me an icen statue at the pole,
Where winds can't carry, and where waves can't roll;
To man, to greedy man, your bard prefers,
White foxes, sables, ermines, cats and bears,
And all the furry monsters GREENLAND can call hers.
          Or is the boon too great for gods to give?
Recal the mighty word that bade me live:
So, in the dust forever shall I shun
That worst of evils that affronts the sun,
A fool whose crimes, or father's, have made great,
Spurning true genius prostrate at his feet.

ROBERT FERGUSSON
(1750–1774)

━━

THE poet Robert Fergusson was born and educated in Edinburgh; he also attended school in Dundee before taking up a scholarship at the University of St Andrews, where he read English literature alongside Greek and Latin, as well as mathematics and moral philosophy. At St Andrews he studied under the vernacular poet William Wilkie, who, like Fergusson, championed a renewed use of Scots in literature. In 1771 and 1772, back home in Edinburgh, he published poems in a local periodical, *The Weekly Magazine*. Under the guidance of the periodical's editor, Walter Ruddiman, *Poems* (1773) soon followed. In the same year, Fergusson produced '*Auld Reekie*', a raucous 300-line celebration of Edinburgh and its people. Shortly after this came Fergusson's *Poem to the Memory of John Cunningham*, for a writer who had died in Newcastle's mental asylum. Severely depressed, Fergusson's own mental and physical health rapidly worsened. In the next year, he was dead, aged just twenty-four.

━━

'*Elegy, on the Death of Scots Music*'

Poems (Edinburgh: Walter & Thomas Ruddiman, 1773).

> *Mark it, Caesario; it is old and plain,*
> *The spinsters and the knitters in the sun,*
> *And the free maids that weave their thread with bones,*
> *Do use to chant it.*
>
> Shakespeare's *Twelfth Night*.

On Scotia's plains, in days of yore,
When lads and lasses *tartan* wore,
Saft Music rang on ilka shore,
    In hamely weid;
But harmony is now no more,
    And *music* dead.

Round her the feather'd choir would wing,
Sae bonnily she wont to sing,
And sleely wake the sleeping string,
    Their sang to lead,
Sweet as the zephyrs of the spring;
    But now she's dead.

Mourn ilka nymph and ilka swain,
Ilk sunny hill and dowie glen;
Let weeping streams and *Naiads* drain
    Their fountain head;
Let echo swell the dolefu' strain,
    Since music's dead.

Whan the saft vernal breezes ca'
The grey-hair'd Winter's fogs awa',
Naebody than is heard to blaw,
    Near hill or mead,
On chaunter, or on aiten straw,
    Since music's dead.

Nae lasses now, on simmer days,
Will lilt at bleaching of their claes;
Nae herds on *Yarrow*'s bonny braes,
    Or banks of *Tweed*,
Delight to chant their hameil lays,
    Since music's dead.

At gloamin' now the bagpipe's dumb,
Whan weary owsen hameward come;
Sae sweetly as it wont to bum,
    And *Pibrachs* skreed;
We never hear its warlike hum;
    For music's dead.

Macgibbon's gane: Ah! waes my heart!
The man in music maist expert,
Wha cou'd sweet melody impart,
    And tune the reed,
Wi' sic a slee and pawky art;
    But now he's dead.

Ilk carline now may grunt and grane,
Ilk bonny lassie make great mane,

Since he's awa', I trow there's nane
      Can fill his stead;
The blythest sangster on the plain!
      Alake, he's dead!

Now foreign sonnets bear the gree,
And crabbit queer variety
Of sounds fresh sprung frae *Italy*,
      A bastard breed!
Unlike that saft-tongu'd melody
      Which now lies dead.

Cou'd *lav'rocks* at the dawning day,
Cou'd *linties* chirming frae the spray,
Or todling *burns* that smoothly play
      O'er gowden bed,
Compare wi' *Birks of Indermay?*
      But now they're dead.

O SCOTLAND! that cou'd yence afford
To bang the pith of Roman sword,
Winna your sons, wi' joint accord,
      To battle speed?
And fight till MUSIC be restor'd,
      Which now lies dead.

'The King's Birth-Day in Edinburgh'

Oh! qualis hurly-burly fuit, si forte vidisses.
                  Polemo-Middinia.

I sing the day sae aften sung,
Wi' which our lugs hae yearly rung,
In whase loud praise the Muse has dung
      A' kind o' print;
But wow! the limmer's fairly flung;
      There's naithing in't.

I'm fain to think the joy's the same
In London town as here at hame,
Whare fock of ilka age and name,
      Baith blind and cripple,

Forgather aft, O fy for shame!
　　To drink and tipple.

O *Muse*, be kind, and dinna fash us
To flee awa' beyont Parnassus,
Nor seek for *Helicon* to wash us,
　　That heath'nish spring;
Wi' Highland whisky scour our hawses,
　　And gar us sing.

Begin then, dame, ye've drunk your fill,
You woudna hae the tither gill?
You'll trust me, mair wou'd do you ill,
　　And ding you doitet;
Troth 'twould be sair agains my will
　　To hae the wyte o't.

Sing then, how, on the *fourth* of June,
Our *bells* screed aff a loyal tune,
Our ancient castle shoots at noon,
　　Wi' flag-staff buskit,
Frae which the soldier blades come down
　　To cock their musket.

Oh willawins! MONS MEG, for you,
'Twas firing crack'd thy muckle mou;
What black mishanter gart ye spew
　　Baith gut an' ga'?
I fear they bang'd thy belly fu'
　　Against the law.

Right seldom am I gi'en to bannin,
But, by my saul, ye was a cannon,
Cou'd hit a man, had he been stannin
　　In shire o' Fife,
Sax lang Scots miles ayont *Clackmannan*,
　　And tak his life.

The hills in terror wou'd cry out,
And echo to thy dinsome rout;
The herds wou'd gather in their nowt,
　　That glowr'd wi' wonder,
Haflins afraid to bide thereout
　　To hear thy thunder.

Sing likewise, Muse, how *blue-gown* bodies,
Like scar-craws new ta'en down frae woodies,
Come here to cast their clouted duddies,
    And get their pay:
Than them, what magistrate mair proud is
    On king's birth-day?

On this great day the city-guard,
In military art well lear'd,
Wi' powder'd pow and shaven beard,
    Gang thro' their functions,
By hostile rabble seldom spar'd
    Of clarty unctions.

O *soldiers!* for your ain dear sakes,
For Scotland's, alias, *Land of Cakes*,
Gie not her *bairns* sic deadly pakes,
    Nor be sae rude,
Wi' firelock or Lochaber aix,
    As spill their blude.

Now round and round the *serpents* whiz,
Wi' hissing wrath and angry phiz;
Sometimes they catch a gentle *gizz*,
    Alake the day!
And singe, wi' *hair-devouring bizz*,
    Its curls away.

Shou'd th' owner patiently keek round,
To view the nature o' his wound,
Dead pussie, dragled thro' the pond,
    Takes him a lounder,
Which lays his *honour* on the ground
    As flat's a *flounder*.

The Muse maun also now implore
Auld wives to steek ilk hole and bore;
If *baudrins* slip but to the door,
    I fear, I fear,
She'll nae lang shank upon all four
    This time o' year.

Next day each hero tells his news
O' crackit crowns and broken brows,

And deeds that here forbid the Muse
    Her theme to swell,
Or time mair precious to abuse
    Their crimes to tell.

She'll rather to the fields resort,
Whare music gars the day seem short,
Whare doggies play, and lambies sport,
    On gowany braes,
Whare peerless Fancy hads her court,
    And tunes her lays.

'Auld Reekie'

The Poetical Works of Robert Fergusson, ed. Robert Ford (Paisley: Alexander Gardner, 1773).

Auld Reekie! wale o' ilka town
That Scotland kens beneath the moon;
Where couthy chiels at e'enin' meet,
Their bizzin' craigs and mous to weet;
And blythely gar auld care gae by
Wi' blinkit and wi' bleerin' eye.
Ower lang frae thee the muse has been
Sae frisky on the simmer's green,
When flowers and gowans wont to glent
In bonny blinks upon the bent;
But now the leaves o' yellow dye,
Peel'd frae the branches, quickly fly;
And now frae nouther bush nor brier
The spreckl'd mavis greets your ear;
Nor bonny blackbird skims and roves
To seek his love in yonder groves.
Then, Reekie, welcome! Thou canst charm,
Unfleggit by the year's alarm.
Not Boreas, that sae snelly blows,
Dare here pap in his angry nose;
Thanks to our dads, whase biggin' stands
A shelter to surrounding lands!
    Now morn, wi' bonny purpie-smiles
Kisses the air-cock o' St. Giles;

Rakin' their een, the servant lasses
Early begin their lies and clashes.
Ilk tells her friend o' saddest distress,
That still she bruiks frae scoulin' mistress;
And wi' her joe, in turnpike stair,
She'd rather snuff the stinkin' air,
As be subjected to her tongue,
When justly censured in the wrong.
          On stair wi' tub or pat in hand,
The barefoot housemaids lo'e to stand,
That antrin fouk may ken how snell
Auld Reekie will at mornin' smell:
Then, wi' an inundation big as
The burn that 'neath the Nor' Loch brig is,
They kindly shower Edina's roses,
To quicken and regale our noses.
Now some for this, wi' satire's leesh,
Hae gien auld Edinburgh a creesh:
But without sourin' nought is sweet;
The mornin' smells that hail our street
Prepare and gently lead the way
To simmer canty, braw, and gay:
Edina's sons mair eithly share
Her spices and her dainties rare,
Than he that's never yet been call'd
Aff frae his plaidie or his fauld.
          Now stairhead critics, senseless fools,
Censure their aim, and pride their rules,
In Luckenbooths, wi' glowrin' eye,
Their neibours sma'est faults descry.
If ony loun shou'd dander there,
O' awkward gait and foreign air,
They trace his steps, till they can tell
His pedigree as weel's himsel'.
          When Phoebus blinks wi' warmer ray,
And schools at noon-day get the play,
Then bus'ness, weighty bus'ness, comes;
The trader glowers—he doubts, he hums.
The lawyers eke to Cross repair,
Their wigs to shaw, and toss an air;
While busy agent closely plies,

And a' his kittle cases tries.
      Now night, that's cunzied chief for fun,
Is wi' her usual rites begun:
Through ilka gate the torches blaze,
And globes send out their blinkin' rays.
The usefu' cadie plies in street,
To bide the profits o' his feet;
For, by thir lads Auld Reekie's fouk
Ken but a sample o' the stock
O' thieves, that nightly wad oppress,
And mak baith goods and gear the less.
Near him the lazy chairman stands,
And wats na how to turn his hands,
Till some daft birkie, rantin' fou,
Has matters somewhere else to do;—
The chairman willing gies his light
To deeds o' darkness and o' night.
      It's never saxpence for a lift
That gars thir lads wi' fu'ness rift;
For they wi' better gear are paid,
And whores and culls support their trade.
      Near some lamp-post, wi' dowie face,
Wi' heavy een and sour grimace,
Stands she, that beauty lang had kenn'd,
Whoredom her trade, and vice her end.
But see where now she wins her bread
By that which nature ne'er decreed,
And sings sad music to the lugs,
'Mang bourachs o' damn'd whores and rogues.
Whene'er we reputation lose,
Fair chastity's transparent gloss!
Redemption seenil kens the name,
But a's black misery and shame.
      Frae joyous tavern, reelin' drunk,
Wi' fiery phiz, and een half sunk,
Behold the bruiser, fae to a'
That in the reek o' gardies fa'!
Close by his side, a feckless race
O' macaronies shew their face,
And think they're free frae skaith, or harm,
While pith befriends their leader's arm.

Yet fearfu' aften o' their maught,
They quat the glory o' the faught
To this same warrior wha led
Thae heroes to bright honour's bed;
And aft the hack o' honour shines
In bruiser's face wi' broken lines.
O' them sad tales he tells anon,
When ramble and when fighting's done;
And, like Hectorian, ne'er impairs
The brag and glory o' his sairs.

      When feet in dirty gutters plash,
And fouk to wale their fitstaps fash;
At night, the macaroni drunk,
In pools or gutters aftimes sunk:
Hegh! what a fright he now appears,
When he his corpse dejected rears!
Look at that head, and think if there
The pomet slaister'd up his hair!
The cheeks observe, where now could shine
The scancin' glories o' carmine?
Ah, legs! in vain the silk-worm there
Display'd to view her eident care;
For stink instead of perfumes grow,
And clarty odours fragrant flow.

      Now, some to porter, some to punch,
Some to their wife, and some their wench,
Retire, while noisy ten hours' drum
Gars a' your trades gae danderin' hame.
Now, mony a club, jocose and free,
Gie a' to merriment and glee;
Wi' sang and glass they fley the power
O' care, that wad harass the hour;
For wine and Bacchus still bear down
Our thrawart fortune's wildest frown:
It maks you stark, and bauld, and brave,
Even when descending to the grave.

      Now some, in Pandemonium's shade,
Resume the gormandising trade;
Where eager looks, and glancin' een,
Forspeak a heart and stamack keen.
Gang on, my lads! It's lang sinsyne

We kenn'd auld Epicurus' line;
Save you, the board wad cease to rise,
Bedight wi' daintiths to the skies;
And salamanders cease to swill
The comforts o' a burning gill.

But chief, oh Cape! we crave thy aid,
To get our cares and poortith laid.
Sincerity and genius true,
O' knights have ever been the due.
Mirth, music, porter deepest dyed,
Are never here to worth denied;
And health, o' happiness to the queen,
Blinks bonny, wi' her smile serene.

Though joy maist part Auld Reekie owns
Eftsoons she kens sad sorrow's frowns.
What group is yon sae dismal, grim,
Wi' horrid aspect, cleedin' dim?
Says Death, "They're mine, a dowie crew,
To me they'll quickly pay their last adieu."

How come mankind, when lacking woe,
In saulie's face their hearts to show;
As if they were a clock to tell
That grief in them had rung her bell?
Then, what is man?—why a' this fraise?
Life's spunk decay'd, nae mair can blaze.
Let sober grief alane declare
Our fond anxiety and care;
Nor let the undertakers be
The only waefu' friends we see.

Come on, my Muse, and then rehearse
The gloomiest theme in a' your verse.
In morning, when ane keeks about,
Fu' blythe and free frae ail, nae doubt,
He lippens no to be misled
Amang the regions o' the dead;
But straight a painted corp he sees,
Lang streekit 'neath its canopies.
Soon, soon will this his mirth control,
And send damnation to his soul:
Or when the dead-deal (awfu' shape!)
Maks frighted mankind girn and gape,

Reflection than his reason sours,
For the neist dead-deal may be ours.
When Sybil led the Trojan down
To haggard Pluto's dreary town,
Shapes waur nor thae, I freely ween,
Could never meet the soldier's een.

      If kail sae green, or herbs, delight,
Edina's street attracts the sight:
Not Covent-garden, clad sae braw,
Mair fouth o' herbs can eithly shaw;
For mony a yard is here sair sought,
That kail and cabbage may be bought,
And healthfu' salad to regale,
When pamper'd wi' a heavy meal.
Glowr up the street at simmer morn,
The birk sae green, and sweet-brier thorn,
Wi' spraingit flow'rs that scent the gale,
Ca' far awa' the mornin' smell,
Wi' which our ladies' flower-pats fill'd,
And every noxious vapour kill'd.
Oh, Nature! canty, blythe, and free,
Where is there keeking-glass like thee?
Is there on earth that can compare
Wi' Mary's shape, and Mary's air,
Save the empurpled speck, that grows
In the saft faulds o' yonder rose?
How bonny seems the virgin breast,
When by the lilies here carest,
And leaves the mind in doubt to tell
Which maist in sweets and hue excel?

      Gillespie's snuff should prime the nose
O' her that to the market goes,
If she wad like to shun the smells
That float around frae market cells;
Where wames o' painches sav'ry scent
To nostrils gie great discontent.
Now wha in Albion could expect
O' cleanliness sic great neglect?
Nae Hottentot that daily lairs
'Mang tripe, and ither clarty wares,
Hath ever yet conceiv'd or seen,

Beyond the Line, sic scenes unclean.
     On Sunday here, an alter'd scene
O' men and manners meets our een.
Ane wad maist trow some people chose
To change their faces wi' their clo'es,
And fain wad gar ilk neibour think
They thirst for goodness as for drink;
But there's an unco dearth o' grace,
That has nae mansion but the face,
And never can obtain a part
In benmost corner o' the heart.
Why shou'd religion mak us sad,
If good frae virtue's to be had?
Na, rather gleefu' turn your face,
Forsake hypocrisy, grimace;
And never hae it understood
You fleg mankind frae being good.
     In afternoon, a' brawly buskit,
The joes and lasses loe to frisk it.
Some tak a great delight to place
The modest bon-grace owre the face;
Though you may see, if so inclined,
The turning o' the leg behind.
Now Comely-garden, and the Park
Refresh them, after forenoon's wark:
Newhaven, Leith, or Canonmills,
Supply them in their Sunday's gills;
Where writers aften spend their pence,
To stock their heads wi' drink and sense.
     While danderin' cits delight to stray
To Castlehill or public way,
Where they nae other purpose mean,
Than that fool cause o' being seen,
Let me to Arthur's Seat pursue,
Where bonny pastures meet the view,
And mony a wild-lorn scene accrues,
Befitting Willie Shakspeare's muse.
If fancy there would join the thrang,
The desert rocks and hills amang,
To echoes we should lilt and play,
And gie to mirth the lee-lang day.

Or should some canker'd biting shower
The day and a' her sweets deflower,
To Holyrood-house let me stray,
And gie to musing a' the day;
Lamenting what auld Scotland knew,
Bien days for ever frae her view.
O Hamilton, for shame! the Muse
Would pay to thee her couthy vows,
Gin ye wad tent the humble strain,
And gie's our dignity again:
For, oh, wae's me! the thistle springs
In domicile o' ancient kings,
Without a patriot to regret
Our palace and our ancient state.

Blest place! where debtors daily run,
To rid themsels frae jail and dun.
Here, though sequester'd frae the din
That rings Auld Reekie's wa's within;
Yet they may tread the sunny braes,
And bruik Apollo's cheery rays;
Glowr frae St. Anthon's grassy height,
Ower vales in simmer claes bedight;
Nor ever hing their head, I ween,
Wi' jealous fear o' being seen.
May I, whenever duns come nigh,
And shake my garret wi' their cry,
Scour here wi' haste, protection get,
To screen mysel' frae them and debt;
To breathe the bliss o' open sky,
And Simon Fraser's bolts defy.

Now gin a lown should hae his claes
In threadbare autumn o' their days,
St. Mary, broker's guardian saunt,
Will satisfy ilk ail and want;
For mony a hungry writer there
Dives down at night, wi' cleedin' bare,
And quickly rises to the view
A gentleman perfite and new.
Ye rich fouk, look na wi' disdain
Upon this ancient brokage lane,
For naked poets are supplied

Wi' what you to their wants denied.
      Peace to thy shade, thou wale o' men,
Drummond! relief to poortith's pain:
To thee the greatest bliss we owe,
And tribute's tear shall gratefu' flow;
The sick are cured, the hungry fed,
And dreams o' comfort tend their bed.
As lang as Forth weets Lothian's shore,
As lang's on Fife her billows roar,
Sae lang shall ilk whase country's dear,
To thy remembrance gie a tear.
By thee, Auld Reekie thrave and grew
Delightfu' to her childer's view;
Nae mair shall Glasgow striplings threap
Their city's beauty and its shape,
While our new city spreads around
Her bonny wings on fairy ground.
      But provosts now, that ne'er afford
The sma'est dignity to lord,
Ne'er care though every scheme gae wild
That Drummond's sacred hand has cull'd.
The spacious brig neglected lies,
Though plagued wi' pamphlets, dunn'd wi' cries;
They heed not, though destruction come
To gulp us in her gaunting womb.
Oh, shame! that safety canna claim
Protection from a provost's name;
But hidden danger lies behind,
To torture and to fleg the mind.
I may as weel bid Arthur's Seat
To Berwick Law mak gleg retreat,
As think that either will or art
Shall get the gate to win their heart:
For politics are a' their mark,
Bribes latent, and corruption dark.
If they can eithly turn the pence,
Wi' city's good they will dispense,
Nor care though a' her sons were lair'd
Ten fathom i' the auld kirkyard.
      To sing yet meikle does remain,
Undecent for a modest strain;

And since the poet's daily bread is
The favour o' the Muse or ladies,
He downa like to gie offence
To delicacy's tender sense;
Therefore the stews remain unsung,
And bawds in silence drap their tongue.
                    Reekie, fareweel! I ne'er cou'd part
Wi' thee, but wi' a dowie heart:
Aft frae the Fifan coast I've seen
Thee towerin' on thy summit green;
So glowr the saints when first is given
A favourite keek o' glore and heaven.
On earth nae mair they bend their een,
But quick assume angelic mien;
So I on Fife wad glowr no more,
But gallop to Edina's shore.

'The Sow of Feeling'

Well! I protest there's no such thing as dealing
With these starch'd poets—with these men of feeling!
                    Epilogue to "The Prince of Tunis."

Malignant planets! do ye still combine
Against this wayward, dreary life of mine?
Has pitiless oppression—cruel case!—
Gain'd sole possession of the human race!
By cruel hands has every virtue bled,
And innocence from men to vultures fled?
          Thrice happy had I lived in Jewish time,
When swallowing pork or pig was doom'd a crime;
My husband long had blest my longing arms,
Long, long had known love's sympathetic charms!
My children too—a little suckling race,
With all their father growing in their face—
From their prolific dam had ne'er been torn,
Nor to the bloody stalls of butchers borne.
          Ah, luxury! to you my being owes
Its load of misery, its load of woes!
With heavy heart I saunter all the day;

Gruntle and murmur all my hours away!
In vain I try to summon old desire
For favourite sports—for wallowing in the mire:
Thoughts of my husband, of my children, slain,
Turn all my wonted pleasure into pain!
How oft did we, in Phœbus warming ray,
Bask on the humid softness of the clay!
Oft did his lusty head defend my tail
From the rude whispers of the angry gale;
While nose-refreshing puddles stream'd around,
And floating odours hail'd the dung-clad ground.
      Near by a rustic mill's enchanting clack,
Where plenteous bushels load the peasant's back,
In straw-crown'd hovel, there to life we came,
One boar our father, and one sow our dam.
While tender infants on the mother's breast
A flame divine in either shone confest:
In riper hours, love's more than ardent blaze,
Inkindled all his passion, all his praise!
No deadly, sinful passion fired his soul,
Virtue o'er all his actions gain'd control!
That cherub which attracts the female heart,
And makes them soonest with their beauty part,
Attracted mine; I gave him all my love,
In the recesses of a verdant grove:
'Twas there I listn'd to his warmest vows,
Amidst the pendant melancholy boughs;
'Twas there my trusty lover shook for me
A shower of acorns from the oaken tree;
And from the teeming earth, with joy, plough'd out
The roots salubrious with his hardy snout.
      But, happiness! a floating meteor thou,
That still inconstant art to man and sow,
Left'st us in gloomiest horrors to reside,
Near by the deep-dyed sanguinary tide,
Where whetting steel prepares the butchering knives,
With greater ease to take the harmless lives
Of cows, and calves, and sheep, and hogs, who fear
The bite of bull-dogs, that incessant tear
Their flesh, and keenly suck the blood-distilling ear!
      At length the day, the eventful day, drew near,

Detested cause of many a briny tear!
I'll weep, till sorrow shall my eyelids drain,
A tender husband, and a brother, slain!
Alas! the lovely languor of his eye,
When the base murderers bore him captive by;
His mournful voice, the music of his groans,
Had melted any hearts, but hearts of stones!
O! had some angel at that instant come,
Given me four nimble fingers and a thumb,
The blood-stain'd blade I'd turn'd upon his foe,
And sudden sent him to the shades below—
Where, or Pythagoras' opinion jests,
Beasts are made butchers—butchers changed to beasts.
     Wisely in early times the law decreed,
For human food few quadrupeds should bleed;
But monstrous man, still erring from the laws,
The curse of Heaven upon his banquet draws!
Already has he drain'd the marshes dry
For frogs, new victims of his luxury;
And soon the toad and lizard will come home,
In his voracious paunch to find a tomb;
Cats, rats, and mice, their destiny may mourn,
In time their carcases on spits must turn;
They may rejoice to-day—while I resign
Life, to be number'd 'mongst the feeling swine.

MAIRIREAD GHRIOGARACH / MARGARET MACGREGOR

(C.1750–C.1820)

———

MARGARET MACGREGOR, from Perthshire, was born around 1750 on the north side of Loch Rannoch, the Slios Mìn ('smooth side') held by Menzies of Weem. In 1775 she married Dòmhnall Ruadh Gobha (Donald Gow) and settled in his small farm at Auchanruidh (Ach' an Ruighe, 'the field on the slope') in Glen Errochty, on the forfeited Jacobite estate of the Robertsons of Struan. They had at least seven children. Mairiread is said to have died about 1820 and been buried in Struan kirkyard. Thirty-four of her songs were published in 1831 by Donncha Mac Intoisich (Duncan Mackintosh), apparently her step-grandson, in a collection which also includes a handful of songs by her half-brother and by her daughter Anna. The song said to have been composed while she briefly attended a school for girls in Perth harks back to previous summers spent dairy farming on the high shieling grounds by Loch Ericht attached to the Slios Mìn farms. At time of publication it was sung to the tune of a well-known Lochaber song from the 1660s, 'Murt na Ceapaich'. 'Song of the Gable' recalls a disastrous storm.

———

'Òran na Tulchainn'

Co-Chruinneach dh' Orain Thaghte Ghaeleach, ed. Duncan Mackintosh (Edinburgh: John Elder, 1831).

> Cha mhór nach eil gruaim orm
>   Bhith luaidh air an driodfhortan,
> Ciod uime 'm bi oirnn smuairean
>   'S an sluagh bhith mar thigeadh dhoibh?
> Thainig gaoth làidir thuathach
>   Le buaireas neo-mhiosarra,

'S ged thearna sinne uaithe,
  Gum b' fhuathasach an clisge e.

An tulchann a bha dìreach,
  Bu ghrinn agus maiseach i,
Chaidh tilg' sìos cho ìosal,
  Cha chiatach ri fhaicinn i;
Ciod uime 'm biodh oirnn mìghean
  Mun nì sin a thachair dhuinn?
Nam bitheamaid ri thiodhlaig,
  Bu sgial ro mhì-thaitneach e.

Chaidh sinne an leaba dhùint',
  Agus chrùbain sinn tiota beag,
Thainig cadal air ar sùilean,
  Chum dùnadh mar thigeadh dhoibh;
Se chiad nì chuir fuathas oirnn
  Am fuaim bh' aig na clisnichean,
'S gum b' ealamh rinn sinn gluasad
  Nuair luasgain ar misneach oirnn.

An sin thòisich a' mhì-riaghailt,
  Chaidh ghrìosach a sgapadh oirnn,
Gum b'e gun deach a sgiabadh
  Sìos fo nar leapaichean,
Ghrad dh'éirich sinne an-aird
  A bhàthadh nan sradagan,
'S bha cùram oirnn an tràth sin
  Gun cailltear an aitreabh.

Cha deach sinn uile air ànradh,
  B'e an t-àm dhol air tapa e,
Na h-uile té bu làmhchar
  Toirt làmh air na plaideachan,
An criobachan nan gamhna
  Gun thàmh sinn gu madainn ann—
'S gum b' fhad' an oidhche gheamhraidh,
  San àm ri chur seachad ann.

Moch an làirne mhàireach
  Bu ghràineil a' mhadainn i—
Le uisge 's le clamhainn
  Cha ghabhadh aon nì cheartach' dhuinn,

Chuir sinn suas am pàillean
  Chum pàirt a chur seachad ann
'S dh'fhuirich sinn mar bhà sinn,
  Cho sàmhach 's bu chleachd leinn.

Ach mochthrath Di-Ciadain
  Bu chiatach a' mhadainn i,
Chaidh fios air feadh na tìr'
  A dh'innseadh mar thachair dhuinn;
Na h-uile fear a chual' e,
  Ba luath gu siubhal e,
Chan fhanadh iad ri'm feudail,
  'S feum an Ach' an Ruighe orr'.

Bhuail Iain Chaluim suas,
  Bu tuasgailte 's ealamh e,
Bha 's Iain Ruadh ga chomhna,
  Cho tròcaireach 's a b' aithne dha
A chur chlachan ás 's fhòidean,
  'S mòran de spairistean—
Bha madainn fhionnar fhuar ann,
  'S cha chuala mi gearain ac'.

Thainig gillean bàn' an Dròbhair,
  Glé sheòlta mar bhuineadh dhoibh,
'S rinn iad móran réiteach'
  Mun robh na slòigh air cruinneach',
Thainig Uilleam Stiùbhart
  Gu sunndach o na Tulacha,
Na gillean tapaidh iùlar,
  Gur sùbailt' ullamh iad.

Thainig clann a' ghobhainn on t-Socaich,
  'S mhosgail iad tre dhuinealas,
Nuair chual' iad gun robh dochair oirn,
  Cha bheag am forsa chumadh iad;
An Dughlasach 's b'e 'm prop dhiubh e,
  A shocrach' na cloich-bhun dhuinn,
'S cha b'e gun robh e doicheallach,
  'S na pocachan sa mhuileann aig'.

Nar thainig Seumas Shandaidh
  Chaidh aird chur air eireachdas—

'N àm cruinneachadh nan cairdean,
   Cha b'e bhiodh air deireadh dhiubh;
Co-dhiùbh ba ghnothach fortanach e,
   Ros'd no cùis dheireasach,
Bu chinnteach Taigh Cheann Drochaide
   Bhith brosnach' anns gach coinnimh leinn.

Thainig Tearlach Iain 'ic Thearlaich,
   San àm sin nar coimhearsnach,
'S Domhnall òg le chéile
   A chur spéid air ar gnothach-sa:
Thog iad dh'aon bheum e,
   Gu reidh is cha b' umhail leo,
Mun d'thainig laighe gréine,
   Gum b' éibhinn bhith coimhead air.

Nuair chaidh iad uile air ionnsaigh,
   Bu tionnsgalach tapaidh iad,
Gach fear a b' fhearr an ionnsach',
   Toirt làmh air a' chlachaireachd,
Gach aon a gheibheadh allsachd,
   Gun tairngte na cabair leis,
Chaidh cuid air buain nam fàl dhiubh
   'S bha dràibhig chairtean ann.

Nuair chluinneas Domhnall Ruadh seo,
   Cha dual gum bi gean air uim',
Cha mhò a bhios air Pàdraig,
   Gun d'thàinig a' charraid oirnn,
Iad fhéin bhith fada thall,
   San àm an robh a' chabhag ann,
'S on tha sinn uile an làthair,
   Gura dàn dhuinn bhith tallach.

Bidh dragh no dhà ri ùine
   Anns a' chùis seo mas maireann oirnn,
Bi deileachan is cùile
   Ri ghiùlan á Rainneach leinn,
Bidh saor ri thoirt gan dlùthadh,
   Mar ùrachadh barantais,
'S bidh pàirt a dharach dùbailt'
   Ri thoirt á bùth nan ceannaichean.

'The Song of the Gable' (translated by Ronald Black)

I'm almost too terrified
    To speak of the calamity,
But why should we be anxious
    When people act appropriately?
A strong wind from the north
    Came with force immoderate,
And although we got out of it,
    The shock of it was terrible.

The gable that was upright,
    It was grand and beautiful,
It was thrown down so low
    That it's a sorry sight to see;
But why should we be sad
    About our bad experience?
It would be (had we been buried)
    A most unpleasant story.

We got into our box-bed
    And crouched there for a while,
Till sleep came over our eyes
    And made them close as they should do;
The first thing that frightened us
    Was the noise the roof was making,
And we moved extremely quickly
    Once our confidence was shaken.

Then confusion began
    With the embers scattered over us,
For they had now been shifted
    To down below our bedsteads;
We got up immediately
    To extinguish all the sparks,
But from then on we were worried
    That the house was now in danger.

We didn't all go into panic,
    For it was time to be lively,
With every quick-thinking female

Going gathering blankets;
In the stalls of the stirks
    We remained until the morning—
We had a long winter's night
    To get through from that moment.

At the dawn of the next day
    It was a dreadful morning—
Setting anything to rights for us
    In rain and sleet was impossible;
We put up a sort of tent
    For some of us to shelter in
And stayed just where we were,
    As quiet as was our custom.

But early on the Wednesday
    It was a lovely morning,
Word went around the district
    To tell of our experience;
Every man who had heard of it
    Was quick to come and see us—
They didn't wait to haggle
    When Auchinrie needed them.

Malcolm's John just got on with it,
    He was lively and quick at it,
With John Roy's assistance,
    And he was so considerate;
Removing stones from it, and sods,
    And a lot of wooden joists—
The morning was crisp and cold
    But I didn't hear them complaining.

The Drover's fair-haired lads came,
    Very able, as befitted them,
And they had cleared away a lot
    Before the masses gathered there;
William Stewart showed up
    In good cheer from the Tullochs—
All lively, sensible fellows
    Who were agile and competent.

There came the smiths from Succoth,
    Spurred on by big-heartedness—

Almost nothing could have kept them
    When they heard of our catastrophe;
Douglas was their mainstay,
    He settled our foundation stone,
And with his meal-bags in the mill
    He was anything but niggardly.

When Alexander's James arrived
    It was time for embellishments—
When the kinsfolk came together
    He would never be the hindmost;
Be it some lucky circumstance
    Or misfortune or detriment,
We could trust Kindrochit House
    To come up trumps in each encounter.

Tearlach Iain 'ic Thearlaich came
    Who at that time was our neighbour
At the same time as young Donald
    To expedite our business:
In one shift they built it up
    With no trouble, most efficiently—
By the time the sun had set
    It was delightful to look at it.

When they all attacked the job,
    They were active, industrious,
Each man who knew best how to
    Would do his share of mason-work;
Each one who'd get a respite
    Would be set to pulling rafters,
Some went to cut the divots
    And there were carts to be driven.

When Domhnall Ruadh comes to hear this
    It's unlikely he'll be pleased with it
And the same will go for Patrick,
    That we suffered such misfortune,
That they were far away from us
    When we were struck by the disaster,
But because we are all present
    We will have a house to live in.

We'll have one or two problems yet
  In this matter if we're spared,
For deals and other timbers
  Must be brought by us from Rannoch,
We'll need a carpenter to fit them
  As renewal of security,
And we'll need a double oaken part
  To be got from the merchants' shop.

'Òran 's i an sgoil am Peart'

Co-Chruinneach dh' Orain Thaghte Ghaeleach, ed. Duncan Mackintosh
(Edinburgh: John Elder, 1831).

'S mi 'm shuidhe an seo fuaghal, 'n uinneag uasail taigh mhòir,
'S mòr gum b' annsa bhith sa bhuail' 'g èisteachd nuallaich nam bò,
Leagadh ghabhar is chaorach, 's crodh laoigh tighinn mun chrò,
Na bhith an seo air mo dhaoidheid 's an shnàthad chaol ann 'm dhòrn.

Thug mi tamall an toiseach gun sprochd orm no sgìos,
Rè an lath' ri fuaghal, gun smuaineach' air nì,
Gus an cual' mi na dearcan bhith gan reic airson fiach,
Ghrad bhuail e am bheachd-sa Coire Bhacaidh nam fiadh.

'S truagh gun bhith an Leitir Dhubh Lachlainn, 's ann a chaisginn
    mo mhiann,
Gheibhte iomadach meas ann, gun neach a' farraid am prìs;
Coir' gaolach mo chridhe am biodh iasg is sitheann gun dìth,
Meadhg is bainne gun airceas, 's cha b' iad na drapagan tì.

Nuair dh'èigheas iad am bainne, bheir mi sealladh a-mach,
'S ann chì mi 'bharaille air a ceangal an cairt;
Ged a thèid mi ga cheannach, Rìgh cha mhilis bhlas!
'S fheàrr am meadhg bhios sa Ghàidhealtachd na bainne blàth bhios
    am Peart.

Cha robh neach air bhith 'g iarraidh orm triall gu machair nan Gall,
Ach thuig mi gum b' fheàrrd mi ràith an t-samhraidh thoirt ann;
'S mòr an stàth tha san ionnsach', bheir e tionnsgal don dràic,
'S neach sam bith ga bheil tùr cha leig à chuimhne e gu bràth.

Ged bu leamsa Siorrachd Pheairt, na bheil mi faicinn ma cuairt,
No h-uile mìr dhen a' mhachair th' eadar Glaschu is Cluaidh,

Bheirinn trian deth Shir Raibeart nan gabhte e uam,
Chan ann am malairt na h-Apann, ach na th' aig' mu thuath.

'A song composed when she was attending a school in Perth' (translated by Michel Byrne)

Sitting here sewing by a grand mansion window
I'd much rather be among the herds, listening to the lowing of
    the cows,
Milking goats and sheep while calves gather about the fold,
Than be idling away the time here, working my slender needle.

I spent a first while neither dejected nor weary,
Sewing all day, not thinking of much,
But then I heard the call of berries for sale
And in a flash I was back in Curving Corrie of the deer.

If I were only on Lachlan's Black Slope, there I'd quench my desire,
I'd find plentiful fruits there with no-one asking their price;
My beloved corrie, abounding in venison and fish,
Milk and whey for the asking, not drippings of tea.

At the call of milk for sale, I look out the window,
And I see the barrel roped up to a cart;
Though I'll go down to buy some, Lord its taste is unpleasant!
Sweeter the whey in the Highlands than warm milk got in Perth.

No one demanded I journey to the Lowlanders' country,
But I realised it would benefit me to spend a summer season there;
Schooling is of great use, it gives ambition to the drudge,
And anyone of intelligence will retain it for life.

Though Perthshire were mine, what I see of it around me,
Or every piece of the plain between Glasgow and Clyde,
I'd give a third of it to Sir Robert Menzies if he would accept,
Not in exchange for Appin of Dull, but for his Rannoch lands
    up north.

LADY ANNE BARNARD

(1750–1825)

━━

LADY ANNE BARNARD (*née* Lindsay) grew up in a Jacobite household of winnowing fortune in Fife. In Edinburgh, in the 1770s, Barnard nevertheless hobnobbed with the leading intellectuals of the day; she relocated to London in 1781, and soon hosted new circles of prominent men and women, including politicians. Henry Dundas, with whom she endured a complicated friendship since their time in Edinburgh, secured Barnard a secretaryship in the recently captured Cape of Good Hope. Upon her return to Britain in 1801, Lady Barnard withdrew from public life, though she briefly emerged to acknowledge her authorship of the anonymous 1771 song 'Auld Robin Gray', at Walter Scott's request. (Scott had included some lines in his 1823 novel *The Pirate*.) The song had appeared in Herd's *Ancient and Modern Scottish Songs* (1776), and other anthologies into the 1810s, but Scott produced the authoritative version, in her name, for the Bannatyne Club in 1825.

━━

'Auld Robin Gray'

Auld Robin Gray; A Ballad (Edinburgh: James Ballantyne and Co., 1825).

I

When the sheep are in the fauld, when the cows come hame,
When a' the weary world to quiet rest are gane,
The woes of my heart fa' in showers frae my ee,
Unken'd by my gudeman, who soundly sleeps by me.

II

Young Jamie loo'd me weel, and sought me for his bride;
But saving ae crown-piece, he'd naething else beside.
To make the crown a pound, my Jamie gaed to sea;
And the crown and the pound, oh! they were baith for me!

III

Before he had been gane a twelvemonth and a day,
My father brak his arm, our cow was stown away;
My mother she fell sick—my Jamie was at sea—
And Auld Robin Gray, oh! he came a-courting me.

IV

My father cou'dna work—my mother cou'dna spin;
I toil'd day and night, but their bread I cou'dna win;
Auld Rob maintain'd them baith, and, wi' tears in his ee,
Said, "Jenny, oh! for their sakes, will you marry me?"

V

My heart it said na, and I look'd for Jamie back;
But hard blew the winds, and his ship was a wrack;
His ship was a wrack! Why didna Jenny dee?
Or, wherefore am I spared to cry out, Woe is me!

VI

My father argued sair—my mother didna speak,
But she look'd in my face till my heart was like to break;
They gied him my hand, but my heart was in the sea;
And so Auld Robin Gray, he was gudeman to me.

VII

I hadna been his wife, a week but only four,
When mournfu' as I sat on the stane at my door,
I saw my Jamie's ghaist—I cou'dna think it he,
Till he said, "I'm come hame, my love, to marry thee!"

VIII

O sair, sair did we greet, and mickle say of a';
Ae kiss we took, nae mair—I bad him gang awa.
I wish that I were dead, but I'm no like to dee;
For O, I am but young to cry out, Woe is me!

IX

I gang like a ghaist, and I carena to spin;
I darena think o' Jamie, for that wad be a sin.
But I will do my best a gude wife aye to be,
For Auld Robin Gray, oh! he is sae kind to me.

AILEAN DÙGHALLACH /
ALLAN MACDOUGALL
(C.1750–1828)

———

BORN in Glencoe, Ailean Dùghallach (Allan MacDougall), or Ailean Dall (Blind Allan), became the poet to Alasdair Ranaldson MacDonell of Glengarry. MacDougall typically composed panegyric verse, but he was also fond of satire. The following poem eulogizes the wooden paddle-steamer named Highland Chieftain, which had been known as the Duke of Wellington until a group of shareholders interested in West Highland routes acquired it in 1820. They sailed from Glasgow to Isle Ornsay in November of that year. After that, the Highland Chieftain had a varied career before it was finally scrapped in Glasgow in 1838.

———

'Slàn gun till na Gàidheil ghasda'

An t-Oranaiche, ed. Gilleasbuig Mac-na-Ceàrdadh (Glasgow: Archibald Sinclair, 1879).

Slàn gun till na Gàidheil ghasda,
Dh'fhalbh Di-màirt air sàil do Ghlaschu,
Leis a' bhàta dhìonach, sgairteil,
 Làidir, acfhainneach gu strì.

'S e h-ainm am Beurla 's an Gàidhlig,
An 'Ceann-fine measg nan Gàidheal';
'S thig i dhùthaich nam beann àrda,
 'S gheibh i càiridean anns gach tìr.

Nuair a dh'fhalbhas i gu h-aotrom,
'S luaithe h-astar na 'n gath-gaiothe;
Cha till fairg' i no sruth caolais,
 Ge b'e taobh don tig an t-sian.

'S ged a dh'èireadh muir gu buaireas,
Snàmhaidh i air bhàrr nan stuaghaibh,

Mar steud-cruidheach 's spuir ga bhualadh,
    Dhol san rèis a bhuannachd cis.

Le cuibhleachaibh air gach taobh dhith,
'S i masgadh fairge le saothair;
Ioghnadh 's motha th' air an t-saoghal,
    A dhcalbh clann-daoine rim linn.

Gu dol an aghaidh na gaoithe,
Le teine gun aon snàthainn aodaich,
Gun ràimh, ach a stiùir ga saoradh,
    Air muir a' taosgadh na glinn.

Sgioba fearail ri àm cruadail,
'S Caiptean Mac-an-Aba, an t-uasal,
Calum Dòmhnallach is Ruairidh
    'S MacCoinnich a tha suairce, grinn.

Caiptean Mac-an-Aba 'n t-àrmann,
A shìol nam fear a sheasadh làrach,
A leagadh aighean agus làn-daimh,
    Anns an fhàsach bràighe ghlinn.

Mu Urchaidh nam buinnean gailbheach,
Aig Eas Chaiteleig nan garbh-shruth,
'S tric rinn do mhorgha marbhadh,
    Air bradan tàrr-gheal fon still.

'A safe return for the Highland gallants' (translated by Donald E. Meek)

A safe return for the Highland gallants
who went, on Tuesday, by sea to Glasgow
on the watertight, valiant vessel,
    equipped and strong to fight the tide.

Her name in English and in Gaelic
is the "Chieftain among Gaels";
she will come to the Highlands,
    and win friends in every clime.

When she sails away so lightly,
her speed is faster than wind-blast;

no heavy sea or current will halt her,
　　whatever side the squall may rise.

And though the sea should swell to tempest,
she will swim upon the wave-crests,
like a hooved steed spurred in earnest
　　to run the race to win a prize.

On each side she carries paddles,
and she churns the sea with ardour;
of world's wonders, this is the greatest
　　that man has devised in all my time—

To sail straight against the wind-storm
with fire, and not a thread of sail-cloth,
without oars, while her rudder saves her,
　　as glens appear in the surging brine.

She has a manly crew in time of hardship,
with Captain MacNab, the noble,
Malcolm MacDonald and Rory
　　and MacKenzie, kind and fine.

Captain MacNab is the stalwart
descended from those who stand fast,
who would fell both hinds and stags,
　　in the heights of the glen that's wild.

About Orchy of the terrible torrents,
at Eas Chaiteilig of the strong streams,
often your sea-spear, beneath the deluge,
　　caught a white-bellied salmon on its tine.

HELEN CRAIK

(1751–1825)

THE novelist Helen Craik was born at Arbigland, a manor house, in Kirkcudbrightshire. Craik enjoyed a correspondence with Burns, who expressed his admiration for her poem 'Helen' (now considered lost). Little poetry attributed to her has survived. Following a scandal, including the possible murder of a groom on the estate, hushed up by her family, Craik exiled herself to their other property, Flimby Hall, in Cumberland. There she published five anonymous novels with Minerva Press, who were specialists in sentimental and Gothic fiction: *Julia de St Pierre* (1796), *Henry of Northumberland, or, The Hermit's Tale* (1800), *Adelaide de Narbonne, with Memoirs of Charlotte de Cordet* (1800), *Stella of the North, or, The Foundling of the Ship* (1802), and *The Nun and her Daughter, or, Memoirs of the Courville Family* (1805). Dated October 1787, the following fragment was written on the reverse of a frontispiece portrait of Burns in an edition of the Ayrshire Bard's poems.

'Here native Genius, gay, unique and strong'

Glenriddell Manuscripts, volume 1, n. 8 (National Library of Scotland).

> Here native Genius, gay, unique and strong,
> Shines through each page, and marks the tuneful song;
> Rapt Admiration her warm tribute pays,
> And Scotia proudly echoes all she says;
> Bold Independence, too, illumes the theme
> And claims a manly privilege to Fame.
> –Vainly, O Burns! wou'd rank and riches shine,
> Compar'd with in-born merit great as thine,
> These Chance may take, as Chance has often giv'n,
> But Pow'rs like thine can only come from Heav'n.

MAIGHREARAD CHAMSHRON /
MARGARET CAMERON (CAMPBELL)
(C.1755–C.1820)

━━━

HAILING from Glen Orchy, Margaret Cameron (*née* Campbell) was a daughter of a tacksman. After the death of her second husband, Donald Cameron, in 1784, Margaret moved to Callander, then still a largely Gaelic-speaking community. In order to make a little money she completed a collection of songs by herself and others, and arranged for them to be published in Edinburgh. They appeared in 1785 as *Òrain Nuadh Ghàidhealach le Marairead Cham'ron*. Alongside eulogies for prominent citizens of Lochaber and elsewhere we find in the collection 'Oran air Clag Chalasraid'. After four years of petitioning, the inhabitants of Callander finally received a bell for their church in 1784. Margaret Cameron was on hand to celebrate the occasion. In 1810 she reinvented herself as the evangelical poet Margaret Campbell, producing a collection of thirty-four spiritual songs of uncompromising severity, *Laoidhean Spioradail, air an Cnuasachadh le Mairearad Chaimbeul*. As for the bell, it tolled merrily until 1985, and may still be seen today in the garden of Callander Kirk Hall. (Thanks to Anne Macleod Hill and Micky Gibbard for information.)

━━━

'Oran air Clag Chalasraid'

Òrain Nuadh Ghàidhealach le Marairead Cham'ron (Inverness, 1785).

Se mór-chomhnadh ar n-uaislean
    Thain' am smuainte san tim seo
'N eaglais mhór a chur suas duinn
    'S clag bhith bualadh 'na stìopall;
Tha mór-mhaith do gach sluagh ann
    Tha mun cuairt oirnn san sgìreachd—
Nuair nì Bhaltair a ghluasad,
    Cluinnear uaith' e seachd mìle.

Seo 'n clag a tha garrachdail,
    Chost mór-airgead don sgìreachd,
Chan eil leithid dheth 'n Albainn,
    'S fad chaidh ainm feadh nan crìochan;
Nì ar dùsg' anns a' mhochthrath
    Dhol do chlachan gu sìobhalt',
Ged bhiomaid fo airsneal
    Bheir dhuinn caismeachd thoil-inntinn.

Nuair a thugadh e dhachaigh
    Nall o Ghlascho na Beurla,
Sann a chruinnich am baile
    Ga fhaicsinn le h-éibhneas,
'S fhad 's bhios duine maireann
    Do'n aithne a leughadh,
Gheibh iad sgrìobht' air a leathtaobh
    Gun deach a bhaisteadh 'An Seumas'.

Cha b'e mhàin a thoirt dhachaigh
    'N raibh an spacadh san àm sin,
Ach daoine bhith sgairteil
    Ga chur am fasta san teampall:
Rinn am ministear innleachd
    Air masìn á Dùn Éideann,
'S chuireadh suas e le Giobsan
    An crochadh le réidh-bheairt.

A dheagh bhuachaill na sgìreachd,
    A nì gu dìreach ar seòladh,
Meud do ghliocais chan innseam
    Ann am mìneachadh sgeòil duinn,
Tha thu sìobhalt' ad' bhruidhinn,
    Tha thu suidhicht' ad' chomhradh,
Tha thu farast' ad' ghluasad—
    Gun uabhar gun mhòrchuis.

Nuair a chruinnicheas do phoball
    Dh'ionnsaigh t' eaglais Di-Domhnaich,
Is fìor dheas-labhrach t' fhacail
    O chridhe reachdar làn sòlais;
Ged a bhiomaid ri lochdaibh
    On a ghineadh o'r n-òig' sinn,

Bu chruaidh bhiodh ar cridhe
    Mur tiomaich briathra do bheòil sinn.

Ach seachd bhuidhe ri m' Athair
    Nach d'rinn thu fhathast ar fàgail,
Gum faic sinn thu romhainn
    Thoirt do chomhairle 's gach càs oirnn;
Guma fada thu maireann
    'Na do thalla mar thà thu
Air do theaghlach mór prìseil
    Gus an cinn iad an airde.

'The Bell of Callander' (translated by Ronald Black)

It's the great help of our gentry
    I've been thinking of just now
In building us a church so big
    With a bell tolling in its steeple;
It's for everyone's benefit
    All around us in the parish—
When Walter starts ringing it,
    It's heard seven miles away!

This bell here is enormous,
    And it cost the parish a packet,
It's unmatched in all Scotland,
    And far-famed everywhere;
It wakes us up in the morning
    To go demurely to church,
And should our spirits be low
    Its ding-dong cheers us up.

When brought across to its home
    From Scots-speaking Glasgow,
The whole village foregathered
    For the pleasure of seeing it,
And as long as anyone's left
    Who is able to read it,
They'll find engraved on its side
    That it's been baptised 'The James'.

The big struggle after that
    Was not just bringing it home,
But men toiling away
    To fix it up in the church—
The minister arranged for
    A machine from Edinburgh,
Then it was hoisted by Gibson
    And most efficiently hung.

O good parish shepherd
    Who keeps us going straight,
I can't describe your great wisdom
    In the course of our story:
You're civil in your discourse
    And grave in your converse
But tolerant in attitude—
    Never haughty nor arrogant.

When your congregation gathers
    In your church every Sunday,
Your words flow with great eloquence
    From a heart strong and joyful;
Should we even have been sinning
    Since conception in childhood,
Our hearts would be hard
    If your words didn't affect us.

But seven thanks to my Father
    That as yet you've not left us,
That we can see you in future
    For your advice with each problem;
Long may you remain there
    In your manse where you are now
With your large precious family
    Till they've grown to be adults.

ANNE GRANT
(1755–1838)

———

ANNE GRANT (*née* MacVicar) came from a Glaswegian military family, which, after the outbreak of the Seven Years' War, took her to New York as an infant. The family returned to Scotland, from Vermont, when Grant was a teenager. Mrs Grant of Laggan (as she was popularly known) had long been an avid reader and aspiring author; Blind Harry and other auld Scottish minstrels were early favourites of hers. When facing financial hardship, after the death of her husband in 1801, Grant prepared a collection of her poems for the press. (Although printed for the author, in Edinburgh, the collection was also sold by major booksellers in London, Glasgow, Perth, Aberdeen, Elgin, and Inverness.) Encouraged by the success of her 1803 *Poems on Various Subjects*, Grant and the antiquary George Chalmers produced her *Letters from the Mountains* (1807). After *Letters* came *Memoirs of an American Lady* (1808), *The Highlanders, and Other Poems* (1808), and *Essays on the Superstitions of the Highlanders* (1811). In addition to further prose works, she translated Gaelic poems.

———

'To Miss Wallis, with a Sprig of Crimson Heath which Grew on the Summit of a Mountain'

Poems on Various Subjects (Edinburgh: Printed for the Author, 1803).

> "Those looks demure that deeply touch the soul,
> Where, with the light of thoughtful Reason join'd,
> Shine lively Fancy, and the feeling heart."
>
> THOMSON.

Muse that lov'st the lonely mountain,
  Cliff abrupt, and rocky glen,
Rushy dell and mossy fountain,
  Free from strife and far from men:

Muse that lov'st to worship Nature
   In her haunts sublimely wild,
Hail the maid whose every feature
   Speaks her Nature's darling child.

Nurs'd on Inspiration's bosom,
   Drest by meek Simplicity,
She in youth's luxuriant blossom
   Truth and Nature loves like thee.

Deck'd with chaste and artless graces,
   While her form adorns the stage,
Fancy pleas'd recals the traces
   Of a former, better age;

When the virgin's sweet suffusion,
   Timid look, and modest air,
Gentle fears, and soft confusion,
   Shrunk before the public stare.

'Tis not that thy tragic sister
   Wraps her in her crimson stole,
Or that comic powers assist her,
   While she fascinates the soul.

'Tis not that applausive thunder
   Shakes the scene when she appears,
That she draws the gaze of wonder,
   And unlocks the spring of tears:

'Tis not that capricious fashion
   Hails her idol of the day;
But that general adulation
   O'er her breast obtains no sway.

That the charities and duties
   Which domestic life endear,
Add new lustre to her beauties,
   Even in wisdom's view severe.

Lovely WALLIS, these are graces
   That awake the Muse's flame;
And to these sequester'd places
   Have convey'd thy honour'd name.

Pattern bright of filial duty,
    Kindest sister; truest friend,
On thy innocence and beauty
    Still may guardian sylphs attend!

Keep and wear this crimson blossom,
    Place it near thy generous heart,
'Tis a charm that from thy bosom
    Can repel detraction's dart.

On yon mountain's summit aerial,
    Far above the clouds it grew,
Fann'd by purest gales ethereal,
    Fed by bright celestial dew.

No voluptuous scents exhaling,
    Deck'd with no luxurious dye,
Fiercest storms in vain assailing,
    Blooming 'midst the wint'ry sky.

Type of virtue's wreaths victorious,
    Flowering on the craggy height,
Those who mount with ardour glorious
    Pay their labour with delight.

'Sonnet [Awful and stern the rugged entrance low'rs]'

The Highlanders, and Other Poems (London: Longman, Hurst, Rees, and Orme, 1808).

Awful and stern the rugged entrance low'rs
    That leads to Caledonia's last retreats,
Where oft in days of yore, contending pow'rs
    On the dark threshold shone in dreadful feats:
Where deep and dark the *Garrie* foams below,
    Erewhile with hostile gore her sanguine course
Distain'd, hoarse thund'ring bore the tale of woe
    To lands far distant from her gloomy source:
Here oft contending chiefs, in ireful mood,
    Bade civil discord rage, like pent up fire:
Here gallant clans, profuse of generous blood,

Indignant, slow, from *Nassau's* troops retire:
Here, oft at eve, their shadowy forms are seen
Like mist slow gliding o'er the mountains green.

'Sonnet [Dear, peaceful cottage!]'

Dear, peaceful cottage! o'er whose humble thatch
   The dewy moss has velvet verdure spread;
Once more, with trem'lous hands thy ready latch
   I lift, and to thy lintel bow my head.
Dear are thy inmates! Beauty's roseate smile,
   And eye soft melting hail my wish'd return,—
Loud clamours infant joy: around meanwhile
   Maturer breasts with silent rapture burn.
Within these narrow bounds I reign secure,
   And duteous love and prompt obedience find:
Nor sigh to view my destiny obscure,
   (Where all is lowly, but each owner's mind
Content), if pilgrims passing by our cell,
Say, "with her sister Peace *there* Virtue loves to dwell!"

ANDREW MACDONALD

(1757–1790)

———

ANDREW MACDONALD (formerly Donald) was born and educated in Edinburgh. Before taking up a tutoring position with the Oliphants in Perthshire, he received deacon's orders in the Scottish Episcopal Church in 1775. In 1782 he published *Velina, a Poetical Fragment*, and shortly after, *The Independent*, a novel. His tragedy *Vimonda* had been performed in Edinburgh to much acclaim, and he resigned his charge in Glasgow to pursue a literary career there. Taking *Vimonda* to London in 1787, he received an encouraging reception, and the play appeared in print less than a year later. Under the Smolletian pseudonym Matthew Bramble, he amused London with poetical burlesques in the manner of Peter Pindar (John Wolcot). But he received little financial reward. Barely in his early thirties, Macdonald died of consumption in the summer of 1790. A posthumous volume of his sermons secured some renewed popularity. A year later appeared Macdonald's *Miscellaneous Works* (1791), which purportedly includes all his known writings.

———

'Minvela—A Fragment. Imitated from the Gaelick'

The Miscellaneous Works of A. M'Donald; including the Tragedy of Vimonda, and those Productions which have appeared under the Signature of Matthew Bramble, Esq. with various other Compositions, by the same Author (London: J. Murray, 1791).

I

Beneath a rock, in rugged fissures torn,
   The Bard of Morven lay at noon reclin'd;
Where, o'er his head, an old fantastic thorn
   Diffus'd its fragrance to the passing wind:
    His harp, in melancholy mood resign'd,
Near, on a blasted branch in silence hung;

While slow he ponder'd in his pensive mind,
The deeds of fame that fir'd his bosom young,
When dauntless Fingal fought, and grey-hair'd Ullin sung.

II

As thus he lay, enrapt in sacred trance,
    And from his dim eyes stole the silent tear,
An aged Hero leaning on his lance,
    With wav'ring steps along the heath drew near;
    'Twas Murno, weeping for his Uran dear,
His gallant son, in fight untimely slain:
    Exulting forth he went to stain his spear
In hostile blood, on Lena's woody plain;
And there, in earth's cold womb, his lifeless bones remain.

III

Rais'd by the old man's woe, the heav'nly fire
    Thro' the mild soul of Ossian rushing flew;
Quick in his raptur'd hands he took the lyre,
    And struck a tender strain in measures new:
    Not softer ever was the breeze that blew
Through Selma's groves, or Cona's streamy vale,
    When to the moon-beams glanc'd the nightly dew,
And ghosts of heroes, clad in misty mail,
With airy maids came hov'ring o'er the mountains pale.

IV

By Luva's streams (the sightless Bard thus sung)
    In his grey tow'r did noble FORLOTH dwell,
For deeds of glory fam'd the chiefs among;
    Many a dark foe beneath his valour fell.
    Nor did his heart in kindness least excel;
Still in his plenteous hall the feast was spread,
    And still went round in joy the sounding shell:
Well knew the stranger where at noon to tread,
And well at night the wand'rer where to rest his head.

V

One maid of beauty blest his life's decline,
    MINVELA, of the dark and glossy hair,

Form'd by kind Nature in her best design,
   And fairest made of Morven's maidens fair.
   Many young chiefs had fought with ardent care,
Matchless Minvela's secret heart to gain,
   No spark of love she felt; but, free as air,
On the green hills, among her virgin train,
Rejoic'd with flying shafts o'er the brown deer to reign.

VI

'Twas then by winding Carron's stream appear'd
   Warriors unknown, and loud our chiefs defy'd.
Fingal's broad shield was struck, his banner rear'd,
   And Forloth's steps of age were by his side.
   They met; they fought; the banks in gore were dy'd.
Heroes unnumber'd pale and bleeding lay;
   And scarce could night the doubtful strife divide,
But Forloth sure had sunk in death that day,
Had not young FINAN turn'd th' impending stroke away.

VII

To Luva's halls the grateful chief convey'd
   The blue-ey'd Finan, in his shining car.
Come forth, he cried, Minvela, brightest maid,
   And hail thy father victor from the war!
   See, on this youth's white breast the bloody scar,
That sav'd me from the valiant stranger's sword:
   Go, range the vale, the piney cliffs afar,
And wat'ry caves, that herbs of health afford,
Till to his wonted strength my hero be restor'd.

VIII

Soon did the youth his wonted strength regain,
   And soon Minvela breathe the secret sigh;
As from her harp she call'd its tend'rest strain,
   In notes scarce heard, that instant fall and die;
   Her bosom heav'd, and from each swimming eye,
Adown her glowing cheek the big tears stole.
   Grey Forloth smil'd. And Finan, list'ning by,
Felt nameless transports darting thro' his soul,
At ev'ry rising swell, and pause of fainting dole.

IX

The maid, this pining grief to drive away,
    Resolv'd her woodland pastimes to renew:
Then on the hill she stood at down of day,
    Her dogs, with feet of wind, swept o'er the dew;
    And sure as death her feather'd arrows flew.
Sudden was heard the boding eagle's cry,
    And from the howling desart wild winds blew;
Black clouds came rolling round the mountains high;
While deep and dreadful thunder rattled o'er the sky.

X

On a white rock hung o'er the crashing wood,
    Sat fair Minvela, leaning on her bow;
Raging, and all in foam, swift Luva's flood
    Boil'd thro' the rocks and broken dens below.
    How o'er it, lovely Huntress, can'st thou go?
For on that rock thou may'st not long remain
    Dishevell'd in the blast, thy dark locks blow;
Cold round thy trembling bosom beats the rain;
And starless night will soon thy fearful steps restrain.

XI

Across the deep dark chasms, where roar'd the stream,
    Its moss-grown arm an aged oak had hung,
And met the rock beyond. There, while the gleam
    Of lightning flash'd, and hills with thunder rung,
    The shiv'ring hunter oft of old had clung,
And o'er the torrent work'd his per'lous way.
    Far, far below, wild caves and shelves among,
The waters roll; and mists, ascending grey,
To bats, and dismal owls, afford a doubtful day.

XII

The pass young Finan knew, and now had seen
    Minvela wand'ring on the bleak hill's side:
Thro' brakes he rush'd, and tangled copses green,
    Till, standing high above the foaming tide,
    Give me thy hand, fair maid, he joyful cried,
And joyful she her white hand smiling gave.

Trembling along the shaking branch they hied.
It cracks, it breaks, it falls—no strength could save.—
Down the dark void they plunge, amid the flashing wave.

XIII

Forloth sat in his hall. The beam blaz'd bright:
    He fann'd its flame, and wish'd Minvela there.
A sharp scream struck his ear. In wild affright
    He rush'd, and saw his young, his lovely pair,
    Wreath'd round the oak together in despair,
And swiftly shouting down the foamy flood.
    With fruitless cries he filled the troubled air,
And all the gloomy night, in frantic mood,
Roamed o'er the wa'try shore, and thro' the groaning wood.

XIV

Wretched old man! I know thy grief too well;
    Too well my harp has learn'd this dreary strain:
In pride of youth my blooming Oscar fell;
    And last of all my race I now remain.
    Once, like a tow'ring tree, I grac'd the plain;
Shoots round me grew, and flow'rs in fragrant rows;
    But soon the winter's wind, and freezing rain,
Nipt each fair bud, blasted each smiling rose,
"And left me naked, bare to ev'ry storm that blows!"

XV

Long by the fatal stream he wander'd slow;
    Long the wild mountain heard his bursting sighs:
His empty hall no more he seem'd to know;
    Dark was to him the earth, and black the skies.
    At length the distant shouts of war arise,
By Luva's bank sad Forloth hears the sound;
    Reckless of life, to arms once more he flies.
His dark ships, launching on the lake profound,
Spread their white sails, and fly to Malta's rocky mound.

XVI

On green Ferarma, in their course, they land,
    Where the dun roes sport on the woody shore;

High on the rock two beams of beauty stand,
 Young benders of the bow, with shafts in store.
 Such was the garb my lov'd Minvela wore,
Cried Forloth, while swift tears bedimm'd his sight,
 And such the crested helm young Finan bore,
When down the stream, on that disast'rous night,
Wrapt in fierce storms, they sank for ever from the light.

XVII

His well-known voice they heard, on this green isle,
 Where by the winged stream they had been borne:
Quick to his arms they spring; and, for a while,
 Their mingled raptures all expressions scorn.
 The old man's heart, by gnawing grief long worn,
Again in purest joy began to bound:
 To Luva's steams in triumph they return;
Once more, with dance and song the hills resound;
And in the hall, once more, the festive shell goes round.

XVIII

'Twas thus, O Murno! thy lamented son,
 Like Forloth's children, left thee in his prime:
But for a season is thy hero gone,
 On his own stream borne to a happier clime.
 And quick, O Murno, hastens on the time,
When thou shalt meet the gallant youth again;
 His course is now on the white clouds, that climb
The moon's clear face, when winds their force restrain,
And free the light ghosts wander o'er the starry plain.

XIX

'Tis there contending warriors meet in peace,
 And on the tempest's wing together ride:
There in the mutual feast all discords cease;
 Lochlin and Morven sitting side by side.
 For what can now their harmony divide,
When round them fly so thick the airy deer,
 When the blue fields of Heav'n extend so wide?
No, happy shades, ye have no foes to fear;
And on your battles past ye drop a pitying tear.

 * * * * * * *

LADY LOUISA STUART

(1757–1851)

━━

A LONG-LIVED and well-connected writer, Lady Louisa Stuart was the youngest child of the soon-to-be prime minister John Stuart, the third earl of Bute, and Mary Montagu, daughter of the author Lady Mary Wortley Montagu. By the age of ten she had begun to take after her maternal grandmother, having embarked upon a French novel and planned a Roman play. Despite her evident talent, Lady Stuart hoped, for reasons of caste as a woman of quality, never to see her name in print. Not until 1895 would her writings be published under her name. One of her correspondents was Walter Scott, who was a professed admirer of her poetry. Lady Stuart also mixed in the same circles as Frances Burney, who memorably described her as forbidding to strangers but lively among friends.

━━

'To Lady Caroline Dawson'

Gleaning from an Old Portfolio, ed. Mrs Godfrey Strong, 3 vols (Edinburgh: David Douglas, 1895–98).

> Dear gentle Friend, within whose happy breast
> Some fav'ring Planet fixed the cheerful guest,
> Oh may contentment long her wonted reign
> O'er that mild region undisturbed retain!
> Bright as the beam that dries a summer show'r,
> May Comfort circle ev'n affliction's hour!
> May wayward Fancy ne'er presume to bring
> One draught of anguish from a distant spring;
> But when kind Fortune grants the prosp'rous day,
> Round present pleasure unaspiring play.
>
> If bliss from worth, if strength from firmness flow,
> Such is the fate thy patience sure shall know.
> Far diff'rent mine—Each bud of seeming joy

The gloomy Presage can betimes annoy,
Deep to my bosom's inmost folds proceed,
Pluck the weak root, and bruise the little seed,
Or if the transient bloom ere then be fled,
Pour fost'ring drops on sorrow's hateful head,
And lest some ray of adverse sun impair,
Shade the night plant with unabating care.

Then let thy heart ('tis asked in Friendship's name)
Forgive the grief thy Reason ought to blame,
Nor think, uncheck'd by mine its rage allowed
To stretch o'er life th' impenetrable cloud;
Faint as she seems, her weak attempt's pursued,
Her sober counsels are each hour renew'd;
Yet She, ev'n she can sometimes tell me too
No cheering prospect glads her utmost view,
That grateful charms, nor winning graces warm
My pensive converse and my faded form,
That past pursuits regret alone supply,
That Hope recedes, and Youth prepares to fly.

Nay, even the Muse, by whose assistance now
These vain complainings may more smoothly flow,
Finds all her arts and all her power defy'd,
Nor feeds my pleasure nor supports my pride,
When sickly spleen no object round can spare
The frequent curse must undeserving bear,
And oft be told that her pernicious hand
Forbade the bliss which Fate might else have planned,
Wove twisted evils Time shall never part,
Or fill'd the cup whose poison slew my heart.

But murmurs cease! nor from my best loved friend
One smiling thought let all your accents rend,
Or if the rent a partial cure bestows,
Take now your last, and here for ever close.
Yes! skill'd to soothe, to soften, and to cheer,
Returning Reason shall again be clear;
Not that her hand may Mem'ry's sigh restrain,
Or stifle Truth when Truth produces Pain.
The Soul let wild Imagination charm
To frantic joy or instantaneous calm,

The sudden flash for one bright moment speed,
Nor care if Night in double gloom succeed
Her placid torch more steady, more serene,
Can chase no feature from the real scene,
But taught by Her, perhaps my strengthened eye
That real scene shall unappall'd descry.
Be this Her task; to make the wasting fire,
The torturing wish, the groundless hope retire,
Bid good already gain'd in virtue rise,
And veil the happiness that Fate denies.

FRANCES CHADWICK
(B.1758)

━━

ATTRIBUTED to a Mrs Chadwick, *Rural and Other Poems* (1828) appears to be the poet's only collection, even though it was published by a group of leading London publishers. Dated 31 December 1827, the dedication to a Dr Chadwick records the poet's 'maternal affection'. The collection itself ranges over an impressive array of genres, including sonnets, hymns, and epistles, as well as the pastoral poems indicated in the book's title.

━━

'A Dream'

Rural and Other Poems (London: Longman, Rees, Orme, Brown, and Green, 1828).

> Quite oppress'd with the sultry gleams,
>   One noon as I strayed through the glade,
> With such force Sol darted his beams,
>   I sought a retreat in the shade.
>
> I saw there a path in the grove,
>   The woodlark was chanting his song,
> I thought down the path I would rove,—
>   A streamlet ran smoothly along.
>
> I looked for a place to recline,
>   Fatigued as I was by the heat;
> A grotto grown round with woodbine,
>   Freely offered a stranger a seat.
>
> But I had not retired there long,
>   Ere Morpheus threw round me his cloak;
> I dreamed that a stream flowed along,
>   And on it a beautiful boat.

A figure in female attire,
　　Held out her white hand while she gazed;
But how was my bosom on fire
　　When a veil the same moment she raised?

She said,—and the voice thrilled my ear,—
　　"My name it is Pleasure! I go
From Discretion, a mistress I fear;
　　Assist me sweet youth then to row,"

My pity I could not express:—
　　"I vowed I would ever befriend
Such loveliness when in distress;
　　Her steps I would ever attend!"

I vaulted then into the boat,
　　And seizing the oar from her hand,
Down the stream we began swift to float,
　　When a maid loudly hailed us from land:

And as she approached to the view,
　　I saw she was lovely and neat;—
Her garb was ceolian blue,—
　　Her aspect majestic and sweet:

"Stay stay! gentle youth!" she exclaimed,
　　"My name is Discretion!" I hied,
"I saw you with Pleasure enslaved,
　　And wished to be Floria's guide:

But if you're determined to sail
　　With her whom you think is so fair,
My counsel will little avail,
　　In her port know destruction is there!"

To leave Pleasure, wholly I tried,—
　　Alas! ev'ry effort was vain;
The thought was too much, and I sighed,—
　　To lose her would give me deep pain.

My fondness Discretion espied;—
　　She found that I loved the fair maid;
So begged that she might be my guide,—
　　My freedom she would not invade.

Fair Pleasure appeared to be vexed;
    My senses I own were afloat;—
I confess that I felt much perplexed;—
    Then Discretion stept into the boat.

What mortal more happy could be!
    I seemed with two angels to sail;—
I wished not again to be free;—
    We sailed with a brisk blowing gale:

This seeming delight was soon o'er,
    I awoke,—and behold 'twas a dream!—
My mind was as never before;—
    Such loveliness never was seen.

I vowed, that henceforward, if e'er
    Fair Pleasure should tempt me to stray,
Discretion should guide!—for I ne'er
    Can the precept forget of that day.

JEAN GLOVER

(1758–1801)

BORN in Kilmarnock, Jean Glover was an actress who, at an early age, joined a band of strolling players. Burns transcribed the only surviving song currently attributed to her, 'O'er the Muir Amang the Heather', after hearing her perform it. The song was published in *The Scots Musical Museum* (1792), set to an earlier tune. From that point onward, this piece regularly reappeared in nineteenth-century collections.

'O'er the Muir Amang the Heather'

The Scots Musical Museum, ed. James Johnson, 6 vols (Edinburgh: James Johnson & Co., 1787–1803).

> Coming through the Craigs o' Kyle,
>   Amang the bonnie blooming heather,
> There I met a bonnie lassie,
>   Keeping a' her ewes thegither.
>
>   O'er the muir amang the heather,
>   O'er the muir amang the heather,
>   There I met a bonnie lassie,
>   Keeping a' her ewes thegither.
>
> Says I, 'My dear, where is thy hame?
>   In muir or dale, pray tell me whether?'
> Says she, 'I tent the fleecy flocks
>   That feed amang the blooming heather.'
>
> We laid us down upon a bank,
>   Sae warm and sunny was the weather;
> She left her flocks at large to rove
>   Amang the bonnie blooming heather.
>
> While thus we lay she sung a sang,
>   Till echo rang a mile and farther;

And aye the burden o' the sang
  Was 'O'er the muir amang the heather!'

She charmed my heart, and aye sinsyne
  I couldna think on ony ither:
By sea and sky she shall be mine,
  The bonnie lass amang the heather!

    O'er the muir amang the heather,
    Down amang the blooming heather:—
    By sea and sky she shall be mine,
    The bonnie lass amang the heather!

CALUM BÀN BOCHANAN /
MALCOLM 'BÀN' BUCHANAN
(1758–C.1828)

═══

CALUM BÀN BOCHANAN (Malcolm 'Bàn' Buchanan), sometimes
referred to as Calum Bàn MacMhannain, was born at Sarsdal in Flodigarry
on the Isle of Skye. Later he emigrated to Canada on board the Polly. Like
his fellow passengers, Malcolm Bàn Buchanan probably made a conscious decision to emigrate in response to the recruiting campaign con-
ducted by Lord Selkirk in the Hebrides during the autumn and winter
of 1802–3. Selkirk's original scheme to locate Highland colonists in
Upper Canada had foundered on opposition from the British government. Three ships, carrying roughly 800 emigrants, were re-routed to
Prince Edward Island. There the emigrants took up lands in the Belfast
area, where they perpetuated their traditions of song and story in their
everyday language, Gaelic, for generations to come. By his own testimony, as recorded in his song 'Imrich nan Eileanach' ('Emigration of
the Islanders'), Buchanan viewed group emigration as a plausible route
to peace and prosperity after the dismantling of clan culture back home.

═══

'Imrich nan Eileanach'

Translator's transcription

I

An àm togail dhuinn fhìn
Mach o chala Phort Rìgh,
'S iomadh aon a bh' air tìr 's iad brònach;
Iad ag amharc gu dlùth
Null 's an sùil air an luing,
'S ise gabhail a-null gu Rònaigh;
Thuirt MacPhàid às an Dìg,
'S e ag èigheach rium fhìn,
" 'S ann a laigheas i sìos gu Tròdaigh;

'S biodh am fear as fheàrr tùr
Nis na shuidh' air an stiùir
Gus an tèid i os cionn an t-Sòthain.

2

Eilean eil' ann da rèir
Agus Sgeir na Ruinn Gèir,
'S bidh muir air a' bhèist an-còmhnaidh;
Tha cnap eil' ann no dhà,
'S ann dhiubh sin Clach nan Ràmh,
'S Bogha Ruadh tha fo Àird 'Ic Thòrlain;
Leac na Buinne seo shuas
'S Rubh' an Aiseig ri cluais,
Mol a' Mhaide 's e cruaidh le dòirneig;
Thoir an aire gu dlùth
Cumail àrd os an cionn—
Seachain sruth Rubh' Hùnais, 's mòr e."

3

Dh'èirich soirbheas on tuath
Dhuinn os cionn Fladaigh Chuain,
'S ann a ghabhadh i 'n uair sin òran;
I a' siubhal gu luath,
'S i a' gearradh ma cluais,
Dol a ghabhail a' chuain 's i eòlach.
Thug mi sùil às mo dhèidh
Null air Rubh' a' Chùirn Lèith
Is chan fhaca mi fhèin ach ceò air;
Sin nuair labhair MacPhàil,
'S e ag amharc gu h-àrd:
" 'S mòr mo bheachd gur h-e bàrr an Stòrr e."

4

Moire, 's minig a bha
Mise treis air a sgàth
Ann an Rig, 's gum b' e 'n t-àite bhò e;
Nuair a thigeadh am Màrt
Bhiodh an crodh anns a' Chàrn,
'S bhiodh na luibhean co-fhàs ri neòinean;
Bhiodh an luachair ghorm ùr
Nìos a' fàs anns a' bhùrn

Fo na bruthaichean cùbhra', bòidheach;
Bhiodh na caoraich da rèir
Ann ri mire 's ri leum,
'S iad a' breith anns a' Chèit' uain òga.

5

Thàinig maighstir às ùr
Nis a-staigh air a' ghrunnd,
Sin an naidheachd tha tùrsach, brònach;
Tha na daoine às a' falbh,
'S ann tha 'm maoin an dèidh searg,
Chan eil mart aca dh'fhalbhas mòinteach;
Chuireadh cuid dhiubh sa mhàl,
'S fhuair cuid eile dhiubh 'm bàs,
'S tearc na dh'fhuirich a' làthair beò dhiubh:
Ciod a bhuinig dhomh fhìn
Bhith a' fuireach san tìr
O nach coisinn mi nì air bhrògan.

6

'S ann a thèid mi thar sàil,
'S ann a leanas mi càch,
Feuch a' faigheamaid àite-còmhnaidh;
Gheibh sinn fearann às ùr
'S e ri ceannach à grunnd,
'S cha bhi sgillinn ri chunntas oirnn dheth;
'S math dhuinn fasgadh nan craobh
Seach na bruthaichean fraoich
Bhiodh a-muigh ann an aodann Ghròbain;
Air na leacan lom, fuar,
Nuair a thigeadh am fuachd,
Sin an t-astar bu bhuaine mòinteach.

7

Moire 's fhada dhuinn fhìn
Rinn sinn fuireach san tìr,
Ged a thogamaid nì gu leòr ann,
'S iomadh dosgainn is call
Thigeadh orra nan àm,
Chuireadh seachad feadh bheann ri ceò iad.
Ged a readh'maid gu fèill,

'S ged a reiceamaid treud,
'S ged a gheibheamaid fèich gu leòr air,
Thig am Bàillidh mun cuairt
Leis na sumanaidh chruaidh,
'S bheir e h-uile dad uainn dheth còmhladh.

8

B' e sin fitheach gun àgh
Tha air tighinn an-dràst',
'S e na Bhàillidh an àite 'n Leòdaich,
Umaidh àrdanach, cruaidh,
'S e gun iochd ris an tuath,
E gun taise, gun truas, gun tròcair;
'S beag an t-iongnadh e fhèin
Bhith gun chàirdeas fon ghrèin,
Oir chan aithne dhomh fhèin cò 's eòl dha,
Ach an Caimbeulach ruadh
O thaobh Asaint o thuath;
'S nam bu fada fear buan dhe sheòrsa!

9

Ach ma thèid thu gu bràth
A-null thairis air sàil,
Thoir mo shoraidh gu càirdean eòlach,
Thoir dhaibh cuireadh gun dàil
Iad a theicheadh on mhàl,
'S iad a thighinn cho tràth 's bu chòir dhaibh;
Is nam faigheadh iad àm
'S dòigh air tighinn a-nall,
'N sin cha bhiodh iad an taing MhicDhòmhnaill;
'S ann a gheibheadh iad àit'
Anns an cuireadh iad bàrr,
'S ro-mhath chinneadh buntàta 's eòrn' ann.

10

'S e seo Eilean an àigh
Anns a bheil sinn an-dràst',
'S ro-mhath chinneas dhuinn blàth air pòr ann.
Bidh an coirc' ann a' fàs,
Agus cruithneachd fo bhlàth,
Agus tuirneap is càl is pònair,

Agus siùcar nan craobh
Ann ri fhaighinn gu saor,
'S bidh e againn na chaoban mòra;
'S ruma dathte, dearg, ùr
Anns gach bothan is bùth,
Cheart cho pailt ris a' bhùrn ga òl ann.

'Emigration of the Islanders' (translated by Iain S. MacPherson)

1

When the time came for us to sail out of Portree harbour, the shore was lined with downcast folk, eyes riveted on the ship as it made for Rona. MacFadyen from Digg called out to me: "Now she'll head down to Trodday; so have the best hand take the helm, at least till she gets above Sothain."

2

"Then there's another island just like it, and Sgeir na Ruinn Gèir: that beast is always covered by sea. And another nook or two, like Clach nan Ràmh and Bogha Ruadh under Àird 'Ic Thòrlain. Then Leac na Buinne further on, and Rubh' an Aiseig close by: and Mol a' Mhaide pebbled hard. Be very careful, keep well above them, and give the Rubh' Hùnais current a miss: it's pounding."

3

A fair wind rose from the north as we sailed past Fladaigh Chuain, and the ship started to sing: hummed along, tacked round, and took to the wide-open, intimate sea. I looked behind me, over to Rubh' a' Chùirn Lèith, and saw nothing: nothing but mist. So MacPhail glanced up and said, "I'm quite sure it's the summit of Stòrr."

4

Mother Mary, how often in Rigg I was under its shade: such a place for the cows. In March the cattle would be in Càrn, the grass keeping pace with the daisies. Fresh green rushes would rise up in clear water under sweet-smelling, beautiful banks. And the sheep would be there, all tearing around, giving birth to young lambs in May.

5

A new master has now come into the land: upsetting, unsettling news.
The people are leaving, their worldly goods all withered. They've not
even a cow for the moor. Some were put to the rent; others were slaugh-
tered. Only a bare few remain. And so what profit for me to stay on the
land when I can't earn a thing from the shoes.

6

So I'll go overseas. I shall follow the rest, try and find ourselves a place
to live. We'll get new land, to be bought from ground up, and not owe
a penny on it. Better for us the shelter of trees than any heathery banks
facing out towards Gròbain. On cold, barren flagstones, when the cold
would come in, that is one endless long moor.

7

Mother Mary, we stayed so long on the land. And though we managed to
make enough to survive, so much misfortune and loss overcame it in time
and was scattered into mountain mist. Though we'd go to the sales; though
we'd sell off a herd; though we'd get a good enough price; still the Factor
comes round, with his hard paper summons, and strips us of every last bit.

8

That's one joyless raven we've been landed with now as Factor in place
of MacLeod: a cruel, arrogant dolt, and no love lost for tenants; no
compassion, no pity, no mercy. Hardly surprising he's single under the
sun; I have no clue who knows him. Except for the red-headed Campbell
from North Assynt; may his kind live long!

9

But if you ever go back overseas, say farewell to my family, my friends;
and invite them to clear off, away from the rents, and come as soon as
they should. For if they found the time, and some way to get over, then
they'd be no longer beholden to MacDonald. Instead they could find
a place and plant crops where potatoes and barley would flourish.

10

We now live in an Island of plenty. And what we plant comes to flower.
Oats grow, wheat ripens, with turnip, cabbage and beans. There's sugar
from trees, free for the taking, in great heaps. And fresh, coloured, red
rum in every cabin and shop, as abundant as water is drunk.

SEUMAS MAC 'ILLE
SHEATHANAICH / JAMES SHAW
(C.1758–C.1828)

═══

JAMES SHAW was a native of Mull who moved to the mainland parish of Ardchattan and obtained the patronage of General Duncan Campbell of Lochnell, from which he became generally known as *Bard Loch nan Eala*, 'Lochnell's Bard'. Shaw begins 'Naidheachd na Frainge' by telling how he dreams of meeting a mysterious stranger, and demands to know the man's credentials: his people were from Morvern and Mull, the stranger reveals. This includes a celebrated witch of Gaelic tradition, *Caiseart Gharbh Nic an Uidhir* ('Coarse Footwear Daughter of Paleface'), as his grandmother. Her sister was *Cas a' Mhogain* ('Footless Stocking'), another celebrated witch. Having established that his is a representative Gaelic voice of considerable prophetic authority, he states his case: his duty is to bring 'French news to England', a clear reference to Jacobinism and the Revolution. The people of the Highlands, he points out, are being turfed out by the rich and replaced with sheep. The prime minister, William Pitt, should be tried and sentenced to death by 'the poor folk of the land'. In a final flourish, the stranger identifies himself as *Gille Naomh Mac an Rùsgaich* ('Holy Lad Son of the Fleece-Wearer'), a character in the narrative tradition of the day who shows how a war of attrition can be waged on incoming Lowland farmers. It is a truly revolutionary song.

═══

'Naidheachd na Frainge'

Adv. ms 50.2.20, ff. 171rv, 187rv (National Library of Scotland).

> Chunna mise a-raoir bruadar
> A dh'fhàg luaineach mi 'm leabaidh
> Leis na chinn mi fo mhulad
> Bho nach b' urrainn mi cadal.
> Thuirt an guth rium mi a dh'éirigh

Chum 's gun éistinn ri a chagar
A thoirt brìgh ás an fhàisneachd
A rinn càch o chionn fhada.

Rinn mi tionndadh gu h-ullamh
A dh'fhaotainn tuille dh'a sheanchas,
Chuir mi ceist air o m' nàdar
Có an t-àit' ás an d'fhalbh e.
Thuirt e rium gun robh cinnt air
O linn na Dìle 's Rìgh Fearghas
Gun robh a chinneadh 's a chairdean
A' gabhail tàmh ann an Albainn.

Thuirt mi ris, "Ciod as aois dhuit,
Na có na daoine dh'am buin thu,
Na có a' chearna den àit' seo
Am bheil do chairdean a' fuireachd?"
Thuirt e rium gun robh dearbh air
Nan creidinn seanchas deagh urrainn
Gun robh a sheanair sa Mhorbhairn'
'S a dhà sheanmhair am Muile.

"Nuair bha mis' an tùs m' òige
Bha mi eòlach san àite sin,
Eadar Forsa tha thallad,
Rubha na Cailliche 's Àras,
Tobar Mhoire 's Caol Ithe
'S gach ceum dhen t-slighe, tha mi 'g ràite,
'S cha chualas guth air do sheanmhair
'S mur eil i marbh, tha i làthair."

"An cuala tusa riamh an seanchas
Air Caiseart Gharbh Nic an Uidhir?
Bha i chomhnaidh an Gleann Forsa
Nuair bha Oisein 'na ghiullan;
Bha i falbh 's i 'na proitseach
Le Cas a' Mhogain a piuthar—
Is mise an truaghan 'nan déigh,
'S gun fhios cia-dé thainig riutha!"

Thuirt mi ris, "Ciod as ceaird duit,
No an duine fìrinneach ceart thu,
No 'm faod mi 'n naidheachd seo innse,

No a bheil brìgh ann ad' fhacail?"
Thuirt e rium ann am mìothlachd,
    "Tha thu gam fhiachainn ro fhada—
Is mis' am post tha san àm seo
    Toirt fios na Frainge gu Sasann.

"Tha na tighearnan fhéin
    A' dol gu béisteileachd ghràineil,
A' cur de mhàl air am fearann
    Nach fhaigh iad gu bràth e,
Iad a' fògradh nan daoine
    'S a' cur chaorach 'nan àite—
'S thig an fhàisneachd gu fìrinn
    Anns gach nì tha mi 'g ràite.

"Ma thig fear á Dùn Éideann
    Le each-sréin agus dìollaid,
Le spuir agus bòtann
    Mar ri sgleò de na briagan,
Ma bhios airgead 'na achlais
    Ged nach mair e ach bliadhna,
Gheibh e cùirt anns an àite
    Nach fhaigh neach a dh'àraicheadh riamh ann.

" 'S iomadh baile math fearainn
    Gheibhte ceathrar mhath thuaithann
Bheireadh biadh do dh'fhear rathaid
    'S casg a phathaidh den uachdar,
Os barr 's deagh leabaidh
    'S gach aon nì math a bhiodh uaithe—
'S chan fhaic mi 'n-diugh ann ach cìobair
    'S a cheann gun chìreadh, làn uaimheil.

"Ach nam biodh Pitt air a dhìteadh
    'S e am prìosan math làidir
An àite dorcha gun solas,
    Bhiodh na donais am pàirt ris;
'S nam faigheadh bochdan na tìre
    Suidh' air binn a thoirt bàis dha,
Gheibheadh 'n anam beatha shuthainn
    A chorp a liubhairt do a nàbaidh."

O'n a bha 'n duine cho deis rium
    'S a cho-fhreagairt an t-seanchais

Gun fhios am faicinn-sa am-feast e,
   Chuir mi ceist ris ciod a b' ainm dha;
Thuirt e rium gun robh cunntas
   Anns gach dùthaich an Albainn
Air Gille Naomh Mac an Rùsgaich,
   'S thionn' e chùl rium is dh'fhalbh e.

'The News from France' (translated by Ronald Black)

Last night I saw a dream
   That left me restless in bed
And made me grow sorrowful,
   Because I couldn't sleep.
The voice told me to get up
   And listen to its whisper,
Giving substance to the prophecy
   Made by others long ago.

I turned around quickly
   To get more of his narrative,
And naturally asked him
   What place he had come from.
He said it was certain
   That his friends and kin lived
In Scotland from the time
   Of the Flood and King Fergus.

I said to him, "How old are you,
   Or who are your people,
Or where in this place
   Do your kinsfolk reside?"
He told me it was proven,
   If I believed good authority,
That he'd a grandfather in Morvern
   And two grandmothers in Mull.

"When I was very young
   I knew that place well,
Between Forsa over there,
   Rubha na Caillich and Aros,

Tobermory and the Sound of Iona
   And every step of the way, I say,
And I've never heard of your grandmother
   But if not dead, she is there."

"Have you ever heard tell
   Of Caiseart Gharbh Nic an Uidhir?
She lived in Glen Forsa
   When Ossian was a lad;
She went around as a girl
   With Cas a' Mhogain her sister—
I'm the wretch who's survived them,
   And who knows what their fate was?"

I said to him, "What's your trade,
   Or are you honest and truthful,
Or can I pass on this story,
   Or is there substance in your words?"
He said to me peevishly,
   "You are trying me sorely—
I work for now as a messenger
   Bringing French news to England.

"The landlords themselves
   Will commit dreadful atrocities,
Imposing rent on their lands
   That they've no hope of getting,
Banishing the people
   And putting sheep in their place—
This prediction will come true
   In every thing that I say.

"If a man comes from Edinburgh
   With bridled horse and saddle,
With his spurs and his boots
   And his tissues of lies,
If he has cash in his oxter,
   Even only a year's worth,
He'll get a welcome in the place
   Got by no one ever reared there.

"There were many fine farms of land
   With four good tenants in them

Who'd give a traveller food
    And cream enough to quench thirst,
With a comfortable bed too
    And every good thing he'd need—
And all I see now's a shepherd
    His hair uncombed, full of sheep-ked.

"But if Pitt had been sentenced
    And in a good strong prison
In a dark unlit place,
    The demons would sort him;
If the poor folk of the land
    Could condemn him to death,
Their souls would live forever
    For delivering his body to his neighbour."

Since the man was so kind to me
    As to engage me in conversation,
Not knowing if I'd see him again,
    I asked him what his name was;
He told me there were stories
    In every district of Scotland
Of Gille Naomh Mac an Rùsgaich,
    Then turned his back and went off.

ELIZABETH HAMILTON
(1758–1816)

———

THE novelist and essayist Elizabeth Hamilton was born in Belfast. In 1762 her widowed mother sent her to live with a paternal aunt and her husband near Stirling; later, in 1772, they moved to Ingram's Crook, near Bannockburn. Discouraged from intellectual pursuits by her aunt, Hamilton apparently produced little literature until 1785, when an essay of hers appeared in Henry Mackenzie's *The Lounger*. More than a decade passed before her first major book, the satirical novel *Translations of the Letters of a Hindoo Rajah* (1796), appeared. *Memoirs of Modern Philosophers* (1800), a satire on radicalism, came four years later, then *Letters on Education* (1801) a year after that. More novels followed: *Life of Agrippina, the Wife of Germanicus* (1804) and *The Cottagers of Glenburnie* (1808) among them. She also wrote Scots poetry, including the once popular 'My Ain Fireside' and the cheerful 'Is that Auld Age that's tirling at the pin?'.

———

'My Ain Fireside'

The Illustrated Book of Scottish Songs. From the Sixteenth to the Nineteenth Century (London: Illustrated London Library, 1852).

> I hae seen great anes, and sat in great ha's,
> Mang lords and fine ladies a' cover'd wi' braws;
> At feasts made for princes wi' princes I've been,
> Whare the grand shine o' splendour has dazzled my een;
> But a sight sae delightfu' I trow I ne'er spied
> As the bonnie blythe blink o' my ain fireside.
> My ain fireside, my ain fireside,
> Oh, cheery's the blink o' my ain fireside!
>   My ain fireside, my ain fireside,
>   Oh, there's nought to compare wi' ane's ain fireside!
>
> Ance mair, Gude be thanket, round my ain heartsome ingle
> Wi' the friends o' my youth I cordially mingle;

Nae forms to compel me to seem wae or glad,
I may laugh when I'm merry, and sigh when I'm sad.
Nae falsehood to dread, and nae malice to fear,
But truth to delight me, and friendship to cheer:
Of a' roads to happiness ever were tried,
There's nane half so sure as ane's ain fireside.
      My ain fireside, my ain fireside,
      Oh, there's nought to compare wi' ane's ain fireside!

When I draw in my stool on my cosey hearthstane,
My heart loups sae light I scarce ken't for my ain;
Care's down on the wind—it is clean out of sight,
Past troubles they seem but as dreams of the night.
I hear but kend voices, kend faces I see,
And mark saft affection glent fond frae ilk ee;
Nae fleetchings o' flattery, nae boastings of pride,
'Tis heart speaks to heart at ane's ain fireside.
      My ain fireside, my ain fireside,
      Oh, there's nought to compare wi' ane's ain fireside!

COINNEACH MACCOINNICH /
KENNETH MACKENZIE
(1758–C.1837)

━━━

KENNETH MACKENZIE (Coinneach MacCoinnich) was born at
Castle Heather near Inverness. His parents were comfortably off, and
gave him a good education. When about seventeen years old he became
a sailor's apprentice, and took to a life at sea with great enthusiasm, as
is clear from our selected song. By the time he had finished sailoring in
1789 he had amassed a substantial body of work. This he published,
with some additions, as *Òrain Ghaidhealach* in Edinburgh in 1792.
'Moladh na Luinge' serves as an appetiser for his greatest poem, the
312-line 'Seònaid: Òran don Luing 's do dh'Fhear Obair a' Chuain'
('Janet: A Song to the Ship and to the Man who Works at Sea'). (It has
never been translated into English.)

━━━

'Moladh na Luinge'

*Sar-Obair nam Bard Gaelach; or, The Beauties of Gaelic Poetry, and
Lives of the Highland Bards*, ed. John MacKenzie, 4th edn (Edinburgh:
Maclachlan & Stewart, 1877).

> *'S beag mo shunnd ris an liunn,*
>   *Mòran buirn 's beagan bracha—*
> *B' annsa leam caismeachd mo rùin*
>   *Air cuan dubhghorm le capall.*

> Ged a tha mi 'n-diugh gun spéis,
>   'S mi 'n Dùn Éideann gun taice,
> 'S tric a bha mi 'm measg nan seòid,
>   Cluich' an òir air na cairtean.

> Bha mi uair bha m' chairdean ann,
>   Dh'fhalbh an t-àm 's chaidh e seachad,
> 'S a-nis chan fhaic iad mi san ròd,
>   O'n tha mo phòca ri acain.

Ged a tha mi anns an àm
    Air mo chrampadh le astar,
'S tric a thug mi greisean garbh
    Air an fhairge ga masgadh.

Greis le beachd a' dèanamh iùil
    'S greis 'cur siùil ann am pasgadh,
Greis air iomairt, 's greis air stiùir
    'S greis air chùl nam ball-acfhainn.

Se mo cheist an capall grinn
    Rachadh leinn air an aiseag
'S taobh an fhuaraidh fos a cinn
    'S muir ri 'slinn taobh an fhasgaidh.

Uair a bhiodh i fada shìos
    Anns an ìochdar 's nach fhaict' i,
'S greis eile 'n àird nam frìth
    'S i 'cur dhìth air a lethtaobh.

'S i nach pilleadh gun cheann-fàth,
    'S i neo-sgàthach gu sracadh—
A' gearradh tuinn le geur rinn
    'S cudthrom gaoith' air na slatan.

Nuair a chuirt' i air a dòigh
    'S a cuid sheòl ris na racan,
Chuirt' a-mach an t-aodach sgeòid—
    Siud a sròn ris an ascaoin!

Bhiodh i turraban gun tàmh,
    'S chluinnte 'g àinich fon t-sac i,
'S bhiodh gach glùn dhith 'dol fillt'
    'S chluinnte bìd aig gach aisinn.

Chite 'm muir 'na thonnan ard'
    'S chluinnt' i gàirich gu farsaing,
'S bheireadh ronn àrd nan steoll
    Buille throm an gach achlais.

Ann an ascaoineachd a' chuain
    'S ann am fuathas na fraise,
Thugaibh faiceall air a' ghaoith—
    "Fheara gaoil, cumaibh rag i!"

Chluinnte faram aig an fhairg',
    Molach garbh anns an aisith—
Beucach, rangach, torrach, searbh,
    Srannach, anabharrach, brais i.

Buill bu treis' den chorcraich ùir,
    Croinn den ghiùthsaich bu daithte,
Éideadh cainb nach biodh meanbh—
    'S chite geala-dhearg a brataich.

Se mo rùin na feara gleust',
    Siad nach tréigeadh an caitean;
Chluinnte langan nam fear òg—
    'S iad nach deònaicheadh gealtachd.

Tha 'n cridheachan farsaing mòr,
    'S tric a dh'òl iad na bh' aca—
Dannsa 's nigheanan is ceòl
    Nuair bu chòir dol gu'n leabaidh.

Bidh iad gu furachair geur
    'N àm don ghréin dol a chadal,
Ceileireach, luinneagach, réidh
    'N àm bhith 'g éirigh sa mhadainn.

An déidh cogaidh thig an t-sìth
    'S an déidh bìdh thig an t-acras,
An déidh na maidne thig an oidhch',
    An déidh eighre thig aiteamh.

'The Praise of the Ship' (translated by Ronald Black)

I take little pleasure in ale,
    Much water and little malt—
I'd prefer my favourite tune
    On dark-blue sea with a mare.

Though I'm unesteemed today,
    Unemployed in Auld Reekie,
I mixed frequently with heroes,
    Playing with gold at the cards.

My friends would come around,
  But that time's past and gone by—
They don't see me in the street now,
  Because my pocket's complaining.

Though I'm here for the time
  Stiff and cramped from travelling,
I've had many a rough moment
  On the ocean being churned.

A while on careful lookout,
  A while folding a sail,
A while rowing, a while steering,
  A while hauling the tackle-ropes.

My darling's the handsome mare
  Who'd take us on the crossing
With the windward side over her
  And sea to her shoulder on the lee.

Sometimes she'd be far down
  In the depths and invisible,
At other times on the hilltops,
  Leaning sideways and spewing.

She being fearless in attack,
  She'd not turn back for no reason—
Her sharp bowsprit splitting waves
  With weight of wind upon the yards.

When she'd been put under way
  With her sails on the travellers,
The corner canvas was unfurled—
  There's her bow in the turmoil!

She'd vibrate uncontrollably,
  You'd hear her panting with asthma,
Every joint of her would bend
  And every rib you'd hear cracking.

You'd see the sea in its high waves
  And you'd hear it roar grandly,
And the high squirt of waterspouts
  Would strike her hard in each collar.

In the harshness of the ocean
    And the horror of the squall,
Please look out for the wind—
    "Me hearties, hold her steady!"

You'd hear the noise of the ocean,
    Rough and shaggy in contention—
Roaring, wrinkled, heaped and bitter,
    It was snorting, riotous and brash.

Strongest ropes of brand-new hemp,
    Masts of best-coloured pinewood,
Canvas sailcloth, far from puny—
    You'd see the red-white of her ensign.

My darlings are the lively men,
    They'd not shirk the springing breeze;
You'd hear young men roar like stags—
    They'd never tolerate cowardice.

Their hearts are generous and large,
    They often drank all they had—
Girls and dancing and music
    When they should have gone to bed.

They'll be sharp-eyed and watchful
    As the sun goes down to rest,
Warbling, tuneful and sublime
    In time of rising in the morning.

After war there comes the peace
    And after food comes the hunger,
After morning comes the night,
    And after ice comes the thaw.

MARGARET CHALMERS

(1758–1827)

THE poet Margaret Chalmers was born at Lerwick in the Shetland Islands. Impelled by severe financial hardship, Chalmers published her *Poems* by subscription at Newcastle in 1813. Badly printed, and with little publicity, the collection reaped little reward for the author. However, Chalmers had a canny gift for self-deprecatory marketing. She called herself the first British Thulian quill, though the younger Dorothea Primrose Campbell had appeared in print first. Like Campbell, Chalmers expresses a mixture of pride and apology about her native land, enthusiastically describing its landscape while doubting whether it was a suitable environment for a poet. While much of Chalmers's material is local, her literary references are largely national. She freely quotes James Thomson, praises Walter Scott, and imitates Robert Burns. Her own voice is frequently witty, even sardonic.

'A Fire-Side Vocal Concert'

Poems (Newcastle: S. Hodgson, 1813).

> The low'ring, leaden-colour'd evening cloud,
> The chilling frost, the billows breaking loud,
> The wish excite, contented to retire,
> "To pause from toil, and trim the evening fire."
> Snowy triangles clothe each window pane,
> The drear outside makes bright the inside scene;
> The kettle on the clean-swept hearth is plac'd,
> The table with the social tea-cups grac'd;
> The needle and the wire now forward brought,
> Employ the fingers, yet leave free the thought.
> A general consultation next takes place,
> Whether, the while, the historic page to trace,
> Or in Udolphean Mysteries engage;
> But to elude the blustering tempest's rage,

'Tis soon agreed to call the power of song,
Which cheats the winter's night though e'er so long.
     Tay, Tweed, and Yarrow's celebrated streams,
Where the pleas'd muses whisper sylvan themes,
Glide thro' the pastoral vale and flowery mead,
Thro' which the passive fancy pleas'd they lead;
And, in their tranquil murmurings, is drown'd
The wild, the wintry roar of Bressa Sound.
Amid these scenes, each Caledonian swain,
Of Royal Mary breath'd the tuneful strain;
Ah! fair unfortunate! who did inspire
The lovers' tender sigh, the poet's lyre,
Who reign'd alike or in the court or grove;
At once a Queen by majesty and love!
          Boreas, for a while, thy howl refrain,
And thou shalt be rewarded by the strain
Of Gallowshiels, where Rizzio vents his flame,
In daring language for the Royal Dame.
Even Italy's musicians, as 'tis said,
To this sweet strain superior suffrage paid.
Let Caledonia compliment again,
That candour which could prejudice disdain,
And gave the plaudit to a foreign strain.
          Let us attend the swain with yellow hair,
Who seeks the hawthorn glen to sing his fair;
And listen, while he doth the balance hold,
'Twixt native charms and those of powerful gold.
Thy Bush, Traquair, the moment now beguiles,
Which blooms and fades, as Peggie frowns or smiles.
          What heavenly strain ascends from Alloa's Grove,
While all the strings of melody do move!
Such powerful pleasure thro' the heart doth glow,
The pulse forgets to beat! the blood to flow!
          Can it be doubted that the lays of Burns,
Through the Domestic Concert take their turns?
But these are touch'd with far superior skill,
By the sweet lyre of tuneful Tannahill.
          A youthful auditor prepares to speak,
While suing smiles adorn her blooming cheek;
"Now, since to each you give the song they chuse;
To me, I hope you will not one refuse."

Her choice demanded, doth in favour go
Of cruel Carpenter; sad tale of woe!
Or love-lorn fair, whose spirit plough'd the main,
In vengeful quest of her perfidious swain,
Who caught, sunk with her in the closing flood,
(Listen, ye swains,) while sailors trembling stood.

    See now o'er-ruling Providence preside,
Conducting Bothwell to his heir and bride;
And through the medium of the ring and glove,
Decide the doubtful object of his love.

    Full many a virtuous pang the heart assails,
And sympathetic tenderness prevails,
While the performer doth the tale unfold
Of the wood-wilder'd babes, betray'd for gold.
Sweet sufferers! lamented by your peers,
Who write your elegy in sighs and tears.

    But, lo! the Historic muse now treads the stage,
See Royal Eleonora's jealous rage,
That wildly spurns humanity's controul,
Arm'd with the dagger and the poison'd bowl.
Ah, fell revenge! could not that beauteous face,
Where youthful charms triumph in blooming grace,
Divert thy purpose dire? Ah! no—they give
New force, and stern forbid the fair to live;
Each avenue to pity these seal up,
The poniard point, and urge the deadly cup.

    Vengeance self-wrought, O most unhallow'd draught,
To human mind with mental poison fraught!
O sated Queen, what treasures wouldst thou give,
These last, these horrid moments to retrieve!
More kind the cup thou gav'st than didst retain,
While pleas'd was seen thy rival victim's pain;
And ghastly paleness chace the lively bloom,
While love-inspiring eyes repose in death's dark gloom.

    The injurer with the injur'd changing part,
Works revolution in the youthful heart;
And even the feelings of maturer age,
All on the side of Rosamond engage;
Who had not sorrow'd for the injur'd wife,
Had she but spar'd her helpless rival's life;
Thus those, who cruelly revenge pursue,

Lose even that sympathy which is their due.
      Not more heart-felt delight can he inspire,
Who "wakes to exstacy the living lyre,"
Than do such lays around the evening fire;
While "virtue's advocates" they prove to youth,
Insinuating still some moral truth;
Alike with pleasure and improvement fraught,
The useful lesson with success is taught.
Obvious the cause, they in amusement's veil
Excite to virtue, yet the drift conceal.
The tale adventurous suits the eager mind,
The strain impressive which the tale doth bind
On the imagination, which retains
The strain, the tale, and 'companying scenes.
      Thus far 'tis well; but, ah! the counterpart,
Impressing terror on the ductile heart;
For 'tis the *supernatural* gives the charm
Coercive, and from whence flows all the harm;
Hence superstition's teeming altars rise,
On which through life the votaries sacrifice.
The bane and antidote so closely link,
To disunite them 'tis in vain we think;
Could they a partial drop from Lethe steal,
Retain the moral and forget the tale,
'Twere well; but these together still unite,
And rouse the mind to weak or wild affright;
But since from youthful hearers 'tis confest,
The nurse gains more attention than the priest,
'Twere to be wish'd she would her power address,
Virtue to aid, but horror to repress.
The dreadful spectre and the beckoning ghost,
Delight the wondering hearers to their cost.
The Fairy system better is design'd
Fancy to please, nor terrify the mind;
Besides, as fiction it they ever view,
But oft believe the goblin story true;
The startled slumber, and the scaring dream,
Too highly tax the legendary theme.

ROBERT BURNS

(1759–1796)

———

THE Ayrshire poet and songwriter Robert Burns has been a global icon since the Kilmarnock edition of his *Poems, Chiefly in the Scottish Dialect* appeared in 1786. By his early teens Burns was familiar with the work of ploughing, though he also spent time in parish schools in Dalrymple, near Maybole, and Kirkoswald. From a young age he read Pope, Thomson, and Shenstone—and later Ramsay, one of his most enduring influences. By 1781 he had become an avid admirer of Robert Fergusson. Burns spent the next few years gathering a commonplace book of poems, songs and observations, avidly honing his craft. In 1786, with the financial backing of local businessmen, Burns was ready to unleash the Kilmarnock edition. Containing forty-four poems, in Scots and in English, the edition's six-hundred copies sold out in a month. An expanded Edinburgh volume of *Poems* (1787) rapidly sold out too—it had a print run of 3,000 copies. Meanwhile, the Edinburgh engraver James Johnson had been collecting Scottish songs for a six-volume anthology with music, *The Scots Musical Museum* (1787–1803). The de facto editor of the endeavour, Burns contributed well over 150 of his own songs and reworkings of others that he had collected. Burns also contributed well over a hundred songs to George Thomson's *Select Collection of Original Scotish Airs* (1793–1841). An expanded, second Edinburgh edition of Burns's *Poems* appeared in 1793. Succumbing to blue-devilism (a phrase borrowed from his idol Fergusson), and chronic ill health, Burns died in 1796. Numerous clubs were formed to honour his memory, beginning with the Greenock Burns Club in 1801; as the century wore on, literally hundreds of other Burns clubs sprang up in Scotland and overseas.

———

'Address to the Deil'

Poems, Chiefly in the Scottish Dialect (Edinburgh: William Creech, 1787).

O Prince! O Chief of many throned Pow'rs,
That led th' embattl'd Seraphim to war—
                    MILTON.

O Thou! whatever title suit thee,
Auld *Hornie*, Satan, Nick, or Clootie,
Wha in yon cavern grim an' sootie,
            Clos'd under hatches,
Spairges about the brunstane cootie
            To scaud poor wretches!

Hear me, auld *Hangie*, for a wee,
An' let poor damned bodies be;
I'm sure sma' pleasure it can gie,
            E'en to a *deil*,
To skelp an' scaud poor dogs like me,
            An' hear us squeel!

Great is thy pow'r, an' great thy fame;
Far kend an' noted is thy name;
An' tho' yon lowin heugh's thy hame,
            Thou travels far;
An' faith! thou's neither lag nor lame,
            Nor blate nor scaur.

Whyles, ranging like a roarin lion,
For prey, a' holes an' corners tryin;
Whyles, on the strong-wing'd Tempest flyin,
            Tirlin the kirks;
Whyles, in the human bosom pryin,
            Unseen thou lurks.

I've heard my reverend *Graunie* say,
In lanely glens ye like to stray;
Or where auld, ruin'd castles, gray,
            Nod to the moon,
Ye fright the nightly wand'rer's way,
            Wi' eldritch croon.

When twilight did my *Graunie* summon
To say her pray'rs, douce, honest woman!
Aft yont the dyke she's heard you bumman,
            Wi' eerie drone;

Or, rustlin, thro' the boortries comin,
    Wi' heavy groan.

Ae dreary, windy, winter night,
The stars shot down wi' sklentan light,
Wi' you, myself, I gat a fright,
    Ayont the lough;
Ye, like a rash-buss, stood in sight,
    Wi' waving sugh.

The cudgel in my nieve did shake,
Each bristl'd hair stood like a stake,
When wi' an eldritch, stoor quaick, quaick.
    Amang the springs,
Awa ye squatter'd like a drake,
    On whistling wings.

Let *warlocks* grim, an' wither'd *hags*,
Tell how wi' you on ragweed nags,
They skim the muirs an' dizzy crags,
    Wi' wicked speed;
And in kirk-yards renew their leagues,
    Owre howket dead.

Thence, countra wives, wi' toil an' pain,
May plunge an' plunge the kirn in vain;
For, O! the yellow treasure's taen
    By witching skill;
An' dawtit', twal-pint *Hawkie*'s gaen
    As yell's the Bill.

Thence, mystic knots mak great abuse,
On young Guidmen, fond, keen, an' croose;
When the best warklum i' the house,
    By cantraip wit,
Is instant made no worth a louse,
    Just at the bit.

When thowes dissolve the snawy hoord,
An' float the jinglin icy-boord,
Then *Water-kelpies* haunt the foord,
    By your direction,
An' nighted Trav'llers are allur'd
    To their destruction.

An' aft your moss-traversing *Spunkies*
Decoy the wight that late an' drunk is:
The bleezin, curst, mischievous monkies
     Delude his eyes,
Till in some miry slough he sunk is,
     Ne'er mair to rise.

When *Masons'* mystic *word* an' *grip*,
In storms an' tempests raise you up,
Some cock or cat your rage maun stop,
     Or, strange to tell!
The youngest Brother ye wad whip
     Aff straught to h-ll.

Lang syne, in *Eden*'s bonie yard,
When youthfu' lovers first were pair'd,
An' all the Soul of Love they shar'd,
     The raptur'd hour,
Sweet on the fragrant, flow'ry swaird,
     In shady bow'r:

Then you, ye auld, snick-drawing dog!
Ye cam to Paradise incog.
An' play'd on man a cursed brogue,
     (Black be your fa'!)
An' gied the infant warld a shog,
     'Maist ruin'd a'.

D'ye mind that day, when in a bizz,
Wi' reeket duds, and reestet gizz,
Ye did present your smoutie phiz,
     'Mang better folk,
An' sklented on the *man of Uzz*
     Your spitefu' joke?

An' how ye gat him i' your thrall,
An' brak him out o' house and hal',
While scabs an' blotches did him gall,
     Wi' bitter claw,
An' lows'd his ill-tongu'd, wicked Scawl,
     Was warst ava?

But a' your doings to rehearse,
Your wily snares an' fechtin fierce,

Sin' that day *Michael* did you pierce,
　　　Down to this time,
Wad ding a' Lallan tongue, or Erse,
　　　In prose or rhyme.

An' now, auld *Cloots*, I ken ye're thinkan,
A certain Bardie's rantin, drinkin,
Some luckless hour will send him linkan,
　　　To your black pit;
But, faith! he'll turn a corner jinkin,
　　　An' cheat you yet.

But, fare you weel, auld *Nickie-ben!*
O wad ye tak a thought an' men'!
Ye aiblins might—I dinna ken—
　　　Still hae a *stake*—
I'm wae to think upo' yon den,
　　　Ev'n for your sake!

'A Man's a Man for a' That'

The Works of Robert Burns; With an Account of His Life, and a Criticism of His Writings, 5th edn, 4 vols (London: T. Cadell and W. Davies; Edinburgh: W. Creech, 1806).

Is there, for honest Poverty
　　That hings his head, an' a' that;
The coward-slave, we pass him by,
　　We dare be poor for a' that!
For a' that, an' a' that,
　　Our toils obscure, an' a' that,
The rank is but the guinea's stamp,
　　The Man 's the gowd for a' that.

What though on hamely fare we dine,
　　Wear hoddin grey, an' a that?
Gie fools their silks, and knaves their wine;
　　A Man's a Man for a' that.
For a' that, an' a' that,
　　Their tinsel show, an' a' that;
The honest man, tho' e'er sae poor,
　　Is king o' men for a' that.

Ye see yon birkie ca'd a lord,
   Wha struts, an' stares, an' a' that,
Tho' hundreds worship at his word,
   He's but a coof for a' that.
For a' that, an' a' that,
   His ribband, star, an' a' that,
The man o' independent mind,
   He looks an' laughs at a' that.

A Prince can mak a belted knight,
   A marquis, duke, an' a' that!
But an honest man's aboon his might—
   Guid faith, he mauna fa' that!
For a' that, an' a' that,
   Their dignities, an' a' that,
The pith o' Sense an' pride o' Worth
   Are higher rank than a' that.

Then let us pray that come it may,
   As come it will for a' that,
That Sense and Worth o'er a' the earth
   Shall bear the gree an' a' that.
For a' that, an' a' that,
   It's comin yet for a' that,
That Man to Man the warld o'er
   Shall brithers be for a' that.

'To a Mouse'

Poems, Chiefly in the Scottish Dialect (Edinburgh: William Creech, 1787).

On turning her up in her Nest, with the Plough, November 1785.

Wee, sleekit, cowrin, tim'rous beastie,
O, what a panic's in thy breastie!
Thou need na start awa sae hasty,
   Wi' bickerin brattle!
I wad be laith to rin an' chase thee,
   Wi' murd'ring *pattle!*

I'm truly sorry Man's dominion
Has broken Nature's social union,

An' justifies that ill opinion,
  Which makes thee startle,
At me, thy poor, earth-born companion,
  An' *fellow-mortal!*

I doubt na, whyles, but thou may thieve;
What then? poor beastie, thou maun live!
A *daimen-icker* in a *thrave*
  'S a sma' request;
I'll get a blessin wi' the lave,
  An' never miss 't!

Thy wee-bit *housie*, too, in ruin!
It's silly wa's the win's are strewin!
An' naething, now, to big a new ane,
  O' foggage green!
An' bleak December's winds ensuin,
  Baith snell an' keen!

Thou saw the fields laid bare an' waste,
An' weary Winter comin fast,
An' cozie here, beneath the blast,
  Thou thought to dwell,
Till crash! the cruel *coulter* past
  Out thro' thy cell.

That wee-bit heap o' leaves an' stibble,
Has cost thee monie a weary nibble!
Now thou's turn'd out, for a' thy trouble,
  But house or hald,
To thole the Winter's sleety dribble,
  An' cranreuch cauld!

But, Mousie, thou art no thy lane,
In proving *foresight* may be vain:
The best-laid schemes o' *Mice* an' *Men*
  Gang aft agley,
An' lea'e us nought but grief an' pain,
  For promis'd joy!

Still thou art blest, compar'd wi' *me!*
The present only toucheth thee:
But, Och! I backward cast my e'e,
  On prospects drear!

An' forward tho' I canna *see*,
        I *guess* an' *fear!*

'To a Louse, On seeing one on a Lady's Bonnet at Church'

Ha! whare ye gaun, ye crowlin ferlie!
Your impudence protects you sairly:
I canna say but ye strunt rarely,
        Owre gauze and lace;
Tho' faith, I fear, ye dine but sparely
        On sic a place.

Ye ugly, creepan, blastet wonner,
Detested, shunn'd by saunt an' sinner,
How daur ye set your fit upon her,
        Sae fine a Lady!
Gae somewhere else and seek your dinner
        On some poor body.

Swith, in some beggar's haffet squattle;
There ye may creep, and sprawl, and sprattle
Wi' ither kindred, jumping cattle,
        In shoals and nations;
Whare *horn* nor *bane* ne'er daur unsettle
        Your thick plantations.

Now haud you there, ye're out o' sight,
Below the fatt'rels, snug an' tight;
Na faith ye yet! ye'll no be right
        Till ye've got on it,
The vera tapmost, tow'ring height
        O' *Miss's bonnet.*

My sooth! right bauld ye set your nose out,
As plump an' grey as onie grozet:
O for some rank, mercurial rozet,
        Or fell, red smeddum,
I'd gie you sic a hearty dose o't,
        Wad dress your droddum.

I wad na been surpris'd to spy
You on an auld wife's flainen toy;

Or aiblins some bit duddie boy,
     On 's wyliecoat;
But Miss's fine *Lunardi*, fye!
     How daur ye do't?

O, *Jenny*, dinna toss your head,
An' sct your beauties a' abread!
Ye little ken what cursed speed
     The blastie's makin:
Thae *winks* an' *finger-ends*, I dread,
     Are notice takin!

O wad some Pow'r the giftie gie us
To see oursels as ithers see us!
It wad frae monie a blunder free us,
     An' foolish notion:
What airs in dress an' gait wad lea'e us,
     An' ev'n Devotion!

'Address to a Haggis'

Fair fa' your honest, sonsie face,
Great Chieftain o' the Puddin-race!
Aboon them a' ye tak your place,
     Painch, tripe, or thairm:
Weel are ye wordy o' a *grace*
     As lang 's my arm.

The groaning trencher there ye fill,
Your hurdies like a distant hill,
Your *pin* wad help to mend a mill
     In time o' need,
While thro' your pores the dews distil
     Like amber bead.

His knife see Rustic-labour dight,
An' cut ye up wi' ready slight,
Trenching your gushing entrails bright,
     Like onie ditch;
And then, O what a glorious sight,
     Warm-reekin, rich!

Then, horn for horn they stretch an' strive,
Deil tak the hindmost, on they drive,
Till a' their weel-swall'd kytes belyve
    Are bent like drums;
Then auld Guidman, maist like to rive,
    Bethankit hums.

Is there that owre his French *ragout*,
Or *olio* that wad staw a sow,
Or *fricassee* wad mak her spew
    Wi' perfect sconner,
Looks down wi' sneering, scornfu' view
    On sic a dinner?

Poor devil! see him owre his trash,
As feckless as a' wither'd rash,
His spindle shank a guid whip-lash,
    His nieve a nit;
Thro' bluidy flood or field to dash,
    O how unfit!

But mark the Rustic, *haggis-fed*,
The trembling earth resounds his tread,
Clap in his walie nieve a blade,
    He'll make it whissle;
An' legs, an' arms, an' heads will sned,
    Like taps o' thrissle.

Ye Pow'rs wha mak mankind your care,
And dish them out their bill o' fare,
Auld Scotland wants nae skinking ware
    That jaups in luggies;
But, if ye wish her gratefu' prayer,
    Gie her a *Haggis!*

'Death and Doctor Hornbook: A True Story'

Some books are lies frae end to end,
And some great lies were never penn'd:
Ev'n Ministers they hae been kenn'd,
    In holy rapture,
A rousing whid, at times, to vend,
    And nail't wi' Scripture.

But this that I am gaun to tell,
Which lately on a night befel,
Is just as true's the Deil's in h-ll,
    Or Dublin city:
That e'er he nearer comes oursel
     'S a muckle pity.

The Clachan yill had made me canty,
I was na fou, but just had plenty;
I stacher'd whyles, but yet too tent ay
    To free the ditches;
An' hillocks, stanes, an' bushes kend ay
     Frae ghaists an' witches.

The rising Moon began to glowr
The distant *Cumnock* hills out-owre;
To count her horns, wi' a my pow'r,
    I set mysel;
But whether she had three or four,
     I cou'd na tell.

I was come round about the hill,
And todlin down on *Willie's mill*,
Setting my staff wi' a' my skill,
    To keep me sicker;
Tho' leeward whyles, against my will,
     I took a bicker.

I there wi' *Something* did forgather,
That pat me in an eerie swither;
An awfu' scythe, out-owre ae shouther,
    Clear-dangling, hang;
A three-tae'd leister on the ither
     Lay, large an' lang.

Its stature seem'd lang Scotch ells twa,
The queerest shape that e'er I saw,
For fient a wame it had ava,
    And then its shanks,
They were as thin, as sharp an' sma',
     As cheeks o' branks.

"Guid-een," quo' I; "Friend! hae ye been mawin,
When ither folk are busy sawin?"

I seem'd to mak a kind o' stan',
    But naething spak;
At length, says I, "Friend! whare ye gaun?
    Will ye go back?"

It spak right howe—"My name is *Death*,
But be na' fley'd."—Quoth I, "Guid faith,
Ye're maybe come to stap my breath;
    But tent me, billie;
I red ye weel, tak care o' skaith,
    See, there's a gully!"

"Gudeman," quo' he, "put up your whittle,
I'm no designed to try its mettle;
But if I did, I wad be kittle
    To be mislear'd;
I wad na' mind it, no that spittle
    Out-owre my beard."

"Weel, weel!" says I, "a bargain be't;
Come, gie's your hand, an' sae we're gree't;
We'll ease our shanks an' tak a seat,
    Come, gie's your news!
This while ye hae been mony a gate,
    At mony a house."

"Ay, ay!" quo' he, an' shook his head,
"It's e'en a lang, lang time indeed
Sin' I began to nick the thread,
    An' choke the breath:
Folk maun do something for their bread,
    An' sae maun *Death*."

"Sax thousand years are near hand fled
Sin' I was to the butching bred,
An' mony a scheme in vain's been laid,
    To stap or scar me;
Till ane Hornbook's ta'en up the trade,
    And faith, he'll waur me."

"Ye ken *Jock Hornbook* i' the Clachan,
Deil mak his king's-hood in spleuchan!
He's grown sae weel acquaint wi' *Buchan*,
    And ither chaps,

The weans haud out their fingers laughin,
      An' pouk my hips."

"See, here's a scythe, and there's dart,
They hae pierc'd mony a gallant heart;
But Doctor *Hornbook*, wi' his art
      And cursed skill,
Has made them baith no worth a f—t,
      D—n'd haet they'll kill!"

" 'Twas but yestreen, nae farther gaen,
I threw a noble throw at ane;
Wi' less, I'm sure, I've hundreds slain;
      But deil-ma-care!
It just play'd dirl on the bane,
      But did nae mair."

"*Hornbook* was by, wi' ready art,
And had sae fortify'd the part,
That when I looked to my dart,
      It was sae blunt,
Fient haet o't wad hae pierc'd the heart
      Of a kail-runt."

"I drew my scythe in sic a fury,
I near-hand cowpit wi' my hurry,
But yet the bauld *Apothecary*
      Withstood the shock;
I might as weel hae try'd a quarry
      O' hard whin-rock."

"Ev'n them he canna get attended,
Altho' their face he ne'er had kend it,
Just sh—in a kail-blade and send it,
      As soon's he smells't,
Baith their disease, and what will mend it,
      At once he tells't."

"And then a' doctor's saws an' whittles,
Of a' dimensions, shapes, an' mettles,
A' kind o' boxes, mugs, an' bottles,
      He's sure to hae;
Their Latin names as fast he rattles
      As A B C."

"Calces o' fossils, earths, and trees;
True Sal-marinum o' the seas;
The Farina of beans and pease,
　　　He has't in plenty;
Aqua-fontis, what you please,
　　　He can content ye."

"Forbye some new, uncommon weapons,
Urinus Spiritus of capons;
Or Mite-horn shavings, filings, scrapings,
　　　Distill'd *per se*;
Sal-alkali o' Midge-tail clippings,
　　　And mony mae."

"Waes me for *Johnie Ged's Hole* now,"
Quoth I, "if that thae news be true!
His braw calf-ward whare gowans grew,
　　　Sae white an' bonie,
Nae doubt they'll rive it wi' the plew;
　　　They'll ruin *Johnie!*"

The creature grain'd an eldritch laugh,
And says, "Ye needna yoke the pleugh,
Kirkyards will soon be till'd eneugh,
　　　Tak ye nae fear:
They'll a' be trench'd wi' mony a sheugh,
　　　In twa-three year."

"Whare I kill'd ane, a fair strae-death,
By loss o' blood or want o' breath,
This night I'm free to tak my aith,
　　　That *Hornbook*'s skill
Has clad a score i' their last claith,
　　　By drap an' pill."

"An honest Wabster to his trade,
Whase wife's twa nieves were scarce weel-bred,
Gat tippence-worth to mend her head,
　　　When it was sair;
The wife slade cannie to her bed,
　　　But ne'er spak mair."

"A countra Laird had taen the batts,
Or some curmurring in his guts,

His only son for *Hornbook* sets,
    An' pays him well,
The lad, for twa guid gimmer-pets,
    Was Laird himsel."

"A bonie lass, ye kend her name,
Some ill-brewn drink had hov'd her wame;
She trusts hersel, to hide the shame,
    In *Hornbook*'s care;
Horn sent her aff to her lang hame,
    To hide it there."

"That's just a swatch o' *Hornbook*'s way,
Thus goes he on from day to day,
Thus does he poison, kill, an' slay,
    An's weel paid for't;
Yet stops me o' my lawfu' prey,
    Wi' his damn'd dirt!"

"But hark! I'll tell you of a plot,
Tho' dinna ye be speakin o't;
I'll nail the self-conceited Sot,
    As dead's a herrin:
Niest time we meet, I'll wad a groat,
    He gets his fairin!"

But just as he began to tell,
The auld kirk-hammer strak the bell
Some wee short hour ayont the *twal*,
    Which rais'd us baith:
I took the way that pleas'd mysel,
    And sae did *Death*.

'Tam o' Shanter: A Tale'

Poems, Chiefly in the Scottish Dialect, 2 vols, 2nd edn (Edinburgh:
W. Creech; London: T. Cadell, 1793).

> *Of Brownyis and of Bogillis full is this Buke.*
> GAWIN DOUGLAS

When chapman billies leave the street,
And drouthy neebors, neebors meet,

As market-days are wearing late,
An' folk begin to tak the gate;
While we sit bousing at the nappy,
And getting fou and unco happy,
We think na on the lang Scots miles,
The mosses, waters, slaps, and styles,
That lie between us and our hame,
Whare sits our sulky sullen dame,
Gathering her brows like gathering storm,
Nursing her wrath to keep it warm.

    This truth fand honest *Tam o' Shanter*,
As he frae Ayr ae night did canter,
(Auld Ayr, wham ne'er a town surpasses,
For honest men and bonny lasses.)

    O *Tam!* hadst thou but been sae wise,
As taen thy ain wife *Kate*'s advice!
She tauld thee weel thou was a skellum,
A blethering, blustering, drunken blellum;
That frae November till October,
Ae market-day thou was nae sober;
That ilka melder, wi' the miller,
Thou sat as lang as thou had siller;
That ev'ry naig was ca'd a shoe on,
The smith and thee gat roaring fou on;
That at the L—d's house, even on Sunday,
Thou drank wi' Kirkton Jean till Monday.
She prophesied that late or soon,
Thou would be found deep drown'd in Doon;
Or catch'd wi' warlocks in the mirk,
By *Alloway*'s auld haunted kirk.

    Ah, gentle dames! it gars me greet,
To think how mony counsels sweet,
How mony lengthen'd sage advices,
The husband frae the wife despises!

    But to our tale: Ae market-night,
Tam had got planted unco right;
Fast by an ingle, bleezing finely,
Wi' reaming swats, that drank divinely;
And at his elbow, Souter *Johnny*,
His ancient, trusty, drouthy crony;
Tam lo'ed him like a vera brither;

They had been fou for weeks thegither.
The night drave on wi' sangs and clatter;
And ay the ale was growing better:
The landlady and *Tam* grew gracious,
Wi' favours, secret, sweet, and precious:
The Souter tauld his queerest stories;
The landlord's laugh was ready chorus:
The storm without might rair and rustle,
Tam did na mind the storm a whistle.

    Care, mad to see a man sae happy,
E'en drown'd himsel amang the nappy;
As bees flee hame wi' lades o' treasure,
The minutes wing'd their way wi' pleasure;
Kings may be blest, but *Tam* was glorious,
O'er a' the ills o' life victorious!

    But pleasures are like poppies spread,
You seize the flower, its bloom is shed;
Or like the snow falls in the river,
A moment white—then melts for ever;
Or like the borealis race,
That flit ere you can point their place;
Or like the rainbow's lovely form
Evanishing amid the storm.—
Nae man can tether time or tide;
The hour approaches *Tam* maun ride;
That hour, o' night's black arch the key-stane,
That dreary hour he mounts his beast in;
And sic a night he taks the road in,
As ne'er poor sinner was abroad in.

    The wind blew as 'twad blawn its last;
The rattling showers rose on the blast;
The speedy gleams the darkness swallow'd;
Loud, deep, and lang, the thunder bellow'd:
That night, a child might understand,
The Deil had business on his hand.

    Weel mounted on his gray mare, *Meg*,
A better never lifted leg,
Tam skelpit on thro' dub and mire,
Despising wind, and rain, and fire;
Whiles holding fast his gude blue bonnet;
Whiles crooning o'er some auld Scots sonnet;

Whiles glow'ring round wi' prudent cares,
Lest bogles catch him unawares:
Kirk-Alloway was drawing nigh,
Whare ghaists and houlets nightly cry.—
　　By this time he was cross the ford,
Whare in the snaw the chapman smoor'd;
And past the birks and meikle stane,
Whare drunken *Charlie* brak's neck-bane;
And thro' the whins, and by the cairn,
Whare hunters fand the murder'd bairn;
And near the thorn, aboon the well,
Whare *Mungo*'s mither hang'd hersel.—
Before him *Doon* pours all his floods;
The doubling storm roars thro' the woods;
The lightnings flash from pole to pole;
Near and more near the thunders roll:
When, glimmering thro' the groaning trees,
Kirk-Alloway seem'd in a bleeze;
Thro' ilka bore the beams were glancing;
And loud resounded mirth and dancing.—
　　Inspiring bold *John Barleycorn!*
What dangers thou canst make us scorn!
Wi' tippeny, we fear nae evil;
Wi' usquabae, we'll face the Devil!—
The swats sae ream'd in *Tammie*'s noddle,
Fair play, he car'd na deils a boddle.
But *Maggie* stood, right sair astonish'd,
Till, by the heel and hand admonish'd,
She ventur'd forward on the light;
And, vow! *Tam* saw an unco sight!
Warlocks and witches in a dance;
Nae cotillion brent new frae *France*,
But hornpipes, jigs, strathspeys, and reels,
Put life and mettle in their heels.
A winnock-bunker in the east,
There sat auld Nick, in shape o' beast;
A tousie tyke, black, grim, and large,
To gie them music was his charge:
He screw'd the pipes and gart them skirl,
Till roof and rafters a' did dirl.—
Coffins stood round, like open presses,

That shaw'd the dead in their last dresses;
And by some devilish cantraip slight
Each in its cauld hand held a light.—
By which heroic *Tam* was able
To note upon the haly table,
A murderer's banes in gibbet-airns;
Twa span-lang, wee, unchristen'd bairns;
A thief, new-cutted frae a rape,
Wi' his last gasp his gab did gape;
Five tomahawks, wi' blude red-rusted;
Five scymitars, wi' murder crusted;
A garter, which a babe had strangled;
A knife, a father's throat had mangled,
Whom his ain son o' life bereft,
The grey hairs yet stack to the heft;
Three Lawyers' tongues, turned inside out,
Wi' lies seamed like a beggar's clout;
Three Priests' hearts, rotten, black as muck,
Lay stinking, vile, in every neuk.

As *Tammie* glow'rd, amaz'd, and curious,
The mirth and fun grew fast and furious:
The piper loud and louder blew;
The dancers quick and quicker flew;
They reel'd, they set, they cross'd, they cleekit,
Till ilka carlin swat and reekit,
And coost her duddies to the wark,
And linket at it in her sark!

Now, *Tam*, O *Tam!* had thae been queans,
A' plump and strapping in their teens,
Their sarks, instead o' creeshie flannen,
Been snaw-white seventeen hunder linnen!
Thir breeks o' mine, my only pair,
That ance were plush, o' gude blue hair,
I wad hae gi'en them off my hurdies,
For ae blink o' the bonie burdies!

But wither'd beldams, auld and droll,
Rigwoodie hags wad spean a foal,
Louping and flinging on a crummock,
I wonder didna turn thy stomach.

But *Tam* kend what was what fu' brawlie,
There was ae winsome wench and wawlie,

That night enlisted in the core,
(Lang after kend on *Carrick* shore;
For mony a beast to dead she shot,
And perish'd mony a bony boat,
And shook baith meikle corn and bear,
And kept the country-side in fear.)
Her cutty-sark, o' Paisley harn,
That while a lassie she had worn,
In longitude tho' sorely scanty,
It was her best, and she was vauntie.—
Ah! little kend thy reverend grannie,
That sark she coft for her wee Nannie,
Wi' twa pund Scots, ('twas a' her riches),
Wad ever grac'd a dance of witches!

But here my Muse her wing maun cour;
Sic flights are far beyond her pow'r;
To sing how Nannie lap and flang,
(A souple jade she was, and strang),
And how *Tam* stood like ane bewitch'd,
And thought his very een enrich'd;
Even Satan glowr'd, and fidg'd fu' fain,
And hotch'd an blew wi' might and main:
Till first ae caper, syne anither,
Tam tint his reason a' thegither,
And roars out, "Weel done, Cutty-sark!"
And in an instant all was dark:
And scarcely had he *Maggie* rallied,
When out the hellish legion sallied.

As bees bizz out wi' angry fyke,
When plundering herds assail their byke;
As open pussie's mortal foes,
When, pop! she starts before their nose;
As eager runs the market-crowd,
When "Catch the thief!" resounds aloud;
So *Maggie* runs, the witches follow,
Wi' mony an eldritch skreech and hollow.

Ah, *Tam!* Ah, *Tam!* thou'll get thy fairin!
In hell they'll roast thee like a herrin!
In vain thy *Kate* awaits thy comin!
Kate soon will be a woefu' woman!
Now, do thy speedy utmost, Meg,

And win the key-stane of the brig;
There at them thou thy tail may toss,
A running stream they dare na cross.
But ere the key-stane she could make,
The fient a tail she had to shake!
For Nannie, far before the rest,
Hard upon noble *Maggie* prest,
And flew at *Tam* wi' furious ettle;
But little wist she Maggie's mettle—
Ae spring brought off her master hale,
But left behind her ain gray tail:
The carlin claught her by the rump,
And left poor *Maggie* scarce a stump.

  Now, wha this tale o' truth shall read,
Ilk man and mother's son, take heed:
Whene'er to drink you are inclin'd,
Or cutty-sarks run in your mind,
Think! ye may buy the joys o'er dear,
Remember *Tam o' Shanter*'s mare.

'Ae Fond Kiss'

The Scots Musical Museum, ed. James Johnson, 6 vols (Edinburgh:
James Johnson & Co., 1787–1803).

Ae fond kiss, and then we sever;
Ae fareweel, and then forever!
Deep in heart-wrung tears I'll pledge thee,
Warring sighs and groans I'll wage thee.—

Who shall say that Fortune grieves him,
While the star of hope she leaves him:
Me, nae cheerfu' twinkle lights me;
Dark despair around benights me.—

I'll ne'er blame my partial fancy:
Naething could resist my Nancy:
But to see her, was to love her;
Love but her, and love for ever.—

Had we never lov'd sae kindly,
Had we never lov'd sae blindly!

Never met—or never parted,
We had ne'er been broken-hearted.—

Fare-thee-weel, thou first and fairest!
Fare-thee-weel, thou best and dearest!
Thine be ilka joy and treasure,
Peace, Enjoyment, Love and Pleasure!—

Ae fond kiss, and then we sever!
Ae fareweel, Alas, for ever!
Deep in heart-wrung tears I'll pledge thee,
Warring sighs and groans I'll wage thee.—

'Holy Willie's Prayer'

Poems Ascribed to Robert Burns, The Ayrshire Bard (Glasgow: Thomas
Stewart, 1801).

> [*And send the Godly in a pet to pray.*
> ALEXANDER POPE]

O Thou, wha in the heavens dost dwell,
Wha, as it pleases best thysel',
Sends ane to heaven and ten to hell,
    A' for thy glory!
And no for ony guid or ill
    They've done afore thee!

I bless and praise thy matchless might,
Whan thousands thou hast left in night,
That I am here afore thy sight,
    For gifts an' grace,
A burnin' an' a shinin' light,
    To a' this place.

What was I, or my generation,
That I should get such exaltation,
I wha deserve sic just damnation,
    For broken laws,
Five thousand years 'fore my creation,
    Thro' Adam's cause.

When frae my mither's womb I fell,
Thou might ha'e plunged me in hell,

To gnash my gums, to weep and wail,
    In burnin' lake,
Whar damned devils roar and yell,
    Chain'd to a stake.

Yet I am here a chosen sample,
To show thy grace is great an' ample;
I'm here a pillar in thy temple,
    Strong as a rock,
A guide, a buckler, an' example
    To a' thy flock.

[O L—d thou kens what zeal I bear,
When drinkers drink, and swearers swear,
And singin' there, and dancin' here,
    Wi' great an' sma';
For I am keepet by thy fear,
    Free frae them a'.]

But yet, O L—d! confess I must,
At times I'm fash'd wi' fleshly lust;
An' sometimes too, wi' wardly trust,
    Vile self gets in;
But thou remembers we are dust,
    Defil'd in sin.

O L—d! yestreen, thou kens, wi' Meg,
Thy pardon I sincerely beg,
O! may it ne'er be a livin' plague
    To my dishonour,
An' I'll ne'er lift a lawless leg
    Again upon her.

Besides, I farther maun avow,
Wi' Lizie's lass, three times I trow;
But, L—d, that Friday I was fow,
    When I came near her,
Or else, thou kens, thy *servant true*
    Wad ne'er ha'e steer'd her.

Maybe tho lets this *fleshy thorn*,
Beset thy servant e'en and morn,
Lest he owre high and proud shou'd turn,

'Cause he's sae *gifted*;
If sae, thy han' maun e'en be born,
    Until thou lift it.

L—d bless thy chosen in this place,
For *here* thou hast a *chosen race*;
But G—d confound their stubborn face,
    And blast their name,
Wha bring thy elders to disgrace,
    An' public shame.

L—d mind Gaun Hamilton's deserts,
He drinks, an' swears, an' plays at carts,
Yet has sae mony takin' arts,
    Wi' great an' sma',
Frae G—d's ain priest the people's hearts
    He steals awa'.

An' when we chasten'd him therefore,
Thou kens how he bred sic a splore,
And set the warld in a roar
    O' laughin' at us;
Curse thou his basket and his store,
    Kail an' potatoes.

L—d hear my earnest cry an' pray'r,
Against that presbyt'ry o' Ayr;
Thy strong right hand, L—d make it bare,
    Upo' their heads,
L—d weigh it down, and dinna spare,
    For their misdeeds.

O L—d my G—d, that glib-tongu'd Aiken!
My very heart an' saul are quakin',
To think how we stood sweatin', shakin',
    An'p—d wi' dread,
While he wi' hingin' lips gaed snakin',
    Held up his head.

L—d, in the day of vengeance try him,
L—d visit him wha did employ him,
An' pass not in thy mercy by 'em,
    Nor hear their pray'r;

But for thy people's sake destroy 'em,
    And dinna spare.

But, L—d remember me and mine
Wi' mercies temp'ral and divine,
That I for gear and grace may shine,
    Excell'd by nane,
An' a' the glory shall be thine,
    Amen, Amen.

JANET LITTLE
(1759–1813)

BORN in Ecclefechan, Janet Little was always a precocious reader. She went into service when still very young, perhaps acquiring some education while with an early employer, Reverend Johnstone. In 1788 she sought a place with Frances Dunlop, one of the patrons and correspondents of her idol Robert Burns. Shortly after this engagement, Little sent some poems to Burns, who was slow and cool in his reply. Unperturbed, the thirtysomething Little published a collection of her poems in 1792, marketing herself in the title as the Scotch Milkmaid. Unfairly dismissed as a mere imitator of Burns, an undoubted influence, Little experimented with a variety of poetic forms, and wrote in both Scots and English. Even the small sample of her canon that follows reveals an original poet attuned to competing literary traditions of the long eighteenth century.

'An Epistle to Mr Robert Burns'

The Poetical Works of Janet Little, the Scotch Milkmaid (Ayr: John & Peter Wilson, 1792).

> Fairfa' the honest rustic swain,
> The pride o' a' our Scottish plain;
> Thou gi'es us joy to hear thy strain,
>   And notes sae sweet;
> Old Ramsay's shade, reviv'd again,
>   In thee we greet.
>
> Lov'd Thallia, that delightful Muse,
> Seem'd long shut up as a recluse:
> To all she did her aid refuse,
>   Since Allan's day,
> Till Burns arose, then did she choose
>   To grace his lay.

To hear thy song, all ranks desire;
Sae well thou strik'st the dormant lyre.
Apollo, wi' poetic fire,
  Thy breast did warm,
An' critics silently admire
  Thy art to charm.

Caesar an' Luath weel can speak;
'Tis pity e'er their gabs should steek:
They into human nature keek,
  An' knots unravel;
To hear their lectures ance a week,
  Ten miles I'd travel.

Thy dedication to G—H—,
In unco bonny, hamespun speech,
Wi' winsome glee the heart can teach
  A better lesson,
Than servile bards wha fawn an' fleech,
  Like beggar's messin.

When slighted love becomes thy theme,
An' woman's faithless vows you blame,
With so much pathos you exclaim,
  In your Lament,
But glanc'd by the most frigid dame,
  She wad relent.

The daisy too, you sing wi' skill;
An' weel ye praise the whisky gill.
In vain I blunt my feckless quill,
  Your fame to raise,
While echo sounds, frae ilka hill,
  To Burns's praise.

Did Addison or Pope but hear,
Or Sam, that critic most severe,
A plough-boy sing, wi' throat sae clear,
  They, in a rage,
Their works wad a' in pieces tear
  An' curse your page.

If I should strain my rupy throat,
To raise thy praise wi' swelling note,

My rude, unpolish'd strokes wad blot
Thy brilliant shine,
An' ev'ry passage I would quote
Seem less sublime.

The task I'll drop; wi' heart sincere
To heav'n present a humble prayer,
That a' the blessings mortals share
May be, by turns,
Dispens'd with an indulgent care
To Robert Burns.

'Given to a Lady Who Asked Me to Write a Poem'

In royal Anna's golden days,
Hard was the task to gain the bays;
Hard was it then the hill to climb;
Some broke a neck, some lost a limb.
The vot'ries for poetic fame
Got aff decrepit, blind, an' lame;
Except that little fellow Pope,
Few ever then got near its top:
An' Homer's crutches he may thank,
Or down the brae he'd got a clank.
        Swift, Thomson, Addison an' Young
Made Pindus echo to their tongue,
In hopes to please a learned age;
But Doctor Johnson, in a rage,
Unto posterity did shew
Their blunders great, their beauties few.
But now he's dead, we weel may ken;
For ilka dunce maun hae a pen,
To write in hamely, uncouth rhymes;
An' yet forsooth they please the times.
        A ploughman chiel, Rab Burns his name,
Pretends to write; an' thinks nae shame
To souse his sonnets on the court;
An' what is stange, they praise him for't.
Even folks, wha 're of the highest station,
Ca' him the glory of our nation.
        But what is more surprising still,

A milkmaid must tak up her quill;
An' she will write, shame fa' the rabble!
That think to please wi' ilka bawble.
They may thank heav'n, auld Sam's asleep;
For could he ance but get a peep,
He, wi' a vengeance wad them sen'
A' headlong to the dunces' den.

      Yet Burns, I'm tauld, can write wi' ease,
An' a' denominations please;
Can wi' uncommon glee impart
A usefu' lesson to the heart;
Can ilka latent thought expose,
An' Nature trace whare'er she goes;
Of politics can talk wi' skill,
Nor dare the critics blame his quill.

      But then a rustic country quean
To write—was e'er the like o't seen?
A milk maid poem-books to print;
Mair fit she wad her dairy tent;
Or labour at her spinning wheel,
An' do her wark baith swift an' weel.
Frae that she may some profit share,
But winna frae her rhyming ware.
Does she, poor silly thing, pretend
The manners of our age to mend?
Mad as we are, we're wise enough
Still to despise sic paultry stuff.

      "May she wha writes, of wit get mair,
An' a' that read an ample share
Of candour ev'ry fault to screen,
That in her dogg'ral scrawls are seen."

      All this and more, a critic said;
I heard and slunk behind the shade:
So much I dread their cruel spite,
My hand still trembles when I write.

'On Seeing Mr—Baking Cakes'

    As Rab, who ever frugal was,
      Some oat-meal cakes was baking,

In came a crazy scribbling lass,
    Which set his heart a-quaking.

"I fear," says he, "she'll verses write,
    An' to her neebors show it:
But troth I need na care a doit,
    Though a' the country knew it.

My cakes are good, none can object;
    The maids will ca' me thrifty;
To save a sixpence on the peck
    Is just an honest shifty.

They're fair an' thin, an' crump, 'tis true;
    You'll own sae when you see them;
But, what is better than the view,
    Put out your han' an' pree them."

He spoke, an' han'd the cakes about,
    Whilk ev'ry eater prized;
Until the basket was run out,
    They did as he advised.

An' ilka ane that got a share,
    Said that they were fu' dainty;
While Rab cri'd eat, an' dinna spare
    For I hae cakes in plenty.

And i' the corner stan's a cheese,
    A glass an' bottle by me;
Baith ale and porter, when I please,
    To treat the lasses slily.

Some ca' me wild an' roving youth;
    But sure they are mistaken:
The maid wha gets me, of a truth,
    Her bread will ay be baken.

'Upon a Young Lady's Breaking a Looking-Glass'

As round the room, with tentless speed,
    Young Delia tripp'd it finely,
A looking-glass, so Fate decreed,
    She broke, but not design'dly.

A looking-glass of ancient date,
  Its fall the belles lamented;
But all their sorrow prov'd too late,
  Its ruin none prevented.

When Anne the British sceptre sway'd,
  'Twas plac'd in firm position;
Nor did a forward chamber-maid
  E'er alter its condition.

No mirror better could descry
  Th' embrio of a pimple;
The rheum on a neglected eye;
  The hoary hair or wrinkle.

Long time it did the chimney grace,
  So awkward now and empty;
Its with a vengeance chang'd its place,
  And broke in pieces twenty.

O Delia! mourn thy direful fate,
  A thousand ills portending!
Black omens now thy stars await,
  'Gainst which there's no defending.

Poor Delia now, bedew'd with tears
  And piti'd by acquaintance,
Resolv'd to spend full fifteen years,
  In doleful, deep repentance.

Do tears these lovely cheeks distain,
  By thousand charms surrounded!
These eyes from weeping do refrain;
  Their glance have many wounded.

T' adorn thy more accomplish'd mind,
  Each radiant grace conspires:
Hence dread thou not their dark design,
  Though rage each demon fires.

Let hope diffuse a gentle ray,
  There magic spells defying:
Let prudence Delia's footsteps sway,
  On virtue still relying.

But know the rake's alluring smile,
  The heedless fair bewitches:
Let no fond youth your heart beguile,
  By soft enticing speeches.

And if good counsel aught avail,
  Attend Diana's classes:
For mind our sex is ever frail,
  And brittle as our glasses.

JOHN MAYNE

(1759–1836)

———

BORN and educated in Dumfries, John Mayne later relocated to Glasgow, then London, where he worked in the publishing industry. He had written poetry while in Dumfries, and after 1777 he occasionally contributed poems to Ruddiman's *Weekly Magazine* in Edinburgh. Between 1807 and 1817 several of Mayne's lyrics appeared in the *Gentleman's Magazine* too. Mayne laboured over a long poem, *Siller Gun*, even after it appeared in print in 1777; expanded versions followed in 1779, 1780, 1808, and 1836 (the year of his death). Scott was a keen admirer. Mayne's 'Hallowe'en', meanwhile, influenced Burns's Gothic poems. Published in the *Glasgow Magazine* in December 1783, 'Glasgow' is a sly riposte to a famous poem written by one of Mayne's main influences, Robert Fergusson's 'Auld Reekie'. Here follows a small extract of a work that runs to sixty stanzas.

———

Glasgow: A Poem *(1803) (an extract)*

The History of Glasgow, From the Earliest to the Present Time with Numerous Illustrations, by Writers of Eminence (Glasgow: John Tweed, 1873).

> Hail, Glasgow! fam'd for ilka thing
> That heart can wish, or siller bring!
> May Peace, wi' healing on her wing,
>   Aye nestle here;
> And plenty gar thy childer sing,
>   The lee-lang year!
>
> Within the tinkling o' thy Bells,
> How mony a happy body dwells!
> Where they get bread, they ken themsels;
>   But, I'll declare
> They're aye bien-like; and, what precels,
>   Ha'e fouth to spare!

If ye've a knacky Son or twa,
To Glasgow College send them a':
Wi' whilk, for Gospel, or for Law,
        Or Classic Lair,
Ye'll find few Places here awa,
        That can compare!

There ane may be for sma' propyne,
Physician, Lawyer, or Divine:
The gem, lang bury'd i' the mine,
        Is polish'd here,
Till a' its hidden beauties shine,
        And sparkle clear!

Nor is it Students, and nae mair,
That climb, in crowds, our College stair:
Thither the learn'd, far fam'd, repair,
        To clear their notions;
And pay to Alma Mater there,
        Their warm devotions.

Led by a lustre sae Divine,
Ev'n Geddes visited this Shrine!
Geddes! sweet fav'rite o' the Nine!
        Shall live in story;
And, like yon Constellation, shine
        In Rays o' glory!

O! Leechman, Hutcheson, and Wight!
Reid fu' of intellectual light!
And Simpson, as the morning, bright!
        Your Mem'ries here,
Tho' gane to Regions o' Delight,
        Will aye be dear!

'Mang ither Names, that consecrate
And stamp a Country gude or great,
We boast o' some that might compete,
        Or claim alliance,
Wi' a' that's grand in Kirk or State—
        In Art or Science!

Here great Buchanan learnt to scan
The Verse that makes him mair than man!

Cullen and Hunter here began
     Their first probations;
And Smith, frae Glasgow, form'd his plan—
     "The Wealth o' Nations!"

In ilka house, frae man to boy,
A' hands, in Glasgow, find employ;
Ev'n little maids, wi' meikle joy,
     Flow'r lawn and gauze,
Or clip, wi' care, the silken soy
     For Ladies' braws.

Their fathers weave, their mothers spin,
The muslin robe, sae fine and thin,
That, frae the ancle to the chin,
     It aft discloses
The beauteous symmetry within—
     Limbs, neck and bozies!

Look through the town, the houses here
Like noble palaces appear;
A' things the face o' gladness wear—
     The Market's thrang,
Bis'ness is brisk, and a's asteer
     The Streets alang!

Clean keepit Streets! sae lang and braid,
The distant objects seem to fade!
And then for shelter, or for shade,
     Frae sun or show'r,
Piazzas lend their friendly aid,
     At ony hour!

O! for the muse o' Burns sae rare,
To paint the groups that gather there!
The wives on We'n'sdays wi' their ware—
     The lads and lasses,
In ferlying crouds, at Glasgow-Fair;
     And a' that passes!

But, oh! his Muse that warm'd ilk clod,
And rais'd up flow'rs where'er he trod!
Will ne'er revisit this abode!
     And mine, poor lassie,

In tears for him, dow hardly plod
    Thro' Glasgow causae!

Wond'ring, we see new Streets extending,
New Squares wi' Public Buildings blending!
Brigs, stately brigs, in arches bending
    Across the Clyde;
And Turrets, Kirks, and Spires, ascending
    In lofty pride!

High ow'r the lave, St. Mungo rears
His sacred Fane, the pride of years;
And, stretching upwards to the spheres,
    His Spire, afar,
To weary Travellers appears
    A Leading Star!

O! happy, happy were the hours
When first, far aff on Crawfurd-Moors,
I hail'd thee bright thro' sunny show'rs,
    As on I came
Frae murm'ring Nith's romantic bow'rs,
    My native Hame!

Blythe days! ow'r happy to remain!
The Sire, wha led my steps, is gane!—
Yet wherefore shou'd the Muse complain
    In dirge-like lines,
When Heaven has only ta'en its ain,
    For wise designs!

Still happy, happy be their hours
Wha journey, Clydesdale, thro' thy bow'rs!
And, blest amang th' angelic pow'rs—
    Blest be the man
Wha sav'd St. Mungo's hallow'd Tow'rs
    Frae ruin's han'!

ISABELLA KELLY

(1759–1857)

A POET and novelist, Isabella Kelly (*née* Fordyce) was born at Cairnburgh Castle, though her parents were cut off by their wealthy families following their clandestine marriage. In her mid-thirties Kelly published her first book, a *Collection of Poems and Fables*, in 1794, though she had written parts of it as a young teenager, by her own claim. Deserted by her husband and seeking a new income stream, she turned to writing Gothic novels, beginning with her first effort, *Madeline* (1794), and following up with nine more between 1795 and 1813. Kelly also wrote educational books, including *Instructive Anecdotes for Youth* (1819). Her last book, *A Memoir of the Late Mrs. Henrietta Fordyce*, was published anonymously in 1823. Despite living for more than thirty years more, Kelly appears to have abandoned her writing career at that point.

'To an Unborn Infant'

Collection of Poems and Fables on Several Occasions (London: W. Richardson, 1794).

> Be still, sweet babe, no harm shall reach thee,
>   Nor hurt thy yet unfinish'd form;
> Thy mother's frame shall safely guard thee
>   From this bleak, this beating storm.
>
> Promis'd hope! expected treasure!
>   Oh! how welcome to there arms!
> Feeble, yet they'll fondly clasp thee,
>   Shield thee from the least alarms.
>
> Lov'd already, little blessing,
>   Kindly cherish'd, tho' unknown,
> Fancy forms thee sweet and lovely,
>   Emblem of the rose unblown:

Though thy father is imprison'd,
    Wrong'd, forgotten, robb'd of right,
I'll repress the rising anguish,
    Till thine eyes behold the light.

Start not, babe! the hour approaches
    That presents the gift of life;
Soon, too soon thoul't taste of sorrow
    In these realms of care and strife:

Share not thou a mother's feelings,
    Hope vouchsafes a pitying ray;
Tho' a gloom obscures the morning,
    Bright may shine the rising day,

Live, sweet babe, to bless thy father,
    When thy mother slumbers low;
Softly lisp her name that lov'd him,
    Thro' a world of varied woe.

Learn, my child, the mournful story
    Of thy suffering mother's life;
Let thy father not forget her
    In a future happier wife.

Babe of fondest expectation,
    Watch his wishes in his face;
What pleas'd in me, mayst thou inherit,
    And supply my vacant place.

Whisper all the anguish'd moments
    That have wrung this anxious breast,
Say, I liv'd to give thee being,
    And retir'd to endless rest.

'The Choice; or, Dull Hour Past'

Heigho! I'm wond'rous dull; in truth I'm wond'rous sad—
Little amusement, and the weather bad;
What shall I do? I'll write—Come, ready friend—
I mean my pen—Good folks, I pray attend:
Still at a loss, I do not wish to teaze;—
My muse, assist me—teach me how to please—

My thoughts are free—then, fancy, take thy range—
I'll write my wish—no choice—pshaw, how I change!
Critics, be dumb—I will the thought impart,
That some kind youth may bid for Anna's heart:
He who aspires this little heart to gain,
Some decent share of merit must attain;
Serene religion must his actions guide,
Bright truth, nice honor, o'er his mind preside;
Prudence to guide him thro' life's busy scene,
Never extravagant, nor ever mean;
Let him have sense designing men to see,
Enough to rule himself and *govern me*;
To feel for human kind—a generous soul,
To me devoted, but polite to all;
His temper kind—of that I must be sure—
A husband's frown I never could endure;
To female weakness mild reproof impart,
But with indifference never chill the heart;
No *foolish* fondness should he ever shew,
But love refin'd, within his bosom glow;
His manner easy, gen'rous, void of art,
Let ev'ry word flow candid from the heart;
His person pleasing, in his taste refin'd,
A face the index of an honest mind;
To jealousy he never must give way,
Trust to my honour, and I'll not betray;
No flatt'ring fribble shall my hand obtain,
Where much is said, there little can remain;
A man for riches I can never prize,—
Let kindness grant what adverse fate denies;
I wish not wealth, nor titles do I claim,
Only let goodness mark his honest name;
To little errors I will kindly bend;
His wish, my law, I never will contend;
And, should he stray (as none faultless be)
Prudence shall veil it; for *I will not see*:
A youth like this to share the cares of life,
Shall find in me a kind and faithful wife.
Ambitious females in their wealth may glee,—
Love, worth, and honor, form the heart for me.
Methinks ye frown—I hear ye loud exclaim,

"To hope so much a female is to blame;
In modern days, do you expect to find
Grace, worth, and goodness, with firm honor join'd?
But if so high are your pretensions, tell
What do you boast? in what do you excel?"
In great sincerity I now step forth,
Confess my merit humble as my worth;
I boast no beauty—I no graces claim,
And all my portion is, a spotless name;
Sincere and artless—Man exert your skill,
With prudent fondness make me what you will.
Blushing, methinks, I hear it said, "No more!
No other claim!—truly your merit's *poor*."
Yet, in life's varying maze, I hope to meet
Some kindred heart, unpractis'd in deceit.
To prove the tender friend—companion—wife,
Will be the sweetest care of Anna's life;
With temper mild, and innocently gay,
Submissive gentleness she'll ever pay.—
My friends, adieu!—my hour is past away.

UILLEAM ROS / WILLIAM ROSS
(1762–?1791)

HAILING from Skye, Uilleam Ros (William Ross) is often called
the greatest Gaelic love poet of the eighteenth century. His mother
was the daughter of John MacKay, the Blind Piper. Displaying his
own musical talent at a young age, Ross moved with his family to
Forres so he could study at the Grammar School there. As a teenager he fell in love with an older, distant relation, Marion Ross,
who inspired many of his love poems. Plagued by ill health for
some time, he died before reaching thirty. A late work, 'Òran Eile,
air an Adhbhar Cheudna' (also known as 'An t-Òran Eile'), refers
to extreme bodily pain. But, ever the love poet, Ross is troubled
less by his physical consciousness (*càil*) than by his spiritual consciousness (*aigne*).

'Òran Eile, air an Adhbhar Cheudna'

*Sar-Obair nam Bard Gaelach; or, The Beauties of Gaelic Poetry, and
Lives of the Highland Bards*, ed. John MacKenzie, 4th edn (Edinburgh:
Maclachlan & Stewart, 1877).

> Tha mise fo mhulad san àm,
> Chan òlar leam dram le sunnd;
> Tha durrag air ghur ann mo chàil
> A dh'fhiosraich do chàch mo rùn;
> Chan fhaic mi dol seachad air sràid
> An cailin bu tlàithe sùil—
> 'S e sin a leag m' aigne gu làr
> Mar dhuilleach o bhàrr nan craobh.
>
> A ghruagach as bachlaiche cùl,
> Tha mise gad ionndrainn mòr;
> Ma thagh thu deagh àite dhut fèin,

Mo bheannachd gach rè g' ad chòir;
Tha mise ri osnaich nad dhèidh
Mar ghaisgeach an dèis a leòn,
Na laighe san àraich gun fheum,
'S nach tèid anns an t-sreup nas mò.

'S e dh'fhàg mi mar iudmhail air treud,
Mar fhear nach toir spèis do mhnaoi,
Do thuras thar chuan fo bhrèid,
Thug bras shileadh dheur om shùil;
B' fheàrr nach mothaichinn fèin
Do mhaise, do chèill 's do chliù,
No suairceas milis do bhèil
As binne na sèis gach ciùil.

Gach an-duin' a chluinneas mo chàs
A' cur air mo nàdar fiamh,
A' cantainn nach eil mi ach bàrd
'S nach cinnich leam dàn as fiach—
Mo sheanair ri pàigheadh a mhàil
Is m' athair ri màileid riamh—
Chuireadh iad gearrain an crann
Is ghearrainn-sa rann ro cheud.

'S fad' a tha m' aigne fo ghruaim,
Cha mhosgail mo chluain ri ceòl,
'M breislich mar ànrach a' chuain
Air bharraibh nan stuagh ri ceò;
'S e iùnndaran d' àbhachd uam
A chaochail air snuadh mo neòil,
Gun sùgradh, gun mhire, gun uaill,
Gun chaithream, gun bhuadh, gun treòir.

Cha dùisgear leam ealaidh air àill',
Cha chuirear leam dàn air dòigh,
Cha togar leam fonn air clàr,
Cha chluinnear leam gàir nan òg;
Cha dìrich mi bealach nan àrd
Le suigeart mar bha mi 'n tòs,
Ach triallam a chadal gu bràth
Do thalla nam bàrd nach beò.

'Another Song on the Same Topic' (translated by Peter Mackay and Iain S. MacPherson)

Now I'm depressed.
I won't happily take a dram—
a maggot festers in my brain
which lets everyone know my desire.
I can't see, going past in the street,
the young woman with the gentlest eye:
this is what's felled my spirit
like leaves from the top of the trees.

O girl of the curliest hair,
I'm badly missing you;
if you chose a good place for yourself,
my blessing on you for all time.
I am sighing for you,
like a warrior who has been wounded,
lying useless in a battlefield,
who won't enter the fray any more.

What's left me astray from the flock,
like one who can love no woman—
your sea journey as a head-dressed bride
that brought torrents of tears from my eyes;
I wish I couldn't notice
your beauty, your sense and your fame,
or your mouth's sweet affability
more tuneful than any music.

Every hater who hears of my plight
claims my nature is flawed,
says that I'm just a poet
who can't make a worthwhile song;
but my grandfather paid his rent
and my father carried his pack—
they could hitch geldings to ploughs,
and I could cut verse with the best.

My spirits have long been clouded,
music doesn't waken my senses;
delirious like a wanderer at sea

on top of the mist-covered waves;
it is missing your humour
that has changed the hue of my sky:
no love-making, mirth or pride,
no excitement, virtue or direction.

I can't wake an ode on beauty.
I can't get a poem to sit true
I can't raise a tune from the stave,
I can't hear the laugh of the young;
I can't climb high mountain passes
cheerfully, as I once did,
but let me go forever to sleep
in the hall of the unliving poets.

AGNES LYON

(1762–1840)

━━

THE comic poet Agnes Lyon (*née* L'Amy or Lammie) was born in Dundee. Apparently written for her own pleasure and that of her family, many of her works focus on domestic subjects. She even directed at her death that her manuscripts should remain unprinted, unless the family needed pecuniary assistance. She remains best known for the song beginning 'You've surely heard of famous Niel', written at the request of the famous fiddler Niel Gow for his air 'Farewell to Whisky'.

━━

'Niel Gow's Farewell to Whisky'

The Scottish Minstrel: The Songs and Song Writers of Scotland subsequent to Burns, with Memoirs of the Poets, ed. Charles Rogers (Edinburgh: William P. Nimmo, 1876).

(Tune: "Farewell to Whisky")

You've surely heard of famous Niel,
The man that play'd the fiddle weel;
He was a heartsome merry chiel',
    And weel he lo'ed the whisky, O!
For e'er since he wore the tartan hose
He dearly liket *Athole brose!*
And grieved was, you may suppose,
    To bid "Farewell to whisky," O!

Alas! says Niel, I'm frail and auld,
And whiles my hame is unco cauld;
I think it makes me blythe and bauld,
    A wee drap Highland whisky, O!
But a' the doctors do agree
That whisky's no the drink for me;
I'm fley'd they'll gar me tyne my glee,
    By parting me and whisky, O!

But I should mind on "auld lang syne,"
How Paradise our friends did tyne,
Because something ran in their mind—
    Forbid—like Highland whisky, O!
Whilst I can get good wine and ale,
And find my heart, and fingers hale,
I'll be content, though legs should fail,
    And though forbidden whisky, O!

I'll tak' my fiddle in my hand,
And screw its strings whilst they can stand,
And mak' a lamentation grand
    For guid auld Highland whisky, O!
Oh! all ye powers of music, come,
For, 'deed, I think I'm mighty glum,
My fiddle-strings will hardly bum,
    To say, "Farewell to whisky," O!

JOANNA BAILLIE
(1762–1851)

———

JOANNA BAILLIE, of Lanarkshire, remains better known for her dramatic works, particularly *De Monfort. A Tragedy* (1798). But she was also a highly accomplished poet. In her early twenties, Baillie, with her mother and sister, relocated to London, where the author accessed literary society through her aunt Anne Hunter, a popular poet in her own right. Under Hunter's guidance, Baillie produced her first major poem, 'Winter Day'. Her first verse collection, *Poems: Wherein it is Attempted to Describe Certain Views of Nature and of Rustic Manners*, appeared in 1790. With the encouragement of the banker poet Samuel Rogers, Baillie later revised a selection of these early pieces for a collection titled *Fugitive Verses* (1840), which also contained some recent compositions. Much to her satisfaction, an authoritative edition of her dramatic and poetical works appeared shortly before her death.

———

'A Disappointment'

The Dramatic and Poetical Works of Joanna Baillie, 2nd edn (London: Longman, Brown, Green, and Longmans, 1851).

> On village green whose smooth and well-worn sod,
> Cross path'd, with many a gossip's foot is trod;
> By cottage door where playful children run,
> And cats and curs sit basking in the sun;
> Where o'er an earthen seat the thorn is bent,
> Cross-armed and back to wall poor William leant.
> His bonnet all awry, his gather'd brow,
> His hanging lip and lengthen'd visage show
> A mind but ill at ease. With motions strange
> His listless limbs their wayward postures change;
> While many a crooked line and curious maze

With clouted shoon he on the sand portrays.
At length the half-chew'd straw fell from his mouth,
And to himself low spoke the moody youth.
      "How simple is the lad and reft of skill,
Who thinks with love to fix a woman's will!
Who every Sunday morn to please her sight,
Knots up his neckcloth gay and hosen white;
Who for her pleasure keeps his pockets bare,
And half his wages spends on pedlar's ware;
When every niggard clown or dotard old,
Who hides in secret nooks his oft-told gold,
Whose field or orchard tempts, with all her pride,
At little cost may win her for his bride!
While all the meed her silly lover gains,
Is but the neighbours' jeering for his pains.
On Sunday last, when Susan's banns were read,
And I astonish'd sat with hanging head,
Cold grew my shrinking frame, and loose my knee,
While every neighbour's eye was fix'd on me.
Ah Sue! when last we work'd at Hodge's hay,
And still at me you mock'd in wanton play—
When last at fair, well pleased by chapman's stand,
You took the new-bought fairing from my hand—
When at old Hobb's you sung that song so gay,
'Sweet William,' still the burthen of the lay,—
I little thought, alas! the lots were cast,
That thou shouldst be another's bride at last;
And had, when last we tripped it on the green,
And laugh'd at stiff-back'd Rob, small thought I ween,
Ere yet another scanty month was flown
To see thee wedded to the hateful clown;
Ay, lucky churl! more gold thy pockets line;
But did these shapely limbs resemble thine,
I'd stay at home and tend the household gear,
Nor on the green with other lads appear.
Ay, lucky churl! no store thy cottage lacks,
And round thy barn thick stand the shelter'd stacks,
But did such features coarse my visage grace,
I'd never budge the bonnet from my face.
Yet let it be; it shall not break my ease;
He best deserves who doth the maiden please.

Such silly cause no more shall give me pain,
Nor ever maiden cross my rest again.
Such grizzled suitors with their taste agree,
And the black fiend may take them all for me!"
          Now through the village rose confused sounds,
Hoarse lads, and children shrill, and yelping hounds.
Straight every housewife at her door is seen,
And pausing hedgers on their mattocks lean.
At every narrow lane and alley's mouth,
Loud-laughing lasses stand, and joking youth.
A bridal band trick'd out in colours gay,
With minstrels blithe before to cheer the way,
From clouds of curling dust that onward fly,
In rural splendour breaks upon the eye.
As in their way they hold so gaily on,
Caps, beads, and buttons, glancing to the sun,
Each village wag with eye of roguish cast
Some maiden jogs, and vents the ready jest;
While village toasts the passing belles deride,
And sober matrons marvel at their pride.
But William, head erect, with settled brow,
In sullen silence view'd the passing show;
And oft he scratch'd his pate with careless grace,
And scorn'd to pull the bonnet o'er his face;
But did with steady look unalter'd wait,
Till hindmost man had pass'd the churchyard gate,
Then turn'd him to his cot with visage flat,
Where honest Lightfoot on the threshold sat.
Up leap'd the kindly beast his hand to lick,
And for his pains received an angry kick.
Loud shuts the door with harsh and thundering din;
The echoes round their circling course begin,
From cot to cot, church tower, and rocky dell,
It grows amain with wide progressive swell,
And Lightfoot joins the coil with long and piteous yell.

'Song [What voice is this, thou evening gale!]'

What voice is this, thou evening gale!
That mingles with thy rising wail;

And, as it passes, sadly seems
The faint return of youthful dreams?

Though now its strain is wild and drear,
Blithe was it once as sky-lark's cheer—
Sweet as the night-bird's sweetest song,—
Dear as the lisp of infant's tongue.

It was the voice, at whose sweet flow
The heart did beat, and cheek did glow,
And lip did smile, and eye did weep,
And motion'd love the measure keep.

Oft be thy sound, soft gale of even,
Thus to my wistful fancy given;
And, as I list the swelling strain,
The dead shall seem to live again!

'Song, Woo'd and Married and a''

The bride she is winsome and bonny,
  Her hair it is snooded sae sleek,
And faithfu' and kind is her Johnny,
  Yet fast fa' the tears on her cheek.
New pearlins are cause of her sorrow,
  New pearlins and plenishing too,
The bride that has a' to borrow,
  Has e'en right mickle ado,
    Woo'd and married and a'!
    Woo'd and married and a'!
  Is na' she very weel aff
    To be woo'd and married at a'?

Her mither then hastily spak,
  "The lassie is glaikit wi' pride;
In my pouch I had never a plack
  On the day when I was a bride.
E'en tak' to your wheel, and be clever,
  And draw out your thread in the sun;
The gear that is gifted, it never
  Will last like the gear that is won.
    Woo'd and married and a'!

Wi' havins and toucher sae sma'!
I think ye are very weel aff,
    To be woo'd and married at a'!"

"Toot, toot!" quo' her grey-headed faither,
    "She's less o' a bride than a bairn,
She's ta'en like a cout frae the heather,
    Wi' sense and discretion to learn.
Half husband, I trow, and half daddy,
    As humour inconstantly leans,
The chiel maun be patient and steady,
    That yokes wi' a mate in her teens.
A kerchief sae douce and sae neat,
    O'er her locks that the winds used to blaw!
I'm baith like to laugh and to greet,
    When I think o' her married at a'!"

Then out spak' the wily bridegroom,
    Weel waled were his wordies, I ween,
"I'm rich, though my coffer be toom,
    Wi' the blinks o' your bonny blue een.
I'm prouder o' thee by my side,
    Though thy ruffles or ribbons be few,
Than if Kate o' the Croft were my bride,
    Wi' purfles and pearlins enow.
Dear and dearest of ony!
    Ye're woo'd and buikit and a'!
And do ye think scorn o' your Johnny,
    And grieve to be married at a'?"

She turn'd, and she blush'd, and she smiled,
    And she looket sae bashfully down;
The pride o' her heart was beguiled,
    And she played wi' the sleeves o' her gown;
She twirled the tag o' her lace,
    And she nippet her boddice sae blue,
Syne blinket sae sweet in his face,
    And aff like a maukin she flew.
    Woo'd and married and a'!
    Wi' Johnny to roose her and a'!
She thinks hersel very weel aff,
    To be woo'd and married at a'!

'Lines to a Teapot'

On thy carved sides, where many a vivid dye
In easy progress leads the wandering eye,
A distant nation's manners we behold,
To the quick fancy whimsically told.

The small-eyed beauty with her Mandarin,
Who o'er the rail of garden arbour lean,
In listless ease; and rocks of arid brown,
On whose sharp crags, in gay profusion blown,
The ample loose-leaved rose appears to grace
The skilful culture of the wonderous place;
The little verdant plat, where with his mate
The golden pheasant holds his gorgeous state,
With gaily crested pate and twisted neck,
Turned jantily his glossy wings to peck;
The smooth-streaked water of a paly gray,
O'er which the checkered bridge lends ready way,
While, by its margin moored, the little boat
Doth with its oars and netted awning float:
A scene in short all soft delights to take in,
A paradise for grave Grandee of Pekin.
With straight small spout, that from thy body fair,
Diverges with a smart vivacious air,
And round, arched handle with gold tracery bound,
And dome-shaped lid with bud or button crowned,
Thou standest complete, fair subject of my rhymes,
A goodly vessel of the olden times.

But far less pleasure yields this fair display
Than that enjoyed upon thy natal day,
When round the potter's wheel, their chins raising,
An urchin group in silent wonder gazing,
Stood and beheld, as, touched with magic skill,
The whirling clay swift fashioned to his will,—
Saw mazy motion stopped, and then the toy
Complete before their eyes, and grinned for joy;
Clapping their naked sides with blythe halloo,
And curtailed words of praise, like ting, tung, too!
The brown-skinned artist, with his unclothed waist

And girded loins, who, slow and patient, traced,
Beneath his humble shed, this fair array
Of pictured forms upon thy surface gay,
I will not stop in fancy's sight to place,
But speed me on my way with quickened pace.
Packed in a chest with others of thy kind,
The sport of waves and every shifting wind,
The Ocean thou hast crossed, and thou mayest claim
The passing of the Line to swell thy fame,
With as good observation of the thing
As some of those who in a hammock swing.

And now thou'rt seen in Britain's polished land,
Held up to public view in waving hand
Of boastful auctioneer, whilst dames of pride
In morning farthingals, scarce two yards wide,
With collared lap-dogs snarling in their arms,
Contend in rival keenness for thy charms.
And certes well they might, for there they found thee
With all thy train of vassal cups around thee,
A prize which thoughts by day, and dreams by night,
Could dwell on for a week with fresh delight.

Our pleased imagination now pourtrays
The glory of thy high official days,
When thou on board of rich japan wert set,
Round whose supporting table gaily met
At close of eve, the young, the learned, the fair,
And even philosophy and wit were there.
Midst basons, cream-pots, cups and saucers small,
Thou stood'st the ruling chieftain of them all;
And even the kettle of Potosi's ore,
Whose ample cell supplied thy liquid store,
Beneath whose base the sapphire flame was burning,
Above whose lid the wreathy smoke was turning,
Though richly chased and burnished it might be,
Was yet, confessed, subordinate to thee.
But O! when beauty's hand thy weight sustained,
The climax of thy glory was attained!
Back from her elevated elbow fell
Its three-tired ruffle, and displayed the swell
And gentle rounding of her lily arm,

The eyes of wistful sage or beau to charm—
A sight at other times but dimly seen
Through veiling folds of point or colberteen.
With pleasing toil, red glowed her dimpled cheek,
Bright glanced her eyes beneath her forehead sleek,
And as she poured the beverage, through the room
Was spread its fleeting, delicate perfume.
Then did bright wit and cheerful fancy play
With all the passing topics of the day.
So delicate, so varied and so free
Was the heart's pastime, then inspired by thee,
That goblet, bowl or flask could boast no power
Of high excitement, in their reigning hour,
Compared to thine;—red wildfire of the fen,
To summer moonshine of some fairy glen.

But now the honours of thy course are past,
For what of earthly happiness may last!
Although in modern drawing-room, a board
May fragrant tea from menial hands afford,
Which, poured in dull obscurity hath been,
From pot of vulgar ware, in nook unseen,
And pass in hasty rounds our eyes before,
Thou in thy graceful state art seen no more.
And what the changeful fleeting crowd, who sip
The unhonoured beverage with contemptuous lip,
Enjoy amidst the tangled, giddy maze,
Their languid eye—their listless air betrays.
What though at times we see a youthful fair
By white clothed board her watery drug prepare,
At further corner of a noisy room,
Where only casual stragglers deign to come,
Like tavern's busy bar-maid; still I say,
The honours of thy course are passed away.

Again hath auctioneer thy value praised,
Again have rival bidders on thee gazed,
But not the gay, the young, the fair, I trow!
No; sober connoisseurs, with wrinkled brow
And spectacles on nose, thy parts inspect,
And by grave rules approve thee or reject.
For all the bliss which china charms afford,

My lady now has ceded to her lord.
And wisely too does she forego the prize,
Since modern pin-money will scarce suffice
For all the trimmings, flounces, beads and lace,
The thousand needful things that needs must grace
Her daily changed attire.—And now on shelf
Of china closet placed, a cheerless elf,
Like moody statesman in his rural den,
From power dismissed—like prosperous citizen,
From shop or change set free—untoward bliss!
Thou rest'st in most ignoble uselessness.

ROBERT LOCHORE
(1762–1852)

━━

BORN in Lanarkshire, Robert Lochore ran a successful shoemaking business in Glasgow, and undertook various philanthropic schemes there. A long-term lover of literature, Lochore befriended Burns, for whom he wrote an elegiac pastoral titled *Patie and Ralph* (1797). In around 1815 Lochore published, anonymously, *Tales in Rhyme, and Minor Pieces; in the Scottish Dialect*. For a time, in about 1817, he edited the *Kilmarnock Mirror*. And he frequently contributed to local periodicals. Dying decades later, Lochore left unpublished an autobiography and various tales and poems, with no clear instructions for what might be done with them. Lochore was a talented songwriter in his own right, but readers seem to have favoured his little pamphlets, particularly in the west of Scotland.

━━

'Marriage and the Care o't'

The Poets and Poetry of Scotland: From the Earliest to the Present Time (London: Blackie & Son, 1876).

> Quoth Rab to Kate, My sonsy dear,
> I've wooed ye mair than ha'f a year,
> An' gif ye'd tak' me ne'er cou'd speer
>   Wi' blateness, an' the care o't.
> Now to the point: sincere I'm wi't,
> Will ye be my ha'f marrow, sweet?
> Shake hands, an' say a bargain be't,
>   An' think na on the care o't.
>
> Na, na, quo' Kate, I winna wed,
> O' sic a snare I'll aye be redd;
> How mony thoughtless are misled
>   By marriage an' the care o't.
> A single life's a life o' glee,

A wife ne'er think to mak' o' me,
Frae toil an' sorrow I'se keep free,
   An' a' the dools an' care o't.

Weel, weel, said Robin, in reply,
Ye ne'er again shall me deny;
Ye may a toothless maiden die
   For me, I'll tak' nae care o't.
Fareweel for ever, aff I hie;
Sae took his leave without a sigh.
Oh! stop, quo' she, I'm yours; I'll try
   The married life an' care o't.

Rab wheel'd about, to Kate cam' back,
And gae her mou' a hearty smack,
Syne lengthen't out a luvin' crack
   'Bout marriage an' the care o't.
Though as she thought she didna speak,
Ah' looket unco mim an' meek,
Yet blythe was she wi' Rab to cleek
   In marriage, wi' the care o't.

JAMES GRAHAME
(1765–1811)

━━

BORN and educated in Glasgow, James Grahame went in 1784 to Edinburgh, where he qualified as Writer to the Signet, and subsequently for the Scottish bar. But his preference had always been for the Church. At the age of forty-four he took Anglican orders. His collections of literature include *Mary Queen of Scots* (1801), *The Sabbath* (1804), *British Georgics* (1804), *The Birds of Scotland* (1806), and *Poems on the Abolition of the Slave Trade* (1810). At the end of his life, Grahame received a derogatory notice in Byron's *English Bards and Scotch Reviewers* (1809), where the 'Sabbath Bard' is described as mangling prose and writing uninspiring verse.

━━

'To a Redbreast, that Flew in at my Window'

The Poems of James Grahame, John Logan, and William Falconer (Edinburgh: John Anderson; London: T. Tegg, and Simpkin & Marshall, 1823).

> From snowy plains, and icy sprays,
> From moonless nights, and sunless days,
> Welcome, poor bird! I'll cherish thee;
> I love thee, for thou trustest me.
> Thrice welcome, helpless, panting guest!
> Fondly I'll warm thee in my breast:—
> How quick thy little heart is beating!
> As if its brother flutterer greeting.
> Thou need'st not dread a captive's doom;
> No: freely flutter round my room;
> Perch on my lute's remaining string,
> And sweetly of sweet summer sing.
> That note, that summer note, I know;
> It wakes at once, and soothes my woe;
> I see those woods, I see that stream,

I see,—ah, still prolong the dream!
Still with thy song those scenes renew,
Though through my tears they reach my view.
     No more now, at my lonely meal,
While thou art by, alone I'll feel;
For soon, devoid of all distrust,
Thou'lt nibbling share my humble crust;
Or on my finger, pert and spruce,
Thou'lt learn to sip the sparkling juice;
And when (our short collation o'er)
Some favourite volume I explore,
Be't work of poet or of sage,
Safe thou shalt hope across the page;
Uncheck'd, shalt flit o'er Virgil's groves,
Or flutter 'mid Tibulius' loves.
Thus, heedless of the raving blast,
Thou'lt dwell with me till winter's past;
And when the primrose tells 'tis spring,
And when the thrush begins to sing,
Soon as I hear the woodland song,
Freed, thou shalt join the vocal throng.

GAVIN TURNBULL
(1765–1816)

━━

By his own claim, the poet and actor Gavin Turnbull was born in one of the border counties washed by the Tweed. As a young man he encountered vernacular poetry in the alehouse where his father, known as Tammy Turnbull, had a reputation for carousing. After brief schooling, Turnbull was set to weaving carpets for the firm of Gregory and Thomson in Kilmarnock; he slept on straw in an unfurnished garret while composing songs and studying the English poets. Turnbull later moved to Glasgow, where *Poetical Essays* was published in 1788. In 1793, a prominent correspondent, Robert Burns, sought to boost Turnbull's career by placing some of his songs with the publisher George Thomson—he was unsuccessful. However, in the following year, *Poems, by Gavin Turnbull, Comedian* (1794) appeared in print. Turnbull probably emigrated to America shortly afterwards, certainly before 1798, when he was mentioned in Alexander Campbell's *Introduction to the History of Poetry in Scotland*. By 1799 Turnbull had settled in South Carolina, where he contributed poems to the local newspapers and acted on the stage until his death in 1816.

━━

'To a Taylor, with Cloth for a New Suit'

Poetical Essays (Glasgow: David Niven, 1788).

> *Braid claith lends fowk an unco heeze,*
> *Makes mony kail-worms butterflies,*
> *Gi'es mony a Doctor his degrees*
> *For little skaith;*
> *In short ye may be what ye please*
> *Wi' good braid claith.*
>
> FERGUSSON

A Poet, tatter'd and forlorn,
Whase coat and breeks are sadly torn,

Wha lately sue'd for aid divine,
Now, Taylor, maun apply for thine;
Soliciting thy useful art,
Its needy succour to impart.
Ance manners could compleat a man,
But now the Taylor only can.

O Taylor, this is true, I ween,
As I've by sad experience seen,
Whatever talents we possess,
Are a' inferior to our dress;
A ragged Bard, however gabby;
Will ay be counted dull and shabby;
And since my coat and breeks turn'd duddy,
I hae been scorn'd by ilka body.

But trust me, Taylor, soon ye'll see
An unco, sudden change on me;
My friends will ken me ance again,
And some what kent na me short syne,
Will my acquaintance strive to gain,
And ca' my dullest verses fine.

See here's the claith, come, cut it out,
A remnant maun be sav'd, nae doubt,
Auld Nick can never want his due,
And will get baith the piece and you;
Then ply your nimble han's wi' speed,
Rattle your sheers and wax your thread,
And mak the utmost haste you can,
To rig me out a gentleman:
If you with these demands comply,
Then, Stitch, your name shall never die.

'Epistle to a Black-Smith'

Dear Sir, if my unnotic'd name,
Not yet proclaim'd by trump of fame,
Has reach'd your lugs, then swith attend,
This essay of a Bard unkend.
An honest man, lang may he thrive,
(And ilka honest man alive)

As we were wheeling round the bicker,
Tald me that he was unco sicker
A' this braid shire, and other three,
Contain'd na sic a chiel as thee;
That ye, tho' thumpin at the study,
Cou'd mak a verse on ony body,
In nipping, slie, satiric stile,
Wi' teeth as sharp as ony file.

　　Bedeen, I gat upo' my shanks,
And gae the carle routh o' thanks,
And sware an aith, e'en b' my sang,
"His metal I shall try e'er lang;
And then I'll tell ye gif the chiel
Be useless ir'n or temper'd steel."

　　It shaws I hae but little gumption,
Tho' no way scanty o' presumption,
To bourd wi' ane of sic engine,
And parts sae far exceeding mine;
For, a' that ken ye can declare,
Your match is scarce in ony where,
But my impatience may excuse me,
Lest ye should for a dult abuse me.

　　O wad my scanty purse but spare,
That I might tak a jaunt to Ayr,
Ae night wi' thee to sing and roar,
And set auld care ahint the door;
Then we shou'd hae a merry bout,
And no sit dumb nor yet cast out.

　　But, lest that we shou'd ne'er forgether,
To get a crack wi' ane anither,
My earnest prayer ay shall be,
For routh o' coals, and ir'n to thee;
That ye may lang be hale and canty,
And ding that cursed carle *want* ay;
That ye may ne'er be scant o' brass,
To synd the spark that's i' yer hause;
That, as ye blaw your smithy fire,
Apollo may your wit inspire,
To gar your easy flowing rhyme,
Just like alternate hammers chime;
And, that your mind be ne'er perplex'd,

But firm as ony anvil fix'd;
That, as your gauds of ir'n ye bow,
Your enemies may yield to you;
May, by the fatal sisters three,
Thy chain of life extended be,
Till unto langest life thy dust,
Stand proof against the teeth of rust;
And, when grim Death, wi' fatal dart,
Shall gar thy saul and body part,
May this thy Epitaph be made,
"Here Vulcan lies, a matchless Blade."

ANNE BANNERMAN
(1765–1829)

THE Edinburgh-born poet Anne Bannerman was a highly esteemed member of a literary circle that also included John Leyden, Thomas Campbell, and Robert Anderson. In the 1790s Bannerman began her career by publishing a range of pieces, pseudonymously, in the *Monthly Magazine*, the *Poetical Register*, and the *Edinburgh Magazine*, the latter of which was edited by her greatest advocate, Anderson. Bannerman's first volume of *Poems* (1800) contains odes, sonnets, translations from Petrarch, and a series of pieces based on *The Sorrows of Young Werther* by Goethe. Introducing her Wertherian sonnets, Bannerman acknowledges a debt to Joanna Baillie's theory of dramatic composition, namely, a unifying focus on a passion. Bannerman's second volume, *Tales of Superstition and Chivalry* (1802), published anonymously, comprises ten Gothic ballads. The deaths of her mother and brother left the poet without any reliable source of income. Reluctantly, she agreed to publish by subscription, thereby freeing up funds up front. However, *Poems: A New Edition* (1807) sold poorly.

'The Dark Ladie'

Poems: A New Edition (Edinburgh: Mundell, Doig & Stevenson, 1807).

> The knights return'd from Holy Land,
> Sir Guyon led the armed train;
> And to his castle, on the sea,
> He welcom'd them again.
>
> He welcom'd them with soldier glee,
> And sought to charm away their toil;
> But none, on Guyon's clouded face,
> Had ever seen a smile!

And, as the hour of eve drew on,
That clouded face more dark became,
No burst of mirth could overpow'r
The shiverings of his frame;

And often to the banner'd door,
His straining eyes, unbidden, turn'd;
Above, around, they glanced wild,
But ever there return'd.

At every pause, all breathless then,
And pale as death, he bent his ear,
Tho' not a sound the silence broke,
He seemed still to hear!

And when the feast was spread, and all
The guests, assembled, were at meat,
There pass'd them by, with measur'd step,
And took the upper seat,
A Ladie, clad in ghastly white,
And veiled to the feet:

She spoke not when she enter'd there;
She spoke not when the feast was done;
And every knight in chill amaze,
Survey'd her one by one:

For thro' the foldings of her veil,
Her long black veil that swept the ground,
A light was seen to dart from eyes
That mortal never own'd.

And then the knights on Guyon turn'd
Their fixed gaze, and shudder'd now;
For smother'd fury seem'd to bring
The dew-drops on his brow.

But, from the Ladie in the veil,
Their eyes they could not long withdraw,
And when they tried to speak, that glare
Still kept them mute with awe!

Each wish'd to rouse his failing heart,
Yet look'd and trembled all, the while;

All, till the midnight clock had toll'd
Its summons from the southern aisle.

And when the last dull stroke had rung
And left behind its deep'ning knell,
The Ladie rose, and fill'd with wine,
Fill'd to the brim, the sparkling shell.

And to the alarmed guests she turn'd,
No breath was heard, no voice, no sound,
And in a tone, so deadly deep,
She pledg'd them all around,
That in their hearts, and thro' their limbs,
No pulses could be found.

And, when their senses back return'd,
They gaz'd upon the steps of stone
On which the Dark Ladie had stood,
They gaz'd—but she was gone!—

Then Guyon rose,—and ah! to rest,
When every weary knight was led,
After what they had seen and heard,
What wonder, slumber fled!

For, often as they turn'd to rest,
And sleep press'd down each heavy eye,
Before them, in her black veil wrapt,
They saw the Dark Ladie.

And then the voice, the tone that stopt
Thro' all their limbs the rushing blood;
The cup which she had fill'd with wine,
The steps on which she stood.

The sound, the tone,—no human voice
Could ever reach that echo deep;
And, ever as they turn'd to rest,
It roused them from sleep!—

The morning dawns—the knights are met,
And seated in the arched hall,
And some were loud, and some spoke low,
But Huart none at all!

"Dost not remember, well (cries one),
When wide the sacred banners flew,
And when, beneath the blessed Cross,
The infidels we slew."

"This same Sir Guyon, erst so brave,
In fight, who ever led the van,
Soon as the Sepulchre he saw,
Grew pale and trembled then?"

"And as the kneeling knights ador'd,
And wept around the holy place,
O God! I've seen the big drops burst
For hours upon his face!"

"And when I nam'd the blessed name,
His face became as livid clay,
And, on his foamy lips, the sounds,
Unutter'd, died away!"

"But O! that Ladie! (Huart cries),—
That Ladie, with the long black veil,
This morn I heard!—I hear it still,
The lamentable tale!"

"I hear the hoary-headed man,
I kept him till the morning dawn,
For five unbroken hours he talk'd,
With me they were as one!"

"He told me he had lived long
Within this castle, on the sea;
But peace, O Heaven! he never had,
Since he saw the Dark Ladie!"

" 'Twas chill, he said, a hazy night,
Just as the light began to fail,
Sir Guyon came and brought with him
The Ladie in the veil:"

"Yes! to this castle on the sea,
The wild surge dashing on its base,
He brought her in that frightful veil
That ever hides her face."

"And many a time, he said, he tried
That ne'er–uncover'd face to see:
At eve and morn, at noon and night;
But still it could not be!"

"Till once! but O! that glaring eye,
It dried the life–blood, working here!
And when he turn'd to look again,
The Ladie was not near!"

"But, sometimes, thro' her curtain'd tower,
A strange uncolour'd light was seen,
And something, of unearthly hue,
Still passed on between:"

"And then aloof its clasped hands
Were wrung, and tossed to and fro!
And sounds came forth, dull, deep, and wild,
And O! how deadly slow!"

"He told me that, at last, he heard
Some story, how this poor Ladie
Had left, alas! her husband's home
With this dread knight to flee:"

"And how her sinking heart recoil'd,
And how her throbbing bosom beat,
And how sensation almost left
Her cold convulsed feet:"

"And how she clasp'd her little son,
Before she tore herself away;
And how she turn'd again to bless
The cradle where he lay."

"But where Sir Guyon took her then,
Ah none could ever hear or know,
Or, why, beneath that long black veil,
Her wild eyes sparkle so."

"Or whence those deep unearthly tones,
That human bosom never own'd;
Or why, it cannot be remov'd,
That folded veil that sweeps the ground?"

'Exile'

Ye hills of my country, soft fading in blue,
The seats of my childhood, for ever adieu!
Yet not for a brighter, your skies I resign,
When my wand'ring footsteps revisit the Rhine:
But sacred to me is the roar of the wave,
That mingles its tide with the blood of the brave;
Where the blasts of the trumpets for battle combine,
And the heart was laid low that gave rapture to mine.

Ye scenes of remembrance that sorrow beguil'd
Your uplands I leave for the desolate wild;
For Nature is nought to the eye of despair
But the image of hopes that have vanish'd in air.
Again ye fair blossoms of flower and of tree,
Ye shall bloom to the morn, tho' ye bloom not for me;
Again your lone wood-paths that wind by the stream,
Be the haunt of the lover—to hope—and to dream.

But never to me shall the summer renew
The bowers where the days of my happiness flew;
Where my soul found her partner, and thought to bestow
The colours of heaven on the dwellings of woe!
Too faithful recorders of times that are past,
The Eden of Love that was ever to last!
Once more may soft accents your wild echoes fill,
And the young and the happy be worshippers still.

To me ye are lost!—but your summits of green
Shall charm thro' the distance of many a scene;
In woe, and in wandering, and deserts return,
Like the soul of the dead to the perishing urn!
Ye hills of my country! farewel evermore,
As I cleave the dark waves of your rock-rugged shore,
And ask of the hovering gale if it come
From the oak-towering woods on the mountains of home.

'To Pain'

Hail! fiercest herald of a Power,
  Whose wide controul the earth obeys!

I call thee, at this fearful hour;
   To thee my feeble voice I raise.
Say, does compassion never glow
Within thy soul, and bid thee know
   The pangs with which thou fir'st the breast?
Or dost thou never, never mourn,
To plant so deep the hidden thorn,
   Forbidding aid, and blasting rest?

Think'st thou my wavering fickle mind
   Requires so much, to break her chain?
Alas! what earthly joys can bind
   The wretch, who sees thy figure, Pain!
For ever fleet before his eyes;
For him, no glories gild the skies;
   No beauties shine in Nature's bound;
In vain with verdure glows the spring,
If, from within, thy gnawing sting
   Bid only demons scowl around.

Too sure, I feel, in every vein,
   With thee soft Pity ne'er can dwell.
Shall pleasure never smile again,
   Or health thro' ev'ry channel swell?
Yes! tho' thy hand hath crush'd the rose
Before its prime, another blows,
   Whose blooms thy breath can ne'er destroy;
Say, can thy keen and cruel chains
Corrode, where bliss seraphic reigns,
   Where all is peace, and all is joy.

Then, wherefore sighs my fearful heart,
   And trembles thus my tottering frame?
Alas! I feel thy deadly dart,
   More potent far than Fancy's flame:
I bend, grim tyrant! at thy throne;
But spare, ah! spare that sullen frown,
   Relax the horrors of thy brow!
O! lead me, with a softer hand,
And lo! I come at thy command,
   And, unrepining, follow through.

HELEN D'ARCY STEWART
(1765–1838)

━━

HELEN D'ARCY STEWART (*née* Cranstoun) was an accomplished and well-connected poet who became an influential literary hostess in Edinburgh. Stewart's own literary reputation rests on her understated and largely sentimental poems and ballads. Some of her poems were printed in the 1792 volume of Johnson's *Scots Musical Museum*. After 1809, Stewart withdrew from her active role in Edinburgh society, following the death of her only son and in consideration of the failing health of her husband. Stewart did not sign her work but her contributions as a poet were sufficiently well known for the *Gentleman's Magazine* to accord her a leading rank in the pantheon of Scottish songwriters in their brief obituary for her.

━━

'The Tears I Shed'

The Modern Scottish Minstrel; or, The Songs of Scotland of the Past Half Century, ed. Charles Rogers, 6 vols (Edinburgh: Adam & Charles Black, 1855).

(Tune: "Ianthe the Lovely")

The tears I shed must ever fall:
    I mourn not for an absent swain;
For thoughts may past delights recall,
    And parted lovers meet again.
I weep not for the silent dead:
    Their toils are past, their sorrows o'er;
And those they loved their steps shall tread,
    And death shall join to part no more.

Though boundless oceans roll'd between,
    If certain that his heart is near,
A conscious transport glads each scene,

Soft is the sigh and sweet the tear.
E'en when by death's cold hand removed,
    We mourn the tenant of the tomb,
To think that e'en in death he loved,
    Can gild the horrors of the gloom.

But bitter, bitter are the tears
    Of her who slighted love bewails;
No hope her dreary prospect cheers,
    No pleasing melancholy hails.
Hers are the pangs of wounded pride,
    Of blasted hope, of wither'd joy;
The flattering veil is rent aside,
    The flame of love burns to destroy.

In vain does memory renew
    The hours once tinged in transport's dye;
The sad reverse soon starts to view,
    And turns the past to agony.
E'en time itself despairs to cure
    Those pangs to every feeling due:
Ungenerous youth! thy boast how poor,
    To win a heart, and break it too!

No cold approach, no alter'd mien,
    Just what would make suspicion start;
No pause the dire extremes between—
    He made me blest, and broke my heart:
From hope, the wretched's anchor, torn,
    Neglected and neglecting all;
Friendless, forsaken, and forlorn,
    The tear I shed must ever fall.

CAROLINA OLIPHANT, LADY NAIRNE
(1766–1845)

━━

THE songwriter Carolina Oliphant, Lady Nairne grew up in a prominent Jacobite household in Gask, Perthshire. Many of her songs were set to traditional tunes, including 'The Land o' the Leal', which was written for her friend Mary Erskine (Mrs Campbell Colquhoun), on the death of her first child in 1797. As Oliphant composed anonymously, the true extent of her corpus, and its links with a vibrant oral tradition in the region, remains unclear. Her songs were regularly anthologized in the nineteenth century; the following pieces come from an ornate London edition of her life and works published a little over one hundred years after her birth.

━━

'The Women are a' gane wud'

Life and Songs of the Baroness Nairne, with a Memoir and Poems of Caroline Oliphant the Younger, ed. Charles Rogers (London: Charles Griffin and Co., 1869).

(Air: "The Women are a' gane wud")

The women are a' gane wud!
   Oh, that he had bidden awa'!
He's turn'd their heads, the lad;
   And ruin will bring on us a'.
I aye was a peaceable man,
   My wife she did doucely behave;
But noo, do a' that I can,
   She's just as wild as the lave.

My wife noo wears the *cockade*,
   Tho' she kens 'tis the thing that I hate;
There's ane, too, *preen'd* on her maid,
   An' baith will tak' their ain gate.
The wild Hieland lads as they pass,
   The yetts wide open do flee;

They eat the very house bare,
   And nae leave's speer'd o' me.

I've lived a' my days in the Strath,
   Now Tories infest me at hame,
And though I take nae side at a',
   Baith sides will gi'e me the blame.
The senseless creatures ne'er think
   What ill the lad wad bring back;
The Pope we'll hae, and his hounds,
   And a' the rest o' his pack.

'Caller Herrin''

Wha'll buy my caller herrin'?
They're bonnie fish and halesome farin';
Wha'll buy my caller herrin',
   New drawn frae the Forth?

When ye were sleepin' on your pillows,
Dream'd ye aught o' our puir fellows,
Darkling as they fac'd the billows,
A' to fill the woven willows?
   Buy my caller herrin',
   New drawn frae the Forth.

Wha'll buy my caller herrin'?
They're no brought here without brave daring;
Buy my caller herrin',
Haul'd through wind and rain.
   Wha'll buy my caller herrin'? &c.

Wha'll buy my caller herrin'?
Oh, ye may ca' them vulgar farin',
Wives and mithers, maist despairing,
Ca' them lives o' men.
   Wha'll buy my caller herrin'? &c.

When the creel o' herrin' passes,
Ladies, clad in silks and laces,
Gather in their braw pelisses,
Cast their heads and screw their faces.
   Wha'll buy my caller herrin'? &c.

Caller herrin's no got lightlie,
Ye can trip the spring fu' tightlie,
Spite o' tauntin', flauntin', flingin',
Gow had set you a' a-singing
      Wha'll buy my caller herrin'? &c.

Neebour wives, now tent my tellin':
When the bonnie fish ye're sellin',
At ae word be in yere dealin'—
Truth will stand when a' thin's failin'.

Wha'll buy my caller herrin'?
They're bonnie fish and halesome farin';
Wha'll buy my caller herrin',
      New drawn frae the Forth?

'The Laird o' Cockpen'

(Air: "When she cam' ben, she bobbit")

The laird o' Cockpen, he's proud an' he's great,
His mind is ta'en up wi' the things o' the State;
He wanted a wife, his braw house to keep,
But favour wi' wooin' was fashious to seek.

Down by the dyke-side a lady did dwell,
At his table head he thocht she'd look well,
McClish's ae dochter o' Clavers-ha' Lee,
A penniless lass wi' a lang pedigree.

His wig was weel pouther'd and as gude as new,
His waistcoat was white, his coat it was blue;
He put on a ring, a sword, and cock'd hat,
And wha could refuse the laird wi' a' that?

He took the grey mare, and rade cannily,
An' rapp'd at the yett o' Clavers-ha' Lee;
"Gae tell Mistress Jean to come speedily ben,—
She's wanted to speak to the laird o' Cockpen."

Mistress Jean she was makin' the elder-flower wine;
"An' what brings the laird at sic a like time?"
She put aff her apron, and on her silk gown,
Her mutch wi' red ribbons, and gaed awa' down.

An' when she cam' ben, he bowed fu' low,
An' what was his errand he soon let her know;
Amazed was the laird when the lady said "Na,"
And wi' a laigh curtsie she turned awa'.

Dumfounder'd was he, nae sigh did he gie,
He mounted his mare—he rade cannily;
An' aften he thought, as he gaed through the glen,
She's daft to refuse the laird o' Cockpen.

'The Land o' the Leal'

(Air: "Hey tutti taiti")

I'm wearin' awa', John
Like snaw-wreaths in thaw, John,
I'm wearin' awa'
    To the land o' the leal.
There 's nae sorrow there, John,
There 's neither cauld nor care, John,
The day is aye fair
    In the land o' the leal.

Our bonnie bairn 's there, John,
She was baith gude and fair, John,
And oh! we grudged her sair
    To the land o' the leal.
But sorrow's sel' wears past, John,
And joy 's a-coming fast, John,
The joy that 's aye to last
    In the land o' the leal.

Sae dear 's the joy was bought, John,
Sae free the battle fought, John,
That sinfu' man e'er brought
    To the land o' the leal.
Oh! dry your glistening e'e, John,
My saul langs to be free, John,
And angels beckon me
    To the land o' the leal.

Oh! haud ye leal and true, John,
Your day it's wearin' through, John,
And I'll welcome you

To the land o' the leal.
Now fare-ye-weel, my ain John,
This warld's cares are vain, John,
We'll meet, and we'll be fain,
    In the land o' the leal.

'Will ye no come back again?'

Bonnie Charlie's now awa',
    Safely owre the friendly main;
Mony a heart will break in twa,
    Should he ne'er come back again.
        Will ye no come back again?
        Will ye no come back again?
        Better lo'ed ye canna be,
        Will ye no come back again?

Ye trusted in your Hieland men,
    They trusted you, dear Charlie;
They kent you hiding in the glen,
    Your cleadin' was but barely.
        Will ye no, &c.

English bribes were a' in vain;
    An' e'en tho' puirer we may be,
Siller canna buy the heart
    That beats aye for thine and thee.
        Will ye no, &c.

We watched thee in the gloamin' hour,
    We watched thee in the mornin' grey;
Tho' thirty thousand pounds they'd gi'e,
    Oh there is nane that wad betray.
        Will ye no, &c.

Sweet's the laverock's note and lang,
    Lilting wildly up the glen;
But aye to me he sings ae sang,—
    Will ye no come back again?
        Will ye no come back again?
        Will ye no come back again?
        Better lo'ed ye canna be,
        Will ye no come back again?

EBENEZER PICKEN
(1769–1816)

THE poet Ebenezer Picken was born in Paisley. After elementary education there, he studied at the University of Glasgow. His *Poems and
Epistles, Mostly in the Scottish Dialect* (1788) appeared while he was still
a teenager. At the Pantheon in Edinburgh he publicly debated with his
friend Alexander Wilson, with a crowd of about five hundred patrons,
on the topic of who had done more to honour Scottish poetry: Allan
Ramsay or Robert Fergusson? Wilson defended Fergusson, Picken
chose Ramsay. The debate, in verse essays, turned into a joint pamphlet,
*The Laurel Disputed, or, The Merits of Allan Ramsay and Robert Fergusson
Contrasted* (1791). After that, Picken took on teaching appointments in
Falkirk and Carron, before becoming a merchant in Edinburgh with
limited success. In 1813 appeared two volumes of his *Miscellaneous
Poems, Songs, &c.*, which included greatly altered versions of the
juvenilia.

'Nappy Ale'

Miscellaneous Poems, Songs, &c. Partly in the Scottish Dialect, 2 vols
(Edinburgh: James Sawers; Glasgow: Brash & Reid; Paisley: Crighton;
London: R. Ogle, 1813).

> Has some kind Muse my breast inspir'd,
> Wi' prayer sae lang an' sair desir'd;
> Or has some wily elf been hir'd
> To mak' me smirkie?
> Na! nae sic trash ye'r breast has fir'd,—
> It's Ale, my Birkie.
>
> Come a' ye wordy helps o' sang,
> Ye Muses Nine, a kindly gang,
> O gar ideas rise, ding dang,
> At gleesome rate,

An' I sal let ye see, or lang,
        Ise no be blate.

Help me to sing the choicest sap
That ever ream'd in glass or cap,
The kindly, sweet, refreshin' Nap,
        That winna fail
To close his e'en that taks a drap
        O' Nappy Ale.

Sound on the cod his pow he sets,
An' quite forleets baith care an' debts,
What wi' thy pith his weason wets,
        An' tak's his Ma't in,
While mony a bonny dream he gets
        O' thy creatin'.

The droukin' rain may fluid the stack,
An' fa' in pailfu's thro' the thack,
Win's roar till ance the kaibers crack,
        An' barn doors rattle,
He's bravely snorin' on his back,
        An' scogs the battle.

Leese me upon the reamin' fare,
Can send Mishap ae hour frae care:
The wretch on warl's dirt sae gair,
        As banns thy brewin',
His dreams are ay o' barn-yairds bare,
        An' scenes o' ruin.

May tempest ne'er thy harvest bauk,
Nor blight e'er blast thee on the stauk,
Our E'enin' club will never crauk,
        While thou's the cap in,
Nor Ale-wife want the ready cauk
        To score the chappin.

By thee the gleefu' carles a'
Float ay their fashous cares awa;
Nae bilts, nor bruises cou'd befa'
        Their head or tail,
That ever can survive a jaw
        O' Nappy Ale.

Foul fa' the chield wha thinks't a faut
To meddle wi' the juice o' maut,
An' can wi' shameless snout misca't;
            The saucy tyke,
Twad be a pity e'er he saw't,
            Be what he like.

O' aughtpence drink! thou saul o' grain,
Thou maks the Bardie blyth an' fain:
Atween us twa', as we're our lane,
            Tak' this frae me,
O' a' the Nine, the foul a ane,
            Inspires like thee.

The snail–slaw hours thou can beguile,
On Sorrow's cheek can raise a smile:
Whan birkies bourd wi' thee a while,
            I ken't for certain,
Round the red ingle, rank an' file,
            They'd ne'er be partin'.

Weel cronies like thy sonsy face,
For thou's possest o' mony a grace,
In ilk kind howf, whan they're in case
            To frolic wi' thee,
Thou disna want the warmest place
            Their wame can gie thee.

Whan care cauld E'enins wad hae cost them,
An' on a sea o' hardships toss'd them,
While o' thy presence they cou'd boast them,
            To clear their noddle,
They didna care what cankers cross'd them
            Ae single bodle.

Yet tho' we bend thee sweetly down,
Let ne'er thy pith our Reason drown;
Whan e'er the house mints to rin roun',
            There let us stap,
Nor taste, tho' 't war to save the crown
            Anither drap,

Than, what we've a spare hour we'll gie't thee,
Wi' praises on thy pith we'll greet thee,

O'er ilka ither browst we'll beet thee,
       Nor hae't to say
A blush wad tinge our cheek to meet thee,
       Be't whar it may.

Let Misers scrape the walth o' China,
I dinna care a yard o' skeenie,
Gie me just fowth for weans, an' Binie,
       O' guid Scots kail,
An' ay the tither yellow Guinea,
       An' Nappy Ale.

JAMES NICOL
(1769–1819)

———

THE Church of Scotland minister and poet James Nicol was born in
Innerleithen, Peeblesshire. He was educated at the parish school before
going on to the University of Edinburgh. After tutoring for several
families, he was licensed to preach by the presbytery of Peebles. Shortly
after that he became the minister of Traquair. Nicol attracted attention
with the publication of *Poems, Chiefly in the Scottish Dialect* (1805).
'Blaw Saftly, Ye Breezes' regularly appeared in Scottish anthologies,
such as John Struthers's *The Harp of Caledonia* (1821). The anthologist
Charles Rogers, from whose *Modern Scottish Minstrel* (1855) the following text comes, rated Nicol highly, though he criticized what he per-
ceived to be excessive imitation of Burns.

———

'Blaw Saftly, Ye Breezes'

*The Modern Scottish Minstrel; or, The Songs of Scotland of the Past Half
Century*, ed. Charles Rogers, 6 vols (Edinburgh: Adam & Charles
Black, 1855).

Blaw saftly, ye breezes, ye streams, smoothly murmur,
　　Ye sweet-scented blossoms, deck every green tree;
'Mong your wild scatter'd flow'rets aft wanders my charmer,
　　The sweet lovely lass wi' the black rollin' e'e.
For pensive I ponder, and languishin' wander,
　　Far frae the sweet rosebud on Quair's windin' stream!

Why, Heaven, wring my heart wi' the hard heart o' anguish?
　　Why torture my bosom 'tween hope and despair?
When absent frae Nancy, I ever maun languish!—
　　That dear angel smile, shall it charm me nae mair?
Since here life 's a desert, an' pleasure 's a dream,
Bear me swift to those banks which are ever my theme,
　　Where, mild as the mornin' at simmer's returnin',
Blooms the sweet lovely rosebud on Quair's windin' stream.

ALASTAIR MACFHIONGHAIN / ALEXANDER MACKINNON

(1770–1814)

━━━

CORPORAL ALEXANDER MACKINNON was born in Morar. He enlisted in the 92nd Regiment (the Gordon Highlanders) when it was raised in 1794. On 11 August 1799 they embarked for Holland as part of a joint British–Russian expedition against the French and Dutch. So began MacKinnon's 'Battle of Holland', usually known as the Battle of Alkmaar or Egmond. It went on for several hours and was fought by both sides with great tenacity. Effectively the battle was a draw, but the allied advance stuttered to a halt amidst bad weather, flooded polders and inadequate provisions. Following the Battle of Castricum (also near Alkmaar) on 6 October the expedition was abandoned, and by 19 November the allies had evacuated the peninsula. MacKinnon was unscathed, but was severely wounded two years later at Alexandria. Transferred to a hospital ship and discharged with a pension, he joined the 6th Royal Veteran Battalion, in which he served for the rest of his life. He died at Fort William in 1814 and was interred with military honours.

━━━

'Blàr na h-Òlaind'

Sar-Obair nam Bard Gaelach; or, The Beauties of Gaelic Poetry, and Lives of the Highland Bards, ed. John MacKenzie, 4th edn (Edinburgh: Maclachlan & Stewart, 1877).

> Air mìos deireannach an fhoghair,
>   An dara là, gur math mo chuimhne,
> Ghluais na Breatannaich on fhaiche
>   Dh'ionnsaigh tachairt ris na naimhdean.
> Thug Eabarcrombaidh taobh na mara
>   Dhiubh le chanain 's mi gan cluinntinn.
> Bha fòirne aig Mùr gu daingeann
>   Cumail aingil ris na Fraingich.

Thriall Eabarcombaidh 's Mùr na féile
  Le'n laoich euchdach chun a' bhatailt.
Tharraing iad gu h-eòlach treubhach
  Luchd na Beurla ri uchd catha.
Nuair a dhlùth na h-airm ri chéile
  Dhubhadh na speuran le'n deathaich
'S bu lìonmhor fear a bha san éisteachd
  Nach do ghluais leis fhéin an athoidhch.

Dh'fhàg iad sinne mar a b' annsa
  Fo cheannardachd Mhorair Hunndaidh,
An t-òg smiorail fearail naimhdeil
  Nan teannadh ainneart gar n-ionnsaigh.
Le bhrataichean sìoda a' srannraich,
  Ri'n cuid chrann a' danns le mùiseig,
'S na fir a' togairt chun nam Frangach,
  B'iad mo rùn-s' a' chlann nach diùltadh.

Bha an leóghann colgarra gun ghealtachd
  Le mhìle fear sgairteil làmh ruinn,
An Camshronach garg on Earrachd
  Mar ursainn chatha sna blàraibh.
Dh'aontaich sinn mar aon sa bhatailt
  Le faobhar lann sgaiteach stàilinn.
Cha bu ghnìomh le'r laoich gun taise
  Fantainn air an ais san làmhach.

Bhrùchd na naimhdean le'n trom làdach
  Air muin chàich a' bàrcadh teine.
Nuair fhuair Sasannaich droch càradh
  Phill iad on àraich 'nar coinne.
Ghlaodh Eabarcrombaidh ri chuid àrmann:
  "Greasaibh na Gàidhil mu'n coinne
'S tionnda'idh iad an ruaig mar b' àbhaist,
  An dream ardanach neo-fhoilleil."

Greasad air an adhart san àraich
  Ghluais na saighdearan nach pillte
Mar iolairean guineach gun choibhneas
  Nach b' fhurasta chlaoidh le mìomhodh.
Thug iad sgrios orra mar bhoillsgeadh
  Dealanaich ri oidhche dhìlinn,

Ri sìor iomain romhp' nan naimhdean
  'S neul na fal' air rinn am pìcean.

Nuair a dh'ionndrainn a chuid chonnspann
  Morair Gordan o uchd buailte
'S a chual' iad gun robh e leòinte,
  Dh'ùraich iad le deòin an tuasaid.
Mar mhaoim de thuil nam beann mòra
  Brùchdadh o na neòil mu'r guaillibh
Lean iad an ruaig le cruaidh spòltadh
  Gu fuilteach, mòrbhuilleach, gruamach.

Bha Camshronaich an tùs a' chatha
  Air an losgadh mar an ciadna.
Leònadh an ceann-feadhna sgairteil
  Ri còmhrag bhatailteach a liath e.
B' eòlach a stiùireadh e an dearcag
  Fo na neòil nach taise na 'n t-iarann.
Mun chrom a' ghrian fo a cleòca taisgte
  Phàigh sinn air an ais na fiachan.

Ged bha na Rìoghalaich o Albainn,
  Na fir ainmeil, mheanmnach, phrìseil,
Fada bhuainn ri uair a' gharbhchath,
  Is buaidh a b' ainm dhaibh ri uchd mhìltean.
Ghreas iad air aghaidh gu colgail
  Nuair a chual' iad stoirm nam pìcean.
Mo chreach luchd nam breacan ballbhreac
  Bhith le lasair marbh 'nan sìneadh.

Tha na Frangaich math air teine
  Gus an teannar goirid uapa.
Sann mar sin a fhrois iad sinne
  Ré deich mionaidean na h-uarach.
Ach nuair fhuair ar laoich gun tioma
  Dhol an àite buille bhualadh,
Bha rinnean stàilinne biorach
  Sàthadh guineideach mu'n tuairmeas.

Gum b'i sin an tuairmeas smiorail,
  Cinnteach, amaiseach, gun dearmad,
Thug na leóghainn bhorba, nimheil,
  Bu cholgail sealladh fo'n armaibh

Ri sgiùrsadh naimhdean mar fhalaisg
    'S driùchdan fallais air gach calg dhiubh.
'S bha na Frangaich brùchdadh fala
    'S an cùl ri talamh anns a' ghainmhich.

Mar neòil fhuilteach air an riasladh
    Le gaoith a b' iargalta séideadh,
Ruith 'nam badaibh ceigeach liathghorm
    An déidh an cliathadh ás a-chéile,
Chìte na naimhdean gun riaghailt
    Teicheadh gu dian o uchd sreupa
'S iad a' leaghadh air am bialaibh
    Mar shneachd am fianais na gréine.

Ged a phill sinn o an dùthaich
    Cha do mhill sinn ar cliù an cruadal.
Bha sinn gach latha gan sgiùrsadh
    Mar chaoirich aig cù gan ruagadh.
Dh'ainneoin an cuid slòigh gun chunntas
    Tighinn on Fhraing as ùr gar bualadh,
Bu leisg ar gaisgich gu tionndadh
    Nuair a chord an Diùc ri'n uaislean.

Nuair a chuireadh am batailt seachad
    'S a dh'àirmheadh ar gaisgich threubhach,
Bha iomadh Gàidheal san deachamh
    Le meud am braise san t-sreupaig.
Fuil a' ruith air lotaibh frasach
    O luchd nam breacanan féilidh
'S i sìor thaomadh leis na glacan.
    'S truagh nach d'fhaod ar gaisgich éirigh.

'S bochd gun sian orra o luaidhe,
    O'n a bha iad cruaidh 'nan nàdar—
Fulangach a dhol san tuasaid,
    Guineideach nuair ghluaist' an ardan.
Cha robh math d'an nàmhaid gluasad
    Dh'iarraidh buaidh orra sna blàraibh.
Chaill iad air an tràigh seachd uairean
    Tuilleadh na bha bhuainn san àraich.

A-nis on chuir iad sinn do Shasann
    Ghabhail ar cairtealan geamhraidh

Far am faigh sinn leann am pailteas
    Ged tha mac-na-praisich gann oirnn,
Òlar leinn deoch-slàint' a' Mharcais,
    Ar gualann taice 's ar ceannard.
Tha sinn cho ullamh 's a b' ait leis
    Dhìon a bhrataichean o ainneart.

'The Battle of Holland' (translated by Ronald Black)

In the last month of autumn,
    The second day, well I remember,
The British marched from parade
    To engage the enemy.
Abercromby took the coast from them
    With his cannon in my hearing.
Moore had troops concentrating
    Close fire on the French.

Abercromby and generous Moore
    Marched their brave heroes to the fray.
They drew up, with courage and experience,
    The English speakers to the breast of battle.
When the two armies met
    The skies were blackened by their smoke
And many men that heard it
    Moved not by themselves when the night came.

They left us as was preferred
    Under Lord Huntly's command,
A young man who was tough, manly and combative
    Whenever action came towards us.
With his silken banners buzzing,
    Dancing menacingly on their standards,
And the men straining to get at the French,
    How I loved those lads who'd never refuse.

The fierce lion without cowardice
    With his thousand eager men was close by us,
Aggressive Cameron of Erracht
    Like a doorpost in the battlefields.

We joined as one to fight the fray
  With the edge of cutting blade of steel.
It was no task of our hardboiled lads
  To hold back when shooting began.

The enemy began with their heavy artillery
  Belching fire on top of the other side.
When some Englishmen got into a bad situation
  They retreated from the battlefield to meet us.
Abercromby shouted at his officers:
  "Move the Highlanders against them fast
And they'll stem the tide as they've always done,
  Proud and untreacherous as they are."

Swiftly forward in the battlefield
  Moved the unturnable soldiers
Like wounding eagles for unkindness
  Hard to defeat with discourtesy.
They attacked them like a flash
  Of lightning on a night of rain,
Steadily driving the foe before them
  With the hue of blood on their bayonet points.

When his fellow warriors missed
  Lord Gordon from the breast of battle
And they heard he was wounded,
  They vigorously renewed the attack.
Like a squall of rain in the high hills
  Bursting out of the clouds round our shoulders
They pursued the rout with a savage hacking
  That was bloody, hard-hitting and cruel.

Camerons in the front of the battle
  Were shot in the very same way.
Their energetic chief was wounded
  In a hand-to-hand fight that turned him grey.
Well did he aim that little grape
  That's as hard as any iron on earth.
Before the sun lay down snug beneath her cloak
  We had paid back all of our debts.

Although the Royals from Scotland,
  Those far-famed, spirited, estimable men,

Were far from us at the moment of battle,
    They'd a name for triumph when facing thousands.
Onwards they pressed in a battle-rage
    When they heard the rattle of arms.
I'm anguished at men wearing tartan plaids
    Being laid out dead by gunfire.

The French are good marksmen
    Till you get close up to them.
That's how they raked *us*
    For ten minutes as well.
But when our brave heroes got forward
    To where a blow could be struck,
There were sharp points of steel
    Thrusting woundingly towards them.

It was a brave onset,
    Certain, well-aimed, not neglectful,
That those wild, deadly lions made,
    Looking fierce behind their arms
As they scourged the foe like heather-fire
    With drops of sweat on all their bristles.
And the French were belching blood
    As they lay on their backs in the sand.

Like bloody clouds tormented
    By a wind whose blast was surly,
Running in ragged clusters of blue
    After being harrowed apart,
The enemy were seen in disarray
    Fleeing crazed from the battle-gap
And melting before them
    Like snow exposed to the sun.

Though we've withdrawn from the country
    We've not harmed our name for courage.
We scourged them every day
    Like sheep being chased by a dog.
Despite their countless reinforcements
    Coming fresh from France to hit us,
Our heroes were loth to turn round
    When the Duke made a pact with their leaders.

When the battle was fought and won
   And our brave heroes were counted,
Many a Gael was in the decimation,
   So great was their valour in the fight.
Blood flowed from prolific wounds
   Over men wearing kilted plaids
And steadily poured down the hollows.
   Sadly our warriors rose not up again.

Too bad they weren't charmed for lead,
   Since they were so tough by nature—
Hardy in entering the fray,
   Wounding when their pride was up.
Their foes could do themselves no good
   By trying to beat them in open fight.
They lost seven times more on the beach
   Than we left behind on the battlefield.

Now that they've sent us to England
   To take up our winter quarters
Where we'll get plenty of beer
   Though the son-of-the-still is in short supply,
We'll drink a toast to the Marquis,
   Our shoulder-support and our chief.
We're as ready as he could ask
   To defend his banners from attack.

JAMES HOGG

(1770–1835)

━━

BORN on a farm in Selkirkshire, James Hogg grew up amid remote
woods and a rich song culture. Working as a shepherd at Blackhouse
in the Yarrow valley, throughout his twenties, Hogg enjoyed free
access to a wide selection of books, and he read voraciously. He also
began to write poems, plays, and songs. These found a ready audience
in Ettrick, earning him the local nickname Jamie the Poeter. Hogg's
first book, *Scottish Pastorals* (1801), was published in Edinburgh, but
attracted little attention. He provided traditional ballads for Walter
Scott's *Minstrelsy of the Scottish Border* (1802–3); a friendship developed between the poets that was to last for the rest of their lives. With
Scott's encouragement two well-received books by Hogg appeared in
1807: *The Mountain Bard* and *The Shepherd's Guide*. Almost forty, in
1810, he pursued a literary career in Edinburgh. There, *The Forest
Minstrel* (1810) sold poorly. Having had earlier success with periodicals,
he launched his own: *The Spy*. It floundered—but it brought him to
the attention of the city's literati. Quickly running to multiple editions, *The Queen's Wake* (1813) finally established the Ettrick Shepherd
as a leading voice among Scottish Romantics. Two new volumes followed in 1816: *Mador of the Moor* and *The Poetic Mirror*. By 1822, the
marketplace was ready for his four-volume *Poetical Works*.

━━

The Queen's Wake *(1813)*, 'Kilmeny'

The Poetical Works of the Ettrick Shepherd, 5 vols (Glasgow: Blackie and
Son, 1838).

> Bonny Kilmeny gaed up the glen;
> But it wasna to meet Duneira's men,
> Nor the rosy monk of the isle to see,

For Kilmeny was pure as pure could be.
It was only to hear the yorlin sing,
And pu' the cress-flower round the spring;
The scarlet hypp and the hindberrye,
And the nut that hung frae the hazel tree;
For Kilmeny was pure as pure could be.
But lang may her minny look o'er the wa'.
And lang may she seek i' the green-wood shaw;
Lang the laird of Duneira blame,
And lang, lang greet or Kilmeny come hame!
     When many a day had come and fled,
When grief grew calm, and hope was dead,
When mess for Kilmeny's soul had been sung,
When the bedes-man had prayed, and the dead bell rung,
Late, late in gloamin when all was still,
When the fringe was red on the westlin hill,
The wood was sere, the moon i' the wane,
The reek o' the cot hung over the plain,
Like a little wee cloud in the world its lane;
When the ingle lowed with an eiry leme,
Late, late in the gloamin Kilmeny came hame!
     "Kilmeny, Kilmeny, where have you been?
Lang hae we sought baith holt and den;
By linn, by ford, and green-wood tree,
Yet you are halesome and fair to see.
Where gat you that joup o' the lily scheen?
That bonny snood of the birk sae green?
And these roses, the fairest that ever were seen?
Kilmeny, Kilmeny, where have you been?"
     Kilmeny look'd up with a lovely grace,
But nae smile was seen on Kilmeny's face;
As still was her look, and as still was her ee,
As the stillness that lay on the emerant lea,
Or the mist that sleeps on a waveless sea.
For Kilmeny had been, she knew not where,
And Kilmeny had seen what she could not declare;
Kilmeny had been where the cock never crew,
Where the rain never fell, and the wind never blew;
But it seemed as the harp of the sky had rung,
And the airs of heaven played round her tongue,
When she spake of the lovely forms she had seen,

And a land where sin had never been;
A land of love, and a land of light,
Withouten sun, or moon, or night;
Where the river swa'd a living stream,
And the light a pure celestial beam:
The land of vision, it would seem,
A still, an everlasting dream.

   In yon green-wood there is a waik,
And in that waik there is a wene,
   And in that wene there is a maike,
That neither has flesh, blood, nor bane;
   And down in yon green-wood he walks his lane.

   In that green wene Kilmeny lay,
Her bosom happ'd wi' flowerets gay;
But the air was soft and the silence deep,
And bonny Kilmeny fell sound asleep.
She kend nae mair, nor opened her ee,
Till waked by the hymns of a far countrye.

   She 'waken'd on a couch of the silk sae slim,
All striped wi' the bars of the rainbow's rim;
And lovely beings round were rife,
Who erst had travell'd mortal life;
And aye they smiled, and 'gan to speer,
"What spirit has brought this mortal here!"—

   "Lang have I journeyed the world wide,"
A meek and reverend fere replied;
"Baith night and day I have watched the fair,
Eident a thousand years and mair.
Yes, I have watched o'er ilk degree,
Wherever blooms femenitye;
But sinless virgin, free of stain
In mind and body, fand I nane.
Never, since the banquet of time,
Found I a virgin in her prime,
Till late this bonny maiden I saw
As spotless as the morning snaw:
Full twenty years she has lived as free
As the spirits that sojourn in this countrye:
I have brought her away frae the snares of men,
That sin or death she never may ken."—

   They clasped her waist and her hands sae fair

They kissed her cheek, and they kemed her hair,
And round came many a blooming fere,
Saying, "Bonny Kilmeny, ye're welcome here!
Women are freed of the littand scorn:
O, blessed be the day Kilmeny was born!
Now shall the land of the spirits see,
Now shall it ken what a woman may be!
Many a lang year in sorrow and pain,
Many a lang year through the world we've gane,
Commissioned to watch fair womankind,
For it's they who nurice the immortal mind.
We have watch'd their steps as the dawning shone,
And deep in the green-wood walks alone;
By lily bower and silken bed,
The viewless tears have o'er them shed;
Have soothed their ardent minds to sleep,
Or left the couch of love to weep.
We have seen! we have seen! but the time must come,
And the angels will weep at the day of doom!
    "O, would the fairest of mortal kind
Aye keep the holy truths in mind,
That kindred spirits their motions see,
Who watch their ways with anxious ee,
And grieve for the guilt of humanitye!
O, sweet to heaven the maiden's prayer,
And the sigh that heaves a bosom sae fair!
And dear to Heaven the words of truth,
And the praise of virtue frae beauty's mouth!
And dear to the viewless forms of air,
The minds that kythe as the body fair!"
    "O, bonny Kilmeny! free frae stain,
If ever you seek the world again,
That world of sin, of sorrow and fear,
O, tell of the joys that are waiting here;
And tell of the signs you shall shortly see;
Of the times that are now, and the times that shall be."—
    They lifted Kilmeny, they led her away,
And she walked in the light of a sunless day:
The sky was a dome of crystal bright,
The fountain of vision, and fountain of light:
The emerald fields were of dazzling glow,

And the flowers of everlasting blow.
Then deep in the stream her body they laid,
That her youth and beauty never might fade;
And they smiled on heaven, when they saw her lie
In the stream of life that wandered bye.
And she heard a song, she heard it sung,
She kend not where; but sae sweetly it rung,
It fell on the ear like a dream of the morn:
"O! blest be the day Kilmeny was born!
Now shall the land of the spirits see,
Now shall it ken what a woman may be!
The sun that shines on the world sae bright,
A borrowed gleid frae the fountain of light;
And the moon that sleeks the sky sae dun,
Like a gouden bow, or a beamless sun,
Shall wear away, and be seen nae mair,
And the angels shall miss them travelling the air.
But lang, lang after baith night and day,
When the sun and the world have elyed away;
When the sinner has gane to his waesome doom,
Kilmeny shall smile in eternal bloom!"—
      They bore her away, she wist not how,
For she felt not arm nor rest below;
But so swift they wained her through the light,
'Twas like the motion of sound or sight;
They seemed to split the gales of air,
And yet nor gale nor breeze was there.
Unnumbered groves below them grew,
They came, they past, and backward flew,
Like floods of blossoms gliding on,
In moment seen, in moment gone.
O, never vales to mortal view
Appeared like those o'er which they flew!
That land to human spirits given,
The lowermost vales of the storied heaven;
From thence they can view the world below,
And heaven's blue gates with sapphires glow,
More glory yet unmeet to know.
      They bore her far to a mountain green,
To see what mortal never had seen;
And they seated her high on a purple sward,

And bade her heed what she saw and heard,
And note the changes the spirits wrought,
For now she lived in the land of thought.
She looked, and she saw nor sun nor skies,
But a crystal dome of a thousand dyes:
She looked, and she saw nae land aright,
But an endless whirl of glory and light:
And radiant beings went and came
Far swifter than wind, or the linkèd flame.
She hid her een frae the dazzling view;
She looked again, and the scene was new.

   She saw a sun on a summer sky,
And clouds of amber sailing bye;
A lovely land beneath her lay,
And that land had glens and mountains gray;
And that land had valleys and hoary piles,
And marlèd seas and a thousand isles;
Its fields were speckled, its forests green,
And its lakes were all of the dazzling sheen,
Like magic mirrors, where slumbering lay
The sun and the sky and the cloudlet gray;
Which heaved and trembled, and gently swung,
On every shore they seemed to be hung;
For there they were seen on their downward plain
A thousand times and a thousand again;
In winding lake and placid firth,
Little peaceful heavens in the bosom of earth.

   Kilmeny sighed and seemed to grieve,
For she found her heart to that land did cleave;
She saw the corn wave on the vale,
She saw the deer run down the dale;
She saw the plaid and the broad claymore,
And the brows that the badge of freedom bore;
And she thought she had seen the land before.

   She saw a lady sit on a throne,
The fairest that ever the sun shone on!
A lion licked her hand of milk,
And she held him in a leish of silk;
And a leifu' maiden stood at her knee,
With a silver wand and melting ee;
Her sovereign shield till love stole in,

And poisoned all the fount within.
   Then a gruff untoward bedes-man came,
And hundit the lion on his dame;
And the guardian maid wi' the dauntless ee,
She dropped a tear, and left her knee;
And she saw till the queen frae the lion fled,
Till the bonniest flower of the world lay dead;
A coffin was set on a distant plain,
And she saw the red blood fall like rain:
Then bonny Kilmeny's heart grew sair,
And she turned away, and could look nae mair.
   Then the gruff grim carle girned amain,
And they trampled him down, but he rose again;
And he baited the lion to deeds of weir,
Till he lapped the blood to the kingdom dear;
And weening his head was danger-preef,
When crowned with the rose and clover leaf,
He gowled at the carle, and chased him away
To feed wi' the deer on the mountain gray.
He gowled at the carle, and gecked at Heaven,
But his mark was set, and his arles given.
Kilmeny a while her een withdrew;
She looked again, and the scene was new.
   She saw before her fair unfurled
One half of all the glowing world,
Where oceans rolled, and rivers ran,
To bound the aims of sinful man.
She saw a people, fierce and fell,
Burst frae their bounds like fiends of hell;
Their lilies grew, and the eagle flew,
And she herkèd on her ravening crew,
Till the cities and towers were wrapt in a blaze,
And the thunder it roared o'er the lands and the seas.
The widows they wailed, and the red blood ran,
And she threatened an end to the race of man:
She never lened, nor stood in awe,
Till caught by the lion's deadly paw.
Oh! then the eagle swinked for life,
And brainzelled up a mortal strife;
But flew she north, or flew she south,
She met wi' the gowl of the lion's mouth.

With a mooted wing and waefu' maen,
The eagle sought her eiry again;
But lang may she cower in her bloody nest,
And lang, lang sleek her wounded breast,
Before she sey another flight,
To play wi' the norland lion's might.
    But to sing the sights Kilmeny saw,
So far surpassing nature's law,
The singer's voice wad sink away,
And the string of his harp wad cease to play.
But she saw till the sorrows of man were bye,
And all was love and harmony;
Till the stars of heaven fell calmly away,
Like flakes of snaw on a winter day.
    Then Kilmeny begged again to see
The friends she had left in her own countrye;
To tell of the place where she had been,
And the glories that lay in the land unseen;
To warn the living maidens fair,
The loved of Heaven, the spirits' care,
That all whose minds unmeled remain
Shall bloom in beauty when time is gane.
    With distant music, soft and deep,
They lulled Kilmeny sound asleep;
And when she awakened, she lay her lane,
All happed with flowers in the green-wood wene.
When seven lang years had come and fled;
When grief was calm, and hope was dead;
When scarce was remembered Kilmeny's name,
Late, late in a gloamin Kilmeny came hame!
And O, her beauty was fair to see,
But still and steadfast was her ee!
Such beauty bard may never declare,
For there was no pride nor passion there;
And the soft desire of maiden's een
In that mild face could never be seen.
Her seymar was the lily flower,
And her cheek the moss-rose in the shower;
And her voice like the distant melodye,
That floats along the twilight sea.
But she loved to raike the lanely glen,

And keepèd afar frae the haunts of men;
Her holy hymns unheard to sing,
To suck the flowers, and drink the spring.
But wherever her peaceful form appeared,
The wild beasts of the hill were cheered;
The wolf played blythly round the field,
The lordly byson lowed and kneeled;
The dun deer wooed with manner bland,
And cowered aneath her lily hand.
And when at even the woodlands rung,
When hymns of other worlds she sung
In ecstasy of sweet devotion,
O, then the glen was all in motion!
The wild beasts of the forest came,
Broke from their bughts and faulds the tame,
And goved around, charmed and amazed;
Even the dull cattle crooned and gazed,
And murmured and looked with anxious pain
For something the mystery to explain.
The buzzard came with the throstle-cock;
The corby left her houf in the rock;
The blackbird alang wi' the eagle flew;
The hind came tripping o'er the dew;
The wolf and the kid their raike began,
And the tod, and the lamb, and the leveret ran;
The hawk and the hern attour them hung,
And the merl and the mavis forhooyed their young;
And all in a peaceful ring were hurled:
It was like an eve in a sinless world!
    When a month and a day had come and gane,
Kilmeny sought the green-wood wene;
There laid her down on the leaves sae green,
And Kilmeny on earth was never mair seen.
But O, the words that fell from her mouth,
Were words of wonder, and words of truth!
But all the land were in fear and dread,
For they kendna whether she was living or dead.
It wasna her hame, and she couldna remain;
She left this world of sorrow and pain,
And returned to the land of thought again.

'Caledonia'

Caledonia! thou land of the mountain and rock,
 Of the ocean, the mist, and the wind—
Thou land of the torrent, the pine, and the oak,
 Of the roebuck, the hart, and the hind:
Though bare are thy cliffs, and though barren thy glens,
 Though bleak thy dun islands appear,
Yet kind are the hearts, and undaunted the clans,
 That roam on these mountains so drear!

A foe from abroad, or a tyrant at home,
 Could never thy ardour restrain;
The marshall'd array of imperial Rome
 Essay'd thy proud spirit in vain!
Firm seat of religion, of valour, of truth,
 Of genius unshackled and free,
The muses have left all the vales of the south,
 My loved Caledonia, for thee!

Sweet land of the bay and wild-winding deeps,
 Where loveliness slumbers at even,
While far in the depth of the blue water sleeps
 A calm little motionless heaven!
Thou land of the valley, the moor, and the hill,
 Of the storm and the proud rolling wave—
Yes, thou art the land of fair liberty still,
 And the land of my forefathers' grave!

'Why Weeps Yon Highland Maid?'

Why weeps yon Highland maid
Over the tartan plaid—
Is it a pledge of care,
Or are the blood drops there?
Tell me, thou hind of humble seeming,
Why the tears on her cheek are gleaming,
Why should the young and fair
Thus weep unpitied there?

Stranger, that Highland plaid
Low in the dust was laid;

He who the relic wore,
He is, alas! no more:
He and his loyal clan were trodden
Down by slaves on dark Culloden.
Well o'er a lover's pall,
Well may the tear-drops fall!

Where now her clansman true,
Where is the bonnet blue,
Where the claymore that broke
Fearless through fire and smoke?
Not one gleam by glen or river,
It lies dropp'd from the hand for ever.
Stranger, our fate deplore,
Our ancient name's no more!

'A Witch's Chant'

Thou art weary, weary, weary,
  Thou art weary and far away,
Hear me, gentle spirit, hear me,
  Come before the dawn of day.

I hear a small voice from the hill,
The vapour is deadly, pale, and still—
A murmuring sough is on the wood,
And the witching star is red as blood.

And in the cleft of heaven I scan
The giant form of a naked man.
His eye is like the burning brand,
And he holds a sword in his right hand.

All is not well. By dint of spell,
Somewhere between the heaven and hell
There is this night a wild deray,
The spirits have wander'd from their way.

The purple drops shall tinge the moon,
As she wanders through the midnight noon;
And the dawning heaven shall all be red
With blood by guilty angels shed.

Be as it will, I have the skill
To work by good or work by ill;
Then here's for pain, and here's for thrall,
And here's for conscience, worst of all.

Another chant, and then, and then,
Spirits shall come or Christian men—
Come from the earth, the air, or the sea,
Great Gil-Moules, I cry to thee!

Sleep'st thou, wakest thou, lord of the wind,
Mount thy steeds and gallop them blind;
And the long-tailed fiery dragon outfly,
The rocket of heaven, the bomb of the sky.

Over the dog-star, over the wain,
Over the cloud, and the rainbow's mane,
Over the mountain, and over the sea,
　　Haste—haste—haste to me!

Then here's for trouble, and here's for smart,
And here's for the pang that seeks the heart;
Here's for madness, and here's for thrall,
And here's for conscience, the worst of all!

'The Minstrel Boy'

The Minstrel Boy to the glen is gone,
　　In its deepest dells you'll find him,
Where echoes sing to his music's tone,
　　And fairies listen behind him.
He sings of nature all in her prime,
　　Of sweets that around him hover,
Of mountains heath and moorland thyme,
　　And trifles that tell the lover.

How wildly sweet is the minstrel's lay,
　　Through cliffs and wild woods ringing,
For, ah! there is love to beacon his way,
　　And hope in the song he's singing!
The bard may indite, and the minstrel sing,
　　And maidens may chorus it rarely;
But unless there be love in the heart within,
　　The ditty will charm but sparely.

ALEXANDER DOUGLAS

(1771–1821)

———

HAILING from Strathmiglo in Fife, the poet Alexander Douglas was largely self-taught. His *Poems, Chiefly in the Scottish Dialect* (1806) enjoyed some success. In the preface to *Poems* it is said that Douglas's parents encouraged his keen reading habits, which he supported by assisting the weavers in the village from a young age. Ramsay and other major Scottish poets were of especial interest to him; he also read Milton, Young, Watts, Harvey, and Thomson. Of the collection's numerous poems and songs, 'Fife, an' a' the Land about it' was particularly popular throughout the country for some time.

———

'Fife, an' a' the Land about it'

Poems, Chiefly in the Scottish Dialect (Cupar: Printed for the Author, 1806).

(Tune: "Roy's Wife of Aldivalloch")

> *Fife, an' a' the land about it,*
> *Fife, an' a' the land about it;*
> *May health, an' peace, an' plenty glad*
> *Fair Fife, an' a' the land about it.*

We'll raise the song on highest key,
    Thro' ev'ry grove till echo shout it;
The sweet enchantin' theme shall be,
    Fair Fife, an' a' the land about it.
    Fair Fife, an' a' the land about it, &c.

Her braid an' lang extended vales
    Are clad wi' corn, a' wavin' yellow;
Her flocks an' herds crown a' her hills;
    Her woods resound wi' music mellow.
    Fair Fife, an' a' the land about it, &c.

Her waters pastime sweet afford
  To ane an' a' wha like to angle,
The seats o' mony a laird an' lord,
   Her plains, as stars the sky, bespangle.
    Fair Fife, an' a' the land about it, &c.

In ilka town an' village gay,
  Hark, Thrift, her wheel an' loom is usin',
While to an' frae each port an' bay,
   See wealthy Commerce briskly cruisin'.
    Fair Fife, an' a' the land about it, &c.

Her maids are frugal, modest, fair,
  As lilies by her burnies growin';
An' ilka swain may here repair,
   Whase heart wi' virt'ous love is glowin'.
    Fair Fife, an' a' the land about it, &c.

In peace, her sons like lammies mild,
  Are lightsome, friendly, an' engagin';
In war they're loyal, bauld, an' wild,
   As lions rous'd, an' fiercely ragin'.
    Fair Fife, an' a' the land about it, &c.

May auld an' young hae meat an' claes;
  May wark an' wages ay be plenty;
An' may the sun to latest days
   See Fife an' a' her bairnies canty.

   Fife an' a' the land about it;
   Fife an' a' the land about it;
   May health, an' peace, an' plenty glad
   Fair Fife an' a' the land about it.

SIR WALTER SCOTT

(1771–1832)

———

BORN in the Old Town of Edinburgh, and trained for the law profession, Walter Scott enjoyed a successful career as a poet before he became the world's bestselling novelist. From a young age he was surrounded by Scottish and other literatures. His aunt Jenny read popular songs to him from works such as Allan Ramsay's *The Tea-Table Miscellany*. At school in Edinburgh and in Kelso he also studied Virgil, Horace, and Terence, among others. And he read Scottish and English poetry, including Shakespeare, Milton, Ramsay, and Pope. Thomas Blacklock encouraged him to study Ossian and Spenser closely. In 1796 Scott translated two Bürger poems into English and, in 1799, some Goethe too. He also contributed three Germanic poems to Matthew Lewis's delayed collection, *Tales of Wonder* (1800). As well as a major editing project of his own—*Minstrelsy of the Scottish Border* (1802-3) —Scott prepared original book-length poems. The first, *The Lay of the Last Minstrel* (1805), was by most standards hugely successful. In the author's lifetime there were twenty-one British editions of the poem. The next, *Marmion* (1808), was even more popular: 8,000 copies were sold in its first year. Following this, *The Lady of the Lake* (1810) sold 20,000 copies within months. Scott wrote two more long poems, *Rokeby* (1813) and *The Lord of the Isles* (1815). They sold very well (10,000 and 13,750 copies in the first year, respectively). But Scott felt the pressure of a new poet on the scene, Lord Byron, whose first two cantos of *Childe Harold's Pilgrimage* (1812) astonished the literary world.

———

The Lady of the Lake *(1810)*, *'The Chase'*

The Lady of the Lake. A Poem, 4th edn (Edinburgh: John Ballantyne and Co.; London: Longman, Hurst, Rees, and Orme, and W. Miller, 1810).

> Harp of the North! that mouldering long hast hung
>   On the witch-elm that shades Saint Fillan's spring,
> And down the fitful breeze thy numbers flung,

Till envious ivy did around thee cling,
Muffling with verdant ringlet every string,—
　O minstrel Harp, still must thine accents sleep?
Mid rustling leaves and fountains murmuring,
　Still must thy sweeter sounds their silence keep,
Nor bid a warrior smile, nor teach a maid to weep?

Not thus, in ancient days of Caledon,
　Was thy voice mute amid the festal crowd,
When lay of hopeless love, or glory won,
　Aroused the fearful, or subdued the proud.
At each according pause, was heard aloud
　Thine ardent symphony sublime and high!
Fair dames and crested chiefs attention bow'd;
　For still the burthen of thy minstrelsy
Was Knighthood's dauntless deed, and Beauty's matchless eye.

O wake once more! how rude soe'er the hand
　That ventures o'er thy magic maze to stray;
O wake once more! though scarce my skill command
　Some feeble echoing of thine earlier lay:
Though harsh and faint, and soon to die away,
　And all unworthy of thy nobler strain,
Yet if one heart throb higher at its sway,
　The wizard note has not been touch'd in vain.
Then silent be no more! Enchantress, wake again!

I

The Stag at eve had drunk his fill,
Where danced the moon on Monan's rill,
And deep his midnight lair had made
In lone Glenartney's hazel shade;
But, when the sun his beacon red
Had kindled on Benvoirlich's head,
The deep-mouth'd blood-hound's heavy bay
Resounded up the rocky way,
And faint, from farther distance borne,
Were heard the clanging hoof and horn.

II

As chief who hears his warder call,
"To arms! the foemen storm the wall,"—

The antler'd monarch of the waste
Sprung from his heathery couch in haste.
But, ere his fleet career he took,
The dew-drops from his flanks he shook;
Like crested leader proud and high,
Tossed his beamed frontlet to the sky;
A moment gazed adown the dale,
A moment snuffed the tainted gale,
A moment listened to the cry,
That thickened as the chase drew nigh;
Then, as the headmost foes appeared,
With one brave bound the copse he cleared,
And, stretching forward free and far,
Sought the wild heaths of Uam-Var.

III

Yelled on the view the opening pack,
Rock, glen, and cavern paid them back;
To many a mingled sound at once
The awakened mountain gave response.
An hundred dogs bayed deep and strong,
Clattered an hundred steeds along,
Their peal the merry horns rung out,
An hundred voices join'd the shout;
With hark and whoop and wild halloo,
No rest Benvoirlich's echoes knew.
Far from the tumult fled the roe,
Close in her covert cowered the doe;
The falcon, from her cairn on high,
Cast on the rout a wondering eye,
Till far beyond her piercing ken
The hurricane had swept the glen.
Faint, and more faint, its failing din
Returned from cavern, cliff, and linn,
And silence settled, wide and still,
On the lone wood and mighty hill.

IV

Less loud the sounds of sylvan war
Disturb the heights of Uam-Var,
And roused the cavern, where 'tis told

A giant made his den of old;
For ere that steep ascent was won,
High in his path-way hung the sun,
And many a gallant, stayed per-force,
Was fain to breathe his faultering horse;
And of the trackers of the deer
Scarce half the lessening pack was near;
So shrewdly, on the mountain side,
Had the bold burst their mettle tried.

V

The noble Stag was pausing now,
Upon the mountain's southern brow,
Where broad extended, far beneath,
The varied realms of fair Menteith.
With anxious eye he wander'd o'er
Mountain and meadow, moss and moor,
And pondered refuge from his toil,
By far Lochard or Aberfoyle.
But nearer was the copse-wood gray,
That waved and wept on Loch-Achray,
And mingled with the pine-trees blue
On the bold cliffs of Ben-venue.
Fresh vigor with the hope return'd,
With flying foot the heath he spurned,
Held westward with unwearied race,
And left behind the panting chase.

VI

'Twere long to tell what steeds gave o'er,
As swept the hunt through Cambus-more;
What reins were tightened in despair,
When rose Benledi's ridge in air;
Who flagged upon Bochastle's heath,
Who shunned to stem the flooded Teith,—
For twice, that day, from shore to shore,
The gallant Stag swam stoutly o'er.
Few were the stragglers, following far,
That reached the lake of Vennachar;
And when the Brigg of Turk was won,
The headmost Horseman rode alone.

VII

Alone, but with unbated zeal,
That horseman plied the scourge and steel;
For, jaded now, and spent with toil,
Embossed with foam, and dark with soil,
While every gasp with sobs he drew,
The labouring Stag strained full in view.
Two dogs of black Saint Hubert's breed,
Unmatched for courage, breath, and speed,
Fast on his flying traces came,
And all but won that desperate game;
For, scarce a spear's length from his haunch,
Vindictive toiled the blood-hounds staunch;
Nor nearer might the dogs attain,
Nor farther might the quarry strain.
Thus up the margin of the lake,
Between the precipice and brake,
O'er stock and rock their race they take.

VIII

The hunter marked that mountain high,
The lone lake's western boundary,
And deemed the Stag must turn to bay,
Where that huge rampart barred the way;
Already glorying in the prize,
Measured his antlers with his eyes;
For the death-wound, and death-halloo,
Mustered his breath, his whinyard drew;
But, thundering as he came prepared,
With ready arm and weapon bared,
The wily quarry shunned the shock,
And turned him from the opposing rock;
Then, dashing down a darksome glen,
Soon lost to hound and hunter's ken,
In the deep Trossachs' wildest nook
His solitary refuge took.
There while, close couched, the thicket shed
Cold dews and wild flowers on his head,
He heard the baffled dogs in vain
Rave through the hollow pass amain,
Chiding the rocks that yelled again.

IX

Close on the hounds the hunter came,
To cheer them on the vanished game;
But, stumbling in the rugged dell,
The gallant horse exhausted fell.
The impatient rider strove in vain
To rouse him with the spur and rein,
For the good steed, his labours o'er,
Stretched his stiff limbs, to rise no more.
Then, touched with pity and remorse,
He sorrowed o'er the expiring horse.
"I little thought, when first thy rein
I slacked upon the banks of Seine,
That highland eagle e'er should feed
On thy fleet limbs, my matchless steed!
Woe worth the chase, woe worth the day,
That costs thy life, my gallant grey!"—

X

Then through the dell his horn resounds,
From vain pursuit to call the hounds.
Back limped, with slow and crippled pace,
The sulky leaders of the chase;
Close to their master's side they pressed,
With drooping tail and humbled crest;
But still the dingle's hollow throat
Prolonged the swelling bugle-note.
The owlets started from their dream,
The eagles answered with their scream,
Round and around the sounds were cast,
Till echo seemed an answering blast;
And on the hunter hied his way,
To join some comrades of the day;
Yet often paused, so strange the road,
So wondrous were the scenes it show'd.

XI

The western waves of ebbing day
Rolled o'er the glen their level way;
Each purple peak, each flinty spire,

Was bathed in floods of living fire.
But not a setting beam could glow
Within the dark ravines below,
Where twined the path, in shadow hid,
Round many a rocky pyramid,
Shooting abruptly from the dell
Its thunder-splintered pinnacle;
Round many an insulated mass,
The native bulwarks of the pass,
Huge as the tower which builders vain
Presumptuous piled on Shinar's plain.
The rocky summits, split and rent,
Formed turret, dome, or battlement.
Or seemed fantastically set
With cupola or minaret,
Wild crests as pagod ever deck'd,
Or mosque of eastern architect.
Nor were these earth-born castles bare,
Nor lacked they many a banner fair;
For, from their shivered brows displayed,
Far o'er the unfathomable glade,
All twinkling with the dew-drop sheen,
The briar-rose fell in streamers green,
And creeping shrubs, of thousand dyes,
Waved in the west-wind's summer sighs.

XII

Boon nature scattered, free and wild,
Each plant or flower, the mountain's child.
Here eglantine embalmed the air,
Hawthorn and hazel mingled there;
The primrose pale, and violet flower,
Found in each cliff a narrow bower;
Fox-glove and night-shade, side by side,
Emblems of punishment and pride,
Grouped their dark hues with every stain,
The weather-beaten crags retain;
With boughs that quaked at every breath,
Grey birch and aspen wept beneath;
Aloft, the ash and warrior oak
Cast anchor in the rifted rock;

And higher yet, the pine-tree hung
His shatter'd trunk, and frequent flung,
Where seemed the cliffs to meet on high,
His boughs athwart the narrowed sky.
Highest of all, where white peaks glanced,
Where glistening streamers waved and danced,
The wanderer's eye could barely view
The summer heaven's delicious blue;
So wondrous wild, the whole might seem
The scenery of a fairy dream.

XIII

Onward, amid the copse 'gan peep
A narrow inlet, still and deep,
Affording scarce such breadth of brim,
As served the wild-duck's brood to swim;
Lost for a space, through thickets veering,
But broader when again appearing,
Tall rocks and tufted knolls their face
Could on the dark-blue mirror trace;
And farther as the Hunter stray'd,
Still broader sweep its channels made.
The shaggy mounds no longer stood,
Emerging from entangled wood,
But, wave-encircled, seemed to float,
Like castle girdled with its moat;
Yet broader floods extending still,
Divide them from their parent hill,
Till each, retiring, claims to be
An islet in an inland sea.

XIV

And now, to issue from the glen,
No pathway meets the wanderer's ken,
Unless he climb, with footing nice,
A far projecting precipice.
The broom's tough roots his ladder made,
The hazel saplings lent their aid;
And thus an airy point he won,
Where, gleaming with the setting sun,
One burnish'd sheet of living gold,

Loch-Katrine lay beneath him rolled;
In all her length far winding lay,
With promontory, creek, and bay,
And islands that, empurpled bright,
Floated amid the livelier light;
And mountains, that like giants stand,
To sentinel enchanted land.
High on the south, huge Benvenue
Down to the lake in masses threw
Crags, knolls, and mounds, confusedly hurled,
The fragments of an earlier world;
A wildering forest feathered o'er
His ruined sides and summit hoar,
While on the north, through middle air,
Ben-an heaved high his forehead bare.

XV

From the steep promontory gazed
The Stranger, raptured and amazed.
And, "What a scene were here," he cried,
"For princely pomp or churchman's pride!
On this bold brow, a lordly tower;
In that soft vale, a lady's bower;
On yonder meadow, far away,
The turrets of a cloister grey.
How blithely might the bugle-horn
Chide, on the lake, the lingering morn!
How sweet, at eve, the lover's lute
Chime, when the groves were still and mute!
And, when the midnight moon should lave
Her forehead in the silver wave,
How solemn on the ear would come
The holy matins' distant hum,
While the deep peal's commanding tone
Should wake, in yonder islet lone,
A sainted hermit from his cell,
To drop a bead with every knell—
And bugle, lute, and bell, and all,
Should each bewildered stranger call
To friendly feast and lighted hall.

XVI

"Blithe were it then to wander here!
But now,—beshrew yon nimble deer,—
Like that same hermit's, thin and spare,
The copse must give my evening fare;
Some mossy bank my couch must be,
Some rustling oak my canopy.
Yet pass we that;—the war and chase
Give little choice of resting-place;—
A summer night, in green-wood spent,
Were but to-morrow's merriment;
But hosts may in these wilds abound,
Such as are better missed than found;
To meet with highland plunderers here
Were worse than loss of steed or deer.—
I am alone;—my bugle strain
May call some straggler of the train;
Or, fall the worst that may betide,
Ere now this faulchion has been tried."—

XVII

But scarce again his horn he wound,
When lo! forth starting at the sound,
From underneath an aged oak,
That slanted from the islet rock,
A Damsel guider of its way,
A little skiff shot to the bay,
That round the promontory steep
Led its deep line in graceful sweep,
Eddying, in almost viewless wave,
The weeping willow twig to lave,
And kiss, with whispering sound and slow,
The beach of pebbles bright as snow.
The boat had touch'd this silver strand,
Just as the Hunter left his stand,
And stood concealed amid the brake,
To view this Lady of the Lake.
The maiden paused, as if again
She thought to catch the distant strain,
With head up-raised, and look intent,

And eye and ear attentive bent,
And locks flung back, and lips apart,
Like monument of Grecian art.
In listening mood, she seemed to stand,
The guardian Naiad of the strand.

XVIII

And ne'er did Grecian chizzel trace
A Nymph, a Naiad, or a Grace,
Of finer form, or lovelier face!
What though the sun, with ardent frown,
Had slightly tinged her cheek with brown,—
The sportive toil, which, short and light,
Had dyed her glowing hue so bright,
Served too in hastier swell to show
Short glimpses of a breast of snow:
What though no rule of courtly grace
To measured mood had trained her pace,—
A foot more light, a step more true,
Ne'er from the heath-flower dashed the dew;
E'en the slight hare-bell raised its head,
Elastic from her airy tread:
What though upon her speech there hung
The accents of the mountain tongue,—
Those silver sounds, so soft, so dear,
The list'ner held his breath to hear.

XIX

A chieftain's daughter seemed the maid;
Her satin snood, her silken plaid,
Her golden brooch, such birth betray'd.
And seldom was a snood amid
Such wild luxuriant ringlets hid,
Whose glossy black to shame might bring
The plumage of the raven's wing;
And seldom o'er a breast so fair,
Mantled a plaid with modest care,
And never brooch the folds combined
Above a heart more good and kind.
Her kindness and her worth to spy,
You need but gaze on Ellen's eye;

Not Katrine, in her mirror blue,
Gives back the shaggy banks more true,
Than every free-born glance confessed
The guileless movements of her breast;
Whether joy danced in her dark eye,
Or woe or pity claimed a sigh,
Or filial love was glowing there,
Or meek devotion poured a prayer,
Or tale of injury called forth
The indignant spirit of the north.
One only passion, unrevealed,
With maiden pride the maid concealed,
Yet not less purely felt the flame;—
O, need I tell that passion's name!

XX

Impatient of the silent horn,
Now on the gale her voice was borne:—
"Father!" she cried; the rocks around
Loved to prolong the gentle sound.
A while she paused, no answer came,—
"Malcolm, was thine the blast?" the name
Less resolutely uttered fell,
The echoes could not catch the swell.
"A stranger I," the Huntsman said,
Advancing from the hazel shade.
The maid alarm'd, with hasty oar,
Pushed her light shallop from the shore,
And, when a space was gained between,
Closer she drew her bosom's screen;
(So forth the startled swan would swing,
So turn to prune his ruffled wing.)
Then safe, though fluttered and amazed,
She paused, and on the Stranger gazed.
Not his the form, nor his the eye,
That youthful maidens wont to fly.

XXI

On his bold visage middle age
Had slightly pressed its signet sage,
Yet had not quenched the open truth,

And fiery vehemence of youth;
Forward and frolic glee was there,
The will to do, the soul to dare,
The sparkling glance soon blown to fire,
Of hasty love, or headlong ire.
His limbs were cast in manly mould,
For hardy sports, or contest bold;
And though in peaceful garb arrayed,
And weaponless, except his blade,
His stately mien, as well implied
A high-born heart, a martial pride,
As if a baron's crest he wore,
And sheathed in armour trode the shore.
Slighting the petty need he showed,
He told of his benighted road;—
His ready speech flowed fair and free,
In phrase of gentlest courtesy;
Yet seemed that tone, and gesture bland,
Less used to sue than to command.

XXII

A while the maid the Stranger eyed,
And, reassured, at length replied,
That highland halls were open still
To wildered wanderers of the hill.
"Nor think you unexpected come
To yon lone isle, our desert home;
Before the heath had lost the dew,
This morn, a couch was pulled for you;
On yonder mountain's purple head
Have ptarmigan and heath-cock bled,
And our broad nets have swept the mere,
To furnish forth your evening cheer."—
"Now, by the rood, my lovely maid,
Your courtesy has erred," he said;
"No right have I to claim, misplaced,
The welcome of expected guest.
A wanderer, here by fortune tost,
My way, my friends, my courser lost,
I ne'er before, believe me, fair,
Have ever drawn your mountain air,

Till on this lake's romantic strand,
I found a fay in fairy land."—

XXIII

"I well believe," the maid replied,
As her light skiff approached the side,
"I well believe, that ne'er before
Your foot has trod Loch-Katrine's shore:
But yet, as far as yesternight,
Old Allan-bane foretold your plight,—
A grey-haired sire, whose eye intent
Was on the visioned future bent.
He saw your steed, a dappled grey,
Lie dead beneath the birchen way;
Painted exact your form and mien,
Your hunting suit of Lincoln green,
That tassell'd horn so gaily gilt,
That faulchion's crooked blade and hilt,
That cap with heron's plumage trim,
And yon two hounds so dark and grim.
He bade that all should ready be,
To grace a guest of fair degree;
But light I held his prophecy,
And deemed it was my father's horn,
Whose echoes o'er the lake were borne."—

XXIV

The Stranger smiled:—"Since to your home,
A destined errant-knight I come,
Announced by prophet sooth and old,
Doomed, doubtless, for achievement bold,
I'll lightly front each high emprize,
For one kind glance of those bright eyes;
Permit me, first, the task to guide
Your fairy frigate o'er the tide."—
The maid, with smile suppressed and sly,
The toil unwonted saw him try;
For seldom, sure, if e'er before,
His noble hand had grasped an oar:
Yet with main strength his strokes he drew,
And o'er the lake the shallop flew;

With heads erect, and whimpering cry,
The hounds behind their passage ply.
Nor frequent does the bright oar break
The darkening mirror of the lake,
Until the rocky isle they reach,
And moor their shallop on the beach.

XXV

The Stranger viewed the shore around;
'Twas all so close with copse-wood bound,
Nor track nor path-way might declare
That human foot frequented there,
Until the mountain-maiden showed
A clambering unsuspected road,
That winded through the tangled screen,
And opened on a narrow green,
Where weeping birch and willow round
With their long fibres swept the ground;
Here, for retreat in dangerous hour,
Some chief had framed a rustic bower.

XXVI

It was a lodge of ample size,
But strange of structure and device;
Of such materials, as around
The workman's hand had readiest found.
Lopped of their boughs, their hoar trunks bared,
And by the hatchet rudely squared,
To give the walls their destined height,
The sturdy oak and ash unite;
While moss and clay and leaves combined
To fence each crevice from the wind.
The lighter pine-trees, over-head,
Their slender length for rafters spread,
And withered heath and rushes dry
Supplied a russet canopy.
Due westward, fronting to the green,
A rural portico was seen,
Aloft on native pillars borne,
Of mountain fir with bark unshorn,
Where Ellen's hand had taught to twine

The ivy and Idaean vine,
The clematis, the favoured flower,
Which boasts the name of virgin-bower,
And every hardy plant could bear
Loch-Katrine's keen and searching air.
An instant in this porch she stayed,
And gaily to the Stranger said,
"On heaven and on thy lady call,
And enter the enchanted hall!"—

XXVII

"My hope, my heaven, my trust must be,
My gentle guide, in following thee."—
He crossed the threshold—and a clang
Of angry steel that instant rang.
To his bold brow his spirit rushed,
But soon for vain alarm he blushed,
When on the floor he saw displayed,
Cause of the din, a naked blade
Dropped from the sheath, that careless flung
Upon a stag's huge antlers swung;
For all around, the walls to grace,
Hung trophies of the fight or chase:
A target there, a bugle here,
A battle-axe, a hunting-spear,
And broad-swords, bows, and arrows store,
With the tusked trophies of the boar.
Here grins the wolf as when he died,
And there the wild-cat's brindled hide
The frontlet of the elk adorns,
Or mantles o'er the bison's horns;
Pennons and flags defaced and stained,
That blackening streaks of blood retained,
And deer-skins, dappled, dun, and white,
With otter's fur and seal's unite,
In rude and uncouth tapestry all,
To garnish forth the sylvan hall.

XXVIII

The wondering Stranger round him gazed,
And next the fallen weapon raised;

Few were the arms whose sinewy strength
Sufficed to stretch it forth at length.
And as the brand he poised and swayed,
"I never knew but one," he said,
"Whose stalwart arm might brook to wield
A blade like this in battle field."—
She sighed, then smiled and took the word:
"You see the guardian champion's sword;
As light it trembles in his hand,
As in my grasp a hazel wand:
My sire's tall form might grace the part
Of Ferragus or Ascabart;
But in the absent giant's hold
Are women now, and menials old."

XXIX

The mistress of the mansion came,
Mature of age, a graceful dame;
Whose easy step and stately port
Had well become a princely court,
To whom, though more than kindred knew,
Young Ellen gave a mother's due.
Meet welcome to her guest she made,
And every courteous rite was paid,
That hospitality could claim,
Though all unasked his birth and name.
Such then the reverence to a guest,
That fellest foe might join the feast,
And from his deadliest foeman's door
Unquestion'd turn, the banquet o'er.
At length his rank the Stranger names,
"The knight of Snowdoun, James Fitz-James;
Lord of a barren heritage,
Which his brave sires, from age to age,
By their good swords had held with toil;
His sire had fallen in such turmoil,
And he, God wot, was forced to stand
Oft for his right with blade in hand.
This morning with Lord Moray's train
He chased a stalwart stag in vain,

Out-stripped his comrades, missed the deer,
Lost his good steed, and wandered here."—

XXX

Fain would the Knight in turn require
The name and state of Ellen's sire.
Well showed the elder lady's mien,
That courts and cities she had seen;
Ellen, though more her looks displayed
The simple grace of sylvan maid,
In speech and gesture, form and face,
Shewed she was come of gentle race;
'Twere strange in ruder rank to find
Such looks, such manners, and such mind.
Each hint the knight of Snowdoun gave,
Dame Margaret heard with silence grave;
Or Ellen, innocently gay,
Turned all inquiry light away.
"Weird women we! by dale and down,
We dwell afar from tower and town.
We stem the flood, we ride the blast,
On wandering knights our spells we cast;
While viewless minstrels touch the string,
'Tis thus our charmed rhymes we sing."—
She sung, and still a harp unseen
Filled up the symphony between.

XXXI SONG.

"Soldier, rest! thy warfare o'er,
    Sleep the sleep that knows not breaking;
Dream of battled fields no more,
    Days of danger, nights of waking.
In our isle's enchanted hall,
    Hands unseen thy couch are strewing,
Fairy strains of music fall,
    Every sense in slumber dewing.
Soldier, rest! thy warfare o'er,
Dream of fighting fields no more;
Sleep the sleep that knows not breaking,
Morn of toil, nor night of waking."

"No rude sound shall reach thine ear,
   Armour's clang, or war-steed champing,
Trump nor pibroch summon here
   Mustering clan, or squadron tramping.
Yet the lark's shrill fife may come
   At the day-break from the fallow,
And the bittern sound his drum,
   Booming from the sedgy shallow.
Ruder sounds shall none be near,
Guards nor warders challenge here,
Here's no war-steed's neigh and champing,
Shouting clans or squadrons stamping."—

XXXII

She paused—then, blushing, led the lay
To grace the stranger of the day;
Her mellow notes awhile prolong
The cadence of the flowing song,
Till to her lips in measured frame
The minstrel verse spontaneous came.

SONG CONTINUED.
"Huntsman, rest! thy chase is done,
   While our slumbrous spells assail ye,
Dream not, with the rising sun,
   Bugles here shall sound reveillie.
Sleep! the deer is in his den;
   Sleep! thy hounds are by thee lying;
Sleep! nor dream in yonder glen,
   How thy gallant steed lay dying.
Huntsman, rest! thy chase is done,
Think not of the rising sun,
For at dawning to assail ye,
Here no bugles sound reveillie."—

XXXIII

The hall was cleared—the Stranger's bed
Was there of mountain heather spread,
Where oft an hundred guests had lain,
And dreamed their forest sports again.

But vainly did the heath-flower shed
Its moorland fragrance round his head;
Not Ellen's spell had lulled to rest
The fever of his troubled breast.
In broken dreams the image rose
Of varied perils, pains, and woes;
His steed now flounders in the brake,
Now sinks his barge upon the lake;
Now leader of a broken host,
His standard falls, his honour's lost.
Then,—from my couch may heavenly might
Chase that worst phantom of the night!—
Again returned the scenes of youth,
Of confident, undoubting truth;
Again his soul he interchanged
With friends whose hearts were long estranged.
They come in dim procession led,
The cold, the faithless, and the dead;
As warm each hand, each brow as gay,
As if they parted yesterday.
And doubt distracts him at the view,
O were his senses false or true!
Dreamed he of death, or broken vow,
Or is it all a vision now!

XXXIV

At length, with Ellen in a grove
He seemed to walk and speak of love;
She listened with a blush and sigh,
His suit was warm, his hopes were high.
He sought her yielded hand to clasp,
And a cold gauntlet met his grasp:
The phantom's sex was changed and gone,
Upon its head a helmet shone;
Slowly enlarged to giant size,
With darkened cheek and threatening eyes,
The grisly visage, stern and hoar,
To Ellen still a likeness bore.—
He woke, and, panting with affright,
Recalled the vision of the night.

The hearth's decaying brands were red,
And deep and dusky lustre shed,
Half shewing, half concealing, all
The uncouth trophies of the hall.
Mid those the Stranger fixed his eye
Where that huge faulchion hung on high,
And thoughts on thoughts, a countless throng,
Rushed, chasing countless thoughts along,
Until, the giddy whirl to cure,
He rose, and sought the moon-shine pure.

XXXV

The wild rose, eglantine, and broom,
Wasted around their rich perfume;
The birch-trees wept in fragrant balm,
The aspens slept beneath the calm;
The silver light, with quivering glance,
Played on the water's still expanse,—
Wild were the heart whose passion's sway
Could rage beneath the sober ray!
He felt its calm, that warrior guest,
While thus he communed with his breast:
"Why is it at each turn I trace
Some memory of that exiled race?
Can I not mountain maiden spy,
But she must bear the Douglas eye?
Can I not view a highland brand,
But it must match the Douglas hand?
Can I not frame a fevered dream,
But still the Douglas is the theme?—
I'll dream no more—by manly mind
Not even in sleep is will resigned.
My midnight orison said o'er,
I'll turn to rest, and dream no more."—
His midnight orison he told,
A prayer with every bead of gold,
Consigned to heaven his cares and woes,
And sunk in undisturbed repose;
Until the heath-cock shrilly crew,
And morning dawned on Benvenue.

'The Bonnets of Bonnie Dundee'

The Christmas Box: An Annual Present for Children, ed. T. Crofton
Croker (London: William Harrison Ainsworth, 1828).

To the Lords of Convention, 'twas Clavers who spoke,
Ere the king's crown go down there are crowns to be broke;
So let each Cavalier who loves honour and me—
Let him follow the bonnet of bonnie Dundee.
   Come fill up my cup, come fill up my can,
   Come saddle my horses, and call up my men;
   Come open the West-port, and let me gae free,
   And it's room for the bonnets of bonnie Dundee.

Dundee he is mounted—he rides up the street,
The bells are rung backwards, the drums they are beat;
But the Provost, douce man, said, "Just e'en let him be,
The Town is weel quit of that deil of Dundee."
   Come fill up, &c.

As he rode down the sanctified bends of the Bow,
Each carline was flyting and shaking her pow;
But some young plants of grace—they look'd couthy and slee,
Thinking "luck to thy bonnet, thou bonnie Dundee."
   Come fill up, &c.

With sour-featured Whigs the Grass-market was pang'd,
As if half the West had set tryste to be hang'd;
There was spite in each face, there was fear in each ee,
As they watch'd for the bonnet of bonnie Dundee.
   Come fill up, &c.

These cowls of Kilmarnock had spits and had spears,
And lang-hafted gullies to kill Cavaliers;
But they shrunk to close-heads, and the causeway left free,
At the toss of the bonnet of bonnie Dundee.
   Come fill up, &c.

He spurr'd to the foot of the high castle rock,
And to the gay Gordon he gallantly spoke—
"Let Mons Meg and her marrows three vollies let flee,
For the love of the bonnets of bonnie Dundee."
   Come fill up, &c.

The Gordon has ask'd of him wither he goes,
"Wheresoever shall guide me the spirit of Montrose,
Your Grace in short space shall have tidings of me,
Or that low lies the bonnet of bonnie Dundee."
    Come fill up, &c.

There are hills beyond Pentland, and streams beyond Forth,
If there's Lords in the Southland, there's Chiefs in the North;
There are wild dunnie-wassals, three thousand times three,
Will cry *Hoigh!* for the bonnets of bonnie Dundee.
    Come fill up, &c.

"Away to the hills, to the woods, to the rocks,
Ere I own a usurper I'll couch with the fox;
And tremble, false Whigs, tho' triumphant ye be,
You have not seen the last of my bonnet and me."
    Come fill up, &c.

He wav'd his proud arm, and the trumpets were blown,
The kettle-drums clash'd, and the horsemen rode on,
Till on Ravelston Craigs and on Clermiston lee,
Died away the wild war-note of bonnie Dundee.
    Come fill up my cup, come fill up my can,
    Come saddle my horses, and call up my men;
    Fling all your gates open, and let me gae free,
    For 'tis up with the bonnets of bonnie Dundee.

JAMES MONTGOMERY
(1771–1854)

THE Irvine native James Montgomery became an accomplished hymn writer and poet, after some fits and starts. Educated in Grace Hill in County Antrim and in Leeds, Montgomery grew up in a Moravian household. By the age of fifteen he had composed three volumes of sacred poems. During a mindnumbing apprenticeship to a baker, and anxious to secure a publisher for his writings, he ran away to London, where he worked for a bookseller. Frustrated with the lack of success, he then moved to Sheffield to take up a position at a newspaper, of which he later became the editor and then owner. Incarcerated on libel charges, he wrote *Prison Amusements* (1797). A volume of essays under the pseudonym Gabriel Silvertongue, *The Whisperer*, followed in 1798. *The Ocean* (1805) made little impact, but *The Wanderer of Switzerland and Other Poems* (1806), following shortly after, finally secured an appreciative readership.

'On Finding the Feathers of a Linnet Scattered on the Ground in a Solitary Walk'

The Poetical Works of James Montgomery (London: Longman, Brown, Green, and Longmans, 1854).

These little relics, hapless bird!
That strew the lonely vale,
With a silent eloquence record
Thy melancholy tale.

Like Autumn's leaves, that rustle round
From every withering tree,
These plumes, dishevell'd o'er the ground,
Alone remain of thee.

Some hovering kite's rapacious maw
Hath been thy timeless grave:

No pitying eye thy murder saw,
No friend appear'd to save.

Heaven's thunder smite the guilty foe!
No:—spare the tyrant's breath,
Till wintry winds, and famine slow,
Avenge thy cruel death!

But every feather of thy wing
Be quicken'd where it lies,
And at the soft return of Spring,
A fragrant cowslip rise!

Few were thy days, thy pleasures few,
Simple and unconfined;
On sunbeams every moment flew,
Nor left a care behind.

In Spring to build thy curious nest,
And woo thy merry bride,
Carol and fly, and sport and rest,
Was all thy humble pride.

Happy beyond the lot of kings,
Thy bosom knew no smart,
Till the last pang, that tore the strings
From thy dissever'd heart.

When late to secret griefs a prey,
I wander'd slowly here,
Wild from the copse an artless lay,
Like magic, won mine ear.

Perhaps 'twas thy last evening song,
That exquisitely stole
In sweetest melody along,
And harmonised my soul.

Now, blithe musician! now no more
Thy mellow pipe resounds,
But jarring drums at distance roar,
And yonder howl the hounds:—

The hounds, that through the echoing wood
The panting hare pursue;

The drums, that wake the cry of blood,
—The voice of glory too!

Here at my feet thy frail remains,
Unwept, unburied, lie,
Like victims on embattled plains,
Forsaken where they die.

Yet could the Muse, whose strains rehearse
Thine unregarded doom,
Enshrine thee in immortal verse,
Kings should not scorn thy tomb.

Though brief as thine my tuneful date,
When wandering near this spot,
The sad memorials of thy fate
Shall never be forgot.

While doom'd the lingering pangs to feel,
Of many a nameless fear,
One truant sigh from these I'll steal,
And drop one willing tear.

REBEKAH CARMICHAEL

(*FL.* 1790–1806)

———

REBEKAH OR REBECCA CARMICHAEL (later Hay) may have been born and raised in Edinburgh. Certainly, in 1790, she arranged for a collection of her *Poems* to be printed there; and she includes a dedication to David Steuart-Moncrieffe that places her in the city. The collection covers an astonishing array of topics across different forms, from lovelorn night scenes to philosophical soliloquies on nature. Sincere and sarcastic in equal measure, her poems reveal an endless variety of moods.

———

'The Tooth'

Poems (Edinburgh: Printed for the Author, 1790).

> O look not, lady, with disdain!
>   Nor fill our hearts with ruth;
> You still may charm some humble swain,
>   Altho' you've lost a tooth!
>
> Thy beaming eyes are black as jet,
>   And pretty is thy mouth;
> No angel ever smil'd so sweet,
>   Before you lost a tooth.
>
> While fondly thus you strive to shine
>   In all the charms of youth;
> Your face and figure e'er divine,
>   But, O! you've lost a tooth.
>
> Ah! why that angry frown? for shame!
>   I only speak the truth:
> It cannot hurt ELIZA's fame
>   To say she's lost a tooth.
>
> But search some hearts, perhaps you'll find
>   A greater fault forsooth;

O! it were well for woman kind
Were all their loss a tooth!

'On the St. Bernard's Canary Birds'

Sweet is the subject of my verse,
Then let the softest notes rehearse
    The simple tale of woe;
Two pretty birds, by love endear'd,
Elate on airy pinions rear'd,
    In mutual flight did go

To yonder grove, where neither strife,
Nor jarring scenes of busy life,
    Could hurt the little pair;
They knew the master good and kind,
Of tender heart, and equal mind,
    And thought to settle there.

In sweetest notes his praise they sung,
In yonder yew bush hatch'd their young,
    Yet shyly shun'd his care;
Around the season seem'd to smile,
They knew not nature could beguile,
    So flew in open air.

Their infant brood had caught the wing,
Their little throats were tun'd to sing,
    When lo! the killing frost
Did on each tender blossom seize;
Chill, helpless 'mong the hoary trees,
    They fell, for ever lost.

Yet shall some pretty babe relate
Their timeless end, but happy fate,
    Too apt to find an urn;
And other songsters, as they fly,
Shall view them with a plaintive eye,
    But envy while they mourn.

ANNE ROSS

(*FL.* 1777–1798)

━━

ANNE ROSS may have been a native of Glasgow. In that city she published *A Collection of Poems*, which ran to three editions by 1798, and
many of her pieces refer to the Clyde and the surrounding areas.
Favouring rhyming quatrains, Ross nevertheless enjoyed experiment-
ing in a variety of forms, from very short epistles to longer, more
thoughtful meditations.

━━

'On Being Desired by a Friend, in the Year 1785, to Make a Poem on a Family Residing Near the Banks of Clyde'

A Collection of Poems, 3rd edn (Glasgow: R. Chapman, 1798).

What shall I do? for me it suits not well,
In verse, the language of my heart to tell;
Tho' happy here, cannot restrain my tears,
When I remember days of other years:
Tho' happy at this time and in this place,
Yet all my past enjoyments I can trace.

The many happy days I spent with you,
They now are gone and never can return;
And when remembrance calls past scenes to view,
Tho' happy here, I cannot help to mourn.

Still may kind Heav'n its choicest influence shower
Upon your serious hours, or hours of mirth;
In every virtue may you happy be,
And bless the honour'd dame who gave you birth.

One son is left, to bless these happy plains,
And, for to sweeten all the joys of life

A num'rous offspring in his house remains;
A virtuous and an amiable wife.

In virtue may her lovely daughters shine,
All worthy of their justly honour'd race.
By the all-ruling powers above, divine,
May num'rous sons live to uphold the place.

MARY MCMORINE

(FL. 1794–1799)

———

ACCORDING to the title page of her collection *Poems, Chiefly on Religious Subjects* (1799), Mary McMorine or MacMorine was a servant-maid, perhaps based in or near to Edinburgh. A handful of the poems are dated 1794 or 1795, but most are left unmarked.

———

'Conflict'

Poems, Chiefly on Religious Subjects (Edinburgh: J. Pillans & Sons, 1799).

Ah! my tumultnous soul, be still,
    Why is my spirit hurried thus?
Silence, O Lord, this noisy storm,
    And speak this tempest into peace.

The raging ocean hears thy voice,
    Submissive to thy high command,
Its roaring billows strive in vain,
    To combat with the yielding sand.

O may thy mighty pow'r prevail,
    To conquer my most stubborn heart!
O calm this fever in my soul,
    Bid this seducing fiend depart.

Thy great salvation I neglect,
    My soul's deceiv'd from day to day;
A heart impure I still retain,
    Still thy salvation's far away.

Sprinkle my heart with water pure,
    And cleanse this guilty soul of mine;
Repair the ruin of the fall,
    And make me in thine image shine.

No peace the wicked can enjoy,
  This by experience I find,
Unhallow'd passions ever jarr,
  And fret and vex my anxious mind.

In mercy, Lord, think on my case,
  Nor leave me to my idols join'd,
Be thou my friend, and I am safe,
  Though earth and hell were both combin'd.

MARY MACLAURIN
(D. 1812)

———

MARY MACLAURIN'S *Poems* appeared in 1812, when the poet was already dead. The title page of the collection signals that she was the daughter of the late Colin Maclaurin, a Professor of Mathematics at the University of Edinburgh. (We might therefore presume that she was born in or near to Edinburgh.) According to a footnote to the final item in the collection, 'Verses Addressed to the Shade of Miss Mary Maclaurin, and respectfully inscribed to Miss Ann Maclaurin, Haddington', the poems were transcribed by James, the son of the poet William Wilkie.

———

'On the Death of Her Nephew, Addressed to his Linnet'

Poems (Haddington: George Miller and Son, 1812).

> Though formed, through air, to soar and swiftly fly,
>   A captive bred, a captive still remain;
> For know, sweet bird! now should'st thou mount on high,
>   Death would pursue, and strike thee down again.
> Thus in the body, toiling and confined,
>   Must still remain a prisoner like thee,
> The soul of man, even his immortal mind,
>   Till death arrives to let the captive free.
> Thou wert the darling of a lovely child,
>   But he, alas! too soon from life was torn;
> His soul was sensible, his temper mild,
>   He soar'd to heaven, and left us here to mourn;
> In blooming health, one morn we saw him rise,
>   How sweetly playful, innocently gay;
> Next morn, how great our anguish and surprise,
>   In death's fell jaws the lovely infant lay.

Ah! then, how languish'd every sprightly grace,
    How sad his eye, how sudden was his doom;
The shades of death o'erspread his beauteous face,
    Pale, pale and wan, he sunk into the tomb.
Methinks all nature while I sadly moan,
    A sympathetic face of sorrow wears;
The hollow winds responsive seem to groan,
    The clouds in sable, shedding floods of tears.
While sad dejected, languishing I lay,
    The gloom dispell'd, reviving hope was given,
Methought a voice celestial seemed to say,
    Cease to bewail, thy darling is in heaven!
He like a beautious flower with sweet perfume,
    Lest this low earth the tender bud should spoil,
Lest storms below should blast its lovely bloom,
    Was soon transplanted to a heavenly soil.
Bright as a seraph never more to die,
    In undecaying bloom he shines above;
Joins the society of saints on high,
    With heavenly harmony, seraphic love.
No more, sweet bird! should anguish fill my heart,
    Nor of captivity should thou complain;
Think not to fly, ah! we must never part,
    With me for life contentedly remain,
Though gay the plumes superior birds display,
    They seem to me less beautiful than thee;
Though sweet the nightingales enchanting lay,
    Still more melodious is thy song to me.

PATRICIA ROLLAND DARLING

(D. 1814)

———

POETICAL PIECES appeared posthumously in Edinburgh in 1817, three years after the author's death, according to 'Monody on the Death of the Author, Who Died suddenly, 14th February, 1814', the first of seven poems by her son, Peter Middleton Darling, that appear at the end of the volume. (The collection also includes pieces by Patricia Rolland Darling's daughter Jessy.)

———

'On Leaving Scotland for America'

Poetical Pieces (Edinburgh: Printed for the Author's Family, 1817).

> Farewell ye lawns, by fond remembrance blest,
>   Witnesses of my gay and happy hours!
> Where fond maternal love my bosom prest,
>   And happy infancy past amongst your bowers!
> Ye romantic plains, and blue heather bells,
>   By Spring's luxuriant hand smiles around!
> Ye flinty rocks and tremendous fells,
>   That frown on him who treads thy mystic ground!
> And oh! ye promis'd happiness, whose voice
>   Deluded fancy heard in ev'ry gloomy grove,
> Bidding this aching fearful heart rejoice,
>   In the bright sunshine of unfading love;
> Tho' lost to me, still may thy smile serene,
> Bless my friend of Scotia's regretted scene.

MARIA FALCONAR

(B. 1771)

THE Falconar sisters, Maria and Harriet, produced two joint collections of poems when they were still teenagers. *Poems* (1788) exhibits the precociousness of the Falconars across a variety of fashionable poetic genres. Among the venerable list of subscribers we find the Duke of Northumberland and leading authors Elizabeth Carter and Helen Maria Williams. Another volume, *On Slavery*, followed in the same year. In 1791 appeared a further collection, *Poetic Laurels*, which was addressed to the future King, George IV. The content of this volume suggests they were preparing for marriage and were aware it might limit their freedom to write more poetry. It is possible that they continued to write under their married names.

'The Dying Rose'

Poems (London: J. Johnson, and Messrs. Egertons, 1788).

> One summer's eve, the fair Myrtilla stray'd
>   To taste the coolness of the western breeze;
> On ev'ry gale ambrosial sweetness play'd,
>   And the soft zephyrs gently fann'd the trees.
>
> Amidst her ev'ning walk, Myrtilla heard
>   A rose, the loveliest of the flow'ry train,
> That once the garden's proudest boast appear'd,
>   In sad admonitory notes complain.
>
> Ah! see, fair nymph, she cry'd, these charms decay.
>   I once was fair and beautiful like thee;
> No fragrant blossom open'd to the day,
>   That equall'd mine, or could compare with me.
>
> Flatter'd and prais'd, I felt my beauty's pow'r,
>   I treated all the flow'ry race with scorn;

Till, 'mid my triumphs, in a lackless hour,
   From yonder bush by Sylvia was I torn.

A few short hours I bloom'd upon her breast,
   Adding new graces to her charming mien;
When (sad reverse!) what tongue can speak the rest;
   She dash'd my faded beauties on the green.

But time her beauties shall, like mine, impair;
   And thou, fair nymph, be warn'd, and mark my doom;
E'en thou, Myrtilla, must this ruin share,
   E'en thy bright charms must lose their boasted bloom.

CHRISTIAN GRAY

(1772–1830)

━━━

BORN in the parish of Aberdalgie in Perthshire, close to the Ochil Hills, Christian Gray came from a farming family. Losing her eyesight as a child, almost certainly as a result of smallpox, Gray learned to compose poetry by memory, over and over, before it could be committed to the page. Well-read in English and Scottish poetry, and religious writing, she particularly admired Milton and Cowper, as well as Ossian; she often imitated their works, in parts and wholes. She also composed ballad responses to Lady Nairne and other leading figures in Scotland. Her first volume of poems, *Tales, Letters, and other Pieces in Verse* (1808), was published in Edinburgh. In 1821 a further volume of poems appeared: *A New Selection of Miscellaneous Pieces in Verse*.

━━━

'Another Extract from Ossian'

A New Selection of Miscellaneous Pieces in Verse (Perth: R. Morison, 1821).

> From grief a kind of joy doth flow,
>   When peace is in the breast;
> Some minds indulge themselves in woe,
>   And love to be distress'd.
>
> Altho' by sad remembrance pain'd,
>   The heart still holds it dear,
> The soft sensation is retain'd,
>   Tho' causing many a tear. –
>
> But sorrow wastes the mournful soul,
>   Its joyless days are few,
> Whose heart of settled sadness full
>   Bids cheerfulnes adieu!—
>
> A willing stranger to delight,
>   It wastes in early bloom,

Like flowers which nightly mildews blight,
   And scorching suns consume.—

The floweret bends its heavy head,
   The killing drops to drink,
So does the mind to pleasure dead,
   In cherish'd sorrow sink.—

But grief doth such in secret waste,
   Their fleeting days are few,
Whose minds by settled gloom possess'd,
   Bid chearfulness adieu!—

CHRISTIAN MILNE
(1773–1816)

───

THE working-class poet Christian Milne (*née* Ross) was baptized in Inverness, though the family later settled in Aberdeenshire, when the poet's widowed father remarried. Briefly schooled at a dame-school in Auchintoul, Milne quickly developed a love for literature. At fourteen, she went out to service and began writing her own poetry. She destroyed most of her early efforts, until she received encouragement from one of her employers who had stumbled across some discarded pages. A volume of her verse was published in 1805. Illness prevented her from doing much writing after 1810, and apparently none of her work except the 1805 volume survives in print.

───

'To a Lady who said it was Sinful to Read Novels'

Simple Poems, on Simple Subjects (Aberdeen: J. Chalmers and Co., 1805).

> To love these Books, and harmless Tea,
>   Has always been my foible,
> Yet will I ne'er forgetful be
>   To read my Psalms and Bible.
>
> Travels I like, and Hist'ry too,
>   Or entertaining Fiction;
> Novels and Plays I'd have a few,
>   If sense and proper diction.
>
> I love a natural harmless Song,
>   But cannot sing like Handel;
> Depriv'd of such resource, the tongue
>   Is sure employ'd—in scandal.

'To a Gentleman Desirous of Seeing My Manuscript'

> I'm gratify'd to think that you
>   Should wish to see my Songs,

As few would read my Book, who knew
  To whom this Book belongs.

My mean estate, and birth obscure,
  The ignorant will scorn;
Respect, tho' distant, from the good,
  Makes that more lightly borne.

Tho' I could write with Seraph pen –
  Tho' Angels did inspire,
None but the candid and humane
  My writings would admire.

The proud wou'd cry, "Such paltry works
  We will not deign to read;
The Author's but a Shipwright's Wife,
  And was a serving Maid."

Inur'd to hardships in my youth,
  If want my age should crown,
I'll never beg the haughty's bread;
  Death's milder than their frown.

You'll think but little of my Songs,
  When you have read them o'er;
But say, "They're well enough from her"—
  And I expect no more.

EÒGHANN MACLACHLAINN /
EWEN MACLACHLAN

(1773–1822)

━━

Ewen MacLachlan (Eòghann MacLachlainn) was a weaver's son from Coruanan in Lochaber. Prodigiously clever, he was educated in the parish school of Kilmallie and at King's College, Aberdeen. He spent his working life in that city, serving as librarian of King's College and successively master of the Parochial School and the Grammar School. A pioneer in Scottish Gaelic paleography and lexicography, he translated most of Homer's *Iliad* into Gaelic. As a poet in his own right he also published original works in Gaelic, Latin, Greek, and English. Employing a large and limpid vocabulary, he is at his best in realistic descriptions of rural labour, seasons, and festivals such as Christmas and New Year.

━━

'An t-Earrach'

Translator's transcription

Thàinig earrach oirnn mun cuairt,
　　Théid am fuachd fo fhuadach cian.
Théid air imrich thar a' chuain
　　Geamhradh buaireasach nan sian:
Ràith sneachdach, reòtach, cruaidh,
　　A dh'atas colg nan luath-ghaoth dian—
Sligneach, deilgneach, feanntaidh, fuar,
　　A lom 's a dh'aognaich snuadh gach nì.

'Nis on thill a' ghrian a-nall,
　　Tréigidh sìde 's annradh garg,
Ìslichear srannraich nan speur
　　'S ceanglar srian am beul nan stoirm.
Sguiridh na builg-shéididh chruaidh

San aibheis àird a b' uaibhreach fearg,
Éighear Sìothchaimh ris gach dùil
'S tionnda'idh iad gu mùthadh foirm.

Iompaichear an uair gu blàths
    Le frasan on àird an-iar;
Leaghaidh sneachd 'na shruithibh luath
    O ghuaillibh nan gruaim-bheann ciar.
Fosglaidh tobraichean a' ghrunnd
    A bhrùchdas 'nan spùtaibh dian
'S deigh gu sgealbach ceillchdeach dlùth
    Le gleadhraich ghairbh ga sgùradh sìos.

Sgapaidh dall-cheò tiugh nan nial
    Ás a-chéile 'n-iar 's an-ear
'Na mheallaibh gibeach, ceigeach, liath,
    Druim-robach, oglaidh, ciar-dhubh, glas;
A' snàmh san fhailbhe mhóir gun cheann
    A-nunn 's a-nall mar luing fo beairt,
'S iadhaidh iad 'nan rùsgaibh bàn
    Mu spiodaibh pìceach àrd nam bac.

Nochdaidh Phoebus duinn a ghnùis
    A' deàlradh o thùr nan speur
Le soillse caoimhneil, boillsgeil, blàth,
    Gu tlusmhor bàidheil ris gach creubh.
Na sgrios a' ghailleann chiùrrach, fhuar,
    Mosglaidh iad a-nuas on eug;
Ath-nuadhaichear a' bhliadhn' as ùr,
    Gach dùil gu mùirneach, sùrd air feum.

Sgeadaichear na lòin 's na blàir
    Fo chòmhdach àlainn lusan meanbh;
Sgaoilidh iad a-mach ri gréin
    An duilleach fhéin fo mhìle dealbh—
Gu gibeach caisreagach fo'm blàth
    Le'n daithibh àillidh, fann-gheal, dearg,
Bileach, mealach, maoth-bhog, ùr,
    Luirgneach, sùghmhor, driùchdach, gorm.

Gur h-ionmhainn an sealladh fonnmhor
    A chìtear air lom gach leacainn;
S cùbhraidh leam na fìon na Frainge

Fàileadh thom, is bheann, is ghlacag—
Mìsleineach, biolaireach, sòbhrach
(Eagach cuach nan neòinein maiseach),
Seamragach, failleineach, brìoghmhor,
Luachrach, dìtheineach, gun ghaiseadh.

Thig muilleinean de shluagh an fheòir
Beò fo thlus nam fann-ghath tlàth,
Le'n sgiathaibh sìoda ball-bhreac òir
'S iad daithte 'm bòidhchead mìos a' Mhàigh—
Ann an tuairneagaibh geal nam flùr
Dùisgidh iad le h-iochd a' bhlàiths
'S measgnaichidh an rìghleadh dlùth
Sa chéitein chiùin nach lot an càil.

Dìridh snodhach suas on fhriamhaich
Throimh cham-chuislean snìomhain bhad-chrann,
Gu maoth-bhlasta, mealach, cùbhraidh,
Sìor-chur sùigh sna fiùrain shlatach;
Bidh an còmhdach gorm a' brùchdadh
Throimh shlios ùr nan dlùth-phreas dosrach—
Duilleach, babach, uasal, sgiamhach
Dreach nam meur as rìomhach coltas.

Bidh eòineinean binn a' chàthair
A' cruinneachadh shràbh gu neadan—
Togaidh iad sna geugaibh uaigneach
Aitribh chuartagach ri taice;
Laighidh gu clùthmhor 'nan tàmh
A bhlàithteachadh nan cruinn-ubh breaca
Gus am brist an t-slige làn,
'S an tig an t-àlach òg a-mach dhaibh.

Thig éibhneas na bliadhn' an tùs
Mun crìochnaich an t-ùr-mhìos-Màirt—
Bheir an spréidh an toradh trom
Le fosgladh am bronn gu làr:
Brùchdaidh minn is laoigh is uain
'Nam mìltibh mun cuairt don bhlàr,
S breac-gheal dreach nan raon 's nan stùc
Fo choisreadh mheanbh nan lùth-chleas bàth.

Bidh gabhair nan adhaircean cràcach,
Stangach, cam, an àird nan sgealb-chreag.

Ròb-bhrat iom-dhaitheach mun cuairt dhaibh,
 Caitein ciar-dhubh gruamach gorm-ghlas,
'S na minneinean laghach, greannmhor
 Le meigeadaich fhann, gan leanmhainn—
S mireineach a' chleasachd ghuanach
 Bhios air pòr beag luath nan gearra-mhinn.

Caoirich cheig-rùsgach fo chòmhdach
 Sgaoilt' air réidhlein lòintean driùchdach
'S uaineinean cho geal ri cainchein
 Air chluaintean nan learg ri sùgradh.
An crodh mór gu lìontaidh, làirceach
 Ag ionaltradh fhàsach ùr-ghorm—
An dream lìth-dhonn, caisfhionn, bàn-bhreac,
 Guaillfhionn, crà-dhearg, màgach, dùmhail.

S inntinneach an ceòl ri m' chluais
 Fann-gheum laogh mun cuairt don chrò,
Ri comh-ruith timcheall nan raon,
 Grad-bhrisg, seang-mhear, aotrom, beò;
Stairirich aig an luirgnean luath
 Sìos mun bhruaich gu guanach òg—
Steach 's a-mach á buailidh làin
 S bras an leum ri bàirich bhò!

'N aimsir ghnàthaichte na bliadhna,
 Sgapar sìol gu biadh san fhearann,
Ga thilgeadh 'na fhrasaibh dìona
 Sna h-iomairean fiara, cama;
Sgalag is eich làidir ghnìomhach
 Ri sraighlich nan cliath gan tarraing
'S tiodhlaicear fon dùslaing mhìn
 An gràinein lìontaidh as brìoghmhor toradh.

Sgoiltear am buntàta cnuachdach
 'Na sgrailleagaibh cluasach bachlach;
Théid an inneir phronn 'na lòdaibh
 Socach trom air chòmhnard achaidh
Le treun-ghearrain chùbach chàrnach,
 Cliathach, spidreach, bràideach, srathrach—
Sùrd air teachd-an-tìr nan Gàidheal
 Dh'fheuch an tàrar e fon talamh.

Nuair a thogas Phoebus àigh
   Mach gu h-àird nan nial a cheann
O sheòmar deàlrach a' chuain,
   Ag òradh air chruach nam beann,
Brùchdaidh ás gach ceàrn an tuath,
   Staigh chan fhuirich, luath no mall—
Inntrigidh air gnìomh nam buadh
   Buntàta 's inneir! Suas an crann!

Théid an inneal-draibh an òrdugh,
   Seann eich làidir mhòr a' tarraing
Nan ionnsramaid gleadhrach, ròpach—
   Beairt 'san lìonmhor còrd is amall,
Ailbheagan nan cromag fiara,
   Socach, coltrach, giadhach, langrach;
Glige-ghlaige crainn is iarainn,
   Sùrd air gnìomh, o'm biadhchor toradh.

Hùis! An t-ùraiche 's am bàn-each,
   Fear air ceann, 's air crann sa chorraig,
Buntàta, 's inneir theth 'na cliathaibh,
   Ga taomadh san fhiar-chlais chorraich
Aig bannal clis, lùthmhor, gleusta,
   Cridheil, aotrom, brisg, gun smalan,
'S gillean òg a' dìol na h-àbhachd,
   Briathrach, gàireach, càirdeil, fearail.

Nuair dh'fholchar san ùir am pòr
   Thig feartan g'ar còir on àird—
Á sgirtean liath-ghlas nan nial
   Frasaidh e, gu ciatach blàth,
Silteach, sàmhach, lìonmhor, ciùin,
   Trom 'na bhrùchdaibh ciùbhrach tlàth:
S mìorbhailteach a' bhraonachd dhlùth,
   Tarbhach, maoth-mhìn, driùchdach, sèamh.

S lìonmhor suaicheantas an earraich
   Nach comas domh 'luadh le fileachd:
Ràith' as tric a' caochladh earraidh,
   'S ioma car o 'thùs gu 'dheireadh,
Ràithe 'n tig am faoilleach feannaidh,
   Fuar chloch-mheallain, stoirm nam peiler,

Feadag, sguabag, gruaim a' ghearrain,
    Crainntidh 'chailleach as beurra friodhan.

Nuair spùtas gaoth lom a' Mhàirt oirnn,
    Nì 'n t–sìd' ud an t–àl a chrannadh—
Mìos cabhagach, oibreach, saothrach
    Nam feasgar slaod-chianail reangach,
Acras a' diogladh nam maodal,
    Blianach, caol-ghlas, aognaidh, greannach;
Deòghlar trian de t' fhìor-liunn-tàth uait
    'S mar ghad snìomhain, tàirnear fad' thu.

Ràithe san tig tùs annlain,
    Liteach, cabhrach, làghan lapach,
Druim-fhionn, ceann-fhionn, brucach, riaspach,
    Robach, dreamsglach, riabhach, rapach,
Càl is feòil is cruinn-bhuntàta
    'S aran corca làidir reachdmhor—
Bog no cruaidh, ma chanar biadh ris,
    Se nach diùlt an ciad nì as faisge.

Nuair thig òg-mhìos céitein chiùin oirnn
    Bidh a' bhliadhna 'n tùs a maise,
'S flathail caoimhneil soillse gréine—
    Mìos geal ceutach, speur-ghorm, feartach,
Flùrach, ciùbhrach, bliochdach, maoineach,
    Uanach, caorach, laoghach, martach,
Gruitheach, uachdrach, càiseach, sùghmhor,
    Mealach, cùbhraidh, driùchdach, dosrach.

'Nis théid earrach uainn air chuairt
    'S thig an samhradh ruaig a-nall.
'S gorm-bhog duilleach gheug air choill,
    Eunlaith 'seinn air bhàrr nan crann;
Driùchdan òir air feur gach glinn
    'S làn-thoil-inntinn sgiamh nam beann—
Théid mi ceum throimhn lòn a-nunn
    'S tàirneam crìoch air fonn mo rann.

'Spring' (translated by Ronald Black)

Spring has come around to us,
    Into faraway exile goes the cold.

Turbulent winter of elements
    Moves its home across the sea:
A snowy quarter, hard and frozen,
    That swells the rage of swift, cruel winds—
Shelly, prickly, cold, and flaying,
    It has bared and wasted away all things.

Now that the sun has come back across,
    Wild weather and storm will go away,
The roar of the skies will be subdued
    And a bridle secured to the mouth of the gales.
The fierce bellows will run out of wind
    In the high abyss of noble rage,
To all the elements Peace will be called
    And they will alter their mode of display.

The weather will be turned into warmth
    With showers arriving from the west;
Snow will melt into tumbling streams
    From the flanks of all the grey gloomy hills.
Underground springs will open up
    And burst forth in turbulent spouts
While ice in tight-packed splinters and blocks
    Will be washed downhill with a savage roar.

The thick dark curtain of misty clouds
    Will drift apart to the west and east
Into ragged, shaggy, silvery lumps,
    Fearful, rough-ridged, tawny and grey;
In the great void without end they will swim
    Like a full-rigged ship going back and forth,
And they'll encircle like sheep's white fleeces
    The high-peaked boggy mountain-tops.

Phoebus reveals to us his face
    Shining from battlements in the skies
With light that's kindly, radiant, warm,
    Tender and loving to all flesh.
All that was crushed by cold brutal storm
    Will waken and rise again from death;
The year will be renewed once again,
    All elements glad, as they're anxious to serve.

The fields and meadows will be adorned
　　With a lovely covering of tiny herbs;
In the sunshine they will spread out
　　Their foliage into a thousand shapes—
Bunched and wrinkled under their blooms
　　With their lovely colours, pale-white, red,
Bladed, honeyed, gently soft, fresh,
　　Long-stalked, sap-filled, dew-covered, blue.

Delightful will be the happy sight
　　To be seen on the brow of every slope;
Sweeter to me than the wine of France
　　Is the scent of hills, and bens, and hollows—
Of meadow grass, of cress, of primrose
　　(Notched is the cup of the lovely daisies),
Of shamrocks, of suckers, and of sap,
　　Of rushes, of flowers, and all unblemished.

The millions of the grassy host are brought
　　Alive by the balm of soft, mild beams,
Their silken golden speckled wings
　　Will be tinged with the loveliness of May—
In the bright cups of the flowers
　　They'll awake to the mercy of the warmth
And mix in close-packed aerial dance
　　For gentle maytime can't wound their strength.

Up through the crooked, winding veins
　　Of clustering trees climbs sap from the roots,
Gentle and sweet, honeyed and scented,
　　Steadily moistening branching boughs;
The rich green covering bursts out
　　Through the fresh flank of the thick-plumed bushes—
Leafy, tasselled, noble and beautiful
　　Is the form of the twigs now lovely in shape.

The little melodious birds of the moss
　　Will all be gathering straws for their nests—
In secluded branches they'll build
　　Well-supported circular homes;
They will settle in downy repose
　　To hatch the rounded, speckled eggs

Until, when the full shell breaks apart,
    Out will come their young brood of chickens.

The joy of the year will first arrive
    Before the young month of March is out—
The stock will yield their heavy fruit
    By opening their wombs to the ground:
Kids, calves and lambs all bursting out
    In their thousands around the plain,
Speckle-white the hue of the fields and hills
    Under footwork of childlike frolicking games.

In the heights of the jagged rocks are the goats
    With their high-rising, curved, antler-like horns.
They wear shaggy coats of many colours,
    Of repulsive grey-black blue-grey fur,
While their lively, adorable little offspring
    Follow them, bleating appealingly—
How funny they are, the crazy pranks
    Of that swift little tribe of diminutive kids.

Sheep matted of fleece when under cover
    Are scattered on plains of dewy meadows
With little lambs as white as cotton-sedge
    Frolicking on the sloping fields.
Great cattle replenished and plump
    Are grazing pastures renewed and green—
The brown-coloured, white-legged, white-speckled tribe,
    White-shouldered, red-footed, short-legged, big.

Delightful music to my ear
    Is the calves' faint lowing around the pen,
Running together around the fields,
    Sudden-brisk, slim-lively, light, and alive;
Their long swift legs go thundering
    Down round the brae in youthful exuberance—
In and out of a fold that's full
    They eagerly jump to the lowing of cows!

In the customary time of year
    Seed is sown in the land for food.
It is broadcast in vehement showers
    Into the crooked, bending rigs;

A servant with strong and willing horses
    Draws the rattling harrows along
And the plump little grain of nourishing fruit
    Is buried under the smooth dark soil.

The lumpy potatoes are well split up
    Into curly ear-shaped parings;
Chopped dung is brought in jagged loads
    On to the level part of a field
By sturdy garrons with sledges and slipes,
    Panniered, tight-pulling, collared, draught-saddled—
So is everything devoted to putting
    The Gael's subsistence into the ground.

When glorious Phoebus raises his head
    Out to the summit of the clouds
From the ocean's shining chamber,
    Gilding the mountain pinnacles,
Joint-tenants burst from every neuk,
    Swift or slow, they don't stay in—
There enter now on productive duty
    Potatoes, dung! Up with the plough!

The dragging machine is put together,
    Large, mature, strong horses pull
The rattling, rope-tied instruments—
    Tackle of multiple cords and whippletrees,
With bent hooks connected up to rings,
    Socked, coultered, iron-banded and chained;
Clink-clank go the shafts and irons,
    Willing work, with food resulting.

Hùis! to the young horse and the white one,
    One man at the head, one at the left plough-stilt,
While potatoes, and hot dung in creelfuls,
    Are dug into the rough crooked furrow
By lively, sturdy, skilful women
    Who're merry, light-hearted, brisk, undaunted,
As young boys parry their jokes,
    Articulate, laughing, affectionate, manly.

When the seed is hidden in the ground
    Powers come to us from high above—

From the silver-grey edges of the clouds
    Come showers, beautiful and warm,
Dripping, silent, copious, calm,
    Heavy in drizzly tranquil bursts:
Marvellous is the persistent rain,
    Profitable, smooth-soft, dewy, mild.

Numerous are the signs of spring
    That I'm incompetent to put into verse:
Quarter that constantly changes clothes,
    With many a twist from start to finish,
Quarter that brings the flaying wolftime,
    Freezing hailstones, storms like bullets,
Whistler, sweeper, cutter's snarl,
    The withering hag whose voice is shrill.*

When the bare March wind breaks out upon us,
    It's weather that shrivels up all offspring—
Month of hurry, of work, and of labour
    Full of long slow lingering evenings,
Of hunger that gnaws into the belly,
    Meagre, skinny-pale, wasted, unkempt;
It sucks from you a third of your strength
    And like a curled willow withy, it pulls you out far.

Season that brings the beginnings of luxury
    With porridge, sowens and pithless flummery,
Whitebacked, whitefaced, speckled, coarse,
    Untidy, mixed-up, brindled, and slovenly,
With kale and flesh and round potatoes
    And oaten bread that's strong and sturdy—
Be it soft or hard, if it is called food,
    No one will scorn the first thing to hand.

When the young month of calm maytime arrives*
    The year will be at the start of its beauty,
Princely and kindly the gleam of the sun—
    Bright month that's lovely, blue-skied, renowned,
Flowery, drizzly, milky, productive,
    Lamby and sheepful, calvy and cowful,
Curdy and creamful, cheesy and sapful,
    Honeyed and scented, dewy, luxuriant.

Now spring will move along on its way
    And summer will come and stay for a while.
Leaves on boughs in the woods will be green and soft,
    And bird-flocks will sing on the tops of the trees;
With dewdrops of gold on the grass of each glen
    The hills' allure gives us pleasure of mind—
I'll go for a walk across the meadow
    And draw to an end my verses' tune.

HARRIET FALCONAR

(B. 1774)

===

THE Falconar sisters, Maria and Harriet, produced two joint collections of poems when they were still teenagers. *Poems* (1788) exhibits the precociousness of the Falconars across a variety of fashionable poetic genres. Among the venerable list of subscribers we find the Duke of Northumberland and leading authors Elizabeth Carter and Helen Maria Williams. Another volume, *On Slavery*, followed in the same year. In 1791 appeared a further collection, *Poetic Laurels*, which was addressed to the future King, George IV. The content of this volume suggests they were preparing for marriage and were aware it might limit their freedom to write more poetry. It is possible that they continued to write under their married names: that trail has gone cold.

===

'On Infancy'

Poems (London: J. Johnson, and Messrs. Egertons, 1788).

> Hail, scenes of life, more lovely than the spring,
>> More beauteous than the dawn of summer's day,
> More gay and artless than the birds that sing
>> Their tuneful sonnets on the leafy spray!
>
> Adieu, ye paths, adorn'd with springing flowers,
>> Oh! could those vernal sweets again be given,
> When guardian angels watch'd my guiltless hours,
>> And strove to guide my erring steps to heaven.
>
> So the first pair in Paradise were blest,
>> Perpetual pleasures open'd to the view;
> Nor guilt, nor fear, disturb'd the peaceful breast,
>> Nor anxious care their happy moments knew.
>
> But, ah! those joys shall fly with winged speed,
>> And leave to busy care the jocund scene;

To innocence shall guilt and pain succeed,
    To lively youth long hours of gloom and spleen.

So shines the sun in orient splendour bright,
    So bloom the roses on a summer's day;
The sun shall sink in dark and chearless night,
    The blooming roses feel a sure decay.

ROBERT TANNAHILL

(1774–1810)

——

THE songwriter Robert Tannahill was born in Paisley, where, aside from stints in Lochwinnoch and Bolton, he worked as a weaver for the rest of his short life. He began to write verses while still at school, and continued to write, at the loom, as an adult. Early pieces appeared in the *Glasgow Courier* and elsewhere. A rapidly sold volume of poems, *The Soldier's Return* (1805), was published by subscription. Tannahill, a founding secretary of the Paisley Burns Club, was strongly influenced by the Ayrshire Bard and, to a lesser extent, by James Thomson and William Shenstone. Deceptively simple, Tannahill's sonorous songs fed the demands of a burgeoning genteel market that set folk pieces to piano and other instruments. However, the poet's hopes for a second edition of his works stalled. Despondent, he destroyed his papers. He died by suicide at the age of thirty-five.

——

'Eild. A Fragment'

The Poems and Songs of Robert Tannahill (Paisley: Alex. Gardner, 1874).

> The rough hail rattles through the trees,
>   The sullen lift low'rs gloomy grey,
> The trav'ller sees the swelling storm,
>   And seeks the ale-house by the way.
>
> But, waes me! for yon widow'd wretch,
>   Borne down wi' years, an' heavy care,
> Her sapless fingers scarce can nip
>   The wither'd twigs to beet her fire.
>
> Thus youth and vigour fends itsel';
>   Its help, recipricol, is sure,
> While dowless Eild, in poortith cauld,
>   Is lanely left to stan' the stoure.

'Written with a Pencil in a Tap-Room'

This warl's a tap-room owre an' owre,
    Whare ilk ane tak's his caper,
Some taste the sweet, some drink the sour,
    As waiter Fate sees proper;
Let mankind live ae social core,
    An' drap a' selfish quar'ling,
An' when the Landlord ca's his score,
    May ilk ane's clink be sterling.

'Barochan Jean'
(Air: "Johnnie M'Gill")

'Tis ha'ena ye heard, man, o' Barochan Jean?
    An' ha'ena ye heard, man, o' Barochan Jean?
How death an' starvation cam' o'er the hale nation,
    She wrocht sic mischief wi' her twa pawkie een.
The lads an' the lasses were deein' in dizzens,
    The tane killed wi love, an' the tither wi' spleen;
The ploughin', the sawin', the shearin', the mawin'—
    A' wark was forgotten for Barochan Jean.

Frae the south an' the north, o'er the Tweed an' the Forth,
    Sic comin' an gangin' there never was seen;
The comers were cheerie, the gangers were blearie,
    Despairin' or hopin' for Barochan Jean.
The carlins at hame were a' girnin' and granin',
    The bairns were a' greetin' frae mornin' till e'en;
They gat naething for crowdie but runts boiled tae sowdie,
    For naethin gat growin' for Barochan Jean.

The doctors declared it was past their descrivin',
    The ministers said 'twas a judgment for sin;
But they looked sae blae, an' their hearts were sae wae,
    I was sure they were deein' for Barochan Jean.
The burns on road-sides were a' dry wi' their drinkin',
    Yet a' wadna sloken the drouth i' their skin;
A' roun' the peat-stacks, an' alangst the dyke backs,
    E'en the win's were a' sighin', sweet Barochan Jean.

The timmer ran dune wi' the makin' o' coffins,
   Kirkyairds o' their swaird were a' howkit fu' clean;
Deid lovers were packit like herrin' in barrels,
   Sic thousan's were deein' for Barochan Jean.
But mony braw thanks tae the laird o' Glenbrodie,
   The grass owre their graffs is now bonnie an' green:
He sta' the proud heart o' our wanton young ladie,
   An' spoiled a' the charms o' her twa pawkie een.

'The Braes of Balquhither'

(Air: "The three carles o' Buchanan")

Let us go, lassie, go
   To the braes of Balquhither,
Where the blaeberries grow
   'Mang the bonnie Highland heather;
Where deer and the rae,
   Lightly bounding together,
Sport the lang Simmer day
   On the braes o' Balquhither.

I will twine thee a bow'r,
   By the clear siller fountain,
And I'll cover it o'er
   Wi' the flowers o' the mountain;
I will range through the wilds,
   And the deep glens sae dreary,
And return wi' their spoils.
   To the bow'r o' my deary.

When the rude wintry win'
   Idly raves round our dwelling,
And the roar of the linn
   On the night breeze is swelling;
So merrily we'll sing,
   As the storm rattles o'er us,
'Till the dear shieling ring
   Wi' the light lilting chorus.

Now the Simmer is in prime,
   Wi' the flowers richly blooming,

And the wild mountain thyme
   A' the moorlands perfuming;
To our dear native scenes
   Let us journey together,
Where glad innocence reigns
   'Mang the braes o' Balquhither.

ROBERT ALLAN
(1774–1841)

———

THE weaver poet Robert Allan hailed from Kilbarchan in Renfrewshire. Early in life he began to write songs, chiefly in Scots. Like Tannahill, a fellow weaver poet who much admired him, he would often compose while working at his loom. Robert Archibald Smith set many of his songs to music and published them in *The Scottish Minstrel* in 1820. Some pieces reappeared in ornate editions such as *The Harp of Renfrewshire*. A volume of Allan's poems finally appeared in 1836, in the author's sixties. He emigrated to America, with his large family, but died barely six days after the voyage.

———

'The Covenanter's Lament'

Evening Hours: Poems and Songs (Glasgow: David Robertson; Edinburgh: Oliver and Boyd; London: Simpkin, Marshall, and Co., 1836).

(Air: "The Martyr's Grave")

There's nae covenant now, lassie!
   There's nae covenant now!
The solemn league and covenant
   Are a' broken through!
There's nae Renwick now, lassie,
   There's nae gude Cargill,
Nor holy sabbath preaching
   Upon the Martyr's Hill!

It's naething but a sword, lassie!
   A bluidy, bluidy ane!
Waving owre poor Scotland
   For her rebellious sin.
Scotland's a' wrang, lassie,
   Scotland's a' wrang—

It's neither to the hill nor glen,
   Lassie, we daur gang.

The Martyr's Hill forsaken,
   In simmer's dusk, sae calm;
There's nae gathering now, lassie,
   To sing the eenin' psalm!
But the martyr's grave will rise, lassie,
   Aboon the warrior's cairn;
An' the martyr soun' will sleep, lassie,
   Aneath the waving fern!

MARGARET MAXWELL INGLIS

(1774–1843)

———

A RELIGIOUS poet, Margaret Maxwell Inglis (*née* Murray) hailed from Sanquhar in Dumfriesshire. Inglis displayed her literary and musical gifts early, but apparently wrote relatively little until late in life. After the death of her second husband, John Inglis, in 1826, she became a prolific author right up until her own death. Under the name M. M. Inglis, *Miscellaneous Collection of Poems, Chiefly Scriptural Pieces* finally appeared in 1838. Here, the poet showcases an extraordinary range of works, from simple tales to elaborate epistles. While the moods shift throughout, the overriding tone is highly meditative.

———

'A Sabbath Morning Walk'

Miscellaneous Collection of Poems, Chiefly Scriptural Pieces (Edinburgh: Charles Ziegler, 1838).

> I've seen the spring's green promise
>   Through the thin soft morning air,
> And all around look lovely,
>   And rich, and sweet, and fair.
>
> I've seen yon gilded turrets
>   Reflect the morning beams,
> And nature's beauty swelling
>   In fields, and lakes, and streams.
>
> My heart has beat responsive
>   To every warbler's voice;
> And a purer glow of feeling
>   Has bid me to rejoice.
>
> But when my wanderings led me
>   To the distant lonely glen,
> And I had pass'd the portals
>   Of rich and honour'd men:—

O, then, indeed, a halo
    Of deep and calm repose
Stole gently, sweetly o'er me,
    As the humble cottage rose.

There melody so touching,
    So simple, yet so pure,
Those patriarchal strains, which speak
    Of David's mercies sure,

Rais'd every nobler feeling,
    To higher, holier things,
Than man can ever taste below
    From earth's polluted springs.

O how the soul is melted
    In extacy of love,
To trace those pure and simple strains
    To heaven's high courts above.

Like incense softly rising,
    While angels catch the song;
And each adoring spirit hears,
    And echoes it along.

This is indeed a Sabbath,
    A Sabbath of delight;
When hearts in humble gladness
    And grateful praise, unite.

O how all earthly greatness
    Flits by like empty air!
While we behold the peasant breathe
    His meek, yet fervent prayer.

This is our noblest treasure,
    This is our highest aim;
More lovely than a brow when wreath'd
    In chaplets green of fame.

This is the highest honour
    To dying sinners given;
Their access to a God of grace,
    Their intercourse with heaven.

JOHN LEYDEN
(1775–1811)

———

THE linguist and poet John Leyden was born in Denholm, near Hawick, in the Scottish Borders, and grew up on a farm in Henlawshiel. Taught to read by his grandmother, he briefly attended the parish school at Kirktown, and later studied under the Reverend James Duncan, a covenanting pastor. Later still, he distinguished himself at the University of Edinburgh, where he displayed a keen interest in Hebrew, Arabic, and Persian, as well as philosophy and theology. At Edinburgh he met the anthologist Robert Anderson, through whom he contributed to the *Edinburgh Literary Magazine*. He also contributed a ballad to Matthew Lewis's *Tales of Wonder* (1801). That year he also met Walter Scott, to whose *Minstrelsy of the Scottish Border* (1802–3) he contributed five poems and other materials. Retaining a lifelong love of linguistics, and travelling extensively in the ensuing decades, Leyden produced numerous essays on an array of Asian and Middle Eastern languages. In 1819, a posthumous collection of his verse appeared.

———

'Written in the Isle of Sky, in 1800'

The Poetical Remains of the Late Dr John Leyden, with Memoirs of His Life (London: Longman, Hurst, Rees, Orme, and Brown, 1819).

> At eve, beside the ringlet's haunted green
> I linger oft, while o'er my lonely head
> The aged rowan hangs her berries red;
> For there, of old, the merry elves were seen,
> Pacing with printless feet the dewy grass;
> And there I view, in many a figur'd train,
> The marshall'd hordes of sea-birds leave the main,
> And o'er the dark-brown moors hoarse-shrieking pass.
> Next in prophetic pomp along the heath

I see dim forms their shadowy bands arrange,
Which seem to mingle in encounter strange,
To work with glimmering blades the work of death:
In fancy's eye their meteor falchions glare;
But, when I move, the hosts all melt in liquid air.

SIR ALEXANDER BOSWELL

(1775–1822)

———

BORN and educated in Edinburgh, Alexander Boswell was a poet, antiquary, and politician. When his father, the biographer James Boswell, died, the teenager continued his legal studies in Leipzig, but soon gave them up. After visits to Dresden and Berlin, he returned to Britain. As a young man, Boswell composed several songs, including 'Jenny's Bawbee' and 'Jenny Dang the Weaver', which were published anonymously in various anthologies after 1790. In 1803 he produced *Songs, Chiefly in the Scottish Dialect*, *The Spirit of Tintoc*, and *Epistle to the Edinburgh Reviewers*. Other book-length poems include *Edinburgh; or, The Ancient Royalty* (1810), *Clan-Alpin's Vow* (1811), and *Sir Albon* (1811). In 1815 he established a private press at Auchinleck, where he published *The Tyrant's Fall* (1815), *Skeldon Haughs* (1816), and *The Woo-Creel* (1816).

———

'Jenny Dang the Weaver'

Songs, Chiefly in the Scottish Dialect (Edinburgh: Manners & Miller, 1803).

> At Willie's wedding o' the green,
>   The lassies, bonny witches,
> Were busked out in aprons clean,
>   And snaw-white Sunday's mutches.
> Auld Maysie bade the lads tak tent,
>   But Jock wad na believe her,
> But soon the fool his folly kent,
>   For—Jenny dang the Weaver.
>
> In ilka countra dance and reel
>   Wi' her he wad be babbin';
> When she sat doun, then he sat doun,
>   And till her wad be gabbin';

Whare'er she gaed, or butt or ben,
  The coof wad never leave her,
Aye cacklin' like a clockin' hen,
  But Jenny dang the Weaver.

Quoth he, "My lass, to speak my mind,
  Gude haith I needna swither,
Ye've bonny e'en, and gif ye're kind,
  I needna court anither."
He humm'd and haw'd—the lass cried pheugh,
  And bade the fool no deave her;
Then crack'd her thumb, and lap, and leugh,
  And dang the silly Weaver.

'To the Memory of Burns'

The Poetical Works of Sir Alexander Boswell, of Auchinleck, Baronet, ed.
Robert Howie Smith (Glasgow: Maurice Ogle & Company, 1871).

Ah! who shall breathe upon the oaten reed
  That pour'd its melody on winding Ayr,
And who shall claim thy mantle as his meed,
  Gift of wild poesy, which thou did'st wear?
    For rude and earthborn wight how little meet
    So rich a mantle, and a note so sweet!

Thee, Bard of Coila, all her echoes mourn,
  Hid in thy silent cave and tuneless grove,
No more the [   ]* on the breeze is borne
  Mirth's jocund carol, or the plaints of love.
    Dark Lugar's stream unheeded laves its bed,
    And all that liv'd to thee seems dull and dead.

But when soft memory of other days
  Steals on the fancy with delusive glow,
And while deep wrapt we ponder on thy lays
  With music not their own the waters flow;
    Thy spirit hov'ring seems to rule the spell,
    And our eyes glisten while our bosoms swell.

LADY BURY, CHARLOTTE SUSAN MARIA CAMPBELL

(1775–1861)

———

LADY CHARLOTTE BURY (*née* Campbell) was born into a Hiberno-Scottish aristocratic family in London. Her first publication, *Poems on Several Occasions*, appeared anonymously in 1797, when she was barely twenty-two years old. Until she was appointed lady-in-waiting to the future Queen Caroline in 1810, Bury spent much of her time in Edinburgh, where she entertained many of the literary celebrities of the day, forming a close bond with the novelist Susan Ferrier. Bury began her career as a novelist at this time, publishing *Self-Indulgence* anonymously in 1812. *Conduct is Fate* followed in 1822, and then a dozen other novels, the last of which, *The Two Baronets*, was published posthumously in 1864. In addition to novels and poems, Bury also wrote *Suspirium Sanctorum, or, Holy Breathings* (1826), a collection of prayers, and her best-known publication, *Diary Illustrative of the Times of George IV* (1838).

———

'On Seeing Some Withered Roses Thrown Away'

Poems on Several Occasions (Edinburgh, 1797).

> These fading flowers too well impart
> A mournful lesson to my heart.
> You pluck'd them beauteous, gay and fair,
> Their perfume scented all the air,
>   And fill'd each passing gale:
> Now withering, languid, almost dead,
> Their freshness and their beauty fled,
>   Their colour sickly pale.
> You throw them with disgust away,
> And as you throw them, seem to say,
> Go, useless flowers, you please no more,
> Your fascinating charms are o'er:
>   Ah! what do charms avail!

But had you wisely kept the flower,
Beyond the limits of an hour,
You might its sweetness have retain'd,
And thence have useful morals gain'd,
    More eloquent than speech.
For, ah! full many a fragrant rose
Is lost, through ignorance in those
    That ne'er its merits reach;
Who ne'er below a surface scann'd,
Pluck flowers with idle, wanton hand;
And when their beauty once is flown,
To them their ev'ry charm seems gone;
    But much to me they teach.

For their sad fate, that heart must prove,
Which hopes from thine eternal love,
Allur'd alone by Beauty's power,
Which is impair'd by ev'ry hour,
    Thy love must soon decrease.
Then, Reason, at thy shrine I bow,
Receive a contrite convert now,
    From grief my soul release;
Oblivion bring to calm the pain,
Else all thy pow'rs will prove but vain;
Then pluck the dart still rankling here,
Wipe off the yet impassion'd tear,
    And turn my heart to peace.

RICHARD GALL

(1776–1801)

———

A DUNBAR native, Richard Gall attended the parish school of Haddington, before taking up an apprenticeship to his maternal uncle, a carpenter and builder. Gall afterwards became a printer's apprentice in Edinburgh, and then a travelling clerk. Quickly recognized as a talented songwriter, he enjoyed the friendship of fellow poets Robert Burns and Thomas Campbell. Several of Gall's songs were set to music. Two of these, 'Farewell to Ayrshire' and 'Now bank an' brae are clad in green', were wrongly attributed to Burns. After a short illness, during which time he kept writing, he died at the tender age of twenty-four. Eighteen years later, an edition of Gall's *Poems and Songs* (1819) finally appeared in his adopted city, Edinburgh.

———

'Farewell to Ayrshire'

Poems and Songs. With a Memoir of the Author (Edinburgh: Oliver and Boyd, 1819).

> Scenes of wo and scenes of pleasure,
>   Scenes that former thoughts renew,
> Scenes of wo and scenes of pleasure,
>   Now a sad and last adieu!
> Bonny Doon, sae sweet at gloamin',
>   Fare thee weel before I gang!
> Bonny Doon, whare, early roaming,
>   First I weaved the rustic sang!
>
> Bowers, adieu! whare love decoying,
>   First enthralled this heart o' mine;
> There the saftest sweets enjoying,
>   Sweets that memory ne'er shall tine.
> Friends, sae near my bosom ever,
>   Ye hae rendered moments dear;

But, alas! when forced to sever,
   Then the stroke, oh! how severe.

Friends, that parting tear, reserve it,
   Though 'tis doubly dear to me;
Could I think I did deserve it,
   How much happier would I be!
Scenes of wo and scenes of pleasure,
   Scenes that former thoughts renew;
Scenes of wo and scenes of pleasure,
   Now a sad and last adieu!

'Now Bank an' Brae are Clad in Green'

Now bank an' brae are clad in green,
   An' scattered cowslips sweetly spring;
By Girvan's fairy-haunted stream
   The birdies flit on wanton wing;
By Cassillis' banks, when e'ening fa's,
   There let my MARY meet wi' me,
There catch her ilka glance o' love,
   The bonny blink o' MARY's e'e.

The chiel wha boasts o' warld's wealth
   Is aften laird o' meikle care;
But MARY she is a' my ain,
   An' Fortune canna gie me mair.
Then let me stray by Cassillis' banks,
   Wi' her, the lassie dear to me,
An' catch her ilka glance o' love,
   The bonny blink o' MARY's e'e.

WILLIAM GILLESPIE

(1776–1825)

THE Church of Scotland minister and poet William Gillespie was born and educated in Kells. He read theology at the University of Edinburgh, where he pursued a secondary interest in medicine. He was also a member of the Academy of Physics, alongside the prominent men of letters Henry Brougham and Francis Jeffrey. While at Edinburgh he wrote 'The Progress of Refinements', which was eventually published in a collection some years later. After ordination, he engaged in little literary activity, aside from occasional contributions to periodicals such as the *Scots Magazine*. In 1815, however, he produced a decently sized volume of poetry, *Consolation, with Other Poems*. As a poet Gillespie enjoyed writing in a variety of forms, from Spenserian dream visions to picturesque sonnets, as well as odes, dirges, ballads, and more.

'The Highlander'

Consolation, with Other Poems (Edinburgh: Archibald Constable and Co.; London: Longman, Hurst, Rees, Orme, and Brown, 1815).

Many years ago, a poor Highland Soldier, on his return to his native hills, fatigued, as it was supposed, by the length of the march, and the heat of the weather, sat down under the shade of a birch-tree on the solitary road of Lowran, that winds along the margin of Loch-Ken, in Galloway. Here he was found dead; and this incident forms the subject of the following verses.

From the climes of the sun, all war-torn and weary,
   The Highlander sped to his youthful abode;
Fair visions of home cheered the desert so dreary,
   Though fierce was the noon-beam, and steep was the road.

Till spent with the march that still lengthened before him,
   He stopped by the way in a sylvan retreat;
The light shady boughs of the birch-tree waved o'er him,
   The stream of the mountain fell soft at his feet.

He sunk to repose where the red heaths are blended,
    One dream of his childhood his fancy past o'er;
But his battles are fought, and his march it is ended,
    The sound of the bagpipe shall wake him no more.

No arm in the day of the conflict could wound him,
    Though War launched her thunder in fury to kill,
Now the Angel of Death in the desert has found him,
    And stretched him in peace by the stream of the hill.

Pale Autumn spreads o'er him the leaves of the forest,
    The fays of the wild chaunt the dirge of his rest;
And thou, little brook, still the sleeper deplores,
    And moistenest the heath-bell that weeps on his breast.

THOMAS CAMPBELL
(1777–1844)

———

BORN and educated in Glasgow, Thomas Campbell was an exemplary
student, and won prizes at the city's university. In 1798 he moved to
Edinburgh, where he met many talented men of letters, Dugald
Stewart and Francis Jeffrey among them. Barely a year later,
Campbell's *The Pleasures of Hope* (1799) appeared to wide acclaim.
By 1807 he was supporting himself with hackwork such as *Annals of
Great Britain* (1807) and acquiring patronage from various admirers.
Gertrude of Wyoming (1809) was not as acclaimed as the name-making
Pleasures of Hope, but it found keen readers. A longstanding project,
Specimens of the British Poets (1819), brought in further funds.
Further editorial work, for *New Monthly Magazine*, persisted until
1830. In this period, he published his last substantial poem, *Theodric*
(1824), but it garnered little praise. Many shorter poems followed,
though. In his later years, despite persistent ill health, Campbell kept
up his career as an author in various areas, including travel writing, as
in *Letters from the South* (1837), and biography, with his *Life of
Petrarch* (1841). Greatly admired throughout Europe, Campbell was
especially loved in Scotland, where he was given the freedom of the
city of Edinburgh, and Glasgow students established a Campbell
Club in his honour.

———

'Song to the Evening Star'

The Poetical Works of Thomas Campbell. A New and Improved Edition
(Edinburgh: Oliver & Boyd, 1837).

> Star that bringest home the bee,
> And sett'st the weary labourer free!
> If any star shed peace, 'tis thou,
>   That send'st it from above,
> Appearing when heaven's breath and brow
>   Are sweet as her's we love.

Come to the luxuriant skies,
Whilst the landscape's odours rise,
Whilst far-off lowing herds are heard,
    And songs, when toil is done,
From cottages whose smoke unstirr'd
    Curls yellow in the sun.

Star of love's soft interviews,
Parted lovers on thee muse;
Their remembrancer in heaven
    Of thrilling vows thou art,
Too delicious to be riven
    By absence from the heart.

'The Last Man'

All worldly shapes shall melt in gloom,
    The Sun himself must die,
Before this mortal shall assume
    Its Immortality!
I saw a vision in my sleep,
That gave my spirit strength to sweep
    Adown the gulf of Time!
I saw the last of human mould,
That shall Creation's death behold,
    As Adam saw her prime!

The Sun's eye had a sickly glare,
    The Earth with age was wan,
The skeletons of nations were
    Around that lonely man!
Some had expired in fight,—the brands
Still rusted in their bony hands;
    In plague and famine some!
Earth's cities had no sound nor tread;
And ships were drifting with the dead
    To shores where all was dumb!

Yet, prophet-like, that lone one stood,
    With dauntless words and high,
That shook the sere leaves from the wood

As if a storm passed by—
Saying, We are twins in death, proud Sun,
Thy face is cold, thy race is run,
   'Tis Mercy bids thee go;
For thou ten thousand thousand years
Hast seen the tide of human tears,
   That shall no longer flow.

What though beneath thee man put forth
   His pomp, his pride, his skill;
And arts that made fire, floods, and earth,
   The vassals of his will;—
Yet mourn not I thy parted sway,
Thou dim discrowned king of day:
   For all those trophied arts
And triumphs that beneath thee sprang,
Healed not a passion or a pang
   Entailed on human hearts.

Go, let oblivion's curtain fall
   Upon the stage of men,
Nor with thy rising beams recall
   Life's tragedy again.
Its piteous pageants bring not back,
Nor waken flesh, upon the rack
   Of pain anew to writhe;
Stretched in disease's shapes abhorred,
Or mown in battle by the sword,
   Like grass beneath the sithe.

Ev'n I am weary in yon skies
   To watch thy fading fire;
Test of all sumless agonies
   Behold not me expire.
My lips that speak thy dirge of death—
Their rounded gasp and gurgling breath
   To see thou shalt not boast.
The eclipse of Nature spreads my pall,—
The majesty of Darkness shall
   Receive my parting ghost!

This spirit shall return to Him
   Who gave its heavenly spark;

Yet think not, Sun, it shall be dim,
   When thou thyself art dark!
No! it shall live again, and shine
In bliss unknown to beams of thine,
   By Him recalled to breath,
Who captive led captivity,
Who robbed the grave of Victory, —
   And took the sting from Death!

Go, Sun, while Mercy holds me up
   On Nature's awful waste
To drink this last and bitter cup
   Of grief that man shall taste—
Go, tell the night that hides thy face,
Thou saw'st the last of Adam's race,
   On Earth's sepulchral clod,
The darkening universe defy
To quench his Immortality,
   Or shake his trust in God!

'The Death-Boat of Heligoland'

Can restlessness reach the cold sepulchred head?—
Ay, the quick have their sleep-walkers, so have the dead.
There are brains, though they moulder, that dream in the tomb,
And that maddening forehear the last trumpet of doom,
Till their corses start sheeted to revel on earth,
Making horror more deep by the semblance of mirth:
By the glare of new-lighted volcanoes they dance,
Or at mid-sea appal the chill'd mariner's glance.
Such, I wot, was the band of cadaverous smile
Seen ploughing the night-surge of Heligo's isle.

The foam of the Baltic had sparkled like fire,
And the red moon looked down with an aspect of ire;
But her beams on a sudden grew sick-like and gray,
And the mews that had slept clanged and shrieked far away—
And the buoys and the beacons extinguished their light,
As the boat of the stony-eyed dead came in sight,
High bounding from billow to billow; each form
Had its shroud like a plaid flying loose to the storm;

With an oar in each pulseless and icy-cold hand,
Fast they ploughed, by the lee-shore of Heligoland.

Such breakers as boat of the living ne'er cross'd;
Now surf-sunk for minutes again they uptossed,
And with livid lips shouted reply o'er the flood
To the challenging watchman that curdled his blood—
"We are dead—we are bound from our graves in the west,
First to Hecla, and then to——." Unmeet was the rest
For man's ear. The old abbey bell thundered its clang,
And their eyes gleamed with phosphorous light as it rang:
Ere they vanished, they stopped, and gazed silently grim,
Till the eye could define them, garb, feature and limb.

Now who were those roamers?—of gallows or wheel
Bore they marks, or the mangling anatomist's steel?
No, by magistrates' chains 'mid their grave-clothes you saw,
They were felons too proud to have perished by law;
But a ribbon that hung where a rope should have been,
'Twas the badge of their faction, its hue was not green,
Showed them men who had trampled and tortured and driven
To rebellion the fairest Isle breathed on by Heaven,—
Men whose heirs would yet finish the tyrannous task,
If the Truth and the Time had not dragged off their mask.
They parted—but not till the sight might discern
A scutcheon distinct at their pinnace's stern,
Where letters, emblazoned in blood-colour'd flame,
Named their faction—I blot not my page with its name.

'Lines on Revisiting a Scottish River'

And call they this Improvement?—to have changed,
My native Clyde, thy once romantic shore,
Where Nature's face is banished and estranged,
And Heaven reflected in thy wave no more;
Whose banks, that sweetened May-day's breath before,
Lie sere and leafless now in summer's beam,
With sooty exhalations cover'd o'er;
And for the daisied green sward, down thy stream
Unsightly brick-lanes smoke, and clanking engines gleam.

Speak not to me of swarms the scene sustains;
One heart free tasting Nature's breath and bloom
Is worth a thousand slaves to Mammon's gains.
But whither goes that wealth, and gladdening whom?
See, left but life enough and breathing-room
The hunger and the hope of life to feel,
Yon pale Mechanic bending o'er his loom,
And Childhood's self as at Ixion's wheel,
From morn till midnight tasked to earn its little meal.

Is this Improvement?—where the human breed
Degenerates as they swarm and overflow,
Till Toil grows cheaper than the trodden weed,
And man competes with man, like foe with foe,
Till Death, that thins them, scarce seems public woe?
Improvement! smiles it in the poor man's eyes,
Or blooms it on the cheek of Labour?—No—
To gorge a few with Trade's precarious prize,
We banish rural life, and breathe unwholesome skies.

Nor call that evil slight; God has not given
This passion to the heart of man in vain,
For Earth's green face, the untainted air of Heaven,
And all the bliss of Nature's rustic reign.
For not alone our frame imbibes a stain
From fetid skies; the spirit's healthy pride
Fades in their gloom—And therefore I complain,
That thou no more through pastoral scenes shouldst glide,
My Wallace's own stream, and once romantic Clyde!

MARY BRUNTON
(1778–1818)

———

THE novelist Mary Brunton (*née* Balfour) was born on Burray, one of the Orkney Islands. She had little formal education, but her mother taught her music, French, and Italian. Late in 1798 she eloped with the Reverend Alexander Brunton. With her husband's support she developed an interest in the philosophy of mind, especially that of Thomas Reid; in history she particularly enjoyed the works of William Robertson. She also stressed the importance of studying ancient languages and mathematics. Brunton's first novel, *Self-Control*, was published in 1811. The next novel, *Discipline* (1814), proved successful (it ran to three editions within two years). For her next venture in prose, she planned a series of domestic tales—and she made some progress. Weakened by a difficult labour to a stillborn son, however, she died less than two weeks later, aged just forty. Taken from a posthumous collection of unfinished pieces, the following poem is one of three included therein.

———

'While thou at eventide art roaming'

Emmeline. With Some Other Pieces (Edinburgh: Manners and Miller, and Archibald Constable and Co.; London: John Murray, 1819).

> While thou at eventide art roaming
> Along the elm-o'ershaded walk,
> Where, past, the eddying stream is foaming
> Beneath its tiny cataract,—
> Where I with thee was wont to talk,—
> Think thou upon the days gone by,
> And heave a sigh!
>
> When sails the moon above the mountains,
> And cloudless skies are purely blue,
> And sparkle in the light the fountains,
> And darker frowns the lonely yew,—

Then be thou melancholy too,
When musing on the hours I proved
With thee, beloved!

When wakes the dawn upon thy dwelling,
And lingering shadows disappear,
And soft the woodland songs are swelling
A choral anthem on thine ear,
—Think—for that hour to thought is dear!
And then her flight remembrance wings
To by-past things.

To me, through every season, dearest;
In every scene—by day, by night,
Thou present to my mind appearest
A quenchless star—for ever bright!
My solitary, sole delight!
Alone—in grove—by shore—at sea,
I think of thee!

JOHN GALT
(1779–1839)

———

JOHN GALT was born in Irvine, on the west coast of Scotland. When he was about nine years old the family moved to Greenock. It was in this corner of Scotland, between these two locations, that Galt was to place a successful series of novels, which he called *Tales of the West*. He spent the next fourteen or fifteen years in Greenock and he retired there for the last five years of his life, having also lived elsewhere in Scotland, England, and Canada. In his thirties he published verse in the *Scots Magazine* and experimented with drama, including a tragedy about Mary, Queen of Scots. A prolific writer in long- and short-form prose and verse throughout his ensuing career, Galt, like Hogg and Scott, and many others, developed his sketch-like style in *Blackwood's Edinburgh Magazine*. As a poet, he wrote in Scots or English. The following poems comprise a loose reworking of a Horatian ode and a passionate meditation on home.

———

'Spring. Suggested by the Fourth Ode of the First Book of Horace'

Poems (London: Cochrane and McCrone, 1833).

I

Wha's yon braw lass, wi' gowan snood,
That's walking o'er the broomy knowe;
She dings the cranreuch frae the wood,
And plaits a garland round the bough?
Her e'en, twa dew-drops, sparkling clear,
Shed love and daffin' as they glance;
The birds wi' canty liltings cheer,
And a' the flow'rs rise frae their trance?
It's bride-maid Spring, whose leilsome art
Gars lightly loup the youthful heart.

II

Thrang frae the misty highland isles,
Whar ghaists in flocks glow'r as they flee,
And Brownie for the Lathron toils,
Wi' barkened sails the kowters see—
By heaps o' timber caps, and plates,
The wark that wile't the winter's drear,
Right snod the kintra carlin waits,
And wearies wha the price will speer.
For a' the lads are on the rig,
And she maun thole the snash and prig.

III

The clachan lucky spreads fu' proud
Her webs and spyniels on the green;
And signs and window cheeks renew'd,
Like the young leaves shine fresh and clean.
But lo! best proof that winter's done,
Auld grannie frae the chumley nook
Late toddling in the afternoon
To kirk, wi' napkin round her book.
In love, or life, or growth, or sense,
All feel the genial influence.

IV

Come then, dear Jamie, while we may
The vernal hours of youth enjoy:
The hope that blooms so fair and gay,
A worm may gnaw, a blast destroy.
But o'er the past, as Horace sings,
Not e'en almighty Jove has power,
And mem'ry still delighted brings
The vision of the happy hour;
That man in joyless age may bear
The wumbling pain, and snuling care.

'Irvine Water. On seeing a Picture of a Favourite Scene of my Boyhood'

The Demon of Destiny; and Other Poems (Greenock: W. Johnston and Son, 1839).

How beautiful!—not childhood's glad blue eyes
Are half so beautiful as shines the skies,
Mirror'd in yonder calm and summer flow—
A radiant vista of a noon below:
As if the Universe—the Infinite—
Were one bright vast of sunshine and delight;
And the great globe, with all that it inherits,
Hung in a halo form'd of glorious spirits.

Why hymns sad Fancy thus on solemn wing?
And Mem'ry back to me would boyhood bring,
Ere care I knew, when I might freely rove
The green Goffields, or sylvan Howmills grove—
The skyey vision in the witches' linn?
I then had visions too—alas! as thin.

But wayward, pensive, more I lov'd to muse—
Tranc'd in the churchyard, and the tombs peruse:—
At one I sadden'd, half inclin'd to flee,
Which spectral said, "Prepare to follow me!"
For I had heard that none in life may know,
To where, with Death, the dead hearefater go,
And often wonder'd, in the grim of night,
To what dread land the dead-man did invite.

The green oblivious grave was then a mound—
Nor kind nor dear had the mute beckon own'd
Of Him that's ever far, yet ever nigh,
Shadow of life, the dumb, black Deity.
And rife around me comrade boys were gay,
Our business pleasure, and our labour play—
Then but to be I thought sufficient bliss,
But now I long for Heaven's unknown abyss.

Well I remember all the golden prime,
When sleep and joy were night and day in time,
That to be drowsy on my mother's knee,
Was almost sweeter than blest liberty—
Oh! how my heart enjoy'd the lov'd caress,
The patted cheek, the fond maternalness;
And that soft blessing, Heaven could not but hear,
While on my neck fell the delightful tear.

Stern Fortitude, proud self-commanding power!
That calmly sat around misfortunes lower,
And ever wears the smiling masque of ease,

As if Affliction could have aught to please,—
Is thine the strength that's rosy, firm, and fair,
Or but the grasp of consciousless Despair?
Canst thou to him, that's begging youth restore—
Restore the associates of the sunny scene,
Unseal the tomb, and wake the who hath been?—
Poor ineffectual hypocrite, begone!
And take life with thee—now an anguish'd moan.

Yet Heaven I thank for making me still see
The good and beauty of His mystery.
The world of terrors, for I have ever found,
But prompts to equanimity around,
Though Hope be dead; and by Thy laws I know
My ails and cares are cureless now below.

They think not wisely, and turn Truth awry,
Who deem that life's as an infectious sigh:—
From me and mine be far that murky thought,
Which Grief for guilt hath to be wretched brought,
And ever shine that blest benignant plan,
Which helps to mitigate all ills to man.

Oft in the trances of my wond'ring youth,
When life was light, and hope believ'd as truth,
On the green hill I lov'd to muse alone,
When gold-ey'd daisies bright around me shone,
And think, in innocence of boyhood, then,
How all was lovely that was made for men.

That young conceit, in Fortune's darkest hour,
Has been the candle of my midnight bower;
And still, while ails on wrongs increasing come,
It is the torch that lights me on to home.

Well do I mind the thrilling gush of bliss
With which the energy of cheerfulness
First came upon me in those simple days,
When discontent could but the boy amaze.

A Sabbath stillness sweeten'd all the air;
The fragrant sunshine of the summer glare,
Visible blessedness, felicity,
Was as if Goodness could partake of glee.
Boundless afar the shining ocean spread,
The azure infinite was over head,
And in her robes maternal Nature smil'd,

As if the world and Heav'n were reconcil'd.
　In that calm noon, as on the grass I lay,
Methought I heard some gentle spirit say:
"Man cag'd in finitude can never know
The happiness of full perfection's glow;
But he may taste, and ever more and more,
Something of what the future has in store":
Ever since then, by compensating Heav'n,
For all of suffering, recompense was given.
　'Twas then I fancied that if hopeful power
Make youth in life, Aurora's orient hour,
Age, the dim vesper, by experience taught,
Hath strength in slights that ne'er by power are wrought.
　But not alone the feeble or the frail
Gain bright equivalents, by lore, for ail;
All, all in life the mystic blessing share,—
The boon of being,—Heaven's spontaneous care;
And since, my pilgrimage has serv'd to prove
The gracious tendence of that unsought love.
Yes, though the finite, ever less or more,
Must own some lack,—a craving or a sore,—
Still each and all that is, or that shall be,
May taste the bliss of my blest reverie;
Ev'n those who feel but misery in breath,
Know there is shelter—they may fly to death.
　But tho' the thought, as boyhood's thought, was crude,
I glow'd with it, as if the sense of good
Was first experience'd then. Oh! many a time,
Amidst dismay, has it appear'd sublime,
Serene and clear, beyond the hurrying strife
Of storms and clouds that aw'd the scene of life;
Oft it has seem'd, o'er streamers glaring red,
The morning's harbinger, forbidding dread.
E'en yet, thank Heav'n, though all be dark and drear.
Around again, and Reason beckon Fear,
The cheerful dream that visited my youth
Smiles beautiful. Oh! beautiful as Truth.
　What though no more I ever shall enjoy
The radiant fancies of the musing boy,
No more partake what Health and Hope impart
To youth unwitting, ere in life we start,—

Still all that come might yet be worse, I say,
And thus the sternest pass as almost gay.

But why is it that in this solemn hour
I can but think of boyhood's nest and bower?—
Around but scenes of love I see. Alas!
All that I see is but in mem'ry's glass.

Oh ! never more must I again behold
Such sunny days as were so bright of old,
When she that's dust embrac'd her wayward own,
And all the claims upon me were unknown.

My native burgh, its window-eyes so bright,
Basks in the noon, and purrs as with delight—
Sweet is the thought, as in that hour of ease,
When all of life was but to play or please.
Mysterious Nature! why should he complain,
Who plays a child in memory's hall again,
Who sees around him, ever bright and fair,
The hopes of life, though but a picture's there;
And with the past, when griefs and cares annoy,
May be again a happy-hearted boy.

CLEMENTINA STIRLING GRAHAM
(1782–1877)

━━

CLEMENTINA STIRLING was born in Dundee. After her mother succeeded to the small estate of Duntrune, near Dundee, the family
adopted the surname of Graham after her ancestor John Graham of
Claverhouse (better known as Viscount Dundee). Spending her time
partly in Edinburgh, in Francis Jeffrey's Whiggish circle, and partly at
Duntrune, Graham was celebrated as a mimic of different social arche-
types. One of her most popular creations was Lady Pitlyal, a countri-
fied old lady with the habits and manners of forty years before. In her
old age, at the request of her friend Dr John Brown, she recorded the
pranks she had played on Jeffrey and others in a little volume titled
Mystifications. Privately circulated in 1859, the volume also included
a few poems and prose sketches accrued over the years. Brown edited the
first published edition of *Mystifications* in 1865 and it remained in print
until 1911. Before that, in 1829, Graham translated from the French
Jonas de Gelieu's *The Bee Preserver*, for which she received a medal
from the Highland Society.

━━

'The Birkie o' Bonnie Dundee'

Mystifications, 4th edn (Edinburgh: Edmonston and Douglas, 1869).

> Ye fair lands of Angus and bonnie Dundee,
> How dear are your echoes, your memories to me!
> At gatherings and meetings in a' the braw toons,
> I danced wi' the lasses and distanced the loons;
> Syne bantered them gaily, and bade the young men
> Be mair on their mettle when I cam' again.
> They jeered me, they cheered me, and cried ane and a',
> He 's no an ill fellow that, now he 's awa.
>
> When puir beggar bodies cam' making their mane,
> I spak them aye cheery, for siller I'd nane;

They shook up their duddies, and muttered, "Wae 's me,
Sae lightsome a laddie no worth a bawbee!"
I played wi' the bairnies at bowls and at ba',
And left them a' greeting when I cam' awa;
Aye! mithers, and bairnies, and lasses and a',
Were a' sobbin loudly when I cam' awa.

I feigned a gay laugh, just to keep in the greet,
For ae bonnie lassie, sae douce and sae sweet,
How matchless the blink of her deep loving e'e,
How soft fell its shade as it glanced upon me.
I flung her a wild rose sae fresh and sae fair,
And bade it bloom on in the bright summer there;
While breathing its fragrance, she aiblins may gi'e
A thought to the Birkie o' bonnie Dundee.

ALLAN CUNNINGHAM
(1784–1842)

———

THE poet and collector Allan Cunningham was born in the parish of
Keir in Dumfriesshire. A voracious reader from a young age, he wrote
early too. When R. H. Cromek travelled to Scotland to collect songs,
Cunningham tricked him into thinking some of his modern compositions were antique. Encouraged by Cromek, Cunningham sought
a literary career in London. *Remains of Nithsdale and Galloway Song*
(1811) appeared within months of his arrival there. Ostensibly an anti-
quarian project, the collection really comprises Cunningham's own
work. Another Cunningham-helmed volume, *Songs, Chiefly in the
Rural Language of Scotland*, came out in 1813. In 1822 appeared two
volumes of *Traditional Tales of the English and Scottish Peasantry*, and
in 1825 four volumes of *The Songs of Scotland, Ancient and Modern*,
which was favourably received. In the following years he produced the
romances *Paul Jones* (1826), *Sir Michael Scott* (1828), *The Maid of
Elvar* (1833), a poem in twelve parts, and *Lord Roldan* (1836). But *The
Works and Life of Burns* (1834), in eight volumes, was the lasting legacy
of this period in his life, along with his numerous volumes of antiqued
songs and tales.

———

'The Thistle's Grown aboon the Rose'

Poems and Songs, ed. Peter Cunningham (London: John Murray, 1847).

> Full white the Bourbon lily blows,
> Still fairer haughty England's rose;
> Nor shall unsung the symbol smile,
> Green Ireland, of thy lovely isle.
> In Scotland grows a warlike flower,
> Too rough to bloom in lady's bower;
> But when his crest the warrior rears,
> And spurs his courser on the spears,

O there it blossoms—there it blows—
The Thistle's grown aboon the Rose.

Bright like a steadfast star it smiles
Aboon the battle's burning files;
The mirkest cloud, the darkest night,
Shall ne'er make dim that beauteous sight;
And the best blood that warms my vein,
Shall flow ere it shall catch a stain.
Far has it shone on fields of fame
From matchless Bruce to dauntless Graeme,
From swarthy Spain to Siber's snows;—
The Thistle's grown aboon the Rose.

What conquer'd aye and nobler spared,
What firm endured, and greatly dared?
What redden'd Egypt's burning sand?
What vanquish'd on Corunna's strand?
What pipe on green Maida blew shrill?
What dyed in blood Barossa hill?
Bade France's dearest life-blood rue
Dark Soignies and dread Waterloo?
That spirit which no tremor knows;—
The Thistle's grown aboon the Rose.

I vow—and let men mete the grass
For his red grave who dares say less—
Men blither at the festive board,
Men braver with the spear and sword,
Men higher famed for truth—more strong
In virtue, sovereign sense, and song,
Or maids more fair, or wives more true,
Than Scotland's, ne'er trode down the dew;
Unflinching friends—unconquer'd foes,
The Thistle's grown aboon the Rose.

'It's Hame, and it's Hame'

It's hame, and it's hame, hame fain wad I be,
An' it's hame, hame, hame, to my ain countree!
When the flower is i' the bud and the leaf is on the tree,

The larks shall sing me hame in my ain countree;
It's hame, and it's hame, hame fain wad I be,
An' it's hame, hame, hame, to my ain countree!

The green leaf o' loyaltie 's beginning for to fa',
The bonnie white rose it is withering an' a';
But I'll water 't wi' the blude of usurping tyrannie,
An' green it will grow in my ain countree.
It's hame, and it's hame, hame fain wad I be,
An' it's hame, hame, hame, to my ain countree!

There's naught now frae ruin my country can save,
But the keys o' kind heaven, to open the grave,
That a' the noble martyrs wha died for loyaltie,
May rise again and fight for their ain countree.
It's hame, and it's hame, hame fain wad I be,
An' it's hame, hame, hame, to my ain countree!

The great now are gane, a' who ventured to save,
The new grass is springing on the tap o' their grave;
But the sun thro' the mirk blinks blythe in my ee:
"I'll shine on ye yet in your ain countree."
It's hame, and it's hame, hame fain wad I be,
An' it's hame, hame, hame, to my ain countree!

'The Mermaid of Galloway'

Sir Marmaduke Maxwell, a Dramatic Poem; The Mermaid of Galloway; The Legend of Richard Faulder; and Twenty Scottish Songs (London: Taylor and Hessey, 1822).

1

There's a maid has sat on the green merse side
    These ten lang years and mair;
An' every first night o' the new moon
    She kames her yellow hair.

2

An' ay while she sheds the yellow burning gowd,
    Fu' sweet she sings an' hie,
Till the fairest bird that wooes the green wood,
    Is charm'd wi' her melodie.

3

But wha e'er listens to that sweet sang,
  Or gangs the dame to see,
Ne'er hears the sang o' the laverock again,
  Nor wakens an earthlie ee.

4

It fell in about the sweet simmer month,
  I' the first come o' the moon,
That she sat o' the tap of a sea-weed rock,
  A-kaming her silk-locks down.

5

Her kame was o' the whitely pearl,
  Her hand like new-won milk,
Her breasts were a' o' the snawy curd,
  In a net o' sea-green silk.

6

She kamed her locks owre her white shoulders,
  A fleece baith bonny and lang;
An' ilka ringlet she shed frae her brows,
  She raised a lightsome sang.

7

I' the very first lilt o' that sweet sang,
  The birds forsook their young,
An' they flew i' the gate o' the grey howlet,
  To listen the sweet maid's song.

8

I' the second lilt o' that sweet sang,
  Of sweetness it was sae fu',
The tod leap'd out frae the bughted lambs,
  And dighted his red-wat mou'.

9

I' the very third lilt o' that sweet sang,
  Red lowed the new-woke moon;
The stars drapp'd blude on the yellow gowan tap,
  Sax miles that maiden roun'.

10

"I hae dwalt on the Nith," quo' the young Cowehill,
    "These twenty years an' three,
But the sweetest sang e'er brake frae a lip,
    Comes thro' the green wood to me."

11

"O is it a voice frae twa earthlie lips,
    Whilk makes sic melodie?
It wad wyle the lark frae the morning lift,
    And weel may it wyle me?"

12

"I dreamed a dreary thing, master,
    Whilk I am rad ye rede;
I dreamed ye kissed a pair o' sweet lips,
    That drapp'd o' red heart's-blede."

13

"Come haud my steed, ye little foot-page,
    Shod wi' the red gold roun';
Till I kiss the lips whilk sing sae sweet,"
    An' lightlie lap he down.

14

"Kiss nae the singer's lips, master,
    Kiss nae the singer's chin;
Touch nae her hand," quo' the little foot-page,
    "If skaithless hame ye 'd win."

15

"O wha will sit on yere toom saddle,
    O wha will bruik yere gluve?
An' wha will fauld yere erled bride,
    I' the kindly clasps o' luve?"

16

He took aff his hat, a' gold i' the rim,
    Knot wi' a siller ban';
He seemed a' in lowe wi' his gold raiment,
    As thro' the green wood he ran.

17

"The simmer-dew fa's saft, fair maid,
    Aneath the siller moon;
But eerie is thy seat i' the rock,
    Washed wi' the white sea faem."

18

"Come wash me wi' thy lilie white hand,
    Below and aboon the knee;
An' I'll kame thae links o' yellow burning gold,
    Aboon thy bonnie blue ee."

19

"How rosie are thy parting lips,
    How lilie-white thy skin,
An' weel I wat thae kissing een
    Wad tempt a saint to sin."

20

"Take aff these bars an' bobs o' gold,
    Wi' thy gared doublet fine;
An' thraw me aff thy green mantle,
    Leafed wi' the siller twine."

21

"An' a' in courtesie, fair knight,
    A maiden's love to win;
The gold lacing o' thy green weeds
    Wad harm her lilie skin."

22

Syne coost he aff his green mantle,
    Hemm'd wi' the red gold roun';
His costly doublet coost he aff,
    Wi' red gold flow'red down.

23

"Now ye maun kame my yellow hair,
    Down wi' my pearlie kame;
Then rowe me in thy green mantle,
    An' take me maiden hame."

24

"But first come take me 'neath the chin,
   An' syne come kiss my cheek;
An' spread my hanks o' wat'ry hair,
   I' the new-moon beam to dreep."

25

Sae first he kissed her dimpled chin;
   Syne kissed her rosie cheek;
And lang he wooed her willin' lips,
   Like heather-honie sweet!

26

"O, if ye'll come to the bonnie Cowehill,
   'Mang primrose banks to woo,
I'll wash ye ilk day i' the new milked milk,
   An' bind wi' gold yere brow."

27

"An' a' for a drink o' the clear water
   Ye 'se hae the rosie wine;
An' a' for the water white lilie,
   Ye 'se hae these arms o' mine."

28

"But what 'll she say, yere bonnie young bride,
   Busked wi' the siller fine;
Whan the rich kisses ye kept for her lips
   Are left wi' vows on mine?"

29

He took his lips frae her red-rose mou',
   His arms frae her waist sae sma';
"Sweet maiden, I'm in bridal speed,
   It's time I were awa."

30

"O gie me a token o' luve, sweet May,
   A leal luve token true."
She crapp'd a lock o' yellow golden hair,
   An' knotted it roun' his brow.

31

"O tie nae it sae strait, sweet May,
    But wi' luve's rose-knot kind;
My head is fu' of burning pain,
    O saft ye maun it bind."

32

His skin turned a' o' the red-rose hue,
    Wi' draps o' bludie sweat;
An' he laid his head 'mang the water lilies—
    "Sweet maiden, I maun sleep."

33

She tied ae link o' her wet yellow hair
    Aboon his burning bree;
Amang his curling haffet locks
    She knotted knurles three.

34

She weaved owre his brow the white lilie,
    Wi' witch-knots more than nine;
"Gif ye were seven times bride-groom owre,
    This night ye shall be mine."

35

O twice he turned his sinking head,
    An' twice he lifted his ee;
An' twice he sought to loose the links
    Were knotted owre his bree.

36

"Arise, sweet knight, yere young bride waits,
    An' doubts her ale will sour;
An' wistly looks at the lilie-white sheets,
    Down spread in ladie-bower."

37

"An' she has preened the broidered silk
    About her white hause-bane;
Her princely petticoat is on,
    Wi' gold can stand its lane."

38

He faintlie, slowlie, turn'd his cheek,
    And faintly lift his ee,
And he strave to loose the witching bands
    Aboon his burning bree.

39

Then took she up his green mantle,
    Of lowing gold the hem;
Then took she up his silken cap,
    Rich wi' a siller stem;
An' she threw them wi' her lilie hand
    Amang the white sea faem.

40

She took the bride ring frae his finger
    An' threw it in the sea;
"That hand shall mense nae ither ring
    But wi' the will o' me."

41

She faulded him i' her lilie arms,
    An' took her pearlie kame;
His fleecy locks trailed owre the sand,
    As she took the white sea-faem.

42

First rose the star out owre the hill,
    An' neist the lovelier moon;
While the beauteous bride o' Galloway
    Looked for her blithe bridegroom.

43

Lightly she sang while the new-moon rose,
    Blithe as a young bride may,
Whan the new-moon lights her lamp o' luve,
    An' blinks the bride away.

44

"Nithsdale, thou art a gay garden,
    Wi' monie a winsome flower;

But the princeliest rose o' that garden
   Maun blossom in my bower.

45

"Oh, gentle be the wind on thy leaf,
   And gentle the gloaming dew;
And bonnie and balmy be thy bud,
   Of a pure and steadfast hue;
And she who sings this sang in thy praise,
   Shall love thee leal and true."

46

An' ay she sewed her silken snood,
   An' sung a bridal sang;
But aft the tears drapt frae her ee,
   Afore the grey morn cam.

47

The sun leam'd ruddie 'mang the dew,
   Sae thick on bank and tree;
The plow-boy whistled at his darg,
   The milk-may answer'd hie;
But the lovely bride o' Galloway
   Sat wi' a tear-wet ee.

48

Ilk breath o' wind 'mang the forest leaves
   She heard the bridegroom's tongue,
And she heard the bridal-coming lilt
   In every bird which sung.

49

She sat high on the tap-tower stane,
   Nae waiting May was there;
She loosed the gold busk frae her breast,
   The kame frae 'mang her hair;
She wiped the tear-blobs frae her ee,
   An' looked lang and sair.

50

First sang to her the blithe wee bird,
 Frae aff the hawthorn green;
"Loose out the love curls frae yere hair,
 Ye plaited sae weel yestreen."

51

An' the spreckled lark frae 'mang the clouds
 Of heaven came singing down;
"Take out the bride-knots frae yere hair,
 An' let these lang locks down."

52

"Come, bide wi' me, ye pair o' sweet birds,
 Come down and bide wi' me;
Ye shall peckle o' the bread an' drink o' the wine,
 And gold yere cage sall be."

53

She laid the bride-cake 'neath her head,
 And syne below her feet;
An' laid her down 'tween the lilie-white sheets,
 An' soundly did she sleep.

54

It seemed i' the mid-hour o' the night,
 Her siller-bell did ring;
An' soun't as if nae earthlie hand
 Had pou'd the silken string.

55

There was a cheek touch'd that ladye's,
 Cauld as the marble stane,
An' a hand cauld as the drifting snaw,
 Was laid on her breast-bane.

56

"O cauld is thy hand, my dear Willie,
 O cauld, cauld is thy cheek;

An' wring these locks o' yellow hair,
  Frae which the cauld draps dreep."

57

"O seek anither bridegroom, Marie,
  On these bosom-faulds to sleep;
My bride is the yellow water lilie,
  Its leaves my bridal sheet!"

ALEXANDER RODGER
(1784–1846)

KNOWN as the Radical Poet, Alexander Rodger was born in East Calder, near Livingston. After local schooling, Rodger moved with his family to Edinburgh, where he spent a year apprenticed to a silversmith. Rodger then settled with relatives in the east end of Glasgow, where he began handloom weaving as a young teenager. In 1803 he joined the Glasgow Highland volunteers, an experience that informed his witty verses about Highland politics. Meanwhile, in Bridgeton, then a suburb of Glasgow, he composed and taught music, a lifelong passion of his. In 1819 Rodger took a staff position at *The Spirit of the Union*, a radical Glasgow newspaper. A frequent contributor to periodicals, he brought out his own collections in the 1820s: *Scotch Poetry* (1821) and *Peter Cornclips* (1827). He collected much of his earlier works, and added new ones, in his large edition of *Poems and Songs* (1838), along with a follow-up, *Stray Leaves* (1842). An abolitionist, anti-monarchist, and revolutionary, Rodger wrote unflinchingly political poems throughout his life. He was even imprisoned on suspicion of sedition. But he kept writing verse both serious and humorous.

'Behave Yoursel' Before Folk'

Poems and Songs, Humorous and Satirical (Glasgow: David Robertson, 1838).

(Air: "Good morrow to your night cap")

> Behave yoursel' before folk,
> Behave yoursel' before folk,
> And dinna be sae rude to me,
> As kiss me sae before folk.
>
> It wadna gie me meikle pain,
> Gin we were seen and heard by nane,
> To tak' a kiss, or grant you ane;

But, guidsake! no before folk.
　　Behave yoursel' before folk,
　　Behave yoursel' before folk;
　Whate'er ye do, when out o' view,
　　Be cautious ay before folk.

Consider, lad, how folk will crack,
And what a great affair they'll mak'
O' naething but a simple smack,
　That's gi'en or ta'en before folk.
　　Behave yoursel' before folk,
　　Behave yoursel' before folk;
　Nor gie the tongue o' auld or young
　　Occasion to come o'er folk.

It's no through hatred o' a kiss,
That I sae plainly tell you this;
But, losh! I tak' it sair amiss
　To be sae teazed before folk.
　　Behave yoursel' before folk,
　　Behave yoursel' before folk;
　When we're our lane ye may tak' ane,
　　But fient a ane before folk.

I'm sure wi' you I've been as free
As ony modest lass should be;
But yet, it doesna do to see
　Sic freedom used before folk.
　　Behave yoursel' before folk,
　　Behave yoursel' before folk;
　I'll ne'er submit again to it—
　　So mind you that—before folk.

Ye tell me that my face is fair;
It may be sae—I dinna care—
But ne'er again gar't blush sae sair
　As ye ha'e done before folk.
　　Behave yoursel' before folk,
　　Behave yoursel' before folk;
　Nor heat my cheeks wi' your mad freaks,
　　But aye be douce before folk.

Ye tell me that my lips are sweet,
Sic tales, I doubt, are a' deceit;

At ony rate, its hardly meet
  To pree their sweets before folk.
    Behave yoursel' before folk,
    Behave yoursel' before folk;
   Gin that's the case, there's time and place,
    But surely no before folk.

But, gin you really do insist
That I should suffer to be kiss'd,
Gae, get a license frae the priest,
  And mak' me yours before folk.
    Behave yoursel' before folk,
    Behave yoursel' before folk;
  And when we're ane, baith flesh and bane,
    Ye may tak' ten—before folk.

'The Answer'

Can I behave, can I behave,
Can I behave before folk,
When, wily elf, your sleeky self
Gars me gang gyte before folk?

In a' you do, in a' ye say,
Ye've sic a pawkie coaxing way,
That my poor wits ye lead astray,
An' ding me doilt before folk!
  Can I behave, can I behave,
  Can I behave before folk,
While ye ensnare, can I forbear
To kiss you, though before folk?

Can I behold that dimpling cheek,
Whar love 'mang sunny smiles might beek,
Yet, howlet-like, my e'elids steek,
  An' shun sic light, before folk?
  Can I behave, can I behave,
  Can I behave before folk,
When ilka smile becomes a wile,
Enticing me—before folk?

That lip, like Eve's forbidden fruit,
Sweet, plump, an' ripe, sae tempts me to't,

That I maun pree't, though I should rue't,
   Aye twenty times—before folk!
     Can I behave, can I behave,
     Can I behave before folk,
   When temptingly it offers me
   So rich a treat—before folk?

That gowden hair sae sunny bright;
That shapely neck o' snawy white;
That tongue, even when it tries to flyte,
   Provokes me till't before folk!
     Can I behave, can I behave,
     Can I behave before folk,
   When ilka charm, young, fresh, an' warm,
   Cries, "kiss me now"—before folk?

An' oh! that pawkie, rowin e'e,
Sae roguishly it blinks on me,
I canna, for my saul, let be,
   Frae kissing you before folk!
     Can I behave, can I behave,
     Can I behave before folk,
   When ilka glint conveys a hint
   To tak' a smack—before folk?

Ye own, that were we baith our lane,
Ye wadna grudge to grant me ane;
Weel, gin there be nae harm in't then,
   What harm is in't before folk?
     Can I behave, can I behave,
     Can I behave before folk,
   Sly hypocrite! an anchorite
   Could scarce desist—before folk!

But after a' that has been said,
Since ye are willing to be wed,
We'll hae a "blythesome bridal" made,
   When ye'll be mine before folk!
     Then I'll behave, then I'll behave,
     Then I'll behave before folk;
   For whereas then, ye'll aft get "ten,"
   It winna be before folk!

WILLIAM TENNANT
(1784–1848)

———

THE linguist and poet William Tennant was born and educated in Anstruther. As a student at the University of St Andrews, Tennant translated poetry and produced light imitations of medieval verse. Published anonymously, *Anster Fair* (1812) was an instant hit—it ran to six editions in the author's lifetime and received a glowing notice from Francis Jeffrey. Appointed parish schoolmaster of Dunino, near St Andrews, Tennant kept up his study of Hebrew, and developed new skills in Arabic, Syriac, and Persian. Further, increasingly prestigious, school appointments in Lasswade and Clackmannanshire followed. Finally, in 1834, he became a languages professor at St Mary's College, St Andrews. Tennant produced more poetry, including the abandoned epic *The Thane of Fife* (1822) and *Papistry Stormed* (1827). And he contributed prose translations from Greek and German to the *Edinburgh Literary Journal* after 1830. His comic poetry, 'Tammy Little' included here, deserves a new audience.

———

'Tammy Little'

Anster Fair, and Other Poems (Edinburgh: William and Robert Chambers, 1838).

> Wee Tammy Little, honest man!
>   I kent the body weel,
> As round the kintra-side he gaed
>   Careerin' wi' his creel.
>
> He was sae slender and sae wee,
>   That aye when blasts did blaw,
> He ballasted himself wi' stanes
>   'Gainst bein' blawn awa.
>
> A meikle stane the wee bit man
>   In ilka coat-pouch clappit,

That by the michty gowlin' wind
    He michtna doun be swappit.

When he did chance within a wood
    On simmer days to be,
Aye he was frichtit lest the craws
    Should heise him up on hie;

And aye he, wi' an aiken cud,
    The air did thump and beat,
To stap the craws frae liftin' him
    Up to their nests for meat.

Ae day, when in a barn he lay,
    And thrashers thrang were thair,
He in a moment vanish'd aff,
    And nae man could tell whair.

They lookit till the riggin' up,
    And round and round they lookit,
At last they fand him underneath
    A firlot cruyled and crookit.

Ance as big Samuel past him by,
    Big Samuel gave a sneeze,
And wi' the sough o't he was cast
    Clean down upon his knees.

His wife and he upon ane day
    Did chance to disagree,
And up she took the bellowses,
    As wild as wife could be;

She gave ane puff intill his face,
    And made him, like a feather,
Flee frae the tae side o' the house,
    Resoundin' till the tither!

Ae simmer e'en, when as he through
    Pitkirie forest past,
By three braid leaves, blawn aff the trees,
    He down to yird was cast;

A tirl o' wind the three braid leaves
    Down frae the forest dang,

Ane frae an ash, ane frae an elm,
  Ane frae an aik-tree strang;

Ane strak him sair on the back neck,
  Ane on the nose him rappit,
Ane smote him on the vera heart,
  And down as dead he drappit.

But ah! but ah! a drearier dool
  Ance hapt at Ounston-dammy,
That heis'd him a' thegither up,
  And maist extinguish't Tammy:

For as he came slow-daunderin' down,
  In's hand his basket hingin',
And staiver'd ower the hie-road's breidth,
  Frae side to side a-swingin',

There came a blast frae Kelly-law,
  As bauld a blast as ever
Auld snivelin' Boreas blew abraid
  To make the warld shiver.

In liftit Tammy aff his feet,
  Mair easy than a shavin',
And hurl'd him half a mile complete
  Hie up 'tween earth and heav'n.

That day puir Tammy had wi' stanes
  No ballasted his body,
So that he flew, maist like a shot,
  Ower corn-land and ower cloddy.

You've seen ane tumbler on a stage
  Tumble sax times and mair,
But Tammy weil sax hundred times
  Gaed tumblin' through the air.

And whan the whirly-wind gave ower,
  He frae the lift fell plumb,
And in a blink stood stickin' fast
  In Gaffer Glowr-weel's lum.

Ay—there his legs and body stack
  Amang the smotherin' soot;

But by a wonderfu' good luck,
   His head kept peepin' out.

But Gaffer Glowr-weel, when he saw
   A man stuck in his lum,
He swarf'd wi' drither clean awa,
   And sat some seconds dumb.

It took five masons near an hour
   A' riving at the lum
Wi' picks (he was sae jamm'd therein)
   Ere Tammy out could come.

As for his basket—weel I wat,
   His basket's fate and fa'
Was, as I've heard douce neighbours tell,
   The queerest thing of a'.

The blast took up the body's creel,
   And laid it on a cloud,
That bare it, sailin' through the sky,
   Richt ower the Firth's braid flood.

And whan the cloud did melt awa,
   Then, then the creel cam' down,
And fell'd the town-clerk o' Dunbar
   E'en in his ain good town.

The clerk stood yelpin' on the street
   At some bit strife that stirr'd him,
Down cam' the creel, and to the yird
   It dang him wi' a dirdom!

The Epitaph for Tammy
Oh Earth! oh Earth! if thou hast but
   A rabbit-hole to spair,
Oh grant the graff to Tammy's corp,
   That it may nestle thair:
And press thou light on him, now dead,
   That was sae slim and wee,
For, weel I wat, when he was quick,
   He lightly prest on thee!

JOHN WILSON
(1785–1854)

———

A HIGHLY accomplished man of letters, the Paisley-born John Wilson remains best known as the chief contributor to the Christopher North series published in *Blackwood's Edinburgh Magazine*, the leading Scottish outlet for creative writing in the period. In 1822 Wilson produced *Lights and Shadows of Scottish Life*, a decent-sized collection of his magazine pieces. This was followed in 1823 by *The Trials of Margaret Lyndsay*, and then his final novel, *The Foresters*, in 1825. Books aside, Wilson thrived in periodical writing. In 1834 alone he contributed more than fifty separate articles. Among his many outputs he produced two substantial collections of poems, both of which mix long narrative verse with sonnets and fragments, among other things—*The Isle of Palms, and Other Poems* (1812) and *The City of the Plague, and Other Poems* (1816).

———

'Melrose Abbey'

The Isle of Palms, and Other Poems (New York: James Eastburn, 1812).

> It was not when the Sun through the glittering sky,
> In summer's joyful majesty,
> Look'd from his cloudless height;—
> It was not when the Sun was sinking down,
> And tinging the ruin's mossy brown
> With gleams of ruddy light;—
> Nor yet when the Moon, like a pilgrim fair,
> 'Mid star and planet journeyed slow,
> And, mellowing the stillness of the air,
> Smiled on the world below;—
> That, MELROSE! 'mid thy mouldering pride,
> All breathless and alone,
> I grasped the dreams to day denied,
> High dreams of ages gone!—
> Had unshrieved guilt for one moment been there,

His heart had turn'd to stone!
For oft, though felt no moving gale,
Like restless ghost in glimmering shroud,
Through lofty Oriel opening pale
Was seen the hurrying cloud;
And, at doubtful distance, each broken wall
Frown'd black as bier's mysterious pall
From mountain-cave beheld by ghastly seer;
It seem'd as if sound had ceased to be;
Nor dust from arch, nor leaf from tree,
Relieved the noiseless ear.
The owl had sailed from her silent tower,
Tweed hush'd his weary wave,
The time was midnight's moonless hour,
My seat a dreaded Douglas' grave!

My being was sublimed by joy,
My heart was big, yet I could not weep;
I felt that God would ne'er destroy
The mighty in their trancèd sleep.
Within the pile no common dead
Lay blended with their kindred mould;
Theirs were the hearts that pray'd, or bled,
In cloister dim, on death-plain red,
The pious and the bold.
There slept the saint whose holy strains
Brought seraphs round the dying bed;
And there the warrior, who to chains
Ne'er stooped his crested head.
I felt my spirit sink or swell
With patriot rage or lowly fear,
As battle-trump, or convent-bell,
Rung in my trancèd ear.
But dreams prevail'd of loftier mood,
When stern beneath the chancel high
My country's spectre-monarch stood,
All sheath'd in glittering panoply;
Then I thought with pride what noble blood
Had flow'd for the hills of liberty.

High the resolves that fill the brain
With transports trembling upon pain,

When the veil of time is rent in twain,
That hides the glory past!
The scene may fade that gave them birth,
But they perish not with the perishing earth,
For ever shall they last.
And higher, I ween, is that mystic might
That comes to the soul from the silent night,
When she walks, like a disembodied spirit,
Through realms her sister shades inherit,
And soft as the breath of those blessèd flowers
That smile in Heaven's unfading bowers,
With love and awe, a voice she hears
Murmuring assurance of immortal years.
In hours of loneliness and woe
Which even the best and wisest know,
How leaps the lighten'd heart to seize
On the bliss that comes with dreams like these!
As fair before the mental eye
The pomp and beauty of the dream return,
Dejected virtue calms her sigh,
And leans resign'd on memory's urn.
She feels how weak is mortal pain,
When each thought that starts to life again,
Tells that she hath not lived in vain.

For Solitude, by Wisdom woo'd,
Is ever mistress of delight,
And even in gloom or tumult view'd,
She sanctifies their living blood
Who learn her lore aright.
The dreams her awful face imparts,
Unhallowed mirth destroy;
Her griefs bestow on noble hearts
A nobler power of joy.
While hope and faith the soul thus fill,
We smile at chance distress,
And drink the cup of human ill
In stately happiness.
Thus even where death his empire keeps
Life holds the pageant vain,
And where the lofty spirit sleeps,

There lofty visions reign.
Yea, often to night-wandering man
A pow'r fate's dim decrees to scan,
In lonely trance by bliss is given;
And midnight's starless silence rolls
A giant vigour through our souls,
That stamps us sons of Heaven.

Then, MELROSE! Tomb of heroes old!
Blest be the hour I dwelt with thee;
The visions that can ne'er be told
That only poets in their joy can see,
The glory born above the sky
The deep-felt weight of sanctity!
Thy massy towers I view no more
Through brooding darkness rising hoar,
Like a broad line of light dim seen
Some sable mountain-cleft between!
Since that dread hour, hath human thought
A thousand gay creations brought
Before my earthly eye;
I to the world have lent an ear,
Delighted all the while to hear
The voice of poor mortality.
Yet, not the less doth there abide
Deep in my soul a holy pride,
That knows by whom it was bestowed,
Lofty to man, but low to God;
Such pride as hymning angels cherish,
Blest in the blaze where man would perish.

MARY EDGAR

(*FL.* 1810–1824)

———

LITTLE can be known with certainty about Mary Edgar beyond what we find in her slim collection *Tranquillity: A Poem, to which are added, Other Original Poems, and Translations from the Italian* (1810), which was expanded in 1824. Printed in Dundee, *Tranquillity* was sold in Edinburgh by the major booksellers Archibald Constable and John Ballantyne, as well as by agents in Glasgow, Aberdeen, and Montrose. The first edition lacks an author's name. Having gained more than one hundred pages, and now containing additional translations from Spanish, the second edition identified the poet as a Miss Edgar. From internal evidence in the title poem we can deduce that her Christian, or preferred, name was Mary. In any case, the poems reveal an author well-versed in the histories of English and Scottish poetry.

———

'On Reading Some Trifling Verse, by a Scottish Poet'

Tranquillity: A Poem, to which are added, Other Original Poems, and Translations from the Italian (Dundee: R. S. Rintoul, 1810).

> Ill-fated bard! thy memory lives
>   Beyond the poetaster's lay:
> Though soon shall fade the wreath he gives,
>   Thy well-earn'd laurels ne'er decay.
>
> The poet's mantle Fancy wove
>   With flowers of never-fading dyes;
> And taught thy early steps to rove
>   Where'er she show'd the beauteous prize,
>
> And where the daisy's drooping crest
>   Inspired a strain of tender, woe,—

Even there, upon thy feeling breast,
  The enchanted folds were seen to flow.

And was that finely tinctured stole,
  Of loveliest texture, left by thee
To lowly bards with happier dole?—
  Not yet the auspicious gift we see.

Though oft an *ignis fatuus'* beam
  Allures and cheats the wilder'd sight,
Illusive as the wandering gleam
  That glares amid the shades of night,—

No kindred genius brightly glows,
  To paint the gayly festive scene,
Or like the lunar lustre throws
  Its light across the sweet serene.

But thou didst quit the beauteous prize,
  To run gay Folly's wild career.
Dire choice! for which thy Coila sighs,
  With every friend of heart sincere.

And who that bears a poet's name
  But from the view dejected turns,
When on the heights of genuine fame
  He sees the tottering steps of BURNS?

Of BURNS! whom Nature's partial care
  Disposed her sweetest scenes among,
To mark her matchless form and air,
  And paint their charms in deathless song.

And long to Nature he was true,
  While from each fragrant field and grove
He cull'd the floweret bright with dew,
  And sung the joys of guileless love;

Or braved the stormy winter sky,
  To catch a wilder, grander grace,
Where'er the rapt enthusiast's eye
  Could wonder-working Nature trace;

Or from sublimer views retired,
  Would sketch the "cotter's" evening scene,

By sweet simplicity inspired,
    Where all is love and joy serene,—

Where pious confidence in Heaven
    Bespeaks the patriarchal sage,
Whose precepts, with example given,
    Insure respect to reverend age.

But here so well the poet knows
    A touching interest to impart,
That all the simple picture glows
    With charms beyond the reach of art.

Yet could Ambition seize his soul,
    And Pleasure's fascinating form
Usurp great Nature's mild control,
    And raise the Passions' powerful storm.

Ah! then, no more the etherial ray,
    The raptured poet's bliss and boast,
Its cloudless radiance could display,
    To clear the path with perils cross'd.

Debased, amid the inglorious throng
    "That led him Pleasure's devious way,"
It yet illumed the poet's song,
    To cheer Misfortune's darkening day.

And those last efforts still shall charm,
    In plaintive air or mirthful sound,
While Nature's voice the breast can warm,—
    While Nature strews her sweets around.

'To the River North Esk'

In museful mood, how frequent here I stray,
When summer smiles illume the lovely scene!
Sweet river! on thy margin, soft and green,
I turn, and oft retrace my winding way;
And often on thy changeful surface gaze,
Where the smooth stream reflects an azure sky,
Red rock, green moss, and shrubs of darker dye,—

Or gayly gleams with bright meridian rays.
Here, scarce a zephyr curves the glassy plain,
And scarce a murmur meets the listening ear:
There, white foam swells the wave, and still we hear
The rushing waters tumbling down amain,
Till, softening in their course, the noiseless tide
Within the enchanting mirror gently glide.

MARGARETTA WEDDERBURN

(FL. 1811)

━━

ACCORDING to the authorial preface, the eponymous work in *Mary Queen of Scots, an Historical Poem, with Other Miscellaneous Pieces* (1811) was a long gestating project. Printed for the author, the book was, according to the title page, sold by booksellers in London, Edinburgh, and Glasgow. In addition to the main poem, the collection includes works in a pleasing variety of forms and styles, such as acrostics, epistles, songs, and hymns. The following poem reveals the poet's connection to Dalkeith, where she evidently spent a happy childhood.

━━

'Dalkeith, on the happy days I have enjoyed within its bonny bounds'

Mary Queen of Scots, an Historical Poem, with Other Miscellaneous Pieces (Edinburgh: Printed for the Author, 1811).

These verses were occasioned by returning to the place where I was brought up (about six miles from Edinburgh) after several years absence.

> In Scotia's isle much lov'd Dalkeith,
> How have I wish'd to see
> Its ancient spire, each lowly cot,
> As it was wont to be.
>
> This wish (in part) accomplished,
> But fill'd my heart with woe,
> The different aspect which it wears,
> Oft cause the tears to flow.
>
> For now where once the dwelling stood,
> Of aunt who did me rear,
> From infant days instruction gave,
> And taught me to revere

Her conduct as a Christian friend,
Which gratitude demands
From me, as long as life doth last,
A stately fabric stands.

Although this structure doth excel
With architect so rare,
In beauty and magnificence,
Few with it may compare.

Yet decorated thus superb,
To me its charms are fled,
For friends are gone, and social mate,
Are number'd with the dead.

Farewell those prospects of delight,
With life's gay morn in view;
Cold apathy no cherish'd guest,
For ev'ry scene was new.

While we with jocund hearts improv'd,
Each pleasure then in store,
And night her sable mantle spread,
E'er we our sports gave o'er.

How oft by moon light on the green,
We danc'd the hours away,
Or tried our skill at some new feat,
We had acquired that day.

As jumping over the mill–dam,
When wheel was going round,
One false step, would have seal'd our doom,
That one had sure been drown'd.

And running o'er the stepping stones,
Just by the hanging leaves,
Or list'ning to the sound they made,
With every passing breeze.

Or travers'd oft the winding path,
That led to iron mill,
O'er wooden bridge, which safe conveyed
To where my friend did dwell.

And often when I there arriv'd,
Would Christiana find,
In the garden wat'ring flowers,
Or arbor cool reclin'd.

For she was wont there to retire,
And leave the giddy throng,
To meditate on matchless works
Of power supreme alone.

Who left this world in early age,
Now shines a saint in light,
Who knew her worth to say with me,
Her memory dear unite.

Whose social converse journeying on,
Remember'd oft I ween,
Thro' life and usual haunts where we
E'er now, have happy been.

For scarcely had the sun arose,
When walking forth to view
The verdant field, the spangled thorn,
Bedeck'd with morning dew.

Or join the great Creator's praise,
With birds from every spray,
Whose tuneful throats, a lesson teach,
To sing the vocal lay.

Or ramble through the woodland scene,
By Lougton or bridgend,
To gather strawberries that grew,
Spontaneous from their stem.

Or when our silk worms did engage
Our search for mulberry leaves,
Their labour in return for food,
Was always sure to please.

Like grain of mustard-seed or spots,
Those insects first appear,
Yet thousands from their silken stores,
Are clothed every year.

Each one retir'd to separate cell,
In work of different dye,
Employ'd, finish'd each web comes forth,
A charming Butterfly.

Example rare for those who would
Excel in useful art,
In solitude the place to learn
To act the brightest part.

Or seek the shade from noon-tide heat,
With unison of mind.
Alternate read historic page,
Till ev'ning rays declin'd.

These summer days sped swift away,
Nor did we think of home
Till town clock bell with usual peal,
Gave warning to return.

And when by winter fire we sat,
And plied our seam, or spun,
While some have told the merry tale,
And others they have sung.

Rosanna fair who died for love,
While all around did weep;
Each task perform'd for bed prepar'd,
And there felt fast asleep.

No lasting grief our youthful minds oppress'd,
For every night, we sunk in calm repose;
Nor carping care, that bane to peaceful rest,
We still with joy to meet each other rose,
Or hail'd the morning dawn.

MARGARET BROWN

(*FL*. 1819)

———

MAINLY comprising epistles to friends (and to creatures and countries), Margaret Brown's *Lays of Affection* (1819) addresses a range of
social issues, including slavery and foreign conflict. The collection
exhibits a persistent patriotism, as we see in the following pair of
poems 'From Scotia'.

———

'From Scotia, to a Lady on Her Eager Desire to Return to Her Native Country'

Lays of Affection (Edinburgh: Waugh and Innes, 1819).

> I love thee that the Land is dear
>   That first awaked thy infant lay,
> But mourn thou long'st the hour were near
>   That bears from Scotia far away.
>
> In the first hour thou met'st my view,
>   No chill indifference I could feel;
> And still the more thy mind I knew,
>   I priz'd thee with a tenderer zeal.
>
> O! how delightful my employ!
>   Thy charms to others view I bring,
> And listen with an eager joy,
>   While holy hearts, Maria, sing.
>
> If envious hate thy worth malign,
>   My looks will tell thee every where,
> 'Tis sweet to gaze on eyes like thine,
>   And feel the Virtue imaged there.
>
> Still as the sacred Seasons roll,
>   They give to Friendship holier zeal;

Within the Temple, all my soul
    Expands in wishes for thy weal.

And can a love like this decline,
    As glides the stream of Life away?
O no! thou dear One! it is mine
    The Friendship that can ne'er decay.

O! let this fond, and faithful zeal
    Be as thy natal Land before;
Or still the pang will Scotia feel,
    She has no power to charm thee more.

'From Scotia, to Friends Never to be Forgotten'

O! list to me.
It is no Siren's song my minstrelsy,
Ye cherish'd of a Sister Land!
I hail'd you here with wishes bland,
For dear is England; I have joy'd to find,
How sage her Daughters are, how lovely, and how kind!

You I recal
Oft to remembrance. Oft I think on all
The bliss which hearts like yours can feel,
So eager for each other's weal.
Ah! that so rarely on the Earth it glows!
Ah! who can name the ills from envious hate that flows?

Ye have no pride,
That feels a pleasure when ye can deride.
Your hearts are form'd delight to know,
Wherever ye can praise bestow.
Sure any Country ye may roam to see
Will find in you a charm, and mingle praise with me.

Ere many Lands
Have seen you with the hope my heart expands,
Ye will return to glad mine eyes,
You, need I say, my Cities prize?
You, will my Woods and Lakes, my every Vale,
My every shelly Shore, and every Mountain, hail!

And, till we meet,
The fond entreaty I will still repeat,
Return, ye cherish'd Ones! return!
And O! with what desire I burn,
Your God may watch forever o'er your weal,
And give you all the bliss "the pure in heart" can feel!

MARY MACQUEEN
(1786–1854)

ALSO known as Mrs Storie, Mary MacQueen left her home in Lochwinnoch, Renfrewshire, to settle in Upper Canada with her labourer husband. Schooled in the oral tradition of storytelling by her grandmother, MacQueen often reworks familiar tropes in ingenious new ways. 'The Hawthorn Green' relies on a deceptively straightforward anaphoric structure to convey a rapid dialogue between a young girl and the hawthorn tree. Fourteen of MacQueen's songs were collected by her close contemporary Andrew Crawfurd.

'The Hawthorn Green'

Andrew Crawfurd's Collection of Ballads and Songs, ed. Emily B. Lyle (Edinburgh: Scottish Text Society, 1975–6).

As lady as fair as fair could be
Sat marvelling under yon hawthorn tree
She marvelled much how things could be
To see the grein leaves on yon hawthorn tree

Then out bespak the hawthorn tree
What makes you marvel sae much at me
The finest dew that ever was seen
Does faw on me and keep me green

What if I wud cut you doun
And carry you hence to yonder town
The next year after ye woudna be seen
To spread forth your leaves baith fresh and green

To cut me down I put nae doubt
But ye dinna cut me by the root
The neist year after I will be seen
To spread my leaves baith fresh and green

But you fair maids you are not so
When ance that your virginity go
The next year after you may be seen
But never to flourish sae fresh again

This fair maid she hearing this
She turned her back to the hawthorn buss
The neist year after she was never seen
To talk onie mair to the hawthorn grein

CATHERINE G. WARD
(1787–c.1837)

═══

CATHERINE G. (GEORGE) WARD was a prolific author of poetry and prose. She acted briefly on the stage in Edinburgh, but by the 1810s she had settled in London. Ward's first work, a small collection of *Poems* (1805) printed in Edinburgh, was sold by subscription. She followed this up five years later with her first novel, *The Daughter of St Omar* (1810). During the four decades in which she published, Ward produced six collections of poetry and twenty-one novels, as well as two unpublished operas and a farce. Despite receiving financial support from notable figures, including royalty, by her own claim, Ward requested financial aid from the Royal Literary Fund on five separate occasions between 1816 and 1832, with some success. By the late 1820s, Ward (now known as Mrs Mason) published less and less, and all but faded away from literary life in 1832.

═══

'Lines Written in Kelsoe Abbey, Scotland'

Miscellaneous Poems (London: Gold and Northhouse, 1820).

> Dear Caledonia! at whose early birth,
> Came blithesome health, and peace, and joyous mirth,
> Genius and strength thy hardy sons first knew,
> And deeds of valor first belonged to you:
> Blest be your hills, for ever blest your shades,
> Your lofty mountains and your peaceful glades,
> Where happy shepherds feed their flocks secure,
> On grounds their aged fathers trod before.
> Many a battle fought, achievement won,
> And glorious feats by gallant Scotsmen done,
> Where youthful warriors felt the glowing flame,
> And gather'd laurels in the field of fame;
> Now springing flowrets o'er their tombs are spread,
> And mingle blossoms with the heroes dead:

Immortal chiefs! though long to dust consign'd,
Ye'll live eternal on the grateful mind!
Fight o'er your battles in your sons again,
And Scotia mourn her chiefs no longer slain.

'On the Author's Visiting the Grave of Robert Burns'

Sweet Bard, to feeling and to virtue dear,
Long shall thy mem'ry claim the pensive tear.
Thy rustic song give transport to my heart,
And own the magic of thy tuneful art.
The fondest pride that Scotia ever knew,
When she gave birth, immortal bard, to you!
Oh could I sound thy own soft thrilling lays,
I'd make each hill and valley echo to thy praise,
And Scotia's hills should echo back again,
And sigh responsive to thy soothing strain.
The flow'rets sweet thy fancy lov'd to trace,
Reflect in scent and hue thy native grace;
For thy sake, dear each blue-bell still shall be,
And gowans ever welcome guests with me.
What though no story'd urn, nor pompous bust,
Adorns the spot where lies thy sacred dust!
Though humble turf be bound upon thy breast,
And not a stone has mark'd thy place of rest!
Thou'rt fled where worth is better understood;
Thy brightest monument is—peace with God.

IAIN MACILLEATHAIN / JOHN MACLEAN
(1787–1848)

===

A NATIVE of Caolas on the island of Tiree, the Gaelic poet Iain MacIlleathain (John MacLean) was a shoemaker by trade. He became an honorary poet to the Laird of the neighbouring island of Coll. MacLean also collected verse, and published an anthology of his own and others' songs in 1818. A year later, he emigrated to Nova Scotia. For the first years outside of Scotland, he struggled to adjust to the new world. Composed no later than 1820, 'Oran do dh' Ameireaga' is outwardly an anti-emigration tract in verse. By 1830, though, MacLean found a wider range in his poetry-making, including a considerable number of hymns, among other things.

===

'Oran do dh' Ameireaga'

Clàrsach na Coille: A Collection of Gaelic Poetry, ed. Alexander Maclean Sinclair (Glasgow: Archibald Sinclair, 1881).

> Gu bheil mi am ònrachd sa choille ghruamaich,
> Mo smaointean luaineach, cha tog mi fonn;
> Fhuair mi an t-àit' seo an aghaidh nàduir,
> Gun thrèig gach tàlant a bha nam cheann;
> Cha dèan mi òran a chur air dòigh ann,
> An uair nì mi tòiseachadh bidh mi trom;
> Chaill mi a' Ghàidhlig seach mar a b' àbhaist dhomh
> An uair a bha mi san dùthaich thall.

> Chan fhaigh mi m' inntinn leam ann an òrdugh,
> Ged bha mi eòlach air dèanamh rann;
> Is e mheudaich bròn dhomh 's a lùghdaich sòlas
> Gun duine còmhla rium a nì rium cainnt;
> Gach là is oidhche is gach car a nì mi
> Gum bi mi cuimhneachadh anns gach àm
> An tìr a dh' fhàg mi tha an taic an t-sàile,
> Ged tha mi an-dràsd' ann am bràighe ghleann.

Chan iongnadh dhòmhsa ged tha mi brònach,
Is ann tha mo chòmhnaidh air cùl nam beann,
Am meadhan fàsaich air Abhainn Bhàrnaidh
Gun dad as fheàrr na buntàta lom;
Mun dèan mi àiteach 's mun tog mi bàrr ann
Is a' choille ghàbhaidh chur às a bonn
Le neart mo ghàirdein gum bi mi sàraichte,
Is treis' air fàilinn mum fàs a' chlann.

Is i seo an dùthaich sa bheil an cruadal
Gun fhios don t-sluagh a tha tighinn a-nall;
Gur h-olc a fhuaras oirnn luchd a' bhuairidh
A rinn le an tuaraisgeul ar toirt ann!
Ma nì iad buannachd cha mhair i buan dhaibh;
Cha dèan i suas iad 's chan iongnadh leam,
Is gach mallachd truaghain a bhios gan ruagadh
Bhon chaidh am fuadach a chur fon ceann.

Bidh gealladh làidir ga thoirt an tràth sin,
Bidh cliù an àite ga chur am meud;
Bidh iad ag ràitinn gu bheil bhur càirdean
Gu sona sàidhbhir gun dad a dh'èis;
Gach naidheachd mheallta ga toirt gur n-ionnsaigh-se
Feuch an sanntaich sibh dol nan dèidh;
Ma thig sibh sàbhailt', nuair chì sibh àdsan,
Chan fheàrr na stàtachan na sibh fèin.

An uair thèid na dròbhairean sin gur n-iarraidh
Is ann leis na briagan a nì iad feum,
Gun fhacal fìrinne bhith ga innse,
Is an cridhe a' dìteadh na their am beul;
Ri cur am fiachaibh gu bheil san tìr seo
Gach nì as prìseile tha fon ghrèin;

An uair thig sibh innte gur beag a chì sibh
Ach coille dhìreach toirt dhibh an speur.
An uair thig an geamhradh is àm na dùbhlachd
Bidh sneachd a' dlùthadh ri cùl nan geug,
Is gu domhain dùmhail dol thar na glùine,
Is ge math an triùbhsair cha dèan i feum
Gun stocainn dhùbailt sa mhocais chlùdaich
Bhios air a dùnadh gu dlùth le èill:

B' e am fasan ùr dhuinn a cosg le fionntach
Mar chaidh a rùsgadh den bhrùid an-dè.

Mur bi mi eòlach airson mo chòmhdaich
Gum faigh mi reòta mo shròn 's mo bheul;
Le gaoith a tuath a bhios nimheil fuaraidh
Gum bi mo chluasan an cunnart geur;
Tha an reothadh fuathasach, cha seas an tuagh ris,
Gum mill e a' chruaidh ged a bha i geur;
Mur toir mi blàths di, gum brist an stàilinn,
Is gun dol don cheàrdaich cha gheàrr i beum.

An uair thig an samhradh 's am mìosa Cèitein
Bidh teas na grèine gam fhàgail fann;
Gun cuir i spèirid sa h-uile creutair
A bhios fo èislean air feadh nan toll;
Na mathain bhèisteil gun dèan iad èirigh
Dhol feadh an treud, is gur mòr an call:
Is a' chuileag ìneach gu socach puinseanta
Gam lot gu lìonmhor le rinn a lainn.

Gun dèan i m' aodann gu h-olc a chaobadh,
Chan fhaic mi an saoghal, 's ann bhios mi dall;
Gun at mo shùilean le neart a cungaidh,
Ro ghuineach drùidheach tha sùgh a teang';
Chan fhaigh mi àireamh dhuibh ann an dànachd
Gach beathach gràineil a thogas ceann;
Is cho liutha plàigh ann 's a bha air rìgh Phàro
Airson nan tràillean, nuair bhàth e an camp.

Gur h-iomadh caochladh tighinn air an t-saoghal
Is ro bheag a shaoil mi an uair bha mi thall;
Bu bheachd dhomh 'n uair sin mun d' rinn mi gluasad
Gum fàsainn uasal nuair thiginn ann;
An car a fhuair mi cha b' ann gum bhuannachd,
Tighinn thar a' chuain air chuairt bha meallt',
Gu tìr nan craobh anns nach eil an t-saorsainn,
Gun mhart, gun chaora, is mi dh' aodach gann.

Gur h-iomadh ceum anns am bi mi an dèislàimh
Mun dèan mi saidhbhir mo theachd-an-tìr;
Bidh m' obair èigneach mun toir mi feum aisd',
Is mun dèan mi rèiteach airson a' chroinn;

Cur sgonn nan teinntean air muin a chèile
Gun do lasaich fèithean a bha nam dhruim,
Is a h-uile ball dhiom cho dubh a' sealltainn,
Bidh mi gam shamhlachadh ris an t-sùip.

Ge mòr an seanchas a bh' aca an Albainn,
Tha a' chùis a' dearbhadh nach robh e fìor;
Na dolair ghorma chan fhaic mi falbh iad,
Ged bha iad ainmeil a bhith san tìr;
Ma nìtear bargain chan fhaighear airgead,
Ged 's èiginn ainmeachadh anns a' phrìs;
Ma geibhear cùnnradh air feadh nam bùthan
Gum pàighear null e le flùr no ìm.

Chan fhaic mi margadh no latha fèille
No iomain feudalach ann an dròbh,
No nì nì feum dhuinn am measg a chèile:
Tha an sluagh nan èiginn 's a h-uile dòigh;
Cha chulaidh fharmaid iad leis an ainbhfhaich,
A' reic na shealbhaicheas iad an còir;
Bidh fear nam fiachan is cromadh cinn air
Ga chur don phrìosan mur dìol e an stòr.

Mun tig na cùisean à taigh na cùirte,
Gun tèid an dùblachadh aig a' mhòd;
Tha an lagh a' giùlan o làimh na jury
Gun tèid a spùinneadh 's nach fiù e an còrr;
Bidh earraid siùbhlach air feadh na dùthcha
Gan ruith le cùnntasaibh air an tòir;
Gur mòr mo chùram gun tig e am ionnsaigh:
Cha ghabh e diùltadh 's bidh diùbhail òirnn.

Chan fhaigh mi innse dhuibh ann am Ghàidhlig,
Cha dèan mo nàdur a chur air dòigh
Gach fios a b' àill leam thoirt do mo càirdean
San tìr a dh' fhàg mi, rinn m' àrach òg;
Gach aon a leughas e, tuigibh reusan,
Is na tugaibh èisteachd do luchd a' bhòsd,
Na fàidhean brèige a bhios gur teumadh,
Gun aca spèis dhibh ach dèidh bhur n-òir.

Ged bhithinn dìcheallach ann an sgrìobhadh
Gun gabhainn mìosa ris agus còrr,

Mun cuirinn crìoch air na bheil air m' inntinn
Is mun tugainn dhuibh e le cainnt mo bheòil;
Tha mulad dìomhair an dèidh mo lìonadh
On is èiginn strìochdadh an seo rim bheò,
Air bheag thoil-inntinn sa choille chruinn seo,
Gun duine faighneachd an seinn mi ceòl.

Cha b' e sin m' àbhaist an tùs mo làithean,
Is ann bhithinn ràbhartach aig gach bòrd,
Gu cridheil sùnndach an comann cùirteil
A' ruith ar n-ùine gun chùram òirnn.
An uair thug mi cùl ribh bha mi gur n-ionndrainn,
Gun shil mo shùilean gu dlùth le deòir,
Air moch Diardaoin a' dol seach an Caolas
Is an long fo h-aodach 's a' ghaoth on chòrs'.

'A Song to America' (translated by Donald E. Meek)

I am so lonely in this gloomy forest;
my thoughts are restless, I can raise no song;
since I found this place which conflicts with nature,
every former talent in my head has gone;
I am unable to construct a song here,
I become despondent when I try my hand;
I have lost my Gaelic as I once had it
when I lived over in that other land.

I cannot put my mind in order
though I knew once how to make a verse;
what has increased my sorrow, and decreased my solace
is having no-one near me with whom I can converse;
each day and night, in each task I do,
I keep remembering time and again
the land that I left hard by the ocean—
though I now live at the top of glens.

I am not surprised that I am doleful—
behind the hills is where I have a roof,
in the middle of a wilderness on Barney's River,
with bare potatoes as my finest food;

before I till the soil there and take crops from it,
and dig the awful forest from its root
by my fore-arm's strength, I'll be exhausted,
and long in decay before I've raised my brood.

This is the land that is filled with hardship,
unknown to those coming across the sea;
what evil tactics were used by those enticers
who, by their yarns, took us over here!
If they make a profit, it will not be lasting,
it will not raise their status, and I wonder not,
since they are pursued by the curse of wretches
who were subjected to an eviction plot.

A firm promise will then be offered,
the reputation of the place will be enhanced;
they will make the claim that all your relations
are happy and wealthy, with no earthly lack;
every misleading story will be laid before you,
to see if you will crave to follow them;
if you arrive safely, when you observe them,
the swells are no wealthier than ourselves.

When those drovers set out to get you,
they succeed only by telling fibs,
without ever uttering a word that's truthful,
while their heart condemns what is on their lips;
they make pretence that this land possesses
the most previous gems beneath the sun on high;
on your arrival, you will see little
but a towering forest blocking off the sky.

When winter comes and the time of darkness
the snow lies packed behind each branch;
deep and thick, it goes over knee-height,
and though the trouser's good it will not suffice
without a double stocking in a ragged moccasin
tight-closed with thongs around the foot:
it was our new fashion to wear it hairy,
as skinned yesterday from the brute.

If I am not careful about my clothing,
my nose and mouth will be found to freeze;

because of the north wind with its biting coldness
a pernicious danger awaits my ears;
the frost is awful, the axe cannot stand it,
it will spoil the blade though it were sharp;
unless I warm it, the steel will fracture—
without going to the smithy, it will cut no mark.

When summer comes, and the month of Maytime,
the heat of the sun will leave me weak;
it will put vigour into every creature
which, in all the holes, has been asleep;
the beastly bears, they too will waken
to go through the herd, causing massive loss,
and the taloned insect, poisonous and snouty,
will wound me profusely with its sharp-tipped lance.

It will make my face come up lumpy,
I'll not see the world, I will be blind;
my eyes will swell through its potent poison,
its tongue's venomous juice is of a penetrating kind;
I cannot enumerate for you in verses
every horrid beast that rears its head,
with plagues as plentiful as came to Pharaoh
because of slaves, when he downed his men.

My world is affected by many adverse changes
which I scarcely imagined when in that isle;
it was then my intention before I left it
that, when I came here, I would reach noble style;
the misfortune that hit me brought me no profit,
coming over the ocean in deception's track,
to the land of trees where there is no freedom,
no cow nor sheep, and few clothes for my back.

In many activities I will lag behind
before my livelihood makes any wealth;
my work will falter before I prosper,
and clear the land to plough the earth;
when stacking log-blocks to use as firewood,
I strained some muscles that were in my back,
and I will be likened to a chimney sweeper,
since every limb of me looks so black.

Though great the talk that they had in Scotland,
matters prove that it was all lies;
the green dollars I do not see tendered,
although they were reputedly n this land;
if one makes contracts, one gets no money,
though it has to be mentioned in the price,
and if, when shopping, you find a bargain,
flour and butter must transact its like.

I see no market or day of selling
or the driving of cattle in a drove,
or anything to help us in our predicament;
the people are in desperation of every form;
they are not to be envied as they are indebted,
selling everything they rightly own;
the shameful debtor must hold his head down
since he goes to prison unless he pays the store.

Before matters are taken from the court house,
at the bar of trial, they will be twice as sore;
the law that's delivered by the hand of the jury
demands he be plundered, as he's worth no more;
a number officer will scour the country
pursuing them with warrants in every place;
my great worry is that he will come my way;
he cannot be refused, and we will lose face.

My Gaelic fails me when I try to tell you,
nor can my nature arrange in form,
all I'd wish conveyed to my relations
in the land I left, where I was once a boy;
each one who reads this, let him heed reason,
and pay no attention to the loquacious pack—
those false prophets who sting you sorely,
and love not you, but the gold in your sack.

Though I should be diligent in my writing,
I would need to spend a month and more,
before I could express all that concerns me,
and present it to you by word of mouth;
a subconscious sorrow has filled my being
since I must submit here all my life long,

with little pleasure in this constricting forest,
and no one asking if I'll sing a song.

That was not my custom when I was youthful—
at every table I loved to chat,
in jovial company, in hearty spirits,
in carefree style, as our time ran fast.
When I turned my back to you, I missed you greatly,
and my eyes wept tears in copious floods,
early on Thursday as we passed Caolas,
the ship under sail and the wind off the coast.

SUSANNA HAWKINS
(1787–1868)

BORN in Dumfriesshire, Susanna (or Susannah) Hawkins spent her youth and young adulthood as a dairymaid. By middle age she had significantly improved upon her basic education and developed a keen interest in poetry. An avid admirer of Hawkins's works, the owner of the *Dumfries Courier* covered the costs of printing them in small volumes with paper covers. By 1861, Hawkins's output of *Poetical Works* had filled nine volumes. For half a century Hawkins took her books across the country, selling copies from door to door.

'Address to Satan'

The Poetical Works (Dumfries: John M'Diarmid and Co., 1829).

December winds did chilly blaw,
Wi' heavy show'rs o' hail and snaw,
Ae gloomy night the cluds did lour,
And mist did on the mountains tow'r;

Auld Satan strove, and did prevail,
To rise in show'rs o' rattling hail;
He in the air took wings and flew,
And strongly he his bellows blew;

He shatter'd ships upon the sea,
And gart their masts and riggin' flee,
And some he drave fast in the sand,
And after that he came to land.

O'er Criffel hill, he loudly roar'd,
O'er Burnswark hill, he wildly snor'd;
Through entries blew wi' sic a birl,
Baith ricks and houses he did tirl;

He tirled mony houses bare,
He took their thack up in the air;
And strong trees out o' root did blaw,
And blew down mony an ancient wa';

Auld carlins wi' their flainen toys,
Did loudly cry, Fye rin out boys!
Auld curls wi' their pirnies red,
Were like to be the younger's dead,

Misca'd them for a lazy set,
When young like you we scarce were bet;
Wi' a strong blast he loud did blaw,
To gather in his brownies a',

Till near about the midnight hour,
He lighted in a haunted tower;
Within the tow'r, a light did rise,
Which did the neighbourhood surprise;

In shape o' man, he there was seen,
Wi' twa large fiery glouring een.
Witches and warlocks ran with speed,
Unto auld Nick, to learn their creed.

Murderers and robbers ran
To get a wag o' his black han';
The liars joining wi' the thieves,
To see if he would sign their briefs;

If he would help them to a post,
Their labour it would not be lost.
The hypocrites wi' blunt-like een,
Were unco laith they should be seen;

Pretended they came out to pray,
But they had wander'd off their way;
At Satan they did gae a tug,
And whisper'd slowly in his lug,

That he might learn them to be sly,
Right cunningly to cheat and lie.
Witches and warlocks got their creed,
To shoot both horse and kye to deed;

Wi' murderers he did agree,
To help them wi' a cruelty.
He likewise did the thieves enlist,
In time o' need they might assist;

He signed the liars their black card,
To be where they would best be heard;
The hypocrites got a receipt,
To wrang their neebors by deceit,

An' envy, slander, sigh, and pray,
An' cheat, an' lie, a' in a day;
Auld Satan did his brownies lead,
To places where they cam' good speed;

Wi' selfish cunning where few saw,
The hypocrites were wurst ava'.
Satan, you are still on ye'r watch,
Ye auld black rogue, ye strive to catch,
And lead the human race astray,
But ye'll be catch'd yoursel' some day.

GEORGE GORDON, LORD BYRON
(1788–1824)

——

ARGUABLY the most gifted poet of his generation, and certainly the most famous, George Gordon, sixth Baron Byron retained a lifelong passion for his maternal home county, Aberdeenshire. Byron's parents settled into the Gordons' estate at Gight, though they briefly moved to the Isle of Wight to evade creditors, and then Paris and London, where the poet was born. A year later, Byron and his mother moved into the city of Aberdeen. After early schooling in Aberdeen, Byron studied at Harrow and Cambridge. Around this time, he worked up his early poems for publication, though most copies of *Fugitive Pieces* were destroyed in response to adverse feedback from friends and family. *Poems on Various Occasions*, a revised collection of early poems, appeared in a small print run early in 1807. A few months later followed *Hours of Idleness*, which received an aggressive notice in the *Edinburgh Review*. Livid, Byron produced a book-length satire in response, *English Bards and Scotch Reviewers* (1809). Having attacked many of the leading poets of the age (the Lake School, the Della Cruscans, romancers like Scott, and more), Byron declared his own genius with the critically acclaimed *Childe Harold's Pilgrimage* (1812). Further major works poured forth, in satire, in various lyric forms, but mostly in the sequence of narratives that began with *The Giaour* and *The Bride of Abydos* (1813) and culminated with *Parisina* and *The Siege of Corinth* (1816). Partly written in the company of the Shelleys in exile, *The Prisoner of Chillon and Other Poems* also appeared in 1816. Within a couple of years, Byron began his unfinished masterpiece, *Don Juan* (1819–24), and scores of other critically acclaimed poems. Dead at thirty-six, his poetic legacy had long been assured.

——

'Lachin y Gair'

The Works of Lord Byron, 14 vols (London: John Murray, 1832).

> Away, ye gay landscapes, ye gardens of roses!
> In you let the minions of luxury rove;

Restore me the rocks, where the snow-flake reposes,
    Though still they are sacred to freedom and love:
Yet, Caledonia, beloved are thy mountains,
    Round their white summits though elements war;
Though cataracts foam 'stead of smooth-flowing fountains,
    I sigh for the valley of dark Loch na Garr.

Ah! there my young footsteps in infancy wander'd;
    My cap was the bonnet, my cloak was the plaid;
On chieftains long perish'd my memory ponder'd,
    As daily I strode through the pine-cover'd glade:
I sought not my home till the day's dying glory
    Gave place to the rays of the bright polar star;
For fancy was cheer'd by traditional story,
    Disclosed by the natives of dark Loch na Garr.

"Shades of the dead! have I not heard your voices
    Rise on the night-rolling breath of the gale?"
Surely the soul of the hero rejoices,
    And rides on the wind, o'er his own Highland vale.
Round Loch na Garr while the stormy mist gathers,
    Winter presides in his cold icy car:
Clouds there encircle the forms of my fathers;
    They dwell in the tempests of dark Loch na Garr.

"Ill-starred, though brave, did no visions foreboding
    Tell you that fate had forsaken your cause?"
Ah! were you destined to die at Culloden,
    Victory crown'd not your fall with applause:
Still were you happy in death's earthy slumber,
    You rest with your clan in the caves of Braemar;
The pibroch resounds, to the piper's loud number,
    Your deeds on the echoes of dark Loch na Garr.

Years have roll'd on, Loch na Garr, since I left you,
    Years must elapse ere I tread you again:
Nature of verdure and flow'rs has bereft you,
    Yet still are you dearer than Albion's plain.
England! thy beauties are tame and domestic
    To one who has roved on the mountains afar:
Oh for the crags that are wild and majestic!
    The steep frowning glories of dark Loch na Garr!

'I would I were a careless child'

I would I were a careless child,
　　Still dwelling in my Highland cave,
Or roaming through the dusky wild,
　　Or bounding o'er the dark blue wave;
The cumbrous pomp of Saxon pride
　　Accords not with the freeborn soul,
Which loves the mountain's craggy side,
　　And seeks the rocks where billows roll.

Fortune! take back these cultured lands,
　　Take back this name of splendid sound!
I hate the touch of servile hands,
　　I hate the slaves that cringe around.
Place me among the rocks I love,
　　Which sound to Ocean's wildest roar;
I ask but this—again to rove
　　Through scenes my youth hath known before.

Few are my years, and yet I feel
　　The world was ne'er designed for me:
Ah! why do dark'ning shades conceal
　　The hour when man must cease to be?
Once I beheld a splendid dream,
　　A visionary scene of bliss:
Truth!—wherefore did thy hated beam
　　Awake me to a world like this?

I loved—but those I loved are gone;
　　Had friends—my early friends are fled:
How cheerless feels the heart alone
　　When all its former hopes are dead!
Though gay companions o'er the bowl
　　Dispel awhile the sense of ill;
Though pleasure stirs the maddening soul,
　　The heart—the heart—is lonely still.

How dull! to hear the voice of those
　　Whom rank or chance, whom wealth or power,
Have made, though neither friends nor foes,
　　Associates of the festive hour.

Give me again a faithful few,
    In years and feelings still the same,
And I will fly the midnight crew,
    Where boist'rous joy is but a name.

And woman, lovely woman! thou,
    My hope, my comforter, my all!
How cold must be my bosom now,
    When e'en thy smiles begin to pall!
Without a sigh would I resign
    This busy scene of splendid woe,
To make that calm contentment mine,
    Which virtue know, or seems to know.

Fain would I fly the haunts of men—
    I seek to shun, not hate mankind;
My breast requires the sullen glen,
    Whose gloom may suit a darken'd mind.
Oh! that to me the wings were given
    Which bear the turtle to her nest!
Then would I cleave the vault of heaven,
    To flee away, and be at rest.

'When I roved a young Highlander'

When I roved a young Highlander o'er the dark heath,
    And climb'd thy steep summit, oh Morven of snow!
To gaze on the torrent that thunder'd beneath,
    Or the mist of the tempest that gather'd below,
Untutor'd by science, a stranger to fear,
    And rude as the rocks where my infancy grew,
No feeling, save one, to my bosom was dear;
    Need I say, my sweet Mary, 'twas centred in you?

Yet it could not be love, for I knew not the name,—
    What passion can dwell in the heart of a child?
But still I perceive an emotion the same
    As I felt, when a boy, on the crag-cover'd wild:
One image alone on my bosom impress'd,
    I loved my bleak regions, nor panted for new;
And few were my wants, for my wishes were bless'd;
    And pure were my thoughts, for my soul was with you.

I arose with the dawn; with my dog as my guide,
　　From mountain to mountain I bounded along;
I breasted the billows of Dee's rushing tide,
　　And heard at a distance the Highlander's song:
At eve, on my heath-cover'd couch of repose,
　　No dreams, save of Mary, were spread to my view;
And warm to the skies my devotions arose,
　　For the first of my prayers was a blessing on you.

I left my bleak home, and my visions are gone;
　　The mountains are vanish'd, my youth is no more;
As the last of my race, I must wither alone,
　　And delight but in days I have witness'd before:
Ah! splendour has raised, but embitter'd my lot;
　　More dear were the scenes which my infancy knew:
Though my hopes may have fail'd, yet they are not forgot;
　　Though cold is my heart, still it lingers with you.

When I see some dark hill point its crest to the sky,
　　I think of the rocks that o'ershadow Colbleen;
When I see the soft blue of a love-speaking eye,
　　I think of those eyes that endear'd the rude scene;
When, haply, some light-waving locks I behold,
　　That faintly resemble my Mary's in hue,
I think on the long flowing ringlets of gold,
　　The locks that were sacred to beauty, and you.

Yet the day may arrive when the mountains once more
　　Shall rise to my sight in their mantles of snow:
But while these soar above me, unchanged as before,
　　Will Mary be there to receive me?—ah, no!
Adieu, then, ye hills, where my childhood was bred!
　　Thou sweet flowing Dee, to thy waters adieu!
No home in the forest shall shelter my head,—
　　Ah! Mary, what home could be mine but with you?

'So, we'll go no more a roving'

I

So, we'll go no more a roving
So late into the night,

Though the heart be still as loving,
    And the moon be still as bright.

II

For the sword outwears its sheath,
    And the soul wears out the breast,
And the heart must pause to breathe,
    And love itself have rest.

III

Though the night was made for loving,
    And the day returns too soon,
Yet we'll go no more a roving
    By the light of the moon.

'She Walks in Beauty'

She walks in beauty, like the night
    Of cloudless climes and starry skies;
And all that's best of dark and bright
    Meet in her aspect and her eyes;
Thus mellow'd to that tender light
    Which heaven to gaudy day denies.

One shade the more, one ray the less,
    Had half impair'd the nameless grace
Which waves in every raven tress,
    Or softly lightens o'er her face;
Where thoughts serenely sweet express
    How pure, how dear their dwelling place.

And on that cheek, and o'er that brow,
    So soft, so calm, yet eloquent,
The smiles that win, the tints that glow,
    But tell of days in goodness spent,
A mind at peace with all below,
    A heart whose love is innocent!

'The Destruction of Sennacherib'

I

The Assyrian came down like the wolf on the fold,
And his cohorts were gleaming in purple and gold;

And the sheen of their spears was like stars on the sea,
When the blue wave rolls nightly on deep Galilee.

2

Like the leaves of the forest when Summer is green,
That host with their banners at sunset were seen:
Like the leaves of the forest when Autumn hath blown,
That host on the morrow lay withered and strown.

3

For the Angel of Death spread his wings on the blast,
And breathed in the face of the foe as he pass'd;
And the eyes of the sleepers wax'd deadly and chill,
And their hearts but once heaved, and for ever grew still!

4

And there lay the steed with his nostril all wide,
But through it there roll'd not the breath of his pride:
And the foam of his gasping lay white on the turf,
And cold as the spray of the rock-beating surf.

5

And there lay the rider distorted and pale,
With the dew on his brow, and the rust on his mail;
And the tents were all silent, the banners alone,
The lances unlifted, the trumpet unblown.

6

And the widows of Ashur are loud in their wail,
And the idols are broke in the temple of Baal;
And the might of the Gentile, unsmote by the sword,
Hath melted like snow in the glance of the Lord!

'Darkness'

I had a dream, which was not all a dream.
The bright sun was extinguish'd, and the stars
Did wander darkling in the eternal space,
Rayless, and pathless, and the icy earth

Swung blind and blackening in the moonless air;
Morn came and went—and came, and brought no day,
And men forgot their passions in the dread
Of this their desolation; and all hearts
Were chill'd into a selfish prayer for light:
And they did live by watchfires—and the thrones,
The palaces of crowned kings—the huts,
The habitations of all things which dwell,
Were burnt for beacons; cities were consumed,
And men were gather'd round their blazing homes
To look once more into each other's face;
Happy were those who dwelt within the eye
Of the volcanos, and their mountain-torch:
A fearful hope was all the world contain'd;
Forests were set on fire—but hour by hour
They fell and faded—and the crackling trunks
Extinguish'd with a crash—and all was black.
The brows of men by the despairing light
Wore an unearthly aspect, as by fits
The flashes fell upon them; some lay down
And hid their eyes and wept; and some did rest
Their chins upon their clenched hands, and smiled;
And others hurried to and fro, and fed
Their funeral piles with fuel, and look'd up
With mad disquietude on the dull sky,
The pall of a past world; and then again
With curses cast them down upon the dust,
And gnash'd their teeth and howl'd: the wild birds shriek'd,
And, terrified, did flutter on the ground,
And flap their useless wings; the wildest brutes
Came tame and tremulous; and vipers crawl'd
And twined themselves among the multitude,
Hissing, but stingless—they were slain for food:
And War, which for a moment was no more,
Did glut himself again;—a meal was bought
With blood, and each sate sullenly apart
Gorging himself in gloom: no love was left;
All earth was but one thought—and that was death,
Immediate and inglorious; and the pang
Of famine fed upon all entrails—men
Died, and their bones were tombless as their flesh;

The meagre by the meagre were devour'd,
Even dogs assail'd their masters, all save one,
And he was faithful to a corse, and kept
The birds and beasts and famish'd men at bay,
Till hunger clung them, or the dropping dead
Lured their lank jaws; himself sought out no food,
But with a piteous and perpetual moan,
And a quick desolate cry, licking the hand
Which answer'd not with a caress—he died.
The crowd was famish'd by degrees; but two
Of an enormous city did survive,
And they were enemies: they met beside
The dying embers of an altar-place
Where had been heap'd a mass of holy things
For an unholy usage; they raked up,
And shivering scraped with their cold skeleton hands
The feeble ashes, and their feeble breath
Blew for a little life, and made a flame
Which was a mockery; then they lifted up
Their eyes as it grew lighter, and beheld
Each other's aspects—saw, and shriek'd, and died—
Even of their mutual hideousness they died,
Unknowing who he was upon whose brow
Famine had written Fiend. The world was void,
The populous and the powerful was a lump,
Seasonless, herbless, treeless, manless, lifeless—
A lump of death—a chaos of hard clay.
The rivers, lakes, and ocean all stood still,
And nothing stirr'd within their silent depths;
Ships sailorless lay rotting on the sea,
And their masts fell down piecemeal; as they dropp'd
They slept on the abyss without a surge—
The waves were dead; the tides were in their grave,
The Moon, their mistress, had expired before;
The winds were wither'd in the stagnant air,
And the clouds perish'd; Darkness had no need
Of aid from them—She was the Universe.

ANNA GHOBHA / ANN GOW
(1788–C.1850)

———

ANNA GHOBHA (Ann Gow), a daughter of the poet Margaret MacGregor, was a native of Glen Errochty in Atholl. She is known to have been a highly skilled weaver of fine tartans whose services were much in demand by the gentry for the production of the specialist fabrics needed for military uniforms and Highland dress. Captain William MacKenzie of Gruinard, the addressee of the song that follows, served in the 72nd Regiment of Foot. In 1820, when living in Edinburgh on half pay, he founded the Celtic Society (known since 1873 as the Royal Celtic Society). Under MacKenzie's supervision, its members played a prominent part in King George IV's visit to Edinburgh in 1822. The following song is set to the air *Ge socrach mo leabaidh, b' annsa cadal air fraoch* ('Though my bed is comfortable, sleeping on heather's better').

———

'Do Chaiptean Uilleam MacCoinnich Ghruinneard'

Co-Chruinneach dh' Orain Thaghte Ghaeleach, ed. Duncan Mackintosh (Edinburgh: John Elder, 1831).

> 'S mi 'm shuidh' an seo 'm ònar
> Ann an seòmar leam fhéin
> A' snìomh éide don òigear
> 'S deise còmhnairde ceum,
> Do Chaiptean MacCoinnich,
> Fear foghainteach, treun,
> 'S chan eil mulad no bròn orm
> Gun duine 'm chòir bheir dhomh sgeul.
>
> Nam b' urrainn mi 'n òran,
> Dheilbhinn còmhradh le rùin
> Mun fhear 's maisich 'm measg còisre
> 'Ga bheil foghlam is iùl—

'S ann a ghabh mi ort eòlas
Aig a' chòmhdhail an tùs
'S bu lìonmhor baintighearn' 's math stoidhle
A bha faighneachd co thù.

'S math thig breacan an fhéilidh
Mu do shléistean gu dlùth,
Osain gheàrr agus gartain
Nach d'thig faisg air a' ghlùin,
Agus còta dhen tartan
Air a bhasadh mu d' chùl
'S ite dhosrach an fhìreoin
'S i gu dìreach á d' chrùn.

Dh'aithnichte cumadh Gàidhil ort
O d' bhràigh gu do bhonn,
Gura math thig dhut armachd,
Clogad 's targaid bhiodh trom
'S claidheamh cinn airgid,
'S e gun chearb, an sonn—
Pìc den iubhar nach lùbadh
'S plasg den fhùdar chruaidh lom.

Air a' choinnimh 'n Dùn Éideann
Measg nan ceud fhuair thu cliù
Aig grinnead do phearsa
'S do dhreas air do chùl;
Cha robh leithid MhicCoinnich
Sa cho-thional an tùs—
Thug Rìgh Deòrsa dha 'n t-urram
Thar gach duine fon chrùn:

Thug e òrdugh dh'fhear-làimh
Dealbh 'n àrmainn chur suas
Ann an deise a' Ghàidhil
Mar a bhà e san uair;
Do chomisean chaidh àrdach'
Gu bhith 'd cheannard air sluagh,
Do chur air thoiseach nan Gàidheal
Chumail 'n àird an t-sròil uain'.

Cha b'i do dhùthchas an cabhsair
No fuaim nan àrd-chlag mar cheòl,

Ach a' siubhal feadh fàsaich
'S do choin a' gàirich ad' chòir;
Dìreadh bheanntan is sgàirnich,
'S tric a rinn thu tàrmach a leòn—
Leis a' ghunna nach diùltadh
Bhiodh fuil air ùdlach nan cròc.

'S tu rachadh an gradachd le d' dhaoine
Nan d'thigeadh maoim air an cùl,
'S tu a b' urrainn gan teàrnadh
Latha blàir no rebhiù;
Le ciall agus seòltachd
Cur gach lòd air an druim,
Cha bhiodh orr' gealtachd ro'n nàimhde
'S an comanndair ri'n cùl.

'S mar an toil-inntinn do d' mhàthair
'S do d' chàirde ra-mhór,
Slat den abhal dh'fhàs thu
Tha cho ard am measg slòigh,
Laoch curanta dealbhach
'S e neo-chearbach 'na dhòigh—
Cha b'ann á crìonach nan crann
Shìnte 'n àird na meòir.

'S làidir lìonmhor do chinneach
Anns gach ionad mu thuath,
Luchd bhòt agus stiorap,
Ge b'e shireadh iad suas—
Clanna Choinnich nan geurlann,
Na fir threuna bha cruaidh,
'S tric a choisneadh buaidh làraich
Nuair bhiodh càch anns an ruaig.

'S leat mo rùn fhad 's as beò mi
A shàr chomhlan 's math dealbh,
'S b'e mo roghainn 's cha stòras
Thu bhith 'd chòirneal air arm—
Leòmhann fuileachdach seòlt'
Dh'fhàs gu connspaideach, garg,
Tha coisinn buaidh do Rìgh Deòrsa
'S cumail còir ri fir Alb'.

'To Captain William MacKenzie of Gruinard'
(translated by Ronald Black)

I'm sitting here alone
   In a room by myself
Spinning clothes for the handsome
   Smooth-stepping hero,
For Captain MacKenzie,
   An able, brave man,
And I don't mind having no one
   Here to give me their news.

If I were able in song,
   I'd talk eagerly of him
Who's the best-looking member
   Of the wise learned society—
I got to know you
   First at the gathering
Where lots of elegant ladies
   Asked who you were.

The kilt and the plaid
   Fit well round your thighs,
Short stockings with garters
   Not too close to the knee,
With a waistcoat of tartan
   Passed round your back
And a plumed eagle's feather
   Rising up from your head.

You've the shape of a Gael
   From your top to your toe,
You're well suited to weapons,
   Heavy target and helmet
And silver-hilted sword,
   The sapling is faultless—
Unbending yew bow
   And hard bare flask of powder.

At the Edinburgh meeting
   You were famed amongst hundreds
For your personal elegance

And the clothes on your back;
There was none like MacKenzie
    To the fore in the gathering—
King George gave him honour
    Over all 'neath the crown:

He ordered an artist
    To paint our man's picture
In the garb of the Gael
    As he was at the time,
And you were promoted
    To be an army commander
At the head of the Gael
    And bear the green satin flag.

No pavement's your heritage,
    No sound of bells is your music,
But tramping the wastelands,
    Your hounds barking beside you;
Climbing mountains and screes,
    You often wounded your target—
With well-functioning gun
    Antlered stag would be blooded.

You'd move fast with your men
    If attacked from behind,
You'd look after them well
    On day of strife or review,
With sense and intelligence
    You'd put each load on their back,
They'd never flee from the enemy
    With their commander behind them.

To the thrill of your mother
    And of your great kindred
You're an apple-tree branch
    That's risen high amongst peoples,
A brave handsome hero
    With no fault in your manners—
From no shrivelled tree
    Were the branches stretched up.

Your kin, strong and numerous
    In every place in the north,

Are folk of boots and of stirrups,
   Whoever might want them—
Sharp-bladed MacKenzies,
   The brave men who were hardy
And frequently victorious
   While the rest ran away.

You have my love all my life,
   My fine handsome companion,
And my choice wasn't wealth but
   Your being colonel of a regiment—
My lion, warlike and clever,
   Who grew up quarrelsome, fierce,
Winning wars for King George
   And justice for Scotsmen.

ANN CUTHBERT KNIGHT
(1788–1860)

——

BORN in Aberdeenshire, the educator and poet Ann Cuthbert Knight (*née* Rae) later lived and died in Canada. She published two books of poetry while still living in Scotland: *Home* (1815) and *A Year in Canada, and Other Poems* (1816). Emigrating to Montreal with her first husband in the summer of 1815, she opened a school for girls. She wrote several pioneering school textbooks, including *First Book for Canadian Children* and *The Prompter*. Taken from *A Year in Canada*, her second collection of verse, 'Geraldine', displays a Coleridgean talent for thrilling, unsettling verse narrative.

——

'Geraldine'

A Year in Canada, and Other Poems (Edinburgh: James Ballantyne & Co., 1816).

I

> Burst from her heart the struggling sigh,
> Her changing cheek turn'd deadly pale;
> But fixt resolve was in her eye,
> And calm, and sad, she said, "Farewell!"
>
> "Farewell! thy vassal's orphan child
> From all the joys of guilt can flee;
> Though she would dwell in desert wild,
> To live to Virtue and to thee."
>
> "Then hear," he said, "this one request.
> In holy fane our vows be giv'n,
> Heard only by th' appointed priest,
> And all-observing ear of Heav'n;
>
> And thine shall be the rural home,
> Where winds the streamlet down the dell."

Fast o'er her cheek's returning bloom
The shower of melting fondness fell.

II

Sir Edward! though her humbler race
Could ill aspire to rank with thine,
For every charm,—for every grace,
The maid might match a nobler line.

Beside thy own, her gallant sire
Had often stemm'd the tide of fight!
With dauntless heart, and eye of fire,
The bravest follower of the knight.

And in Sir Richard's latest field,
When widely waved the Danish sword,
Still, still his place the warrior held,
And fought,—and fell,—beside his lord!

He fell, and gave one dear bequest,
A fair, a young, an orphan child;
And by the aged knight carest,
Sweet in his hall the cherub smiled,

Till the cold hand of Death consign'd
His well-loved consort to the tomb,
And to the sister's care resign'd,
A convent hid the orphan's bloom.

At distance then, in fields of death,
The gallant heir of Elmsdale fought,
But through her glades loud rumour's breath,
Full oft his deeds of valour brought.

III

The rose may blush in cloister'd cell,
It dyes the cheek of Geraldine;
But, ere she took the hallow'd veil,
Quick summon'd from the convent scene,

Fondly to Elmsdale's towers she flew,
To watch her guardian's last repose,
And duteous came Sir Edward too,
To sooth the pangs of nature's close.

Amid the scene of fun'ral gloom,
The knight has mark'd her dark-blue eye;
Her lip, the heath-flower's op'ning bloom,
Unfolding to the summer's sigh.

Whether the shower of sorrow flow,
Or o'er her cheek soft blushes move;
The sparkling tear, the deep'ning glow,
Still fan the kindling fire of love:

But he, whose soul serene and bright,
Inspired a form of manly grace,
Rose on the young enthusiast's sight,
A being of superior race.

There is a love, though seldom seen,
Stronger than passion's headlong swell;
That round the heart of Geraldine
Had lock'd its soul-entrancing spell.

IV

The oath-bound priest to silence bought,
The appointed hour of midnight peal'd;
Nor has it crost the father's thought,
Whose was the hand Sir Edward held.

Through painted glass, the moonbeams throw
Their trembling light o'er pillars pale,
And scarce the knight his bride might know
All shrouded in the snowy veil.

But ne'er a form more sweetly fair,
In monarch's glitt'ring court shall shine,
Nor purer—fonder bosom e'er
Rise softly at the hallow'd shrine.

V

No sprightly rout with minstrel lay
Has graced Sir Edward's nuptial morn,
Nor costly feast, nor revel gay,
Fair Elmsdale's lofty halls adorn.

And lone are now fair Elmsdale's towers,
But where its brook's wild waters fall,

Or gaily bloom the summer flowers,
And sweetly smiles the sylvan hall.

No tapestry decks the lady's bower,
Nor waves the banner on the wall;
Green rushes strew the rural floor,
The red-deer's antlers grace the hall;

Nor broider'd zone, nor diamonds sheen,
Blaze on her light robe's graceful fold,
But o'er the vest of simple green
Her ringlets fall in waving gold.

Yet lends the harp its soothing sound,
One aged minstrel loves the scene;
And one—a fair and fav'rite hound,
Fawns on the hand of Geraldine.

Well loves the knight, when morning's dawn
Gleams on the blue lake bright and clear,
To urge his courser o'er the lawn,
Or rouse the trembling forest deer.

Well loves the knight in sultrier hour,
With musing hermit-step to rove,
Where mingling beech and pine-trees tower,
And Nature frames the wild alcove.

But when the west, with crimson glow,
Welcomes the radiant orb of day,
Sweetly the minstrel's numbers flow,
And sweeter still the lady's lay.

There be round Hymen's sacred ties,
Who Love's luxuriant wreath can twine;
And hadst thou known the charm to prize,
Sir Edward! all that bliss was thine.

Yet ne'er had Art her lesson taught,
That bosom sway'd by Nature's law;
That heart with tender feeling fraught,
And watchful love, and modest awe.

Still o'er her cheek the varying dye
Spreads quick from Feeling's throbbing shrine,

And still the soul-enchanting eye
With soften'd sweetness beams on thine.

VI

Soft falls the blossom from the broom,
On August's bosom fades the rose,
But rich and deep the heather bloom
O'er all the empurpled mountain glows.

'Tis past!—September's evenings mild
Have closed on many a harvest day;
And ruder breezes sweep the wild,
And faintly gleams the solar ray;

And darkly on yon mountain's brow,
November's louring glooms repose;
And in the shepherd's cot below,
The evening faggot brightly glows.

And leaves the knight his lone retreat?
Love may not bind him longer there,
Afar he goes his peers to meet,
The lists to grace—the banquet share.

But while stern winter closes round,
O will the fair all lonely stay,
Left in the wild wood's dreary bound,
With youthful page and minstrel grey!

No selfish wish that heart may wear,
She strives to hide the pearly shower;
Yet "wilt thou, 'mid the gay and fair,
Think sometimes on thy forest bower?"

VII

His followers range in order gay,
To meet their lord on castle-lawn;
With heavy heart and sleepless eye,
The lady watch'd the unwelcome dawn.

Though deep her struggling bosom's swell,
No murmur chill'd the fond adieu;
But cold her heart—her cheek grew pale,
As through the glade his courser flew.

She cross'd the hall's deserted bound,
The fav'rite dog in slumber lay,
Ah! dream not that the horn shall sound,
To call thee to the chase to-day!

All darkly lours the wintry sky,
And thick the stormy showers descend,
And, waving to the wild wind's sigh,
With sullen sound the branches bend.

Chill blows the blast—fast falls the shower,
But in the hall the fire burns gay,
And oft, to steal the wintry hour,
The aged minstrel pours the lay.

VIII

The storm has raged its strength away,
In soften'd gales the south wind blows,
With spiry leaf the crocus gay
Peeps sweetly through the melting snows.

Hark!—is not that his courser's tread?
'Twas but the breeze that swept the rill,
The appointed day is come and fled,
The knight of Elmsdale lingers still.

IX

"And haste thee back, my boy," she said;
Yet, yet the page has tarried long,
Though gleams the castle through the glade,
Where lone she waits with bosom wrung.

Where, where was Honour's guardian power?
No vain report the tidings spread,
From Brankden's hall to Elmsdale's bower,
A courtly bride the knight has led.

Oh, Edward! though her dower had strove
With Persian sceptre's rubied glow,
What was it to thy injured love,
What to thy Heav'n-attested vow!

Unnoticed round the lonely bower
The unfolding sweets of spring shall blow;

No hand is there to crop the flower,
No eye to mark its beauties now.

The page—the minstrel—join the train,
In Elmsdale's courts of festive joy.
And can Sir Edward ask again,
"How fares thy mistress—say, my boy?"

"When Night her shadowy curtain spread,
The lady wept in sylvan bower;
When morning tinged the skies with red,
I waked,—but she was there no more."

Pause not, Sir Knight,—amid the halls
The guests are set—the attendants wait;
Pause not, Sir Knight,—the banquet calls,
And thou hast found a nobler mate.

And all is splendour, pomp, and pride,
And all in Pleasure's guise is drest,
For richly flows the golden tide;
But oh!—if Elmsdale's lord be blest.

Ev'n when the banquet sparkles high,
And soft the sounds of music flow,
As meets that page his master's eye,
What passing cloud o'ercasts his brow?

Why does he still the chase forsake,
If seek the deer yon beechen grove?
Why may the minstrel never wake
The lay that plains of faithless love?

X

Fond Fortune's child—in vain carest:—
And can Sir Edward's bride repine?
Oh! where is now that faithful breast,
Whose every wish was lost in thine?

How oft amid the louring storm,
Of sullen pride and peevish spleen,
Shall mem'ry paint the peerless form,
And gentle heart of Geraldine!

XI

No heir has blest Sir Edward's bed,
To gild with smiles the castle's gloom;
Three sullen summers slowly sped,
The fourth shone o'er his lady's tomb!

Remembrance wakes more fond, more keen,
For "where is now that lovely flower,
Who well might grace the gayest scene,
In lofty hall or lordly bower?"

"It came—the dream of wealth and power—
A rainbow form that charm'd to flee;
Ill was it worth one blissful hour
Thy once loved Edward pass'd with thee."

The faithful page has sought in vain,
In lonely cot or village bower,
In sylvan shade or flowery plain,
The Rose of Elmsdale blooms no more.

XII

Pensive the knight,—the morn was fair,
He cross'd his steed at early dawn,
And musing rode, unheeding where,
By forest deep, and verdant lawn,

Till o'er a stream-embowering glade,
Where high surrounding mountains swell,
His courser's fleeting pace he staid,
To mark the beauties of the dell.

A winding pathway threads the vale,
O'er fragrant birch the pine-trees tower,
The wild rose blushes to the gale,
Twined with the woodbine's fringing flower.

The summer sun shone high and clear,
When bounding fast by brake and tree,
A milk-white hound came fawning near,
And fawning sought Sir Edward's knee.

Conjecture flash'd through sorrow's gloom,
For soon the faithful dog he knew;

When lo! a boy in infant bloom,
In tend'rer meaning, fixt his view!

Ah! fond yet faithless! well I ween
May'st thou the blooming infant know;
He wears the smile of Geraldine,
Thy eagle glance and lordly brow.

With wild surmise—with fearful joy,
Th' unconscious child Sir Edward eyed;
"And who art thou, my lovely boy,
Or what thy father's name?" he cried.

"My name is Edward of the dell,"
The answering cherub blush'd and smiled,
"And dost thou seek the hermit's cell,
For I am Father Bertrand's child?"

Alighting from his sable steed,
He gain'd the monk's sequester'd cell,
Age shed its honours o'er his head,
His mien was mild, his cheek was pale.

"Oh! tell me, father, tell me true!
Who is it in this sylvan wild
That owns that hound of milky hue,
And who the parent of the child?"

"But, gallant stranger! who art thou
Whose steps have sought the lonely dell?
For but to one I may avow—
To one on earth—the mournful tale."

"If rumour e'er the glade explored,
Sacred to solitude and thee;
Thou may'st have heard of Elmsdale's lord."
"I have,"—"and, father, I am he."

"Then rest, Sir Knight—the glen's wild flowers
Have thrice adorn'd the summer ray,
Since, where you aged elm-tree towers,
I mark'd a lovely stranger stray.

'Tis not to share in Nature's joy,
'Tis not to pluck the budding rose,

For, fondling o'er her infant boy,
The shower of tender sorrow flows.

Oft had she silent pass'd and slow,
Till once, when thunder shook the vale,
She came—the pensive child of woe
Was welcome still to Bertrand's cell.

I strove to sooth, but ill can paint
The grief whose vainly smother'd sigh
Disdain'd the murmur of complaint,
And shunn'd the probe of sympathy.

But from the radiant throne on high
Had mercy shed its sweetest beam,
The hope of immortality,
And well the mourner loved the theme.

Still, still her placid eyes betray
The settled sorrow, deep but meek,
And the bright ensign of decay
Waves fluttering on her fading cheek.

Another winter swept the glade,
And summer rose array'd in bloom,
While she in lone retirement's shade
Was slowly sinking in the tomb.

'Twas in a peasant's widow's shed
That child first drew his infant breath,
And there my pensive steps were led
To watch his parent's couch of death.

Pass we the church's mystic rite,
The wonted bead and hallow'd prayer,
Ere life's faint torch was set in night,
To me she gave her earthly care.

A jewell'd cross, in glittering pride,
Depending from a pearly band,
Around the infant's neck she tied
With tearful eye and trembling hand.

"Father," she said, "when I am fled,
Oh! wilt thou take this friendless child,

And let him share thy mossy bed,
Thy peaceful cell and counsel mild?"

"Though left forlorn in cottage bower,
That infant bears no peasant's name;
Where Elmsdale rears her lofty tower,
My son a noble sire may claim."

"Yet thou in sacred silence keep
The secret trusted to thy breast,
And let the tale unnoticed sleep
Which only coming death could wrest."

"But, ah! if ever fate should bring
Sir Edward Eldin to thy view,
Then give to him this glittering ring,"—
The token forth the hermit drew,—

"Haply it may recall once more
A sacred rite, a solemn scene,
In holy church at midnight hour
It cross'd the hand of Geraldine!"

"And should the throb of feeling move,
Lead to his knee his youthful son,
The tender pledge of wedded love,
For I am guiltless, though undone."

"Yet, yet if vain regret should sting,
And wild remorse for broken truth
His breast with keener anguish wring,
Thine be the care that grief to sooth."

"Blest be that word, from Heaven above
I deem'd the wish of meekness came,
Alas! it sprung from earthly love,
The triumph of no common flame."

"For oh! should time retreating move,
And give those hours for ever lost,
Scarce might I yield his fatal love
For all the joy that life can boast."

And yet, in spite of sorrow dear,
Death's icy hand alone can chill

The cherish'd wish warm glowing here,
To live beloved in mem'ry still.

Yes, I have seen his wak'ning ruth
And late repenting sorrow flow,
And knelt and pray'd to Heaven to sooth,
And weeping shared his fancied woe.

If true the dream, may'st thou be near,
And with its fond forgiveness join
This heart's last wish, Oh! bid him bear
The contrite grief to Mercy's shrine.

So shall a ray of passive joy
Gleam sweet o'er sorrow's ebbing tide;
So may he view his blooming boy
With all a father's conscious pride.

And think how swift the summer flew
In sylvan bower, in forest green,
And many a tender hour review
That past with love and Geraldine.

And say "still faithful, still the same
She lived to bless, and blessing died.
Ill, ill were given so dear a claim
For all that earth could boast beside."

"Yet stay, my child;—by him above
Oh be the tender crime forgiven,
But thou with more than idol love
Hast paid to man the dues of Heaven."

"Father, I know,"—one contrite tear
Roll'd gently o'er her visage mild,
But Faith, and Hope, and Peace, were there,
And soft the parting spirit smiled.

Remembrance thrill'd the old man's soul,
Where Pity reign'd with aspect meek,
And the bright dews of feeling stole
In silver current down his cheek.

But dark remorse in furious glare
Had fix'd Sir Edward's tearless eye,

And the cold stupor of Despair
Lock'd in his breast the dormant sigh.

The hermit mark'd his brow of gloom,
And strove to burst the dark'ning spell,
"Oh wouldst thou see the lowly tomb
Of one who loved thee passing well?"

With hurried step the path he trod,
An infant birch-tree's fragrant bough
Hangs weeping o'er that verdant sod,
The slumb'ring dust lies cold below.

He kneels, but oh! that gloomy eye!
Stay, stay thy lips! no hallow'd prayer,
Some rash, some dreadful oath is nigh,
Some frantic purpose louring there.

"Oh stay, thy bosom's tumult rein,
Say wouldst thou slight the last request,
The tomb of her thou lov'dst profane,
Or rouse the ashes of the blest."

"To injured love the tear, the sigh
Of fond remembrance well is due,
But Heaven has call'd her to the sky,
And thou hast duties yet to do:"

"Then stay—thy bosom's tumult rein;
Say, wouldst thou slight the last request,
The tomb of her thou lov'dst profane,
Or rouse the ashes of the blest?"

Fell on his heart the mild appeal,
The blood in quicker circles flow'd,
But, torn with grief's convulsive swell,
His struggling bosom prest the sod.

The rising throb the hermit eyed,
He saw the bursting torrent flow,
Nor strove to check the welcome tide,
But blest the hour of soften'd woe.

He saw the combat half was won,
And placed the child his arms between,
"Oh kindly rear thy infant son,
'Tis all that lives of Geraldine!"

HERMIONE BALLANTYNE
(D.1854)

———

HAILING from Kelso, Hermione Ballantyne (*née* Parker) married into a prominent family of printers. Widowed in 1821, she received continued support from one of the trustees of John Ballantyne's will, Walter Scott. In turn, she wrote endearing memoirs of Scott and his circle, which appeared in *Chambers's Edinburgh Journal* late in 1843. In addition to securing some financial aid, Scott encouraged Ballantyne to write poetry. First published in 1832, *The Kelso Souvenir: or, Selections from Her Scrap-Book* brought together her early and most recent efforts. Many of the poems pay homage to Scott's poetic interests, such as the Germanic ballads translated by Scott and others in the 1790s. Other works echo Coleridge and De Quincey, among other favourites of the period. Others reach back into older traditions, such as the fables of Robert Henryson.

———

'Lines to a Spider'

The Kelso Souvenir: or, Selections from Her Scrap-Book (Edinburgh: W. Blackwood; Kelso: Walter Grieve, 1832).

> If it be true, as bards have shewn,
>   That thou wert once a "blooming Miss,"
> Thou surely must have undergone
>   A woful metamorphosis!
>
> And what thy *Miss*-deeds must have been,
>   I blush but merely to surmise,
> That 'tis thy destiny to spin—
>   For ages—in *this* sad disguise!
> But work away, I beg of thee,
>   I scorn to touch, or to displace,
> A thread of thy machinery,
>   Though it were flapping in my face!

So stick thy fly-traps far and wide,
    And spread thy banners up aloof,
Ensigns armorial—they will hide
    The dirt depending from my roof.
But never near the *rich and great*
    Must thou thy busy shuttle ply,
Nor venture to contaminate
    The gilded domes of Majesty!
For some eradicating broom
    Would to thy trade soon put a stop,
If thou the palace shouldst presume
    To turn into a weaver's shop!
But thou mayst take thy swing for *me*,
    Thy webs may serve to keep me warm,—
Though truly, to be plain with thee,
    There's ample reason for "Reform."

'Stanzas Occasioned by Observing a Bee at Work on a Rose'

How merrily the mountain bee
    Passes her summer hours,
Humming her deep-toned minstrelsy
    Among the fairest flowers!
Rock'd on the bosom of the rose,
    Or some sweet cowslip bell,
She steals the treasure which o'erflows
    Her wond'rous waxen cell—
That masterpiece, whose curious plan,
    (With all his pride and state,)
Short-sighted, vain, presumptuous man,
    Could never imitate!
He walketh proudly on the earth
    In purple and in gold;
But soon that body, nothing worth,
    Manures its native mould!
Man buildeth palaces and towers,
    Which in the sunbeam shine,
But greedy earth, which all devours,
    Says—"These shall soon be mine—

Thee and thy treasures ALL I'll have,
　　Thy day will soon be o'er—
There's no device within the grave,
　　There thou shalt scheme no more.
Prepare thee for eternity,
　　Or ere the morning gloom—
Cold, dark, and drear, the night will be—
　　The silent, sunless tomb!"
Thus saith the earth—each fading flower—
　　Our bodies' slow decay:
Still we neglect the present hour,
　　We work not *while 'tis day!*

'Lines, Occasioned by Seeing the Well Known Spectre Peatcart Horse, of St Andrews, Led by its Owner'

There's famine in thy very face,
I see it in that hollow eye,
In each imploring glance I trace
Despair, and woe, and misery!
Perchance when young and strong of yore,
Thy daily pittance was but scant,
But now, when thou canst work no more,
'Tis hard indeed to die of want!
Have those bare ribs no shelter found,
No cov'ring from the piercing cold?
Thy bed the damp, unwholesome ground,
Thus lean, and lame, and blind, and old!
For *this* hast thou thine owner serv'd,
So duteously, by day and might,
And never from hard labour swerv'd—
To die in this most dismal plight?
Relentless man! thy prayer in vain,
In time of thy distress may be—
Nor dare thou, miscreant! to complain,
If thus *thy* master deal with THEE!

MRS M. A. REID

(*FL*. 1827)

━━

PUBLISHED in Edinburgh, *The Harp of Salem* (1827) comprises a series of powerful poems adapted from scripture, along with reflective pieces on the biggest questions of all, about life and death and God. The following pieces showcase different facets of Mrs M. A. Reid's versifying. Written in rhyming quatrains, 'Happiness in Death', the first, conveys a defiance in the face of death. The second, 'Where is He?', reworks Job 14:10.

━━

'Happiness in Death'

The Harp of Salem: A Collection of Historical Poems, from the Scriptures. Together with Some Reflective Pieces (Edinburgh: James Taylor Smith and Co., 1827).

Stretch'd upon the bed of death,
   See the ransom'd sinner lies;
Faint and fault'ring is his breath—
   Dim and ghastly are his eyes.

Tis the last, the dreadful hour,—
   Friends are weeping, hope is fled:
What can be the unseen power
   That supports yon feeble head?

See, unto that livid cheek
   One triumphant smile is given;
Mark that hand so pale, so weak,—
   Its silent movement points to heav'n.

Hush! the final sigh is o'er—
   Sweetly seems the dead to sleep:

Sin or suffering can no more
   Cause those closed eyes to weep.

Where, O Death! is here thy sting?
   Where, O Grave! thy triumph here?
That freed spirit spreads its wing
   Far beyond your narrow sphere.

'Where is He?'

Job xiv, 10.

Where is he?—In the land of graves
His pallid, mould'ring clay is laid;
O'er his lone home the rank grass waves,
And whistles o'er his low-laid head.

But that bright spark which lit his eye,
And sparkled there, a mental light—
Oh! can that heavenly radiance lie
Extinguish'd in eternal night?

The dust which now in silence sleeps
In the lone church-yard's narrow bed,—
Is't that o'er which fond mem'ry weeps,
And soft affection hangs her head?

Was it not something nobler far
That bound the bosom to its friend,—
Which shone thro' life love's guiding star,
Or bless'd us when we sooth'd its end?

Yes, the gay rosy blush which plays
On beauty's cheek may win our smile;
Fair earthly forms attract our gaze,
And charm the fetter'd mind a while:

But that which beam'd in heavenly light,
Illum'ning lip, and brow, and eye,
Glow'd on the cheek serenely bright,
Or swell'd the bosom with a sigh:

'Twas that we lov'd—'tis that we mourn;
Tis for its loss our sorrows rise;

Tis gone, alas!—nor will return,
And where is it?—'Tis in the skies.

Then wipe each selfish drop that streams
For those belov'd ones that are gone;
On high the immortal spirit beams
In holiness before the throne.

DAVID VEDDER

(1789–1854)

THE Orcadian poet David Vedder was largely educated by his widowed mother. Orphaned at the age of twelve, he went to sea as a cabin boy; at the age of twenty-two he became captain of a Greenland whaler. Later, while still in his twenties, he was appointed first officer of an armed cruiser and, five years after that, became a tide surveyor, officiating successively at Montrose, Kirkcaldy, Dundee, and Leith. From a young age Vedder wrote and translated verse. Nearing forty, he published *The Covenanters' Communion, and other Poems* (1828). A prose and verse miscellany, *Orcadian Sketches*, followed in 1832. In addition to writing a popular *Memoir of Sir Walter Scott*, he edited the life and works of the Kirkcaldy poet Robert Fraser. His own *Poems, Legendary, Lyrical, and Descriptive* came out in 1842. In addition to these and further books, Vedder contributed to many anthologies and magazines in his adopted home city of Edinburgh.

'To Orkney'

Orcadian Sketches; Legendary and Lyrical Pieces (Edinburgh: William Tait, 1832).

> Land of the whirlpool—torrent—foam,
> Where oceans meet in madd'ning shock;
> The beetling cliff—the shelving holm—
> The dark insidious rock:
> Land of the bleak, the treeless moor—
> The sterile mountain, sered and riven;
> The shapeless cairn, the ruined tower
> Scathed by the bolts of heaven:
> The yawning gulf—the treacherous sand—
> I love thee still, my native land.
>
> Land of the dark—the Runic rhyme—
> The mystic ring—the cavern hoar;

The Scandinavian seer—sublime
In legendary lore:
Land of a thousand Sea-kings' graves,
—Those tameless spirits of the past,
Fierce as their subject Arctic waves,
Or hyperborean blast;
Tho' polar billows round thee foam,
I love thee! Thou wer't once my home.

With glowing heart, and island lyre,
Ah! would some native bard arise
To sing with all a poet's fire
Thy stern sublimities;
The roaring flood—the rushing stream,
The promontory wild and bare,
The pyramid where sea-birds scream
Aloft in middle air;
The Druid temple on the heath
Old, even beyond tradition's breath.

Though I have roamed thro' verdant glades,
In cloudless climes, 'neath azure skies;
Or plucked from beauteous orient meads
Flowers of celestial dyes;
Though I have laved in limpid streams,
That murmur over golden sands;
Or basked amid the fulgid beams
That flame o'er fairer lands;
Or stretched me in the sparry grot,—
My country! Thou we'rt ne'er forgot.

WALTER SHOLTO DOUGLAS /
MARY DIANA DODS
(1790–1830)

———

RAISED at Dalmahoy House, near Edinburgh, the author Walter Sholto Douglas (born Mary Diana Dods) was admired by the Byron–Shelley circle but died before fulfilling their potential. Mary Shelley secured false passports for Douglas and Isabella Robinson so they could emigrate to Paris as husband and wife, with little intention of returning to Scotland. Under the pseudonym of David Lyndsay, Douglas contributed dramas, essays, and stories to *Blackwood's Edinburgh Magazine*, literary annuals, and gift books throughout the 1820s. Perpetually ill, and imprisoned for chronic debts, Douglas died sometime between November 1829 and November 1830, not yet forty years old. As Lyndsay, Douglas produced two books, *Dramas of the Ancient World* (1821–2) and *Tales of the Wild and the Wonderful* (1825). 'The Owl' contains scenes of extreme violence.

———

'The Owl'

Blackwood's Edinburgh Magazine, 20 (July 1826).

> There sat an Owl in an old Oak Tree,
> Whooping very merrily;
> He was considering, as well he might,
> Ways and means for a supper that night:
> He looked about with a solemn scowl,
> Yet very happy was the Owl,
> For, in the hollow of that oak tree,
> There sat his Wife, and his children three!
>
> She was signing one to rest,
> Another, under her downy breast,
> 'Gan trying his voice to learn her song,
> The third (a hungry Owl was he)
> Peeped slyly out of the old oak tree,

And peer'd for his Dad, and said "You're long,"
But he hooted for joy, when he presently saw
His sire, with a full-grown mouse at his claw.
Oh what a supper they had that night!
All was feasting and delight;
Who most can chatter, or cram, they strive,
They were the merriest owls alive.

What then did the old Owl do?
Ah! Not so gay was his to-whoo!
It was very sadly said,
For after his children had gone to bed,
He did not sleep with his children three,
For, truly a gentleman Owl was he,
Who would not on his wife intrude,
When she was nursing her infant brood;
So not to invade the nursery,
He slept outside the hollow tree.

So when he awoke at the fall of the dew,
He called his wife with a loud to-whoo;
"Awake, dear wife, it is evening gray,
And our joys live from the death of day."
He call'd once more, and he shudder'd when
No voice replied to his again;
Yet still unwilling to believe,
That Evil's raven wing was spread,
Hovering over his guiltless head,
And shutting out joy from his hollow tree,
"Ha—ha—they play me a trick," quoth he,
"They will not speak,—well, well, at night
They'll talk enough, I'll take a flight."
But still he went not, in, nor out,
But hopped uneasily about.

What then did the Father Owl?
He sat still, until below
He heard cries of pain, and woe,
And saw his wife, and children three,
In a young Boy's captivity.
He follow'd them with noiseless wing,
Not a cry once uttering.

They went to a mansion tall,
He sat in a window of the hall,
Where he could see
His bewilder'd family
And he heard the hall with laughter ring.
When the boy said, "Blind they'll learn to sing."
And he heard the shriek, when the hot steel pin
Through their eye-balls was thrust in!
He felt it all! Their agony
Was echoed by his frantic cry,
His scream rose up with a mighty swell,
And wild on the boy's fierce heart it fell;
It quailed him, as he shuddering said,
"Lo! The little birds are dead."
—But the Father Owl!
He tore his breast in his despair,
And flew he knew not, recked not, where!

But whither then went the Father Owl,
With his wild stare and deathly scowl?
—He had got a strange wild stare,
For he thought he saw them ever there,
And he scream'd as they scream'd when he saw them fall
Dead on the floor of the marble hall.

Many seasons travelled he,
With his load of misery,
Striving to forget the pain
Which was clinging to his brain,
Many seasons, many years,
Number'd by his burning tears.
Many nights his boding cry
Scared the traveller passing by;
But all in vain his wanderings were,
He could from his memory tear
The things that had been, still were there.

One night, very very weary,
He sat in a hollow tree,
With his thoughts—ah! all so dreary
For his only company—
—He heard something like a sound

Of horse-hoofs through the forest bound
And full soon he was aware,
A Stranger, and a Lady fair,
Hid them, motionless and mute,
From a husband's swift pursuit.

The cheated husband passed them by,
The Owl shrieked out, he scarce knew why;
The spoiler look'd, and, by the light,
Saw two wild eyes that, ghastly bright,
Threw an unnatural glare around
The spot where he had shelter found.—
Starting, he woke from rapture's dream,
For again he heard that boding scream,
And "On—for danger and death are night,
When drinks mine ear yon dismal cry"—
He said—and fled through the forest fast;
The owl has punish'd his foe at last—
For he knew, in the injured husband's foe,
Him who had laid his own hopes low.

Sick grew the heart of the bird of night,
And again and again he took to flight,
But ever on his wandering wing
He bore that load of suffering!—
Nought could cheer him!—the pale moon,
In whose soft beam he took delight,
He look'd at now reproachfully,
That she could smile, and shine, while he
Had withered 'neath such cruel blight.
He hooted her—but still she shone—
And they away—alone! alone!—

The wheel of time went round once more,
And his weary wing him backward bore,
Urged by some strange destiny
Again to the well-known forest tree,
Where the stranger he saw at night,
With the lovely Lady bright.

The Owl was dozing—but a stroke
Strong on the root of the sturdy oak
Shook him from his reverie—

He looked down, and he might see
A stranger close to the hollow tree!
His looks were haggard, wild, and bad,
Yet the Owl knew in the man, the lad
Who had destroyed him!—he was glad!

And the lovely Lady too was there,
But now no longer bright and fair;
She was lying on the ground,
Mute and motionless, no sound
Came from her coral lips, for they
Were seal'd in blood; and, as she lay,
Her locks, of the sun's most golden gleam,
Were dabbled in the crimson stream
That from a wound on her bosom white—
(Ah! that Man's hand could such impress
On that sweet seat of loveliness)—
Welled, a sad and ghastly sight,
And ran all wildly forth to meet
And cling around the Murderer's feet.

He was digging a grave—the Bird
Shriek'd aloud—the Murderer heard
Once again that boding scream,
And saw again those wild eyes gleam—
And "Curse on the Fiend!" he cried, and flung
His mattock up—it caught and hung—
The Felon stood a while aghast—
Then fled through the forest, fast, fast, fast!

The hardened Murderer hath fled—
But the Owl kept watch by the shroudless dead,
Until came friends with the early day,
And bore the mangled corse away—
Then, cutting the air all silently,
He fled away from his hollow tree.

Why is the crowd so great to-day,
And why do the people shout "huzza"?
And why is yonder Felon given
Alone to feed the birds of Heaven?
Had he no friend, now all is done,
To give his corse a grave?—Not One!

Night has fallen. What means that cry?
It descends from the gibbet high—
There sits on its top a lonely Owl,
With a staring eye, and a dismal scowl;
And he screams aloud, "Revenge is sweet!"
His mortal foe is at his feet!

MARGARET DOUGLAS-MACLEAN-CLEPHANE, LADY COMPTON

(1791–1830)

———

BORN into an aristocratic song-collecting family based in Torloisk on the Isle of Mull, Margaret Douglas-Maclean-Clephane, Lady Compton was a favourite of Walter Scott. Even though her poetry was praised by Wordsworth and other leading authorities, for its simplicity, pathos, and energy, it went unpublished during her lifetime. A posthumous collection was edited by her husband, Spencer Compton, the second marquess of Northampton, and printed privately in 1833. Barely two weeks after the birth of their sixth child, Lady Compton died suddenly, in her late thirties.

———

'To Mrs Douglas Maclean Clephane'

Irene, A Poem, in Six Cantos. Miscellaneous Poems (London: Mills, Jowett, and Mills, 1833).

To you, whose praise my verse did first expand,
I send this web, the fabric of my brains,
Sure that you will not take a broom in hand
To sweep it down like cobwebs for my pains.
And were it the best lay whose inky stains
Had ever blotted paper, 'twere your due:
Nay here and there perhaps a trace remains
In fancy's airy wanderings, not a few
Of things which, little changed, I've ta'en or stol'n from you.

As for our king of critics, he whose eye
Train'd in the doubting science of the laws,
Sharp as a sportsman doth his game espy,
And pounces on poor wretches' faults and flaws:—
Tell him I will not trust his teeth and claws,
Which, ruthless, would unfledge each Sylphid wing;

Moreover, like those martyrs of their cause
Who bade defiance to Assyria's king,
Tell him, I do not care to please him in this thing.

For the whole story's tissued out of lies,
Improbable, impossible, and full
Of such anachronisms as must surprise
The order'd inside of a reasoning skull.
Well; who says otherwise? There's room to cull
As perfect faults as critic could desire:
Bad rhymes, bad lines—but yet it is not dull—
Or, if it is, for Heaven's sake ne'er inquire
Into its faults or charms, but lodge it in the fire.

DOROTHEA PRIMROSE CAMPBELL
(1792–1863)

━━

A NATIVE of Shetland, Dorothea Primrose Campbell was a poet and novelist. Her first volume, *Poems* (1811), came out when she was still a teenager. The influential critic Francis Jeffrey admired the volume immensely. A teacher by 1812, Campbell opened her own school at Lerwick in 1813. In 1816 she published an enlarged volume of *Poems*, now dedicated to Walter Scott, with whom she corresponded. However, the publisher's bankruptcy dashed any hopes of profit. Campbell kept teaching after her own school foundered. She turned to fiction with her next publication, *Harley Radington* (1821). After that, it's likely she turned to magazine publication. Throughout her writing we can trace a diverse range of influences, whether the canonical Chaucer and Shakespeare, the still fashionable Goldsmith, or fellow Scots like Anne Bannerman.

━━

'An Address to Zetland'

Poems. By Miss D. P. Campbell, of Zetland (London: Baldwin, Cradock, and Joy, 1816).

> "The land of Cakes" has oft been sung,
>   In many a poet's strain;
> But never might "the land of Fish"
>   Such proud distinction gain.
>
> Then I will lift the voice of praise;
>   To thee my strains belong;—
> Thy misty hills, and humid vales,
>   First woke my infant song.
>
> Oft wand'ring by thy sea-beat shore
>   I woo'd the pensive Muse;
> Nor will the Genii of thy rocks
>   This votive lay refuse.

Long be thy banks, romantic Sound!
   Industry's happy seat;
And long thy fame remember'd be;—
   First trod by princely feet!

May commerce oft with spreading sail,
   To Lerwick's coast repair;
And gentle peace, on halcyon plume,
   For ever linger there.

And long the nymphs of Lerwick shine,
   Devoid of modish art;
With beauty deck'd, and ev'ry charm
   That wins the gallant heart.

And fertile prove your barren fields,
   Adorn'd with waving grain,
Where nought but noisome weeds,
   And dreary desert plain.

And many that source of half your wealth,
   The ocean's finny race,
Reward the honest fisher's toil,
   And long long your tables grace.

And, oh! ye Zetland lairds be kind,
   And shield th' industrious poor
From hard oppression's iron rod,
   And tyranny of pow'r.

Oh! think how noble 'tis to smooth
   The couch of want of care;
To bid the honest tenant smile,
   And sweet contentment share.

Oh! think what fond and fervent zeal
   Shall sanctify your cause,
When never forc'd by pining want
   To break your rigid laws.

How sweet the meed of conscious worth,
   More dear than public fame!
How sweet the blessings that repose
   Upon a good man's name!

Then rule with mercy—so shall Heav'n
    Your fondest wishs speed;
And joy, and peace, and plenty reign
    From Scaw to Sumburghead.

Oh! Laxford, dear! thy barren hills
    Fond mem'ry still must love;
To thee my wand'ring fancy turns,
    Where'er my footsteps rove.

Oh! scenes by happy childhood bless'd,
    When grief was all unknown—
But dearer now, and treasur'd more,
    Your joys for ever flown.

'Twas there, oh, Scott! thy presence cheer'd
    Thine hospitable hall;
'Twas there thou gav'st with friendly smile
    A welcome unto all.

Beneath thy roof each wand'rer found
    A refuge from the storm;
And frequent hast thou shelter'd there
    The orphan's trembling form.

Now in the cold and silent tomb
    Thy mould'ring dust is laid,
And yet no marble stone is rear'd
    To point thy lowly bed.

But, oh! within the grateful breast
    Thy mem'ry long shall dwell;
Nor ask of art its feeble aid,
    Thy honour'd name to tell.

And thou whom sorrow's chilling breath
    Destroy'd in beauty's bloom,
How oft shall friendship's sacred tear
    Bedew thy early tomb!

Oh, Isabella! ever dear,
    How oft has fancy rov'd
With thee by Laxford's moonlight stream,
    And all the haunts we lov'd!

With thee I never more shall rove
   By Laxford's bounding wave—
Thy spirit sought its kindred skies,
   Thy form its peaceful grave.

When o'er thy bed a husband hung,
   And dropt the fruitless tear;
When thy lov'd infant's feeble voice
   Rung on thy dying ear;

With all the eloquence of sighs,
   And all the warmth of pray'r,
The kneeling friends around thy bed
   Besought of Heav'n to spare.—

'Twas in vain—thy blameless course was run,
   The blow of death was giv'n;
And angels hover'd o'er thy head,
   To waft thy soul to heav'n.

Adieu to thee, and all the friends
   That happy childhood knew;—
By absence some, yet more by death,
   Snatch'd sudden from my view!

And Laxford's winding stream, adieu!
   Adieu, thy sea-beach wild,
Where oft I rov'd with careless feet,
   Untutor'd nature's child!

I dream'd not that a fairer spot
   On earth's broad bosom lay;
Nor ever wish'd my wand'ring feet
   Beyond its bounds to stray.

And when I read of fairer fields
   Beyond the northern main;
And tow'ring trees, whose leafy arms
   Spread o'er the flow'ry plain;

Of rivers, through the verdant vale
   Meandering smooth and clear;
Or where cascades their torrents dash
   O'er precipices drear:

I read—and fancy cloth'd thy steps
   With darkling groves of pine;
Bright bloom'd thy flow'rs, smooth flow'd thy streams,
   And ev'ry charm was thine.

Soft on the weedy sea-beach stole
   The wave with murmur low;
And o'er the undulating tide
   Serener zephyrs blow.

And there the moon, in radiance pale,
   Her mildest lustre threw;
Silv'ring the rocks of Tuinna-taing,
   And Ocean's bosom blue.

The fields of Hammerslain were gay
   With flow'rs of simple dye;
And primrose there and daisy bloom'd
   Beneath a brighter sky.

Oh, Laxford! once my happy home,
   Farewell thy rocky shore!
The wand'rer that has fled from thee
   Returns, alas! no more.

Oh! Hammerslain's romantic fields,
   Take, take my last farewell!—
Another now shall rove your banks,
   And in Scott's-Hall shall dwell;

Another now shall nurse the flow'rs
   I rear'd with anxious care;
Another range the sandy beach,
   And cull the sea-shells there.

Another, by the burn reclin'd,
   O'er some sad tale shall weep;
Or list'ning to its murm'ring voice,
   Be softly lull'd to sleep.

Another now by Severspool
   At purple dawn shall stray,
And on the mossy ward-hill mark
   The sportive lambkins play.

Farwell, ye scenes of dear delight,
  A long, a last adieu!
For never more your distant charms
  These aching eyes shall view.

And, Laxford! thou my once lov'd home,
  A long farewell to thee—
The blissful hour of sweet return
  Shall never smile on me!

Yet mem'ry oft with pious tear,
  As changing seasons roll,
Shall consecrate thy parted joys,
  And bind thee to my soul.

JOANNA BELFRAGE PICKEN
(1798–1859)

▬

THE Edinburgh-born poet and teacher Joanna Belfrage Picken was the daughter of the Poet of Paisley, Ebenezer Picken. With her sister Catherine she ran a boarding-school in Musselburgh, but it failed, reportedly because of Joanna's satires on local figures. In 1842, after the death of their mother, Joanna and Catherine joined their brothers in Canada. In Montreal Joanna supported herself by teaching music. Today she is best remembered for her comic poem, 'An Auld Friend wi' a New Face', which appeared in the *Glasgow Courier* before she emigrated. Written in a familiar twelve-line stanza, it parodies the refrain of an old song long associated with Joanna Baillie ('Song, Woo'd and Married and a''), which also features in the present collection. During her life in Canada Picken continued to publish in such periodicals as the *Montreal Transcript, and Commercial Advertiser*, typically under the pseudonym Alpha.

▬

'An Auld Friend wi' a New Face'

The Poets and Poetry of Scotland, ed. John Grant Wilson, 2 vols (New York: Harper & Brothers, 1876).

> A queer kind o' lott'ry is marriage—
> Ye never ken what ye may draw,
> Ye may get a braw hoose an' a carriage,
> Or maybe get nae hoose ava.
> I say na 'tis *best* to be single,
> But ae thing's to me unco clear:
> Far better sit *lane* by the ingle
> Than thole what some wives hae to bear.
> > It's braw to be dancin' and gaffin'
> > As lang as nae trouble befa'—
> > But hech! she is sune ower wi' daffin'
> > That's woo'd, an' married, an' a'.

She maun labour frae sunrise till dark,
An' aft tho' her means be but sma',
She gets little thanks for her wark—
Or as aften gets nae thanks ava.
She maun tak just whatever may come,
An' say nocht o' her fear or her hope;
There's nae use o' lievin' in Rome,
An' tryin' to fecht wi' the Pope.
     Hectored an' lectured an' a,
     Snubbed for whate'er may befa',
     Than *this*, she is far better aff—
     That never gets married ava'.

Oh, then come the bairns without number,
An' there's naething but kisses an' licks—
Adieu then the sleep an' to slumber,
An' the Pa is as cross as twa sticks.
A' the week she is makin' their parritch,
An' turnin' auld frocks into new;
An' on Sunday she learns them their carritch,
Puir wife! there's nae rest-day for you.
     Warkin' an' fetchin' awa,
     Saturday, Sunday, an' a':
     In troth she is no that ill aff
     That never gets married ava.

In nae time the cauld an' the wheesles
Get into your family sae sma',
An' the chincough, the croup, or the measles
Is sure to tak' aff ane or twa.
An' wi' them gang the puir mither's joys,
Nae comfort seems left her ava—
As she pits by the claes an' the toys
That belanged to the wee things awa'.
     Doctors an' drugs an' a',
     Bills an' buryin's an' a',
     Oh surely her heart may be lichter
     That never was married ava.

The married maun aft bear man's scornin',
An' humour his capers an' fykes;
But the single can rise in the mornin',

An' gang to her bed when she likes;
An' when ye're in sickness and trouble,
Just tell me at wha's door ye ca';
It's no whar ten bairns mak' a hubble,
But at *hers* that has nae bairns ava.

    Usefu', an' peacefu', an' cantie,
    Quiet, an' canny, an' a',
    It's gude to ha'e sister or auntie
    That never was married ava.

A wife maun be humble an' hamely,
Aye ready to rise, or to rin;
An' oh! when she's brocht up a family,
It's then her warst sorrows begin;
For the son, he maun e'en ha'e a wife;
An' the dochter a hoose o' her ain;
An' then, thro' the battle o' life,
They ne'er may forgather again.

    Cantie, an' quiet, an' a',
    Altho' her bit mailin be sma',
    In truth she is no that ill aff
    That never gets married ava.

It's far better still to keep single
Than sit wi' yer face at the wa',
An' greet ower the sons and the dochters
Ye've buried and married awa'.
I fain wad deny, but I canna,
Altho' to confess it I grieve,
Folks seldom care muckle for grannie,
Unless she has something to leave.

    It's nae that I seek to prevent ye,
    For that wad be rhyme thrown awa';
    But, lassies, I pray, just content ye,
    Altho' ye're ne'er married ava.

IAIN MACCOINNICH / JOHN MACKENZIE
(1806–1848)

━━

THE poet and anthologist John MacKenzie was born at Mellon Charles in Gairloch, Ross-shire, his father being hereditary tacksman of all the lands on the north side of Loch Ewe that belonged to MacKenzie of Gairloch. In his 1838 *Cruiteara Gàëlach*, a collection of love songs, he included 'Òran Sùgraidh' with a note stating he wrote it in 1830 for Miss Mary S—. This was Mary Sudge, a Wick innkeeper's daughter. It is difficult to know how seriously to take the courting song. In any case, John never married, and liked nothing better than wandering the Highlands with chapbooks for sale, picking up songs, stories, and subscriptions to whatever works were in his pipeline. Based first in Inverness, then Glasgow, then Edinburgh, he found himself increasingly tied to publishers' desks as the demand for Gaelic reading-matter increased. His many books include *Sar-Obair nam Bàrd Gaelach; or The Beauties of Gaelic Poetry, and Lives of the Highland Bards* (1841)—probably the most influential secular work ever printed in Gaelic (that is to say, the poems are in Gaelic, but the biographies are in English). In addition to *Sar-Obair*, he was the editor or translator of thirty-two publications, including the songs of Alastair, mac Mhaighstir Alastair, Duncan Ban Macintyre, and William Ross, a history of the '45, a satirical magazine, and an English–Gaelic dictionary that was still in use until recently.

━━

'Òran Sùgraidh'

Translator's transcription

> Hoireann ò gur mì tha tùrsach,
> Thriall mo mhànran, dh'fhàg mo lùgh mi,
> Chan eil càil agam gu sùgradh
> Gus am faic mi rùn mo chéile.

'S truagh nach robh mo chaileag ghreannar
Mar rium fhéin fo sgéith nam beanntan

Far am biodh a' chuthag shamhraidh
    Seinn sa ghleann an àm dhuinn éiridh.

Laighinn oidhch' sa choill ri ceò leat
Far nach cluinneadh Goill ar comhradh,
Barrach nan crann ga nar comhdach
    Gus an éireadh deò na gréin' oirnn.

Bheirinn ruaig a bhuain nan cnò leat,
A ghuanag a' ghluasaid mhodhair,
Far am bi coileach na smeòraich
    A' cur fàilt' air an lò sna geugan.

Tha do ghruaidh mar shnuadh nan ròsan—
Cha chuir sin ort uaill no mórchuis,
Ged as gil' thu, luaidh, na 'n t-eòinean
    'S na canach nan lón sa Chéitean.

B'e mo mhiann is trian de m' ailgheas
Teannadh dian ri bial do mhànrain—
Chan eil ciall no rian nach fhàg mi
    Mura tarr mi bhon a' chléir thu.

Tha thu aoidheil, caoimhneil, cairdeil,
Gun ghiamh gun uabhar gun ardan,
Ged a fhuair mi 'm measg na gràisg thu
    Bhiodh san t-sàil' a' tarraing éisg ás.

Gun dh'fhuadaich iad mi 's tu, àraig,
Gu còsan nan creag mar fhardach,
'S bu cheòl duinn fuaim nan tonn gàireach
    A' ruith gu tràigh gu càirgheal beucach.

'S trom mo chridh' an-diugh gad fhàgail
Aig na Gallaich—b'e mo chàs e,
'S nach earbainn thu ri mo bhrathair,
    Ge h-e mac mo mhàthar fhéin e.

Ged a tharr mi nise triall bhuat,
Air m' fhacal cha b'e mo mhiann e—
B' fhearr leam thu na nighean iarla
    Gun dad ga do dhìon ach léine!

Ach, a rùin, cha d'toir mi fuath dhut
A dh'aindeoin na their an sluagh rium—

Ged a thogadh iad ort tuaileas,
> Their mise gur buaitheam bréig e.

'A Courting Song' (translated by Ronald Black)

Hoireann ò it's I who am sorry,
My joy has gone, my strength has left me,
I cannot have the desire for amusement
> *Until I can see the one whom I love.*

O what a shame that my beautiful lass
Was not with me in the shade of the mountains
Where the summertime cuckoo would sing
> In the glen when we were arising.

I would lie with you for a night in the woods
Where Lowlanders could not hear us talking
With nothing but branches of trees to cover us
> Till the gleam of the sun would arise upon us.

I'd forage with you to harvest the nuts,
O my fun-loving girl who's gentle in movement,
In the place in which the cock of the song-thrush
> Will bid the day welcome amongst the branches.

Upon your cheek is the colour of roses—
That does not make you vain or conceited,
Although you are whiter, my love, than the daisy
> And than the bog-cotton of meadows in May.

It's my desire and a third of my wishes
To be thrusting against your flirtatious mouth—
I will take leave of my senses and faculties
> If I cannot get the clergy to marry us.

You are welcoming, kind and friendly,
Without fault or vainglory or surfeit of pride,
Although I found you amongst the rabble
> Who spent their time pulling fish from the sea.

They drove us away from them, you and me, darling,
To take to the holes in the rocks as a dwelling,
With the sound of the murmuring waves as our music,
> Running foam-white and roaring upon the strand.

My heart is heavy today to be leaving you
With the Caithness men—it was painful for me,
As I would not trust you to be with my brother
        Although he is my own mother's son.

Although I have now been obliged to leave you,
Upon my word it's not what I wanted—
I'd rather have you than an earl's daughter
        With nothing protecting you but a shirt!

But, my love, I can never despise you
Despite all that people have said to me—
No matter how much they may try to miscall you,
        I'll say that it's nothing but blustering lies.

CAROLINE OLIPHANT THE YOUNGER
(1807–1831)

===

A NIECE of the poet Lady Nairne, the younger Caroline Oliphant
was born in Perthshire. As a child she also lived in Durham, and
spent substantial time in Marseilles, Hyères, Florence, and Rome.
Oliphant wrote poetry from a young age—at thirteen, according to
the memoir given in the posthumous collection of her poems (and
that of her famous aunt): *Life and Songs of the Baroness Nairne, with
a Memoir and Poems of Caroline Oliphant the Younger*. The memoir
also describes her family as keen readers of Byron and Scott. As
a teenager and twentysomething, Oliphant sojourned in Clifton,
Gloucestershire, and Ireland, with infrequent visits to her home-
town. After something like nine months of bed-bound illness, she
died aged just twenty-four.

===

'The Garden at Gask'

*Life and Songs of the Baroness Nairne, with a Memoir and Poems of Caroline
Oliphant the Younger*, ed. Charles Rogers (London: Charles Griffin and
Co., 1869).

> Fain would I linger here, as I have seen
> The sun reposing on this mossy green,
> That well might tempt his chariot-wheels to stay,
> And check his coursers in their fiery way.
> Speed on, thou Sun, thy home is in the west;
> I too must speed, for this is not my rest.
>
> Like thee, bright orb! my further path is trac'd,
> And to my going down, I too must haste,
> For on my pilgrim path no Gibeon's hill
> Invites my weary spirit to stand still.
> Thou hast returned and brought the shadow back;
> I may not, would not, turn me from my track.

Still o'er these mossy walks thy circuit make,
Still in these bowers thy bright siesta take;
On me the gate hath closed, and I must go
Forth from this Eden thro' a vale of woe;
Diverse our path, yet both our God hath blest;
Heav'n spreads a couch for each—a glorious golden rest.

EXPLANATORY NOTES

23 *wolftime*: A period of rough weather generally reckoned to lie two weeks on either side of *Latha Fhéill Brighde*, St Brigid's Day (1 February).

33 *Judas*: Maj.-Gen. John Campbell of Mamore, who served in 1745–6 as commander-in-chief of government forces in the West of Scotland.

35 *grunting*: Due to the boar in their armorial bearings, Campbells were routinely called pigs in Gaelic verse.

80 *that attemper'd Hero*: Timoleon. [Note in the original]

the Theban twain: Pelopidas and Epaminondas [Note in the original]

104 *No smearing will save you*: As protection against parasites, before the advent of dipping, sheep were smeared annually with a mixture of tar, butter, and grease.

113 *HYGEIA*: The goddess of health.

135 *The Jews . . . nor any missing*: Exodus 16:17–18.

140 *Rhymer*: Thomas the Rhymer, whose thirteenth-century prophecies were as well known in the Highlands as in the Lowlands.

George and William: King George and William, Duke of Cumberland.

168 *That man who introduced the Act*: The Lord High Chancellor, Philip Yorke, 1st Earl of Hardwicke, was responsible for the disarming and disclothing legislation.

178 *They started weeping and hand-clapping*: In Gaelic tradition hand-clapping was an expression of grief at funerals.

188 *ORAN*: Oran is a fictitious name; under which our author meant to conceal the object of her affections. He was an Irishman of distinction. On his return from Edinburgh to his own country by sea, he was unfortunately drowned. The recollection of this disastrous event was too deeply impressed on the writer's mind, to be erased by time. It set the colour of her life, saddened her future prospects, and produced its influence on her writings. For it disposed her to prefer the mournful Elegy; where disappointed lovers are permitted to complain, and where the tears of sorrow may be shed without reprehension. [Note in the original]

197 *The hosts were deployed . . . Fife*: Possibly a reference to the old prophecy that the last great battle would be fought in Fife.

243 *Cuchullin*: [James Macpherson, hereafter M]: Cuchullin, or rather Cuth-Ullin, *the voice of Ullin*, a poetical name given the son of Semo by the bards, from his commanding the forces of the Province of Ulster against the Ferbolg or Belgae, who were in possession of Connaught. Cuchullin when very young married Bragela the daughter of Sorglan, and passing over into Ireland, lived for some time with Connal, grandson by a daughter

to Congal the petty king of Ulster. His wisdom and valour in a short time gained him such reputation that, in the minority of Cormac the supreme king of Ireland, he was chosen guardian to the young king, and sole manager of the war against Swaran king of Lochlin. After a series of great actions he was killed in battle somewhere in Connaught, in the twenty-seventh year of his age. He was so remarkable for his strength that to describe a strong man it has passed into a proverb, "He has the strength of Cuchullin." They shew the remains of his palace at Dunscaich in the Isle of Skye; and a stone to which he bound his dog Luath goes still by his name.

243 *Cairbar*: [M]: Cairbar or Cairbre signifies a strong man.

the scout: [M]: We may conclude from Cuchullin's applying so early for foreign aid that the Irish were not then so numerous as they have since been; which is a great presumption against the high antiquities of that people. We have the testimony of Tacitus that one legion only was thought sufficient, in the time of Agricola, to reduce the whole island under the Roman yoke; which would not probably have been the case had the island been inhabited for any number of centuries before.

Moran the son of Fithil: [M]: Moran signifies many; and Fithil, or rather Fili, *an inferior bard*.

244 *the king*: [M]: Fingal the son of Comhal, and Morna the daughter of Thaddu. His grandfather was Trathal, and great grandfather Trenmor, both of whom are often mentioned in the poem.—Trenmor, according to tradition, had two sons: Trathal, who succeeded him in the Kingdom of Morven, and Conar, called by the bards *Conar the great*, who was elected king of all Ireland, and was the ancestor of that Cormac who sat on the Irish throne when the invasion of Swaran happened. It may not be improper here to observe that the accent ought always to be placed on the last syllable of Fingal.

Malmor: [M]: Meal-mór—*a great hill*.

Cabait: [M]: Cabait, or rather Cathbait, grandfather to the hero, was so remarkable for his valour that his shield was made use of to alarm his posterity to the battles of the family. We find Fingal making the same use of his own shield in the 4th book.—A horn was the most common instrument to call the army together before the invention of bagpipes.

Curach: [M]: Cu-raoch signifies *the madness of battle*.

Crugal's: [M]: Cruth-geal—*fair-complexioned*.

Cuthon: [M]: Cu-thón—*the mournful sound of waves*.

245 *Cromla*: [M]: Crom-leach signified a place of worship among the Druids. It is here the proper name of a hill on the coast of Ullin or Ulster.

On Lena's dusky heath . . . mist: [M]: So when th' embattled clouds in dark array, | Along the skies their gloomy lines display; | The low-hung vapours motionless and still | Rest on the summits of the shaded hill. POPE.

Innisfail: [M]: Ireland, so called from a colony that settled there called Falans.—Innis-fail, *i.e.* the island of the Fa-il or Falans.

Connal: [M]: Connal, the friend of Cuchullin, was the son of Cathbait prince of the Tongorma or the *island of the blue waves*, probably one of the Hebrides. His mother was Fion-coma the daughter of Congal. He had a son by Foba of Conachar-nessar, who was afterwards king of Ulster. For his services in the war against Swaran he had lands conferred on him, which, from his name, were called Tir-chonnuil or Tir-connel, *i.e.* the land of Connal.

Erin: [M]: Erin, a name of Ireland; from *ear* or *iar* West, and *in* an island. This name was not always confined to Ireland, for there is the highest probability that the *Ierne* of the ancients was Britain to the North of the Forth.—For Ierne is said to be to the North of Britain, which could not be meant of Ireland. STRABO, 1. 2. & 4. CASAUB. 1. 1.

Calmar: [M]: Cálm-er, *a strong man.*

Lochlin: [M]: The Galic name of Scandinavia in general; in a more confined sense that of the peninsula of Jutland.

Inis-tore: [M]: Innis-tore, *the island of whales*, the ancient name of the Orkney islands.

246 *Duchomar*: [M]: Dubhchomar, *a black well-shaped man.*

Fergus: [M]: Fear-guth,—*the man of the word*; or a commander of an army.

comest thou like a roe: [M]: Be thou like a roe or young hart on the mountains of Bether. SOLOMON's Song.

Four stones: [M]: This passage alludes to the manner of burial among the ancient Scots. They opened a grave six or eight feet deep: the bottom was lined with fine clay; and on this they laid the body of the deceased, and, if a warrior, his sword, and the heads of twelve arrows by his side. Above they laid another stratum of clay, in which they placed the horn of a deer, the symbol of hunting. The whole was covered with a fine mold, and four stones placed on end to mark the extent of the grave. These are the four stones alluded to here.

narrow house: [M]: The grave.—The house appointed for all living. JOB.

Morna: [M]: Muirne or Morna, *a woman beloved by all.*

Torman: [M]: Torman, *thunder.* This is the true origin of the Jupiter Taramis of the ancients.

247 *thou art dark*: [M]: She alludes to his name—*the dark man.*

Moina: [M]: Moina, *soft in temper and person.*

Let them ride around: [M]: It was the opinion then, as indeed it is to this day, of some of the highlanders, that the souls of the deceased hovered round their living friends; and sometimes appeared to them when they were about to enter on any great undertaking.

As rushes a stream: [M]: As torrents roll encreas'd by numerous rills | With rage impetuous down the ecchoing hills; | Rush to the vales, and pour'd along the plain, | Roar thro' a thousand channels to the main. POPE. *Aut ubi decursu rapido de montibus altis, | Dant sonitum spumosi amnes, & in aequora currunt, | Quisque suum populatus iter.* VIRG.

248 *rustling winds*: [M]: As when the hollow rocks retain | The sound of blustering wind. MILTON.

249 *As autumn's*: [M]: The reader may compare this passage with a similar one in Homer. *Iliad.* 4. v. 446. Now shield with shield, with helmet helmet clos'd, | To armour armour, lance to lance oppos'd, | Host against host, with shadowy squadrons drew, | The sounding darts in iron tempests flew; | With streaming blood the slipp'ry fields are dy'd, | And slaughter'd heroes swell the dreadful tide. POPE. Statius has very happily imitated Homer. *Jam clypeus clypeis, umbone repellitur umbo, | Ense minax ensis, pede pes, & cuspide cuspis, &c.* Arms on armour crashing, bray'd | Horrible discord, and the madding wheels | Of brazen chariots rag'd, &c. MILTON.

Sithallin: [M]: Sithallin signifies *a handsome man*,—Fiöna, *a fair maid*;—and Ardan, *pride.*

isle of mist: [M]: The Isle of Sky; not improperly called the *isle of mist*, as its high hills, which catch the clouds from the western ocean, occasion almost continual rains.

Dusronnal: [M]: One of Cuchullin's horses. Dubhstron-gheal.

Sifadda: [M]: Sith-fadda, *i.e. a long stride.*

maid of Inistore: [M]: *The maid of Inistore* was the daughter of Gorlo king of Inistore or Orkney islands. Trenar was brother to the king of Iniscon, supposed to be one of the islands of Shetland. The Orkneys and Shetland were at that time subject to the king of Lochlin. We find that the dogs of Trenar are sensible at home of the death of their master, the very instant he is killed.—It was the opinion of the times that the souls of heroes went immediately after death to the hills of their country, and the scenes they frequented the most happy time of their life. It was thought too that dogs and horses saw the ghosts of the deceased.

250 *two clouds*: [M]: As when two black clouds | With heaven's artillery fraught, come rattling on | Over the Caspian. MILTON.

It was . . . placed the deer: [M]: The ancient manner of preparing feasts after hunting is handed down by tradition.—A pit lined with smooth stones was made; and near it stood a heap of smooth flat stones of the flint kind. The stones as well as the pit were properly heated with heath. Then they laid some venison in the bottom, and a stratum of the stones above it; and thus they did alternately till the pit was full. The whole was covered over with heath to confine the steam. Whether this is probable I cannot say; but some pits are shewn, which the vulgar say, were used in that manner.

Kinfena: [M]: Cean-feana, *i.e. the head of the people.*

251 *Ossian*: [M]: Ossian the son of Fingal and author of the poem. One cannot but admire the address of the poet in putting his own praise so naturally

into the mouth of Cuchullin. The Cona here mentioned is perhaps that small river that runs through Glenco in Argyleshire. One of the hills which environ that romantic valley is still called Scornafena, or the hill of Fingal's people.

In other days: [M]: This episode is introduced with propriety. Calmar and Connal, two of the Irish heroes, had disputed warmly before the battle about engaging the enemy. Carril endeavours to reconcile them with the story of Cairbar and Grudar; who, tho' enemies before, fought *side by side* in the war. The poet obtained his aim, for we find Calmar and Connal perfectly reconciled in the third book.

Golbun's: [M]: Golb-bhean, as well as Cromleach, signifies *a crooked hill*. It is here the name of a mountain in the county of Sligo.

Lubar's: [M]: Lubar—a river in Ulster. *Labhar*, loud, noisy.

Brassolis: [M]: Brassolis signifies *a woman with a white breast*.

Pleasant is thy . . . calm shower: [M]: But when he speaks, what elocution flows! | Like the soft fleeces of descending snows. POPE.

252 *The ghosts*: [M]: It was long the opinion of the ancient Scots that a ghost was heard shrieking near the place where a death was to happen soon after. The accounts given, to this day, among the vulgar, of this extraordinary matter, are very poetical. The ghost comes mounted on a meteor, and surrounds twice or thrice the place destined for the person to die; and then goes along the road through which the funeral is to pass, shrieking at intervals; at last, the meteor and ghost disappear above the burial place.

Lutha: [M]: Lutha, *swift stream*. It is impossible, at this distance of time, to ascertain where the scene here described lies. Tradition is silent on that head, and there is nothing in the poem from which a conjecture can be drawn.

Malvina: [M]: Mal-mhina, *soft or lovely brow*. *Mh* in the Galic language has the same sound with *v* in English.

Son: [M]: Tradition has not handed down the name of this son of Alpin. His father was one of Fingal's principal bards, and he appears himself to have had a poetical genius.

Pleasant: [M]: Ossian speaks. He calls Malvina a beam of light, and continues the metaphor throughout the paragraph.

253 *the dwelling*: [M]: The description of this ideal palace of Fingal is very poetical, and agreeable to the notions of those times, concerning the state of the deceased, who were supposed to pursue, after death, the pleasures and employments of their former life. The situation of Ossian's heroes, in their separate state, if not entirely happy, is more agreeable, than the notions of the antient Greeks concerning their departed heroes. See Hom. Odyss. I. II.

My aged son: [M]: Ossian; who had a great friendship for Malvina, both on account of her love for his son Oscar, and her attention to his own poems.

253 *The maids*: [M]: That is, the young virgins who sung the funeral elegy over her tomb.

The sons of little men: [M]: Ossian, by way of disrespect, calls those, who succeeded the heroes whose actions he celebrates, *the sons of little men*. Tradition is entirely silent concerning what passed in the north, immediately after the death of Fingal and all his heroes; but it appears from that term of ignominy just mentioned that the actions of their successors were not to be compared to those of the renowned Fingalians.

Toscar: [M]: Toscar was the son of that Conloch, who was also father to the lady, whose unfortunate death is related in the last episode of the second book of Fingal.

the last sound: [M]: Ossian seems to intimate by this expression that this poem was the last of his composition; so that there is some foundation for the traditional title of *the last hymn of Ossian*.

Berrathon: [M]: Barrathón, *a promontory in the midst of waves*. The poet gives it the epithet of sea-surrounded, to prevent its being taken for a peninsula in the literal sense.

254 *But the memory*: [M]: The meaning of the poet is that Fingal remembered his own great actions, and consequently would not sully them by engaging in a petty war against Uthal, who was so far his inferior in valour and power.

we often half-unsheathed our swords: [M]: The impatience of a young warrior, going on their first expedition, is well marked by their half-drawing their swords. The modesty of Ossian, in his narration of a story which does him so much honour, is remarkable; and his humanity to Nina-thoma would grace a hero of our own polished age. Though Ossian passes over his own actions in silence, or slightly mentions them; tradition has done ample justice to his martial fame, and perhaps has exaggerated the actions of the poet beyond the bounds of credibility.

the maid: [M]: Nina-thoma the daughter of Torthóma, who had been confined to a desart island by her lover Uthal.

Finthormo: [M]: Finthormo, the palace of Uthal. The names in this episode are not of a Celtic original; which makes it probable that Ossian founds his poem on a true story.

255 *I rejoiced over the blood*: [M]: Ossian thought that his killing the boar, on his first landing in Berrathon, was a good omen of his future success in that island. The present highlanders look, with a degree of superstition, upon the success of their first action, after they have engaged in any desperate undertaking.

Thou art fallen: [M]: To mourn over the fall of their enemies was a practice universal among Ossian's heroes. This is more agreeable to humanity than the shameful insulting of the dead, so common in Homer, and after him, servilely copied by all his imitators, the humane Virgil not excepted, who have been more successful in borrowing the imperfections of that great poet than in their imitations of his beauties. Homer, it is probable, gave the manners of the times in which he wrote, not his own sentiments: Ossian also seems to keep to the sentiments of his heroes. The reverence, which the most barbarous highlanders have still for the remains of the deceased, seems to have descended to them from their most remote ancestors.

257 *Such were my deeds . . . such were*: [M]: Ossian speaks.

The aged oak: [M]: Here begins the lyric piece, with which, tradition says, Ossian concluded his poems.—It is set to music, and still sung in the north, with a great deal of wild simplicity, but little variety of sound.

But thy steps: [M]: This magnificent description of the power of Fingal over the winds and storms, and the image of his taking the sun, and hiding him in the clouds, do not correspond with the preceding paragraph, where he is represented as a feeble ghost, and no more the TERROR OF THE VALIANT; but it agrees with the notion of the times concerning the souls of the deceased, who, it was supposed, had the command of the winds and storms, but in combat were not a match for valiant men.

It was the immoderate praise bestowed by the poets on their departed friends that gave the first hint to superstition to deify the deceased heroes; and those new divinities owed all their attributes to the fancy of the bard who sung their elegies.

We do not find that the praises of Fingal had this effect upon his countrymen; but that is to be imputed to the idea they had of power, which they always connected with bodily strength and personal valour, both which were dissolved by death.

258 *like the leaves*: [M]: Mr. Pope falls short of his original; in particular he has omitted altogether the beautiful image of the wind strewing the withered leaves on the ground.—Like leaves on trees the race of men are found, | Now green in youth, now with'ring on the ground; | Another race the following spring supplies; | They fall successive, and successive rise. POPE.

Ryno: [M]: Ryno, the son of Fingal, who was killed in Ireland, in the war against Swaran, was remarkable for the beauty of his person, his swiftness and great exploits. Minvane, the daughter of Morni, and sister to Gaul so often mentioned in Ossian's compositions, was in love with Ryno.—Her lamentation over her lover is introduced as an episode in one of Ossian's great poems. The lamentation is the only part of the poem now extant, and as it has some poetical merit, I have subjoined it to this note. The poet represents Minvane as seeing, from one of the rocks of Morven, the fleet of Fingal returning from Ireland.

She blushing sad, from Morven's rocks, bends over the darkly-rolling sea. She saw the youths in all their arms.—Where, Ryno, where art thou?

Our dark looks told that he was low!—That pale the hero flew on clouds! That in the grass of Morven's hills, his feeble voice was heard in wind!

And is the son of Fingal fallen, on Ullin's mossy plains? Strong was the arm that conquered him!—Ah me! I am alone.

Alone I will not be, ye winds! that lift my dark-brown hair. My sighs will not long mix with your stream; for I must sleep with Ryno.

I see thee not with beauty's steps returning from the chace.—The night is round Minvane's love; and silence dwells with Ryno.

Where are thy dogs, and where thy bow? Thy shield that was so strong? Thy sword like heaven's descending fire? The bloody spear of Ryno?

I see them mixed in thy ship; I see them stained with blood.—No arms are in thy narrow hall, O darkly-dwelling Ryno!

When will the morning come, and say, arise, thou king of spears! arise, the hunters are abroad. The hinds are near thee, Ryno!

Away, thou fair-haired morning, away! the slumbering king hears thee not! The hinds bound over his narrow tomb; for death dwells round young Ryno.

But I will tread softly, my king! and steal to the bed of thy repose. Minvane will lie in silence, near her slumbering Ryno.

The maids shall seek me; but they shall not find me: they shall follow my departure with songs. But I will not hear you, O maids: I sleep with fair-haired Ryno.

258 *Alpin*: [M]: Alpin is from the same root with Albion, or rather Albin, the ancient name of Britain; Alp, *high*, in *land*, or *country*. The present name of our island has its origin in the Celtic tongue; so that those who derived it from any other betrayed their ignorance of the ancient language of our country.—*Britain* comes from *Breac't in, variegated island,* so called from the face of the country, from the natives painting themselves, or from their party-coloured cloaths.

259 *Minona*: [M]: Ossian introduces Minona, not in the ideal scene in his own mind, which he had described; but at the annual feast of Selma, where the bards repeated their works before Fingal.

Salgar: [M]: Sealg-'er, *a hunter.*

Colma: [M]: Cul-math, *a woman with fine hair.*

260 *Morar*: [M]: Mór-ér, *great man.*

261 *It is thy father*: [M]: Torman, the son of Carthul, lord of I-mora, one of the western isles.

Armin: [M]: Armin, *a hero.* He was chief or petty king of Gorma, *i.e. the blue island*, supposed to be one of the Hebrides.

Carmor: [M]: Cear-mór, *a tall dark-complexioned man.*

262 *Fura*: [M]: Fuar-a, *cold island.*

the son of the rock: [M]: By *the son of the rock* the poet means the echoing back of the human voice from a rock. The vulgar were of opinion that this repetition of sound was made by a spirit within the rock; and they, on that account, called it *mac-talla; the son who dwells in the rock.*

Thick bend the thongs: [M]: The poet here only means that Erath was bound with leathern thongs.

263 *the voice*: [M]: Ossian is sometimes poetically called *the voice of Cona.*

264 *To louder notes . . . vocal reed*: [Alexander Geddes, hereafter G]: IMITATION. *Paulo majora canamus.* [Virgil]

265 *THOMAS the True*: [G]: Thomas of Lermount, commonly called Thomas the Rymer [or Rhymer].

the RAVEN: [G]: The Ravenscroft arms.

the ROOK: [G]: The crest of the armorial bearings of the Traquaire family.

the Sun . . . nuptial bed: [G]: IMITATION. *Tanquam sponsus procedens de thalamo suo.*

like a giant . . . his force: [G]: IMITATION. *Exultavit, ut gigas, ad currendam viam suam.*

266 *Yet still remain . . . former times*: [G]: IMITATION. *Pauca, tamen, suberunt Priscae vestigia fraudis.* [Virgil]

267 *No pois'nous herb . . . pregnant ewes*: [G]: IMITATION. *Non infueta graves tentabunt pabula foetas.* [Virgil]

568 *the flaying wolftime . . . is shrill*: The terms *faoilleach* 'wolftime', *feadag* 'whistler', *sguabag* 'sweeper', *gearran* 'cutter', and *cailleach* 'hag' are windnames which feature in many traditional rhymes once used to determine the proper time for each item of spring labour.

When the young . . . maytime arrives: *Céitean* ('maytime') is the name given to the period on either side of 1 May, the traditional beginning of summer.

583 *No more the [   ]*: Robert Howie Smith finds the word in the manuscript is unintelligible, but two suggestions have been offered. *The Mercury* (29 January 1816) has 'descant'; the *Glasgow Chronicle* (1893) has 'pennant'.

INDEX OF POETS